S

To my old
Frank
with &
Michael D Mueller
3 iii 1994

Thus far with rough and all unable pen
The bending author hath pursued the story
In little room confining mighty men
Mangling with starts the full course of their
                                                    glory.

                    Prologue Henry $\overline{V}$

MARINE
WAR
RISKS

LLOYD'S SHIPPING LAW LIBRARY

Time Charters
third edition
by Michael Wilford, Terence Coghlin
and John D. Kimball
(1989)

The Ratification of Maritime Conventions
edited by The Institute of Maritime
Law, University of Southampton
(1990)

Laytime and Demurrage
second edition
by John Schofield
(1990)

The Law of Shipbuilding Contracts
by Simon Curtis
(1991)

EC Shipping Law
by Vincent Power
(1992)

Admiralty Jurisdiction and Practice
by Nigel Meeson
(1993)

Marine Environment Law
by John H. Bates and
Charles Benson
(1993)

Ship Sale and Purchase
second edition
by Iain Goldrein
et al.
(1993)

Voyage Charters
by Julian Cooke, Timothy Young,
Andrew Taylor, John D. Kimball,
David Martowski, LeRoy Lambert
(1993)

Contracts for the Carriage of Goods
by David Yates *et al.*
(1993)

Marine War Risks
second edition
by Michael D. Miller
(1994)

MARINE WAR RISKS

BY

MICHAEL D. MILLER

SECOND EDITION

LONDON   NEW YORK   HAMBURG   HONG KONG
LLOYD'S OF LONDON PRESS LTD.
1994

Lloyd's of London Press Ltd.
Legal Publishing Division
27 Swinton Street
London WC1X 9NW

USA AND CANADA
Lloyd's of London Press Inc.
Suite 308, 611 Broadway
New York, NY 10012 USA

GERMANY
Lloyd's of London Press GmbH
59 Ehrenbergstrasse
2000 Hamburg 50, Germany

SOUTH EAST ASIA
Lloyd's of London Press (Far East) Ltd.
Room 1101, Hollywood Centre
233 Hollywood Road
Hong Kong

©
Michael D. Miller
1990, 1994

First published in Great Britain 1990
Second edition 1994

British Library Cataloguing in Publication Data
A catalogue record for
this book is available from the
British Library

ISBN 1–85044–516–8

Text set in 10 on 12pt Linotron 202 Times by
Interactive Sciences
Gloucester.
Printed in Great Britain by
WBC Print Ltd., Bridgend, Mid-Glamorgan

Acknowledgments

The first edition of this work acknowledged the contributions of a great number of people of many nations who had each given something to the knowledge and experience upon which I have freely drawn—judges, barristers, solicitors, ship-owners, ship masters and ships officers, club members, club directors, club managers, club correspondents, insurance brokers, shipbrokers, underwriters, civil servants, average adjusters, military and naval officers. So it is with the second edition, and it is impossible to thank them all in fitting terms, except to say that without their contributions, this work would never have seen the light of day. Even so, there are a number of people to whom especial thanks, and one apology, are due: to Mr. Alan Jackson, whose name was (quite inexcusably) omitted from the first edition, who with his Technical and Clauses Committee laboured so long and so hard to re-draft the Institute Clauses in the early 1980s; to the late Mr. Donald O'May, the solicitor who advised them; to Mr. Jorgen Hojer of the Baltic and International Maritime Council (BIMCO) and to Mr. Hans Levy and Mr. Nicholas Hambro of the Skuld and Nordisk Associations respectively who, under my chairmanship, redrafted the CONWARTIME and VOYWAR 1993 Clauses; to the many members of the Documentary Council who made such detailed suggestions; to the chairman of the Documentary Council, Mr. Nils-Gustav Palmgren, whose quiet determination and encouragement helped our work so much; to Mr. Peter Tudball, the chairman of the Baltic Exchange, who still found time from a busy life putting together the Baltic Exchange after it had been destroyed by a terrorist bomb, to take an interest and to make suggestions; to Mr. Peter Stone and Mr. Nicholas Spratt of Miller Marine, who have dealt tirelessly with various obscure points with a clamness and patience that few can match; to Professor Rhiddian Thomas, and to the people who attend the seminars which he chairs, who, whilst professing no knowledge of the subject, still managed to shed welcome light into dark corners; to Mr. Charles Hassell, who unlocked the secrets of the lordly word-processor and made it into the humble servant it should properly be; and last, but by no means least, to Jill my wife, whose never failing patience and extrovert nature were sorely tried, but were never found wanting.

Every book should be dedicated. This work can be dedicated to the Benches of the High Court, the Court of Appeal, and the House of Lords, with a sympathy as profound as it is respectful.

M.D.M.

Preface

In the first edition of this work, a ship was described as being of enormous value, and the ship of today may require as much capital to build and to run as a modern factory. The same is true of a cargo which may well be of even greater value than the carrying ship herself; a full cargo of crude oil on board a VLCC or a ULCC, even when the price of this commodity is not at one of its periodic peaks, requires the sort of figures to describe it as are otherwise only to be found in astronomy. Individual containers are valuable objects, and one of the big container ships, carrying perhaps 2,500 containers, has a king's ransom on board in the containers alone, let alone their contents. It is a brave fellow who entrusts so much money to the inconstant element of the sea, which is not only cold, wet and grey, but restless as well, and given to sudden and vicious outbursts of rage, when its power can lead to catastrophic consequences to life, limb, and property. Even nowadays, when the coasts of the whole world are well charted and most of the hazards are known, danger lurks in shoals, rocks, and sandbanks, which are always ready to claim a victim, and a moment's inattention or carelessness, to which all human beings are prone, can lead to disaster.

The financial risks which the sea's dangers pose can be guarded against by marine insurance. Such is the demand for this safeguard that the industry is now a gigantic player on the World's stage, and is readily available to those who wish to engage in foreign commerce and so entrust their wealth to the sea. There is however something more than the natural dangers of the sea. Generally speaking, marine insurance can be divided into three separate aspects. There are the perils posed by Mother Nature herself (which include the negligence, or worse, of those in charge of the ship) to the ship and all on board her; this is safeguarded by the "marine clauses". There are the liabilities which the ship incurs, or "what the ship does to other people"; these are safeguarded by the Protection and Indemnity insurance in one of the P. & I. Clubs. Lastly, there is the damage or destruction to the ship and all on board her by people from outside the ship, or, broadly speaking, "what other people do to the ship"; these are safeguarded by the War and Strikes clauses, and since this damage or destruction can also affect her freight, cargo and containers as well, these too need War and Strikes clauses of their own.

It is with this last aspect that this work is concerned. The owner of a factory or a large building has the chance to weigh the political situation and the effectiveness, or otherwise, of the local forces of law and order before he invests his money. It is of course true that he cannot readily remove them should things turn out for the worse. A ship, being mobile by nature, does have this chance, and can often (if not always) remove herself and all that goes with her out of harm's way. That said, the seas have never been, and probably never will be, policed as effectively as a city street. Even in the years between 1800 and 1950, when the Royal Navy, unrestrained by the liberal thinking that has since become fashionable, was for all practical purposes the policeman of the seas, dealing with troublemakers by the time honoured means of hard blows followed by a hanging, was this so. The seas are an ideal hiding place for those who wish to harm commerce, and they can lurk almost without fear of detection until their chance should appear. An added factor is the withdrawal of the former colonial powers to their own countries, because with them went the concept of the rule of law and the peaceful determination of disputes, dealt with by judges of undoubted impartiality. This has posed many local dangers ashore which previously did not exist, but which cannot be discounted.

The dichotomy between the three types of insurance for trading by sea is not so clear that a work of this nature can deal only with one and ignore the other two. Cases on the marine clauses have a clear bearing on the war risks clauses which do not always have decisions of their own on the particular point. It is necessary to trespass into the field of the marine clauses to reach them, while resisting the temptation to write a treatise on the marine clauses themselves. This has not always been easy, and the reader's patience is sometimes abused. It may seem strange that piracy, an insured peril of the marine clauses, should be brought well to the fore whilst there is no chapter on barratry. Piracy was regarded as an insured peril for the war risks clauses between 1937 and 1983, and is still so regarded by the Mutual War Risks Associations. Barratry on the other hand has always been an insured peril of the marine clauses. It is hoped however this will not cause confusion to those who consult this work.

City of London, September 1993   MICHAEL MILLER

Contents

CONTENTS

CONTENTS

CONTENTS

CONTENTS

xiii

CONTENTS

CONTENTS

Table of cases

Table of legislation

CHAPTER 1

The history of the War Risks Policy

1.1 The picturesque and archaically worded S.G. Form which was used by the London market up to 1983, had its origins in the bond or document by which 17th century merchants and shipowners (in those days there was rarely the distinction that now exists between them), meeting together in Lloyd's Coffee House, bound themselves one to another to make good any loss which any of them might suffer. This, in the course of time, emerged as a policy whereby one or several of them took all the risks in consideration of a premium. The S.G. Form was not a planned document and never during the whole of its long life did it acquire this characteristic. Risks and exceptions were added on an *ad hoc* basis as the demands of the insured shipowners, the practices of the market, and the decisions of the courts indicated were necessary. It was issued with the relevant clauses attached, usually by no more than a paperclip. For instance, an agreement to insure hulls or freight against marine risks would have required the attachment to the S.G. Form of the Institute Time Clauses, Hulls or Freight and an agreement to insure a ship against war risks, the attachment of the Institute War and Strikes Clauses. Insured risks, exceptions and limitations were dotted about in the S.G. Form itself and in the attachments and often required experience and persistence to find them. Agreements varying the terms of the policy, whether made at the time that the Agreement to insure was made or subsequently, were evidenced by endorsement slips which were stuck on with paste. Sometimes clauses bore the puzzling words stamped on them with a rubber stamp "deleted". The policy itself, particularly when compared with a conveyance of real property or a mortgage of a ship, had an untidy and unworkmanlike appearance. It was drawn up by the brokers who placed the risk and was then checked and signed by the Lloyd's Policy Signing Office from the broker's slip, hardly a paragon of neatness and order in itself. This recorded each underwriter's agreement to provide the insurance and his agreed proportion or percentage. The slip, being the only document that the underwriter ever signed to bind himself to the risk, is the evidence of the actual agreement to give insurance and the policy, when it came to be prepared, reflected its terms. When an underwriter has signed a slip, the brokers use the expression that he has "scratched" it, an expression which is more descriptive of the slip's appearance than many would care to agree.

1.2 That said, it must be appreciated that the pre-eminence of the London market in marine insurance is founded on the S.G. Form. If an individual insured shipowner did not understand what insurance it provided (in the author's experience, he frequently needed no help in doing so), there were plenty of average adjusters, brokers, solicitors and counsel to help him. If he had to go to law, he found judges on the benches of the High Court and the Appellate courts who were well acquainted with its terms, and who could give judgment based on their own profound knowledge obtained from their own experience whilst practising at the Bar and from case law, going back to the start of the 18th century. It did not require the wisdom of some secret, closed and remote society to unlock its secrets. Untidy and unworkmanlike in appearance the policy may have been but it proved on many occasions how flexible it could be, and by its changes, even though on an *ad hoc* and unplanned basis, how well it could respond and adapt to changing requirements.

1.3 Much to the disgust of those who had grown accustomed to its ways and to the dispair of the nostalgic, the S.G. Form was swept away in 1983 to be replaced by the new form of Lloyd's Marine Policy (in the case of the Institute of London Underwriters, the Companies Marine Policy) known as the MAR form which is the first policy for marine risks ever issued by the London market as a comprehensively planned document. No doubt over the years changes will be made to it but there is a great difference to changing a document which has been planned as a whole from changing one which grew on an *ad hoc* basis. No doubt some measure of untidiness will remain because endorsements will still have to be added and the relevant clauses attached so that the paperclip and the paste will retain their essential use. An examination of the MAR form will, however, reveal how systematic it is. It begins with a declaration that in consideration of the payment of the agreed premium, insurance is provided against "loss, damage, liability or expense"—surely a most comprehensive definition—and makes it clear that each underwriter's liability is confined to his agreed proportion. There follows a page devoted to the individual description of the subject matter insured and the agreed (insured) value with a space for the endorsements and another page to identify the underwriters who have accepted the risk and the proportions of the risk they have agreed to accept. Most importantly of all, and essential if the MAR form is to be used for all marine insurances, be they hull and machinery, freight, cargo, or war risks, or whatever variation the insurance is to assume, attached clauses, in our case the Institute War and Strikes Clauses, contain the insured risks, or perils, set out in a comprehensive list with the exclusions and other conditions also printed in their respective places in an easy-to-read format. No doubt questions will arise on some of the terms which are used and litigation will ensue, but it would be wrong not to pay tribute to Mr. Alan Jackson and to his Committee whose members laboured long and hard to produce some readable and comprehensive documents in which clarity is the main objective and which, in themselves, do much to assist the London market to retain the preeminence that it has already won for itself. Some criticisms of the drafting will follow, but they will be made with the recognition of the sound nature of the Committee's work.

1.4 We cannot, however, dismiss the S.G. Form from our consideration. Much of the London market's practice grew up on its basis and the huge body of existing case law judicially defined its terms. The Marine Insurance Act 1906, which codified the law existing at that date with only minor alterations, was founded on the S.G. Form which is set out in a schedule to the Act itself. During its life of some 80 years, the Act has given rise to many legal decisions. Moreover the MAR form, whilst it does introduce some welcomed clarifications, does not set out to make substantial alterations to the marine insurance hitherto provided by the London market.

1.5 It is difficult for anyone now living to remember that the very firm and concise distinction between marine and war risks which is so well known to us today has existed only since 1898. Before that date the distinction, whilst it had existed to a greater or lesser degree for many years, was nothing like so clear and the degree to which it did exist at any particular moment is best appreciated from the history of the F.C. & S. Clause which follows. The reader will find it helpful to compare the date of the case he is studying with this history.

1.6 From the start of the use of the S.G. Form in the 17th century, marine and war risks were insured by the same policy. No less than 12 (some would say more) of the perils we would today describe as war risks were insured by the same policy which also insured such marine risks as "perils of the seas". Underwriters sometimes wished to exclude war risks and an early example of this is *The Charming Peggy*.[1] In 1739 there was even greater tension than usual in the relations between the United Kingdom and France, so "capture and seizure" were excluded from the perils insured by the policy. Wars in the 18th and 19th centuries were fought on the seas as much as they were on the land and made the enemy's seaborne trade an especial target. Even though Britannia ruled the waves, the powerful and omnipresent Royal Navy was never able to obviate entirely the depredations of skilled, determined and resourceful enemy seafarers. The Seven Years' War, the American War of Independence, the 1812 War and the Napoleonic Wars emphasised that there was a real distinction to be made between marine and war risks, and a variety of exclusions were then added to the policies by endorsement as the chapters on war, capture and seizure will show. A particularly favoured exclusion, which seems to have been directed at excepting risks to ships in European ports which may have been affected by Napoleon's Continental system read: "Free of capture and seizure in the ship's port of discharge." This has a familiar ring and can be said to have been the beginnings of the F.C. & S. Clause as it later appeared. The perils thus excepted could be insured by underwriters willing to write war risks. They seem to have found the business very profitable, although several were ruined by the disaster in 1780, when only eight British ships out of a convoy of 63 escaped capture. By the time of the *Ionides* case[2] the F.C. & S. Clause in common use read: "Warranted free from capture, seizure and detention, and all the consequences thereof, or any attempt thereat, and free from all consequences of hostilities, riots, or commotions."

1.7 In 1883, the underwriting community of the United Kingdom assembled at Lloyd's wanted "warlike operations" added to this list. The Royal Navy had the year before bombarded Alexandria; apparently there was no state of war, and it was merely aiding a friendly State to put down a rebellion. In 1889 the Clause is recorded as reading: "Warranted free from capture, seizure and detention, the consequences thereof, or of any attempt thereat, unless arising from piracy or barratry, and from all consequences of hostilities or warlike operations, whether before or after declaration of war."

---

1. *Green* v. *Brown* (1743) 2 Strange 1199. See para. 30.68.
2. *Ionides* v. *The Universal Marine Insurance Co.* (1863) 14 C.B. (N.S.) 259. See paras. 14.5–14.10.

In 1893 there was a further amendment to add the "consequences of riots and civil commotions", which had appeared in a slightly different form in the 1863 version, to "hostilities and warlike operations". This gave rise to much opposition, so that the 1898 version omitted them.

1.8 During the 1890s, war risks came to be viewed with some disfavour by the London market, and this led to pressure for changes for an organised and uniform method to be used by the entire market.

The ancients who lived at the time told us this was a golden age of peace and plenty. The history books tell us a very different story. This was a time of great tension between the United States of America and the United Kingdom which could have led to a war, and of a crisis between the United Kingdom and France over the Fashoda incident which very nearly did. Both the United States and France possessed powerful navies, which, even if numerically inferior to the Royal Navy of the time, could have caused enormous damage to the United Kingdom's maritime commerce.

1.9 The Imperial German Navy was, at the time, of little consequence, but, as Robert K. Massie's interesting book *Dreadnought* shows, the Kaiser had ambitions to build a large and powerful fleet, and it could be anticipated that he would succeed in doing so. The memory of the 1812 war in particular, when the infant United States Navy had wreaked havoc in spite of all that the mighty Royal Navy could do to prevent it, was still green. In 1895 the London Assurance Company wrote to the Committee of Lloyd's suggesting that there should be separation of marine and war risks perils, and that the latter should be insured by a separate policy. This should have its own rating which would be separate from the rating of the Marine Policy. It is not known why the Committee returned a chilling answer that it was not in a position to dictate to the Lloyd's underwriters how they should conduct their business, but the companies were not then looked upon with much favour by the Lloyd's underwriters and a suggestion of this nature from such a source may not have been welcome.

1.10 There was soon to be a change of heart. In addition to *Dreadnought*, there is Thomas Pakenham's equally interesting *The Scramble for Africa* which also describes in vivid detail the tense relations that existed between Great Britain, France, Germany, Russia, and to a lesser extent only, the United States of America. On 15th June, 1898, a General Meeting of Lloyd's decided that marine risks and war risks would be insured by separate policies. In 1899, spurred on no doubt by the tense situation caused by the Fashoda incident in the previous September, it was further resolved that all marine policies should include an F.C. & S. Clause excluding war risks peril unless otherwise specifically agreed. The companies followed suit. From this date onwards, it has been the practice of the London market (an expression which in this book will include both the Lloyd's underwriters and the companies) to insure marine risks and war risks under separate policies. This is still the practice today, even though, as we shall see at para. 1.23, the F.C. & S. Clause is no longer used. The important point is that in 1898, the totally different nature of marine and war risks was recognised to the extent that, from thenceforth, they had to be separately insured.

1.11 It is easy to be critical of the method chosen in 1898 to effect this division between marine and war risks. It must be borne in mind that the draftsmen, whose job it was to give effect to the decision, did not have the experience that we have today with two World Wars, the Spanish Civil War, the Sino-Japanese War, the Iran/Iraq War and numerous small but dangerous wars since the Second World War, all of which have had a considerable impact upon merchant shipping. To a great extent, they were bound by precedent to the forms of exclusion which were used in the 18th and 19th centuries. They were particularly concerned not to exclude unwittingly existing cover which an error in drafting might have done and thus, unintentionally, have deprived the Assured of cover which he previously enjoyed. The 1898 F.C. & S. Clause which was to be so used read as follows: "Warranted nevertheless free of capture, seizure and detention, and of the consequences thereof, or any attempt thereat, piracy excepted, and also from all consequence of hostilities or warlike operations, whether before or after the declaration of war." ("Nevertheless" is recorded by some writers but not by others. Its effect in any case appears negligible.)

1.12 In 1901 a further attempt was made to exclude from the Marine Policy "riots and civil commotions". Although on this occasion the opposition was not quite so forceful as it had been in 1893, it was still powerful enough to compel abandonment of the attempt. The clause was still in the same form on the outbreak of war in 1914 with only minor changes; there was now a comma after "seizure" and the attempt provision now read: "or of any attempt thereat". The *Sanday* case,[3] however, drew attention to the proper character of "restraint" as a war risk. In 1916 the F.C. & S. Clause was again altered to: "Warranted free of capture, seizure, arrest, restraint, or detainment, and the consequences thereof or of any attempt thereat, piracy excepted, and also from all consequences of hostilities or warlike operations whether before or after the declaration of war."

1.13 In a 1921 case, this clause is quoted with some differences; there were commas after "thereof" and "warlike operations", and "piracy excepted" was in brackets (in some versions it already was). These differences could have had an important consequence in the interpretation of the clause. It appears, however, that there was no case where these differences became important so there is no point in discussing them here. The troubles of the world between the wars led to further redefinitions of marine and war risks so that in 1937 the 1916 version was changed to: "Warranted free of capture, seizure, arrest, restraint or detainment, and the consequences thereof or of any attempt thereat; also from the consequences of hostilities or warlike operations, whether there be a declaration of war or not, civil war, revolution, rebellion, insurrection or civil strike arising therefrom, or piracy."

1.14 It is very puzzling that Arnould's 12th edition (1939)[4] quotes the clause somewhat differently: "Warranted free of capture, seizure, arrest, restraint, or detainment, and the consequences thereof, or of any attempt thereat, piracy excepted, and also from all the consequences of hostility or warlike operations, whether before or after declaration of war." The great similarity between Arnould's text and the 1916 version leads to the belief that this may have been an oversight by the learned authors of the 12th edition in 1939 that the 1916 version was still the current text in use at the time. There are substantial differences in the

---

3. *Sanday* v. *British & Foreign Marine Insurance Co.* [1915] 2 K.B. 781. See paras. 13.17–13.26.
4. *The Law of Marine Insurance and Average* (Stevens).

two texts, particularly as the 1937 version puts piracy firmly into the field of war risks. This belief is strengthened by the facts that *The Coxwold*[5] was contested on the text of the 1937 version, and the 1937 version seems to have been the baseline for the 1943 (and last) version to which we must now come.

1.15 The *Coxwold* decision of the House of Lords was not received with any enthusiasm by the London market. The underwriters saw it as obfuscating the clear distinction between marine and war risks for which they had striven. Mr. William NcNair K.C. (later McNair J.) was instructed to draft the 1943 version. It read:

"Warranted free of capture, seizure, arrest, restraint or detainment, and the consequences thereof or of any attempt thereat; also from the consequences of hostilities or warlike operations, whether there be a declaration of war or not; but this warranty shall not exclude collision, contact with any fixed or floating object (other than a mine or torpedo), stranding, heavy weather or fire unless caused directly (and independently of the nature of the voyage or service which the vessel concerned or, in the case of a collision, any other vessel involved therein, is performing) by a hostile act by or against a belligerent power; and for the purpose of this warranty 'power' includes any authority maintaining naval, military or air forces in association with a power.

Further warranted free from the consequences of civil war, revolution, rebellion, insurrection, or civil strife arising therefrom, or piracy."

This is a very tangled clause, but again precedent prevented any thought of the "clean sweep" which would have made more easily comprehensible the London market's wish that marine and war risks perils should be separate from each other. Even so, the draftsmen of all these clauses did achieve their object to insure war risks under insurance which was separate from that which covered the marine risks and did so in such a way that no insurance cover which had previously been given was inadvertently excluded. The two policies complemented one another by a process which has been referred to as "dovetailing". On the other hand, a slightly ludicrous situation arose because the Marine Policy stated in its main body that it insured a risk, for instance pirates, and then excluded that risk by the F.C. & S. Clause so that it was insured by another policy, the War Risk Policy. This method of doing things drew some adverse comments from the judges whose views were expressed with some asperity in 1970 by Mr. Justice Mocatta. In *Panamanian Oriental SS Corporation* v. *Wright* (*The Anita*)[6] his Lordship said:

"It is probably too late to make any effective plea that the traditional method of insuring against ordinary marine risks and what are usually called war risks should be radically overhauled. The present method, certainly as regards war risk insurance, is tortuous and complex in the extreme. It cannot be beyond the wit of underwriters and those who advise them in this age of law reform to devise more straightforward and easily comprehended terms of cover. However, the form taken by the war risk cover here, since Clause 1 of the Institute Clauses only covers the risks excluded from the S.G. Form by the F.C. & S. Clause, requires one to see what cover is given by the S.G. Form on the facts, which would then be excluded from it by the F.C. & S. Clause, for it is only in respect of such exclusions that the plaintiffs can recover under the present [War Risks] Policy."

1.16 His Lordship was protesting at the mental gyrations which this process involved. When dealing with a claim under a risk which was imported into the War

5. *Yorkshire Dale Steamship Co. Ltd.* v. *Ministry of War Transport (The Coxwold)* (1942) 73 Ll.L.Rep. 1; [1942] A.C. 691; [1942] 2 All E.R. 6. See paras. 40.10–40.17.
6. [1970] 2 Lloyd's Rep. 365 at p. 371. See paras. 13.35–13.44.

Risk Policy by the F.C. & S. Clause, the court was first of all obliged to consider whether the risk was insured by the Marine Policy and, if it was, whether it was then excluded from that policy by the F.C. & S. Clause. Only if both questions could be answered in the affirmative was the court able to move to the primary duty which an action on the War Risk Policy imposed upon it, namely that of deciding whether the loss arose from a risk insured by that policy. Surely the wit of the underwriters and their legal advisers was equal to the task of finding a less labyrinthine way of providing insurance?

1.17 If that was not enough, criticism appeared from another source, the United Nations Conference on Trade and Development (UNCTAD) which reported very comprehensively on the world's marine insurance methods for both ships and cargo on 20th November, 1978. Much of this report was, and still is, regarded as very controversial, suggesting as it does some very simplistic solutions to very complex situations which, if adopted, would themselves introduce further complications and do little or nothing to resolve the problems which it identifies. There can, however, be no disagreement with what it has to say about the method of insuring war risks in its paragraph 123:

"The very concept of granting an insurance cover and excluding it in the same document (the S.G. Form), and then excluding it again in attached clauses, which override the first document in any case, and then granting it again (either in another document or as an additional attachment) by reinstating the original exclusion, is so complicated and contorted that the uninitiated is confused by the very procedure of insurance without even considering the complicated draftsmanship. The very complexity of the subject matter calls for the most simple and straightforward procedures."

1.18 This method simply confused those who had no expert knowledge or advice available to them; where there should be complete clarity, there was organised chaos and confusion. A suggested improvement is set out in paragraph 191(4). Whilst the suggestion that there should be all risks coverage with specific exceptions is probably impracticable, the general tenor of the "suggested improvement" can only be regarded as sound:

"The antiquated Lloyd's S.G. Form should be revised and updated. Specifically, the perils clause should be revised to be comprehensible in modern day context as well as to eliminate war risks terminology. Furthermore, the perils clause should be combined with other appropriate institute clauses so that the designated risks appear in one unified risks clause. Consideration should be given to altering the method of granting insurance coverage from the enumeration of perils method to an all risks grant of coverage minus specific exceptions. Consideration should also be given to facilitate the method of granting war risks insurance. All these reforms are designated to make the insurance coverage easier to understand and to interpret, particularly in view of its international use."

1.19 This was not the end of the problems of the War Risk Policy written on the S.G. Form, and there were others which Mocatta J. had no reason to touch upon, although UNCTAD, being under no similar restraints, did. It did for instance make a particularly scathing attack upon "warlike operations" as being imprecise. In addition to the insured perils imported from the Marine Policy into the War Risk Policy by the F.C. & S. Clause were a number of insured perils which were specifically insured as follows:

"Loss or damage to the property hereby insured caused by:—
    (a) Hostilities, warlike operations, civil war, revolution, rebellion, insurrection, or civil strife arising therefrom;
    (b) Mines, torpedoes, bombs or other engines of war;
    loss of or damage to the property hereby insured caused by strikers, locked out workmen, or persons taking part in labour disturbances, riots or civil commotions; destruction of or damage to the property hereby insured caused by persons acting maliciously."

1.20 This caused some duplication, never a desirable feature of any insurance policy, with the insured perils imported into the War Risk Policy by the F.C. & S. Clause even if it enlarged upon some of them. There was also the puzzling result of the wholesale incorporation of the Institute Time Clauses from the Marine Policy. Most of these dealt with the methods of claims adjustment, and the situations which could arise from total losses and with sister ships, but one, Clause 7, was the "Inch-maree" Clause which could properly be described as an insured perils clause, or a clause which provided insurance cover. The exact result of its inclusion in this way appears not to be subject to judicial review. Finally, there was the clause which resulted from the attachment of a limpet mine to the *Granwood* in 1964 whilst the ship was in Miami. It was possibly attached by Cuban exiles, although this was never certain. Because of this uncertainty, the marine underwriters were persuaded by the ship's Mutual War Risks Association that they should accept the claim for the damage which the vessel suffered. Determined that no further claim should arise from such a source, the marine underwriters inserted into the Institute Time Clauses a new clause, Number 24, in the following words:

"Warranted free from loss, damage, liability or expense arising from:
    (a) The detonation of an explosive.
    (b) Any weapon of war.
and caused by any person acting maliciously or from a political motive."

1.21 This clause, sometimes known as the Malicious Damage Clause, was imported into the War Risk Policy by slightly different wording from that used in the case of the F.C. & S. Clause in a way which raised anxious doubts in the minds of the learned editors of Arnould's *Law of Marine Insurance and Average*, 16th edition, paragraph 880.

1.22 Such vigorous criticism from the High Court and from UNCTAD, that the S.G. Form and method of insurance defied easy comprehension, required action to give both the radical overhaul they so clearly needed. It was a most welcome development that Mr. Alan Jackson and his Committee, assisted by the late Mr. Donald O'May, the solicitor who advised them, addressed themselves to this task. A new form of policy document appeared in the shape of the MAR form. New Institute Time Clauses were also produced, both for Marine Risks and for War Risks, those for cargo taking effect on 1st January, 1982, and those for ships and freight on 1st October, 1983. Whilst containers had to wait until 1987, they too were similarly treated. Special cargo insurances also received attention. Altogether it was a gigantic task.

1.23 If the Marine and War Risks insurances were still to complement one another, then the Committee had to start with the marine policy and decide which war risks were to be excluded from it. If we take the ships as an example, it will be seen from Appendix C that they are excluded from the marine insurance by Clauses 23 to 26 which are headed, and will no doubt become generally known as, the War Exclusion (23), the Strikes Exclusion (24), the Malicious Acts Exclusion (25), and the Nuclear Exclusion (26). They are set out in the Institute Clauses with the somewhat commanding heading: "The following clauses shall be paramount and shall override anything contained in this insurance inconsistent therewith." The War and Strikes insurance (Appendix D) gives insurance for these risks, except for the nuclear exclusion, in almost identical terms. There are differences, and the following chapters will attempt to explore them. The nuclear risks are not, in general, insured by either policy, but, as will be seen, in some cases, this is not an absolute concept.

1.24 By setting out the marine insured perils and the war insured perils in separate policies, it can be said that Mr. Alan Jackson and his Committee achieved with the MAR form a solution which met the complaint made by Mr. Justice Mocatta and that it is no longer necessary to refer to another document, the Marine Policy, before deciding whether the peril is insured by the War Risks Policy. But it would not be correct to say that in all cases no further reference need be made to the Marine Policy, particularly where, as in the days of the S.G. Form, the aim is that both policies should complement one another and provide an insured shipowner with the full range of cover that he requires without gaps between the two policies which could, in some cases, leave him without any insurance at all. For instance, a fire on board a ship often raises very difficult questions of how it was caused and these difficulties are increased immeasurably when the fire causes the loss of the ship in deep water where it becomes impossible, or prohibitively expensive, to examine the evidence. Was the fire caused accidentally or was it caused by a weapon of war set off by a terrorist or by a person acting maliciously or from a political motive? Was that person a member of the crew so that questions of barratry arise? In *Pan American Airways Inc.* v. *The Aetna Casualty and Surety Co.*[7] and *Spinney's (1948) Ltd. and Others* v. *Royal Insurance*[8] the courts found immense difficulty in defining the motives of the people who caused the loss, even where, in the *Pan American* case, the names of those people were known. The plaintiff claimant might find that he had no other course, as in *Munro Bryce* v. *War Risk Insurance Ltd.*,[9] but to sue both marine and war risk underwriters at the same time and arrange to have the actions heard together. This would allow the same court to decide whether "on the balance of probabilities"(Chapter 30) one or the other of the underwriters should meet his claim and avoid the situation, which could otherwise easily arise, that separate courts should hear separate actions and reach opposing conclusions on the same evidence, that both, or neither, underwriters should pay. Suing both sets of underwriters at the same time can involve the plaintiff claimant in the penalty of paying the costs of the successful underwriter and it can only be hoped that an insured shipowner would have the financial support of his Freight, Demurrage and Defence Association in the proceedings. This type of difficulty is not one that can be answered by draftsmen, however skilled, depending as it does on minute details of the facts of any particular case, and Mr. Jackson's Committee wisely refrained from any such attempt.

7. [1974] 1 Lloyd's Rep. 207; [1975] 1 Lloyd's Rep. 77. See paras. 6.16–6.26, 8.13, 8.30, 8.31, 17.13, 17.24–17.26.
8. [1980] 1 Lloyd's Rep. 406. See paras. 7.7–7.16, 8.17–8.18, 17.27–17.29.
9. [1918] 2 K.B. 78. See paras. 30.70–30.80.

CHAPTER 2

The underwriters

2.1 War risk insurance is highly specialist and the dangers of insuring the consequences of what other people do to ships contain so many imponderable factors, which are less easy to quantify than insurance against marine risks, that the number of underwriters who are willing to undertake such insurance is limited. Moreover the number of underwriters who are willing to "lead" a risk which others will follow is very small indeed. The well-recognised "leaders" are to be found in the London insurance market among the syndicates at Lloyd's, and the insurance companies who are members of the Institute of London Underwriters who are willing to give war risk insurance to merchant ships. In case it should be thought from this bare description that the capacity of the London market to give war risk insurance is limited, or that there is a monopoly among a small number of underwriters in the London market to provide it, two points should be made. The capacity of the London market is so huge, particularly when the reinsurance treaties are added to the primary war risk insurance given by the underwriters, that the London market could give war risk insurance to all the ships in the world if required to do so. Any increase in the rates will, as we have recently seen, induce other underwriters to overcome their caution and themselves enter the war risks field. This was particularly evident during the first half of the 1980s. In 1984 an attempt was made by the Committee of London War Risk Underwriters, consisting of the known leaders, to raise the annual rates of premium. This very rapidly foundered, because others saw their opportunity to enter the field by reducing rates below those agreed by the Committee, thereby attracting much business in their direction. This, incidentally, was one of the causes which led to the disbandment of the Committee in October of that year.

2.2 In this we can see an example of the efficiency of the London market, particularly where the assured is concerned. The war risk underwriters of the London market may be small in number, but their capacity to provide war risk insurance is colossal, and the forces of competition which exist in any market which is free of artificial restrictions and restrictive practices will ensure that they are never in a position to enforce a monopoly, either in the provision of the insurance or the premiums which are paid for it. A broker, attempting to place war risk insurance on behalf of a shipowner, will find no difficulty in completing his "slip" for the full amount of the insurance which he requires as soon as a leader has "scratched" the "slip" and indicated the rate of premium which he agrees with the broker.

2.3 The London market as above described, a term which we shall use throughout this work, underwrites on the MAR form with the respective Institute War and

11

Strikes Clauses attached. This form of policy against war risks for ships is found in Appendix D. It is important to appreciate that there is no requirement that the risks must be written on this form. The individual underwriters are free to make their own bargain with the insured shipowner, and frequently they do so when re-insuring risks from other underwriters or from foreign markets. In practice there is a measure of restraint upon them. A "slip" which excludes, for instance, the Automatic Cancellation and Termination of Cover Clause would not be looked upon favourably by other underwriters, who are going to be asked to follow a leader, and a "slip" which does so might not be completed. An exception to this general rule is where a large reinsurance treaty is being underwritten from a foreign market or a mutual association, both of which will require reinsurance for their original risks. Other insurers abroad also afford war risk insurance to ships, particularly in the United States, France, Germany, Italy, Norway and Japan, in the latter case by means of a consortium of underwriters. These issue their own policies. Their capacity is so limited that they find it necessary to reinsure their risks in the London market, or in some cases to give insurance for only a minimal proportion of the amount required by the shipowner. Whilst there is not total uniformity between their policies and those issued by the London market, the willingness of the London market to give war risk cover outside the Institute War and Strikes Clauses is itself very limited, and the wish of a foreign underwriter to give cover for a risk for which he does not have reinsurance is correspondingly inhibited.

2.4 Some nationalities of shipowners have followed the practice of the Protection and Indemnity Associations, and have formed Mutual Associations to give war risk cover to the members who enter their ships for insurance with these Associations. The essential difference between a market underwriter and a Mutual Association is that in the latter case, it is the individual shipowners, who are the members of the Association, who actually provide the cover on a mutual basis to any one of their number who, during the policy year, is unfortunate enough to suffer a casualty. If this should happen, then all the members of the Association will bear a share of the loss. The directing body of the Association is the Board of Directors, who are elected by the members from among their own number. The managers of the Association, who manage the day-to-day affairs, are paid a fee for their services, and are responsible to the Board of Directors and through them to the membership as a whole. The point that we must note is that the Associations are underwriters who consist of the insured shipowners, a characteristic which enables them, provided that they can retain the confidence of the market underwriters who reinsure them, to control the costs of the insurance and the claims which are paid. In other words, they provide insurance to the shipowners in accordance with the shipowners' requirements, and also manage the Association on their behalf. A shipowner who insures his war risks with an Association is given a certificate of entry which incorporates the Rule Book of the Association. These two documents together form the basis of the legal contract between the Association and the member and, in the event of a dispute, are the documents which will be considered by the courts. The Rules themselves are extremely lengthy and, because they deal in great detail with the relationship between a shipowner member and the Association, there is no purpose in burdening the reader with their provisions apart from the Rules which actually provide the insurance cover. The Rules used by the British War Risks Associations are set out in Appendix N as an example of the insurance cover which is covered by the Mutual War Risks Associations to their shipowner members. These are described at greater length in Chapter 23.

2.5 A comprehensive list of the Mutual War Risks Associations which presently provide war risk insurance cover to shipowners is:

A. The London Group of War Risk Associations. This is a pool of nine Associations providing war risk cover for British shipowners, namely:

> The Britannia Steam Ship Insurance Association Limited.
> The Liverpool and London War Risks Insurance Association Limited.
> The London Steamship Owners Mutual Insurance Association Limited.
> The Newcastle War Risks Indemnity Association Limited.
> The North of England Protecting and Indemnity Association Limited.
> The Standard Steamship Owners Mutual War Risks Association Limited.
> The Sunderland Steamship Mutual War Risks Association Limited.
> The United Kingdom Mutual War Risks Association Limited.
> The West of England Mutual War Risks Association Limited.

These Associations insure British flag and British-owned flagged-out ocean-going ships. Another Association which is outside the Group insures British-owned vessels of smaller size, such as coasters, salvage tugs and fishing vessels. As in the P. & I. field, it is considered that such vessels, which have very specialist requirements, are better served by an independent Association of their own.

B. The Hellenic Mutual War Risks Association (Bermuda) Limited.
> This Association insures Greek flag and Greek owned ships, mostly ocean-going.

C. Den Norske Krigsforsikring for Skib.
> This Association insures Norwegian flag and Norwegian–owned flagged-out ships, mostly ocean-going.

D. Krigsforsikringen for Danske Skibe.
> This Association insures Danish flag and Danish–owned flagged-out ships, mostly ocean-going.

E. Sveriges Ångfartygs Assurans Förening.
> This Association insures Swedish flag and Swedish flagged-out ships, mostly ocean-going.

F. The Canadian Shipowners Mutual Assurance Association.
> This Association insures Canadian-owned ships, some ocean-going but mostly coastal and lakers.

2.6 In addition, War and Strikes insurance is given on mutual terms by the Through Transport Mutual Insurance Association Ltd. and the Through Transport Mutual Insurance Association of Europe Ltd. to containers, trailers, and handling equipment. This includes some insurance for War Risks on Land. The insurance given by these two Associations is described in Chapter 39.

2.7 The reader is asked to note two points. In former times, the Associations only insured ships of their national flags. With the modern tendency to "flag-out", and the establishment of open registers, such a clear distinction is no longer possible. The Associations now cover ships which are owned by the nationals of their country, mostly regardless of the flags that they fly, in addition to those which fly the flags of their own nationalities. In a chapter which is only intended to indicate who are the principal insurers who give insurance cover to ships against war risks and the forms of policy which they use, and in a book which is designed to describe and comment upon that insurance cover, there is little point in commenting upon the detailed characteristics of the Mutual War Risks Associations. This is a subject which would require a volume on its own.

CHAPTER 3

The premiums

3.1 If an underwriter were to assess his premiums for the war risk insurance to merchant ships on a comprehensive or whole basis, he would have to remember that losses will occur during the following periods:

(a) A conflict between the super-powers which is most likely to be a world war or,

(b) a period of peace between the super-powers, in areas of the world which can be described by the relative term of peaceful or,

(c) a period of peace between the super-powers, in areas of the world where there are local wars or where there is a marked danger of a violent attack upon, or interference with, merchant ships.

3.2 If an underwriter were to take such an overall picture of the risks he was insuring, he would have to take into account the consequences of a world war and the stupendous losses that could be expected. His charge of premium would therefore be correspondingly high. Even if he could persuade the insured shipowners to pay it without fear of being undercut by competitors, two exceedingly doubtful propositions, he would amass an enormous sum of money with, if the prospect of a world war was remote, no apparent or immediate purpose. The presence of such money would itself pose formidable problems. Any attempt to establish it as a reserve would be challenged by the names of a Lloyd's syndicate or by the shareholders of an insurance company who would want it distributed as a profit, and also by the taxation authorities who would question whether it was a reserve for a genuine purpose. A failure to convince them would give rise to an assessment to tax. Even if these difficulties could be overcome, the additional difficulties of forecasting the possibility of a world war and its probable duration would bring into question whether this reserve was adequate to meet the expected losses. Last, but by no means least, is the consideration that possibly not even the enormous capacity of the London market would suffice to meet the claims arising from a world war, either with or without such a reserve. It is considered that only some governments, or combinations of governments bound together by treaty to one another, possess this capability.

3.3 For these reasons, the underwriter and the insured shipowner agree to concentrate on the peacetime war risk insurance as described in (b) and (c) above and to exclude from the war risk policy any insurance of risks during a world war. This is achieved in the policy, not perhaps entirely satisfactorily, by the notice of cancellation and automatic termination of cover clause, 5.2.2 (Chapter 4).

15

3.4 Confining the insurance to periods of peace between the great powers leaves two other considerations. Many ships will trade only between peaceful places where even the recently-increased risks of terrorism, piracy and confiscation by third world countries can to a great extent be contained or confined either to certain limited areas of the world, or by sensible and reasonable precautions taken on board the ship, or in the event of a casualty, by diplomatic representations, or on occasion by police or military action. Other ships will trade to areas of the world which are dangerous at the time the insurance is underwritten or which subsequently become dangerous at some time during the currency of the policy.

3.5 By the normal methods of insurance, the underwriter is required to assess his premium against his risk at the time that the insurance contract is made and cannot subsequently vary his premium until the renewal of the risk, even though the risk itself should suddenly and unexpectedly increase in a way that was never foreseen. It would, however, scarcely be welcome to the insured shipowners whose ships trade solely between such peaceful places as South Africa to the United Kingdom, Canada to Rotterdam or Western Australia to Japan to have their premiums increased at the time the contract is made because of the underwriters' fear, which may or may not turn out to be justified, that some other part of the world to which they do not trade is dangerous or should suddenly become dangerous to merchant ships at any time during the period of the insurance.

3.6 Out of these considerations, therefore, has been born the concept of two premiums. The first premium is paid for the whole period of the insurance, which will be paid for war risk insurance cover to the insured ship throughout the world. The second premium is the additional premium for visits which are made by the insured ship to geographically-defined areas which have a high element of danger to her. It contains no surprises when such areas can be agreed between the parties when the contract of insurance is made or is renewed, even if there is some surprise that the amount of the additional premium or premiums to be charged for such visits during the period of the insurance is not then agreed. What will come as a considerable surprise to many readers who come fresh to war risk insurance is the right that the underwriter reserves to himself to designate a new area at any time during the period of the insurance, which is not among the areas that were agreed at the time the insurance contract was made, and, by giving seven days' notice, require additional premiums to be paid for visits to that area. Moreover, he can also require that special terms and conditions should be applied to the insurance whilst the insured ship is within the area. The reader will object that this is nothing more than a unilateral alteration of the agreed terms of the insurance which can only be justified if there is a clear provision in the war risks policy or if there is a custom of the market which permits this; also it appears to be an imposition upon the insured shipowner which gives him little time to consult his professional advisers or his mortgagees, which he may be obliged to do.

3.7 Before coming to the explanation of why this is a long-accepted practice, it should be noted that Clause 5.1, which on its own is known as the Notice of Cancellation Clause, seems remarkably ill fitted for its purpose, bearing in mind that it must be strictly construed against the underwriter who, in all but the most exceptional circumstances, is the only party who is likely to make use of it. The first sentence seems clear enough to require no comment. The second sentence, however, would appear to confirm that the underwriter, having given the seven days' notice, must restore the cover on terms which bind him for the remaining period of the contract as to premiums and conditions of insurance. No doubt such a strict interpretation of the second sentence could be overcome by a subsequent notice every time the underwriter felt it necessary to alter the premiums and conditions to reflect either an increased or decreased degree of danger within the area concerned. This would present formidable administrative problems and a most unwelcome degree of confusion both to the underwriter and to the insured shipowner in circumstances where the need for absolute clarity is paramount.

3.8 There is also a tendency in the London market to refer to visits of the insured ship to areas which have been declared dangerous and thus require the payment of an additional premium or premiums, as "breaches of warranty" and to the premiums so payable as "breach of warranty premiums". This is an inaccurate description of the provision; whilst it is open to the underwriter to introduce additional warranties by using the machinery of Clause 5.1, this is only rarely done in practice, and it would indeed be a most unwelcome development if it was commonly done. In the context of marine insurance, warranties must be exactly complied with as will be seen from Chapter 26. It is thus a most undesirable practice to use the terms "breach of warranty" and "breach of warranty premiums" to areas which have been declared more than usually dangerous by the underwriters and to the extra premiums which are charged to visits to those areas and not only because such descriptions are inaccurate.

3.9 It appears, however, as a study of the cases which follow will confirm, that it is well understood by the underwriters of the London market, by the insured shipowners and by the courts, that the use of Clause 5.1 of the War Risk Policy is a long and well-accepted device for surcharging the owners of insured ships who trade to such areas and for imposing extra terms and conditions whilst they are within those areas in order to fulfil the requirements which appear in the earlier part of this chapter. Such expressions as "breach of warranties" and "breach of warranty premiums" can still give rise to misunderstandings, and the final reason which persuaded the mutual war risk associations to adopt in 1977 different provisions, which reflect more accurately the purpose for which Clause 5.1 is intended, can be briefly described.

3.10 Shortly after the reopening of the Suez Canal in 1975, a ship was chartered to load grain in New Orleans for discharge in Bombay and Calcutta, a voyage which could have required two to three months to perform. At the time the Suez Canal area, which would have needed little more than 16 hours to go through, was subject to additional premiums because of the fear of terrorist action against ships transiting the Canal by those persons who disapproved of its use. No other part of the voyage presented more than the usual hazards. It was for a time contended that additional premiums were payable for the whole period of the voyage. Fortunately the view of the mutual war risk association concerned was finally accepted that the premium was payable only in respect of the time spent during the passage through the Canal. In order to make the position absolutely clear, the mutual war risk associations have adopted provisions in their rules which depend upon two new and further concepts, the additional premium area and the additional premium. Their directors can, if they feel that an area is becoming more than usually hazardous, or if they find that they are required to do so by the provisions of any reinsurance treaty, declare any areas, defined as "any ports, places, countries, zones or areas (whether of land or sea)" to be "additional premium areas" seven days after notice of any such declaration is given by the association to its insured members. An additional premium area needs to be geographically defined with some degree of precision, which gives rise to no especial difficulty. If an insured ship "shall proceed to or be or remain within any additional premium area" a premium "to be arranged" is payable and there are powers for the association to stipulate terms and conditions whilst the insured ship is within the additional premium area. The insured shipowner has power to suspend his cover whilst the insured ship is within the additional premium area if he decides that he does not wish to have insurance cover with his mutual war risk association during this time. This latter provision is aimed at preventing the uncertain position arising from being "held covered" which gave rise to such difficulty in *The Litsion Pride*,[1] and also in preventing the insured owner from being forced to accept the payment of a premium and the imposition of further conditions against his will. It is suggested that the mutual war risk associations' provisions are a more accurate reflection of the arrangements, and indeed the practice of the London market, of charging the additional premiums for visits to dangerous areas than is Clause 5.1 of the War Risk Policy.

3.11 The cases referred to previously in this chapter are the most recent cases which have come before the courts on additional premiums, because there would be no point in setting out the many previous cases in any detail. The facts of *The Litsion Pride*[2] are shown at paras. 28.11–28.13. Expert advocates on each side contested it bitterly and took every conceivable point that it was possible to take. Hurst J. described them at great length in his judgment and they make the most interesting reading, being a testimonial of the skill and persistence of the English Bar. Clearly the plaintiffs would have preferred a judgment that found that they were not liable to pay additional premiums at all. But not even their highly experienced counsel considered that such a point could be taken with the remotest chance of success. *Telfair Shipping Corporation* v. *Athos Shipping Company S.A. (The Athos)*[3] was a case where the *Athos* had been withdrawn from her charter because of non-payment of amounts due from the charterer under the terms of the charterparty. In fact these were additional premiums for visits to additional premium areas which, under the terms of the charterparty, the charterers were obliged to reimburse to the owners. Neill J. ruled against the shipowners—a judgment later upheld by the Court of Appeal—but only on the grounds that the withdrawal had taken place too early. The charterers again would have preferred a position where the owner was not obliged to pay additional premiums at all, but not even his very competent legal advisers felt able to challenge that additional premiums were a fact of insurance life. Neill J. made some other findings, which were not challenged before the Court of Appeal and which are of great interest:

1. The charterer challenged the insured value of the ship which was $8.76m, whereas on a poor freight market her true value was $4m only. The court

---

1. *Black King Shipping Corporation and Wayang (Panama) S.A.* v. *Mark Ranald Massie (The Litsion Pride)* [1985] 1 Lloyd's Rep. 437. See paras. 28.11–28.13.
    2. [1985] 1 Lloyd's Rep. 437.
    3. [1981] 2 Lloyd's Rep. 74.

held that the owner could insure his ship for what value he reasonably considered right and proper.

2. The charterer challenged the cost of the insurance, pointing out that the hull and machinery of the ship could have been insured for .01%, whereas the owner had effected some extra cover and the total cost was .06%. The court held that the owners had acted prudently and were entitled to demand reimbursement for their total additional premiums.

3. The charterer objected to the freight cover, which was part of the $8.75m. The court held that since the freight insurance would be recovered in full in the event of the ship's total loss, it was properly regarded as part of the insurance of the corpus of the ship herself.

3.12 Lastly, the charterers in *Ocean Star Tankers S.A.* v. *Total Transport Corporation (The Taygetos)*[4] did not feel able to challenge the principle that some additional premiums were properly due for a visit to an additional premium area. They merely contested the amount of the additional premiums. Bingham J. ruled against them for the same reasons as Neill J.

SOME OTHER CASES ON RECOVERY OF ADDITIONAL PREMIUMS

3.13 It is not the practice of shipping to seek to recover additional premiums from voyage charterers, and there are commonly no provisions in voyage charters permitting this; additional premiums charged by the underwriters for trading to dangerous areas are supposed to be met from the freight which the shipowner receives for the discharge of his primary obligation of carrying the cargo from the loading to the discharging port, and of overcoming the obstacles placed in his way. The rights of shipowners to recover additional premiums is confined to time charterparties, and such rights will depend upon the terms of the time-charter. These will be construed by the courts with the same precision as any other agreement. In the words of Goff J. in the *Oinoussian Virtue* case: "Everything turns on the words used in the particular clause." Some notes on recent cases will serve to show how the courts have interpreted such provisions.

3.14 Marine Transport Overseas GmbH v. Unitramp and Others (The Antaios)[5]

The charterparty read:

"40. Any increase in War risks premiums for the vessel, officers and crew, after delivery to be notified . . . and the (Charterers) to pay the increase."

Goff J. agreed with the arbitrators that the charterers were liable to reimburse the shipowners only in respect of increases in the rates of additional premiums which had taken place after the delivery of the ship to the time-charterers. The case

4. [1982] 2 Lloyd's Rep. 272.
5. [1981] 2 Lloyd's Rep. 284.

went to appeal, but the Court of Appeal's judgment was purely concerned with the procedural obstacles to an appeal, and made no substantive findings.

3.15 Schiffahrtsagentur Hamburg Middle East Line GmbH v. Virtue Shipping Corporation (The Oinoussian Virtue) (No. 2)[6]

The charterparty read:

"Any additional war risk insurance premium over and above normal war risks insurance premiums . . . to be for Charterers account."

Goff J., again agreeing with the arbitrator, held that "normal" in this context meant the ordinary rate of war risks insurance as contrasted with additional premiums which related to a ship's entry to an additional premium area.

3.16 Pacific Navigation Corporation of Monrovia v. Islamic Republic of Iran Shipping Lines (The El Champion, El Challenger and El General)[7]

The charterparties were in common form (save for the omission from the *El General's* charter of the words "Persian Gulf") and read:

"68. Basic War risk insurance premium to be always for owner's account. Any extra war risks insurance premium on Hull and Machinery due to vessels trading Persian Gulf to be for Charterers account . . . "

Staughton J., overruling the arbitrator, held that Clause 68 required the charterers to reimburse the owners for additional premiums payable because the ships entered an additional premium area on their voyages to Bandar Abbas. In principle, he was willing to consider that the increased value insurance which the owners had effected came within the expression "Hull and Machinery". He felt unable to make an immediate decision on this point, as the case had to be remitted to the arbitrator for further findings on the facts.

3.17 Islamic Republic of Iran Shipping Lines v. P. & O. Bulk Shipping (The Discaria)[8]

The *Discaria* had been chartered to carry anhydrous ammonia from Qatar to Iran, and was thus going to sail entirely within an additional premium area for a considerable time. Her normal war risks insurance had been cancelled, and in its place her owners had arranged a special insurance which insured, besides the usual war risks, blocking and trapping insurance, and also loss of earnings. It was to last for 356 days at a premium of $16,000 per day. The charterparty read:

"N4. All additional war risks premiums and blocking and trapping insurance together with war risks bonus payable to officers and crew to be for Charterers account."

Staughton J. held that Clause N4 gave the owners the right to recover from the charterers the additional war risks premiums which it specifically described. They

6. [1981] 2 Lloyd's Rep. 300.
7. [1985] 2 Lloyd's Rep. 275.
8. [1985] 2 Lloyd's Rep. 489/493.

could also recover the cost of the blocking and trapping insurance, because this too was specifically described. They could not recover the cost of the loss of earnings insurance which they had never had in the past; Clause N4 did not stretch that far.

3.18 Empresa Cubana de Fletes v. Kissavos Shipping Company S.A. (The Agathon) (No. 2)[9]

The charterparty was on the Baltime Form and the relevant part of Clause 21(B) read:

" . . . the Owners to be entitled from time to time to insure their interests in the vessel and/ or hire . . . as they shall think fit, the Charterers to make a refund of the premiums."

Hobhouse J. held that this was wide enough to include the whole of the Hellenic Association's insurance, for hull and machinery, for freight, for detention, for war P. & I. and for sue and labour. He declined the charterers' plea that the Clause was only wide enough to include the insurance of the actual ship herself.

3.19 World Magnate Shipping Ltd. v. Rederi A/B Soya[10]

The charterparty, which was made in 1975 for a vessel being built especially for it, was to last for 10 years on the New York Produce Exchange Form. It read:

"47 If at any time during the currency of this Charterparty the Owners are required to pay extra premiums in respect of war risks insurance over and above that being paid at the time of delivery to the Charterers . . . Charterers are to reimburse the actual costs of such premiums to the Owners."

Donaldson J. held that it made more sense, particularly in a 10-year time-charter, that this provision should refer to increases in the liability of the owners for war risks insurance as compared with full war risk insurance covering the whole of the trading limits which they either effected, or should have effected, when the ship was delivered.

3.20 Phoenix Shipping Company v. Apex Shipping Corporation (The Apex)[11]

The charterparty read:

"53 Premium for basic war risks insurance on hull and machinery and crew always to be for owner's account but any additional premium and/or crew bonus in respect of these risks arising from the vessel proceeding at Charterer's request to areas currently or subsequently designated as excluded areas by vessel's war risk underwriters to be for time-charterer's account . . . "

Mustill J. held that this too was wide enough to include the whole of the Hellenic War Risks Association's insurance. The freight insurance in particular was included because this constituted part of the insurance of the ship herself.

9. [1984] 1 Lloyd's Rep. 183.
10. [1975] 2 Lloyd's Rep. 498.
11. [1982] 2 Lloyd's Rep. 407.

3.21 Islamic Republic of Iran Shipping Lines v. Zannis Compania Naviera S.A. (The Tzelepi)[12] and Seavision Investments S.A. v. Norman Thomas Evenett and Others (The Tiburon)[13]

These cases are often quoted as being among the cases which define the extent of the liability of the time-charterers to reimburse the owners for war risks premiums, but this is not correct. The first of these cases relates to the offer by the Iranians to give insurance through their own insurance company Bimeh, which was frequently made during the Iran/Iraq War. The case is purely concerned with the extent of the authority given to the charterers to arrange insurance while the ship was in the additional premium area of the Gulf, and properly belongs to the law of agency. The second case is concerned with whether the *Tiburon* was properly included as a German-owned ship in the special insurance arranged for German owners.

CLAUSE ADOPTED BY BIMCO MAY, 1993

3.22 The Baltic and International Maritime Council (BIMCO) has recently adopted the CONWARTIME 1993 War Clauses to replace some very out-of-date war clauses, some of which date back for more than 50 years and no longer reflect modern conditions. The clause which defines the time-charterers' liability to reimburse the owners reads:

"4(a) The Owners may effect war risks insurance in respect of the Hull and Machinery of the vessel and their other interests (including, but not limited to, loss of earnings and detention, the crew and their protection and indemnity risks), and the premiums and/or calls therefor shall be for their account.
4(b) If the underwriters of such insurance should require payment of premiums and/or calls because, pursuant to the charterers orders, the vessel is within, or is due to enter and remain within, any area or areas which are specified by such underwriters as being subject to additional premiums because of war risks, then such premiums and/or calls shall be reimbursed to the owners at the same time as the next payment of hire is due."

12. [1991] 2 Lloyd's Rep. 265.
13. [1991] 2 Lloyd's Rep. 265.

CHAPTER 4

Cancellation and Automatic Termination Clause

4.1 This clause reads:

"This insurance may be cancelled by either the underwriters or the assured giving seven days' notice (such cancellation becoming effective on the expiry of seven days from midnight of the day on which notice of cancellation is issued by or to the underwriters). The underwriters agree however to reinstate the insurance subject to agreement between the underwriters and the assured prior to the expiry of such notice of cancellation as to the new rate of premium and/or conditions and/or warranties.

Whether or not such cancellation has been given this insurance shall TERMINATE AUTOMATICALLY.

Upon the occurrence of any hostile detonation of any nuclear weapon of war . . . wheresoever or whensoever such detonation may occur and whether or not the vessel/container/insured-object may be involved.

Upon the outbreak of war (whether there be a declaration of war or not) between any of the following countries:

United Kingdom, United States of America, France, The Union of Soviet Socialist Republics, The People's Republic of China.

In the event of the vessel/container/insured-object being requisitioned, either for title or use."

4.2 The Cancellation and Automatic Termination Clause appears in the following clauses:

Clauses	*Clause No.*
Institute War and Strikes Clauses Hulls—Time 1.10.83	5
Institute War and Strikes Clauses Cargo stored afloat in mechanically propelled vessels 1.6.82	14
Institute War and Strikes Clauses Containers—Time 1.1.87	7
Institute War and Strikes Clauses Freight—Time 1.10.83	5

4.3 The clause does not appear in the War and Strikes insurance for cargo. It does however appear in a slightly different form in The Rules of the Through Transport Mutual Insurance Association Ltd. and the Through Transport Mutual Insurance Association of Europe Ltd. Part 1, Sections 1 to 4, Rules 2.4.5(b), 8.5.3(b), 9.5.3(b) and 6.4.5(b) respectively where it reads:

"(b) Insurance under this paragraph . . . shall in any event terminate automatically upon:
(1) the occurrence of any hostile detonation of any nuclear weapon of war wheresoever

23

such detonation may occur and regardless of whether the insured equipment is involved;

(2) the outbreak of war (whether there be a declaration of war or not) between any of the following countries:
France, the People's Republic of China, the Union of Soviet Socialist Republics, the United Kingdom, the United States of America."

4.4 What should be noted here is that the Through Transport insurance does not terminate automatically upon requisition either for title or use. Moreover, it is only the War and Strikes insurance which terminates; the non-War and Strikes insurance is not affected.

4.5 It may seem odd that a work on War and Strikes insurance should include in one of its earlier stages a description of how the insurance shall come to an end. Since it is almost unique in that its provisions can bring an agreed insurance to an end without the expiry of the agreed period of time, without the fault of the assured, or even without his agreement, it does seem appropriate that its provisions, and its complementary provisions, should be discussed here. The clause itself contains four separate parts which can easily be distinguished.

OUTBREAK OF WAR

4.6 The Cancellation and Automatic Termination Clause is complemented by Clause 4.1.2 (using the numbers of the ship's War and Strikes insurance). This reads:

"4 Exclusions
This insurance excludes
    4.1 loss damage liability or expense arising from
    4.1.2 the outbreak of war (whether there be a declaration of war or not) between any of the following countries: United Kingdom, United States of America, France, the Union of Soviet Socialist Republics, the People's Republic of China."

4.7 This paragraph appears in the following clauses:

Clauses	Clause No.
Institute War and Strikes Clauses Hulls—Time 1.10.83	4.1.2
Institute War and Strikes Clauses Cargo stored afloat in mechanically self-propelled vessels	3.9
Institute War and Strikes Clauses Containers—Time	5.1.2
Institute War and Strikes Clauses Freight—Time 1.10.83	4.1.2

4.8 The two Through Transport Associations have similar provisions in Part 1, Sections 1 and 4 where insurance is given against "War Risks" (definitions, para. 39.7), the Rules being numbered 2.4.4(b) and 6.4.4(b) respectively.

4.9 It can therefore be said that the combination of the Cancellation and Automatic Termination Clause, and Clause 4.1.2 means that not only is the insurance automatically terminated on the outbreak of war between the named powers, but the loss which may be caused or the damage that may be done in the incident which causes the outbreak of war is not insured either. Whether a state of war does or does not exist when the loss or damage is done may be a very moot point and this must depend on the circumstances. The question of "war" is addressed in Chapter 6.

4.10 Cargo is in a different position. Neither the Cargo War nor the Cargo Strikes insurances contain the Cancellation and Automatic Termination Clause. Consequently their insurance continues despite the outbreak of hostilities between the named powers. This is understandable, because cargo insurance is on a voyage- and not a time-basis. In addition, the cargo clauses do not contain any equivalent to Clause 4.1.2. It is true that the Institute Strikes Clauses (Cargo) dated 1.1.82 exclude "loss damage or expense caused by war . . . " (Clause 3.10) and that this exclusion is carried through the Cargo Strikes Clauses for special cargoes; this is not of importance to cargo, because the Institute War Clauses (Cargo 1.1.82) give insurance against "war", and since there is no relevant exclusion, this must mean that insurance is given for war between the named powers.

4.11 There remains the separate question of the two Through Transport Association's Part 1, Sections 2 and 3, where insurance is given against "Strikes Riots and Terrorists Risks" (but not "War Risks") (definitions, para 39.7). Rules 8.5.2 and 9.5.2 respectively exclude strikes, riots and terrorists risks arising from war. This seems wide enough to include any conflict between the named powers.

4.12 It would appear that shortly after the Second World War, it was thought fit to bring the policy to an end on the outbreak of a war between any of the five permanent members of the Security Council of the United Nations, on the basis that any such war would rapidly develop into a world war which, for the reasons explained in Chapter 3, is beyond the ability of the Lloyd's market to cover under its peacetime arrangements. It presently seems most unlikely that the United Kingdom and France would repeat their habits of past centuries and now go to war, being as they now are members of the NATO Alliance and the European Union. At one stage, it did seem likely that the U.S.S.R. and the People's Republic of China might engage in some form of hostilities over a minor frontier dispute in the Far East. Even though such hostilities would be very limited in nature, they could, if they had amounted to a "war" in the legal sense (Chapter 6), have brought the insurance to an abrupt end. In 1962 the People's Liberation Army of The People's Republic of China invaded North East India to seize disputed territory in the area of the frontier and in doing so they engaged the Indian armed forces. Some savage fighting ensued with considerable losses on each side. Although there was little possibility that this would ever be anything more than some fighting within the area of the border, and that China never intended a full-scale invasion of India, there could be no doubt that a state of war existed between the two countries. Under the Automatic Termination Clause as it then existed, the war risk cover came to an end, and there was no such insurance when immediately afterwards, a very dangerous situation developed in the Western Atlantic and the Caribbean which is known to history as the Cuba crisis. The United States demanded that Russian missiles, situated in Cuba and targeted on American cities, should be removed forthwith. This was eventually done, but in the meantime a very tense situation, with all the possibilities of a serious war risk claim, existed. The China/India conflict had thus caused the clause to operate and deprive the shipowners of their war risk insurance cover just when they most needed it in the Atlantic and Caribbean in a way that was never intended and was not justified. Fortunately, the Lloyd's underwriters agreed on request that the clause should not operate to terminate the cover. This, incidentally, is a practical example and an object lesson of how the London market works, and how the wording of the policy, which may have unfortunate and unseen results, can be dealt with by invoking the good sense and the integrity of the Lloyd's underwriters of the London market.

4.13 The wish of the underwriters to bring to an end the War and Strikes insurance on the outbreak of a global conflict must be understood and respected. It is impossible for them to insure such risks (Chapter 3), and less than honest to pretend that they can; probably only governments, or conglomerations of governments such as NATO, possess the necessary capacity. In the first edition of this work (1990), it was suggested that the insurance should terminate only upon the outbreak of hostilities between NATO and the Warsaw Pact, because at that time such a conflict presented the only realistic prospect of a world war. Now, happily, this suggestion is itself out-of-date because the Warsaw Pact has disappeared down the corridors of history. Again happily, it is most unlikely that any conflict will arise between the named powers, but if it did, then it could be expected to spread over the whole globe or at least a large part of it.

4.14 It is therefore suggested that, even though there will continue to be anomalies of the type described above, the underwriters would be quite justified in leaving the outbreak of war provision as it is, except for one change. The Union of Soviet Socialist Republics now no longer exists, and should be replaced by "The Russian Federation". This is the only part of The Commonwealth of Independent States that has any chance of engaging in a global war, and it would have the added advantage of maintaining the principle that the named states should be the five Permanent Members of the Security Council of the United Nations.

NUCLEAR DETONATION

4.15 The use of different wording in the various clauses to exclude nuclear detonations and their consequences can lead to anomalies. These are described at paras. 36.11–36.25. The purpose of this part of Chapter 4 is to set out the wording used in different instances, and to draw attention to the interaction between the exclusion clauses and the Cancellation and Automatic Termination clause where it is included in the particular insurance.

Ships and freight

4.16 The Cancellation and Automatic Termination Clause is included in the Institute War and Strikes Clauses—Time 1.10.83 and the Institute War and Strikes Clauses Freight—Time 1.10.83 which also include an exclusion clause, in each case numbered 4.1.1. It reads:

"*4. Exclusions*

This insurance excludes

4.1   loss damage liability or expense arising from
4.1.1 any detonation of any weapon of war employing atomic or nuclear fission and/or
      fusion or other like reaction or radioactive force or matter.''

4.17 It therefore seems that the insurance comes to an immediate end if a detonation is hostile, wherever in the world it may occur, but it will continue unaffected by a practice or accidental detonation. There is however no insurance for any loss of or damage done to the ship and her freight whether the detonation is hostile, in practice, or accidental.

Containers insured by the London market

4.18 The Institute War and Strikes Clauses—Containers—Time 1.1.87 contain the Cancellation and Automatic Termination Clause and a similar exclusion (Clause 5.1.1) to Clause 4.1.1. The position is exactly the same as it is for ships and for freight.

Containers insured mutually

4.19 Clauses very similar to the Cancellation and Automatic Termination Clause appear in Part 1, Sections 1 to 4 of the Rules of the Through Transport Mutual Insurance Association Limited and the Through Transport Mutual Insurance Association of Europe Limited. There are, however, different exclusions for loss or damage caused by a nuclear detonation.
4.20 In Part 1, Sections 1 and 4, Rules 2.4.4(a) and 6.4.4(a) respectively:

"You are not insured for any War Risks arising from the hostile detonation of any nuclear weapon of war.''

In Part 1, Sections 2 and 3, Rules 8.5.2 and 9.5.2 respectively:

"You are not insured for Strikes Riots and Terrorists Risks arising from . . . any hostile act by or against a belligerent power.''

4.21 The effect of these provisions is discussed more fully at paras. 39.25–39.27. Briefly, it can be said that a hostile detonation of a nuclear weapon will bring the insurance given for "War Risks" and "Strikes Riots and Terrorists Risks" to an immediate end wherever in the world it may occur, and there will be no insurance if the hostile nuclear detonation causes loss or damage to the insured object. On the other hand, a practice or an accidental detonation will not bring the insurance to an end, and neither will any loss or damage which it may cause be uninsured.

Cargo stored afloat

4.22 The Institute War and Strikes Clauses—Cargo stored afloat in mechanically propelled vessels 1.6.82 contain the Cancellation and Automatic Termination Clause. In addition, there is the following clause which reads:

"*Exclusions*

3. In no case shall this insurance cover
3.8 Loss damage or expense arising from any hostile use of any weapon of war employing
    atomic or nuclear fission and/or fusion or other like reaction or radioactive force or
    matter.''

4.23 Thus the insurance will come to an immediate end upon the hostile detonation of a nuclear weapon wherever in the world it may occur, and any loss or damage that it may cause will not be insured. The insurance will not be affected by a practice or an accidental explosion, and any loss or damage which it may do will be insured.

Cargo—War Clauses, Additional Expenses

4.24 Neither the Institute War Clauses (Cargo) 1.1.82, nor the War Clauses for Special Cargoes, and nor the Institute Additional Expenses Clauses (Cargo—War Risks) 1.7.85, contain the Cancellation and Automatic Termination Clause. The War Clauses (and also the War Clauses for Special Cargoes) contain an exclusion which reads:

"*Exclusions*

3. In no case shall this insurance cover
3.8 loss damage or expense arising from any hostile use of any weapon of war employing atomic or nuclear fission and/or fusion or other like reaction or radioactive force or matter."

The Additional Expenses Clauses have a similar exclusion in Clause 11.

4.25 A nuclear detonation wherever it may occur in the world does not affect the currency of the insurance whether it be hostile, in practice, or accidental, but any loss or damage which a hostile nuclear detonation may cause to the insured object will not be insured. A practice or an accidental detonation is however within the insurance.

Cargo—Strikes

4.26 The Institute Strikes Clauses (Cargo) 1.1.82, and the Strikes Clauses for Special Cargoes, do not contain the Cancellation and Automatic Termination Clause. They (and the Strikes Clauses for Special Cargoes) contain the following exclusion which reads:

"*Exclusions*

3. In no case shall this insurance cover
3.9 loss damage or expense arising from the use of any weapon of war employing atomic or nuclear fission and/or fusion or other like reaction or radioactive force or matter."

4.27 The detonation of any nuclear weapon, wherever it may occur, will not affect the currency of the insurance, whether it be hostile, in practice, or accidental. The word "use" gives rise to some difficulty since "use" must denote "purposeful use". If any such detonation should take place, and cause loss or damage to the insured cargo, Clause 3.9 seems sufficient to exclude hostile or practice detonations, because these are purposeful use. An accidental detonation cannot come within the definition of purposeful use, and is probably not excluded from the insurance. This matter is discussed in greater detail at paras. 36.11–36.25.

4.28 There is a lack of uniformity in the nuclear detonation clauses which do not seem to reflect the general desire of the underwriters to exclude all nuclear incidents from the scope of the insurance which they give. This also is commented on in greater detail at paras. 36.11–36.25.

REQUISITION

4.29 Most countries have powers of requisition in time of need of their own subjects' property either for title or for use. Requisition for title transfers the property to the requisitioning state, whereas requisition for use leaves the property in the hands of its original owner but allows the state to use it as it wishes. Requisition must be distinguished from Angary, which allows the state to compel a neutral to allow the state to use his property in the way it sees fit. These matters are described in greater detail in Chapter 21.

4.30 Requisition (but not Angary) can bring the insurance to an end. The justification for this is that a totally new position arises because a new person, the requisitioning authority, is introduced, and the underwriter may not wish to contract with him. Furthermore, a new set of risks become apparent which were never contemplated when the insurance contract was made.

Ships and freight

4.31 The Institute War and Strikes Clauses Hulls—Time 1.10.83, and the Institute War and Strikes Clauses Freight—Time 1.10.83 both contain the Cancellation and Automatic Termination Clause. They also contain the following exclusion clause which reads:

"*Exclusions*

This insurance excludes
4.1   loss damage liability or expense arising from (in the case of the freight insurance—loss (total or partial) or expense arising from)
4.1.3 requisition or pre-emption."

Thus the insurance comes to an end on the requisition of the ship, and there is no insurance for any loss caused by the requisition.

Containers—insured by the London market

4.32 The Institute War and Strikes Clauses Containers—Time 1.1.87 contain the Cancellation and Automatic Termination Clause. They also contain the following exclusion which reads:

"*Exclusions*

5. This insurance excludes
5.1   loss damage liability or expense arising from
5.1.3 requisition or pre-emption"

4.33 The Cancellation and Automatic Termination Clause makes it clear that it is only the insurance for the requisitioned container which terminates; the insurance for the other containers continues unaffected. The exclusion clause can only refer to the container which is requisitioned. With this sole exception, the position is the same as that for ships and freight.

29

Containers insured mutually

4.34 The Rules of the Through Transport Mutual Insurance Association Limited and the Through Transport Mutual Insurance Association of Europe Limited both contain in Part 1, Sections 1 to 4 their own version of the Cancellation and Automatic Termination Clause. This does not terminate the insurance upon requisition. There are the following exclusions which read:

Part 1, Sections 1, 2, 3, and 4, Rules 2.3.2(c), 8.3.3(3)(d), 9.3.3(3)(d), and 6.3.2(c) respectively: "You are not insured for . . . physical loss arising from nationalisation, requisition or pre-emption", and in Rules 2.3.3(b), 8.3.4(b), 9.3.5(a), and 6.3.3(b) respectively: " . . . after it has been requisitioned."

4.35 Thus the insurance will continue after the requisition comes to an end, if at that time the insurance is still current. There is no insurance for the fact of requisition of the insured item, or for any loss or damage it may suffer during the period of the requisition.

Cargo stored afloat

4.36 The Institute War and Strikes Clauses—Cargo stored afloat in mechanically self-propelled vessels 1.6.82 contain the Cancellation and Automatic Termination Clause in a slightly modified form. This reads:

"14.1.1.3 in the event of the subject matter insured or the named storage vessel being requisitioned either for title or use."

There is no exclusion dealing with loss or damage suffered by the fact of requisition. The insurance does however come to an end if the stored cargo or the vessel in which it is stored should be requisitioned.

Cargo—War and Strikes

4.37 Neither the Institute War Clauses (Cargo) 1.1.82, nor the Institute Strikes Clauses (Cargo) 1.1.82 contain the Cancellation and Automatic Termination Clause, and furthermore, there is no exclusion which deals with the fact of requisition. This pattern is carried through the War and Strikes Clauses for Special Cargoes. The insurance of cargo is thus unaffected by requisition.

CANCELLATION

4.38 The first clause of the Cancellation and Automatic Termination Clause will strike the reader as being most peculiar, and indeed draconian, in its form. How is it that the insurer, for it is principally he who will use its powers, can cancel insurance or impose different premiums and terms before it has run its course? Chapter 3 describes it, and also the ample justification, which is not apparent from its words, which lies behind it as a device for charging additional premiums when the ship enters a dangerous area.

THE MUTUAL WAR RISKS ASSOCIATIONS

4.39 Whether or not their insurance is to continue after the hostile detonation of a nuclear weapon, the outbreak of a war between the United Kingdom, the United States of America, France, the Union of Soviet Socialist Republics, or the People's Republic of China, or requisition, largely depends on whether reinsurance is available to them after such momentous events. For instance, the Hellenic (Bermuda) Association, being unable to get reinsurance without the Cancellation and Automatic Termination Clause from the London Market, or a reinsurance from its own government which is similar to that of the British Mutual War Risks Associations (Appendix P), includes this clause in Rule 4. They also include in their Rules general exclusions, which apply to the whole insurance of the Association. These read:

"3.1 Exclusion of claims arising out of war between major powers

An Owner is not insured for any loss, damage, liability, cost or expense arising out of the outbreak of war (whether there be a declaration of war or not) between any of the following countries:
3.1.1 The United Kingdom of Great Britain and Northern Ireland.
3.1.2 The United States of America.
3.1.3 France.
3.1.4 The Union of Soviet Socialist Republics.
3.1.5 The People's Republic of China.

3.2 Exclusion of certain nuclear risks

An Owner is not insured for any loss, damage, liability, cost or expense arising out of any detonation of any weapon of war employing atomic or nuclear fission and/or fusion or other like reaction or radioactive force or matter.

3.4 Exclusion of claims arising out of requisition or pre-emption

An Owner of an Entered Ship is not insured for any loss, damage, liability, cost or expense arising out of requisition of the ship, whether for title or use, or pre-emption."

4.40 In these respects therefore, the ships and freight entered with the Hellenic (Bermuda) Association for insurance are in exactly the same position as ships and freight insured by the London market. In the days of the Cold War, they, and other ships similarly placed, looked to NATO to provide their War Risks insurance. (Chapter 41).

4.41 The insurance given by the Rules of the British War Risks Associations will, however, continue after the outbreak of a war involving the five named powers. There is no equivalent of the Cancellation and Automatic Termination Clause in these Rules, and furthermore, there are no exclusions of loss or damage caused by nuclear detonations or the outbreak of war between the five named powers. On the contrary, Rule 2, Part A sets out the insurance given for losses liabilities costs and expenses caused by the "Queen's Enemy Risks", which are the risks which must arise out of war or other hostilities involving the United Kingdom. The "Queen's Enemy Risks" insurance is continuous, even when the Queen has no enemies, and are reinsured by Her Majesty's Government (Appendices N and O).

4.42 Requisition is placed on a different basis. Rule 4F.6 reads:

"4F.6 Requisition

The Association shall not be liable for any losses, liabilities, costs or expenses arising from the requisition, whether for title or use, of the Entered Ship by or on behalf of the country or the Government of the country where the Entered Ship is owned or registered or by the Government of the United Kingdom;

4F.6.1 PROVIDED ALWAYS that:

if the Insured Owner shall continue to have an insurable interest in the Entered Ship after the date of such requisition and if the Insured Owner shall thereafter sustain some further losses, liabilities, costs or expenses (such loss or damage not being the direct consequence of the requisition and not being proximately caused thereby) then nothing herein contained shall prevent recovery by the Insured Owner of such further losses, liabilities, costs or expenses."

4.43 The result of this Rule is that there is no insurance for the actual fact of requisition. If however requisition is only for use (and not for title), the insurance of the requisitioned ship continues. Rule 4F.6 was redrafted and made clearer so as to give it the interpretation placed upon its forerunner, which many complained was obscure and difficult to read during the South Atlantic War (1982), when many merchant ships were requisitioned to support the Task Force in the re-possession of the Falkland Islands. This interpretation may be summarised:

1. The owner of a ship which is requisitioned for title by the government of the country where she is owned or registered, or by the government of the United Kingdom, so that the ownership passes to the requisitioning government, has no claim for her loss because of this requisition. This applies particularly to the Detention insurance (Chapter 23). The insurance of the insured ship ceases under Rule 33.2 because the insured owner parts with her possession.

2. If a ship is requisitioned for use only (at the time, following the normal practice of Her Majesty's Government, all the ships requisitioned to support the Task Force were so requisitioned), then the insured owner has no claim because she has been requisitioned; the insurance does however continue so that she is insured for loss or damage which she may suffer during the period of requisition.

WHAT OF THE FUTURE?

4.44 The Cancellation and Automatic Termination Clause was very appropriate when it was drafted and put into use shortly after the Second World War, and it remained so during the whole period of the Cold War. A conflict which spread over the whole globe, or at least a large part of it, was only realistically likely if the five named powers entered into hostilities with each other. They alone formed the so-called "Nuclear Club" because only they possessed nuclear weapons. The provision relating to the detonation of a nuclear weapon was, in effect, only another way of describing a war between them.

4.45 In one sense, the position has greatly changed for the better in the last three years. It was not generally appreciated by the people of the West during the 1970s and early 1980s what a real and dreadful danger there was of a conflict between NATO and the Warsaw Pact. Such knowledge was only apparent to those who, like the author, were privileged to render some services to NATO. Undeniably, it was a great relief when the Eastern threat disappeared. Even if, happily, the possibility of a global conflict has much diminished, such possibility as there is, is well provided for by the "outbreak of war" provision in the Cancellation and Automatic Termination Clause. The underwriters have to have this for the reasons explained in Chapter 3 and earlier in this chapter. One alteration does need to be made. The Union of Soviet Socialist Republics no longer exists, and needs to be replaced by "The Russian Federation". Of all the States of the Commonwealth of Independent States, the former Soviet Union, only the Federation could possibly undertake a global conflict.

4.46 In another sense, the position is less happy. Nuclear proliferation has taken place. Countries such as Israel and South Africa certainly have nuclear weapons, while other countries such as North Korea, India, Pakistan, Argentina, Egypt, Iran, Iraq, Libya and Brazil either have them already or are close to having them. The provision of the Cancellation and Automatic Termination Clause, that the insurance should cease altogether on the hostile detonation of a nuclear weapon is likely to cause severe problems if it remains in the insurance. Since any use of such weapons is likely to be local (apart from the five named powers using them on each other), it could produce a very onerous and totally unnecessary result o a ship, or any other insured object, which was far from the scene. If for instance Israel should use a nuclear weapon on Iraq, it would produce great hardship for a ship, and her cargo, which was in the Pacific at the time.

4.47 It is suggested that the detonation of a nuclear weapon provision could be deleted from the clause without any adverse results on the underwriters. If the five named powers should use such weapons on each other, this would undoubtedly be war, and "war" is adequately provided for in the "outbreak of war" provision. If a nuclear weapon was used by one of the lesser powers on its neighbour, then the existing exclusion of loss or damage arising from the use of a nuclear weapon would suffice.

Representations have been made to Lloyd's on these lines. It remains to be seen if they will bear fruit before the publication of this work.

CHAPTER 5

The insured perils—some preliminary remarks

5.1 As is stated in Chapter 30 on the proximate cause, a claim against a war risk underwriter will succeed only if the loss was "proximately caused" by one of the perils for which insurance is given by the policy. In other words, the insured must show that the facts surrounding the casualty which the insured object has suffered lead to the conclusion that the loss or damage was caused by one (or more) of the perils against which the policy gives insurance cover. These perils are risks which are interpreted as a matter of law and the purpose of this and the following chapters is to consider the decisions which have been made by the courts and, where appropriate, the practices of the London market in relation to each of them.

5.2 There has been much discussion whether there is any difference between "insured perils", perhaps the older and more traditional description favoured by the MAR form and the Marine Insurance Act, or "risks covered" (sometimes simply "risks"), the terms used by the Mutual War Risks Associations. This matter is dealt with in detail in Chapter 32 but, for the purposes of this and the following chapters, it should be noted that section 2 of the Marine Insurance Act 1906 defines "maritime perils". On the other hand, several cases have dealt with "all risks" or simply "risks" and have defined how far the all embracing expression of "all risks" actually extends to give insurance cover. It is suggested that where the insurance policy sets out in well-defined lists the misfortunes which the insured object may encounter, as do the Institute Clauses and the Rules of the Mutual War Risks Associations, and states clearly that insurance cover is given in case they are encountered and the terms upon which it is given, there is no substantial difference between the two expressions. The misfortunes themselves are now well defined by a large body of case law and it can now be assumed that the meaning and extent of each separate misfortune are well-known to the parties to the insurance contract when they make it. It is further suggested that so far as insurance of ships is concerned, the concept of "marine adventure" is now much less important than it once was. In *The Bamburi*[1] Staughton J. commented at some length upon the present position (paras. 13.63–13.72) and it would appear that the concept is of importance only in such matters as general average and salvage. In modern conditions, this is not really surprising. In the days when the expression was coined, shipowners and merchants (they were often the same persons) would join together in a form of partnership to despatch a ship loaded with cargo to some far distant place where the captain or supercargo (often a partner in the venture) sold the cargo for what it would fetch

1. [1981] 1 Lloyd's Rep. 312.

and loaded other cargo which he thought would be suitable to the home market and would earn the venture a profit. There was no means of communicating with his employers or his partners and he was very much on his own. Nowadays ships are more reliable and they have the advantages of electronic navigation, better communications and better knowledge of the weather patterns. Moreover, liner and container cargoes are "booked" by the conferences' agents at the loading port and are simply loaded on to the next ship of the conference which, according to the timetable, is due to sail from that port. Bulk carriers and tankers are chartered to those requiring the carriage of cargoes, either in a contract made on an exchange or between the respective offices ashore, and the captain is simply given instructions by his head office to go to a port to load and to another port to discharge. Ships no longer engage in a "venture" or an "adventure"; they provide a service to such clients who need it on the basis that those who provide the best service at the cheapest cost will be given the business. This suggestion must not be taken as reflecting on the insurance of cargo, where the concept is, subject only to the effects of Clause 3.7 of the Institute War Clauses—Cargo (Edition 1.1.82), very much alive.

5.3 In the United Kingdom, there has been a move to codify the ancient common law on criminal offences into modern statutes on a far greater scale than was previously the case. This is not a new tendency; the Treason Act 1351 and the Statute of Forcible Entry 1381 (sometimes described as the Forcible Entry Act 1381) were similar steps taken for similar reasons in the 14th century. The first of these statutes is still law, whilst the second was only repealed in 1977 so that it could be replaced by a wider and more comprehensive measure. The legislature is naturally concerned to furnish the means to prevent and punish anti-social behaviour of a modern kind and to make sure that the forces of law and order are not increasingly frustrated because ancient law does not suffice to deal with modern misdeeds. In any case the criminal law, like the civil law, must broadly reflect the public expectation at the time of what it ought to be if it is to be acceptable and effective in a free and democratic society. To these ends there has recently been a spate of Criminal Justice Acts, which have contained substantive changes to the criminal law besides dealing with its administration, and such measures as the Theft Act 1968 and the Public Order Act 1986 are typical. The substitution of the rather more pliable rules of the common law for the rigidity of statutory definition does pose problems with the interpretation of insured perils. Many of the insured perils of the War Risk Policy involve the criminal liability of the perpetrator, and this must be so in any insurance which gives cover against what other people do to the insured object. A definition of a criminal offence at common law was not rigidly binding on a court which was considering the same offence as an insured peril in an insurance policy, where the judges felt free to give it the meaning that the two parties to the contract must have intended it to mean. Piracy (Chapter 20) has definite requirements for the proof of the criminal offence of piracy, but the rules for the proof of the insured peril of "piracy" are more general and less rigorous. Before 1987, there was greater similarity between the criminal offence of riot and the insured peril of "riot", but even here the American courts in the *Pan Am* case[2] felt justified in breaking

2. *Pan American World Airways Inc.* v. *The Aetna Casualty & Surety Co.* [1974] 1 Lloyd's Rep. 207. See paras. 6.16–6.26, 8.13, 8.30, 8.31, 17.13, 17.24–17.26.

away from the "ancient formula" when the contract of insurance concerned an air-craft, and considering what the parties to the contract must have had in mind when they agreed to the insurance of a Boeing 747. Now there is the Public Order Act 1986 (Chapter 17), which was enacted to deal more effectively with football and street hooliganism and the deplorable habit of organised gangs terrorising innocent citizens, particularly in public places. The need in the United Kingdom for this stat-ute as a criminal measure cannot be doubted, but is it to govern the insured peril of "riot" particularly when it is contained in a contract of insurance which has an international application? This would seem to lead to some strange, and possibly very unsatisfactory results. In places where riots are common there may be no diffi-culty, because such riots often involve hundreds of people intent upon mayhem to both persons and property and their very aspect can be calculated to terrify. The question could become acute where the "rioters" are small in number, possibly less than twelve. MacGillivray and Parkington on *Insurance Law*, 8th edition, Chapter 28, paragraphs 1931–1933 contains an interesting dissertation on the effects of stat-utes on insured perils and concludes:

"There is thus some conflict in the Authorities on the question whether criminal offences which are the subject of insurance should, in the absence of any definition in the policy, be defined in accordance with the definition settled in the criminal law. Thus it has been doubted whether the words 'larceny' or 'forgery' in a policy of insurance should be given their technical meaning; but the better view is probably that where terms to which the criminal law has given a technical meaning are used in a policy which offers no further definition or elaboration, such terms should be given the same meaning as that assigned to them by the criminal law."

5.4 This would seem to be a little too sweeping, even though the author does suggest that "persons acting maliciously" are more akin to those committing crimes than anything else (paras. 19.1–19.11). Even so, it is surely preferable that in deal-ing with an insured peril in an insured policy, the courts should continue to construe the policy in the light of what the parties intended should or should not be insured. It is true that in many cases the obvious intention of the parties would lead straight back to the criminal definition, but this need not necessarily be so, and neither should it be assumed to be so.

5.5 Pickford J. in the *Republic of Bolivia* case[3] seems to have been the first judge to have made a clear distinction between a criminal offence and an insured peril, whilst Goddard J. in the *Kawasaki* case[4] called for construction in "a commonsense way" having regard to the general tenor and purpose of the document which des-cribes the parties' intentions. It can only be hoped that the courts will continue to have regard to these principles, and will not regard themselves as being rigorously bound in all cases by criminal definitions.

5.6 In the chapters which follow, the main subdivisions of the insured perils of the Institute War and Strikes Clauses and the Rules of the Mutual War Risks Associations each have a chapter devoted to them, and then each insured peril is described individually. This is regarded as essential by the author because the proximate cause of any loss must be established by the insured with a considerable

3. *Republic of Bolivia* v. *Indemnity Mutual Marine Insurance Co. Ltd.* [1909] 1 K.B. 785. See paras. 20.19–20.25.
4. *Kawasaki Kisen Kabushiki Kaisha* v. *Bantham Steamship Co. Ltd. (No. 2)* (1939) 63 Ll.L.Rep. 155; [1939] 2 K.B. 544. See paras. 6.6–6.10.

degree of certainty. On the other hand it is inevitable that where a policy contains so many insured perils with a considerable degree of overlapping between them, it may well be thought that one particular example used to illustrate one insured peril may be equally appropriate to describe another. It is essential to know the facts of each case and, to avoid burdening the reader with repetition, cross-references are given to the place where the story is set out. Many of the decisions turn on questions of fact and with them the formation of the law. It is also necessary to appreciate that it is not always possible to divide the insured perils into hard and fast categories. For instance it would be very convenient if "seizure" and "detention", which is more akin to "arrest, restraint or detainment", could be regarded as so separate from one another than never the twain shall meet. The judges have not always treated them as such, and where the meanings of insured perils overlap, it is understandable that the language they have used in their judgments can blur the strict distinctions which exist. This is not unnecessarily unhelpful to the definition by the law of the insured perils or of the cover given. It does not, however, aid the reader's ready understanding where the author has divided the cases into hard and fast divisions to illustrate each insured peril, and it can only be hoped that the aim of clarity will be achieved without introducing confusion of an unwelcome nature. The mention of "military and usurped power", which is not now an insured peril, will inevitably confuse. The modern law, particularly on "revolution", "rebellion", "insurrection" and "civil commotion" so greatly depends for its evolution on the cases dealing with "military and usurped power" that it cannot be left out. Likewise, mention of "warlike operations" cannot be omitted. Subject to many and varying interpretations by the courts so that the result of any case was completely unforeseeable, and execrated by UNCTAD (para. 1.19), Mr. Jackson's Committee considered in 1983 that its intended purposes and functions would be better served by the wholly new insured perils of "war" (Chapter 6), and by "or any hostile act by or against a belligerent power" (Chapter 10) put into a different setting from its original place in the F.C. & S. Clause. Undoubtedly these new provisions, even though difficulties will arise in their interpretation, are more precise and thus more satisfactory to insurer and assured alike. Whilst "warlike operations", with all its uncertainties of what was insured and what was not insured, has thankfully disappeared from the War Risk insurance, it had an influence on the formulation of the law during the 100 years of its existence (1883 to 1983) and it cannot be entirely ignored.

5.7 A description is given of cases before the English courts with some measure of ease because there is only one High Court and cases concerning insurance policies are usually heard by the Commercial Court or the Admiralty Court, which are part of the Queen's Bench Division. All appeals go to the Court of Appeal and to the House of Lords which also hears appeals from the Scottish courts and, before Eire became a Sovereign State, appeals from the Irish courts. There is a considerable measure of uniformity in cases emanating from the United Kingdom. The same is not totally true of cases decided in the United States of America. Cases are heard either in the District or State Courts as courts of first instance depending upon a complex set of rules contained in the Constitution which govern whether some cases should be heard by the Federal Courts or by the State Courts. Appeals from the District Courts go to the Circuit Courts of Appeal within the geographically-defined jurisdiction of the District Court which heard the case; for instance the 2nd Circuit hears appeals from District Courts in New York and the eastern seaboard (including Puerto Rico), the 5th Circuit hears appeals from the southern states, and the 9th Circuit deals with appeals from District Courts on the west coast. The Circuit Courts of Appeal do not necessarily regard themselves as being bound by decisions made by each other, although they naturally take them into account when making decisions on similar points. Where a case is heard in the State Courts as courts of first instance, any appeals go to their own State Courts of Appeal. It is very difficult to appeal to the only court which deals with appeals from all over the country, the Supreme Court of the United States. The Supreme Court does not have jurisdiction to hear all appeals and will only hear appeals with leave which is only rarely given. Most of the pleadings before it are made in written briefs and oral presentation of argument is limited by time.

5.8 Australia and Canada also have federal systems, although their methods of pleading are more akin to the English, and their systems of appeal are differently organised to those of the United States. The South African courts too, although they pay more attention to the Roman–Dutch law than the common law, hear a substantial number of cases on marine insurance. All these courts frequently take into account the decisions of foreign courts and use them for guidance. Their decisions are regarded as authoritative, and the author has felt free to quote them.

CHAPTER 6

War

6.1 It will be noted that "war" is expressed as an insured peril only since the MAR form was introduced in 1983 and thus it is a new peril to the War Risks Policy. "War" was not expressed in the S.G. Form of the War Risks Policy as an insured peril although it was clearly the intention that casualties resulting from a war should be insured by that Policy. Clause 2(a) of the S.G. Form sets out as insured perils "hostilities" and "warlike operations"; F.C.& S. Clause imported into the War Risks Policy "consequences of hostilities or warlike operations, whether there be a declaration of war or not". These words gave rise to almost unimaginable difficulties of interpretation which are described in Chapter 40. The alteration to the F.C. & S. Clause in 1943 (para. 1.15) was in response to the House of Lords' judgment in *The Coxwold*[1] and was intended to ensure that only in the clearest cases would casualties, which could have been payable by either the Marine or the War Risks Policies, be paid by the war risk underwriters.

6.2 War is described in the *Oxford English Dictionary* as: "Hostile contention by means of armed forces, carried on between nations, states or rulers, or between parties in the same nation or state; the employment of armed forces against a foreign power, or against an opposing party in the state", and hostile as: "of, or pertaining to, or characteristic of an enemy; pertaining to or engaged in actual hostilities", and hostility as: "The state of fact of being hostile; hostile action exercised by one community, state, or power against another."

6.3 In *Driefontein Consolidated Gold Mines Ltd.* v. *Janson*[2] Mathew J. quoted with approval *Hall on International Law*, 4th edition, page 63:

"When differences between states reach a point at which both parties resort to force, or one of them does acts of violence, which the other chooses to look upon as a breach of the peace, the relation of war is set up, in which the combatants may use regulated violence against each other, until one of the two has been brought to accept such terms as his enemy is willing to grant."

6.4 Halsbury's *Laws of England*, Vol. 49, paragraph 101, gives the following definition: "At common law, there is no state of war between the United Kingdom and a foreign State unless the Crown has declared war or hostilities have commenced by the Crown's authority." It will be borne in mind that Halsbury confines himself to describing a war involving one State only, the United Kingdom. Never-

---

1. *Yorkshire Dale Steamship Co., Ltd.* v. *Minister of War Transport* (1942) 73 Ll.L.Rep. 1; [1942] A.C. 691; [1942] 2 All E.R. 6. See also Chap. 40.
2. [1900] 2 Q.B. 339 at p. 343.

theless this definition of war has some bearing, although only a limited one, on our considerations.

6.5 Over a series of cases, the courts have made it clear that when they are considering a commercial document such as a war risks policy, they are not going to be bound by narrow definitions, even those as authoritative as the ones which are quoted above. They are only willing to consider the intention of the parties as disclosed by the documents and then proceed to give the documents the meaning which the parties obviously intended they should have. If the parties include "war" in their contract and provide that certain consequences are to follow, "war" will be given its normal and popular meaning. This must mean that these definitions will have a persuasive effect only and will not be a binding authority which allows for no deviation. The individual facts of any case will be closely considered.

6.6 Two cases in particular will serve to show the view which the English courts will take and it is worth while to go into them in considerable detail. The first is *Kawasaki Kisen Kabushiki Kaisha* v. *Bantham Steamship Company Ltd. (No. 2).*[3] The court was considering a charterparty, which gave both parties the "liberty of cancelling this charterparty if war breaks out involving Japan". After the date of the charterparty, the Sino-Japanese War broke out and, on 18th September, 1937, Bantham, by notice, withdrew the ship, thus cancelling the charterparty. Kawasaki claimed that this cancellation and withdrawal were wrongful and commenced arbitration proceedings. The case made its way as a case stated to the High Court and the Court of Appeal.

6.7 On 15th August, 1937, Japan had charged China with making war preparations against her and stated that her patience was exhausted. Certain elements of the Chinese army had entertained aggressive intentions towards her and must be "chastised". The Nanking Government must be impressed with the necessity to reconsider its attitude towards Japan which stated that it had no territorial designs. The umpire (the arbitrators having failed to agree) found as facts that:

(1) There had been no declaration of war by either side,

(2) diplomatic relations between the two countries had not been severed; both countries maintained their Embassies in each other's capitals,

(3) by 19th September, 1937, 50,000 Japanese troops, backed by their fleet and airforce, had engaged 1,500,000 Chinese troops in the neighbourhood of Shanghai, and that 100,000 Japanese troops with artillery and aircraft had engaged 300,000 Chinese troops in northern China. Over 50 battles, mostly of a ferocious nature, had been fought with many killed and injured on each side,

(4) the Japanese Navy had blockaded the Chinese coast,

(5) the United States had appealed to both sides not to resort to war (Kawasaki claimed that the U.S. Neutrality Act had not been invoked although there was no finding to this effect), and

(6) on 29th August and 2nd September, 1937, Japan had further described her purpose. She desired to obtain a drastic improvement in China's attitude and to purge aggressive intentions, mostly in the Chinese army, towards her. China deserved to be "beaten to her knees" and thereafter

3. (1939) 63 Ll.L.Rep. 155; [1939] 2 K.B. 544.

governed by Japan. There was not a state of war between the two parties but merely "a major conflict".

On all this, the umpire found that there was a "war" subject to the decision of the courts.

6.8 In the High Court, Goddard J. approved this finding and dealt with the quotation of Mathew J. which is set out above. He did not consider this quotation as exhaustive. Some people chose to think that China had not chosen to look on Japan's actions as a breach of the peace and, indeed, she had not so declared. On the other hand, the resistance of her armies indicated that she so regarded it. The parties to a contract are not concerned with the niceties of international law. They "intended the word 'war' to be construed as war in the sense in which an ordinary commercial man would use it".

He considered that the same principles of construction applied as those applied by Pickford J. in *Republic of Bolivia* v. *Indemnity Mutual Marine Insurance Company*.[4] He also dealt with the certificate of H.M. Foreign Office, a point which was also pleaded before the Court of Appeal.

6.9 On appeal, Kawasaki pleaded three points. First, "war" does not have a loose or popular meaning but a technical meaning which is to be found in the principles of international law. Secondly, the courts are bound by the opinion of the Foreign Secretary whether a state of war exists between two Sovereign States and must accept his certificate as conclusive. Thirdly, there can be no war unless there is *animus belligerendi* between the two States. The unanimous judgment of the Court of Appeal was given by Lord Greene M.R. in the robust fashion one comes to expect from such a source. International lawyers speak with many tongues and his Lordship had no idea what were the principles of international law. He dismissed this " . . . to say the English law recognises some technical and ascertainable description of what is meant by 'war' appears to me to be an impossible proposition".

6.10 *Animus belligerendi* received similarly short shrift. The court had heard argument but was none the wiser. When armies were locked together in battle, there must be *animus belligerendi* whatever this might happen to be. Regarding the Foreign Secretary's certificate, its terms were far from conclusive. The Foreign Secretary had declined to express a view one way or the other and had added a pithy comment that it was not for him to decide the rights or wrongs of a commercial contract. For our purposes we need to note the final conclusion of the court: " . . . in the particular context in which the word 'war' is found in this charterparty, that word must be construed, having regard to the general tenor and purpose of the document, in what may be called a commonsense way".

6.11 The second case which needs full consideration is *Pesquerias y Secaderos de Bacalao de España S.A.* v. *Beer*.[5]

The plaintiffs were the owners of six ocean-going fishing trawlers based on Pasajes in North Western Spain. On 3rd July, 1936, they effected an insurance

---

4. [1909] 1 K.B. 785. See paras. 20.19–20.25. This principle has also been followed in *National Oil Company of Zimbabwe (Private Ltd. and Others* v. *Sturge* [1991] 2 Lloyd's Rep. 281; the *Mozambique* case (paras. 8.22–8.26) and in *Athens Maritime Enterprises Corporation* v. *Hellenic Mutual War Risks Association (Bermuda) Ltd.* [1982] 2 Lloyd's Rep. 483—*The Andreas Lemos* case (paras. 20.33–20.38).
5. (1945–46) 79 Ll.L.Rep. 417; (1946–47) 80 Ll.L.Rep. 318; (1948–49) 82 Ll.L.Rep. 501; [1949] 1 All E.R. 845.

policy with the defendant underwriters (represented in the proceedings by Mr. Beer) containing the following clause:

"This insurance is only to cover loss or damage to the within insured interest caused by strikers, locked out workmen or persons taking part in labour disturbances or riots or civil commotions arising from incendiarism, use of explosive bombs or other engines of destruction or from any other malicious act whatsoever by any persons, including general average, salvage and salvage charges as a direct result of malicious damage not recoverable under the Marine Policies. Excluding war risks and excluding all other risks ordinarily covered under the vessel's marine policy."

It will be noted from the account which follows that the policy was effected after the disturbances of the Spanish Civil War had commenced. It seems that neither party took any point on this fact.

6.12 In February, 1936, the Spanish General Election returned the Republican Government, which contained many extreme left-wing elements, to power. The Government seems to have lost no time in declaring (17th February, 1936) a "state of alarm" which had the effect of suspending certain laws. It is not clear from the judgments if the unrest preceded this declaration or only resulted from it and no points in the House of Lords' decision turn upon it. On the 18th July, 1936, General Franco landed in Spain from Spain's African colonies and by a *pronunciamiento* declared that a state of war existed. Nearly all the military commanders in Spain rose in his support as did most of the regular police. In particular General Mola, the army commander in Pamplona, declared for Franco and set about the conquest of the north-western provinces of Spain in his name. The garrison at San Sebastian rose in his support although the Government later managed to subdue it. By the end of July, 1936, General Mola's troops were within 10 to 15 kilometres of Pasajes and San Sebastian. He was also making considerable progress in his first military aim, namely to cut this part of Spain off from France, although he only achieved this fully by the capture of the frontier towns in the first week of September, 1936.

6.13 Faced with the defection of all but a few of the regular armed forces of the State and the police of the country, the Government had no choice but to raise a militia from its citizens if it was to continue to exist. At first the militia had few arms and no uniforms other than armbands. The Government attempted to impose military discipline upon its militia but, at least in the early stages, with many criminal elements among its ranks, even such limited restraints as military discipline manages to impose on trained and regular troops in scenes of retreat and armed political upheaval were conspicuously absent. This goes far to explain the facts of this case and the nature of the pleadings of the plaintiffs. Nevertheless, the civil governors of the provinces did have some success in resisting General Mola's men and in maintaining some form of law and order in the territory under their control although, in the nature of things, this was only of a limited nature. They also had considerable difficulty in controlling their men, and formal requisition to furnish them with what they needed to fight a war, observing the forms required by the law, was beyond them. The Government was fighting for its life and its often unruly men took what they needed. Besides taking what could justifiably be required for military purposes, there was a considerable amount of looting and violence to those who opposed them. The scenes in the plaintiff's fish processing factory in Pasajes where four of the trawlers were berthed can be imagined when the trawlers were required for Government service. There was no polite if firm service of a requisition order by a naval officer or a ministry official; a large and angry mob took what it needed with a minimum of explanation.

6.14 Other factors also weighed with the court. On 6th August, 1936, one trawler was sent from Pasajes to Bilbao where she was fitted with a naval gun. On 17th August, 1936, Bilbao was shelled by a Franco warship and the coast was being patrolled by other warships which had sided with him. In early September, 1936, San Sebastian was bombed and was also shelled by a Franco cruiser. On 8th September, 1936, the day that General Mola's troops entered Pasajes, the remaining three trawlers were despatched to Bilbao carrying militiamen, military stores and refugees. General Mola further captured San Sebastian on 13th September, 1936. On 5th March, 1937, the armed trawler was sunk in a battle with a Franco warship. Another trawler was scuttled, being later raised and handed back to her owners. The remaining two trawlers eventually escaped to a French port, whence they were returned to their owners with the loss of much of their gear.

6.15 In the High Court, Atkinson J. found on the facts that a loss had arisen on the policy and gave judgment in favour of the plaintiffs. This judgment was unanimously reversed by the Court of Appeal and in the subsequent further appeal to the House of Lords, the judgment of Lord Greene M.R. in the Court of Appeal was cited with much approval. In the House of Lords, Lord Porter delivered the main speech with which the other Lords, with only minor variations, unanimously agreed. Lord Porter found it necessary to draw different conclusions from the facts from those drawn by the trial judge and meticulously did so. The following passages from his speech are of concern to us:

"The crux of the matter is, was there a civil war or not? In my view there plainly was . . . "

"Finally it was argued that civil war was not excepted from the risk on the grounds that the word 'war risk' did not include war between nationals of the same country. So far as the Court of Appeal was concerned the argument was untenable, the contrary having been decided in *Curtis & Sons* v. *Matthew* [1919] 1 K.B. 425."

" . . . In my opinion, the exclusion of 'war risks' applies. It is common ground that this phrase is not a term of art. I am prepared, for present purposes, to interpret it in what appears to me to be the narrowest sense of which it is capable, namely, as excluding the risk of loss or damage of which the proximate cause is war. I see no grounds whatever for excluding civil war from the scope of that expression. The suggestion that there was no civil war, or that if there was anything resembling civil war, it did not attain to that size or intensity necessary to bring it within the exception, I have already dealt with sufficiently in my examination of the facts . . . It was the war that was in each case the proximate cause of the taking [of the trawlers]."

From these cases, it would seem that the insured peril of "war" is reasonably well settled in English law even though it has only been an insured peril in the War Risk Policy since 1983 and there are so far no decisions of the English courts which consider it in that context.

6.16 American decisions have been expressed in a somewhat different way and it is worth examining in some detail *Pan American World Airways Inc.* v. *The Aetna Casualty and Surety Co.*[6]

---

6. The District Court's decision is to be found in [1974] 1 Lloyd's Rep. 207 and the Circuit Court of Appeals' decision in [1975] 1 Lloyd's Rep. 77.

On 6th September, 1970, two men, Diop and Gueye, attempted to buy air tickets on El Al's flight from Amsterdam to Tel Aviv. El Al's staff became suspicious and refused to sell them. They then bought tickets on Pan Am's 747 flight from Brussels and Amsterdam to New York. Pan Am's staff seem to have been equally suspicious but, after searching them, sold them tickets and allowed them to board their aircraft. How they managed to smuggle weapons on board is not clear but 45 minutes after take off, whilst over London, they had the means to coerce the crew into flying the plane to Beirut. Their original intention was to land the plane at Dawson's Field, an airstrip in the desert in the northern part of Jordan, where their colleagues had already assembled or were in the process of assembling three other hijacked planes belonging to T.W.A., Swissair, and B.O.A.C. They were persuaded by the plane's captain that it was impractical to land a 747 at Dawson's Field and, with some difficulty, the Lebanese authorities were persuaded to let the plane land in Beirut. There Diop and Gueye were joined by eight or nine other men who placed explosive charges on board the plane and wired them together. After refuelling, and with one of the Beirut men accompanying them, they forced the crew to fly to Cairo. There the passengers and the crew were allowed to disembark and the three men then destroyed the plane by detonating the explosives.

6.17 It was found as a fact that Diop and Gueye were members of the Popular Front for the Liberation of Palestine (P.F.L.P.). The court further found as facts that the P.F.L.P. was a radical political group dedicated as its name implies to the recovery of Palestinian land in Israel and the expulsion therefrom of the Israelis. It was not a "State", and Diop and Gueye were not acting on the authority of any of the States where the Front was based, if only because these States disapproved of hijacking. For the most part it was based in Jordan, whence it carried out raids on Israel. Its relationship with the Jordanian authorities was not a happy one. Shortly after the hijackings referred to the P.F.L.P. was expelled from Jordan by the Jordanian Army, which proved that it was willing to use very considerable force to achieve this objective. During the Pan Am flight the following announcement was made and leaflets were handed out to the passengers:

"P.F.L.P. is speaking. Why do we take the airoplane? We took the American airplane because the government of America helps Israel daily—the government of America gives Israel fantom airoplanes which attack our camps and burn our village. We—the group of AKA—which is following for p.f.l.p. know that by warning the people of America for the crimes and murders which is committed always on Palestine and Vitnam—make him feel how his government helps the Zionism.

We left our homes, and our lands 20 years old. Every day the Jews attack us—in our camps—we think that by our work make you know the truth.

We are sorry for what we make of disturbance but you must understand us."

6.18 Pan Am was insured by Aetna under an "all risks" policy with the following exclusion:

"C. This policy does not cover anything herein to the contrary notwithstanding loss or damage due to or resulting from:–
  1. Capture, seizure, arrest, restraint or detention or the consequences thereof or any attempt thereat, or any taking of the property insured or damage to or destruction thereof by any government or governmental authority or agent (whether secret or otherwise) or by any military, naval or usurped powers, whether any of the foregoing be done by way of requisition or otherwise or whether in time of peace or war and

whether lawful or unlawful (this subdivision 1 shall not apply, however, to any such action by a foreign government or foreign governmental authority following the forceful diversion to a foreign country by any person not in lawful possession or custody of such insured aircraft and who is not an agent or representative, secret or otherwise, of any foreign government or governmental authority).

2. War, invasion, civil war, revolution, rebellion, insurrection or warlike operations, whether there be a declaration of war or not.

3. Strikes, riots, civil commotion.''

(Both the District Court and the Circuit Court of Appeals noted that by 1970 ''hijacking clauses'' had been drafted and were in use, but that they were not used in the insurance contracts in this case.)

6.19 A war risks policy was effected to cover Pan Am in respect of these excluded risks, the cover being given by London underwriters and by the U.S. Government. Aetna took every possible point on the perils excluded by this exclusion clause that it could do including some that seemed to have only the remotest chance of success. Their assertions were vigorously contested by the war risk underwriters and by the U.S. Government and the result was that the District Court and the Circuit Court of Appeals were obliged to make a whole-scale review on the law relating to most of the perils insured by war risks policies. Such a recent review by such senior and well-respected courts is of the greatest value.

6.20 First, both courts addressed themselves to the insured perils of ''war'' and ''warlike operations''. From the judgments it seems that neither court made separate distinctions between the two insured perils, and it must be borne in mind that the two hearings took place in 1974 and 1975, nearly 10 years before the MAR form appeared in 1983, and at a time when the necessity for separate distinctions was not as apparent as it is today. For the reasons set out in Chapters 30 and 40 in particular, it would be absolutely essential that, in any similar case that is heard today, the important necessity for separate and clear distinctions should be urged upon the court which should be discouraged from equating them, or regarding them as broadly similar in the way that the District and Circuit Courts of Appeal felt justified in doing. The Circuit Court's judgment was given by Circuit Judge Hays who noted with approval the District Court's judgment: ''The term 'war' has been defined almost always as the employment of force between governments or entities essentially like governments at least *de facto*'' and added his own finding: ''The cases establish that 'war' is a course of hostility engaged in by entities that have at least significant attributes of sovereignty.''

The Circuit Court noted with approval the following cases:

6.21 Vanderbilt v. Travellers Ins. Co.[7]

Mr. Vanderbilt effected a life policy which excluded death by ''war''. In 1915 he was drowned when a U-Boat sank the *Lusitania*. Germany, whose naval forces sank the *Lusitania*, was undoubtedly a Sovereign State. Even though Mr. Vanderbilt was not a combatant, his death was caused by ''war''.

---

7. 112 Misc. 248; 184 N.Y.S. 54 (S.C. N.Y.C., 1920).

6.22 Welts v. Connecticut Mutual Life Insurance Company[8]

During the American Civil War, Mr. Welts was working with a repair gang on a railroad 30 miles to the rear of General Thomas's Union Army. Four men armed with revolvers but wearing no uniforms or military insignia robbed the gang and killed Mr. Welts. It seems that the underwriters were held to have failed to prove their case that the four men were members of the Confederate Army. Had they succeeded in doing so the findings of the court would probably have been that Mr. Welts was killed as a result of "war". In the circumstances, the court found that the proximate cause of his death was highway robbery.

6.23 Schneiderman v. Metropolitan Casualty Company[9]

Mr. Schneiderman was killed by artillery fire in Egypt after the cease-fire enforced by the United Nations upon Israel, the United Kingdom, France and Egypt following the fighting around the Suez Canal in 1956. His death, since it occurred after the cease-fire, was held not to be due to "war". (In the circumstances this does seem to be rather a surprising decision.)

The Circuit Court also noted the following decisions in connection with "warlike operations":

6.24 Swinnerton v. Columbian Insurance Company[10]

The vessel *Lawrence Waterbury* was seized and sunk in Hampton Roads in 1861. A marine policy contained a form of F.C. & S. Clause. The fighting between the Union (the North) and the Confederacy (the South) had not yet broken out, although it did so shortly afterwards. The court held that there was in fact a "war", even though war had not been declared and that, at the time, there was a *de facto* government in the south.

Three other cases arising out of the American Civil War seem relevant under the heading of "war" but since they are mainly concerned with "military or usurped power" they are dealt with under this heading and are simply noted here. They are of particular interest because the courts recognised that, during the Civil War, the Confederacy was governed by a government which had at least *de facto* status.

6.25 Barton v. Home Insurance Co.[11]; Insurance Company v. Boon[12]; Portsmouth Insurance Co. v. Reynolds[13]

Another more modern case needs to be noted:

8. 48 N.Y. 34 (1871).
9. 14 App. Div. 2d 284; 220 N.Y.S. 947 (1961).
10. 35 N.Y. 174 at pp. 186–188 (1867).
11. 42 Mo. 156 (1868). See para. 8.14.
12. 95 U.S. (5 Otto) 117 (1877).
13. 73 Va. (32 Gratt.) 209 (1880). See para. 8.14.

6.26 Hamdi and Ibrahim Mango Company v. Reliance Insurance Company[14]

Hamdi's automotive parts were destroyed by mortar fire during the battle for Haifa. It seems that this was a casualty of the 1948 battles when the Arab powers were seeking to subdue and destroy the infant State of Israel. The District Court and the Circuit Court of Appeals, relying on *Swinnerton* v. *Columbian Insurance Company*, both held that the loss was due to "hostilities and warlike operations". It would also seem that whilst the State of Israel was not yet fully formed with a fully *de jure* government, both courts were satisfied that, at the time, Israel was ruled by a government which could at least be described as having *de facto* status.

Applying the tests and the cases which are quoted above, the Circuit Court of Appeals held in the *Pan Am* case that the loss of the 747 was not due to a "warlike operation", and by inference a "war", in the following terms:

"There is no basis whatever for any claim that the insured, Pan American, was involved in a 'warlike operation'. It carried no cargo of military stores. It carried no cargo destined for a theatre of war. Its owner was not the national of any middle eastern belligerent. Pan Am serves no routes to any middle eastern belligerent. When the loss occurred, the aircraft was not near or over the territory of any belligerent or any theatre of war."

Clearly the Circuit Court felt it had already adequately dealt with Diop and Gueye and the P.F.L.P; in spite of their protestations to the contrary, they also were not at war in the sense that the insured peril of "war" is understood in an insurance policy.

6.27 It may however be dangerous simply to assume the insured peril of "war" can be compared in all respects to an elephant, very easy to recognise in any of its separate breeds but very difficult to define in a totally comprehensive and inclusive fashion to someone who has never seen one, when one considers the courses that some of the recent wars have followed and their natures. The following examples are offered for consideration:

6.28 (1) On 3rd September, 1939, the United Kingdom declared war on the German Reich. The fighting came to an end on 8th May, 1945, and in 1948 and 1955 peace treaties were signed respectively with what are now the States of the Federal Republic of Germany and Austria. No peace treaty was signed with the German Democratic Republic, which in 1939 was part of the German Reich, until 1978. Long before that date, however, the two countries were trading with each other and were exchanging trade delegations. A nationalised German Democratic Republic company fought at least one case in the English courts. The ships of each country visited each other's ports. Businessmen came and went. Visas were issued to U.K. citizens, at first argumentatively but later freely. It would be difficult to contend that, after the Armistice in May, 1945, which was signed by German representatives whose authority extended to what, until 1990, was the German Democratic Republic, there was a "war" between the two countries except in the most narrow and legalistic sense of the kind which the courts in the *Kawasaki*[15] case refused to accept. The observations of the courts in *Board of Trade* v. *Hain Steamship Com-*

14. 291 F 2d 437 (1961).
15. *Kawasaki Kisen Kabushiki Kaisha* v. *Bantham Steamship Co. Ltd.(No. 2)* (1939) 63 Ll.L.Rep. 155; [1939] 2 K.B. 544. See paras. 6.6–6.10.

pany Limited,[16] that there could not be a loss by "hostilities" after an armistice, tends to reinforce this view, even though Lord Buckmaster, Viscount Dunedin, Viscount Sumner and Lord Warrington recognised that the Armistice on 11th November, 1918, was no more than a temporary cessation of hostilities, and that the First World War was not at an end when the casualty happened on 25th December, 1918.

6.29 (2) In 1950, North Korea invaded South Korea and in answer to a resolution of the Security Council of the United Nations several countries came to the aid of South Korea. Most prominent among these was the United States but there were also contingents from (amongst others) the United Kingdom, Australia, New Zealand, India, Greece, Belgium and Turkey. Subsequently, China came to the aid of North Korea. The troops of all these countries (excepting India) were heavily engaged in some savage battles; Indian troops were not engaged in any of the fighting, the Indian contingent consisting only of non-combatant troops in a field hospital. Throughout, the British Embassy in Beijing remained open and British ships, some of them in a liner service, visited Chinese ports. Greek ships also visited Chinese ports. No ships were interfered with by the Chinese authorities. From start to finish nobody declared war on anyone else and the fighting came to an end with an armistice in 1953. It would seem doubtful if there was a war between any of these nations, with, of course, the exception of North and South Korea, in the sense that the word is normally understood, other than in the immediate area of the fighting.

6.30 (3) In 1948, the Egyptian armed forces invaded the infant State of Israel and were repulsed. There were some savage battles when Israel invaded Egypt in 1956 and 1967 and Egypt attempted to recover lost territory in 1973, but these conflicts were of short duration only. In between there were periods of uneasy calm punctuated only by border raids on each side. Yet, until the final Peace Treaty in 1979, each side considered itself at war with the other and did not hesitate to inflict economic damage on the other when the opportunity arose. Israeli ships were not allowed through the suez Canal. Egypt would not allow ships of other nations which had visited Israel into her ports. It is suggested that throughout the entire period from 1948 to 1979 the two countries were at "war" in the sense with which we are concerned, if only because they both considered themselves to be at war and acted accordingly.

6.31 (4) From the start of the 20th century, Argentina laid claim to the Falkland Islands, becoming particularly insistent in the period following the Second World War. Her claim embraced all the territories which were administered under the title of the Crown Colony of the Falkland Islands and its Dependent Territories. Such territories included the Falkland Islands themselves, South Georgia and the South Sandwich Islands. During the 1970s Argentina established a research and scientific station on South Thule in these latter islands. This drew forth a protest from the United Kingdom but nothing more. It is not necessary to go into all the details of the respective claims of the two countries except to note that, as the successor of some of the territory of the former Spanish empire, Argentina's claim to the Falkland Islands, which she had been dissuaded from exercising by the threat of force in

16. [1929] A.C. 535.

1833, was not devoid of legal merit. A claim to the other territories was at best doubtful; the Spanish empire was not even aware of their existence and they were discovered and claimed for the United Kingdom by Capt. Cook in the 1770s. On the other hand, it could be said that the United Kingdom had acquiesced in the occupation of South Thule. When Argentina invaded the Falkland Islands on 2nd April, 1982, quickly overcoming the determined resistance of the small British garrison stationed there, she could claim that she was doing no more than ejecting trespassers and was using no more than reasonable force in a way that the law permits. There was a similar brisk action on South Georgia during which an Argentine warship was badly damaged. British soldiers taken prisoner were not interned in prisoner-of-war camps but were promptly sent home. No promise was obtained from them by their Argentine captors that they would not serve in any further hostilities against her; indeed, some of them actually did so.

At this, the United Kingdom protested vigorously. A strong military and naval force was promptly despatched with the object of regaining possession of the disputed territories. Having 8,000 miles to cover and some formidable logistic problems to overcome, it would be some time before it could reach the scene. In the meantime, the United Kingdom undertook a vigorous diplomatic offensive and asserted her own very strong legal claim to the territories before the Security Council, with the aim of securing the departure of unwelcome visitors by diplomatic means rather than by warfare. The United States' Secretary of State engaged in "shuttle diplomacy" between Washington, London and Buenos Aires. This took almost the whole of April, 1982, and, during this time, there was always doubt whether the British armed forces would ever engage their Argentine opposite numbers; either they would not be able to overcome the obstacles posed by distance and the imminent onset of winter, or there would not be the political will in the United Kingdom to undertake hostilities, or world opinion would frown upon such an undertaking to the extent of making it impossible.

Any such doubts were dispelled when on 25th April, 1982, the British armed forces compelled the surrender of the Argentine garrison on South Georgia, in the process sinking an Argentine submarine. The United Kingdom had previously drawn a "total exclusion zone" around the Falkland Islands requiring all others to keep outside it. This zone did not touch the neighbouring Argentine coast. The inference was that attacks on Argentina's armed forces would only take place inside it, although in early May, 1982, a British submarine sank the *General Belgrano* whilst she was a short distance outside it. On 1st May, the British armed forces bombed the Argentine garrison on Port Stanley airfield. Shortly afterwards, there were further air attacks and each side sank the other's warships. On 21st May, the British armed forces landed on the Falkland Islands and on 28th May engaged in the first of a series of land battles which culminated in the Argentine armed forces' surrender on 14th June, 1982. During the whole period from 2nd April onwards, there was no interference with British ships which happened to be in Argentine ports at that date and no action was ever taken against British subjects in Argentina, of which there was a considerable colony. British journalists came and went in and out of Buenos Aires during May and June, 1982, and even interviewed some senior Argentine political and military figures.

6.32 The difficulty here is to decide when a state of war existed and what was its geographical extent. It would appear that there was undoubtedly a state of war between 25th April, 1982, (the British attack on South Georgia) and 14th June, 1982 (the date of the Argentine surrender in Port Stanley). Furthermore that this state of war existed between these dates only within the total exclusion zone around the Falkland Islands and in the neighbourhood of South Georgia. It could also be said that a state of war also existed in the neighbourhood of the South Sandwich Islands on the 19th June, 1982, when the British armed forces compelled the evacuation of the Argentine research and scientific station on South Thule. It is suggested, however, that there was no state of war along the Argentine coast which (apart from some rumoured operations by specialist troops which may or may not have taken place) the British armed forces studiously refrained from attacking. Nor was there ever an all-out war with Argentina in the sense of the two World Wars. Whilst no peace treaty has ever been signed, and will not be signed until some solution on the disputed territory can be agreed between the two nations, it is further suggested that there has not been a state of war in any area of the world between the United Kingdom and Argentina since 14th June, 1982. The two countries trade with one another (albeit through intermediaries) and visas are granted for British and Argentine nationals to visit one another's countries, even though neither allows visits by the ships of each other to their ports and the national airlines of each country have not yet been allowed to resume their previous services.[17]

6.33 (5) The Gulf War 1990 to 1991 did not present quite the same difficulties as are demonstrated by the previous examples of determining whether a state of war existed between Iraq and the States of the Alliance that was formed against her; the difficulty here is determining when the state of war came into being and when it ended (if indeed it has yet ended) and who were the parties. On 2nd August, 1990, Iraq invaded Kuwait and, rapidly overcoming some determined resistance by the Kuwaiti armed forces, occupied the entire country. A series of resolutions by the Security Council ordered her to leave at once, and when these were disregarded, authorised the imposition of sanctions. An armada of ships belonging to a large number of states was assembled to enforce them. This amounted to a naval blockade which commenced in early August. Even the port of Akaba was blockaded to prevent supplies, whether for military or civilian use, reaching Iraq through Jordan. Meanwhile, fearing that the aggressive Iraqis were about to invade Saudi Arabia, a huge military and air force was assembled in that country to prevent any such attempt. Primarily, these came from the United States, although they were complemented by substantial contingents from, amongst others, the United Kingdom, France, Italy, Syria, Egypt, and Pakistan, besides of course Saudi Arabia and such of the Kuwaiti armed forces which had managed to escape. Its primary purpose was, until mid-November, 1990, purely defensive. The embassies in the respective capitals and Baghdad remained open, and a limited amount of travel to Baghdad was possible, even though Iraqi Airways were forbidden to fly anywhere other than to Jordan. A number of distinguished visitors, such as Edward Heath and Willi Brandt, visited Baghdad to intercede with the Iraqi Government. The Iraqis retaliated by forcing the closure of foreign embassies in Kuwait, which they eventually

17. A peace treaty has eventually been signed and normal relations between the two countries restored. The text of the first edition has been left unchanged, as it represents the actual position between 1982 and 1990.

succeeded in doing, and in seizing hostages from the nationals of Western countries. Later the Iraqis relented, and they were released. Diplomatic missions came and went in an effort to resolve the crisis.

By November, 1990, it was clear to President Bush that nothing was going to remove the Iraqis from Kuwait other than force, and further resolutions were obtained from the Security Council authorising its use, providing that diplomatic means were first tried and that force would only be employed if these turned out to be fruitless. From this point on, the armed forces assembled in Saudi Arabia ceased being a defensive array, and became one intended for offensive operations. The Generals were not ready for such an operation, and needed further time to prepare for it. A deadline was set for hostilities to begin on 16th January, 1991, if the Iraqis had not left Kuwait of their own accord by this date. There were further diplomatic attempts to defuse the situation, largely through the medium of President Gorbachev, right up until the very last moment, and the embassies in the respective capitals only closed shortly before the deadline expired.

The attack, when it started a few minutes into 16th January, was ferocious. Naval and air bombardment of Iraq's cities and military installations continued without intermission for nearly six weeks. As always, there was no public certainty about the date that American and British special forces began ground operations inside Iraq, making their primary target Iraq's missile sites. Iraq retaliated by launching missiles against Riyadh, and also Israeli cities. With the very greatest difficulty, the Israelis were dissuaded from the sort of reaction that comes naturally to them. The ground attack by the Alliance's ground forces, begun in late February, was so successful that the fighting came to an end by the end of the month. An armistice has been signed, but no peace treaty has been concluded.

From that day to this, sanctions have continued against Iraq, who cannot export her oil or import any commodity except for some essential medicines. Sanctions are set to continue until Iraq complies with the United Nations Resolutions. United Nations teams are busy inside Iraq dismantling, with variable success, her war machine. Western aircraft, primarily American, British and French, patrol two zones, one in the north of Iraq and one in the south, to keep the Iraqi airforce from attacking their Kurdish and Shi'ite minorities.

It is not always an easy question whether a state of war existed between the individual nations who were members of the Alliance and Iraq so that the insured peril of "war" could be said to arise. The question is best considered by referring to separate periods of time:

2nd August, 1990–end February, 1991. A state of war existed between Iraq and Kuwait during the whole of this time. The Kuwaiti Government did not surrender, but instead went into exile. Such members of the Kuwaiti armed forces who managed to escape joined the armed forces of the Alliance.

16th January–end February, 1991. Likewise, there cannot be any question that the United States, the United Kingdom, France, and Saudi Arabia were at war with Iraq. They all provided naval, air, and ground forces, and took an active part in the aerial bombardment and the land battle. The same is true of Italy; although she provided no ground troops, she provided warships and her planes took part in the bombing. It must also be true of Syria and Egypt, who provided substantial ground forces, and took an active part in the ground operations. The same can be said of Australia, who provided warships. All these countries and many others were actively supporting the Alliance, and their armed forces were committed to obey the orders of its Supreme Command in whatever way it might require.

It is, however, extremely doubtful if Israel was ever at war with Iraq. It is true that her cities were being bombarded by missiles and her citizens were being killed and injured, and this itself is an act of war. On the other hand, she studiously refrained from replying in kind with a quality of restraint which does not come naturally to her. She did not take part in any of the fighting.

2nd August, 1990–16th January, 1991. This is a more difficult question. The purpose of the Alliance's armed forces was, at least until mid-November, purely defensive. Even so, Iraq was being blockaded, and a blockade is itself an act of war, particularly when there lurks behind it the ultimate threat of force. The view is tentatively advanced that all the countries supplying warships to enforce this blockade were engaged in a war with Iraq during this time.

End February, 1991–to date. This is the most difficult question of all. The United Nations' teams are, with varied success, attempting to disarm a defeated foe. The planes of the former Alliance, mainly American but with contingents from Britain and France, still fly over areas of Iraq, trying to protect some minorities which the Government of Iraq would like to exterminate. There has been some bombing, notably of the Iraqi Security Headquarters in retaliation for a plot to assassinate President and Mrs. Bush. The aircraft have fired upon Iraqi anti-aircraft batteries who have locked their radar onto them. The blockade is still being maintained to enforce the United Nations Sanctions. As has already been said, a blockade is an act of war.

With very great hesitation, it is suggested that the countries engaged in these military operations are still in a state of war with Iraq, and that the insured peril of "war" still arises. There is a measure of support for this view in the *Hain Steamship* case, because no peace treaty has yet been signed, and it will not be until Iraq complies with the United Nations Resolutions. The contrary can still easily be argued, but it is unlikely that the matter will ever be judicially decided. If a casualty should happen, it is more likely that another insured peril would be more easily established than that of "war".

6.34 In seeking to draw conclusions from the decided cases, it should be borne in mind that there are two prerequisites to a claim upon the War Risk Policy. First, the insured peril of "war" must have arisen. Secondly, loss or damage must have resulted. This chapter is only concerned with the first of these requirements when asking what lessons are to be drawn from the decided cases so that they can be applied to the modern types of war, examples of which are set out above. The following propositions are put forward:

  (i) The word "war" in a commercial contract such as an insurance policy is given its normal and popular meaning. Any technical meanings which the word may have in international law are not relevant.

  (ii) The insured peril of "war" will only arise where there is a conflict between two or more nations whose governments have committed them to warfare, either by aggression or by defence thereto.

(iii) Such a government (or governments) may be *de jure* or *de facto*. For the narrow purposes of the insured peril of "war", it is not necessary that a *de facto* government should have all the attributes which might otherwise be required, such as some measure of international recognition by other nations; it is sufficient if it has at least to some substantial degree the character of a Sovereign State and has the will and ability, either by persuasion or compulsion, to lead the people over whom it rules into active hostilities.

(iv) The insured peril of "war" can arguably arise where two or more nations consider themselves to be at war in the popular sense with each other even though no military operations against each other are currently in process. It will not, however, arise where two nations who have been at war consider themselves to be at peace with each other and act accordingly, even though they have signed no peace treaty.

(v) The insured peril of "war" can also arise where two or more nations are at peace, but are conducting military operations against each other within a limited area only; in such an event, the insured peril will only arise within that limited area and such extensions thereof which are within the ranges and abilities of the various weapons which are employed, for instance patrolling aircraft and warships.

(vi) A declaration of war is not a requisite to the insured peril of "war" arising. It will be enough if one nation makes an attack upon another which seeks to repel that attack.

(vii) It is not a requisite to the insured peril of "war" arising that a ship should fly the flag of one of the belligerents or should be owned by their nationals. The property of neutrals, whether it be a ship or anything else, can be lost or damaged by the insured peril of "war".

CHAPTER 7

Civil war

7.1 In the *Pesquerias*[1] case, the House of Lords saw no essential difference between "war" and "civil war". Lord Porter regarded the matter as settled by the decision of the Court of Appeal in *Curtis and Son* v. *Mathews*[2] when the Court of Appeal was considering the W. and B. (War and Bombardment) Clause which read:

"W. and B. Clause. This policy to cover risk of loss and/or damage to the property hereby insured directly caused by war, bombardment, military or usurped power, or by aerial craft (hostile or otherwise), including bombs, shells, and/or missiles dropped or thrown therefrom or discharged thereat and fire originating on the premises insured or elsewhere. No claim to attach hereto for delay, deterioration, and/or loss of market, or for confiscation or destruction of the government of the country in which the property is situated, or for breakage of glass due to concussion. Only to pay hereon if not recoverable under any other existing policy of insurance."

7.2 The premises insured were in Dublin. On 24th April, 1916, some 2,000 men, describing themselves as the armed forces of the self-styled Provisional Government of the Irish Republic, occupied the Post Office and other buildings in Dublin in an event known to history as the "Easter Rising". The British armed forces attempted to suppress the insurgents and there was some vigorous street-to-street fighting. The G.P.O. itself was shelled by artillery. This started a fire which spread through several intervening buildings until it destroyed the plaintiff's premises. The fire brigade was unable to put it out because of the shooting by the insurgents. The court noted with approval the finding of Roche J. when giving judgment for the plaintiffs: "I am satisfied that Easter week in Dublin was a week not of mere riot but of civil strife amounting to warfare waged between military and usurped powers and involving bombardment."

7.3 In the Court of Appeal, Bankes L.J. made the following observations on usurped power: "Usurped power seems to me to mean something more than the action of an unorganised rabble. How much more I am not prepared to define. There must be action by some more or less organised body with more or less authoritative leaders." (We shall return to this quotation under the heading "Military or Usurped Power".)

7.4 Following the *Pesquerias* case,[3] which was decided in 1949, it could reason-

---

1. *Pesquerias y Secaderos de Bacalao de España S.A.* v. *Beer* (1945) 79 Ll.L.Rep. 417; (1947) 80 Ll.L.Rep. 318; (1948–49) 82 Ll.L.Rep. 501; [1949] 1 All E.R. 845.
2. [1919] 1 K.B. 425.
3. Footnote 1, above.

ably be concluded that the English courts saw no essential difference between "war" and "civil war" other than the obvious one that wars are fought between nations and civil wars between the citizens of a State.

There is now confirmation of this in the recent *Mozambique* case (paras. 8.22–8.26), which was decided in 1991, where Saville J., applying the principle that in commercial documents words must be given their ordinary everyday meaning said: "In this context 'civil war' means a war with the special characteristic of being civil—i.e. being internal rather than external."

7.5 When dealing with the *Somoza* ships case (paras. 7.17–7.23) in 1983, the U.S. District Court and the U.S. Court of Appeals 2nd Circuit did not deal in any detail with the meaning of "civil war". They treated the fighting in Nicaragua in the late 1970s and early 1980s, when the Sandinistas sought, and eventually achieved, the ousting of the Dictator General Somoza, as a self-evident fact that "civil war" existed. Had they had Saville J.'s dictum before them, there can be little doubt that they would have approved it.

7.6 From the American courts came the insistence which was repeated in the *Pan Am*[4] case that both kinds of war must be between governments which are *de jure* or at least *de facto*. American law was clearly governed by the decisions in the Civil War cases (noted under "War" and "Military or Usurped Power") and there was never any real doubt that the Confederacy (the South), although usually referred to as "the rebels", was governed by a government which had *de facto* status. From the start of the American Civil War, the Confederacy consisted of a very large tract of territory, it passed and enforced laws, it had its own currency and it had the ability to lead its people into war; even though most of the regular army had sided with the Union (the North), the Confederates won most of the early battles. There is less noticeable insistence in the *Somoza* ships case (paras. 7.17–7.23) that the Sandinistas should have at least *de facto* status, but it seems clear that the U.S. courts were satisfied that, at the time of the casualties, they self-evidently did have it, and possibly *de jure* status as well. It seems that the issue whether General Franco's Government had at least a *de facto* status was not argued with any force in the *Pesquerias*[5] case although if it had been, it is suggested that the courts would have had little hesitation in finding that it too had at least this standing. The General commanded a considerable force which he brought with him from Africa, the regular army in Spain itself and the police mostly declared in his favour, his *pronunciamiento* attracted a large part of the civilian population, and at a very early stage he held sway over considerable tracts of territory. This factor is not so clear in the *Curtis* case although it can be said that in the "Easter Rising", there was certainly the political aspiration to form a government backed by a powerful and determined armed force. The *Pan Am*[6] case is not helpful in giving guidance on "civil war" because there was an agreement between the parties that if an "insurrection" could not be proved, then there was no chance of proving that a "civil war" existed; if the lesser could not be proved then neither could the greater.[7]

4. *Pan American World Airways Inc* v. *The Aetna Casualty and Surety Co*. [1974] 1 Lloyd's Rep. 207; [1975] 1 Lloyd's Rep. 77. See paras. 6.16–6.26, 8.13, 8.30, 8.31, 17.13, 17.24–17.26.
5. Footnote 1, above.
6. Footnote 4, above.
7. See paras. 8.2, 8.3.

7.7 A most authoritative case on "civil war" is *Spinney's (1948) Ltd. and Others* v. *Royal Insurance*[8] because in this case the facts were complicated in the extreme, and they received a thorough and exhaustive analysis from Mustill J. The judgment deserves to be regarded as essential reading for the students of Lebanon's political and social history in 1975 and 1976. No easy assumptions could be made whether any of the separate parties had *de facto* or *de jure* status.

7.8 Spinney's ran a retail supermarket business selling mostly food, and their business in West Beirut (a Moslem enclave) was conducted from two shops and a tower block which seems to have contained their Head Office and a considerable quantity of food awaiting distribution to retail outlets. Their property was insured with the Royal Exchange Assurance under conditions of great complexity. In order not to burden the reader with more length and detail than is absolutely necessary, it will serve for our purposes to list the perils concerned, whether as insured or excepted perils, which the High Court was called upon to consider: Civil War, Usurped Power, Invasion, Rebellion; Insurrection, Hostilities; Warlike Operations, Civil Commotion, and the specific exclusion which read: " . . . Any act of any person acting on behalf of or in connection with any organisation with activities directed towards the overthrow by force of the government *de jure* or *de facto* or to the influencing of it by terrorism or violence."

7.9 The court found as facts from the evidence given to it that the Lebanon's population consisted of about 3.5m people (the exact figure was not known) made up by about 1.6m Christians, 1.6m Moslems, and 350,000 Palestinians, mostly refugees who had left the State of Israel upon its formation in 1948. Of these, only the Palestinians had any pretence of unity. The Christians consisted of several individual religious persuasions, the Maronites (the majority), Greek Orthodox, Greek Catholics and some other smaller sects, all of whom were divided by deep and divisive doctrinal differences. The Moslems also were similarly divided by equally deep and divisive doctrinal differences and here the court felt able to give proportions. Of every 11 Moslems five were Sunnis, four were Shi'ites and two were Druze. In order to govern the country, the National Pact of 1943 had divided the centres of power so that the President of the Republic was a Maronite Christian, the President of the Chamber of Deputies was a Shi'ite Moslem, the Prime Minister was a Sunni Moslem and the C.-in-C. was a Maronite Christian. The Chamber of Deputies was divided so that there were six Christian to five Moslem seats. The arrangement worked quite efficiently if not to the entire satisfaction of all concerned and Lebanon became a very prosperous and fairly peaceful country. By 1975, however, the increase in the Moslem proportion of the population to that of the Christians led to an expectation of a rearrangement in the Moslems' favour, and the Moslem population was not immune to the tide of Moslem nationalism which swept the Middle East during the 1960s and 1970s. This expectation and the demands which accompanied it were resisted by the Christians in a way which ensured that trouble was bound to ensue.

7.10 The facts of the case are best presented in a diary form:

Pre-February 1975

A deteriorating political and security situation leads to feuds and violence between the various sects. There are also clashes between the regular army and the Palestinians whose presence is greatly resented

8. [1980] 1 Lloyd's Rep. 406.

by the Christians. There are further clashes between the paramilitary forces maintained by the various Christian and Moslem factions, sometimes involving the Palestinians. The most powerful of these forces are maintained by the Maronite Christians (the Phalange), the Shi'ite Moslems, the Druze and the Palestinians themselves.

1975

February

The government presently consists of:
       The President—Suleman Franjieh (Maronite Christian)
       The Prime Minster—Rashid-Al-Sulh (Sunni Moslem)
       Cabinet Ministers—Various representatives of the Phalange, other Christian political parties and groups, and Jumblattist Shi'ites.
There is an *ad hoc* opposition consisting of two Moslems, Mr. Said Salan and Mr. Karami, and a Maronite Christian, M. Raymond Edde. These three gentlemen are highly respected political figures who lead their own followers to take more moderate courses than those favoured by the Phalange and the Jumblattists both of whom are far more extreme.

26th February

A strike and a demonstration by fishermen in Sidon over an industrial dispute leads to a riot and the death of one of the local leaders. Demonstrations in sympathy in Sidon and Beirut are put down by the army with more deaths. The army is praised by the Christians and execrated by the Moslems.

13th April

M. Gemeyal (the Maronite Christian leader) attends the consecration of the new church and gunmen kill four of his attendant supporters. The Phalange murder Palestinians in a bus. Moslem and Christian suburbs exchange rocket and small arms fire. A ceasefire is arranged.

26th April

The Jumblattists withdraw from the government and refuse to serve in any future government which includes the Phalange.

15th May

The Prime Minister resigns and the government falls. The Jumblattists refuse to serve in any government that includes the Phalange, which refuses to support any government that does not include it. Some military officers are appointed to run the government until the deadlock can be resolved but have to resign after three days. There is much shooting and sporadic violence.

30th June

Mr. Karami forms a government which includes M. Chamoun, a moderate Christian leader, but excludes the Phalange and the Jumblattists. Two months of uneasy calm follow.

End August

A gaming dispute in Zamleh, a Christian village enclave, leads to shooting which spills over into Tripoli.

7th September

The Christians murder a busload of Moslems and Christian property in Tripoli and the north of Lebanon is looted.

15th September

There is some violent fighting in Beirut and the Christians bombard the Souk.
At this point, the court finds:

     (1) The violence is basically sectarian.
     (2) The Palestinians are hardly involved, if at all.
     (3) Mr. Karami is doing all that he can to resolve matters peaceably and without violence.
     (4) Except for the bombardment of the Souk, fighting is in the traditional areas of tension between the Christians and the Moslems (this seems to indicate that up to now there is no invasion of enclaves, but sporadic shooting from one enclave into another).

End September

Syria now intervenes on the basis that she cannot tolerate disorder on her borders which might tempt the Israelis to intervene themselves. The Foreign Minister comes to Lebanon to mediate and manages to

persuade the politicians to form a "Government of National Reconciliation". It includes both the Maronites and the Jumblattists, but soon breaks down because the Jumblattists continue to insist on being
given more posts in the Civil Service and the Army which they consider to be too pro-Christian. The
Arab League also attempts to mediate but fails. The President's and the Prime Minister's supporters
fight in Tripoli.

October/November

There is gunfire and looting in Beirut. A ceasefire fails to last. The Christian militias, apparently with
some support from the Palestinians, now invade the Moslem enclaves in West Beirut. The court regards
this as a turning point, in that fighting is no longer from fixed positions and, for the first time, there is
wholescale invasion of an enclave. There is an exodus of refugees and the fighting, punctuated by cease-
fires, dies down.

November

Mr. Karami makes political moves to form a new committee. At first he meets with no success but later
things seem more hopeful. The Syrian President invites Gemeyal to Damascus for talks.

6th December

The worst violence so far breaks out in Beirut. In what appears to be a reprisal, the Phalange murders
200 Moslems. The Moslem militias drive the Phalange out of West Beirut. Moslems and radical politicians rejoin a "Higher Co-ordinating Committee". Another uneasy peace begins.

1976

Early January

The Palestinians block a bridge which is vital to Christian communications. The Phalange engages them
and besieges some Palestinian camps. The Palestinians seek to raise the sieges. Fighting also resumes
between Christian East Beirut and Moslem West Beirut. The Lebanese air force attacks the Moslems.
There is fighting in other parts of the country.

15th–18th January

The Phalange occupies, with little resistance, two large working-class Moslem suburbs and the refugees
flee to West Beirut, setting up camps along the beach in the neighbourhood of Spinney's shops and
tower block.

19th–20th January

Syria again intervenes and moves a regular brigade, the Yarmouk Brigade, which consists of Palestinians recruited into the Syrian army, into the Bekaa Valley.

20th January

A Syrian political delegation arrives and manages to form a joint Lebanese-Syrian-Palestinian Military
Commission to end the fighting. At about this time, Syrian troops enter Beirut and make their presence
felt on the streets.

7.11 This is only a very short description of the court's findings and the reader
who wishes a fuller account (which continues after January 1976) should read pages
412 to 425 of the judgment. It is, however, most important to appreciate the situation which existed at the time Spinney's loss took place. There was no hard and
fast division of Christian against Moslem and the more moderate and less radical of
the elements of each religion often supported the other, at least politically. Whilst
there were enclaves, these were scattered throughout the country in suburbs, vil-
lages and small towns. There was no similarity to the American Civil War where
the Confederacy controlled from the start a large tract of territory, or the Spanish
Civil War where General Franco very rapidly gained control over a large tract of
territory shortly after hostilities started. Apart from the Lebanese regular army,
which rapidly disintegrated and took sides in accordance with each soldier's
religious and political beliefs, there were no regular forces. There were various

militias. The Palestinians had a large armed militia which was intended for use against the Israelis. The Phalange had a large and powerful militia of its own which owed allegiance to the Phalange's leaders. Likewise the Jumblattist Shi'ites had a similar militia which owed allegiance to its own political leaders. There were several other smaller but well armed militias which owed allegiance in various directions. Alliances were made and broken with bewildering rapidity. It was not unknown for Moslems and Christians to unite to fight other Moslems or Christians, and it would be going too far to say that all Christians lined up on one side and all Moslems on the other.

7.12 Between 18th and 23rd January, 1976, Spinney's two shops and the tower block were broken into and looted. All the edible stock was removed. Some fixtures, fittings and furniture in the offices and shops were taken and the rest were smashed. Some minor internal and external damage of the buildings was caused. There was a small fire in the basement of the tower block, but this seems to have been caused by the looters lighting torches to see their way to the basement food-stores rather than to an attempt to set the building on fire. The identity of the looters was not established with any certainty. Spinney's had previously been presented with demands from some Moslem sects for food and money to feed the refugees on the beach, and had in part met these demands. The looters were described as being of no one particular economic class and some were obviously well-to-do. Some people loaded their cars with stolen goods. For a time one sect, the Nasserite militants or Moribitoun, provided a guard to prevent looting until sent away by the watchman who feared an outbreak of shooting. The judge's findings were:

(1) During the looting there was some shooting between the looters themselves and between the looters and such persons who attempted to prevent it. The shooting was sporadic and unorganised.
(2) Only small arms were used and the buildings were not fired upon.
(3) The Palestinians were not involved in the looting and when present they tried to prevent it.
(4) Probably such shooting as there was came from members of various militias who were present.
(5) A number of people were acting in concert with one another and they may have been organised, but there was no evidence of an overall organisation to loot.
(6) Many people—particularly women and children—took advantage of the situation to loot.
(7) There was no sectarian motive for the attack on Spinney's although the looters seemed mainly to have been Moslems.
(8) Possibly some looters came from the refugees camped on the beach, but they did not initiate the looting or form an organised body to loot.
(9) If there was a common origin, there was no basis to decide what that common origin was.

7.13 Before moving on to the tests applied by the court to decide whether the loss was due to "civil war", the judge's decisions on the following points should be noted:

On treason being a necessary ingredient to civil war (as opposed to "military or usurped power"): "The expression 'civil war' . . . is part of the contemporary speech, and I cannot see any reason to suppose that it was introduced into this policy with the intent of calling up the ancient doctrine of constructive treason", and on public international law: "The words [i.e., civil war] under construction are to be given their ordinary business meaning, which is not necessarily the same as they bear in public international law"; on the nature of civil war as opposed to war: "In my judgment the ordinary and literal meaning of the words are the same; a civil war is a war which has the special characteristic of being civil—i.e., internal rather than external. This special characteristic means that certain features of an international war are absent. Nevertheless a civil war is still a war. The words do not simply denote a violent internal conflict on a large scale."

7.14 In this work, the author suggests conclusions and the factors which should be applied to see if a particular insured peril has arisen in the circumstances of any casualty. Besides recommending the three above quotations, it is suggested that the three tests applied by the court in *Spinney's* case[9] are particularly appropriate, even though the court was at pains to emphasise that it was not attempting a general definition:

(1) Can it be said that the conflict was between opposing sides?

It must be possible to say of each fighting man that he owes allegiance to one side or the other and it must also be possible to identify each side by reference to a community of objective leadership and administration. Complete identity is not necessary and some allies bear considerable animosity to each other. But: " . . . there must be some substantial community of aim which the allies have banded together to promote by use of force". A civil war is not necessarily restricted to two sides but too many sides can become: "A melee without a clear delineation of combatants which is one of the distinguishing features of a war."

(2) What were the objectives of the "sides" and how did they set about pursuing them?

The first question is whether the party's aim was to seize dominion over a whole or a part of the State. If not, it may still be a civil war but: " . . . it will then be necessary to look closely at the events to see whether they display the degree of coherence and community of purpose which helps to distinguish a war from a mere tumultuous upheaval". Participants can be activated by tribal, racial or ethnic purposes, or even by a desire to change a government's policies rather than the government itself.

(3) What was the scale of the conflict, and its effect on public order and on the life of the inhabitants?

It is not correct to say that each faction must hold a substantial proportion of territory. Even though this principle is qualified by the court to some extent as appears below, it is a move away from the American decisions arising out of the American

9. [1980] 1 Lloyd's Rep. 406.

Civil War, where there was never any question that each side held substantial tracts of territory from the outset, and possibly from the *Pesquerias* case[10] as well, although the question was not raised in that case. This could give rise to some differences between future American and English decisions although it is respectfully suggested that the High Court's decision in the *Spinney's*[11] case is more appropriate and more in line with the modern forms that civil war now takes.

7.15 The judge noted that in *Curtis* v. *Mathews*[12] the rebels held little land, that they were united in an explicit purpose to produce far reaching changes. They possessed a high degree of discipline and skill at arms with powerful modern weapons. Matters which need consideration to see if internal strife has reached the considerable scale that "civil war" requires are:

The number of combatants.
The number of casualties, both military and civilian.
The amount and nature of arms employed.
The relative sizes of territory occupied.
The extent to which it is possible to delineate territory.
The degree to which the populace as a whole is involved.
The duration and degree of continuity of conflict.
The extent to which public order and administration of justice has been impaired.
The degree of interruption of public services and private life.
The question of whether there have been movements of population as a result of the conflict.
The extent to which each faction purports to exercise an exclusive legislature, and administrative and judicial powers over the territory which it controls.

7.16 The court clearly did not intend that the scale of the conflict should be judged by these factors alone, or that other relevant factors should be excluded from consideration. Neither did it intend that all the listed factors should exist to a substantial degree. It is, however, clearly essential that a large number of the listed factors must exist, and moreover must exist to a substantial degree, before the scale of the conflict can be serious enough to warrant the conclusion that a civil war exists.

In conclusion, it can be said that in applying these tests to *Spinney's* case,[13] the judge found that at the time of the looting in January 1976 "civil war", in the sense that it is used in a war risks policy, did not exist.

7.17 The American courts dealt with the *Somoza ships* case where the facts were very much less complicated and therefore much more easily established. *O.P.E. Shipping Ltd. and El Porvenir Shipping Company Inc.* v. *Allstate Insurance Company Inc. and Others*[14] was heard by the U.S. District Court for the Southern District of New York and by the U.S. Court of Appeals 2nd Circuit. The Dictator

10. *Pesquerias y Secaderos de Bacalao de España* S.A. v. *Beer* (1945) 79 Ll.L.Rep. 417; (1946) 80 Ll.L.Rep. 318; (1948) 82 Ll.L.Rep. 501; [1949] 1 All E.R. 845. See paras. 6.11–6.15.
11. [1980] 1 Lloyd's Rep. 406 (1948).
12. [1919] 1 K.B. 425. See paras. 7.1–7.5.
13. [1980] 1 Lloyd's Rep. 406.
14. [1983] A.M.C. 22, [1983] A.M.C. 30.

of Nicaragua, General Somoza, owned four ships, the *Hope* which flew the Nicaraguan flag, and the *El Salvador*, the *Honduras*, and the *Managua* all of which were registered in Panama. Allstate gave insurance for marine risks, whilst Lloyd's underwriters insured the War and Strikes risks. Events took the following course:

1979

15th May

The insurance is placed.

1st June

The Sandinistas, who have been fighting General Somoza for a long time, decide the time has now come to topple him.

4th June

A general strike with this end in view begins.

17th June

The *Hope*, whose crew are Sandinista sympathisers, take over their ship and sail her to Cuba, which is sympathetic to the Sandinista cause.

22nd June

The *El Salvador*'s crew, also Sandinista sympathisers, seize her in Panama, which is also friendly. During the next few days, she is joined by the *Honduras* and the *Managua*.

6th July

Allstate's policy terminates, possibly because the premiums are not paid.

9th July

The Nicaraguan registry of all four ships is "cancelled", presumably by the owner.

10th July

All the ships are transferred to the Cayman Island's flag. The War Risks insurance is continued by agreement.

20th July

Revolutionary government comes to power in Nicaragua. All General Somoza's property is seized by decree.

Later

All four ships return to Nicaragua.

1980

By now the ships have incurred some large bills for port expenses in Nicaragua. An unsuccessful attempt is made to sue the Cayman Island companies. The ships are then sold to pay the port dues.

7.18 The marine policy gave insurance for barratry, but excluded civil war, revolution, rebellion, insurrection, and civil strife arising therefrom. The War and Strikes policy gave insurance for these exclusions, but had an exclusion of its own. There was to be no insurance for:

"Capture, seizure, arrest, restraint, detainment, or confiscation by the Government of the United States or of the country in which the vessel is owned or registered."

7.19 Both Pollack D.J. in the District Court and the Court of Appeals thought that the crews had been guilty of barratry. The District Court found Lord Ellenborough's definition of barratry in *Earle* v. *Rowcroft*[15] persuasive:

15. (1806) 8 E 126/138.

" . . . a fraudulent breach of duty by the Master in respect of his owners; or, in other words, a breach of duty in respect to his owners with a criminal intent, or *ex maleficio*, is barratry."

7.20 In the Appeals Court, van Graafeiland C.J. pointed to an American decision, *Marcardier* v. *Chesapeake Insurance Company*[16]:

"An act committed by the Master or mariners of a ship, for some unlawful or fraudulent purpose, contrary to their duty to their owners, whereby the latter sustain an injury."

7.21 Both courts felt that there may have been barratry, but this could not be considered in isolation to all else that had been going on. What had been the "predominant and determining" or "real efficient" cause of the loss of the ships by the assured?[17] Taken all in all, it was the civil war in Nicaragua that was the proximate cause of the loss.

7.22 Such findings excused the marine underwriters, Allstate, but with the War Risks insurance there was a more complex position. The District Court thought that the ships had been seized by the government of the country in which they were owned or registered, because the ships had already been taken from General Somoza's possession by the Sandinistas when the transfer to the Cayman Island flag was made. It was influenced by the doctrine of "relating back" which is described in the English case *Civil Transport Inc.* v. *Central Air Transport Corporation*.[18]

"Subsequent recognition *de jure* of a new government as the result of a successful insurrection can in certain cases annul a sale of goods by a previous government. If the previous government sells goods which belong to it but are situated in territory effectively occupied at the time by insurgent forces acting on behalf of what is already a *de facto* new government, the sale may be valid if the insurgents are afterwards defeated and possession of the goods is regained by the old government. But if the old government never regains the goods and the *de facto* new government becomes recognized . . . as the *de jure* government, purchasers from the old government will not be held in Her Majesty's Courts to have a good title after that recognition."

7.23 The District Court therefore found in favour of the War and Strikes underwriters, but this part of its judgment was reversed by the Court of Appeals. The ships were lost by the insured peril of "civil war" when they were taken by their crews. In any case, the transfer to the Cayman Island flag had taken place on 10th July, 1979, whereas the decree seizing General Somoza's property was not promulgated until 20th July, and the sale of the ships did not happen until 1980. The War and Strikes underwriters were accordingly judged to be liable.

7.24 This work attempts to reach conclusions which, it is hoped, will be of general guidance to the reader. In the case of civil war, this is often easily recognisable, as the courts found in the *Mozambique* (paras. 8.22–8.26) and the *Somoza ships* cases. Where however the position is more indeterminate, and it is not so easy to say whether a "civil war" exists or not, it is suggested that the tests prescribed by Mustill J. in the *Spinney's* case, (paras. 7.7–7.16) should be applied.

16. [1814] U.S. 39/49.
17. These expressions are frequently used by the American courts in connection with the proximate cause of the casualty—see para. 30.13.
18. [1952] 2 Lloyd's Rep. 259, [1953] A.C. 70.

CHAPTER 8

Revolution, rebellion, insurrection . . .

8.1 Considered in the strict order in which the insured perils are set out in the War Risks Policy, "revolution, rebellion and insurrection" are the next insured perils to be considered. They are, however, so very close to each other in meaning and also to the meanings of "riots and civil commotions" which appear as insured perils in other paragraphs, that they should be considered together rather than separately.

8.2 It has been suggested that where an insurance policy sets out no less than five types of civil disorder in carefully graduated degrees, beginning with the most serious and ending with the least, and moreover includes a generalised provision about civil strife arising from any of them, then any kind of civil disorder which is within the bracket between the most and least serious disorders is insured by the War Risks Policy even though it is not named as an insured peril by the policy. This suggestion seems to have arisen from the *Pan Am* case,[1] where it seems that there was an agreement between the parties that if the insured peril of "insurrection" could not be proved then the more serious disorders of rebellion, revolution and civil war could not arise. The 2nd Circuit Court of Appeals describes this agreement:

"All parties agree that if loss was not caused by insurrection then it could not have been caused by any [other] terms relating to civil disorder. Insurrection presents the key issue because rebellion, revolution and civil war are progressive stages in the development in civil unrest, the most rudimentary form of which is insurrection."

8.3 An agreement of this nature between the parties to a civil case would effectively prevent the court from taking another view. At the same time it does not signify approval by the court that this suggestion represents the law. It is submitted that more compelling authority is required before the above-mentioned suggestion is accepted as an exception to the rule that the proximate cause of a casualty must come within the explicit terms of at least one of the insured perils of the policy as a condition which is precedent to any liability on the part of the underwriter.

It has also been suggested that where an insured peril such as "civil commotions" is insured by the policy, and another insured peril of greater gravity is excluded such as "war", and the loss is held to be due to "war", then the loss is not covered by the insurance and that the authority for this proposition is the *Pesquerias* case. The general proposition is felt to be correct if only to give effect to the intention of

---

1. *Pan American World Airways Inc.* v. *The Aetna Casualty & Surety Co.* [1974] 1 Lloyd's Rep. 207; [1975] 1 Lloyd's Rep. 77. See paras. 6.16–6.26, 8.13, 8.30, 8.31, 17.13, 17.24–17.26.

the parties that losses due to the proximate cause of "war" are not to be insured by the policy and that a lesser peril which is insured cannot have its meaning extended so that it includes a greater peril and thus defeats this intention. What is disputed is that the *Pesquerias* case[2] is such an authority. A study of the terms of the insurance (paras. 6.11–6.15) will show that the insurance given for "civil commotions" was heavily qualified in a way which is not usual in war risks policies, and it is extremely doubtful that the losses suffered by the plaintiff in that case can ever have met the terms of these qualifications. Moreover, the terms of the insurance excluded "war risks" which in market parlance is a generic term which could have been held to exclude a lot more perils than "war" including, let it be said, "civil commotions" other than the qualified cover which the policy expressly stated that it gave. The case in any event centred on "war" and "civil war" alone, and it is suggested that it is an autority for these insured perils only.

8.4 Revolution is defined in the *Oxford English Dictionary*: "A complete overthrow of the established government in any country or state by those who were previously subject to it; a forcible substitution of a new ruler or form of government" and rebellion: "Organised armed resistance to the ruler or government of one's country; insurrection, revolt; open or determined defiance of, or resistance to, any authority or controlling power" and insurrection: "The action of rising in arms or open resistance against established authority or governmental restraint; an armed rising, a revolt; an incipient or limited rebellion."

8.5 Even if insured perils or risks must be interpreted "in the sense which an ordinary man would use [them]"—the approach of Goddard J. in the *Kawasaki* case[3]—these interpretations must be approached with some caution. One is still tempted to adopt the approach of the learned authors of Hudson and Allen, *The Institute Clauses Handbook*, page 189, and consider a rebellion as becoming a revolution as soon as it succeeds. The upheavals known to history as the French and Russian Revolutions began not as attempts to change the Governments of France and Russia, but to change the Governments' policies, albeit in far-reaching and fundamental ways. They only became revolutions when the new Governments were substituted for the previous Governments after it eventually became clear that the previous Governments were incapable of the desired changes. The Peasants' Revolt of 1381 has always been wrongly described even though its participants were armed and adopted a threatening manner. There was never the intention to change the Government of England, but only to seek the redress of grievances which the participants believed lay in the power of the King. Having obtained promises from him, they dispersed to their homes, and did not reassemble even when those promises were not fulfilled and their trust in the King's word was rudely abused.

8.6 Under this heading will be considered the cases on "Military or Usurped Power". These are not insured perils in the modern Institute War and Strikes Clauses although they appear as such in insurance policies on other objects and

---

2. *Pesquerias y Secaderos de Bacalao de España S.A.* v. *Beer* (1945) 79 Ll.L.Rep. 417; (1946) 80 Ll.L.Rep. 318; (1948) 82 Ll.L.Rep. 501, [1949] 1 All E.R. 845. See paras. 6.11–6.15.
3. *Kawasaki Kisen Kabushiki Kaisha* v. *Bantham Steamship Company Ltd. (No. 2)* (1939) 63 Ll.L.Rep. 155; [1939] 2 K.B. 544. See paras. 6.6–6.10.

in the *Pan Am*[4] and *Spinney's*[5] cases were excluded perils. The relevant cases will continue to have some influence on future decisions, particularly on rebellion and insurrection to which there is some similarity.

8.7 Consideration must begin with the Treason Act 1351 which made it an offence to wage war against the sovereign in his realm. The Act did not cover all the doings of our turbulent and unruly ancestors and by the 16th century the doctrine of constructive treason had become firmly established. In *Bradshawe v. Burton*[6] and in *R. v. Messenger*,[7] the distinction appears that a rebellious mob asserts "usurped power" and is guilty of high treason, whilst a common mob commits only felonies. High treason was an offence against the Monarch and is to be compared with petit treason which was an offence by a junior against a senior, such as a wife against her husband or a servant against his master. "Usurped power" referred to a subject seizing and exercising power which only the constitutional government, namely the Monarch, and later the Monarch and Parliament, could lawfully use. Lord Mansfield C.J. refined this further in *R. v. Gordon*[8] in which the chief proponent of the Gordon riots was prosecuted: " . . . If this multitude assembled with intent, by acts of force or violence, to compel the legislature to repeal a law, it is high treason."

8.8 It was always a necessary ingredient to the offence of high treason that the subject should have arrogated to himself powers which properly belong to the King alone or, at least, that he should have attempted to do so. It was not, however, treasonable unless the offenders were in "a posture of war"—bearing arms was enough to prove a treasonable intent—and neither was it treasonable to seek, although armed for the purpose, the redress of private grievances.

8.9 In *Drinkwater* v. *The Corporation of the London Assurance*[9] Mr. Drinkwater's malting house in Norwich was insured by a fire policy with the following exclusion clauses: "Burnt by any invasion of foreign enemies, or any military or usurped power whatever."

8.10 On 27th September, 1766, a mob in Norwich protested at "the high price of provisions" (in modern parlance the high cost of living) and despoiled divers quantities of flour. The magistrates read the Riot Act 1714 and the mob, no doubt suitably impressed by its draconian penalties, dispersed peaceably to their homes. The next day, the 28th September, their indignation having overnight surmounted their fears of the Riot Act, they reassembled and this time Mr. Drinkwater's malting house was burnt down. They do not seem to have been very determined or destructive since they only attacked two bakers and one miller and were put to flight by 30 law abiding citizens without apparently too much difficulty. The court, by a majority of three to one, gave judgment in favour of Mr. Drinkwater. Gould J. (the dissenting judge) considered that it was "usurped power" to attempt to alter by force the laws and the price of victuals and wanted to sign judgment in favour of the defendant underwriter. Clive J. considered that "usurped power" must amount to

4. *Pan American World Airways Inc* v. *The Aetna Casualty & Surety Co.* [1974] 1 Lloyd's Rep. 207; [1975] 1 Lloyd's Rep. 77. See paras. 6.6–6.26, 8.13, 8.30, 8.31, 17.13, 17.24–17.26.
5. *Spinney's (1948) Ltd. and Others* v. *Royal Insurance* [1980] 1 Lloyd's Rep. 406. See paras. 7.7–7.16, 8.17, 8.18, 17.27–17.29.
6. (1597) 79 E.R. 1227.
7. (1668) 84 E.R. 1087.
8. (1781) 21 St. Tr. 485.
9. (1767) 2 Wils. K.B. 363.

high treason and not, as here, a mere felonious riot and considered that judgment should be signed in the plaintiff's favour. The more influential decisions were given by the remaining two judges, both of whom favoured the plaintiff. Bathurst J. considered: "Usurped power can only mean an invasion of the kingdom by foreign enemies, to give laws and usurp the government thereof, or an internal armed force in rebellion assuming the power of government, by making laws, and by punishing for not obeying those laws." He did not consider this to be the case here.

8.11 Wilmot C.J. said: "My idea of the words, burnt by a usurped power, from the context, that they mean burnt or set on fire by occasion of an invasion from abroad, or of an internal rebellion, when armies are employed to support it, when the laws are dormant and silent, and firing of towns is unavoidable, these are the outlines of the picture drawn by the idea which these words convey to my mind."

He further considered that an essential feature of a rebellious mob, which was guilty of high treason was: " . . . A universality, a purpose to destroy all houses, all enclosures, all bawdy-houses. Here they fell upon two bakers and one miller . . . to abate the price of provisions in a particular place; this does not amount to a rebellious mob."

8.12 Another English case from the 18th century is *Langdale* v. *Mason*,[10] where Lord Mansfield was the presiding judge. It arose out of the Gordon Riots in 1780 where the mob's fear and fury were directed at the Roman Catholics under the all embracing cry of "no popery", although in their later stages the riots degenerated into wanton destruction. The government suppressed the riots with some difficulty and in London the troops had to fire on the mob to restore order. A great deal of damage was done to property and, amongst other destruction Mr. Langdale's brewery was burnt down. It was insured against fire by the Sun Fire office whose policy excluded damage arising from: "Civil commotion and military or usurped power."

Lord Mansfield directed the jury in the following terms:

"What is meant by military or usurped power? They are ambiguous and they seem to have been the subject of a question and determination [a reference to the *Drinkwater* case[11]] . . . They must mean rebellion where the fire is made by authority; as in the year 1745, when the rebels (led by Charles Edward Stuart) came to Derby; and if they had ordered any part of the town, or a single house to be set on fire, that would have been by authority of a Rebellion. That is the only distinction in this case—it must be a rebellion, got to such a head, as to be under authority . . . Usurped power takes in rebellion, acting under usurped authority."[12]

8.13 In the *Pan Am* case[13] the Circuit Court of Appeals adopted a different approach. It dismissed Aetna's pleadings based on the 1597 and 1688 cases somewhat brusquely by saying that the pleadings were based on a false reading of English cases and were shot through with *non sequiturs*. It held:

" . . . that in order to constitute a military or usurped power, the power must be at least that of a *de facto* government. On the facts of this case, the P.F.L.P was not a *de facto* government in the sky over London when the 747 was taken. Thus the loss was not 'due to or resulting from' a 'military . . . or usurped power'."

10. (1780) 1 Bennett's *Fire Insurance Cases* 16.
11. (1767) 2 Wils. K.B. 363.
12. A clear definition of "military and usurped power" emerges by 1780—see para. 8.32.
13. *Pan American World Airways Inc.* v. *The Aetna Casualty & Surety Co.* [1974] 1 Lloyd's Rep. 207; [1975] 1 Lloyd's Rep. 77. See paras. 6.16–6.26, 8.13, 8.30, 8.31, 17.13, 17.24–17.26.

In another part of the judgment, the court held that not even in Jordan, where the main elements of the P.F.L.P. were to be found, did the P.F.L.P. have the characteristic of a *de facto* government.

8.14 The same view is also noticeable in the American cases of *Insurance Company* v. *Boon*.[14] The Supreme Court of the United States was considering a case of damage to property by fire caused by the fighting between the Union and the Confederate armies around the town of Glasgow during the American Civil War. It must be remembered that the victorious North (the Union) always considered that the vanquished South (the Confederacy) were rebels and frequently referred to them as such, even though being prepared to recognise that the Confederacy was ruled by a *de facto* government. (The ability of the Confederacy to pass laws and wage war etc. has already been referred to at para. 7.6.) The Supreme Court, situated in the north, was not immune from this line of thought when it held that the Confederacy exercised a usurped power and that a usurped power is either the power exerted by invading foreign enemies, or an internal armed force in rebellion: "Sufficient to supplant the laws of the land and displace the constituted authorities".

The subsequent American decisions in *Barton* v. *Home Insurance Company*[15] (which arose out of the same battle) and *Portsmouth Insurance Company* v. *Reynold's Administratrix*,[16] were on similar lines, both drawing much support for their decisions from Chief Justice Wilmot in the *Drinkwater* case.[17]

8.15 Until the *Spinney's* case[18] the English courts did not give further close analytical attention to "military or usurped power" but two further cases should be noted. In *Rogers* v. *Whittaker*[19] Sankey J. considered whether the expression included foreign military forces. He was considering a case where a Zeppelin had dropped a bomb on a warehouse. He decided that "military power" included the exercise of a foreign military power in time of war: "Military or usurped power suggests something more in the nature of 'war' and 'civil war' than 'riot' and 'tumult'."

8.16 In the *Curtis* case[20] Bankes L.J. said: "Usurped power seems to me to mean something more than the action of an unorganised rabble . . . There must probably be action by some more or less organised body with more or less authoritative leaders." And added on the *Drinkwater*[21] case: "The acts were the acts of a common mob dispersed in less than an hour acting feloniously and not treasonably."

8.17 We can thus see why in *Spinney's* case[22] Mustill J. declined to follow the American view that "military or usurped power" can be exercised only by a government with at least *de facto* status and felt that here the English and the American laws diverged:

"Returning to the English cases, they clearly establish the proposition that one of the tests for a usurped power is whether the acts in question amount to constructive treason . . . The

---

14. 95 U.S. (5 Otto) 117 (1877).
15. 42 Mo. 156 (1868).
16. 73 Va. (32 Gratt) 209 (1880).
17. *Drinkwater* v. *The Corporation of the London Assurance* (1767) 2 Wils. K.B. 363. See paras. 8.9–8.11.
18. *Spinney's (1948) Ltd. and Others* v. *Royal Insurance* [1980] 1 Lloyd's Rep. 406. See paras. 7.7–7.16, 8.17, 8.18, 17.27–17.29.
19. [1917] 1 K.B. 942.
20. *Curtis & Son* v. *Matthews* [1919] 1 K.B. 425. See para. 7.1–7.5 (if wanted).
21. *Drinkwater* v. *The Corporation of the London Assurance* (1767) 2 Wils. K.B. 363.
22. Footnote 18, above.

usurpation consists of the arrogation to itself by the mob of a law-making and law-enforcing power which properly belongs to the sovereign."

The author considers that the reason for this divergence is explained (paras. 7.6, 8.14) and can be traced to the previous American decisions arising out of the American Civil War. In English law, *Spinney's* case[23] clearly points to the mob arrogating to itself the sovereign's powers as the proper test and it is not necessary that it should have attained the status of a *de facto* government before it exercises "usurped power".

8.18 Mustill J. then applied the English test to *Spinney's* case,[23] and also dealt with universality of purpose thus: " . . . One must ask oneself whether those participating in the events which appeared at the time in question had a sufficiently warlike posture, organisation and universality of purpose to constitute them an usurped power" and found that the answer in the case of the casual looters was "no". On the other hand, he answered the question with a "yes" in the case of the militias and their civilian allies. It is true that there was not complete identity of purpose in their many and varied motives but there was universality of purpose in that they were all arrogating to themselves the power of government and were therefore exercising an usurped power: "By side-stepping the government and proceeding to direct actions, the citizen groups arrogated to themselves the proper functions of the State and thereby exercised (or constituted) an usurped power . . . "

8.19 This lengthy excursion into "military or usurped power", which is not even an insured peril or risk in the War Risks Policy is made necessary for two reasons. Most of the decided cases deal with it rather than with "revolution", "rebellion" and "insurrection". Until *Spinney's* case,[23] there was the temptation to equate all these expressions as indistinguishable and if a casualty should arise, it may be difficult indeed to disentangle the actual events so that there is a clear pointer in one direction or the other. Nevertheless the distinction does exist and Mustill J. indicated this in the *Spinney's* case[23]: " . . . Are there other requirements ('military or usurped power'); in particular that the events should have amounted to a rebellion or insurrection? It seems to me that in the particular context the answer must be no."

Even if in the *Langdale* case[24] there was some indication that "usurped power" connotes "rebellion" or "insurrection", Mustill J. regarded Lord Mansfield as not necessarily equating them and this seems to be the modern view, however fine the distinction may be in practice.

8.20 Returning now to the insured perils of the War Risks Policy, Mustill J. adopted as a definition of "rebellion" that given by the *Oxford English Dictionary*: " . . . Organized resistance to the ruler or government of one's country; insurrection, revolt" and added something more: " . . . The purpose of the resistance must be to supplant the existing rulers or at least to deprive them of authority over part of their territory."

8.21 Regarding "insurrection" he again turned to the *Oxford English Dictionary* which to him indicated an incipient or limited rebellion with a lesser degree of

23. Footnote 18, above.
24. *Langdale* v. *Mason* (1780) 1 Bennett's *Fire Insurance Cases* 16. See para. 8.12.

organisation. He emphasised, however, that, in both "rebellion" and "insurrection", there must be action against the government with a view to supplanting it.

8.22 In 1981, Mustill J. did have the advantage of considering the judgment of Magruder C.J. in the *Davila* case (paras. 8.27–8.29), but did not have before him the judgment of Saville J., given in 1991, where "insurrection" was directly in point. It seems that *National Oil Company of Zimbabwe and Others* v. *Sturge*[25] is the first reported case to have reached the courts after the new forms of insurance for cargo and for ships were adopted in 1982 and 1983 respectively. The plaintiffs ("the Others" included B.P., Mobil, Caltex and Total) owned the gasoil and the mogas being transported through the Beira-Feruka pipeline which carried oil from the coast to landlocked Zimbabwe, formerly Rhodesia. Mr. Sturge was the representative underwriter of the insurance of the oil which incorporated the Institute Strikes Clauses (Cargo) 1.1.82. The material parts of the insurance read:

"Risks covered

This insurance covers, except as provided in Clauses 3 and 4 below, loss of or damage to the subject-matter insured caused by
  1.1 Strikers, locked-out workmen, or persons taking part in labour disturbances, riots or civil commotions
  1.2 any terrorist or any person acting from a political motive."

whilst the important exclusion read:

"Exclusions
  3. In no case shall this insurance cover
  3.10 loss damage or expense caused by the war civil war revolution rebellion insurrection, or civil strife arising therefrom or any hostile act by or against a belligerent power."

The material events can be set out:

1962

The Front for the Liberation of Mozambique (Frelimo) is founded. Its object is to gain independence from Portugal by violent means.

September 1974
Independence is granted and Frelimo begins to turn the country into a Marxist/Leninist state. There is wholesale nationalisation of land, villagers are moved to new homes, objectors are thrown into prison, and some people are sent off for "re-education".

March 1976
The previous permission to the Rhodesian armed forces to cross the frontier in "hot pursuit" is withdrawn. Sanctions against Rhodesia are now applied.

1976 to 1980
The Mozambique National Resistance Movement (Renamo) is founded. At first it is ineffective, but rapidly gains in importance. It opposes Frelimo by violent means. A radio station is established in Rhodesia.

February 1980
Rhodesia gains independence as the new state of Zimbabwe. South Africa takes Rhodesia's place as the main supporter of Renamo, and the radio station is moved there.

Late 1980
Renamo, much more effective than formerly, is now a formidable guerilla force. It engages in operations against road, rail, water and electricity services, and there are frequent ambushes of government troops besides many instances of murder of Frelimo supporters. By now it controls considerable stretches of territory, and can field up to 8,000 men against the government's army of about 20,000.

25. [1991] 2 Lloyd's Rep. 281.

July 1982

Renamo attacks the pipeline, and between this date and January 1983 carries out altogether five attacks upon it. A considerable quantity of Gasoil and Mogas is lost. By this time Renamo is able to carry out many daring acts of sabotage over the whole country, and the position is so serious that the President, Samora Machel, has to postpone a visit to London.

8.23 The underwriters were prepared to accept that the losses fell within the insured perils, but contended that Clause 3.10 excluded any claim. The question arose whether Renamo was engaged in a civil war, a rebellion, or an insurrection.

8.24 It is very noticeable that only the *Spinney's* case and the *Davila* case were quoted by counsel for the consideration of the court, and this confirms the dearth of judicial authority which has been remarked upon in this chapter. Saville J. gave judgment that:

" 'Rebellion' and 'insurrection' have somewhat similar meanings to each other. To my mind, each means an organised and violent internal uprising in a country with, as a main purpose, the object of trying to overthrow or supplant the Government of that country, although insurrection denotes a lesser degree of organisation and size than 'rebellion'."

8.25 It did not matter what the motives of Renamo were, whether they were moved by high altruistic motives such as the establishment of a democratic regime, or by simple greed and the desire for power for themselves, provided that their purposes were clear. The underwriters had made out their case, and were entitled to judgment in their favour.

8.26 The court did not feel that it was necessary to go into the questions whether Renamo's activities had become a "rebellion" or a "civil war", but Saville J. clearly considered these to be higher degrees of disorder. Continuing the approach adopted by Pickford J. and the Court of Appeal in the *Republic of Bolivia* case (paras. 20.19–20.25), by Goddard J. and Lord Greene in the *Bantham* case (paras. 6.6–6.10), and by Staughton J. in the *Andreas Lemos* case (paras. 20.33–20.38), he added:

"In the context of a commercial contract such as the policy under discussion, the expression 'civil war' 'rebellion' and 'insurrection' bear their ordinary business meanings."

and on the subject of "civil war":

"In this context, 'civil war' means a war with the special characteristic of being civil—i.e. being internal rather than external."

8.27 It would seem that the insured peril "insurrection" has only received close attention in one other case, namely *Home Insurance Company of New York* v. *Davila*,[26] a decision of the 2nd Circuit Court of Appeals. Mr. Davila owned buildings at Jayuy in Puerto Rico which were insured with the Home Insurance Company of New York against fire risks with the following exclusion clause: "Ex loss or damage caused by insurrection". On 30th October 1950, Puerto Rican nationalists undertook violent actions at various places in Puerto Rico. Four carloads of nationalists arrived at Jayuy and hoisted the nationalist flag. They set fire to several buildings and engaged in a violent gun battle with the police. The fire brigade was prevented from attending to the fires by the shooting of the nationalists and Mr. Davila's property was seriously damaged. The court described the affair: "as an incident of the uprising staged . . . by a little band of extremists calling themselves the Nationalist Party of Puerto Rico". Apparently, they had a rudimentary military

26. 212 F. (2d) 731 (1952).

organisation with officers, cadets and a training programme. The size of their resources can be judged by the fact that they devoted only four carloads of men to the City of Jayuy.

8.28 The judgment of the 2nd Circuit was given by Magruder C.J. The court was not making a finding whether an "insurrection" had arisen; it was only concerned with the District Court's direction to the jury. It considered that the jury could find that there was an "insurrection" if it was satisfied that the nationalist leaders had as their "maximum objective" the overthrow of the government. Since apparently the District Court had not so directed the jury, the case was remitted for a new trial.

8.29 Subsequently, in the *Pan Am* case,[27] the 2nd Circuit added further to its judgment on the *Davila* case[28]: "Under *Davila*, revolutionary purpose need not be objectively reasonable. Any intent to overthrow, no matter how quixotic, is sufficient" and approved the description given by the District Court that an "insurrection" means:

(1) A violent uprising by a group or movement [which is]
(2) acting for the specific purpose of overthrowing the constituted government and seizing its powers.

8.30 In applying these principles to the *Pan Am* case[29] itself, it is scarcely surprising that the 2nd Circuit Court of Appeals found: "All risks insurers did not support the burden of proving that at the time of the loss the P.F.L.P. intended to overthrow King Hussein [of Jordan]; if the P.F.L.P. was fighting Hussein, it was fighting for survival rather than Hussein's overthrow. Alternatively insurrection did not cause the loss", and made a further, and reassuring, finding that in London at that time there was no insurrection.

8.31 The reader may wish to compare the contents of this chapter with Chapter 17 which is devoted to the insured perils of "riots" and "civil commotions". These are totally separate insured perils and must be treated as such, even though the actual events of any casualty may, in spite of the most careful analysis, appear to cross the strict boundary lines which must be drawn around each separate insured peril. Before he does so, however, it is suggested that he notes the conclusions that can be drawn on "revolution", "rebellion" and "insurrection":

8.32 As conclusions, it is suggested:

(1) The meaning of "military or usurped power" became clear with the *Langdale* case in 1780. It could only arise if there was treasonable intent, or at least that of constructive treason. This in turn meant that the objects of the mob had to include the unseating of the government or coercing it by force.
(2) The reference to 1745 was to the Rising to place Bonnie Prince Charlie, the Young Pretender, on the throne as the heir of James II, and to send the Hanoverian King back whence he had come. This was a treasonable intention. If any houses had been burnt (including presumably any

27. *Pan American World Airways Inc.* v. *The Aetna Casualty & Surety Co.* [1974] 1 Lloyd's Rep. 207; [1975] 1 Lloyd's Rep. 77. See paras. 6.16–6.26, 8.13, 8.30, 8.31, 17.13 17.24–17.26.
28. Footnote 26, above.
29. Footnote 27, above.

"bawdy-houses") by the Young Pretender's followers, the loss would have been due to "military or usurped powers".

(3) The mobs in the *Drinkwater* and *Langdale* cases were not seeking to displace or coerce the government. The first mob did not like paying so much for its food, and thought that a tumultuous assembly would be helpful. The second mob did some terrible things, but its aim was to lynch any unfortunate Catholic it could lay hands upon, and to destroy his property. In neither case was there any question of "military or usurped power".

(4) "Military or usurped power" are no longer insured perils or excluded risks of the Institute War and Strikes Clauses. Mustill J. found some difficulty in equating "military and usurped power" with their modern equivalents "revolution", "rebellion" and "insurrection". There are however some common characteristics, and these include the intention to replace the government or to coerce it.

(5) There is always a danger of distortion in describing insured perils in a descending order of gravity; nevertheless, it is felt that such an order can, broadly speaking, be drawn up in the order of "revolution", "rebellion" and "insurrection". Moveover, Saville J. would have been quite justified in making a finding of a more serious disorder in the *Mozambique* case.

(6) "Revolution", as an insured peril, does not appear to have been judicially defined in the war risks context. The *Oxford English Dictionary* gives it this meaning:

"It is necessary that there must be a complete overthrow of the established government by the people over whom it formerly ruled, and a successful and complete substitution by another form of government which rules over and controls the territory in question and the people who live there. An element of forcible substitution is required although it is sufficient if the substitution is achieved without force provided that there is the threat of force, either actual or implied."

(7) "Rebellion" as an insured peril means the organised, armed and forcible resistance to the government of the country by its subjects, even though assisted from without. An essential aim is the intention to supplant the government, even though in all the circumstances that aim may appear unlikely or impossible of achievement.

(8) "Insurrection" as an insured peril is difficult to distinguish from "Rebellion" whose characteristics it shares and in particular the aim to supplant or coerce the existing government. A possible distinction is that it can include an upheaval with a lesser degree of organisation, or which is less widespread.

(9) The modern tendency of the courts is to seek after the proximate cause and to define it strictly. "Revolution", "Rebellion" and "Insurrection" are listed as separate insured perils. It can therefore be expected that in future cases, the courts will seek stricter definitions than presently exist.

(10) In the *Davila* case, the jury would have been quite justified if it found that Mr. Davila's property was damaged by an "insurrection." The violence was there, as also was the intention to overthrow the Government of Puerto Rico.

8.33 To take two more modern examples, it is questionable, and possibly even far fetched, to describe the miners' strike in the United Kingdom (1984–85) as an "insurrection". It is true that its leaders, the National Union of Mineworkers, made no secret of their loathing of the government of the day and their desire to replace it with a left-wing government which was more to their liking. To this end, they described the miners as "the shock troops of the working class". The union leaders openly congratulated themselves on the overthrow of Mr. Heath's government (1970–74), and regarded it as very desirable to repeat this triumph with Mrs. Thatcher's government. The overthrow of the government was not however the main object of the strike; this was to prevent a programme of pit closures which, if withdrawn by their employers, would have brought the strike to an immediate end. It is moreover, extremely doubtful if many of the individual members of the miners' union, although prepared to engage in violent battles with the police to prevent mines being closed, subscribed to the idea of overthrowing the government by these means. Considerations of this long drawn out strike belongs to Chapter 17 which deals with riots. It will be dealt with there.

8.34 If it is accepted that the Sarajevo Government is the *de jure* Government of Bosnia, then the Bosnian Serbs and the Bosnian Croats have, throughout 1992 and 1993, been engaged in a rebellion against it. This is not necessarily true of the Serbs and Croats who have come to the help of their ethnic brethren in Bosnia from outside. They have never been Bosnian subjects.

CHAPTER 9

. . . or civil strife arising therefrom . . .

9.1 There appear to be no decided cases on this insured peril, apart from some indications in *Spinney's* case.[1] It is clear from the terms of the policy that this insured peril is intended to cover situations of civil disorder which arise during a war, civil war, revolution, rebellion or insurrection,[2] or which continue after the war etc. is over; it can be expected that civil disorder of some kind can be expected to arise either during, or after, such traumatic events, and, provided that the civil disorder can factually be linked to war etc. in the sense that it "arises" from them, or from one of them, a claim will arise in respect of an insured object which is lost or damaged as a result.

9.2 "Civil" is defined in the *Oxford English Dictionary*: "Of or pertaining to citizens; of or belonging to citizens; consisting of citizens or men dwelling together in a community; also of the nature of a citizen" and "strife": "The action of striving together or contending in opposition; a condition of antagonism, enmity or discord; contention, dispute; in a state of discord or contention; by force or violence (also appropriate to a situation without violence)."

9.3 Following the indications in the *Spinney's* case,[3] it is suggested that such "civil strife" must be of a most serious nature amounting at least to a "civil commotion"[4] and nothing less than this will cause this insured peril to operate on its own. This does not mean that other disturbances of a lesser nature, which are insured perils in their own right, are excluded from the insurance cover. These insured perils will not separately cease to become complete simply because this insured peril will only operate where serious disturbances are involved.

---

1. *Spinney's (1948) Ltd. and Others* v. *Royal Insurance* [1980] 1 Lloyd's Rep. 406. See paras. 7.7–7.16, 8.17, 8.18, 17.27–17.29.
2. See Clause 1.2, Appendix D.
3. Footnote 1, above.
4. See Chapter 17.

CHAPTER 10

. . . or any hostile act by
or against a belligerent power

10.1 These words were not included in the F.C. & S. Clause until the 1943 version, and then only in a heavily qualified form (para. 1.15). The reasons for the decision of Mr. Alan Jackson's Committee in 1983 to exclude "warlike operations" from the new MAR form are described at para. 1.19. Its place was taken by the wholly new insured peril of "war", which in turn was reinforced by "or any hostile act by or against a belligerent power", promoted for the first time to the full standing of an insured peril in its own right from its previously obscure position. Whilst, as noted in Chapter 6, there are still a number of unanswered questions about "war" as an insured peril, it can still be regarded as definite and precise. Whilst there are few judicial definitions of the insured peril which this chapter considers, there are sufficient to suggest the view that it, too, is definite and precise with a well-defined field of application.

10.2 The *Oxford English Dictionary* defines "hostile" as: "Of pertaining to, or characteristic of an enemy; pertaining to or engaged in actual hostilities" and "hostility" as: "The state or fact of being hostile; hostile action exercised by one community, State or power against another."

10.3 Jowitt's *Dictionary of English Law* (1959 edition) defines "belligerent" as a noun rather than an adjective: "A nation or party of persons carrying on war according to the law of nations, as distinguished from irregular combatants who have no rights under the law of nations." Therefore even before the eye reaches the word "power" a distinct flavour is introduced of warlike actions by or against a State or at the very least an organised body of persons. In connection with "power", it should be noted that the F.C. & S. Clause contained an explanation: "and for the purpose [of the F.C. & S. Clause] power includes any authority maintaining naval, military or air forces in association with a power". This phrase has been left out of the MAR form, no doubt because it was felt to be unnecessary and added nothing to the insurance cover given.

10.4 Matters were put on to an even firmer and more definitive basis by Bailhache J. in *Atlantic Mutual Insurance* v. *King*.[1] The *Tennyson* sailed from Bahia bound for New York in February 1916 loaded in number 4 hold with a cargo of hides and skins. Five days after sailing, on 18th February, 1916, a bomb exploded in the hold, seriously damaging the after end of the ship and the hides and skins in number 4 hold, killing three seamen and starting a fire. It was clearly a very powerful weapon, and it turned out that it was planted there by Herr Niewerth, a

---

1. [1919] 1 K.B. 309.

German citizen living in Bahia, and a shadowy accomplice with several aliases. Niewerth was an electrical engineer and the manager of a local factory. His house was the centre of German activities in Bahia and he never made any secret of his patriotic feelings. In due course, he was tried and convicted for what he had done by the Brazilian Criminal Courts. Atlantic, who were the primary insurers, paid the claim of the owners of the cargo, and looked to Mr. King to reimburse them under the reinsurance policy. This document contained an exclusion clause: "Warranted free from all consequences of hostilities or warlike operations . . . "

10.5 On "hostilities", Bailhache J. had this to say:

"In one sense, it is plainly true that the fire was due to a hostile act, but the plaintiffs say rightly, as I think, that the word 'hostilities' as used in the Clause, means hostile acts by persons acting as the agents of sovereign powers, or such organized or considerable forces as are entitled to the dignified name of rebels as contrasted with mobs or rioters, and does not cover the act of a merely private individual acting entirely on his own initiative, however hostile his actions may be."

If matters had rested there, the plaintiff would have won his case because the conclusion must have been that Niewerth was acting on his own and not on the orders of his government. The court seems not to have been too impressed with the defendant's list of 27 similar instances, or the expressed policy of Germany to wage war, not only by means of her armed forces but: " . . . by all her subjects wherever found who were willing to help her by doing . . . mischief . . . "

10.6 What seems to have clinched the matter in the defendant's favour was the production of a circular to all the German naval attachés in Germany's overseas embassies that they were to spare no effort to recruit "destruction agents". The chief targets were to be munitions for the United Kingdom, France, Canada, the United States and Russia. Bombs were to be placed on board. Trouble was to be fermented in the ports. The use of anarchists and criminals was sanctioned. Funds would be made available. Whilst there was no evidence that Niewerth ever saw the circular, it was reasonable to assume that a man of his character was the servant, or agent, of Germany. There was no subsequent ratification of his actions by Germany, and he was not an agent in the business sense, but:

"I am disposed to think that a man is acting in such a case as this as the agent of his government when knowing that the settled and concerted policy of that government is to avail itself of the efforts of all its subjects . . . he uses such opportunity as presents itself under that policy."

Niewerth could thus be regarded as a German agent as fully as though he was a member of the German armed forces and wore their uniform.

10.7 Two years later, in 1921, Bailhache J.'s views received the support of the Court of Appeal and the House of Lords in *The Petersham*[2] and *The Matiana*.[3] Atkin L.J. considered that "hostilities" implied enemy nations at war with one another. Lord Atkinson added to this: "I concur with Atkin L.J. thinking that the word 'hostilities' connotes the idea of belligerents properly so called, enemy

---

2. *Britain S.S. Co.* v. *Rex* (*The Petersham*) (1920) 3 Ll.L.Rep. 163, 205; (1920) 4 Ll.L.Rep. 245; [1921] 1 A.C. 99 (H.L.). See para. 40.5.
3. *Green* v. *British India Steam Navigation Co.*, *British India Steam Navigation Co.* v. *Liverpool & London War Risks Association* (*The Matiana*) (1920) 3 Ll.L.Rep. 205; (1920) 4 Ll.L.Rep. 245; [1921] 1 A.C. 99 (H.L.). See para. 40.4.

nations at war with one another and is used to describe the operations, offensive, defensive, or possibly protective of the one against the other in the conduct of the war."

10.8 Lord Wrenbury used different words, but in spite of an initial impression of divergence, it is suggested that he meant the same:

"All the decisions have, I think, proceeded, and in my judgment have rightly proceeded, upon the footing that the word 'hostilities' does not mean 'the existence of a state of war' but means 'acts of hostility' or (to use the noun substantive which follows[4]) 'operations of hostility'. The sentence may be read 'all consequences of the operations of hostility (of war) or operations warlike (similar to operations of war) whether before or after declaration of war.' To attribute to the word the larger meaning—namely 'all consequences of the existence of a state of war'—would give the expression a scope far beyond anything which one can conceive as intended."

10.9 This view of "hostilities" and "hostile act" received much support in *International Dairy Engineering Company of Asia* v. *American Home Assurance Company*.[5] The court's decision really turned on the "consequences" point but it is clear that the court would have been equally prepared to sign judgment in the underwriter's favour because the loss was due to "a hostile act by or against a belligerent power" which was similarly excluded from the insurance cover. Sweigert D.J. held:

"The term 'hostilities' and 'hostile act' . . . has been defined as actual operations of war, either offensive, defensive or protective by a belligerent. It has also been held that the hostile act need not involve the overt use of a weapon which is, in itself, capable of inflicting harm; it can be an operation such as the extinguishment of a navigational light or the outfitting of ship—if done for a hostile purpose."

10.10 The Vietcong could not be described as a nation but: " . . . [The] National Liberation Front [Vietcong] were engaging in hostilities with the Republic of South Vietnam and as such insurgents had taken control of many regions of South Vietnam . . . " Undoubtedly Bailhache J. would have accorded the Vietcong "the dignified name of rebels" and likewise considered them as "belligerent".

10.11 As conclusions, it can be said:

1. The words "hostile", "belligerent" and "power" all point in the same direction, that the agency which destroys or damages the insured ship must be a government or, at the very least, rebels.
2. Such a government could have either *de jure* or *de facto* status, such as the Confederates in the American Civil War or the Nationalists in the Spanish Civil War.
3. Rebels need to have the same status as is indicated for "rebellion" and "insurrection" (Chapter 8). It will not be sufficient if the persons causing the destruction or damage to the insured ship are engaged in a mere civil commotion or a riot, serious as both of these incidents are.
4. The indications are that as things stand at present, this insured peril can only arise in the context of a "war" or "civil war". The possibility that it extends the insurance cover beyond them should not be entirely excluded.

---

4. In the phrase "consequences of hostilities or warlike operations".
5. [1971] A.M.C. 1001. See paras. 14.22–14.24.

It is tempting to think that if the highjackers in the *Pan Am* case[6] had been employed by a State at war with another State, in which the United States was neutral, or had been rebels, then the loss of the 747 would have been covered by this insured peril. So far, this line of thinking has not been sanctioned by the authority of judicial decision, and until such a decision is given, this proposition must be treated with caution.

---

6. *Pan American World Airways Inc.* v. *The Aetna Casualty & Survey Co.* [1974] 1 Lloyd's Rep. 207; [1975] 1 Lloyd's Rep. 77. See paras. 6.16–6.26, 8.13, 8.30, 8.31, 17.13, 17.24–17.26.

CHAPTER 11

Capture

DIFFERENCES BETWEEN "CAPTURE" AND "SEIZURE"

11.1 Whilst "capture" and "seizure" both involve depriving the insured ship-owner of his property, they are nonetheless distinct and separate insured perils. Definitions of insured perils must always be approached with caution, and whilst "capture" can be defined quite easily, "seizure", which can be effected by a number of different persons who are acting for a wide degree of motives, is less easy to describe comprehensively. The following descriptions are helpful. Channell J., when giving judgment in *Andersen* v. *Marten*[1] in 1907 quoted from Emerigon when defining "capture": "A taking by the enemy as prize, in time of open war, or by way of reprisals, with intent to deprive the owner of all dominion or right of property over the thing taken."

11.2 Lord Fitzgerald in the House of Lords hearing of *Cory & Son* v. *Burr*[2] contrasted "capture" with "seizure":

"Capture would seem properly to include every act of seizing or taking by an enemy or belligerent. 'Seizure' seems to be a larger term than 'capture' and goes beyond it, and may reasonably be interpreted to embrace every act of taking forcible possession either by lawful authority or by overpowering force."

11.3 Hilbery J., when giving judgment in *Middows* v. *Robertson*[3] contrasted "capture" with "takings at sea", an insured peril which no longer appears in the Institute War and Strikes Clauses but which to some extent is co-extensive with "seizure":

"Capture is a taking by the enemy as prize in time of open war with intent to deprive the owners of their property and the goods. It is a belligerent act. A taking at sea is something less, and it may be a taking at sea although at the time there is no intention thereby to deprive the owner of his property and the ship, but merely the intention to take the ship in for an adjudication. It is the lesser thing included in the greater which is capture."

This definition was noted with much approval by Kerr L.J. in *The Salem*.[4]

---

1. [1907] 2 K.B. 248. See paras. 11.27–11.30.
2. (1883) 8 App. Cas. 393. See paras. 12.12, 12.13, 12.16–12.19.
3. *Forestal Land, Timber & Railways Company* v. *Rickards (The Minden); Middows* v. *Robertson (The Wangoni); W.W. Howard, Bros. & Co.* v. *Kann* (1940) 67 Ll.L.Rep. 484; (1940) 68 Ll.L.Rep. 45 (C.A.); (1941) 70 Ll.L.Rep. 173; [1942] A.C. 50 (H.L.). See paras. 13.27–13.34.
4. *Shell International Petroleum Co. Ltd.* v. *Caryl Antony Vaughan Gibbs (The Salem)* [1981] 2 Lloyd's Rep. 316; [1982] 2 W.L.R. 745; [1982] 1 Lloyd's Rep. 369; [1982] Q.B. 946 (C.A.); [1983] 1 Lloyd's Rep. 342; [1983] 2 W.L.R. 271 (H.L.). See paras. 12.54–12.63.

THE IMPORTANCE OF THE DATE OF THE ISSUE OF THE WRIT

11.4 Actual Total Loss, Constructive Total Loss and Notice of Abandonment are the subjects of Chapter 27. It is hoped that the following brief description will be of help to the reader.

11.5 The natural corollaries to capture are a claim upon the underwriters, Notice of Abandonment, and, if the claim is not accepted, the issue of a writ which commences legal proceedings. The date of the issue of the writ or, if the normal practice is followed, the date that underwriters reject the Notice of Abandonment and "put the shipowners in the same position as though a writ had been issued", is of the utmost importance as the following example will show:

Monday	*Thursday*
The ship is captured.	The writ is issued.
Tuesday	*Friday*
Notice of Abandonment is tendered to the underwriters.	The ship is released.
Wednesday	
The Notice of Abandonment is rejected.	

11.6 The rule of the law is that the position of the unlikelihood of recovery of the ship must be judged by the circumstances as they exist on the Thursday, or if the underwriters have placed the shipowner in the same position as though he had issued a writ, on the Wednesday. If *at that time* the circumstances were such that it was unlikely that the assured would recover his ship within a reasonable time, then he would be entitled to claim that his ship was a constructive total loss under section 60 of the Marine Insurance Act (paras. 27.7, 27.15, 27.39). It would make no difference that on Friday, the captors quite unexpectedly relented and released the ship, or that she was equally unexpectedly recaptured by friendly armed forces, or escaped by the exertions of her crew. This is of course a very extreme example and in practice it is highly unlikely that events would take this course. Nevertheless, the effect of this rule of law should be fully understood, and also its application to other insured perils appreciated, particularly "seizure", "arrest", "restraint", "detainment", "confiscation" and "expropriation" as *The Anita* and *The Bamburi*[5] cases illustrate. Distinction should be made between a constructive total loss to which this rule applies, and an actual total loss where it has no application. If another natural corollary should also follow, condemnation by an enemy Prize Court, a usual but not inevitable course, it could be said that the transfer of ownership which such condemnation involves has irretrievably deprived the assured of his ship so that, under section 57 of the Marine Insurance Act, she is an actual total loss. Whilst not ignoring this possibility, this work will concentrate on the more likely position that, in the case of "capture" (and more particularly in the case of the other insured perils) the ship will be a constructive total loss and this rule of law will have to be taken into account.

5. *Panamanian Oriental Steamship Corpn.* v. *Wright (The Anita)* [1970] 2 Lloyd's Rep. 365; *The Bamburi* [1982] 1 Lloyd's Rep. 312. See paras. 13.35–13.44 and 13.63–13.72.

11.7 This rule of law grew only slowly over a long period of time as the cases quoted in this chapter will show. It is particularly (although not exclusively) relevant to war risks cases. It can be particularly severe on the underwriter, and it is surprising that the Institute War and Strikes Clauses contain no provision to offset its sometimes extreme effect. As will be seen (paras. 23.24–23.33) the Rules of the Mutual War Risks Associations contain provisions aimed at producing not only a less arbitrary effect, but one which is fairer and more equitable between the underwriter and the insured alike.

THE CASES DESCRIBING THE INSURED PERIL

11.8 The earliest case which concerns us is *Goss* v. *Withers*,[6] which arose out of the Seven Years' War. The case concerned the *David and Rebeccah* and her cargo of fish which was loaded in Newfoundland for Spain and Portugal. Whilst they were separately insured under different policies, the court seems to have made no distinction between them, presumably because the ship and the cargo were owned by the same interests. Furthermore, there seems to have been no exclusion of war risks from the policy.

1756

November/December

The ship sails. She is damaged by a violent storm and needs extensive repairs to continue the voyage.

23rd December

The ship is captured by a French privateer. The crew is removed except for an apprentice and a landsman and the ship is directed to a French port with a prize crew on board.

31st December

The ship is retaken by a British privateer.

1757

18th January

The ship arrives in Milford Haven. Notice of Abandonment is given to the underwriters. The cargo of fish goes bad but it is not clear from the report if this is the result of the prolonged voyage or the lengthy delays in Milford Haven.

11.9 Lord Mansfield, the presiding judge, made a clear distinction between the positions of the underwriter who insures the ship on the one hand and any vendee or recaptor on the other. Where the ship has not been condemned by an enemy Prize Court so that her legal ownership is transferred from her true owner, a vendee or recaptor has no title against the owner of the ship who retains his property in her. He noted two cases from the 17th century as authority for this proposition. In the first case, the ship was recaptured by an English privateer after 14 weeks in the enemy's possession without being condemned. In the second case, *Assievedo* v. *Cambridge*,[7] there was long possession by the enemy, which included two sales and

6. (1758) 2 Burr. 683.
7. (1712) 10 Mod. Rep. 77.

several voyages, but again no condemnation before the ship was recaptured by an English warship. The court held in both cases that the original owners still had the best title. Regarding the underwriters, however Lord Mansfield said:

"But whatever rule ought to be followed, in favour of the owner, against a recaptor or vendee, it can in no way affect the case of an insurance between the insurer and insured . . . The ship is lost by the capture . . . and the insurer must pay the value. Capture by a pirate or capture under a commission where there is no war do not change the property. Yet between the insurer and insured, they are just upon the same foot as capture by an enemy."

11.10 In the *Goss* case[8] the court judged that the *David and Rebeccah* and her cargo were total losses but it would appear that the storm damage to the ship, coupled with the salvage and other charges attending her recapture led in any event to what we would now call a constructive total loss apart, of course, from the cargo which, as has already been noted, was an actual total loss. What we need to note is that the actual capture by the French privateer gave rise to the insured peril of "capture" and it was not necessary that the ship and her cargo should first be condemned by a French Prize Court.

11.11 Lord Mansfield did find it necessary to emphasise that the mere fact of a capture might not necessarily justify an abandonment to the underwriter and a claim for a total loss, using these words:

"There might be circumstances under which a capture would be but a small temporary hindrance to the voyage; perhaps none at all; as if the ship was taken, and in a day or two, escaped entire, and pursued her voyage. These are circumstances under which it would be deemed an average loss; if a ship taken is immediately ransomed by the Master and pursues her voyage, there the money paid is an average loss."

11.12 However emphatic Lord Mansfield was in the *Goss* case,[9] he soon found himself making exactly the same points three years later in *Hamilton* v. *Mendes*.[10] The *Selby* was loaded with tobacco in Virginia for London.

1760

28th March

The ship sails.

6th May

The French privateer *Aurora of Bayonne* captures the ship and removes the crew except for the Mate and one man. A prize crew is put aboard to take the ship to a French port.

23rd May

The ship is retaken off Bayonne by H.M.S. *Southampton*.

6th June

The ship arrives in Plymouth where the salvor apparently has a right to one-eighth of the value.

23rd June

A letter is written to the underwriters abandoning the ship to them.

26th June

Notice of Abandonment is tendered. The underwriters say that they do not think that they are bound to take the ship. They are, however, ready to pay salvage and other expenses.

8. (1758) 2 Burr. 683.
9. (1758) 2 Burr. 683.
10. (1761) 2 Burr. 1198.

19th August

The ship arrives in London where the cargo is discharged.

11.13 The question for the court was whether the plaintiff had the right to abandon the ship on 26th June. It was held that he did not have this right or the right to claim for a total loss. The underwriters' attitude was the correct one, and the shipowner was entitled to no more than the relatively minor expenses which arose directly from the insured peril. In this case there was little, if any, damage to the ship or to the tobacco. Lord Mansfield added by way of explanation to what he had said in the *Goss* case[11]:

"It does not necessarily follow, that, because there is a recapture, therefore the loss ceases to be total. If the voyage is absolutely lost, or is not worth pursuing; if the salvage is very high; if further expense is necessary; if the insurer will not engage, in all events, to bear that expense, although it should exceed the value or fail of success; under these and many other like circumstances the insured may disentangle himself and abandon, notwithstanding there has been a recapture."

11.14 In the middle of the 18th century, it seems to have been assumed that the shipowner's entitlement to a total loss payment was to be judged at the date that the Notice of Abandonment was given. In this work, we refer to the more peremptory modern practice of giving notice to the underwriter although it would seem from the reports that a more courteous procedure was in vogue at the time of offering abandonment to the underwriter. Possibly the assumption went even further, that the insured owner was entitled to a total loss payment on the date that the notice was given. Lord Mansfield found it necessary to correct this in two passages from his judgment in the *Hamilton* case[12]:

"The plaintiff's demand is for an indemnity. His action then must be founded upon the nature of his damnification as it really is at the time that the action is brought. It is repugnant, upon a Contract of Indemnity, to recover as for a total loss when the final event is decided that the damnification in truth is an average, or perhaps no loss at all."

and

"I desire it may be understood that the point here determined is that the plaintiff upon a policy can only recover an indemnity according to the nature of his case at the time of the action brought or, at most, at the time of his offer to abandon."

11.15 Lord Mansfield declined to give any guidance on the position that would arise if the ship and the goods were restored safely between the dates of the Notice of Abandonment and the issue of the writ (apart of course from that which he actually gave) or between the dates of the issue of the writ and the giving of the judgment. Furthermore he wanted no inferences to be drawn in case the ship or the goods should be restored after the payment of the total loss or whether the insurer could in such a case compel a refund of the money in exchange for the restored ship or goods.

11.16 It is not clear why, in spite of the clear directions given by Lord Mansfield, there should have been a spate of cases arising out of the Napoleonic Wars or the 1812 War between the United Kingdom and the U.S.A. It is true that he left some matters open and possibly some misunderstanding arose from the last 11 words of

11. (1758) 2 Burr. 683.
12. (1761) 2 Burr. 1198.

89

the last quotation which is mentioned above. Some of them should be mentioned here if only to emphasise the rule that has developed that it is the date of the commencement of proceedings that matter, not the date that Notice of Abandonment is given.

11.17 Bainbridge v. Neilsen[13]

The *Mary* was insured with a valued policy of £6,000 on her hull and another policy of £4,000 on her freight.

1807

August

The ship sails from Jamaica bound for Liverpool.

21st September

The ship is captured by a French privateer.

25th September

The ship is recaptured by a British privateer and taken to Loch Swilley.

30th September

The shipowner first hears of her capture (but not of her recapture).

1st October

Notice of Abandonment is given to the underwriters.

2nd October

The news of the ship's capture is confirmed.

6th October

The news of the ship's recapture is first heard and is passed to the underwriters.

Later

The ship completes her voyage.

Lord Ellenborough C.J. and three other judges held that the Notice of Abandonment was properly given but that it did not confer any rights on the plaintiffs and of itself make a total loss out of a partial loss. The date of the issue of the writ cannot be quoted with certainty but it would appear that it was some time between 1st October and the arrival of the ship in Liverpool, and thus after the recapture of the ship. Lord Ellenborough C.J. in saying that he was dealing with a case on which Lord Mansfield had declined to give any guidance, where the ship or goods were safely restored between the dates of the Notice of Abandonment and the issue of the writ:

"The true effect of a Notice of Abandonment is only this, that if the offer to abandon turns out to have been properly made upon the supposed facts, which turn out to be true, the assured has put himself in a condition to insist upon his abandonment. But it is not enough that it was properly made upon facts supposed to exist at the time, if it turns out that circumstances existed, unknown to the parties, which did not entitle the owner to abandon."

Here there was no question of huge expenses of recovery which might have arisen

13. (1808) 10 East 329.

from an insured peril and thus lead to a total loss being payable. The expenses were trifling and a partial loss only was held to be justified.

11.18 Patterson v. Ritchie[14]

Goods to the value of £1,400 were loaded on the *Dispatch*, namely 31 puncheons of rum, 120 tons of salt, a quantity of coal and some mats.

1814

10th August

The ship sails from Liverpool for Quebec.

27th September

The ship is captured by an American privateer.

13th October

The crew returns home and notifies the owner what has happened. A Notice of Abandonment is given to the underwriters. A total loss payment is requested but is refused.

27th October

The ship and cargo are recaptured by a British privateer and taken to Halifax. Eleven puncheons of rum are sold to pay the cargo's proportion of salvage.

1815

May

The ship reaches Quebec. The remaining cargo, although pilfered to a minor extent, is in good condition.

   The underwriters paid all amounts due on the basis of a partial loss. It was held that whilst the cargo was probably a total loss at the date that the Notice of Abandonment was given, the circumstances had altered before the writ was issued and a partial loss was all that was due.

11.19 Brotherton v. Barber[15]

The *Fanny* was the ship in question.

1814

8th March

The ship sails from Maranham in Brazil for Liverpool.

9th April

The ship is captured off the coast of Ireland by an American privateer. The crew is transferred to a Portuguese ship bound for Liverpool.

25th April

The crew make a full report to the owner and Notice of Abandonment is given to the underwriters.

12th May

The ship is recaptured by H.M.S. *Sceptre*.

---

14. (1815) 4 Mau. & Sel. 393.
15. (1816) 5 Mau. & Sel. 418.

15th June

News of the recapture reaches the shipowners and the underwriters.

24th June

The ship reaches Gravesend.

29th September

The ship reaches Liverpool.

10th November

The shipowner issues a writ against the underwriters.

In giving judgment that the loss was only a partial loss and not a total loss, Lord Ellenborough said:" . . . It seems to me that these plaintiffs must stand, in regard to their claim for indemnity in the position in which subsequent events have placed them at the time when they came to demand it; that is when this action is brought." and Abbott J. added a comment about one of the foremost writers of the 18th century indicating that he gave the courts little by way of firm guidance in any direction.: "Upon referring to Emerigon, who collects almost all that is to be found upon the subject in the foreign writers, I observe that there is a great contrariety of opinion to the cases in which abandonment is to be deemed absolute." (Presumably so absolute that a total loss is payable.)

11.20 Naylor v. Taylor[16]

Goods were loaded on to the *Monarch* for carriage from Liverpool to the River Plate. The insurance policy contained a liberty that in the event of a blockade, or the ship being ordered out of the River Plate, they may be discharged at another port.

1826

2nd February

The *London Gazette* notifies Brazil's blockade of the River Plate.

11th March

The ship sails from Liverpool.

22nd May

The ship arrives in the River Plate.

23rd May

The ship and the cargo are captured by a Brazilian frigate.

21st July

The ship's crew overpower the Brazilian prize crew and the ship and cargo escape.

28th May

Notice of Abandonment is given to the underwriters and refused.

20th September

The ship and the goods reach Liverpool.

16. (1829) 9 B. & C. 718.

1827

Hilary term

A writ is issued against the underwriters claiming a total loss of the goods.

Lord Tenterden C.J. held there was no total loss: "If the abandonment is to be viewed with regard to the ultimate state of facts, as appearing before action brought, according to the opinion of the court in *Bainbridge* v. *Neilson*[17] there has not . . . been a total loss."

11.21 Rodocanachi v. Elliott[18]

Silks are despatched from Shanghai to London and are sent overland by rail from Marseilles. The Franco-Prussian War breaks out during the voyage.

1870

10th September

The Prussian armed forces cut the rail links between Paris and the north Channel ports.

13th September

The silks reach Paris and are warehoused.

19th September

The Prussian armed forces complete the encirclement of Paris.

7th October

Notice of Abandonment is given and, on the underwriters refusing to accept it, a writ is issued shortly afterwards.

1871

30th November

The silks arrive in London.

During the siege of Paris by the Prussian armed forces, the silks were shut up inside the city. At the time the writ was issued, there was no realistic hope that they would be delivered in London at a time that could be regarded as reasonable.

The position was complicated by the sale of the silks on 2nd September, 1870, subject to their being delivered within four months. In the event, the buyers accepted delivery, paying the contract price of £9,362 12s. 6d. The plaintiffs were nonetheless held to be entitled to receive a total loss (presumably less the proceeds of sale) on the basis that at the date of the issue of the writ, the goods could be regarded as being lost for an indefinite time.

11.22 Before we leave the ancient cases two further cases should be noted. In case it should be thought that the rule, enunciated by Lord Mansfield and followed by Lords Ellenborough and Tenterden, that the position between the insured and the underwriter must be judged at the date of the commencement of proceedings only applied to war risk cases, the same law was applied by Bayley J. in *Holdsworth*

17. (1808) 10 East 329. See para. 11.17.
18. (1873) L.R. 8 C.P. 649.

v. *Wise*.[19] The *Westbury*'s crew abandoned her believing that she was on the point of sinking and were rescued by the *Columbia*. The next day the *Bolivar* found the *Westbury* abandoned and took her to New York. She was repaired and sent back to Liverpool where, before the expiry of the policy, she suffered further damage in the last stages of her voyage. Whilst the court admitted the owners' claim for a total loss, it made it clear that it did so on the basis that all the expenses exceeded her insured value; had this not been the case the owners would have recovered a partial loss only.

11.23 *Cologhan* v. *The Governor and Company of the London Assurance*,[20] a case which went against the general trend, could be distinguished on its facts. In 1812 the *Friendship* sailed from Quebec bound to Tenerife with a cargo of wheat, fish and barrel staves. She was separated from her convoy by a storm and was captured by an American privateer. The privateer took some of the cargo for her own use and sent her with a prize crew to an American port. On the voyage she was recaptured by H.M.S. *Shannon* and sent to Bermuda. Bermuda at the time was short of food and an embargo was placed upon the wheat and the fish from leaving the island. This was eventually permitted but only on the basis that the cargo, together with an additional quantity of flour, should be taken to Madeira for the use of the British garrison stationed there. This was safely achieved. In an action for the total loss of the cargo some doubts are noticeable on the part of some of the judges, but the court gave judgment in favour of the owners for the reasons given by Bayley J.:

"The destination is to Tenerife; the ship, with the cargo, is captured; recapture follows, but not so as to enable the ship to proceed to Tenerife; for she is sent to Bermuda, where she is placed under an embargo, from which she is never released, except upon condition of altering her destination to Madeira. Therefore there has been no restitution of any part of the cargo, as it regards the risk insured to Tenerife."

11.24 Whilst these points are not relevant to the matter which we have to study, the case is an extremely interesting one for those who wish to see or learn about what captains were required to do, and in fact did, in the days before the miracle of modern communications. They were very much on their own and in the event of a mishap, they had to act as they thought best in the interests of those who owned the ship and the cargo.

11.25 The rule first enunciated by Lord Mansfield C.J. in *Goss* v. *Withers*[21] and followed by the courts since then, notably by Lords Ellenborough C.J. and Tenterden C.J., was thus firmly established by 1872. It is not necessary that there should be condemnation before the insured peril of capture can arise and the time to judge whether or not there is a total loss is the date that the action is brought, namely the date the writ is issued, not the date that Notice of Abandonment is given. *Ruys* v. *Royal Exchange Assurance Corporation*[22] concerned a case of undoubted capture and thus answered any questions on this score which were left open by *Rodocanachi* v. *Elliott*.[23] The *Doelwyk* was insured on a valued policy against war risks on 7th

---

19. (1828) 7 B. & C. 794.
20. (1816) 5 Mau. & S. 47.
21. (1758) 2 Burr. 683. See paras. 11.8–11.11.
22. [1897] 2 Q.B. 135.
23. (1873) L.R. 8 C.P. 649. See paras. 11.25, 11.26.

August, 1896. She was carrying arms for the Emperor of Abyssinia with whom Italy was then at war.

1896

8th August

The *Doelwyk* is captured by an Italian cruiser.

14th August

Notice of Abandonment is given to the underwriters and refused.

21st August

The shipowners issue a writ against the underwriters claiming that the ship is a total loss.

12th December

The Prize Court in Rome condemns the ship in prize. The war being over, it does not order confiscation. With the agreement of all parties the ship is disposed of by the underwriters on a "without prejudice" basis.

11.26 The court first dealt with some preliminary issues, notably the shipowners' knowledge at the time that the insurance was placed. Collins J. noted the line of authorities which are quoted above and gave judgment that on 21st August the ship was a total loss.

"Much might be said for the view of several . . . that the rights of the parties should be finally ascertained upon a proper abandonment. But, the object of litigation being to settle disputes, it is obvious that some date must be fixed upon which the respective rights of the parties may be finally ascertained, and the time of the Writ may be regarded as a time of convenience which has been settled by uniform practice for at least seventy years."

11.27 The *Ruys* case was followed by *Anderson* v. *Marten*[24] and together the two cases can be taken as authority that the flag or nationality of the insured ship, or the nationality of her owners, is immaterial to the insured peril of capture; the words in the definitions "taking by the enemy" do not refer to the enemy of the insured ship's flag or her nationality or that of her owners, although it seems necessary that the captor himself is in the service of a belligerent. The disbursements of the *Romulus*, a German ship, were insured under a policy for one year commencing on 12th January, 1905. The policy contained the following clause: "Warranted free from capture, seizure and the consequence of hostilities . . . "

1904

11th December

The *Romulus* sails from Cardiff bound for Vladivostok with a cargo of coal. It is the time of the Russo-Japanese War. She is supplied with false papers and instructed to follow a circuitous route to her destination to avoid Japanese warships.

1905

21st February

Whilst in the Urup Strait the ship is badly damaged by ice. The crew obliges the master to sail for Hakodati to do repairs.

26th February

Whilst in the Tsugaru Strait and only forty miles from Hakodati, the ship is stopped by a Japanese cruiser and boarded by a naval party. The Japanese Captain is unimpressed by the false papers, puts a

24. [1907] 2 K.B. 248.

prize crew aboard, and orders the ship to proceed to Yokosuka, which is a greater distance away but where there is a Prize Court.

27th February

Bad weather arises and the ship is beached to prevent her sinking. She breaks her back.

2nd March

The crew is taken to Yokosuka where the Prize Court investigates the circumstances of the capture.

Early May

A surveyor examines the ship and announces she is an actual total loss.

16th–17th May

The ship is condemned in prize.

11.28 There was no doubt in the minds of the judges of the Queen's Bench Division, the Court of Appeal or the House of Lords, that the *Romulus* had been captured on 26th February. Was she lost by "capture" (an excluded peril) on that date or by bad weather on the following day? All were unanimous that she was lost by "capture" for the following reasons: Channell J., after noting with approval Arnould's definition of "capture" and Shee J.'s writings in *Abbott on Shipping*, (11th edition, 1867):

" . . . Although mere capture in itself when there is no condemnation does not divest the property, when there is an adjudication of a Prize Court which is an adjudication in rem binding on all the world, it is a decision not merely that the property has passed at the date of the decision, but that it did pass at the time of capture and its effect therefore may be described as relating back."

The ancient cases upon which Shee J. based this decision are *Stevens* v. *Bagwell*,[25] *Morrough* v. *Comyns*[26] and *Alexander* v. *The Duke of Wellington*.[27]

11.29 In the Court of Appeal, Cozens-Hardy M.R. with the support of the other judges adopted Channell J.'s reasoning: "I think that most people, looking at the matter from a commonsense point of view and apart from the technicalities, would say that under the circumstances the owner lost his ship by 'capture', and that the Japanese captors afterwards lost their prize by shipwreck." He also drew attention to the ancient case of *Hahn* v. *Corbett*[28] where the ship was first lost by being driven on to a sandbank and afterwards captured. Here it was held that she was lost by perils of the seas.

11.30 The House of Lords agreed with the two lower courts. Loreburn L.C., after noting that the ship was employed transporting contraband of war by fraud: "I think the reasonable and true way of regarding what actually occurred is that there was, in fact, a total loss by capture on 26th February, though its lawfulness was not authoritatively determined until May 16th following" and Lord Halsbury: " . . . Given the facts . . . it would have been impossible in an English court to deny there was a total loss to the owner on 26th February . . . the rightfulness of the seizure and consequently the change of property related back to the time of capture."

25. (1808) 15 Ves. 139.
26. (1748) 1 Wils. K.B. 211.
27. (1831) 2 Russ. & M. 35.
28. (1824) 2 Bing. 205. See para. 30.17.

WHAT IS MEANT BY UNLIKELIHOOD OF RECOVERY?

11.31 The cases quoted thus far explain two propositions on the insured peril of "capture", namely that it is complete when the actual physical capture takes place irrespective of any subsequent decision by a Prize Court, and that matters between the plaintiff shipowner and the defendant underwriter must be judged as they stand at the time that the action against the underwriters is commenced. There is a further element that must be considered which did not arise in either the *Ruys*[29] or the *Rodocanachi*[30] cases, because at the time that the actions were commenced, there seemed to be no possibility of recovery of the insured property. The further element, which is given greater prominence in the subsequent cases, particularly on seizure, is that at the time that the action is commenced, what is the possibility that the ship or the goods will be returned? We have not considered the line of cases before 1906 when this element was expressed as whether or not on the facts the "ultimate release from capture was a matter of uncertainty". The Marine Insurance Act 1906, section 60, which defines constructive total loss, reads in subsection (2)(i): "In particular there is a constructive total loss—where the insured is deprived of the possession of his ship or goods, a peril insured against, and (a) it is unlikely that he can recover the ship or goods as the case may be . . ."

11.32 It will be appreciated that this subsection has a wider application than capture alone and also applies to "seizure, arrest, restraint, detainment, confiscation or expropriation" as well. It will be seen that "uncertainty" has been substituted by "unlikely". The test is thus somewhat stricter as is shown by *Polurrian Steamship Co. Ltd. v. Young*.[31]

11.33 In 1912 the *Polurrian* loaded a cargo of Welsh coal for carriage to Istanbul. On sailing, the Captain was aware that a war had broken out between Italy and Turkey but he was not aware that Greece and Turkey had also gone to war, a development which had occurred during the voyage. Subsequent events took place:

1912

25th October

A Greek destroyer intercepts the *Polurrian* off Tenedos. The Master's evidence was that "the Greek Captain said he had orders to seize us; that he would convey us to Mudros Bay, Lemnos."

26th October

Notice of Abandonment is given to the underwriters and refused. The shipowners are put in the same position as though a writ has been issued. This date is thus agreed as the date of the commencement of the action.

27th October

Discharge of the coal into the Greek flag ship begins. Subsequently all the cargo is so taken by various units of the Greek fleet. The Master meets the Greek Admiral who, in spite of the Master's denials, forms the view that the Master knew of the hostilities between Greece and Turkey. Later the Master criticises the interpreter, whose English is poor, and it is quite possible that a misunderstanding arises because of language difficulties. After consulting with his government, the Admiral orders the *Polurrian* to Piraeus to be dealt with by the Prize Court, a suggestion which emanates from the British Ambassador.

29. *Ruys* v. *Royal Exchange Assurance Corporation (The Doelwyk)* [1897] 2 Q.B. 135. See paras. 11.25, 11.26.
30. *Rodocanachi* v. *Elliott* (1873) L.R. 8 C.P. 649. See para. 11.21.
31. [1915] 1 K.B. 922.

28th November

Discharge now completed, the *Polurrian* accordingly sails to Piraeus.

29th November

The *Polurrian* arrives in Piraeus.

1st December

An armed guard is put aboard and the *Polurrian* is taken to the naval base in Salamis.

8th December

The Greek Government, by now convinced that the Master did not in fact know of the outbreak of war between Greece and Turkey and that he had conveyed a wrong impression on this point to the Admiral, releases the *Polurrian*.

11.34 Kennedy L.J. gave the judgment at the Court of Appeal with which the other two members of the court agreed. On the facts, he considered that as the law stood before 1906, the shipowner would have been entitled to recover a constructive total loss; on 26th October the owner's loss might have been permanent and was, at any rate, of uncertain continuance. At the date of the trial, however, "uncertainty of recovery" had been substituted by "unlikelihood of recovery".

"The owners now had to establish fully that:
    (i) at the date of the commencement of the action they were deprived of the possession of the *Polurrian*,
    (ii) it was not merely uncertain whether they could recover her within a reasonable time, but that the balance of probability was that they could not do so."

He found that they were unable to prove the second of these two requirements and judgment was accordingly signed for the underwriters.

11.35 Whilst the test of "unlikelihood of recovery" is now firmly established, the above-mentioned quotation is authority for adding the words "within a reasonable time" to the end of the quotation of section 60(2)(i) which is given above. This also applies to the other insured perils where section 60(2)(i) is relevant.

11.36 In the *Forestal*[32] cases Lord Wright in the House of Lords approved Kennedy L.J.'s judgment and added:

"There is a real difference in logic in saying that a future happening is uncertain and saying that it is unlikely. In the former, the balance is even; no one can say one way or the other. In the latter, there is some balance against the event. If on the test of uncertainty, scales are level, any degree of unlikelihood would seem to shift the balance, however slightly; it is not required that the scale should spring up and kick the beam."

APPREHENSION OF CAPTURE

11.37 There is a remarkable paucity of cases arising out of the First and Second World Wars when capture, particularly in the early stages of each conflict, must have been common enough. If the facts are known "capture" is one of the easiest of the insured perils to establish or to disprove and there should be no necessity for proceedings. There are two other aspects of this insured peril which need to be considered.

32. *Forestal Land, Timber & Railways Co. Ltd.* v. *Rickards (The Minden); Middows* v. *Robertson (The Wangoni); W.W. Howard, Bros. & Co.* v. *Kann* (1940) 67 Ll.L.Rep. 484; (1940) 68 Ll.L.Rep. 45 (C.A.); (1941) 70 Ll.L.Rep. 173; [1942] A.C. 50 (H.L.). See paras. 13.27–13.34.

11.38 The first of these is that in English law, loss or damage arising out of the fear of "capture" is not included within the compass of the insured peril as the following cases will demonstrate. In *Hadkinson* v. *Robartson*[33] a cargo of pilchards was loaded on to the *Pascaro* in Penzance for Naples. The pilchards were insured that they were: " . . . Warranted free from average unless general or the ship should have stranded." There was also a liberty to sail in convoy from Falmouth.

1800

19th October

The ship, having completed loading, sails to Falmouth for her convoy.

1801

24th January

The ship sails in convoy with H.M.S. *Seahorse.*

18th February

The convoy shelters in Lisbon from bad weather.

2nd March

The convoy sails from Lisbon.

5th March

The convoy receives news that all British ships are debarred from entering the ports of the Kingdom of Naples.

16th March

The Commodore orders the ship not to proceed to Naples but to go to Port Mahon in Minorca for further news.

25th March

The ship arrives in Port Mahon where the news is confirmed. Under the directions of the Vice-Admiralty Court, the cargo is surveyed and then sold for a very small sum.

Later intelligence reveals that France and the Kingdom of Naples have signed a treaty excluding all ships under British colours from Naples. To sail for Naples would be to invite confiscation of ship and cargo.

23rd April

Notice of Abandonment is tendered and refused.

11.39 In the subsequent proceedings, a jury found for the defendant underwriters. Under the procedures of the time the plaintiff obtained an order that the defendant should show cause why the verdict should not be set aside and a new trial ordered. The verdict was, however, found to be correct as Lord Alvanley C.J., noting that the policy covered "capture" and "detention of Princes", explained:

"But it has appeared to me that where the underwriters have insured against capture and restraint of Princes, and the Captain, learning that if he enters the port of his destination the vessel will be lost by confiscation, avoids that port, whereby the object of the voyage is defeated, such circumstances do not amount to a peril operating to the total destruction of the thing assured . . . I think that the detention of the cargo on board the ship at a neutral port in consequence of the danger of entering the port of destination cannot create a total loss within the meaning of the policy, because it does not arise from a peril insured against . . . The plaintiff cannot recover, unless the . . . article be totally lost by a peril within the policy; and such peril must act directly and not collaterally on the thing insured."

33. (1803) 3 Bos. & Pul. 388.

11.40 Lord Alvanley's judgment was given on 20th May, 1803. On 16th July, 1803, Lord Ellenborough C.J. heard the case of *Lubbock* v. *Rowcroft*[34] which concerned a very similar case. Twenty bags of pepper bound for Messina on board the *Nelly* also arrived in Minorca. Messina was blockaded by French warships (a surprising way to treat a treaty partner) and the Master decided not to risk certain capture. The case never got properly under way because a belated examination of the bills of lading revealed that the pepper had been endorsed over to a receiver in Minorca. This resulted in the plaintiff being "non-suited", but not before his Lordship made it perfectly clear that, even though he did not refer to the *Hadkinson* case,[35] he would have reached a similar decision to Lord Alvanley C.J.

11.41 *Kacianoff* v. *China Traders Insurance Co. Ltd.*[36] dealt with a different situation. The plaintiffs were Russian merchants importing various goods, in this case large quantities of salt beef, into Eastern Russia and Siberia from San Francisco. The Russo-Japanese War had broken out on 8th February, 1904, and the first two shipments, loaded on the *Coptic* and the *Corea* and bound for Vladivostok and Port Arthur respectively, had been captured by the Japanese navy. The underwriters had accepted these losses as proper claims. The third shipment was insured for total loss only for, amongst other risks, "capture, seizure". It was in the process of being loaded on to the *China* for carriage to Vladivostok via Nagasaki, and the ship was due to sail on 26th February, 1904, when the underwriters sent a cable to the merchant's agents in San Francisco pointing out that if the shipment went ahead, the point would be taken that the insured merchants had deliberately caused its loss. They justified this very high-handed action by pointing to the indisputable fact that Japanese warships were known to be stopping and capturing ships and cargoes and, indeed, had already done so with the plaintiffs' goods. Very surprisingly the agents accepted this because they were unwilling to cause further loss to the underwriters and they did not take any of the points which seem to have been open to them. The goods were discharged and sold to Shanghai. Notice of Abandonment was given and refused.

11.42 The plaintiffs claimed for a constructive total loss, giving credit for the sale proceeds. Judgment was given for the underwriters by Pickford J. in the High Court, and by Lord Reading C.J., Phillimore L.J. and Lush J. in the Court of Appeal. All four judges were in agreement that no insured peril had begun to operate. There were very reasonable grounds to expect that the cargo would be lost, in fact its "capture" was almost certain. On the other hand, the prospective instruments of the "capture", the Japanese warships, were many thousands of miles away at the time of the plaintiffs' loss and "capture" could not be said to be its proximate cause. One is left with the feeling, perhaps unjustifiably, that the plaintiffs' agents adopted a remarkably supine stance towards the underwriters. Surely a firmer attitude taken at the time and a claim under the Sue and Labour Clause might have served the plaintiffs better than a direct challenge of the nature which they actually made. The reports do not show such a claim being made even in the alternative. For the purposes of this work however, the decisions are very clear on the point whether or not the insured peril of "capture" had caused the loss.

34. (1803) 5 Esp. 50.
35. (1803) 3 Bos & Pul. 388. See paras. 11.37–11.41.
36. [1914] 3 K.B. 1121.

11.43 No doubt encouraged by the decisions in the *Sanday* case,[37] the plaintiffs pursued the case of *Becker Gray & Co. Ltd.* v. *London Assurance Corporation*.[38] The facts were:

1914

June

Beckers, a British firm, sells 500 bales of jute to German buyers. Property is not to pass until the goods arrive in Hamburg and are paid for there.

6th/7th July

218 bales are loaded in Calcutta on to the *Kattenturm*, a German ship which sails shortly afterwards.

28th July

The plaintiffs effect war risk insurance with British underwriters on the goods. The insured perils include: "Men of war . . . enemies . . . takings at sea, arrests, restraints and detainments of all Kings, Princes and people of what nation, condition or quality soever."

1st August

The ship arrives in Malta.

3rd August

The ship sails from Malta.

4th August

The United Kingdom declares war on Germany.

6th August

The ship puts into Messina, later shifting to Syracuse.

1st September

Notice of Abandonment is given, the goods being described as a constructive total loss through the consequences of hostilities.

2nd September

The underwriters reject the Notice and put the plaintiffs in the same position as though a writ had been issued.

28th October

The Italian Government, by decree, forbids the export of jute.

11th November

The plaintiffs, through the British Consul in Rotterdam, asks the shipowners, Hansa Lines, to deliver the goods.

20th November

Hansa replies that the German Government has forbidden its delivery.

17th December

Following the rejection of a second Notice of Abandonment a writ is issued. The jute is sold in Italy on a "without prejudice" basis.

1915

28th June

The Admiralty confirms by letter, which is accepted by both sides, that at the time any enemy steamer would have been at the risk of capture. The letter does not, indeed cannot, say that the ship would have been captured. Given the strength of the Royal Navy and the French Navy in the Mediterranean at the time, and particularly in the neighbourhood of Gibraltar, the inference must be that the risk of capture is a high one.

---

37. *Sanday* v. *British & Foreign Marine Insurance Co.* [1915] 2 K.B. 781. See paras. 13.17–13.26.
38. [1918] A.C. 101.

11.44 In the High Court, Bailhache J. held that the goods were not lost by a peril insured against but from steps taken by the Captain to avoid an insured peril which had not begun to operate. This finding was unanimously upheld by the Court of Appeal. On appeal to the House of Lords, all five Law Lords, Lords Loreburn L.C., Atkinson, Wrenbury, Dunedin and Sumner, were unanimous that even though the ship would have been in peril of capture, this was not enough for the plaintiffs' case. The plaintiffs could not prove "capture", Lord Dunedin saying: "If I had to decide positively I should decide as Bailhache J. did, that the Captain went into Messina to avoid a peril and not under the stress of an actual peril."

11.45 He noted that one of the main writers, Phillips, thought otherwise and that the result under American law and Continental law might have been different. English law followed the course set by the *Hadkinson*[39] and *Kacianoff*[40] cases and he considered this to be correct. He distinguished the *Sanday* case[41] where British shipowners suddenly found that the declaration of war made continuation of their voyages illegal. There was nothing illegal (at least in English law) in the German Master continuing his voyage. Lord Sumner agreed, making the point that for all the House knew, the ship might have succeeded in evading capture.

11.46 With the benefit of hindsight from the *Forestal* cases,[42] it does seem strange that the courts were not invited to consider the position of the German Master, who no doubt had orders from his government, as the Hansa letter indicates, or the Italian Government's decree which was surely a "restraint". Perhaps the plaintiffs might have succeeded in taking these points.

11.47 But it must not be thought that a "capture" must have taken place before the insured peril of "capture" arises. *Butler* v. *Wildman*[43] is often quoted that "capture" is complete if property is lost or destroyed when actual "capture" is imminent and this case can be distinguished on its facts from the *Hadkinson*,[44] *Lubbock*[45] and *Becker*[46] cases. A large quantity of Spanish dollars was insured on the S.G. Form for carriage from Cadiz to La Guaira via Cuba. It was the time of the South American rebellions, which resulted in the formation of the South American countries we know today. The defendant underwriters knew that the King of Spain was at war with, in the court's words: " . . . Certain persons exercising the powers of government in parts beyond the sea in South America, formally part of the Spanish Empire."

11.48 Whilst it was not stated in so many words, there seems to have been no doubt in the minds of the judges that these persons had the status of *de facto* governments. A ship of war carrying a letter of marque gave chase to Captain Jose Lopez and his ship which she eventually captured. Before she did so but whilst she was still in hot pursuit, Captain Lopez threw the dollars into the sea. He did so as a

---

39. (1803) 3 Bos. & Pul. 388.
40. [1914] 3 K.B. 1121.
41. Footnote 37, above.
42. *Forestal Land, Timber & Railways Co. Ltd.* v. *Rickards (The Minden); Middows* v. *Robertson (The Wangoni); W.W. Howard, Bros. & Co.* v. *Kann* (1940) 67 Ll.L.Rep. 484; (1940) 68 Ll.L.Rep. 45 (C.A.); (1941) 70 Ll.L.Rep. 173; [1942] A.C. 50 (H.L.). See paras. 13.27–13.34.
43. (1820) 3 B. & Ald. 398.
44. (1803) 3 Bos. & Pul. 388.
45. *Lubbock* v. *Rowcroft* (1803) 5 Esp. 50.
46. *Becker Gray & Co. Ltd.* v. *London Insurance Corporation* [1918] A.C. 101.

loyal Spanish citizen to prevent so large a sum of money falling into the hands of his country's enemies. Abbott C.J. and Bayley J. considered this to be a loss by jettison which they thought had a wider application than to general average alone. Abbott C.J. could not distinguish the case from setting fire to a ship to prevent her falling into the enemy's hands, for which the writers Emerigon and Pothier thought the underwriters liable. Bayley J. thought there was a loss by enemies similar to a destruction of the ship by fire, the enemy being the proximate cause. Best J. was particularly impressed by previous French decisions quoted by Pothier which had been given in the plaintiff's favour. "Enemies", without the general words "and of all other perils, losses, and misfortunes that had or should come, to the hurt, detriment, and damage of the said goods . . . " would include only the actual taking and destruction. The general words, which are discussed later in Chapter 14, give cover in this instance for risks which are *ejusdem generis* to the specific perils insured by the policy: " . . . By including all losses which are the consequences of justifiable acts done under certain expectation of capture or destruction by enemies." Holroyd J. gave a concurring judgment.

11.49 The court gave judgment for the plaintiff. It can be questioned if, after throwing the dollars overboard, the result would have been the same if Captain Lopez had managed to make good his escape. It is suggested that, provided the evidence indicates that a reasonable man could have concluded that capture was imminent at the time of the jettison, and this must depend on the evidence before the court, the judges would still have given judgment in the plaintiff's favour. This is not, however, a full description of the judge's reasons, and these are dealt with more fully in Chapter 14 where the "consequences and attempt" provision is discussed.

11.50 *Butler's* case[47] does not seem to determine precisely whether the general words are essential to include a loss of the nature that occurred there. Abbott C.J. Holroyd J. and Bayley J. would appear to have been satisfied that the "general words" were not necessary, whereas Best J. seems to have been quite certain that they were. Subsequent judgments seem to tend towards Best J.'s view in preference to the views of the other three judges. There is, however, the little known or quoted case of *Gordon* v. *Rimmington*[48] which indicates that Lord Ellenborough L.C. seems to have been quite certain that they were not so essential. The *Reliance* sailed in 1804 from Bristol to West Africa, whence she was due to sail to the West Indies. The nature of the voyage raises some questions in the mind as to the exact nature of her employment, but this was not pertinent to the case. She arrived in the River Gambia in June, 1804, and there she was chased by a much more powerful and much faster French privateer. She tried to escape, but the privateer was rapidly overhauling her. The crew fired the guns into the hatchways to set her on fire and escaped in the boats. She was completely burnt. Only sketchy details of the insurance are given in the report, but the shipowners are shown as pleading that she was lost by fire to prevent her and her cargo falling into the hands of the King's enemies. The judgment is very short and to the point:

"This case is new; but I am clearly of the opinion that the plaintiff is entitled to recover. Fire

---

47. *Butler* v. *Wildman* (1820) 3 B. & Ald. 398.
48. (1807) 1 Camp. 123.

is expressly mentioned in the policy, as one of the perils against which the underwriters undertake to indemnify the assured; and if the ship is destroyed by fire, it is of no consequence whether this occurred by common accident, or by lightning, or by an act alone in duty to the State. Nor can it make any difference whether the ship is thus destroyed by third persons, subjects of the King, or by the Captain and crew acting with loyalty and good faith. Fire is still the *causa causans* and the loss is covered by the policy."

11.51 The report does not mention a jury, but ends with a laconic statement "verdict for the defendant". This is surprising in view of Lord Ellenbrough L.C.'s robust direction. There is however a footnote:

"Although this point of insurance law being new to England, it has long been decided in foreign countries that, as the Master is justified in burning the ship under such circumstances, the insurer is liable for the loss. It has even been held abroad justified, and the underwriter liable, when the ship has been burnt to prevent plague from spreading."

11.52 Possibly the distinction is that the insured peril of "fire" does cover such a loss as that of the *Reliance* to avoid her capture by the enemy, whereas destruction of property by means which are not included in an insured peril requires the aid of the general words to bring them within the cover afforded by the underwriter. So long as the general words are included in the policy, the point is probably of no real importance, and here reference is particularly made to "attempt thereat" (Chapter 14).

PRIZE AND SEARCH CASES

11.53 The second of the two aspects is the cases which the Prize Court has dealt with which are often quoted in relation to the insured perils of "capture" and "seizure". Whilst on the facts there can be little difference between "capture" and "seizure" as an insured peril, or for the purposes of consideration by the Prize Court, particularly in the case of neutral vessels, it must be borne in mind that these are Prize Court cases and that it could be very misleading to quote them as fully binding in the field of insurance. There are distinctions of an important nature as Bankes and Scrutton L.JJ. pointed out in *The Sommelsdijk* case.[49] There are a great number of cases but three will serve to demonstrate the point.

11.54 A belligerent nation has long had the right to visit and search neutral vessels at sea, and during the First World War this was extended to allow searches in port because of the impossibility of searching a large vessel at sea and the risk posed by lurking submarines. This right must be used properly. Sir Arthur Channell described it thus in *The Bernisse*[50]:

" . . . So little suspicion is required to justify a search that their Lordships are not prepared to say that if a boarding officer were to state that finding a cargo to be in bulk he thought something may be hidden under it, and therefore directed a search, his conduct would be so unreasonable as to subject the Crown to a liability for damages."

The suspicion must, as always, be an honestly held suspicion even if others could criticise it as being unjustified.

49. *Netherlands American Steamship Co.* v. *H.M. Procurator-General* (1925) 22 Ll.L.Rep. 358; (1925) 23 Ll.L.Rep. 119; [1926] 1 K.B. 84.
50. [1920] P. 1; [1921] A.C. 458.

11.55 In the cases of *The Bernisse* and *The Elve*[51] neutral Dutch shipowners claimed damages from the Crown for the loss of one ship and the damage to the other. In May, 1917, both ships sailed from Rufisque in French Colonial Africa carrying ground nuts for Rotterdam. They had French clearances and should not therefore have been required to obtain British clearances as well, known at the time as the "green clearance". They were stopped by H.M.S. *Patria* near the Faroe Islands and were required to go into Kirkwall to obtain green clearances. The Masters protested that this would take them through the danger area where they were liable to be attacked by U-boats. They received an answer to the effect that their voyages would take them through the danger area in any event, and one U-boat more or less would make little difference. Royal Navy officers and ratings sailed with them to make sure that they went to Kirkwall. Both were torpedoed, the *Elve* being sunk and the *Bernisse* severely damaged. the Prize Court and the Privy Council held that this was a wrongful use of the right to visit and search, and awarded damages to the Dutch owners.

11.56 *Netherlands American Steamship Company* v. *H.M. Procurator-General, The Sommelsdijk*,[52] concerned an appeal by the Crown to the Court of Appeal against an award of compensation by the War Damages Court, established under the Indemnity Act 1920 to deal with compensation to people whose interests had suffered by the exercise of His Majesty's Royal Prerogative during the First World War. In 1915, the *Sommelsdijk*, a Dutch ship, loaded grain in Buenos Aires for Sweden. She was visited and searched off The Downs by H.M. Naval Patrols who sent her into London for a full search. A naval party was put on board her and she was escorted by a torpedo boat. After six weeks' search when no contraband was found, she was released. Her owners claimed damages. During the hearing, the terms "capture" and "seizure" were freely used but it is essential to appreciate them in their true context.

11.57 Bankes L.J. posed the two important questions. Is a visit and search effected under the Royal Prerogative? Is such a claim within the jurisdiction of the Prize Court? If it was in the Prize Court's jurisdiction, then the terms of the Indemnity Act excluded it from the jurisdiction of the War Damages Court. His Lordship went on: "The question for decision . . . is whether . . . the right of visit and search constitutes a seizure within the commission . . . " The commission of the Prize Court authorised it to deal with: "All manner of captures, seizures, prizes and reprisals of all ships . . . and to hear and determine the same."

11.58 The Prize Court exercised exclusive jurisdiction, and awarded compensation and judged responsibilities by applying "internationally the rules of international law" which differed from the normal rules of law. Bankes L.J. considered that the appeal should be allowed for these reasons alone without making any decision on the Prerogative point.

11.59 Scrutton L.J. noted Oppenheim's view that: "Seizure is effected by securing possession of the vessel through the captor sending an officer and some of his own crew on board" and added: "I cannot doubt that what happened here was a seizure, the legality of which could be investigated in the Admiralty sitting in

51. [1920] P. 1; [1921] A.C. 458.
52. (1925) 22 Ll.L.Rep. 358; (1925) 23 Ll.L.Rep. 119; [1926] 1 K.B. 84.

Prize . . . " That legality would be judged not by the rules of common law, but the more general law which is the law of nations and which is applied by the Prize Court. Finally there could not be any question of the Royal Prerogative. That gave the King power over his own subjects only and did not extend to those who owed him no allegiance. Atkin L.J. gave similar judgment and the appeal was allowed.

11.60 The last case that needs to be considered is *The Min*.[53] The *Min* was a Norwegian ship and Norway was a neutral country at this stage of the Second World War.

1939

11th August

The ship is chartered to carry grain from Australia to a wide range of European discharging ports, among them Hamburg.

3rd September

The United Kingdom declares war on Germany.

14th October

The ship bunkers in Las Palmas. By this time the cargo has been sold to the Norwegian Grain Monopoly. The charterparty has been "cancelled" and the ship is instructed to sail around the north of Scotland and to discharge at Vaksdal.

31st October

The ship is stopped and visited by a boarding party from H.M.S. *Colombo* north-west of the Faroe Islands. Suspicions stem from the original range of destinations and the circuitous route being sailed. The ship is ordered into Kirkwall for a search following a route prescribed by the boarding officer with his party on board. On the way, she strands on Reefdyke, north of Ronaldshay and is a total loss.

11.61 The plaintiffs pleaded that the boarding party was responsible for the navigation, and that if the Master was negligent, the ship's officers had become the defendants' agents. Furthermore, the defendants were wrongly in possession and were therefore responsible for the ship's loss. Hodson J. held that there was nothing exceptionally dangerous in the prescribed route and the plaintiffs failed on this point. There was no ulterior motive in sending the ship to Kirkwall and the rights of visit and search were properly conducted. The boarding officers' suspicions were perfectly justified. On the Court of Appeal's findings in *The Sommelsdijk*[54] he noted that the Court of Appeal was considering the jurisdiction of the Prize Court:

" . . . and rejected the argument that a mere temporary detention in exercise of the right of visit and search was, for the purposes of the definition, inconsistent with capture. This use of the word 'seizure' is no doubt in a sense wider than that normally used by international lawyers."

11.62 He thought "seizure" was not an appropriate description of what had happened to the *Min*, and that the sole question was whether the Crown's actions were rightful or wrongful. He decided that they were rightful and the plaintiffs' claim therefore failed.

11.63 It seems that, until *The Min* case, there was no English case that dealt directly with these points. There was, however, an American case, *Wilcocks and*

53. [1947] P. 115.
54. Footnote 52, above.

Others v. *Union Insurance*,[55] which on similar facts went the other way. The distinction was made that in the *Wilcocks* case, the crew were held to be in the hands of the captors who had seized the ship. Such a finding could be expected to lead to a different conclusion.

11.64 When drawing conclusions on "capture", comparisons must be made with the similar conclusions on "seizure", which themselves lead on to further comparisons with "arrest, restraint or detainment" (para. 13.76). "Capture" has the following characteristics:

1. There is now a great deal of authority that "capture" can only be effected by an enemy or belligerent in wartime.

2. There is no doubt that "capture" can take place where the armed forces of a belligerent government, having *de jure* or *de facto* status, carry out the necessary military or naval operation necessary to take physical possession of the insured ship. "Capture" will also take place where nationals of a belligerent *de jure* or *de facto* government, although not members of its armed forces, effect the equivalent of a "citizen's arrest" of the insured ship, provided that their actions are subsequently ratified, or at least are not disavowed, by their government. It is suggested, however, that "capture" will not take place where a terrorist group, even if owing allegiance to a pretender government without either status, take physical possession of her. It is further suggested that such an action would be "seizure", but as long as both "capture" and "seizure" are insured together as they presently are, the difference will not be important; it will only become so and possibly make necessary close judicial definition, if an exclusion clause should exclude from the cover one or other of the two perils.

3. Whilst the captor must be a belligerent, it is not necessary that the insured ship should also be a belligerent; she can be a neutral ship.

4. Whilst "capture" envisages the intention of the captor to acquire the property and legal ownership of the insured ship either on behalf of himself or his government, for the purposes of the insured peril "capture" is complete as soon as the military or naval operation finishes which leaves the captor in physical possession. It is not necessary that it should be confirmed by a Prize Court or by some other legal process, but if this takes place, the transfer of ownership to the captors dates from the time that they physically possess themselves of the insured ship.

5. "Capture" of the insured ship will not necessarily mean that she is a total loss, although the presumption that she is a total loss will be enhanced if legal proceedings in the courts of the captor subsequently condemn her in prize and so transfer the title and property in her to another. An early release (particularly without condemnation) could indicate a partial loss only.

6. If, however, a writ has been issued, or the modern practice has been followed where the underwriters refuse to accept a Notice of Abandonment and put the insured in the same position as if a writ has been issued, the date that either of these two procedures takes place is the time when it is

---

55. (1810) 1 Binn. 574.

judged that the owner is either irretrievably deprived of the insured ship so that she is an actual total loss, or it is unlikely that she can be recovered within a reasonable time so that she is a constructive total loss.

7. "Capture" envisages the presence of force or at least its threat. On the authority of the *Robinson* case, and particularly what was said by the judges in that case[56] and the *Miller* case,[57] it is suggested that actual force need not be used or deployed; it is enough if it is there, even if it is remote to the scene.

8. The remote fear of being captured does not constitute the insured peril of "capture", however well-founded that fear might be. Where, however, the prospect of being captured is manifestly immediate and imminent, the insured peril of "capture" has been found to arise.

---

56. *Robinson Gold Mining Company & Others* v. *Alliance Insurance Company* [1901] 2 K.B. 919; [1902] 2 K.B. 489 (H.L.). See paras. 12.22–12.28.

57. *Miller & The Law Accident Insurance Co.* [1902] 2 K.B. 694; [1903] 1 K.B. 712; [1904] A.C. 359. See paras. 13.11–13.15.

CHAPTER 12

Seizure

DIFFERENCES BETWEEN "CAPTURE" AND "SEIZURE"

12.1 Definitions of some insured perils must be approached with caution. Whilst "capture" can be defined quite easily, "seizure", which can be effected by a number of different persons acting for a wide degree of motives, is less easy to describe comprehensively. There are helpful definitions by Hilbery J. and Kerr L.J.[1] if "seizure" can be equated with "takings at sea" as to some extent it must. The most comprehensive definition of all appears to be that given by Lord Fitzgerald in the House of Lords hearing in *Cory & Son* v. *Burr*[2]:

"Capture would seem properly to include every act of seizing or taking by an enemy or belligerent. Seizure seems to be a larger term than capture and goes beyond it, and may reasonably be interpreted to embrace every act of taking forcible possession either by lawful authority or by overpowering force."

12.2 "Seizure" also overlaps to some extent "restraint" and "detainment" and it is noticeable from the decided cases that the judges do not always find it necessary to draw hard and fast distinctions between them. Its nature is better described in the decided cases.

12.3 The earliest cases which still appear in recent reports where "seizure" is at issue are two cases which seem to have only a slight connection with it. In *Green* v. *Young*,[3] the ship was insured for a voyage from Jamaica to London and one of the insured perils was "detention of Princes". The government in Jamaica laid an embargo upon her, proposing to turn her into a fire-ship and offering to pay for her. Did this excuse the insurers? Holt C.J. thought that it would not because the government's actions were within the compass of the insured peril. If the government had proceeded with its intention, one is tempted to think that the embargo was the least of the worries surrounding the ship. The report is very brief, Holt C.J. gives no absolute opinion, and the decision of the jury which he was directing is not recorded.

12.4 *Touteng* v. *Hubbard*[4] was a charterparty case. In 1800 the *Economy of Stockholm*, a Swedish ship, was chartered to load fruit at Ponte del Gada for carriage to London. The charterparty contained a clause "restraint of Princes and Rulers during the said voyages always excepted". In late December, 1800, the ship sailed from London but was driven back by heavy weather and in January, 1801, took refuge

---

1. See para. 12.64.
2. (1881) 8 Q.B.D. 313; (1882) 9 Q.B.D. 463; (1883) 8 App. Cas. 393. See paras. 12.12, 12.13, 12.16–12.19.
3. (1702) Raym. 840.
4. (1802) 3 Bos. & Pul. 291.

in Ramsgate. There she was embargoed by the British Government's embargo on all Swedish vessels, and she remained in Ramsgate until June, 1801, when the embargo was lifted. The Captain was willing to perform the voyage but the charterer refused on the grounds that there was no point in sailing to load fruit at that time of the year. The shipowner sued for his whole freight (£748 2s. 6d.) and his expenses during the detention (£397 6s. 6d.). Lord Alvanley C.J. found only one prior decision to help the court in a complex charterparty case, namely a decision of Marshall J. in what seems to have been an insurance case: " . . . If a British ship be arrested or seized by the authority of the British Government from State necessity, this shall be a detention within the meaning of the policy for which the insurer is liable."

Again, the result of the case is not known but it is suggested that the meaning was clear enough, and that Lord Alvanley C.J. considered that the ship's flag made no difference.

12.5 With an insured peril of such a wide nature, it is inevitable that some cases should often find their way into the reports even though close examination reveals only the loosest connection. Two have already been noted. Two more are *Rohl* v. *Parr*[5] and *Jones* v. *Schmoll*,[6] both cases of a repulsive nature concerning as they do cargoes of slaves. The first case dealt with the application of a deductible upon loss and second with a mutiny among the slaves so that their connection with the insured peril of "seizure" is not obvious. Another case which is frequently quoted, again without appearing to be fully relevant, is *Court Line* v. *Dant and Russell*.[7] This case concerns the frustration of a charterparty when the Yangtze River was closed by a boom during the China-Japan War in the 1930s.

THE CASES DESCRIBING THE INSURED PERIL

12.6 Cases more directly on "seizure" as an insured peril include two of a particularly interesting nature. In *Powell* v. *Hyde*,[8] the court heard that on 17th March, 1854, the *Bedlington* sailed from Galatz bound for London. Her policy on the S.G. Form included a warranty: "Warranted free from particular average, unless stranded, sunk or burnt; also from capture and seizure, and the consequences of any attempt thereat."

12.7 Before reaching the mouth of the Danube, she had to pass a Russian fort which was firing on Turkish troops. She flew the British flag which the Russians said they mistook for the Turkish flag when they fired upon her. The court thought this to be an unlikely excuse. The United Kingdom was at the time neutral, only later being engaged in the Crimean War. The crew took to the boats, being later rescued by the Russians, and the ship was sunk. Lord Campbell found on the evidence that the Russians intended to detain the ship and gave judgment:

"Capture is not confined to lawful capture but includes any capture in consequence whereof the ship is lost to the insured . . . When they had fired on the ship, and the crew had left her, and she was at the mercy of the Russians, I am of opinion that she was seized by them; that there was, not only an attempt at seizure, but an actual seizure."

5. (1796) *The Times,* 10 March; 1 Esp. 445.
6. (1785) 1 Term Rep. 130.
7. (1939) 64 Ll.L.Rep. 212; 161 L.T. 35; 44 Com. Cas. 345.
8. (1855) Ed. & Bl. 607.

12.8 Coleridge J. thought that it was a capture by lawful authority and the intention was to seize her. Wightman J. held that if the exception was confined just to legal actions, illegal actions could not be within the insured perils. To him seizure could be either legal or illegal. He further held that it was either a seizure or an attempt at one. In signing judgment for the underwriters, the court did not feel it necessary to make a clear distinction between capture and seizure as both were excepted. The inference from the judgment appears to be that if the Russians had succeeded in stopping the ship, they would either have retained her, thus capturing her, or would have seized her temporarily before releasing her.

12.9 A clearer distinction appears in *Johnson & Co.* v. *Hogg.*[9] The *Cypriot* was insured on the S.G. Form with the following clause: "Warranted free of capture and seizure and the consequences of any attempt thereat".

On 7th October, 1879, the ship ran aground in the Brass River. On the following day, natives chased away the Master and the crew and took possession of her. They did so much damage to the ship that both parties agreed that she was a constructive total loss. The jury found that the natives intended to plunder the cargo but did not intend to keep the ship. The plaintiff shipowners contended that to constitute "seizure", there must be taking with intent to keep the ship as one's own and not merely to plunder her. This plea was based on an American case, *Black* v. *Marine Insurance*,[10] where the court ruled: "Seizure may in general be applicable to a taking or detention for the violation of some municipal regulation."

12.10 One of the writers at the time, Phillips, quoted this case as support for the view: "A seizure is equivalent to a capture, as it is made with the intention of depriving the owner of his property in the subject." "Capture" itself was broad enough to comprehend any forcible "seizure", "arrest" or "detention" which may be lawfully insured against.

12.11 Cave J. rejected this view, adding that he had great difficulty in reconciling the writers Phillips, Marshall and Parsons. On reading the policy: "I cannot find any indications that the word seizure is used in any but its ordinary and general signification." Even though the natives did not intend to keep the ship, and lost interest in her as soon as they had plundered her, the court held that it was still a "seizure" and judgment was signed for the underwriters.

12.12 One of the leading cases on "seizure" is *Cory & Sons* v. *Burr*[11] when no less than nine judges in the High Court, the Court of Appeal and the House of Lords ruled that, for virtually the same reasons throughout, there was a "seizure". Four earlier cases were frequently quoted in the courts in connection with "seizure" and it is necessary to consider them. The first, *Havelock* v. *Hancill*,[12] and a similar American case, *American Insurance Company* v. *Dunham*,[13] can both be distinguished quite easily on the wording of the policies. The third case, *Livie* v. *Janson*,[14] was a decision on proximate cause and belongs to a later chapter.[15] None of these three cases seems appropriate to "seizure". A fourth case, *Archangelo* v.

9. (1883) 10 Q.B.D. 432.
10. 11 John N.Y. 287.
11. (1881) 8 Q.B.D. 313; (1882) 9 Q.B.D. 463; (1883) 8 App. Cas. 393. See paras. 12.12, 12.13, 12.16–12.19.
12. (1783) 3 Term Rep. 277.
13. 2 Wend. N.Y. 463.
14. (1810) 12 East 648.
15. Chapter 30, para. 30.16.

Thompson,[16] is rather closer. In *Havelock* v. *Hancill*,[17] the *Economy* was insured for 12 months to engage in "any lawful trade". The insured perils included barratry of the Master and mariners "and all other perils, losses and misfortunes that had or should come to the hurt, detriment or damage of the said ship".

12.13 In March, 1785, the ship sailed from Ostend bound for Sunderland. The Master put into Shields to smuggle ashore a large quantity of brandy and other liquors which belonged to him. The Customs promptly seized the ship and, but for the prompt payment of £408 by the owner, a large sum in those days, would have forfeited her. The underwriter pleaded that the policy only covered the Master's barratry whilst engaged in a lawful trade and this trade was unlawful. Lord Kenyon C.J. gave judgment for the shipowner: "If the owner of the ship conducts himself with propriety, he is entitled to be indemnified against all the perils insured . . . Now in the present case, the owner is not engaged in any unlawful trade."

12.14 In *American Insurance Company* v. *Dunham*,[18] a ship was seized and detained on facts which were very similar to the *Havelock*[19] case. Prohibited goods were found on board which the Master intended to smuggle. The insurance policy appears to have contained a clause freeing the underwriter from liability for "seizure" or "detention" arising from an illicit or prohibited trade. The American courts held, in a decision which can also be distinguished on the wording of the policy from the *Cory* case, that this clause only applied where the illicit or prohibited trading took place with the owner's knowledge and consent. The shipowners were awarded judgment.

12.15 The *Archangelo* case[20] is, as has already been said, rather closer to the *Cory* case (even though it is concerned with capture rather than seizure) because the question of barratry also arose. In 1797 a ship, warranted to be Danish, was insured for a voyage from Trieste to Hamburg. There was no F.C. & S. Clause in the policy. Shortly after leaving Trieste and apparently following a prior agreement which the Danish Captain had made with the French Captain, she was captured by a French privateer and taken to Venice where both ship and cargo were condemned in prize. Underwriters' counsel objected that the loss was from barratry, whereas the plaintiff claimed it arose from "capture". Lord Ellenborough C.J. answered him thus:

"The plaintiff was not party to the barratrous agreement under which the ship was taken. As to him, the loss actually arose from the capture. He might have recovered under a court laying the loss by barratry; but the ship was actually taken by a French privateer, I think this declaration, laying the loss by capture, is sustained by the evidence."

12.16 In the *Cory* case,[21] however, there was a warranty against: "Capture and seizure and the consequences of or any attempt thereat" in the S.G. Form on which the *Rosslyn* was insured. In May, 1879, the Master loaded eight tons of tobacco in Gibraltar with the intention that it should be trans-shipped surreptitiously at sea on

---

16. (1811) 1 Camp. 620.
17. (1783) 3 Term Rep. 277.
18. 2 Wend. N.Y. 463.
19. (1783) 3 Term Rep. 277.
20. (1811) 1 Camp. 620.
21. (1881) 8 Q.B.D. 313; (1882) 9 Q.B.D. 463; (1883) 8 App. Cas. 393. See paras. 12.12, 12.13, 12.16–12.19.

to a coaster which should then smuggle it into Spain. For this he was bribed £30. It was commonly agreed that he was guilty of barratry so this question did not arise for determination by the court. Instead of the coaster, two Spanish revenue cutters appeared out of the night and seized the ship. She was taken to Cadiz where the Master and crew were put in jail and proceedings to condemn and forfeit the ship were commenced. The owner had to pay a large sum to get her released and the action was for its recovery.

12.17 In the High Court,[22] on a special case, Field and Cave JJ. gave judgment for the underwriters. In view of the warranty, it is not difficult to appreciate why the plaintiff strained every nerve to prove that the loss was caused by barratry. He advanced this view, quoting the second edition of Arnould as authority, that loss arising from barratry was in a class of its own in that the barratry need not be the proximate cause of the loss; it was sufficient that it was a remote cause. That being so, the seizure off Cadiz was the result of the barratry in Gibraltar. Not even the judges who were prepared to accept Arnould's view, notably Field J., who considered that a barratrous act "hardly ever is" the proximate cause of a loss, and Cotton L.J., would agree that the loss was caused by barratry in this case. Field J. joined Cave J. in deciding that the loss was caused by "seizure".

12.18 The case went to the Court of Appeal[23] and to the House of Lords.[24] The Earl of Selbourne L.C. summed up the views of all the judges. It was urged by the plaintiffs that "capture and seizure" were belligerent acts only, and whilst this might be true of "capture", "seizure" was a much wider expression which included non-belligerent "seizure" such as "seizure" by Revenue authorities. Moreover: "It is quite manifest that the object of this warranty is and must be to except such losses otherwise covered by the policy, otherwise coming within the express terms of the policy, as arise out of and are losses occasioned by capture and seizure."

12.19 Whilst this was not said in so many words, a distinction can be drawn between the *Archangelo*,[25] the *Dunham*[26] and the *Cory* cases[27] apart from the fact that there was no warranty in the two former cases. In the *Archangelo* case, it is suggested that the barratrous act considered of letting the privateer capture the ship, virtually handing her over. In the *Cory* case, the barratrous act was the loading of the tobacco in Gibraltar with intent to smuggle it. As Field J. recognised, the plot would have succeeded and there would have been no loss to the owners but for the appearance of the Spanish revenue cutters and the "seizure" which they then effected. Finally, it is worth noting a comment of Brett L.J. that, but for the warranty, the shipowner could have sued either in barratry or seizure. He was careful to add however: " . . . It is a warranty against seizure whether by an enemy or by piracy and, as so enlarged, there is nothing to prevent it from applying to a seizure which is the result of barratry."

For this work, we should note that there was a "seizure" by the Spanish Customs Authorities. It can only be supposed that if there had been an F.C. & S. Clause in

22. (1881) 8 Q.B.D. 313.
23. (1882) 9 Q.B.D. 463.
24. (1883) 8 App. Cas. 393.
25. (1811) 1 Camp. 620.
26. *American Insurance Co.* v. *Dunham*, 2 Wend. N.Y. 463.
27. (1881) 8 Q.B.D. 313; (1882) 9 Q.B.D. 463; (1883) 8 App. Cas. 393.

the *Archangelo* case,[28] then, even though the barratry and the capture were apparently simultaneous, the underwriters would have been excused.

12.20 Another case, *Banque Monetaca and Carystuiaki and Others* v. *Motor Union Insurance Company Ltd.*[29] involved very fine distinctions whether or not the ship was lost by seizure or by piracy. Because of the political and military motivation of those affecting the seizure seemed to be the dominant motives, even though those of personal gain were undoubtedly strong, this was held to be a "seizure" by Roche J. (paras. 20.26–20.29).

THE PRESENCE OF FORCE

12.21 How much force is required to effect a seizure? At first sight the word itself indicates a considerable degree of force is required with persons occupying a ship in numbers that cannot be resisted, and having at their disposal sufficient strength to repel any attempt at repossession by the rightful owner. Two cases in particular, *Robinson Gold Mining Company and Others*. v. *Alliance Assurance Company*,[30] and *Miller* v. *The Law Accident Insurance Company*[31] are decisions indicating a great deal less force than this may be sufficient. *Miller*'s case concerns "restraint" and is dealt with under that heading.[32] Both cases should be read together because they have been used as guides on the degree of force that is necessary, particularly on "restraint", in cases subsequent to 1903 which currently end with *The Bamburi*, heard in 1981.[33]

12.22 *Robinson*'s case,[34] which owes much to *Cory*'s case[35] (and to the earlier cases which led to that decision) concerned a shipment of gold made on the eve of the outbreak of the Boer War. Robinson Gold Mining Company was incorporated in the Republic of South Africa and the gold emanated from that territory as it was before the start of the war. On 2nd October, 1899, the gold was loaded on to a train at Johannesburg for Cape Town where it was to be loaded for shipment for London. On the same day, it reached the frontier station at Vereeniging. Whilst it was still within the Republic's territory, the Resident Justice, acting on the instructions of the Republic's Attorney-General, ordered the railway company to unload the gold. The railway company complied and armed guards accompanying the gold did not attempt to resist. On 9th October, 1899, more of Robinson's gold was seized on the orders of the Republic's government whilst it was in a bank in Johannesburg. Again there was no resistance. On 11th October, 1899, the Republic declared war on the United Kingdom.

The gold was insured against: " . . . arrests, restraints and detainments of all Kings, Princes and people of what nation, condition or quality soever." The policy

28. (1811) 1 Camp. 620.
29. (1923) 14 Ll.L.Rep. 48.
30. [1901] 2 K.B. 919; [1902] 2 K.B. 489 (H.L.).
31. [1902] 2 K.B. 694; [1903] 1 K.B. 712 (C.A.); [1904] A.C. 359 (H.L.).
32. See paras. 13.11–13.15.
33. [1982] 1 Lloyd's Rep. 312.
34. Footnote 30, above.
35. Footnote 27, above. See paras. 12.12, 12.13, 12.16–12.19.

contained an F.C. & S. Clause, the material parts of which read: "Warranted free of capture, seizure and detention . . . "

12.23 At the trial, expert evidence was given that before these events the commandos had already been embodied to defend the Republic against a feared invasion and the Executive Council had power to requisition gold and other property to defend the country. In addition, the country's Parliament, the *Volkraad*, had passed a resolution, which had the force of law, vesting legislative power in the Executive. Apart from wagons and cattle, the Republic's government was not bound to give any compensation, but the owners of any requisitioned property had the right to share in any booty that was captured. At the trial, Phillimore J. found that, however strange the law appeared to be, it nonetheless existed and he thought the taking was constitutionally and lawfully made. He rejected the idea that the taking was an "ordinary judicial process" and was more persuaded by *Aubert* v. *Gray*.[36]

12.24 Phillimore J. seems to have been satisfied that what happened was a "seizure" which was expressly excluded by the F.C. & S. Clause. That being so, he did not think it necessary to go in any depth into whether there was an insured peril under the policy. He also answered some further questions. Did capture, seizure or detention require a hostile taking? This was probably so in the case of capture but: "Seizure is an additional word. It means more than capture, and in good sense and according to the precedents it should cover this case. So I think of detention."

12.25 Does seizure imply force? There was sufficient force here even though it was not deployed, because the Republic had all the resources of a State to enforce its orders. Does seizure exclude the operation of the law? Sir Walter Scott (later Lord Stowell) disposed of this idea in *The Maria*,[37] which Phillimore J. cited with approval: "It is a wild conceit that wherever force is used, it may be forcibly resisted; a lawful force cannot be lawfully resisted . . . " (except the enemy's force in time of war).

12.26 Judgment was signed for the defendent underwriters and the plaintiff appealed. Collins M.R. went even further than Phillimore J. He recognised the plaintiffs' difficulty when they argued that there was no "seizure" but only a "restraint" which was not excluded by the F.C. & S. Clause, and furthermore when there was no force. Nevertheless it plainly was a "seizure" within the normal meaning of the word and:

"The suggestion that a subject or resident of the Transvaal owing allegiance to its Government or to all events subject to and under the protection of its laws, in so rendering so large a share of his property is not yielding to force and that the act of taking possession of his property is not a seizure on the part of the authorities, seems to me incapable of serious argument."

In his view, capture pointed to a belligerent capture. Seizure was used to let in other seizures as suggested by Cotton L.J. in the *Cory* case.[38] Seizure seemed to be a larger term than capture, and went beyond it. It could reasonably be interpreted to embrace every act of taking forcible possession, either by lawful authority or by overpowering force.

36. (1863) L.R. Q.B. 50; (1862) 32 L.J.Q.B. 50.
37. (1799) 1 C. Rob. 340 at 360.
38. (1881) 8 Q.B.D. 313; (1882) 9 Q.B.D. 463; (1883) 8 App. Cas. 393 See paras. 12.12, 12.13, 12.16–12.19.

12.27 Mathew L.J. went even further than this. By analogy to the result if the goods had been taken at sea, he was prepared to hold that there was a "capture" besides there being a "seizure": "Here there was a capture, for which no force was necessary. . . . " There is no explanation in the report but presumably he meant that force was not necessary because the taking had the backing of the law. He went on: " . . . and there was a seizure, unaccompained by any violence; nobody was set upon or injured in defence of this gold . . . The other suggestion, that violence is absolutely indispensable, is far fetched and is certainly not indicated by the language of the warranty itself."

12.28 Cozens-Hardy L.J. simply noted his agreement. Since in the report this follows Mathew L.J.'s judgment, he presumably agreed with that judgment which includes a finding that a "capture" had occurred. The Court of Appeal affirmed Phillimore J.'s judgment for the underwriters. The House of Lords later dealt very briefly with the case as all five Lords considered that the Court of Appeal was plainly right. The Earl of Halsbury L.C. made it plain, and the other Lords concurred with this, that he considered the gold to have been lost because of a "seizure" and he did not think that it mattered at all whether that "seizure" was lawful or unlawful; it was still a "seizure".

12.29 Two very similar "seizure" cases should be noted here, namely *Dreifontein Consolidated Gold Mines* v. *Janson*[39] and *West Rand Central Gold Mines Company Ltd.* v. *de Rougement*.[40] We are indebted to these cases for one of the authoritative definitions of "war". Driefontein was a company formed in the Republic of South Africa and was thus an alien enemy at the time that the case was heard, whilst West Rand was a British company. The gold was insured under terms which did not include the F.C. & S. Clause. It was similarly seized at the frontier by the South African authorities on 2nd October, 1989. The cases were heard during the continuance of the Boer War. Did the war extinguish Driefontein's claim? It is true that enemy property cannot be insured in wartime but Matthew J. decided: "The supposed principle contended for by the defendants (the underwriters) would wholly override the well-known rule of law, that where the Contract of Indemnity and the loss are before hostilities, the declaration of war only suspends the remedy whilst the war lasts." The "seizure" was complete on 2nd October. The plaintiffs would only have to wait until the conclusion of the war to commence suit.

12.30 *Nesbitt* v. *Lushington*[41] is often quoted in connection with "seizure", but it is a case which is singularly difficult to understand. It had however a great influence on the *Société Belge*[42] case. The *Industry* was loaded with wheat and coal for carriage from Youghall to Sligo. Bad weather forced her to take shelter in Elly Harbour. At the time, there was much distress in that part of Ireland and the mob from ashore took control of the ship, weighed her anchor so that she went aground, and forced the Captain to sell the wheat at a sum which was about three-quarters of its invoice value. This they removed from the ship leaving only 10 tons which, being damaged in the stranding, was thrown overboard. This ship subsequently com-

39. [1900] 2 K.B. 339.
40. [1900] 2 K.B. 339.
41. *Nesbitt* v. *Lushington*, (1792) 4 Term Rep. 783.
42. *Société Belge des Bétons S.A.* v. *London & Lancashire Insurance Co. Ltd.* (1938) 60 Ll.L. Rep. 225; [1938] 2 All E.R. 305; 158 L.T. 352. See paras. 12.31–12.33.

pleted the voyage with the coal alone. The cargo was insured on the S.G. Form and it is strange to see that the case for the goods' owners was pleaded on the alternative bases that the loss was due to arrests, restraints or detainments "by people" or to "pirates". The report contains no explanation why loss by "assailing thieves" was not pleaded. There was no F.C. & S. Clause but a complicating factor for the plaintiffs was a warranty that the wheat was "free from average unless general or the ship be stranded". The report does not say so but it appears to have been generally accepted that the 10 tons left on board reduced the loss to a partial loss only, particularly as one of the three judges was prepared to find that there was a "capture by pirates". As will be seen from the chapter on piracy, this finding may not be easy to sustain nowadays. A finding of most immediate importance was given by Lord Kenyon C.J. with which the other two judges agreed: "This was not arrests, restraints, and detainment of Kings, Princes and people. The meaning of the word 'people' . . . means the ruling power of the land." Buller J. added to this: "People means the supreme power . . . the power of the country whatever it might be."

12.31 The *Nesbitt* case[43] led on to *Société Belge des Bétons S.A.* v. *London and Lancashire Insurance Co. Ltd.*[44] The terms of insurance were unique in that they were effected on the S.G. Form with the F.C. & S. Clause deleted. There was thus insurance cover for "arrest, restraints, and detainments of all Kings, Princes and people" on a form of policy which was not first and foremost a war risks policy. It was also a case where the court, in a tendency which has sometimes arisen, did not feel justified in drawing a strict difference in "seizure" and "restraint".

12.32 At the start of the Spanish Civil War, two Belgian companies were engaged on harbour works in Valencia through their wholly-owned subsidiary, Iberica, which seems to have owned the equipment and the barges engaged on the work.

1936

18th July

The Spanish Civil War begins. The civil population of Valencia is loyal to the Republican government, but entertains fears that the local garrison will declare for the Nationalists.

20th July

A strike begins, led by the main communist, syndicalist and anarchist unions who arm their members. The garrison is subdued.

The Popular Executive Committee (P.E.C.) is formed "from the very entrails of the people." It seems to have had some measure of encouragement from the governor, Col. Arin, who appears to have accepted it in place of the normal organs of government, namely the provincial deputation and the City Council.

22nd July

The central government forms the Barrios Commission which leaves the P.E.C. in control. It accepts that by early August, the P.E.C. is the *de facto* government of Valencia and is well on the way to becoming the *de jure* government as well.

18th August

The workers' management committee notifies Iberica's manager, Mr. Ceresa, that he is to make no management decisions without first informing it.

43. Footnote 41, above.
44. Footnote 42, above.

2nd September

By now, the P.E.C. is issuing *"incautaciones"* wholesale, thus confiscating the property in the objects concerned. This is to be contrasted with an *"occupacion"* which is a temporary taking only and does not transfer the property. Fearful for their jobs, the workers take over Iberica's business.

4th September

Mr. Ceresa sees the governor who refuses to help him. He is sent back to the works where a document is served upon him to the effect that the works are being taken over. He is threatened with death if he stays and departs for his home in France.

14th September

The plaintiffs receive Mr. Ceresa's report.

6th October

Notice of Abandonment is tendered. The underwriters refuse to put the plaintiffs in the same position as if a writ had been issued and refer them to the Belgian Foreign Office.

6th November

The P.E.C. grants an *incautacion* of Iberica's property.

10th November

The plaintiffs issue a writ.

December

The government replaces the P.E.C. whilst confirming all its previous *incautaciones*.

12.33 In the High Court, Porter J. paid a handsome tribute to Mr. Ceresa who had done all that he could, in circumstances of great difficulty and some personal danger, to protect the property of his employers. He found that on 10th November it was unlikely that the barges or other property would be recovered within a reasonable time and posed the question "Was there a seizure by peoples?" In a passage which may be misunderstood if it is applied to the more usual form of war risk policy, either on the S.G. Form or the MAR form: "It was undoubtedly a seizure, but it is established law that a seizure by the governing power of the country is necessary in order that the assured may recover under this head." Originally it was a seizure by the workers to keep out other elements and so protect their livelihoods, but it had the support of the P.E.C. whose acts were later acquiesced in and confirmed by the government. Judgment was signed in the plaintiffs' favour on the ground that the loss was by a "restraint of peoples".

12.34 A seizure case which is much easier to understand is *Lozano* v. *Janson*.[45] In April 1854, Pinto Perez chartered the *Newport*, owned by Le Sueur of Jersey, to carry lawful produce to Ambriz or Luanda and then African produce to Europe. Pintos were acting for a Senhor Flores, a Brazilian subject living in Luanda who enjoyed an unenviable reputation as a slave trader. The outward bound cargo consisted of packs of staves for making up barrels and other items for barter, and was insured on the S.G. Form for £7,000 (approximately its actual value). There was no F.C. & S. Clause. By 1854, with Brazil's help, the slave trade had been largely suppressed although there were some unconfirmed reports of shipments being made to Cuba.

45. (1859) 2 El. & El. 160.

1854

8th June

The ship sails from the U.K. bound for Luanda.

21st September

A short distance from Luanda, the ship is stopped by H.M.S. *Philomel* and boarded. *Philomel's* Commander, Captain Skeene, concludes that the ship is engaged in the slave trade and sends her to St. Helena under the command of Lt. de Robeck and three naval ratings. Neither Flores, Le Sueur or Pinto are advised of the seizure; nor are they served with any notice of the subsequent proceedings in St. Helena.

8th October

The ship arrives in St. Helena and proceedings are started before the Vice-Admiralty Court. They are described as being mostly *ex parte* apart from the Master.

20th November

The ship is pronounced as forfeited for being engaged in the slave trade and she and the perishable goods are subsequently sold by the court. Pintos are ordered to pay double the value of the cargo (nearly £13,000) and the goods are held by the court until the penalty is paid.

13th December

Whilst the plaintiffs have still no knowledge of the order of the St. Helena Vice-Admiralty Court, Notice of Abandonment is given to the underwriters.

12.35 An appeal was made to the Privy Council against the judgment of the St. Helena Vice-Admiralty Court and the Council gave its judgment in 1858. It strongly condemned the St. Helena Court as being guilty of many irregularities. The evidence before the court was muddled and inconclusive, and a proper enquiry would have established that the barrel staves had previously been used for shipping another commodity which would have made them unsuitable for carrying water. There was no proper service of notice of the proceedings on the shipowners or the cargo owners. Whilst the Privy Council did not say so, the impression is gained from reading the report that Captain Skeene and the Vice-Admiralty Court both concluded from their personal knowledge that Flores, who was well-known to them as a slave trader, was up to his old tricks again. Armed with this knowledge, they seem to have dispensed with the necessary proof that the ship and the goods were in fact engaged in, or intended for, the slave trade. The possibility that Flores may have mended his ways and engaged in an honest living seems not to have crossed their minds.

12.36 Returning to the proceedings against the underwriters, represented by Mr. Janson, Lord Campbell C.J. delivered the court's judgment. Was there an insured peril? Yes there was. The policy covered: "Takings at sea, arrests, restraints and detainments of all Kings, Princes, and people of what nature, condition or quality soever" and: "If this was a lawful taking at sea by a British cruiser, the underwriters would not have been liable; but it must now be definitely considered to have been a wrongful taking; and, this being so, the nationality of the captors becomes immaterial."

12.37 The Notice of Abandonment received some interesting treatment. Whilst the Vice-Admiralty Court's decree was unknown to the plaintiffs at the time it was given, its existence, although wrongful, would have been evidence of illegality and a bar to his action against the underwriters, at least until it was overruled by the Privy Council. The Privy Council's treatment of the decree removed any invalidating effect it would have. The court considered that the plaintiff had suffered a total loss, although it was open to the underwriters to prove that it was a partial loss only. In tones reminiscent of *The Wangoni* case,[46] Lord Campbell C.J. approved Bayley J.'s finding in *Holdsworth* v. *Wise*[47]: " . . . The subject of the insurance must be in existence under such circumstances that the assured may, if they please, have possession, and may reasonably be expected to have possession of it" and added: "and if, before action brought, the goods had been restored to the assured, or he had the means of getting possession of them, under such circumstances as ought to have induced a prudent man to take possession of them, his claim could now only have been made for a partial loss."

SEIZURE BY THOSE ON BOARD

12.38 Can a ship suffer "seizure" by those on board her? This question now seems to be reasonably well settled, even though the recent and tragic events of the *Achille Lauro* and the *City of Poros* have not yet been judicially considered.

Naylor v. *Palmer*[48] is a convenient starting point. This case is often wrongly referred to as *Palmer* v. *Naylor*.[49] These proceedings were on "a writ of error" (in modern parlance, an appeal) in *Naylor* v. *Palmer* and, as Coleridge J. affirmed the judgment of Pollock C.B., are of no interest. This work must concentrate on *Naylor* v. *Palmer*.

12.39 The *Victory* was to carry 360 Chinese coolies from Cumsingmoon (Canton) to Callao. The monies laid out on provisions and goods for the coolies were insured by British underwriters on the S.G. Form but without an F.C. & S. Clause. At some time during the voyage, the coolies "piratically and feloniously" murdered the Captain and several of the crew and took over the ship. They landed on the nearest land and made good their escape. The ship was not damaged and the Mate and the rest of the crew could have completed the voyage; in fact they never did. Pollock C.B. considered and dismissed the defendant's pleas that the loss arose out of the coolies' unwillingness to go to Peru, which seems to have been unattractive to them, and decided:

"The act of seizure of the ship, and taking it out of possession of the Master and crew by the passengers, and so within the express words of the policy or if not of that quality, because it was not done *animo furandi*, it was a seizure *ejusdem generis* analogous to it . . . falling within the general concluding words of the perils enumerated by the policy."

(The general words are considered in more detail in Chapter 14).

12.40 Hard on its heels came *Kleinwort* v. *Shepard*.[50] The *Henriette Marie*, a Dutch ship, was to carry 350 Chinese coolies from Macao to Havana. She and the provisions for the voyage were insured on the S.G. Form, which included "pirates" as an insured peril, but this time there was an F.C. & S. Clause: "Warranted free from capture and seizure, and the consequences of any attempt thereat."

12.41 Again, some, but not all, of the coolies "piratically and feloniously"

46. *Forestal Land, Timber & Railways Co. Ltd.* v. *Rickards* (*The Minden*); *Middows* v. *Robertson* (*The Wangoni*); *W.W. Howard, Bros. & Co.* v. *Kann* (*The Halle*) (1940) 67 Ll.L.Rep. 484; (1940) 68 Ll.L.Rep. 45 (C.A.); (1941) 70 Ll.L.Rep. 173; [1942] A.C. 50 (H.L.). See paras. 13.27–13.34.
47. (1828) 7 B. & C. 794. See para. 11.22.
48. (1853) 8 Ex. 739.
49. (1854) 10 Ex. 382.
50. (1859) 1 El. & El. 447.

assaulted the Captain and some of the crew, and by force stole, took and carried away the ship and provisions from the Captain and the crew's custody. They too made good their escape, although on this occasion, nobody seems to have been seriously hurt. The court was only concerned with construction and the many other issues arising out of the case were due to be heard elsewhere. The plaintiff pleaded that "seizure" could only arise if caused by a belligerent, or by persons from without the ship, and excluded everything done by those lawfully on board her. Lord Campbell C.J. giving the court's judgment, could find no case or usage which so restricts "seizure". Whist the loss came within the enumerated perils, it could not be doubted that in the English language this was a "seizure" within the meaning of the F.C. & S. Clause. Moreover: "We clearly think it would extend to a capture or seizure by pirates."

12.42 The court noted that Holland was at peace with the world and was not presently likely to go to war with anyone. The contracting parties cannot have thought that "seizure" was restricted to a belligerent "seizure". The underwriters had wished to include the F.C. & S. Clause with *Naylor* v. *Palmer*[51] in mind. For an extra premium, which the insured refused to pay, they would have omitted it. Whilst this may be a reason to distinguish the case, it is suggested that these points played little, if any, part in the court's decision, so firm is the language of the judgment.

12.43 The scene shifts to the United States where two very authoritative decisions deal with the misdeeds of the crew. Both are decisions of the Circuit Court of Appeals and, although nearly a century apart, should be considered together. *Greene* v. *Pacific Mutual Life Insurance Company*[52] concerned a case of a whaler where the crew killed the Master and the Mate and badly wounded the other officers. The ship was also badly damaged and the voyage had to be abandoned. She was insured for "barratry" but "seizure" was excluded by the American form of F.C. & S. Clause. Bigelow C.J. gave the court's decision: "In as much as barratry is one of the risks assumed by the assured* [sic], unless particular Acts are clearly excepted in terms which leave no doubt as to their meaning, the general words of the policy must have full operation."

12.44 The court did, however, put the matter on to a more substantial basis. "Seizure" consists of taking the ship out of the possession of those lawfully entitled to it: "Capture and detention are both risks which can arise only from acts of persons having no connection with the ship, who take her out of the possession of the Master and mariners forcibly, either without right or by the authority of law."

12.45 The Master cannot seize that which is entrusted to his possession by the owners. He can, however, betray the trust reposed in him which is the essence of barratry. The same is true of the crew who are also in a position of trust even though they are subject to the Master's orders: "If they violate their duty and disobey the Master, displace him from command and assume entire control of the vessel, it is a breach of trust rather than a seizure."

Bigelow J. distinguished *Kleinwort's* case.[53] Passengers are incapable of commit-

---

51. (1853) 8 Ex. 739.
52. (1864) 91 Mass. (9 Allen) 217.
* (The word "assured" must be a mistake for "insurer").
53. (1859) 1 El. & El. 447. See paras. 12.40–12.42.

ting barratry because they have no care and custody of the ship and stand in no relation of trust to the owner. On these grounds, judgment was signed for the plaintiffs.

12.46 The District Court of Maryland and the U.S. Circuit Court of Appeals (4th Circuit) heard the case of *Republic of China, China Merchants Steam Navigation Co. Ltd. and the United States of America* v. *National Union Fire Insurance Company of Pittsburg, Pennsylvania, The Hai Hsuan*.[54] At the end of the Second World War, the United States sold to the Nationalist Government of China thirteen Liberty-type vessels and assumed the position of mortgagee. The vessels were entrusted for their management to China Merchants. Civil war broke out in China, and by the end of 1949 the Communists had established the People's Republic of China. The Nationalists were confined to the Island of Taiwan only. A complicating factor throughout was the recognition by the United Kingdom in January 1950 of the Communist Government as the *de jure* Government of China. This played some part in the actions of the crews and the refusal of the Singapore police and the Singapore and Hong Kong courts to assist the mortgagees. The facts concerning six of the ships in Hong Kong (the Hong Kong ships) were:

1949

November

All six ships are in Hong Kong.

13th November

First orders are given by China Merchants' office (which by this time was established in Taiwan) that the ships should sail for Taiwan. Many subsequent orders to the same effect are given and at one stage an option is given to sail to the Philippines. All such orders are disobeyed.

1950

13th January

The Manager and the office staff of China Merchants' Hong Kong branch office declare for the People's Republic. They remain working in the office, carrying out their duties. The Red Flag is raised over the building.

16th January
The Masters raise the Reg Flag on the ships.

October
The ships sail for Canton.

12.47 During all this time, the wages were paid by the Hong Kong office, first with money from Taiwan and later from the People's Republic. The courts accepted that whilst agitators were no doubt active, there was no evidence of any activity or presence from the People's Republic apart from a warning in the Beijing *People's Daily* indicating that those in charge of ships should guard the property of the People's Republic. No nationalisation decrees were ever made by the People's Republic and no formalities were undertaken with the Hong Kong authorities to change the flags formally. The older men among the crews were concerned about their families in mainland China and the possible effect that going to Taiwan might have on them. The younger men were afraid of being conscripted in Taiwan.

54. [1957] 1 Lloyd's Rep. 428; [1958] 1 Lloyd's Rep. 351.

12.48 The facts relating to the *Hai Hsuan* (whose name was given to the case) were:

1950

January

The ship is at sea in the Indian Ocean, bound from Spain to Japan with a cargo of salt. The crew hears of the British recognition of the People's Republic.

The Master receives orders to go to Taiwan. The crew objects and the Chief Officer leads a demand that the ship should put into Singapore. The illness of a fireman is used as an excuse. The Hong Kong office also issue orders to go to Singapore.

A meeting takes place on board. There is no violence but the atmosphere is threatening. The Master insists that his orders are obeyed.

The crew's attitude is mutinous. The Chief Officer threatens to stop the engines. The Master, who has been several days without food, falls ill. He informs China Merchants' office in Taiwan but does not include a description of the situation on board. China Merchants, unaware of the situation, instructs the Chief Officer to assume command.

24th January

The Chief Officer brings the ship into Singapore. The Master goes to hospital where he remains for a month.

26th January

The Red Flag is raised.

1st February

Captain Paulsen with a skeleton crew arrives from China Merchants' office in Taiwan to take over the ship. He asks the Singapore police to help him but is refused. Captain Paulsen boards the ship but leaves again when personal violence is threatened.

Throughout the time that the ship is in Singapore the wages are paid by the Hong Kong office.

12.49 Thomsen C.J. gave the judgment of the District Court. He approved the definition of barratry given by Lord Ellenborough C.J. in *Earl* v. *Rowcroft*[55]: " . . . A fraudulent breach of duty by the Master in respect of his owners; or in other words, a breach of duty in respect to his owners, with a criminal intent, or *ex maleficio*, is barratry." This definition was also approved by the Circuit Court which considered that Rule 11 of the Marine Insurance Act gave helpful guidance. The District Court went on to consider "seizure" and applied three tests:

1. Can there be a "seizure" of the vessel by her Master, officers or crew? Are "barratry" and "seizure" mutually exclusive? This question seemed to be answered by the *Greene* case[56] and he noted what Bigelow C.J. said: "Exception of a loss by seizure does not include the risk of mutiny of the mariners and the forcible taking of the ship from the control of the officers." There was no difficulty in distinguishing the *Kleinwort*,[57] *Greene*[58] and *Forestal*[59] cases.

---

55. (1806) 8 East 126.

56. *Greene* v. *Pacific Mutual Life Insurance Co.* (1864) 91 Mass. (9 Allen) 217. See paras. 12.43–12.45.

57. (1859) 1 El. & El. 447.

58. Footnote 56 above.

59. *Forestal Land, Timber & Railways Co. Ltd.* v. Richards (*The Minden*) (1940) 67 Ll.L.Rep. 484; (1940) 68 Ll.L.Rep. 45 (C.A.); (1941) 70 Ll.L.Rep. 173; [1942] A.C. 50. See paras. 13.27–13.34.

2. Is the use or threat of force a necessary element of "seizure"? On the authority of the *Robinson*,[60] *Forestal*[61] and *Cory*[62] cases the answer is, plainly, No.

3. Is action by a government department or its authorised representatives a necessary element of "seizure"? On the authority of the *Kleinwort*[63] and *Johnson*[64] cases, the answer is, again, No.

12.50 Applying these tests, the court awarded judgment to the plaintiffs in respect of the Hong Kong ships, which it held were lost by barratry, and to the defendants in respect of the *Hai Hsuan* which the court held was lost by "seizure". The reasoning of the judgment is hard to follow but it would seem that the court may have misread the *Cory* case: "If 'barratry' and 'seizure' are not mutually exclusive terms, the F.C. & S. warranty excludes from the coverage of the Marine Policy barratrous acts which amount to a 'seizure' or are followed by a 'seizure' as the ultimate cause of the loss." whereas a true reading of the *Cory* case is that the proximate cause of the loss was not "barratry" but "seizure" for the reasons given by the House of Lords.

12.51 Both sides appealed and the 4th Circuit held that all ships were lost by barratry. The court accepted the *Greene* case as establishing: " . . . The term 'seizure' does not include a violent taking of possession of the ship by a mutinous crew" and the crew could not rid themselves of their obligations to the owner by displacing the Master. On the contrary, they would increase them. On a final note, the possibility of the crew of the *Hai Hsuan* being "pirates" was not raised, presumably because of the strong element of their political motivation throughout. The possibility that they were "pirates" should not be dismissed.

12.52 *The Jupiter (No. 3)*[65] is often quoted in the context of barratry, but it is suggested that this is erroneous. The *Jupiter* was a Russian ship owned by a Russian company before the Revolution which had escaped from Russia after the Revolution and was currently in possession of administrators appointed by the French courts. The administrators employed the Master who, in Dartmouth, handed her over to the representatives of the U.S.S.R. for sale. The subsequent action for possession in the High Court ended in a judgment in favour of the French administrators, largely because Hill J. found the Russian Nationalisation Decrees were ineffective. No finding of barratry was made—indeed none was called for—but the court made the point: "Captain Lepine may have acted as a loyal subject of the U.S.S.R. but he betrayed his trust to his employers. *Prima-facie*, the act of Lepine was wrongful." This is very close to the language of the *Greene*[66] judgment.

12.53 As a last word, the *Hai Hsuan*[67] is a remarkable case in showing as it does how much the courts of England and the United States rely upon each other's judgments.

---

60. *Robinson Gold Mining Co. & others* v. *Alliance Insurance Company* [1901] 2 K.B. 919; [1902] 2 K.B. 489 (H.L.). See paras. 12.22–12.28.
61. See footnote 59, above.
62. *Cory & Sons* v. *Burr* (1881) 8 Q.B.D. 313; (1882) 9 Q.B.D. 463; (1883) 8 App. Cas. 393. See paras. 12.12, 12.13, 12.16–12.19.
63. (1859) 1 El. & El. 447. See paras. 12.40–12.42.
64. (1883) 10 Q.B.D. 432. See para. 12.9.
65. [1927] P. 122.
66. Footnote 56, above.
67. Footnote 54, above.

Before coming to the conclusions mention should be made of "takings at sea" even though this is no longer an insured peril. It is hoped that the reader will bear with this diversion on the basis that "takings at sea" has played its part in the formulation of the law on "capture" and "seizure".

TAKINGS AT SEA

12.54 Even though such insured perils as "takings at sea" have not been transferred from the S.G. Form to the new Institute War and Strikes Clauses, and have thus disappeared from the list of insured perils, no consideration of capture and seizure is complete without a description of the recent decisions concerning this insured peril. This arose in *Shell International Petroleum Co. Ltd. v. Caryl Anthony Vaughan Gibbs (The Salem).*[68]

12.55 Although the judgments go back to the mid-18th century, there is now no point in reciting them in detail. We can take as a useful starting point the *Forestal* case[69] where a wrongful reading of its judgments, particularly the judgment of Lord Wright, led to the Court of Appeal's judgment in *Nishina Trading Co. Ltd. v. Chiyoda Fire and Marine Insurance Co. Ltd. (The Mandarin Star).*[70] In this case, the Court of Appeal (reversing the High Court) held that there was a "taking at sea" where a shipowner left Kobe with cargo on board to exercise a lien in Hong Kong. Denning M.R. gave the main judgment. In the *Salem* case,[71] the Court of Appeal doubted the correctness of the *Mandarin Star* and the House of Lords overruled it for the reasons which follow.

12.56 Anxious to obtain crude oil in spite of the ban imposed by the Gulf producers, the South African Strategic Fuel Fund found sellers who were willing to sell them 1.5 million barrels of Saudi (later Kuwaiti) crude oil. It was necessary to purchase a tanker for its carriage and South African interests advanced the money for this purpose against repayment from the purchase price of the oil. Events followed rapidly:

1979

26th November

The Strategic Fuel Fund opens its Letter of Credit.

3rd December

The *South Sun* is purchased and renamed *Salem*.
The *Salem* is chartered to Pontoil of Lausanne to load 200,000 tons of Kuwaiti crude oil for carriage to Italy.
   Pontoil makes a declaration to its insurers to insure the cargo. They have a form of open cover on the Lloyd's S.G. Form with the Institute Cargo Clauses (F.P.A) and Institute strikes, riots and civil commotions clauses attached.

5th December

The *Salem* arrives in Kuwait where her crew is changed. She loads and sails for Italy as soon as loading is completed. The Master signs bills of lading for 195,000 tons.

---

68. [1981] 2 Lloyd's Rep. 316; [1982] 1 Lloyd's Rep. 369 (C.A.); [1983] 1 Lloyd's Rep. 342 (H.L.).
69. *Forestal Land, Timber & Railways Co. Ltd. v. Rickards (The Minder)* (1940) 67 Ll.L.Rep. 484; (1940) 68 Ll.L.Rep. 45 (C.A.); (1941) 70 Ll.L.173; [1942] A.C. 50 (H.L.). See paras. 13.27–13.34.
70. [1969] 1 Lloyd's Rep. 293; [1969] 2 Q.B. 449.
71. Footnote 68, above.

27th December

The *Salem* (by this time bearing the name *Lema*) arrives off Durban and moors to a buoy one-and-a-half miles off shore. She discharges ashore 180,392 tons of crude oil. 15,840 tons cannot be discharged due to trouble with the ship's pumps and this quantity remains on board.

1980

2nd January

The *Salem* sails with the remaining cargo. She is ballasted with sea water to give her the appearance of being a loaded tanker.

15th January

The Strategic Fuel Fund makes payment under its letters of credit.

16th January

The *Salem* is sunk in deep water off Dakar and her crew is rescued by the *British Trident* whose Master films the sinking. The oil slick is noted to be a slight one only, and much less than could be expected from a cargo of 200,000 tons.

12.57 Subsequent investigations revealed that the Strategic Fuel Fund, Pontoil and Shell, who bought the cargo from Pontoil, were the innocent victims of a gigantic swindle. The actual perpetrators are not named in the law reports and were obviously few in number around the shipowning interest. The case was not concerned with this, but only whether the cargo underwriters, represented by Mr. Gibbs, should pay for the loss of the cargo under their policy.

12.58 Mustill J. heard the case in the Commercial Court. Clearly he felt bound by the *Nishina* decision when he held that there was a "taking at sea" by the shipowners when the ship altered course for Durban, and that this required him to sign judgment for Shell in the full amount of its claim. Such a decision did not require a separate decision on the cargo lost off Dakar; the "taking at sea" was the taking of the full cargo at that stage. The trial judge also noted that, if the cargo owners wanted full cover, insuring against all forms of fortuitous losses in transit, they could have effected cover on the Institute Cargo Clauses (all risks form). To appreciate the limited form of insurance effected, see paras. 33.5–33.8.

12.59 In the Court of Appeal, different views were expressed although the end results were the same. Denning M.R. felt that his decision in *The Mandarin Star*[72] case was wrong and had caused the present troubles: "I read Lord Wright as saying that it was sufficient if the German Captain of his own head—without any attornment—changed the character of his possession. This was wrong." (It will be recalled that Lord Wright was giving judgment in the *Forestal* case.[73] The "attornment" was the order of the German Government which was held by the court to alter the entire basis of the Captain's possession of the goods). This later prompted Lord Roskill to remark "even though repentance came late, it was none the less welcome".

12.60 Denning M.R. went on to say: "There must be a change in possession— not merely a change in the character of it. In our present case there was not change in possession when the ship changed course. The goods in *Salem* remained in possession of the owners throughout . . . " He considered there was a "taking" in

72. Footnote 70, above.
73. Footnote 69, above.

Kuwait where there was "larceny by a trick" and also there was a "taking" at Durban. Both of these were, in spite of the buoy's position, in port and not at sea.

12.61 May L.J. approached the matter differently. First, he doubted if *The Mandarin Star*[74] was wrongly decided. He declined to be guided by the criminal law and said: "There was a taking of the cargo of oil when there was wrongly appropriation of it by the shipowners." There was the tort of conversion of the oil, which was inconsistent with the rights of its true owners, when it was pumped ashore in Durban. If this "taking" had happened "at sea", which was not the case, it would have been a "taking at sea".

12.62 Kerr L.J. disagreed with both and came to the conclusion, which was in line with the later conclusion reached by the House of Lords: "Takings at sea cannot in my view apply to a taking by shipowners of the cargo or—if one can conceive this—of a taking of a ship by the cargo owner, but only to a taking of some outsider of both ship and cargo." If there was a "taking" at all it was in port at Durban.

This led to the Court of Appeal reversing Mustill J.'s judgment so that Shell recovered nothing in respect of the oil put ashore at Durban. The oil still in the ship when she sank was, however, lost by "perils of the seas" and Shell were awarded its value.

12.63 The House of Lord's judgment was given unanimously and shortly. It was delivered by Lord Roskill, who firmly declared that *The Mandarin Star*,[75] was wrongly decided and must be overruled. If the cargo owners had wanted all risks cover, they could have obtained it. They had not done so, and: "Your Lordships may think that this House should take the opportunity of firmly declaring that the standard Lloyd's S.G. Policy does not cover wrongful misappropriation of cargo by a shipowner."

That clearly indicated that in the House of Lords' view there was no such thing as a "taking at sea" of the cargo by the shipowner. In the event, even though it disagreed with its reasoning, the House of Lords considered that the Court of Appeal's award on the rights of the respective parties was the correct one.

12.64 If the writer may venture a view after such weighty authority has made itself felt, the judgment of Hilbery J. in *Middows v. Robertson*,[76] which was quoted with approval by Kerr L.J. in *The Salem*,[77] is still appropriate and worthy of note:

"Capture is a taking by the enemy as prize in time of open war with intent to deprive the owners of their property and the goods. It is a belligerent act. A taking at sea is something less, or it may be a taking at sea although at the time there is no intention thereby to deprive the owner of his property in the ship, but merely an intention to take the ship in for an adjudication. It is the lesser thing included in the greater which is capture. If I am right in thinking that here there was capture, there was also a 'taking at sea' immediately before the ship was scuttled."

12.65 As a last and final point on *The Salem*, it is the leading case which confirms the ancient cases on the law of barratry with very firm declarations by each court that barratry can only be committed against shipowners' interests, not against the

74. Footnote 70, above.
75. *Ibid.*
76. (1940) 67 Ll.L.Rep. 484. See paras. 13.27–13.34.
77. Footnote 68, above.

interests of others. Where it is judged that the shipowners were themselves involved in the wrongdoing, as happened here, barratry cannot arise.

12.66 A comparison with these conclusions on "seizure" should be made with those on "capture"[78] in order to appreciate that "seizure" is, as has often been said, of a wider nature than "capture". Comparison should also be made with the conclusions on "arrest, restraint and detainment" with which "seizure" is often linked in the decided cases.

12.67 "Seizure" has the following characteristics:

1. "Seizure" consists of taking over the entire control of the insured ship, either with or without connivance of those lawfully in charge of her, or of those who own her, and requiring her to obey the wishes of those who seize her.

2. It is not necessary that those who "seize" a ship intend to acquire her legal ownership, or, if this is their original intention, that they should persist in it. "Seizure" is complete at the moment that their control of her is complete whatever their motives might be.

3. "Seizure" may be lawful or unlawful. It may be lawfully effected as in the *Cory* case[79] or it may be effected by the wrongful use of legal proceedings as in the *Lozano* case.[80] It can also be effected without any lawful right.

4. "Seizure" may be effected without the intention to take permanent control of the insured ship, either at the time of seizure or at any subsequent time.

5. Whereas "capture" can only be effected by a belligerent *de jure* or *de facto* government in wartime, or by those properly acting in its name, "seizure" can be effected by anyone, such as a government or governmental agency which is acting properly, or even improperly, under its laws, or arbitrarily, or by a political faction, a terrorist group, or even an unorganised gang.

6. "Seizure" like "capture" envisages the presence of force or at least its threat. Where "seizure" is effected under the law, force need not be used or deployed; the law must be obeyed, and submission to its requirements without the vestiges of force being present will not prevent "seizure" becoming complete. It is suggested that submission to what are stated to be its requirements, provided that they can reasonably be regarded as such, at the behest of those who it later transpires are acting unlawfully, will not prevent a "seizure" from becoming complete.

7. "Seizure", unlike "capture", usually leaves open the possibility that the insured ship will be restored to its owner, and it is not likely (although not impossible) that she will become an actual total loss because her owner is irretrievably deprived of her possession. It is far more likely that she will become a constructive total loss because it is unlikely that she can be recovered within a reasonable time. As with "capture", the date that the writ is issued, or the date that the underwriters have refused to accept Notice of Abandonment and put the shipowner in the same position as if a

---

78. See paras. 11.64.

79. *Cory & Son* v. *Burr* (1881) 8 Q.B.D. 313; (1882) Q.B.D. 463; (1883) 8 App. Cas. 393. See paras. 12.12, 12.13, 12.16–12.19.

80. *Lozano* v. *Janson* (1859) 2 El. & El. 160. See paras. 12.34–12.37.

writ had been issued, is the time when it is judged whether it is unlikely that the insured ship can be recovered within a reasonable time.

8. Whilst passengers may "seize" a ship, she cannot be "seized" by the Master or crew to whom she has been entrusted. Any such action by them will be a breach of the trust reposed in them and will probably constitute barratry, which is a peril insured by the Marine Policy and not the War Risk Policy. They may be pirates (Chapter 20).

9. "Seizure" is a wider term than "taking at sea"; it can be effected in port, whereas "taking at sea" can only take place at sea.

CHAPTER 13

arrest, restraint, detainment . . .

GENERAL

13.1 From the way that these three insured perils are set out in the MAR form and the Rules of the Mutual War Risks Associations, they would appear to be separate and distinct from each other. In the decided cases, however, they have been given their normal everyday meanings with the natural result that there is such a considerable degree of overlap between them that any distinctions that may exist have become blurred to the extent that they are, for all practical purposes, non-existent. It is quite possible that in future cases some distinctions may be drawn on the facts of particular cases. As things stand at the time of writing, they must be treated as being broadly repetitive of each other and it is hoped that the cases which follow will illustrate this.

13.2 Insurance on the S.G. Form was given under two parts of the policy. The form itself contains the insured peril "arrests, restraints, and detainments of all Kings, Princes and people, of what nation, condition or quality soever". This was added to by the Institute War & Strikes Clauses attached to the policy which contained the insured perils "arrest, restraint or detainment" with the addition "and consequences thereof or any attempt thereat". The Marine Insurance Act 1906 contained in the "Rules for construction of policy":

"10. *Restraint of Princes*
    The term 'arrests, restraints, and detainments of all Kings, Princes and people' refers to political or executive acts, and does not include a loss caused by a riot or ordinary judicial process."

(Riots were a separate insured peril set out elsewhere in the Institute War & Strikes Clauses.)

13.3 The MAR form with the Institute War & Strikes Clauses attached has the simpler and wider form of insured peril providing simply "arrest, restraint or detainment" (Clause 1.2). Because there is no mention of "Kings, Princes and people" Rule 10 can no longer apply. The same effect is achieved by an express provision (Clause 4.1.6): "This insurance excludes . . . the operation of ordinary judicial process, failure to provide security . . . .". "Ordinary judicial process" is dealt with in Chapter 25.

13.4 When there are no widespread hostilities, such as a world war, "restraint" and "seizure" are the commonest form of war risk losses. Again, there appears to be a degree of overlap between them, but if a distinction is to be drawn, a "restraint", as against a "seizure" which is described at paras. 12.1, 12.39, 12.64, appears to be the prevention of a shipowner from carrying on a course of action upon which he is embarked without, however, laying claim to, or depriving him of, his property. Even this distinction is not totally satisfactory because *The Anita* case[1] was treated as a "restraint" case and so were the Angolan cases,[2] when the Vietnamese and Angolan authorities could be taken to intend the confiscation of the owner's property in the ships. Likewise it could be said that the *Rodocanachi* case[3] should be looked on as a "restraint". Nevertheless this definition will serve as a proper guide provided that it is borne in mind that it is not totally definitive or strictly applied.

THE CASES ILLUSTRATING THE INSURED PERIL

13.5 There are now so many more recent cases which describe this insured peril that there is no point in examining the ancient cases in detail. It was at one time thought that every subject consented to, and adopted as his own, every act of his government and this was so decided in *Conway* v. *Gray*.[4] This being so, a claim could not be made for the restraints of a subject's own Prince. This was firmly over-ruled by the Court of Exchequer Chamber in *Aubert* v. *Gray*.[5] In 1859, 30 bales of carpets were insured on the S.G. Form for shipment from London to Alicante on board the *Jovellanos*. The shipowner and the cargo owner were both Spanish subjects. The policy contained the insured perils of: "Arrests, restraints, and detainments of all Kings, Princes and people of what nation, condition or quality soever". There was no F. C. & S. Clause.

13.6 In Corunna, the ship was embargoed by the Queen of Spain to carry troops to fight in the current war between Spain and Morocco. The cargo was discharged during bad weather and was unceremoniously dumped on the quayside. The weather continued wet and rainy and the carpets were severely damaged. All four judges were unanimous with the judgment read by Erle C.J.: "The restraint of a Prince caused the loss; the assured have used the words which expressed that they are to be indemnified against any restraint from any Prince;" and: "The assertion that the act of the government is the act of each subject of that government is never really true. In representative governments, it may have a partial semblance of truth; but in despotic governments it is without that semblance."

13.7 *Rotch* v. *Edie*[6] had a very big influence on "restraint", deciding as it did a number of matters which were previously open to question. It must be borne in mind that the case was decided at a time when it was accepted that a policy on a ship insured not only the loss of the ship but the loss of the adventure as well. This is no longer the case, and the modern Institute War and Strikes Clauses insure only the loss and damage to the ship. The history of how this change came about and the reasons for it were traced by Staughton J. in *The Bamburi*.[7]

---

1. *Panamanian Oriental Steamship Corpn.* v. *Wright* (*The Anita*) [1970] 2 Lloyd's Rep. 365. See paras. 13.35–13.44.
2. See para. 13.57.
3. *Rodocanachi* v. *Elliott* (1873) L.R. 8 C.P. 649. See para. 11.21.
4. (1809) 10 East 536.
5. (1862) 32 L.J.Q.B. 50.
6. (1795) 6 Term Rep. 413.
7. [1982] 1 Lloyd's Rep. 312. See paras. 13.63–13.72.

13.8 The facts of *Rotch* v. *Edie* were: in 1792, three whaling ships, *Adelaide*, *Adele*, and *Victor* were insured "at or from L'Orient" for voyages to "all ports, seas and places between the Cape of Good Hope and Cape Horn" until their return to L'Orient. The policy was on the S.G. Form and insured against: "Arrests, restraints and detainments of all Kings, Princes and people of what nation, condition or quality soever and against all other perils, losses and misfortunes that should come to the hurt, detriment or damage of the said ships."

Events took the following course:

1793

27th January

The *Adelaide* sails from L'Orient. Bad weather forces her to return first to Port-Louis and later to L'Orient.

30th January

The Minister of Merchant Marine in Paris instructs the Admiralty Court in L'Orient to lay an embargo on all French ships. The reason for the embargo is not clear but it is the time of the upheavals caused by the French Revolution.

5th February

The Admiralty Court executes this order on the *Adelaide* (when she returns to L'Orient) and on the *Adele* and the *Victor* which never left that port. Clearances and passports are not granted so the perishable stores are sold off and the crews discharged.

26th February

Notice of Abandonment is given and refused.

18th March

The embargo remains in force on ships in L'Orient and Port-Louis. It becomes clear that it applies to ships on long voyages but not ships engaged on short voyages.

August

Further Notice of Abandonment is given.

13.9 The plaintiff, an American who resided in the United Kingdom and in France, who was in partnership with a Frenchman resident in L'Orient, sued for total losses. The four judges who heard the case unanimously signed judgment in his favour, dismissing the points raised by the defendants which were expressed by the court:

> The plaintiff cannot plead restraint of his own Princes.
> The embargo at the loading port was not within the policy.
> The wording of the insured perils applied them to hostile operations of a foreign State only.
> The plaintiff was entitled to an indemnity from the French Government and should not look to the underwriters.
> No loss of the subject matter was suffered and no abandonment was justified.
> It was impolitic to provide funds to an actual or a potential enemy.

13.10 These points received very short shrift from the court. Lord Kenyon C.J. thought there was ample precedent in the plaintiff's favour, particularly the *Goss* case,[8] that an arrest or an embargo by a Prince, not an enemy, was insured by the

8. *Goss* v. *Withers* (1758) 2 Burr. 683, See paras. 11.8–11.11.

policy: "The plaintiff has, in fact, lost the voyage; the ships have been detained either by Kings, Princes, or people, the governing power of the country where [they are]." and Ashhurst J., holding that there was no evidence of usage or law to restrain their meaning: "The very words of the policy are sufficiently extensive to include this case", and Grose J., pointing out that the policy expressly covered "at or from L'Orient and holding that a possible French Indemnity was no answer to the insurance policy: "All these vessels were protected at the loading port by the terms of this insurance", and Lawrence J., pointing out that to refuse to insure an American neutral would be tantamount to saying that it would be illegal to insure a neutral's property in a foreign port: " . . . and if the voyage be defeated, it is the same thing for this purpose as if the ship be lost . . . "

The court was particularly impressed by Lord Mansfield's judgments in the *Goss* case[9]:

"I cannot find a single book, ancient or modern, which does not say that, in case of a ship being taken, the insured may demand for a total loss and abandon . . . and what proves the proposition most strongly is that by the general law he may abandon in the case merely of an arrest or an embargo by a Prince, not an enemy."

THE INSURED PERIL AND THE CASES—FORCE

13.11 The very word "restraint" indicates some degree of power to prevent the insured shipowner from carrying on with a course of action on which he is properly embarked. How much force needs to be employed to restrain him? The answer seems to be given by two cases, *Robinson Gold Mining Company* v. *Alliance Assurance Company*[10] and *Miller* v. *The Law Accident Insurance Company*.[11] The *Robinson* case is, strictly speaking, one of seizure, and it is dealt with under that heading. Whilst the word "seizure" of itself connotes a degree of forcible taking, it was held in *Robinson's* case that the degree of force necessary to constitute the insured peril of "seizure" can be the same as that needed to constitute the less alarming insured peril of "restraint". *Miller's* was a "restraint" case but *Robinson's* case was quoted as an authority for the decision that was reached. The degree of force which is necessary has been better developed in the "restraint" cases and it will be dealt with under that heading. Before studying the *Miller* case and the cases which follow in time on the insured peril of "restraint", the reader will find it useful first to look at *Robinson's* case at paras. 12.22–12.28.

13.12 Moving now to *Miller's* case,[12] the events took place in 1900 when the *Bellvue* carried a cargo of bulls from Liverpool to Buenos Aires. Before the shipment, an Argentine decree had forbidden the import of diseased animals into Argentina, and also the import of animals from countries where certain diseases were prevalent. The bulls were insured under a policy which covered: " . . . arrests, restraints or detainments of all Kings, Princes and people of what nation, condition, or quality soever". There was also a general clause which covered: " . . .

9. *Ibid.*
10. [1901] 2 K.B. 919; [1902] 2 K.B. 489 (H.L.). See paras. 12.22–12.28.
11. [1902] 2 K.B. 694; [1903] 1 K.B. 712 (C.A.)
12. *Ibid.*

and all other perils, losses and misfortunes that have or shall come to the hurt, detriment or damage of the said goods and merchandises or any part thereof". There was also an F.C. & S. Clause the material of which read: "Warranted free of capture, seizure or detention . . . "

13.13 On 10th September, 1900, the *Bellvue* arrived in Buenos Aires. On inspection the bulls were found to be diseased and the Argentine authorities ordered the vessel to leave the port. Transhipment of the bulls was permitted provided that this took place outside the limits of the port. On 11th September, 1900, the Argentine Government passed a further decree forbidding the import of cattle from the United Kingdom. The bulls were transhipped into lighters where they spent some days and from thence to the *Sallust*. They were taken to Montevideo where, after 40 days' quarantine, they were sold at a considerable financial loss.

Bigham J. considered that there was no restraint of people. In terms which found some echo in Swinfen-Eady L.J.'s judgment in *Sanday's* case[13]:

"It is sufficient to say that the mere operation of an ordinary municipal law affecting or preventing the delivery of the insured goods at their destination is no 'restraint of people' within the meaning of the policy. As in the case of perils of the seas, there must be something violent or out of the ordinary course of things . . . "

13.14 He appears to have been much influenced by the *Finlay* case[14] and distinguished the *Rodocanachi* case[15] on the grounds that there was there a violent act by the Prussian army which prevented the goods from reaching their destination. In view of this finding his treatment of the F.C. & S. Clause was brief. Whilst "restraint" was not mentioned by the clause, he considered that it was clear that the words which were used were sufficient to include it as an exception. Judgment was signed for the underwriters.

13.15 On appeal by the plaintiffs, his finding on the F.C. & S. Clause was unanimously upheld and this alone justified the dismissal of the appeal. The Court of Appeal did, however, overrule the High Court on one important matter. All three judges considered the actions of the Argentine Government to be a "restraint of people". Vaughan Williams L.J. thought it to be an act of State and thus there was no analogy with detention to enforce the rights of an individual. Stirling and Mathew L.JJ. both considered that the proceedings in Buenos Aires amounted to an exercise of force by the Argentine Government, and if no force was actually used, it was because the Master submitted to the orders of that government's servants; the Argentine State had plenty of force in reserve to enforce its wishes should its use be necessary. In the *Cory* case,[16] an intervention to enforce revenue laws had been held to be a peril within the terms of the policy. Regarding the force available to a State, there was also the then very recent *Robinson Gold Mining Co.* case.[17] The Court of Appeal also distinguished the *Hadkinson* case[18] because in the

13. *Sanday v. British & Foreign Marine Insurance Co.* [1915] 2 K.B. 781. See paras. 13.17–13.28.
14. *Finlay v. The Liverpool & Great Western Steamship Co.* (1870) 22 L.T. 251. See para. 25.3.
15. *Rodocanachi v. Elliot* (1873) L.R. 8 C.P. 649. See para. 11.21.
16. *Cory & Son v. Burr* (1881) 8 Q.B.D. 313; (1882) 9 Q.B.D. 463; (1883) 8 App. Cas. 393. See paras. 12.12, 12.13, 12.16–12.19.
17. Footnote 10, above.
18. *Hadkinson v. Robartson* (1803) 3 Bos. & Pul. 388. See paras. 11.37–11.41.

Miller case,[19] the Master went as far as he could go before he came up against the Argentine prohibition. Had he not entered the port, but "continued his voyage" (by this the court presumably means that he had gone elsewhere to discharge his cargo), the insured perils of "restraint of people" could not have arisen.

13.16 The *Miller* case [20] was followed by *St. Paul's Fire & Marine Insurance Co.* v. *Morice*.[21] An American insurance company had insured a bull for carriage from New York to Buenos Aires on board the *Merchant Prince*. On arrival, it was found to be infected by foot and mouth disease and was slaughtered by the Argentine authorities on board the ship. St. Paul's had paid their assured under the primary policy which contained a mortality clause and claimed against their reinsurers who were Lloyd's underwriters. Kennedy J. found some difficulty with the mortality clause, which seemed to him to cover fortuitous or accidental death or death by disease, but not death by slaughter. However that might be, he made a similar finding to the *Miller* case,[22] that the actions of the Argentine authorities were excluded from the policy by the F.C. & S. Clause. Judgment was accordingly signed for the reinsurance underwriters.

13.17 A "restraint of Princes" was held to arise, not without some judicial doubts on the question, in *Sanday* v. *British and Foreign Marine Insurance Company*[23] where both the High Court and Court of Appeal judgments are set out. In July, 1914, linseed was loaded into two British ships, the *St. Andrew* and the *Orthia* in Argentina for carriage to Hamburg. It was sold on C.I.F. terms but property was not to pass until delivery in Hamburg. This never took place, and so the property in the linseed remained in the plaintiffs throughout. On 4th August, 1914, the United Kingdom declared war on Germany and proclamations were made by Her Majesty's Government prohibiting trade between British subjects and Germany on 5th August and 9th September, 1914. On 9th August, the *St. Andrew*, when off the Lizard, first heard of the war from a French warship which suggested she should seek orders from her own government. The Naval Control Officer in Falmouth sent her to Liverpool to discharge which she duly did. The *Orthia* was warned by her owners whilst in a bunkering port of the outbreak of war and of the Admiralty's suggestion that she should proceed to a British port. She duly did so and discharged her cargo in Glasgow. Besides there being no prospect of the linseed being sent on to Hamburg within any reasonable time, it also suffered substantial physical damage.

13.18 By policies written on the S.G. Form and dated 31st July, 1914, the linseed was insured on both vessels against the perils of: " . . . Takings at sea, arrests, restraints, and detainments of all Kings, Princes, and people of what nation, condition, or quality soever." The free of capture and seizure clause was deleted from the policy. On 7th September, 1914, Notice of Abandonment was given and refused, no point being taken that the Notice was late.

13.19 The plaintiffs claimed for a constructive total loss of the goods on the

19. Footnote 11, above.
20. *Ibid.*
21. (1906) 11 Com. Cas. 153.
22. Footnote 11, above.
23. [1915] 2 K.B. 781.

grounds that the adventure had been terminated by a "restraint". Were they entitled to recover? The case produced some very interesting points when it came before Bailhache J. in the High Court. His judgment was substantially agreed by the majority judgments of the Court of Appeal, namely Lord Reading C.J. and Bray J., that there was a restraint and that the plaintiffs were entitled to recover for a constructive total loss. This, being the majority view, prevailed, but there was a strong dissenting judgment given by Swinfen-Eady L.J. which, since he was in substantial agreement with Bigham J., the trial judge in the *Miller* case,[24] should be noted.

13.20 The defendant underwriters took four points. There was no loss, or if there was a loss it was not caused by an insured peril; the peril insured against was not the proximate cause of the loss; if loss was claimed because of any action by the United Kingdom authorities, then such actions would not amount to "taking at sea" etc.; after the declaration of war on 4th August, 1914, the policy became illegal. The High Court and the majority of the Court of Appeal found against the underwriters on all points. There was a loss because the adventure was lost. In spite of the way the policy was worded, it gave cover for the physical loss or damage of the goods and, quite independently, for the loss of the adventure. This was dealt with more fully in the *Forestal* cases[25] where this characteristic of an insurance on goods, as opposed to a policy upon a ship, was emphasised. There was a loss by a peril insured against, namely "restraints of Princes". The judges followed the Court of Appeal in the *Miller* case[26] that force need not be present, Bailhache J. saying: "No force was used, but restraint of Princes does not necessarily involve the use of force; any authoritative prohibition on the part of a governing power, or the operation of a municipal law, is sufficient", and Lord Reading C.J.: "The Executive has the power of compelling obedience to its orders by the exercise of force if necessary; the force need not be actually present when the Master of the vessel submits to an order of the Executive."

13.21 Lord Reading C.J. went out of his way to define "restraints of Kings, Princes and people". Besides the definition quoted in the *Forestal* cases[27] he noted the *Rodocanachi* case[28] where Brett J. had found that a hostile force, although not used directly against the goods or those persons who had their custody, had prevented the goods being "carried to their destination". He regarded restraints of Kings, Princes and people in an insurance policy as meaning the same as it did in charterparty cases, quoting with particular approval the judgment of Cockburn C.J. in *Geipel* v. *Smith*[29]: "Is a blockade a restraint of Princes? I think it is. It is an act of a Sovereign State or Prince . . . In such a case, the obstacle arises from an act of State of one of the belligerent sovereigns and consequently constitutes a restraint

---

24. *Miller* v. *The Law Accident Insurance Co.* [1902] 2 K.B. 694; [1903] 1 K.B. 712 (C.A.). See paras. 13.11–13.15.
25. *Forestal Land, Timber & Railways Co. Ltd.* v. *Rickards* (*The Minden*); *Middows* v. *Robertson* (*The Wangoni*); *W.W. Howard, Bros. & Co.* v. *Kann* (*The Halle*) (1940) 67 Ll.L.Rep. 484; (1940) 68 Ll.L.Rep. 45 (C.A.); (1941) 70 Ll.L.Rep. 173; [1942] A.C. 50 (H.L.) See paras. 13.27–13.34.
26. Footnote 24, above.
27. Footnote 25, above.
28. *Rodocanachi* v. *Elliott* (1873) L.R. 8 C.P. 649. See para. 11.21.
29. (1872) L.R. 7 Q.B. 404.

of Princes." Moreover, Rule 10 of the Marine Insurance Act for the construction of the policy refers particularly to political or executive acts which includes acts of State, for which force is not necessary.

Bray J. agreed with the view that "restraints of Kings, Princes and people" in an insurance policy has the same meaning as it does in a charterparty, adding to *Geipel* v. *Smith*[30] the case of *Nobel's Explosives Company* v. *Jenkins*.[31]

13.22 It is particularly noticeable that the High Court and the majority of the Court of Appeal regarded the outbreak of war as the restraining factor rather than the two proclamations. Lord Reading C.J. said:

"Both ships were proceeding on the voyage and were compelled to abandon it because the Government intervened by the declaration of war. That act of the Sovereign was in itself, by the operation of the common law, a prohibition to trade with the enemy; the voyage to Germany immediately became illegal and if persisted would doubtless have been prevented by force."

13.23 Bray J. regarded the outbreak of war as being a violent departure from the ordinary course of events. What would happen if a war started without any declaration of war? This would make no difference, it would still be a political act: "A state of war cannot exist without the act of the State either in commencing hostilities or in using the Naval or Military Forces to resist acts of violence committed by the enemy." He also regarded there being quite enough force present to compel submission. A determination to continue the voyage would have resulted in prosecution, prison and confiscation of the goods, and the underwriters would then have pleaded that the goods were lost by an illegal act entitling them to avoid liability. Was this not enough? Plainly it was.

13.24 Regarding the actions of the British authorities, the High Court and the majority of the Court of Appeal regarded the words of the policy as being quite wide enough to include them, and the courts were unable to find any custom of the trade or any part of the law merchant that the policy should be read in any other way than its clear text indicated. Bailhache J. found the *Lozano* case[32] particularly persuasive (and seems to have distinguished it from "ordinary judicial process"). On illegality there was common agreement that there was nothing illegal when the voyages commenced or when the insurance contracts were made as both these took place well before the outbreak of the war. If there had been, the courts would not have heard the plaintiffs' claim. The supervening event of the declaration of war would have made the further continuance of the voyage illegal and of the insurance ineffectual, but there was no attempt to continue the voyage in either case. Judgment in both the High Court and the Court of Appeal was therefore given for the plaintiffs on their plea that there had been a constructive total loss of the venture. This dealt with the damage to the linseed, which was not separately considered. This finding was later affirmed unanimously by the House of Lords, where great emphasis was laid on the declaration of war as being the "restraint" because it brought into operation other laws which forbade trading with the enemy.

30. *Ibid.*
31. [1896] 2 Q.B. 326.
32. *Lozano* v. *Janson* (1859) 2 EL. & EL. 160. See paras. 12.34–12.37.

13.25 It is necessary to consider the dissenting judgment of Swinfen-Eady L.J. who, as it has been remarked, was in agreement with Bigham J. in the *Miller* case[33] on several aspects. There is now little or no prospect, particularly since the *Forestal* cases,[34] of these judgments being followed, but such senior judgments ought not to be ignored. Bigham had held that the words "arrests, restraints or detainments of Kings, Princes or people" do not cover the operation of the ordinary law of the land, but relate only to some violent departure from the ordinary course of things. He added: " . . . but the force of any country, which compels obedience to its ordinary municipal law, is not a restraint of Kings, Princes and people in the plain, ordinary, popular sense of these words occurring in a marine policy to describe perils insured against."

To this Swinfen-Eady L.J. added:

"In my opinion the outbreak of war, whereby the further continuance of a voyage to a port, which has become an enemy port, has become impossible, is not an arrest, restraint, or detainment, either within the ordinary meaning of those words or within any meaning which the custom of merchants or the usages of trade have affixed to those words when used in a policy of marine insurance."

13.26 He considered that force was readily present in the *Goss* case,[35] the *Rotch* case[36] and the *Rodocanachi* case,[37] in the latter case in the shape of the Prussian army. But in the *Sanday* case,[38] it was not present. It appears that he was particularly influenced by the *Hadkinson*[39] and *Lubbock*[40] cases.

This case is also very notable for the authoritative decisions by Swinfen-Eady L.J. and Bray J. regarding the impact of the Marine Insurance Act 1906 on the previous common law and law merchant. This belongs more properly to the chapter on the Act itself (Chapter 26). Lastly, it should be noted that a warranty was added to the cargo policies as a result of this case, and that this warranty was considered in the *Forestal* cases.[41] This warranty has been further refined to a direct exclusion from the Institute War Clauses (Cargo), 1.1.82:

"In no case shall this insurance cover . . .
3.7   Any claim based upon loss of or frustration of the voyage or adventure."

13.27 Three most important cases on "restraint of princes" arose in 1940 and 1941. There is a degree of confusion about them because their names are often quoted separately without reference to the other two cases. All three were heard together in the High Court, the Court of Appeal and the House of Lords. It would be helpful to set out their names as they are quoted from the House of Lords report. The names of the three ships concerned are added although they are not part of the headings:

33. Footnote 24, above.
34. Footnote 25, above.
35. *Goss* v. *Withers* (1758) 2 Burr. 683. See paras. 11.8–11.11.
36. *Rotch* v. *Edie* (1795) 6 Term Rep. 413. See. paras. 13.7–13.10.
37. Footnote 28, above.
38. *Sanday* v. *British & Foreign Marine Ins. Co.* [1915] 2 K.B. 781.
39. *Hadkinson* v. *Robartson* (1803) 2 Bos. & Pul. 388. See paras. 11.37–11.41.
40. *Lubbock* v. *Rowcroft* (1803) 5 Esp. 50. See para. 11.40.
41. Footnote 25, above.

13.28 Forestal Land, Timber & Railways Co. Ltd. v. Rickards (The Minden); Middows, Ltd. v. Robertson (The Wangoni); W.W. Howard Bros. & Co. Ltd v. Kann (The Halle).[42]

Mr. Rickards, Mr. Robertson and Mr. Kann were Lloyd's underwriters. Like the plaintiffs, they were British. The three ships concerned were German. All three cases were test cases and many other claims turned upon the decision of the courts.

13.29 Just before the outbreak of the Second World War, all three plaintiff firms shipped goods on to the three German ships. All three ships had sailed in August 1939, the *Minden* from Buenos Aires for Durban, where the cargo was to be transhipped to China, the *Wangoni* from Bremen for Cape Town and the *Halle* from Australia for London. They would not reach any of these ports until after the outbreak of war on 3rd September, 1939, but at the time of sailing the pre-war crisis between the United Kingdom and France on the one hand and Germany on the other was at its height. The exact date and form of the orders given by the German Government to the Masters of German ships was not known at the dates of the hearings, but it was accepted that the German Government had taken control of all German shipping and had instructed the Masters that they should take refuge in neutral ports and if possible return to Germany. They were to avoid capture by Allied warships and, as a last resort, they were to scuttle their ships. In compliance with these orders, the *Minden* took refuge in Rio de Janeiro, the *Wangoni* in Vigo and the *Halle* in Bissao. Subsequently all three ships left their ports of refuge to return to Germany. In September and October 1939 respectively, the *Minden* and the *Halle* were challenged at sea by Allied warships and were scuttled with the loss of their cargo. The *Wangoni* managed to reach Hamburg in March 1940. Only the Master of the *Wangoni*, through the medium of neutral agents, offered to land the cargo and restore it to the plaintiffs, first in Vigo and later in Hamburg. He first required some very onerous conditions to be met on payment of freight and discharging costs and the giving of guarantees.

13.30 The three cases came before Hilbery J. in the High Court. He found that the three Masters, on sailing from their ports of refuge for Germany, were exercising the German Government's restraint on the goods as the agents of that government. The *Sanday* case[43] had indicated that, in cases of restraint, force was not necessary; it was enough that the Masters, as German citizens, were obliged to obey the orders of the German Government. He noted what Lord Reading said in the *Sanday* case:

"The words arrest, restraint and detainment of all kings, princes and people to my mind also imply some intervention of a fortuitous character, some interference out of the ordinary course of events by the governing authorities who have the force of the State behind them to compel submission to their authoritative decrees."

13.31 The plaintiffs, however, had other difficulties and these led to judgment being signed in favour of the underwriters. The policies contained, as was usual in policies for insurance of goods, a frustration clause: "Warranted free of all claims based upon loss of, or frustration of, the insured voyage or adventure caused by

---

42. The references of the High Court, the Court of Appeal and the House of Lords are: (1940) 67 Ll.L.Rep. 484, (1940) 68 Ll.L.Rep. 45 (C.A.), (1941) 70 Ll.L.Rep. 173, [1942] A.C. 50 (H.L.)
    43. Footnote 37, above.

arrests, restraints of kings princes peoples usurpers or persons attempting to usurp power." Whilst the goods were insured, so was the adventure which was frustrated. To his Lordship, the two were indivisible. The frustration clause contained exclusions and: "It has been decided that, where there are shown to be two causes of the one loss, one of which is a peril insured against and the other of which is a peril of which the policy is warranty free, the insured cannot recover."

Here there had not only been a loss of the goods but frustration, and therefore loss of the adventure as well by the perils which were excepted by the frustration clause. The plaintiffs could therefore not recover for a constructive total loss.

13.32 On the alternative claim by the plaintiffs for the actual total loss of the cargo when the *Minden* and the *Halle* were scuttled, his Lordship felt that in any attempt to run the Allied blockade, both ships were engaged in a warlike operation. Perhaps there was even the risk of capture by Allied warships. But were the goods insured at all at that stage? Neither ship, nor for that matter the *Wangoni*, was employed on the voyage for which the goods were insured after they had sailed from their ports of refuge. There was a "held covered" clause in the policy which permitted diversion or a change of voyage and there was also section 45 of the Marine Insurance Act 1906, but the voyages actually undertaken without the consent of the cargo owners or an additional premium to the underwriters were totally different from the voyages contemplated in the insurance contract. The German Masters substituted, for a common adventure, a warlike operation with a military objective. Regarding the *Wangoni* cargo, the plaintiffs, even if they surmounted the difficulty of providing that the insurance still existed, could have recovered their cargo by paying the costs demanded by the shipowners. They could not therefore show that it was more unlikely than not that they would recover their goods within a reasonable time.

13.33 The plaintiffs appealed. The Court of Appeal reversed the High Court's judgment for reasons which appeared in the further appeal to the House of Lords. There was general agreement in the House of Lords on the following points:

(1) At the latest on the dates that the ships sailed from their ports of refuge, when the German Captains obeyed their government's orders and by so doing acted as their government's agents, there was a "restraint of princes and people", and that this led to constructive total losses. In Viscount Simon's words: " . . . and held the goods as the subject and servant of that government instead of holding as if the bailee of the insured", and Lord Wright's:

"It was in both courts (the High Court and the Court of Appeal), in my opinion, rightly held that the act of the Masters in sailing [for ports of refuge] constituted a restraint of princes within the words of the policy 'capture, seizure, arrest, restraint or detainment . . . ' These words were intended to repeat what is repeated in the body of the policy 'enemies . . . takings at sea, arrest, restraints and detainments of all kings, princes and people'."

(2) In the cases of the *Minden* and the *Halle,* there was always an "unlikelihood of recovery" of the goods. Because of the German Government's orders, the goods would either be taken back to Germany or sunk to the bottom of the sea. In the case of the *Wangoni*, the plaintiff was only

required to act reasonably, and the conditions for the goods to be discharged and returned to their owners, either from Vigo or from Hamburg, were so onerous that it would be unreasonable to expect the plaintiff to have to comply with them, even supposing he could get a licence from the Treasury to trade with the enemy. All plaintiffs had satisfied the court that the requirements of section 60(2)(i) of the Marine Insurance Act 1906 were fulfilled. Lord Wright approved the test applied by Kennedy L.J. in *Polurrian Steamship Co. Ltd.* v. *Young*[44] and added:

> "There is a real difference in logic in saying that a future happening is uncertain and saying that it is unlikely. In the former, the balance is even; no-one can say one way or the other. In the latter, there is some balance against the event. If on the test of uncertainty, the scales are level, any degree of unlikelihood would seem to shift the balance however slightly; it is not required that the scale should spring up and kick the beam."

(3) Whilst on the subject matter of insurance of the goods, the trial judge had erred in holding that loss or damage to the goods and the loss of the adventure were indivisible. They were two separate insurances. In Viscount Maugham's words: "The contract is an insurance against loss of two different kinds in relation to the goods. The first involves loss or damage to the goods themselves. The second involves merely that they have not reached their destination although they may be perfectly safe."

Viscount Maugham felt it necessary to distinguish between the insurance of goods and the insurance of ships. Since this is a work on war risk insurance of merchant ships we should note: "It is now well settled, contrary to the opinion of Lord Mansfield in *Milles* v. *Fletcher*[45] . . . that the loss of the voyage has nothing to do with the loss of the ship."

(4) The trial judge had again erred in holding that the insurance of the goods came to an end when the three Masters left the courses of their voyages by putting into ports of refuge or trying to get back to Germany, thus abandoning the insured voyages or deviating from or changing them. Such deviation or change of the voyage was caused by orders from the German Government and was beyond the control of the Masters and their employers. It was thus excused by section 49(1)(*b*) of the Marine Insurance Act 1906. Likewise, the insurers were not discharged from their liability under section 45 because that section only contemplates changes which are voluntary. These changes were involuntary and were made by each Master in obedience to orders which: "morally as a good subject, he ought not to have resisted".

13.34 Here Lord Porter was guided by the judgment of Lord Ellenborough in *Phelps* v. *Auldgo*.[46] He considered that this also answered the underwriters' claim that at least they were entitled to substantial additional premium under the "held covered" clause saying: "As in my view, the deviation is excusable and there has been no change of voyage, no extra premium is payable."

44. [1915] 1 K.B. 922.
45. (1778) 1 Doug. K.B. 231.
46. (1810) 2 Camp. 350.

It would appear possible that as the House of Lords did not consider that the insurances had come to an end, it would have been prepared to find that there were actual total losses of the *Minden's* and the *Halle's* cargoes. This was not in fact done, presumably because the House was satisfied that, at the latest date when ships left their ports of refuge to return to Germany, the cargoes were already constructive total losses.

SMUGGLING—RESTRAINT BY COURT ORDER

13.35 A case on "restraint" with a distinct measure of difference was *Panamanian Oriental Steamship Corporation* v. *Wright*,[47] often referred to as *The Anita* which was the name of the ship involved.

The *Anita* arrived in Saigon on 7th March, 1966, during a particularly dangerous time of the Vietnamese War. The Government of the Republic of South Vietnam was very anxious to stamp out corruption, which took many forms. Customs officers found a large quantity of wristwatches, transistor radios and other dutiable goods most carefully concealed in various parts of the ship with the obvious intention of smuggling them ashore. The Customs could have proceeded against the ship under the Customs Code, which dated from 1931 when France governed Indo-China. This code provided for the more usual penalties of fines, moderate terms of imprisonment and confiscation of smuggled goods. Shortly before the time of the *Anita's* arrival, the government had set up a Special Court to stamp out corruption and had armed it with extreme powers. Its judges were army officers who were: " . . . vouched for from all points of view as to integrity and who, above all, had an exact idea and a profound comprehension of the higher interests of the Nation and the people at the present time".

13.36 They sat wearing red judicial robes over their army uniforms, and were intended to deal with "dishonest merchants, the disturbers of economy, traders on influence, officials guilty of misappropriation of public funds, extortion". There was no appeal from the court's findings. Its draconian powers were well illustrated by its very first case where it ordered the public execution of a trader guilty of malpractice. It was before this court that the Master and some of the crew were charged. There was no criticism of the court's procedures, which seemed to have been conducted perfectly fairly, or of any lack of consideration of its findings which took two hours to reach. The Special Court acquitted the Master, sentenced some of the crew to terms of imprisonment which were out of all proportion to the trivial nature of the offence, and ordered the confiscation of the ship. There were some genuine doubts whether it had jurisdiction to order confiscation, although arguably this did lie within its powers.

13.37 The *Anita* was insured on the Lloyd's S.G. Form with the Institute Warranty & Strikes Clause attached. It gave cover for "restraints of Kings, Princes and People". It also contained a clause which excluded: "loss . . . arising from . . . arrest, restraint or detainment by reason of infringement of any Customs regulations", and the underwriters' main defence rested on this exclusion.

13.38 In the High Court, Mocatta J. found for the plaintiffs. He rejected the

47. [1970] 2 Lloyd's Rep. 365; [1971] 1 Lloyd's Rep. 487 (C.A.).

suggestion that the proceedings of the Special Court were "ordinary judicial process" for the reasons which appear in the chapter devoted to that subject (Chapter 25). He found that, in ordering the confiscation, the Special Court was exceeding its jurisdiction. State officials had seized the ship and had indicted the Master and crew and then held the ship under the Special Court's order. The insured peril of "arrests . . . of people" therefore arose: "The interposition of a decision of a court between the act of an official of the State in initially restraining a ship and the subsequent retention of the ship pursuant to that decision cannot prevent the acts of the officials from being executive acts."

13.39 Moreover, it made no difference that such of the crew who were not in jail (and later the owner's watchmen) remained on board the ship. The owner was still deprived of her possession after 25th June, 1966. At the date of the first Notice of Abandonment on 29th September, 1966, it was not unlikely that the shipowner would recover his ship within a reasonable time; at the dates of the two subsequent Notices of Abandonment (12th May and 10th August, 1967), and on 29th August, 1967, when the writ was issued, it was "unlikely", and the unlikelihood became even greater as time went on. The exception apart, the owners had successfully made out their case for a constructive total loss.

13.40 Could the underwriters plead the exception? No authorities were cited to the court (and it would seem that there were none before this case) but the exception was clearly intended to include all Customs' regulations however harsh their effect. Whatever the effect of its finding, the Special Court had exceeded its jurisdiction in ordering the vessel's confiscation when it was seeking to punish an infringement of the Customs' regulations. Mocatta J. favoured the following test:

"If the order is made *bona fide* and is strictly due to an error of construction, I think it would be 'a loss by reason of infringement of Customs regulations'. If, however, the order was made arbitrarily in that it was made on the instructions of the government of the time without any genuine belief in the court, that it had jurisdiction to make the order, then I think the conclusion would be different . . . "

13.41 This case really turned on the burden of proof because Mocatta J. held that, to prove the exception, the underwriters had to prove that there was an infringement of the Customs' regulations and that the Special Court had acted honestly. The shipowners had shown, though not conclusively even though there were many strong pointers in this direction, that the order of confiscation was made on the government's instructions. To counter this the underwriters, if they wished to prove an infringement of Customs' regulations, had to show that the court was acting in a *bona fide* way. They had not done so and on the "balance of probabilities" the shipowners were entitled to judgment in their favour.

13.42 Mocatta J.'s judgment was unanimously overturned by the Court of Appeal but only on the question that the trial judge had wrongly applied the burden of proof. The question of whether there was a "restraint of people" was not gone into in any detail although Lord Denning M.R. at least seemed disinclined to question Mocatta J.'s findings on this point. It is possible that the court felt constrained by the agreement of the parties that the *Anita* should be regarded as a constructive total loss. What needs to be noted in this context is the test described by Fenton-Atkinson L.J. with whom Lord Denning M.R. and Sir Gordon Willmer seem to have been in agreement: "Was the decision of the Special Court to order confiscation of the *Anita* a *bona fide* and independent exercise of its powers or what it honestly believed was its powers?" or was it a case that: " . . . the Special Court was not acting *bona fide* as an independent judicial body but merely acting as a puppet court following directions of the Government, or knowingly exceeding its powers . . . "

13.43 On the face of it, the Special Court was acting properly as a court should act, although it was open to the shipowners to prove otherwise. The burden of proof was on them to show that the Special Court had acted improperly with the certainty required to justify a finding that this was so, once the underwriters had proved that there was a smuggling offence and that the Vietnamese court had confiscated the ship as a result. The underwriters had so proved, and the shipowner had failed to discharge the burden of proof in a way which would have justified the court in holding that the Special Court had acted improperly. This justified allowing the appeal of the underwriters.

13.44 The case is interesting for two further matters. Mocatta J. held that the ship was not an actual total loss because she was not "irretrievably lost" within the meaning of section 57 of the Marine Insurance Act 1906. He found this requirement to be far greater than the requirement of "unlikelihood", required by section 60. The point was not gone into deeply because of his finding that the ship was a constructive total loss, and the finding could be open to future question. Lord Denning M.R., in his judgment, made the point that the underwriters had pleaded that there was an "arrest, restraint or detainment" within the meaning of the policy's exclusion clause. The shipowners had replied that this was "confiscation" which is not a peril excluded by the wording of that clause. On this point, he clearly considered that the underwriters were correct. This is another example, to be added to the *Robinson Gold Mining* case,[48] where, particularly when an exceptions clause is being considered, the courts have not always considered themselves as strictly bound to interpret the words used as they would when considering whether or not a peril is insured; in these instances, they would be more inclined to give the words a more general and usual meaning, always provided that they consider they are giving effect to the intention of the parties. The modern tendency, however, is to search diligently for the proximate cause (Chapter 30), and this tendency could lead to a more precise finding on exactly which excluded risks excused the underwriters from liability.

DETAINMENT BY CUSTOMS AUTHORITIES

13.45 *Ikerigi Compania Naviera S.A. and Others* v. *Palmer and Others*[49] was a case typical of many where the charterers fail to honour their commitments for one reason or another, and although this is often for reasons outside their control, the effect on the shipowning interests can be disastrous. In theory, proceedings can be taken against the charterers for breach of contract. In practice, this is frequently impossible, because the charterer is without means or else lives in a place where no confidence can be placed in the judicial system.

48. [1901] 2 K.B. 919; [1902] 2 K.B. 489. See paras. 12.22–12.28.
49. [1991] 1 Lloyd's Rep. 400.

13.46 Ikerigi represented the shipowning interests. Mr. Palmer was a representative Lloyd's underwriter and one of the insurances which he gave was on the Institute War and Strikes Clauses Freight—Time 1.10.83. It contained the following exclusions clauses which read:

"4 Exclusions

This insurance excludes
4.1　　loss (total or partial) or expense arising from
4.1.5　arrest restraint detainment confiscation or expropriation under quarantine regulations or by reason of infringement of any customs or trading regulations
4.1.6　the operation of ordinary judicial process, failure to provide security or to pay any fine or penalty or any financial cause."

13.47 On 4th February, 1987, the *Wondrous* was chartered to load a full cargo of molasses in Bandar Abbas. She arrived on 10th March, and on the 18th March she began loading. It was a very slow process. The cargo was brought alongside by road tankers at spasmodic intervals, and the difficulties of transferring the cargo to the ship's tanks were extreme. Twice, on 12th May and 5th July, she was ordered off the berth by the port authorities. On 14th July the shipowners, pointing out that the 40 days of laytime had long since expired, accepted that the charterers had repudiated the charterparty by their behaviour. The charterers nonetheless continued to send cargo to be loaded, and by 14th August, 1987, the ship had loaded all the cargo she was going to get, altogether 23,014.42 tons. A full and complete cargo would have been some 30,000 tons. The remaining 7,000 tons was never provided.

13.48 It was the charterer's duty to comply with some customs regulations pertaining to the export of the cargo, and this was not done. Without their completion, the ship could not get clearance to sail. She remained in the port until 17th October, 1988, when she was finally allowed to leave. The main engine was by this time inoperative, and the bottom of the ship was very foul. She had to be towed by a tug to Fujairah, where sufficient repairs were done so that she could proceed to Aarhus to discharge the cargo. There were no further mishaps, and she duly earned her freight.

13.49 Hobhouse J. found that the ship was not detained because of any judicial process. The delay was caused because some purely administrative customs formalities were not completed as they should have been, and there did not appear to be any political motive for this failure. He found there was a "detainment" from 1st October, 1987 onwards, but then there was also Clause 4.1.5. The insured peril of "detainment" and the exclusion had to be looked at in the same way:

"The words 'restraint' and 'detainment' have to be given a wide commercial interpretation . . . but by the same token the exclusion must be read in the same way. In a commercial sense she was detained by reason of infringement of customs regulations. She was only detained because, if she had tried to leave, she would have been infringing customs regulations and would have been stopped by force; therefore the reason for her detention was infringement of customs regulations."

Judgment was signed in favour of the underwriters. Subsequently this judgment was upheld by the Court of Appeal.[50]

50. [1992] 2 Lloyd's Rep. 566. (See also, Chapter 22 on Freight.)

MUTUAL WAR RISKS ASSOCIATIONS—PRACTICE

13.51 It is convenient to deal with four cases at this stage concerning the actions which the Mutual War Risks Associations took to deal with cases of "arrest, restraint or detainment" and to note the very different factors which the directors of the Mutual Associations, as practical shipowners, took into consideration as opposed to those which weighed with the courts. Even if one of these cases pre-dated the judgment in *The Anita*,[51] that case had a profound effect on the remaining three.

13.52 In June, 1967, the Suez Canal was closed during the Six Day War between Egypt and Israel. A convoy was going through the Canal when it was closed on 5th June, 1967, and it had to anchor in the Great Bitter Lakes. Subsequently the Canal became blocked by sunken ships at each end and the 14 ships of several nationalities were imprisoned until the Canal's reopening in June, 1975. It is worthy of note that one German vessel was then able to complete her voyage under her own power and arrived in Hamburg to an emotional reception. Between June, 1967 and October, 1973 when the Egyptian Army drove them from a large section of it, the Israeli Army lined the whole of the eastern bank. There were sporadic artillery duels between the two sides. During the whole of this time that the ships remained imprisoned, there was no claim to the possession of the ships themselves. The Egyptian authorities gave every encouragement and assistance to the owners in maintaining them, including effecting periodical changes of their crews. The Israelis put no hindrance in the owners' way.

13.53 The owners of the four British ships made claims for constructive total losses upon their War Risk Associations. Leading counsel (several were instructed) were unanimous that a "restraint" had occurred. Was there deprivation of possession? Counsel knew of no case of a "restraint" where the Master and crew remained on board and there was no claim by anyone to the ship or any attempt by anyone to prevent her from doing something which she would otherwise normally have done. He distinguished *Polurrian Steamship Co. Ltd.* v. *Young*[52] case where the crew remained on board because the Greek Admiral was claiming that the ship was a lawful prize. This remained the position until *The Bamburi*.[53] As time went on, it became noticeable that the opinion of the various leaders tended to diverge. In August, 1968, at least one leader considered that deprivation of possession had then taken place and it is understood that others agreed with this view. A longer period of time indicated that the owners were "deprived of possession" in the sense that they "ceased to be in possession of the ships" in all senses of the word although the courts had never previously sanctioned this line of thought. Was there "unlikelihood of recovery within a reasonable time"? There were a number of peace initiatives throughout, some of them limited to the release of the ships, any one of which could have succeeded. In June, 1969, counsel thought that the ships were arguably constructive total losses, but pointed out that the owners still faced considerable difficulties in proving that they were deprived of possession, and that if the ships were released before the hearings of the courts took place, the courts

---

51. Footnote 47, above.
52. [1915] 1 K.B. 922. See paras. 11.32–11.34.
53. [1982] 1 Lloyd's Rep. 312. See paras. 13.63–13.72.

would most likely find that the ships were not constructive total losses but partial losses only. The War Risk Associations, feeling that the owners had not had the use of their ships for over two years, and that there was no reasonable likelihood of their recovery, accepted their claims for constructive total losses in 1969.

13.54 Equally difficult questions arose in respect of a Greek ship which was chartered in 1974 to load sugar and timber in Bangkok for discharge in Berbera and Hodeidah. No sugar was loaded and the Captain was told by the charterer that the sugar cargo had "fallen through". He was instructed by the charterer to sail with the timber alone and did so. Upon arrival in Berbera in October, 1974, the Somali Government, which had purchased the sugar, asked what had happened to it. They did not believe that none had been loaded and detained the ship. They were convinced that it had been discharged wrongfully somewhere on the route although a comparison with the ship's service speed, the time she took to complete the voyage and the distance involved showed that this could not have happened. Criminal proceedings were taken against the Captain and he was finally sentenced to four years in prison although he was released after a few months under a general amnesty. The Somalis took no action to possess the ship, their attitude simply being that the ship stayed in Berbera until the sugar was delivered or their money was returned. Proof that the shipper had defrauded them and had obtained payment of the full purchase price from the Somalis' bank in Singapore, using a forged bill of lading and other spurious documents to prove that shipment had taken place, merely increased their suspicions that the shipowner had, in some way, been party to the deception practised upon them, although investigations showed that this could not have been the case. Undoubtedly the insured peril of "arrest, restraint or detainment" had arisen. Was the shipowner deprived of the possession of the ship? If so, could he recover it within a reasonable time?

13.55 The directors of the Mutual War Risk Association considered in all the circumstances that the shipowner had been deprived of the effective possession of his ship, because he had been denied the use of her for the purposes for which she was intended, namely earning freight, for a considerable time. *The Anita*[54] had made it clear that it made no difference that the crew was on board the ship and later the owner's watchmen. Regarding the unlikelihood of recovery within a reasonable time, it seemed that it was most unlikely that the Somalis would ever release the ship. They were not willing to discuss the matter with the Association's managers or its lawyers and only responded with reluctance to the Greek and British Ambassadors to whom they made their position clear. Either the sugar was delivered or their money was returned. If either happened the ship could leave but not otherwise. Since neither prospect was even remotely possible, the directors accepted in July, 1975 that the ship was a constructive total loss.

13.56 From the cases quoted above, it will be appreciated that, in doing this, the directors of the Mutual War Risk Associations went considerably beyond what the courts would have ordered them to do had the cases appeared before them. To a practical shipowner "deprivation of possession" could mean not only that the ship was taken away from the shipowner by confiscation or by transfer of her title, it could also mean that he was deprived of her use for the purpose intended. On

---

54. Footnote 47, above.

unlikelihood of recovery within a reasonable time, they were prepared to accept that the attitude of the Somali Government, and its aloof refusal to discuss the matter which was only briefly penetrated by the two diplomats, and the criminal proceedings instituted against the Master, indicated clearly enough what in a practical sense the prospects of release were at any time.

13.57 The same Mutual War Risk Association was soon faced with other problems of ships being "arrested, restrained or detained" and on each occasion they similarly brought their practical shipowning expertise and knowledge to the resolution of the problem rather than the fixed and sometimes over-rigid principles of the law which were drawn from precedent. In April, 1977 the Angolan Government wanted to purchase a considerable quantity of ground nuts from Mozambique. Bills of lading were signed to show that they had been shipped on board five ships, none of which were in Mozambique at that time. In one case the bills of lading were presented to the Angolans' bank in Zurich the day after they were signed in Mozambique, a practical impossibility as the airline schedules revealed. In fact, no ground nuts were ever shipped and, like the Somalis, the Angolans were the victims of an elaborate fraud. The Angolan Government started to make enquiries, and to put it off the scent the charterer, who seems to have instigated the fraud, loaded ground nut husks at various ports. These, without the valuable nuts inside them, were of little value. This subterfuge was unsuccessful. On their arrival in Luanda the five ships were detained. One managed to escape. Of the remaining four, three were insured by the same Mutual War Risk Association. Rather curiously the Angolan Government started civil proceedings against the owners and the possibility arose of taking the defence that the detention of the ship was due to "ordinary judicial process" (Chapter 25). It took a long time to establish satisfactorily that the proceedings were not in fact *bona fide* proceedings, and that the Civil Courts in Angola were most likely acting on the instructions of the Angolan Government. Following the lead given by Mocatta J. and Fenton-Atkinson L.J. in *The Anita*[55] the directors decided in May 1979 that the claims for constructive total loss should be settled. Needless to say, they only reached their decision on being satisfied by extensive enquiries that the owners were in no way involved in the fraud.

13.58 The same Mutual War Risk Association was concerned with casualties arising from the Iran/Iraq War. Of the 75-odd ships in Iraqi ports at the outbreak of the war on 22nd September, 1980, 13 ships were insured by the Association; three of them were actual total losses, being either bombed or shelled, whilst the remaining 10 were undamaged. Were they constructive total losses?

13.59 On 22nd September, 1980, the Iraqi Government issued decree No. 23 which forbade merchant ships either to enter or to leave Iraqi ports. All attempts to obtain this decree were unavailing because such decrees are not published in Iraq. The harbour masters at each port visited each ship and told the Captains of its existence, its contents and their effect. On some occasions the Captains were allowed to read an English translation but none of them were allowed to keep a copy. The existence of the decree and its effect were communicated by Iraqi officials to the Association's representative when he went to visit them in Baghdad but his request for a copy was refused. Ships in Basrah could not have sailed because two ships, the

55. Footnote 47, above.

Uljanik and the *Olanesti*, were sunk athwart the stream at Khorramshahr. The Karun Bar below Khorramshahr would have silted up without continuous dredging which was impossible in wartime, and so would the mouth of the river. Ships at Fao at the mouth of the river could possibly have sailed but again the silting could have been a problem. No such physical hindrances would have prevented the sailing of the ships at Umm Qasr or Khor-al-Zubeir. An Iraqi gunboat was anchored in the stream and, whilst the matter was never put to the test, it was thought that she would have intervened to prevent any attempt to sail without the permission of the Harbour Master. The Iraqi authorities put no hindrance in the way of the owners visiting their ships and in changing their crews or, after their repatriation, the engagement of watchmen. They were allowed to do everything that they wished with their ships except to sail them.

13.60 When the directors of the Association considered the owners' claims for constructive total losses, they found no difficulty in accepting that a restraint had taken place. Decree No. 23 was never put before them, but there was a mass of circumstantial evidence which indicated clearly enough its existence and its effect. They found much more difficulty in answering the two questions "Were the owners deprived of their possession?" and "Was it unlikely that they could recover their possession within a reasonable time?"

13.61 They felt, as practical shipowners rather than as lawyers, that the situation justified them in taking a broad view of both questions. The owners had been deprived of the use of their ships for the only purpose for which they intended them, namely the earning of freight. They had the advantage of leading counsel's opinion, and whilst *Rotch* v. *Edie*[56] would have steered them away from such a decision, there was support for their view in *Arnould on Marine Insurance*, 16th Edition, paragraph 1188, even though the contents of this paragraph had been criticised by Mocatta J. in *The Anita* judgment.[57] There was further support in *Hall* v. *Hayman*[58] and in *Court Line* v. *The King*.[59] Nevertheless, it was as practical shipowners themselves that they took the view that they did. They found much more difficulty with the second question because, at the time (May, 1981), there were a number of peace moves and had these been effective, the ships could have been released. The most promising of these was the imminent departure of the United Nations' Special Commissioner, Mr. Olof Palme, to Baghdad and Tehran, and they therefore adjourned any decision until Mr. Palme's mission had taken place. Further consideration of the owners' claims would take place once the result of that mission was known.

13.62 The Association's Managers were able to see Mr. Palme a few days before the first meeting. Mr. Palme told them that he had only the faintest hopes of success, and in the event his mission never took place. On hearing this, the directors of the Association concluded that there was no likelihood that the shipowners would recover their ships within a reasonable time, and in June, 1981, the Association accepted that the ships were constructive total losses. They also took into consideration (and here they were far away from any of the factors that the courts would

56. (1795) 6 Term Rep. 413. See paras. 13.7–13.10.
57. Footnote 47, above.
58. [1912] 2 K.B. 5.
59. (1945) 78 Ll.L. Rep. 390. See para. 27.21.

have considered) that there was no reasonable prospect that the shipowners would recover the ships that they had lost; prolonged lay-up in such conditions would cause massive deterioration in the condition of the ships, and the values of the ships recovered could be, and on a deteriorating freight market would be, very different from the values when they were first detained. To a shipowner whose ship was at liberty, there would have been a chance to do something to prevent a loss to himself from this cause. To a shipowner whose ship is imprisoned, there is no such opportunity. To a lawyer who must have regard for precedent, these were not factors to be taken into account. To a practical shipowner, they were matters of the utmost importance.

THE BAMBURI DECISION

13.63 Whilst the Mutual Associations dealt with claims before them in this manner, the Market underwriters preferred that the issue should be defined in a test case. A judicial arbitration was therefore held before Staughton J. on one ship, The *Bamburi*.[60] Whilst he decided that the *Bamburi* was a constructive total loss as a result of "restraint", he had to follow precedent, and was not permitted to take into account the factors which influenced the directors of the Mutual Associations.

13.64 The *Bamburi* was a cement carrier insured against war risks on the S.G. Form with the Institute War & Strikes Clauses attached. In August, 1979, the area north of latitude 24°N., which was the Persian Gulf, had been declared a "breach of warranty" area which could only be entered on payment of an additional premium. She duly declared her entry and the additional premiums paid between September, 1980 and the date of the arbitration award amounted to DM. 887, 575:

1980

11th September

The ship sails from Mombasa bound for Khor-al-Zubeir.

20th September

The ship arrives in the Shatt Roads.

21st September

The ship proceeds to Khor-al-Zubeir with a pilot on board.

22nd September

Iraq invades Iran and the resultant war, which lasts for eight years, begins.

22nd September

The ship berths and commences discharge. Several explosions are heard in the distance.

23rd September (a.m.)

Several bombs fall in the vicinity of the ship. The harbour master tells the Captain that if he wishes, he may sail without a pilot.

Late the same night

The harbour master visits the ship (he visits all the ships in the port) and tells the Captain that "all movement of merchant shipping is prohibited" and he cannot sail. This is an obvious reference to Decree No. 23 (para. 13.59) although it appears not to have been described as such.

60. *The Bamburi* [1982] 1 Lloyd's Rep. 312.

24th September

The ship completes discharge. A further request, one of a number which were subsequently made, for permission to sail is refused.

28th–29th September

Due to air-raids on the port, the crew is sent home. The officers remain in Basrah for a few days before they too go home.

22nd December

The Chief Engineer returns to the ship. A few weeks later, other members of the crew join him.

1981

30th September

Notice of Abandonment is given. This is refused, the underwriters placing the owners in the same position as if a writ had been issued.

14th October

Notice of Abandonment is again given and appears to have been similarly treated.

13.65 Staughton J. regarded the date of the start of proceedings as being immaterial as between the two dates and posed the following points for consideration:

1. Had the detention of the ship been proximately caused by a peril insured against? The underwriters pleaded that the Iraqis were motivated by concern about the safety of the *Bamburi* and the other ships and that the matter was similar to the position dealt with by Bailhache J. in *Bulchow Vaughan and Co.* v. *Compania Minera*.[61] In that case, the court had ruled against shipowners who had pleaded "restraint of Princes" when, during the First World War, the Royal Navy required all ships to follow a specified route between the Isle of Wight and the North-East coast to avoid attacks by German warships. This had caused delay but the court had held that it was not a "restraint of Princes". If anything it was an encouragement and an aid to safe navigation. The underwriters also pleaded that the shipowners had not addressed themselves to the right question. On 8th August, 1981, the British Ambassador had written to the Iraqi Foreign Office which had replied on 20th October. This was followed by a further communication from the Iraqi Embassy in London to the British Foreign Office on 26th October. These communications indicated that, provided the Iranians would grant safe conduct, consideration would be given to allowing the ship to sail. To Staughton J. this did not seem to show an altruistic motive. On the contrary, it seemed to be a statement of the Iraqis negotiating position *vis-à-vis* the Iranians and on this basis could be distinguished from the *Bulchow* case. Here there was a "restraint" whatever the motives, which were probably the avoidance of political embarrassment resulting from ships being sunk, and:

"So far as concerns 'restraint of Princes' it is clear and was not disputed that if there is an order of an executive government, backed by the power of the State, it is unnecessary that actual force should be used. These conditions were fulfilled when the vessel was originally detained."

The detention of the *Bamburi* had commenced on 23rd September, 1980, and had continued until the date of the hearing; throughout this time it was proximately caused by "restraint or detainment of people".

2. Had the owners been deprived of possession? The Iraqis had not made any

61. (1916) 32 T.L.R. 404.

claim to the ship, neither had they sought to acquire her ownership and neither had they occupied her. The owners' crew was still on board. In the sense that nobody had taken the ship away from them, they were not deprived of possession. Staughton J. found however: " . . . that the owners have been wholly deprived of the free use and disposal of their vessel. All movement of the ship is prohibited."

13.66 It will be noted from the *Forestal* cases[62] that a cargo policy insured (at least until 1983) not only loss of the insured goods but loss of the venture as well. This used to be true of an insurance policy on a ship, and *Rotch* v. *Edie*[63] and *Peele* v. *The Merchants Insurance Co.*[64] were decided on this basis. In *Peele*, an American case, Storey J. reviewed the law on what later became known as constructive total loss. He found the right of abandonment had been held to exist when the owner was forcibly dispossessed or deprived of the free use of the ship by embargoes, blockades and arrests by sovereign authority and, in a passage which Staughton J. regarded as the origin of the free use and disposal test added, after noting that it was not necessary that the ship should be destroyed: "It may technically exist when the thing is in safety but is for the time being lost to the owner, or taken from his free use and possession. Such are the common cases of total loss by capture, by embargoes, and by restraints and detainments of Princes."

13.67 *Arnould on Marine Insurance* noted in the second edition (1857) that by that date the loss of adventure theory on a ship policy "had expired". On the authority of these two cases, however, Arnould then concluded:

" . . . There can be no doubt that arrest, detention, or embargo of the ship, whether by a hostile or friendly government, gives a *prima facie* right of abandonment in all cases where there is an apparent probability that the owner's loss of the free use and disposal of his ship, once total, by the arrest or embargo, may be long or, at all events, of a very uncertain continuance."

(This passage still appears as paragraph 1188 in the 16th edition.)

13.68 It was possible that by 1857 the law had taken a wrong turning but even if this was so it was now too late to correct any error. Cases since the Marine Insurance Act 1906 tended to support the "free use and disposal" construction rather than to oppose it and there was also the recent authority of *The Anita*,[65] even if Mocatta J. thought that Arnould expressed his views too widely. Applying this test, Staughton J. considered the answer to the second question was that the owner had been deprived of the possession of the *Bamburi*.

3. Is it unlikely that the owners can recover their ship within a reasonable time? Staughton J. made the point: " . . . Time is counted from no earlier date than the Notice of Abandonment. It is then, under the Act, that a vessel must be a constructive total loss for the notice to be valid. It is then that recovery must be unlikely within a reasonable time."

13.69 It will be noted that the Iraqis' replies to the British Ambassador's communications were only received after the second Notice of Abandonment.

---

62. *Forestal Land, Timber & Railways Co. Ltd.* v. *Rickards* (*The Minden*); *Middows* v. *Robertson* (*The Wangoni*); *W.W. Howard, Bros & Co.* v. *Kann* (*The Halle*) (1940) 67 Ll.L. Rep. 484; (1940) 68 Ll.L.Rep. 45 (C.A.); (1941) 70 Ll.L.Rep. 173; [1942] A.C. 50 (H.L.). See para. 13.28.
63. (1795) 6 Term Rep. 413. See paras. 13.7, 13.8.
64. (1822) 3 Mason 27.
65. [1970] 2 Lloyd's Rep. 365; [1971] 1 Lloyd's Rep. 487 (C.A.). See para. 13.35.

Staughton J. had to ask himself: " . . . whether a well-informed observer would have considered it likely, at the date of either Notice of Abandonment, that some such communication would shortly be received from the Iraqi Government" and drew attention to Sir Raymond Evershed's judgment in *Atlantic Maritime Company* v. *Gibbon*[66]: "What happens afterwards may assist in showing what the possibilities really were if they had been reasonably forecast."

13.70 The assured expected to be paid in weeks or months. The underwriters contended that several years was the appropriate length of time, perhaps to the extent of half the expected lifetime of the ship. Staughton J. disagreed with both and thought that 12 months from the date of the Notice of Abandonment was, in the context of this case and on its facts, the appropriate length of time. Since there was no reasonable prospect of a release by October, 1982, it was, in October, 1981, unlikely that the ship would be recovered within a reasonable time.

13.71 An award was signed in the shipowners' favour and Staughton J. moved on, as he was requested to do, to deal with the position of the ships in Basrah. This gave him much difficulty because much of the evidence was so uncertain. Rather curiously, no evidence of the facts which were easiest to prove, namely the sinking of the *Uljanik* and the *Olanesti* across the river at Khorramshahr was produced to him (para. 13.59). He found the evidence of the silting of the Karun Bar and the mouth of the river, and the evidence of unexploded shells on the river bed, too indefinite to support any conclusions. He found, however, that these ships also were total losses through "restraint" and in view of this finding felt it unnecessary to go any further than this. Although leave to appeal was given the case was not taken any further than this.

13.72 This is a judgment of supreme importance particularly as "restraint" is presently the most common cause of loss under the War Risk Policy, and it is the first time that the vexed question of "deprivation of possession" is directly dealt with in relation to this insured peril. It is suggested that the many problems previously posed to counsel, to the Market underwriters and to the Mutual War Risks Associations, how section 60 of the Marine Insurance Act should be interpreted and applied in the case of "restraint" are now resolved in a very firm and definitive judgment.

LOSS IN THE GULF WAR 1990–1991

13.73 A ship, entered for insurance in one of the Mutual War Risks Associations, was loading in Kuwait on 2nd August, 1990, when the Iraqis invaded the country and occupied it. For a few days the ship was forbidden to continue loading or to leave. The Iraqis then took over the ship and sent the crew home. At some unknown time, they moved her to Umm Casr where she stayed for the rest of the war. The fighting ended at the end of February, five months later, and the ship should have been permitted to leave. At first there were outright refusals to let her do this, but later the Iraqi Authorities relented and gave permission for her to leave. This was not the end of the story because, as is so common with bureaucracies such as Iraq's, another arm of the government refused to allow what one had

66. [1954] 1 Q.B. 88. See paras. 22.46–22.51.

sanctioned. This went on for so long that the anniversary of the ship's detention came and went. Under the provisions of the 12-month Clause (see below), the Association paid a constructive total loss. Later, when the promises to let her depart were at last honoured, she was towed to Dubai and sold there. The proceeds of the sale were treated by the Association as salvage.

THE 12-MONTH CLAUSE

13.74 Directly as a result of the *Bamburi* decision, the Detainment Clause was included into the Institute War and Strikes Clauses for containers and ships. This Clause has been in existence for many years but before 1982, was scarcely used. It reads:

"In the event that the . . . shall have been the subject of capture, seizure, arrest, restraint, detainment, confiscation or expropriation, and the assured shall thereby have lost the free use and disposal of the . . . for a continuous period of twelve months then for the purpose of ascertaining whether the . . . is a constructive total loss, the assured shall be deemed to have been deprived of the possession of the . . . without any likelihood of recovery."

13.75 The Institute War and Strikes Clauses for freight contain a similar provision, although the wording is slightly different. The Detainment Clause is discussed in greater detail at paras. 23.28 and 39.15. For immediate purposes, it should be noted that, when the 12 months have passed, the assured is excused from the onus of proof, which has always been a difficult one to discharge that, at a set point of time, it was unlikely that the insured object could be recovered.

CONCLUSIONS

13.76 As it has already been noted in the conclusions of "capture" and "seizure", a comparison of the conclusions of these two insured perils with those on "arrests, restraints or detainments" should be made (paras. 11.64, 12.67). "Arrests, restraints or detainments" have the following characteristics:

1. Although they are set out as three separate insured perils, there is no substantial difference between them and the courts have so far made no serious attempt to draw them, although it can be said that "arrests" seems to indicate some form of legal process taking place whereas the other two do not.
2. It is not necessary that there should be any intention to acquire the ownership of the insured ship or control of her. This does not necessarily exclude an occupation of an insured ship, although if this happens, questions may arise if there is a "seizure", or possibly a "capture". The resolution of these questions will depend upon the individual facts.
3. "Arrests, restraints or detainments" essentially consist of prevention, whether by legal or other means, of the insured ship from carrying out a course of action which, in the normal way, would be perfectly proper.
4. Such prevention can be effected by the provisions of the law, or by the refusal to grant some permission which is required, or by an embargo to enter or leave a port, or by a prohibition to follow a desired route. Whilst this

appears not to have been judicially decided, several leading counsel have expressed the opinion that the trapping of ships as a consequence of a war can constitute "restraint" whatever the attitude of the local governments may be.

5. The Institute War and Strikes Clauses give insurance against loss or damage to the hull and machinery to the insured object only, and does not cover delay, which is likely to be the commonest cause of any loss from "arrest, restraint or detainment". These insured perils usually result in constructive total loss but a claim for a partial loss only, such as the fouling of a ship's bottom during a lengthy delay before release takes place, can also be anticipated.

The same is true of the hull and machinery sections of the Mutual War Risks Associations. They provide additional insurance to cover delay which may arise from a separate set of insured perils (Chapter 23).

6. It is most unlikely that an insured ship will ever become an actual total loss because her owner is irretrievably deprived of her by reason of "arrest, restraint or detainment". A loss is much more likely to be a constructive total loss, based on acceptance that it is unlikely that her owner can recover her within a reasonable time, a point which is likely to be reached at a much earlier date. As with "capture" and "seizure", the date that the writ is issued, or the date that the underwriters have refused to accept Notice of Abandonment and put the shipowner in the same position as if a writ had been issued, is the time when it is judged whether it is unlikely that the insured ship can be recovered within a reasonable time.

7. "Arrest, restraint or detainment", like "capture" and "seizure", may result from force or the threat of force, but this is not an essential element. With "capture" and "seizure", it may not be possible to occupy a ship, unless she is already abandoned, against the wishes of those lawfully in possession of her, and a peaceable occupation is only likely if those people are first over-awed or otherwise convinced of the futility of any resistance. The degree of force necessary for "arrest, restraint, and detainment" may be of a much lesser degree, possibly even to the extent that there is no force at all, or if there is, that it is much more remote to the actual scene.

8. Where "arrest, restraint, or detainment" is effected under the law, force need not be used or deployed; the law must be obeyed and submission to its requirements without the vestiges of force being present will not prevent "arrest, restraint, or detainment" being complete. It is suggested that submission to what are stated to be its requirements, provided that they can reasonably be regarded as such, at the behest of those who it later transpires are acting unlawfully, will not prevent "arrest, restraint, or detainment" from becoming complete.

CHAPTER 14

. . . and the consequences thereof or any attempt thereat

14.1 The Institute War and Strikes Clauses read: "Capture seizure arrest restraint or detainment, and the consequences thereof or any attempt thereat" whereas the rules of the Mutual War Risks Associations read: "Capture, seizure, arrest, restraint or detainment, and the consequences thereof or any attempt thereat".

14.2 The possibility has been raised of arguing that, because there is only one comma after "detainment" in the modern Institute War and Strikes Clauses, the "consequences and attempt" provision applies to "detainment" alone, whereas in the Mutual War Risks Associations' rules, it is undoubtedly a separate provision in its own right and refers to all the preceding insured perils. It is suggested that in spite of the different formats adopted, both provisions have the same effect, and that the "consequences and attempt" provision applies in each case to each of the immediately preceding insured perils. It is certainly the intention that it should.

14.3 It is interesting to note that before 1983 the F.C. & S. Clause imported into the War Risks Policy a provision, commas and all, which read in the same way as the Mutual War Risks Associations' Rules are set out today. Mr. Alan Jackson's Committee proposed that this cover should be continued, this time by including specific insured perils in the War Risks Policy, and avoiding the roundabout methods which the F.C. & S. Clause previously employed (paras. 1.22–1.24). Moreover the "consequences and attempt" provision, by retaining its previous form, would apply to all the immediately preceding insured perils the body of case law which already existed, and that there would be no step into the unknown that a revised provision would have entailed.

14.4 There are a number of decided war risk cases on "consequences" but all these arise out of the F.C. & S. Clause of the S.G. Form. They have thus been decided in the context of an exception of a peril, which would otherwise have been insured by the Marine Policy, or an excepted peril which is turned into an insured peril in the War Policy. The reader who is puzzled by this seemingly inconsistent statement, which on its own is not easy to comprehend, will find a fuller explanation of how this entangled situation arose in Chapter 1. At the date of writing, there have been no cases decided on the modern Institute War and Strikes Clauses which set out the "consequences and attempt" provision in a straightforward fashion. It is possible that the courts will in future conclude that the cases so far decided were distorted by the intellectual gyrations necessary to give effect to the F.C. & S. Clause, and that a straightforward provision should be otherwise construed.

It is suggested, however, that there are no grounds for doing this, and that the cases already decided give firm guidance.

14.5 *Ionides* v. *The Universal Marine Insurance Company*[1] concerned 6,500 bags of coffee loaded on board the *Linwood* in Rio de Janeiro bound for New York with calls in Belize and New Orleans. The coffee was insured on the S.G. Form with the following exclusion clause: " . . . Free from capture, seizure, and detention; and all the consequences thereof, or any attempt thereat, and free from all consequences of hostilities, riots, or commotions."

14.6 On 17th July, 1861, after the American Civil War had broken out, the ship was 35 miles to the eastward of Cape Hatteras, on which there was a lighthouse. Unbeknown to the Captain, he was 50 miles out in his reckoning and thought that he was far further east and thus further out to sea than was the case. This was not unusual or of great concern in the days of sail, and no doubt the Captain wished to get an accurate fix on the lighthouse; otherwise it is difficult to see why he should have altered course to the west when he had a fair southerly wind for a northerly course. He was not to know that the Confederates (the South) had extinguished the light to rob the Union (the North) ships of its help. Had it been lit, those on board would have become aware that they were much closer to the shore line than they thought and of their imminent danger. Still looking for a light which was in fact unlit, they ran the ship hard aground. On 18th July Confederate officers made the Captain prisoner and took him and his papers ashore. The rest of the crew followed him on 19th July. On that day 150 bags of coffee were landed and seized by the Confederates and, if the Confederate troops had not prevented it, another 1,000 bags could have been safely landed. On 20th July the ship broke up in bad weather and the remaining coffee was lost.

14.7 The court went to considerable lengths to consider "consequences", this time of hostilities. Erle C.J. thought it was undoubtedly a hostile act to extinguish the light but: "Was the putting out of the light . . . so immediately connected with the loss of the ship as to make the one the consequence of the other?"

14.8 On the facts, he considered the two too distantly connected with each other to stand in relation to cause and effect. He went on to give examples. It must be remembered that he was dealing with an exclusion clause, whereas it is more usual nowadays that the "consequences" provision relates to insured perils. In the examples, the position is therefore reversed to those the modern reader would expect to see. The following would be losses which would be excluded from the insurance cover by the exceptions clause:

1. A hostile attempt is made to take the ship. In her endeavours to escape she goes aground. This is a loss by the "consequences of hostilities".
2. The ship is chased by an enemy warship and, in trying to avoid being taken, she becomes "embayed" (i.e., forced into a bay from which the wind will not let her escape). The wind drives her ashore. This loss results from an "attempt at capture".
3. There are two channels to a port, only one of which is mined. In ignorance, the Master uses the mined channel and the ship is mined. The proximate cause of the loss can be described as the "consequences of hostilities".

1. (1863) 14 C.B. (N.S.) 259.

Two other situations would not be excluded from the insurance by the exceptions clause:

4. A ship is chased into a bay from which she escapes on a change of wind. She is later lost in a storm which, but for the chase and the resultant delay, she would have avoided. It may be said that but for the hostile attempt at seizure the loss would not have happened, and the consequence of the attempt at seizure was the proximate cause; but at the time of the loss, its proximate cause is perils of the seas, not an attempt at seizure.
5. The Master, aware of mines in one channel, uses the other and runs the ship aground by bad navigation. This is not a loss proximately connected with the consequences of hostilities, but with a peril of the seas.

14.9 On this basis Erle C.J. considered that the ship was wrecked as a result of "perils of the seas", but that only 5,350 bags of coffee were lost by this cause. One thousand bags could have been landed but for the hostile actions of the Confederate troops. The underwriters were excused paying for these because of the exception and also for the 150 bags which were actually landed because these were taken by the troops.

14.10 Willes J. agreed. The light being extinguished may have been a cause but: " . . . It was not the proximate and absolute certain cause of the loss," which was the ship being off course and going on the rocks. On "consequences" he had this to say: "I apprehend it is a fallacy to say that a larger sense is to be given . . . by reason of the use of the word 'consequences' than if the word used had been 'effects' . . . We can only look to the proximate consequences of hostilities," and: " . . . The word 'consequences' is to be dealt with according to the ordinary rule as meaning proximate consequences only." Byles and Keating JJ. agreed. Judgment was signed in the manner suggested by Erle C.J.

14.11 *Pink* v. *Fleming*[2] considered a cargo of fruit which had to be discharged into lighters so that the carrying ship, which was damaged in a collision, could be repaired. In the handling, the delicate oranges and lemons were damaged, and on delivery, much of the fruit had gone bad. It was insured for damage: " . . . consequent on collision with any other ship".

Lord Esher M.R. gave judgment in the Court of Appeal:

"The question can only arise where there is a succession of causes, which must have existed in order to produce the result. Where that is the case, according to the law of marine insurance, the last cause only must be looked to and the others rejected, although the result would not have been produced without them."

14.12 This was a case of collision, followed by the necessity to do repairs, which in turn necessitated the handling. The plaintiffs could not go back two steps, and they lost their case. The learned authors of Arnould, 16th Ed., have criticised the "great severity" of this decision and have given the opinion that subsequent cases have somewhat eased the plaintiff's burden. On the other hand, Chapter 40 on "Consequences of Hostilities and Warlike Operations—'*The Coxwold*' " will leave the reader in no doubt just how difficult it can be to prove that a loss is due to "consequences".

2. (1880) 25 Q.B.D. 397.

14.13 Whilst Chapter 40 describes "consequences" (of hostilities and warlike operations) and its attendant difficulties in detail, one particular wartime case, *Ocean Shipping Company* v. *Liverpool and London War Risks Insurance Association Limited*[3] deserves to be studied in detail if only because of the differences which arose between Scott L.J. in the Court of Appeal and Lords Wright and Porter in the House of Lords. The events took place in 1942 before the alteration of the F.C. & S. Clause in 1943.[4] The *Priam* was due to sail from Liverpool to Alexandria via the Cape of Good Hope with a cargo of war stores. Although the Master objected to loading deck cargo when his prescribed course would take him far out into the North Atlantic in winter time, a tank weighing 21 tons and two crates containing aircraft were loaded on top of No. 2 hatch in the forward well-deck. During the Second World War, ships as fast as the *Priam*, $17\frac{1}{2}$ knots, often sailed without convoy, relying on their speed to avoid U-boats. Few if any U-boats could catch them even when on the surface. This did mean that they had to steam a zig-zag course at full speed whatever the weather; there was little opportunity to take the normal seamanlike precautions in heavy weather of reducing speed or altering course to allow the ship to lie in a more comfortable condition and avoid damage to herself and her cargo. This added to the hazards. Events took place:

1942

7th December

The ship sails from Liverpool. Almost immediately she runs into very bad weather. She maintains full speed although she is taking water over the forecastle and well-deck.

8th December

The weather is now so bad that speed has to be reduced. A big sea hits the aeroplane containers and smashes them. The tarpaulins over the hatches are seen to be torn and damaged. On the weather moderating, full speed is again resumed.

9th December

The tarpaulins on No. 2 hatch are seen to be badly torn with hatchboards missing. There is 11 ft. of water in the hold which the pumps, clogged by wood shavings from the cargo's packaging, cannot pump out. The ship is noticeably down by the head. She maintains full speed.

10th December

Again, bad weather forces a reduction in the speed. The windlass motor-room is flooded.

12th December

In very bad weather, the tank comes adrift seriously damaging the tarpaulins and the hatchboards on No. 2 hatch. More water enters the hold and the ship is now 11 ft. 7 ins. down by the head. The well-deck is awash.

14.14 The ship eventually reached Freetown, discharged the cargo in No. 2 hold and repaired the damage which amounted to £1632 10s. 0d. The plaintiff shipowner claimed the damage was "the consequences of warlike operations", and the defendant underwriter claimed that it was due to "perils of the seas" which concerned the marine underwriter. Atkinson J. in the High Court held that the effective and predominant cause of the damage was the open hold of the ship due to the breaking loose of the deck cargo where the position was aggravated by the necessity to maintain a high speed. He gave judgment for the shipowners.

3. [1946] K.B. 561.
4. See para. 1.15.

14.15 The underwriters appealed first to the Court of Appeal,[5] and also to the House of Lords.[6] The judgments are extremely lengthy and, for the purposes of this work, it is only necessary to note the treatment of the word "consequences" by Scott L.J. and Lords Wright and Porter. Scott L.J. in the Court of Appeal:

"In strict logic, it may be said that the additional mention of any numbers of species adds nothing to the genus, and therefore that the words 'the consequences' add nothing to 'hostilities' 'and warlike operations'. But the draughtsman may have been a businessman and not a logician and thought it safer that everything consequential on either of the generic perils should be covered as a specific peril. At any rate that seems to me the natural sense of the language used. If so, it follows that the word 'consequences' does not mean effects or results of a war peril. This question of construction is important just because it is so easy to slip unconsciously into treating the word 'consequences' in the phrase 'consequences of hostilities and warlike operations' not of itself a named peril, but as the loss or damage consequential on—i.e., caused by—a named peril.

Once the true intention is recognised, namely that the word 'consequences' in the established phrase is descriptive of perils and therefore that <u>every happening which arises out of hostilities or warlike operations and every act or thing done for these purposes constitutes a specific war peril 'consequential' on generic perils named</u>, the causal nexus between peril and loss becomes clearer, just because the particular happening, or act, is nearer the loss; the cause is more obviously 'proximate' i.e., the sense given to that word by the decided cases."

14.16 At first sight, the temptation arises to think that Scott L.J. meant that syntax alone required "consequences" to be added to "hostile operations" and "warlike operations" before they could be fitted into the grammar of the F.C. & S. Clause. The underlined words however show that he did not intend this; on the other hand it is difficult indeed to distinguish the practical results of the underlined words from the meaning that he specifically rejects, namely loss or damage caused by a named peril.

14.17 In the House of Lords, Lord Wright, who seems to have rejected Scott L.J.'s views, adopted a different and simpler approach:

"In the present case, I think that the damage in the way of No. 2 hold is, though due to a marine peril, a loss recoverable under the war risk insurance, not simply because it was sustained whilst the vessel was on a warlike operation . . . but because of the particular fact that an integral element of the operation involved a specific and special war peril and that the loss resulted therefrom. This was *the* cause."

(In the report "*the*" is in italics to show Lord Wright's emphasis on the word.)

14.18 Lord Wright noted Willes J.'s judgment in the *Ionides* case[7] that, in considering the exception, he felt he should only look at the proximate consequences which, to Willes J., were equivalent to effects. Willes J. went on to say: "It seems to me that the loss was a consequence of the perils of the seas, and not a consequence of hostilities", which, to Lord Wright, negatived Scott L.J.'s views which Lord Wright quoted as: "Consequences in the F.C. & S. Clause means causes or perils, not effects, and expands the scope of the words."

Lord Wright finished: "I do not think it would necessarily matter which meaning was given to them, but in my opinion 'hostilities' denotes the peril and 'consequences' the resultant loss."

5. [1946] K.B. 561.
6. [1948] A.C. 243.
7. Footnote 1, above. See paras. 14.5–14.10.

Lord Porter added: "In my opinion the true effect of the language used is to insure the shipowner against loss due to hostilities and warlike operations of all kinds . . .".

14.19 It will be of interest to note that the shipowner recovered in respect of the damage to the hatches and hatch covers of No. 2 hold and for that hold's flooding. He was not entitled to the flooding of the compartment below the forecastle, caused by the gun on the fo'c'sle working loose through the constant battering it received from the seas, or for the damage caused to cargo shifting on the after well-deck. These were judged to be perils of the seas, and thus marine perils.

14.20 The views of Lords Wright and Porter, which themselves confirm the judgment in the *Ionides* case[8] in preference to the views of Scott L.J. received further confirmation from the High Court in *Costain-Blankevoort (U.K.) Dredging Co. Ltd. v. Davenport (The Nassau Bay).*[9] In December, 1974, the *Nassau Bay* was dredging in the English Channel and Rivulet Terre Rouge area of Mauritius. Some 20mm Oerlikon shells were sucked into the machinery and exploded, thus removing a sizeable proportion of the discharge pumps casing. The engineer on duty stopped the suction pump but left the discharging pump running in the belief that this would empty the pumproom of water. It had the opposite effect of flooding the ship and she sank to the bottom of the sea leaving only her upperworks showing. The shells were of Italian and French manufacture, and it seemed unlikely that they would have been used by the only armed forces stationed in Mauritius during World War II, namely British coastal artillery and heavy artillery regiments. Cyclones to which Mauritius is prone could have moved them into the area of the *Nassau Bay's* operations. Mr. Davenport was an Inspector of Taxes pursuing a claim by the Inland Revenue for £607,433 under the Capital Allowances Act 1968. The Act provided that if the ship was lost by a war risk peril under the F.C. & S. Clause, no liability for tax could arise, and this involved consideration of whether the loss was due to "the consequences of hostilities or warlike operations". The Special Commissioners had ruled in favour of the Inland Revenue and the shipowners appealed to the High Court. The Special Commissioners found as a fact that the shells had been dumped by the British armed forces after the end of the Second World War, a finding which was reluctantly accepted by Walton J. in the High Court, although he made many scathing remarks on the slight and unsatisfactory evidence which supported it. On the main point of "consequences", Walton J. decided:

"One must here be careful, because the word 'consequences' is intended to refer, and does refer, only to the effects of the hostilities or warlike operations; it does not, in any way whatever, enlarge the excepted perils. Thus it does not deal at all with the consequences of the consequences of hostilities."

14.21 The Crown, which throughout had made great play upon the difficulties of proof facing the shipowner, had argued that the dumping of ammunition was not a warlike operation, so:

"The only kind of dumping that can be presumed is dumping at the end of the war, after it was all over and our forces were being withdrawn from Mauritius, and the ammunition was no longer of any practical use to anyone. I find it impossible to classify such dumping as a

8. Footnote 1, above. See paras. 14.5–14.10.
9. [1979] 1 Lloyd's Rep. 395.

warlike operation. Anyway, even though dumping of ammunition could be a 'warlike operation' there was no evidence to show that in this case it was."

The shipowners' appeal against the charge for tax was dismissed.

14.22 An American case, *International Dairy Engineering Company of Asia* v.
American Home Assurance Company,[10] is of great interest. The U.S. District
Court for the North District of California considered a case of a parachute flare
which burnt down and destroyed a milk processing plant in Thu Duc village in 1967
during the Vietnamese War. The plant was insured on what is described as the
Standard Marine Transit form with land and fire risks added. The policy contained
an exclusion clause:

" . . . Warranted free from the consequences of hostilities and warlike operations (whether
there be a declaration of war or not) . . . fire . . . caused directly . . . by a hostile act by or
against a belligerent power . . . Further warranted free from the consequences of civil war,
revolution, rebellion, insurrection, or civil strife arising therefrom, . . . ".

14.23 Sweigert D.J., in a judgment which has the welcome echoes of the straightforward and commonsense approach of the *Ionides* case[11] and of Lords Wright and
Porter, found as facts that American aircraft dropped flares at night to illuminate:

1. Crashed aircraft to rescue survivors and warn off attackers.
2. The air base to assist incoming aircraft.
3. Enemy forces in combat areas.
4. Enemy forces attempting to infiltrate the air base.

On the occasion in question, the flares were dropped for this last purpose, as were
90% of all flares dropped. This led to his conclusions: "In our pending case the
dropping of the flares was, itself, a hostile act of one belligerent against another and
was clearly the dominant, effective, proximate, direct cause of the loss regardless of
whether the hostile act was negligently performed."

14.24 Was the loss in question a consequence of "civil war etc."? Yes, on the
facts it plainly was, and this justified judgment being signed in favour of the underwriters. It is very noticeable that whilst guidance was taken from a number of English cases, particularly on the negligence point, no reference was made to the
English cases on "consequences" (other than the *Ionides* case).[12] The court
appears to have reached an independent conclusion on the same principles as those
which guided Lords Wright and Porter, and which would have guided them had
they been judging the case.

14.25 Whilst "attempt thereat" has for many years figured in the War Risk
Policy, there is not the wealth of decided cases as there is with "consequences".
There are two very useful pointers in the direction that, provided the danger is
immediate or imminent, and not distant and remote as it was in the *Hadkinson*,[13]
Lubbock[14] and *Becker*[15] cases, the insured perils might still arise, or alternatively it

10. [1971] A.M.C. 1001.
11. *Ionides* v. *The Universal Marine Insurance Co.* (1863) 14 C.B.N.S. 259. See paras. 14.5–14.10.
12. *Ibid.*
13. *Hadkinson* v. *Robartson* (1803) 3 Bos. & Pul. 388. See paras. 11.37–11.41.
14. *Lubbock* v. *Rowcroft* (1803) 5 Esp. 50. See para. 11.40.
15. *Becker Gray & Co. Ltd.* v. *London Insurance Corporation* [1918] A.C. 101. See paras.
11.43–11.46.

could be an "attempt thereat". The first of these is *Butler* v. *Wildman*,[16] the facts of which are set out at paras. 11.47–11.49. The four judges in that case also considered the general words of the policy "and of all other perils, losses and misfortunes, that have or shall come to the hurt, detriment, or damage of the [insured object]", and they might well have had to deal with a situation where, after throwing the dollars overboard, Captain Lopez managed to make good his escape. It would only have needed a broken mast or spar, a torn sail or parted rigging, not uncommon with sailing ships, to incapacitate his pursuer. It is very noticeable that three of the judges, Abbott C.J., Bayley J. and Holroyd J. considered that the insured perils of "capture" "enemies" and "jettison" had already arisen, Bayley J. going so far as to say that Captain Lopez's acts amounted to jettison *ex justa causa*. They also considered that the plaintiff's claim could have succeeded under the general words which are quoted above. Best J. confined himself to saying that the plaintiff succeeded under the general words although, with some apparent reluctance, he conceded: " . . . It may be observed that such a loss would fall within the other words, takings at sea, men of war, letters of mart and counter-mart."

14.26 It is suggested that, had the four judges been considering "attempt thereat", they would have ruled that the loss was due to an attempt at "capture", although Best J. might have been a little slower than the others to reach such a conclusion.

14.27 *The Knight of St. Michael*[17] was a case of freight insurance where the ship had sailed from Newcastle, New South Wales, bound for Valparaiso with a cargo of Australian coal which began to heat. The Captain returned to Sydney and discharged a large proportion of the cargo to prevent the coal catching fire. Gorell-Barnes J. accepted that this was a reasonable precaution to prevent spontaneous combustion and, because the danger was immediate and imminent, signed judgment in favour of the shipowners for the freight lost on the discharged cargo, even though there never was an actual fire. He expressed himself in the following terms: "The danger was present, and if nothing had been done spontaneous combustion and fire would have followed in the natural course. That means that the peril [of fire] had begun to operate."

14.28 This case led to the other pointer, *Symington & Co.* v. *Union Insurance Society of Canton Limited*.[18] In February, 1920 the plaintiffs gathered cork for shipment on the jetty at Algeciras. A fire started in the neighbourhood. It never reached the cork because the Spanish authorities made a firebreak by throwing some of the cork into the sea and dowsing the rest with sea water. This caused the cork serious damage. The arbitrator made an award in favour of the plaintiffs, and in the High Court, Roche J. affirmed it. The underwriters appealed to the Court of Appeal. Scrutton L.J. thought:

"The test seems to be as is stated in *The Knight of St. Michael*[19] and in the *Kacianoff*[20] cases. Is it a fear of a peril that will happen in the future or had the peril already happened or is so imminent that it is immediately necessary to avert the danger by action?"

---

16. (1820) 3 B. & Ald. 398.
17. [1898] P. 30.
18. (1928) 34 Com. Cas. 23.
19. Footnote 17, above.
20. *Kacianoff* v. *China Traders Insurance Co. Ltd*. [1914] 3 K.B. 1121. See paras. 11.41, 11.42.

14.29 The action taken to prevent the fire spreading was a proximate consequence of "fire" and the general words meant that the plaintiffs could recover. Sankey L.J. considered that the peril had begun to operate and found that Lord
Reading C.J. in the *Kacianoff* case[21] supported him:

"It would have been a totally different state of things if the vessel had left and then, outside,
had been met and threatened by a Japanese vessel, or, if approaching Nagasaki, she had
been in some danger. No doubt there may be circumstances in which judges may differ as to
when the particular peril did begin to operate, but there must be the beginning before the
judge can exercise his judgment upon it."

He particularly approved Gorell-Barnes J.'s judgment which is quoted above.
Greer L.J. delivered a concurring judgment and the appeal was dismissed.

14.30 It is suggested therefore that, provided the insured peril had "begun to
operate" in the senses indicated in the *Kacianoff*,[22] *The Knight of St. Michael*[23] and
Symington[24] cases, an "attempt thereat" by somebody else, even if unsuccessful,
will allow the shipowner to recover from the War Risk underwriter his losses which
are insured under the immediately preceding insured perils. Conclusions can be
given but with some hesitation because there has so far been no case on the new
Institute War and Strikes Clauses; unlike the S.G. Form they set out the "consequences and attempt" provision in a straightforward fashion, but so far it has not
received any judicial consideration:

1. It is tempting to regard "consequences" and "attempt" as two separate
   insured perils in their own right simply because of their position in the
   policy. It is, however, quite wrong to do this; they relate to insured perils.
2. The insured perils to which "consequences" and "attempt" relate are capture, seizure, arrest, restraint or detainment. They do not broaden the
   meaning of these insured perils, although they may extend the measure of
   loss which the insured shipowner can recover.
3. Without "attempt" the measure of loss that could be recovered would be
   that which flowed from the insured peril once it became complete; where,
   however, there is an attempt, for instance to capture the insured ship,
   which does not succeed, it could be questionable (in spite of the indications
   in the decided cases) if the insured shipowner would have any claim for loss
   suffered as a result of the unsuccessful attempt. The existence of "attempt"
   does however allow him a greater measure of recoverable loss and to
   recover such losses if the insured peril is so imminent and immediate that it
   has "begun to operate" in the sense described in the decided cases.
4. Without "consequences" the measure of loss that could be recovered
   would be that which flowed from the insured peril when it was actually
   operating; as soon as it ceased to operate, the loss that could be recovered
   could also cease. The existence of "consequences" does however widen the
   measure of loss that can be recovered. For instance, in the case of the ships
   trapped in the Great Bitter Lake,[25] neither the Egyptian nor the Israeli

21. *Ibid.*
22. *Ibid.*
23. Footnote 17, above. See para. 14.27.
24. Footnote 18, above.
25. See para. 13.52.

authorities put any restriction on the ships trapped after the Six-Day War came to an end. Both sides said that the ships were free to leave so far as they were concerned. Leading counsel regarded the fact that they were trapped long after the fighting finished as a "consequence" of the earlier restraint.

5. Neither "attempt" nor "consequences" extends the measure of loss that can be recovered indefinitely. The remoteness rules still apply. Even if Lord Esher M.R. could be regarded as being too strict in the *Pink* case,[26] his decision can still be regarded as an indication that the courts will put a limit on the extension that will be permitted.

26. (1880) 25 Q.B.D. 397. See paras. 14.11, 14.12.

CHAPTER 15

Mines, torpedoes, bombs and weapons of war

GENERALLY

15.1 Loss or damage caused by mines, torpedoes, bombs or other weapons of war now poses special difficulties. These do not arise from the law itself, since the establishment of the claim will concern issues of fact only. They arise from the wording of the policy and in particular the inclusion of the word "derelict". Where the suggestion for the use of this word came from, or why it was included, is not known but it is interesting to note that the earlier drafts of the new Institute War & Strikes Clause with the new MAR form did not include it. As will be seen it poses a problem of no mean order. The Mutual War Risks Associations have attempted to avoid this problem by insuring the consequences of these weapons being used, both in respect of unqualified mines and other weapons, and "derelict" mines and other weapons.

15.2 Before 1983, there were attempts to argue that the F.C. & S. Clause excluded the risk of contact with mines and torpedoes from the Marine Policy in only certain, but not all, circumstances. These attempts were never pleaded in court and thus put to the test, if only because of the well-known practice of the London market to cover loss or damage arising from mines and torpedoes under the War Risk Policy. This policy as has already been noted earlier in Chapter 1, included "mines, torpedoes, bombs or other engines of war" as specific insured perils and this, it is suggested, would have defeated any serious attempt to plead that in some circumstances the Marine Policy on the S.G. Form would have covered loss or damage caused by such weapons. Before 1983, therefore, it could be said that loss or damage caused by such weapons were at least traditionally regarded as matters for the War Risk Policy and were accepted as such, although as mentioned earlier,[1] the marine underwriters accepted the claim on the *Granwood* in circumstances that might have justified a refusal to do so. In the early 1960s, mines had been attached to the hulls of British ships in Miami by Cuban exiles to express their disapproval of British ships trading to Cuba.

15.3 Since 1983, the new Institute Time Clauses have excluded from their insurance only "derelict mines, torpedoes, bombs or other derelict weapons of war" and the new Institute War Clauses include these as insured perils word for word in the same form. This seems to beg the question that the underwriters of the Marine Policy intend to bear at least some of the risks of mines and other weapons which

---

1. See para. 1.20.

cause loss of or damage to the insured object. In the absence of an authoritative decision by the courts, the author will attempt some analysis of the possible results. The descriptions of the insurance will be very brief. Fuller details will be found in the chapters devoted to ships, cargo and containers.

15.4 The word "derelict" is defined in the *Oxford English Dictionary* as meaning: "Forsaken, abandoned, left by the possessor or guardian; especially of a vessel abandoned at sea; land left dry by the recession of the sea; a piece of property abandoned by the owner or guardian especially a vessel abandoned at sea. A person abandoned or forsaken." It is suggested that these definitions will, at the best, give only marginal help to the court which has to decide what is meant by "derelict mines, torpedoes, bombs or other derelict weapons of war" and whether, in the particular circumstances that exist between the Marine Policy and the War Risk Policy, indeed if either policy, should bear the risk of loss or damage that may be caused. This will apply particularly where the Marine Policy is on a different form to the MAR form and has a simple exclusion of all mines and other weapons from its cover regardless of whether or not they are "derelict" in any sense of the word.

15.5 At the seminar held in October, 1983 to introduce the new MAR form, the question was put to the members of Mr. Alan Jackson's Committee—what was intended by the expression "derelict"? No clear answer was forthcoming. The learned authors of Hudson & Allen, *The Institute Clauses Handbook*,[2] suggest that the word has been added to reverse the effect of the decision in *The Nassau Bay*.[3] The British armed forces stationed in Mauritius during the Second World War had, on the conclusion of the conflict, rather carelessly dumped their unwanted ammunition in shallow water off the coast of Mauritius. Subsequently the *Nassau Bay*, engaged in dredging operations, was badly damaged by an explosion. The High Court held that this was not the result of a "warlike operation".

15.6 The learned authors go on to express the view that if the mine is sown or the weapon is fired so that one of the risks in Clause 1.1 of the War Risk Policy is involved (dealing for the moment with just the ship's insurance), then a claim for loss or damage would be paid under that clause. Equally if such a weapon was used by a striker, or somebody engaged in a civil commotion, or a terrorist, then the war risks underwriters would have to meet the claim under the War Risk Policy, Clause 1.4 or 1.5, whichever is appropriate.

15.7 If this is the correct view, then the draftsmen of the War Risk Policy appear to have considered that the sowing of mines and the firing of weapons would only take place during a war, or some other lesser upheaval, which is an insured peril provided for in Clauses 1.1, 1.4. and 1.5 of the War Risk Policy, so that, in order to give comprehensive insurance, it was only necessary to make special provision for "derelict mines". In this way, they intended that the War Risk Policy would give insurance cover in all instances where such weapons cause loss of or damage to the insured ship; either the loss or damage would be caused by an insured peril specifically provided for in Clauses 1.1, 1.4 and 1.5 of the War Risk Policy or by "derelict" weapons in circumstances similar to the *Nassau Bay*.

There are, however, some serious flaws to this line of reasoning.

2. Lloyd's of London Press Ltd., 1986.
3. *Costain-Blankevoort (U.K.) Dredging Co. Ltd.* v. *Davenport (The Nassau Bay)* [1979] 1 Lloyd's Rep. 395. See para. 14.20.

15.8 These insured perils, war, strikers, terrorists or whatever else, do not exhaust the possibilities in which such weapons, derelict or otherwise, may be encountered. Weapons have been known to be discharged accidentally, an incident occurring in 1985 where a Danish warship accidentally fired a shell into a holiday camp. Mines were reported to be sown off the Libyan coast in 1973 by the Libyan authorities who gave proper notice that they had done so. Libya was not then at war with any country. It would be difficult to impute malice, political motives or even terrorism to a government which appeared to be anxious to protect its own coastline from the possibly harmful attentions of others, however unreasonable its fears might be, and to require any approaches to its ports or its coastline through designated channels which its own armed forces could all the more easily watch.

SHIPS AND FREIGHT

15.9 Ships are insured by the marine clauses for a set number of insured perils only which do not include mines and other weapons. It is arguable that the insured perils of "fire, explosion" (Clause 6.1.2) could be stretched to insure explosions caused by mines and other weapons, but it is suggested that this clause insures internal explosions only. Derelict mines and other weapons are excluded from the marine clauses (Clause 23.3), and are insured by the war clauses (Clause 1.3). The same is true of freight, although the clause numbers are 7.1.2, 17.3, and 1.1.3 respectively. It is thus possible to say that ships and freight have insurance for derelict mines and other weapons, but not for these weapons when the appellation "derelict" cannot be applied.

15.10 There is not the same problem with the insurance given by the Mutual War Risks Associations. Their rules give insurance for "mines" and other weapons, and also "derelict mines" and other weapons. Even though there may be a problem with the insurance given by the London Market, recent history has shown how it has been resolved in a practical way.

15.11 In 1984, 16 ships were damaged by mysterious explosions in the Red Sea. Such factors as the short space of time within which the explosions occurred, the depth of water at the sites of the explosions, the many different ports which the affected ships had come from, the nature of the damage to the bottoms of the ships and the interesting fact that four ships were damaged at positions in a straight line, all pointed in the direction of mines sown from a moving craft as the only possible cause. Although suspicion centred on one particular ship, the culprit was never traced with any certainty and this fact alone would have made it impossible to say whether the actual sowing of the mines was in pursuance of a naval operation in connection with a war, or whether it was the work of a terrorist or somebody acting from malice or from a political motive. In fact, the chief suspect was a ship supposedly under Libyan control. If these suspicions were justified, again Libya was not at war with anyone and it would be difficult to see what appellation could be applied to her from the risks insured by the War Risk Policy. In the subsequent sweeping operations, the Royal Navy recovered a mine of recent Soviet manufacture which was obviously freshly sown. Lying on the bottom of the sea as it was designed to do, there seemed to be no question of it having broken adrift and drifted from elsewhere. While there was nothing determinative to connect it with the mines which had damaged the ships, there was at least a strong indication that the mines which had caused the damage to the ships were not "derelict" in the normal sense that the word is used.

15.12 Many will find astonishing the assertion that where there are casualties that could involve the War Risk Policy, there are often difficulties, sometimes of a most extreme nature, in ascertaining with any degree of certainty how the casualty happened and what were the motives or reasons for any human agency that was involved. Whether or not a particular casualty should be paid for by the Marine Policy or the War Risk Policy (or both or neither) will depend not so much upon fine consideration and interpretation of the clauses of each policy as on the establishment of the actual facts; it is not impossible to foresee the plaintiff insured shipowner faced with enormous difficulties in establishing that his casualty comes within one of the insured risks of the War Risk Policy, and the defendant marine underwriter encountering equally grave difficulties in showing that he is entitled to the benefit of the exclusion clauses of the Marine Policy. Proximate cause is considered in Chapter 30, but the opinion can be advanced here that the redesignation of the former insured risk of mines and other weapons as "derelict" has, perhaps inadvertently, immeasurably increased such difficulties.

15.13 In advance of any judicial decisions on the point, it is submitted that the better view is that, in all circumstances, the War Risk Policy should pay for any loss or damage caused by any such weapons because:

(i) The views advanced by Hudson & Allen as described above are a correct interpretation of the intentions of the draftsmen and will in any case cover most situations where mines are sown or other weapons are fired.

(ii) Traditionally the War Risk Policy has insured loss or damage caused by mines, torpedoes, bombs and other weapons and it is intended that it should go on doing so.

(iii) There was a ready acceptance by the London market that the War Risk Policy should meet the claims arising from the Red Sea mines.

(iv) There has been an equally ready acceptance to meet the claims arising from mines, which cannot be described as "derelict" in the sense the word is normally used, in the Arabian Gulf during the Iran/Iraq War, even though in this instance there is evidence that the mines were sown as a "hostile act by or against a belligerent power", namely Iran.

15.14 Whether or not the courts will feel able to resolve any difficulties in this way remains to be seen. It is a normal rule of interpretation of documents such as insurance policies that the courts should be guided solely by their wording, and it is not normally allowed that further evidence should be given to show that the parties to the contract had intended a different effect or result or that the words of the contract should be given a different meaning to that normally attributable to them.

CONTAINERS

15.15 Containers are insured on the London market for marine risks on an "all risks" basis, but there is a qualification regarding their machinery; this is only insured for "fire, or explosion" which originates "externally to the machinery" (Clause 4.2.1). Derelict mines and other weapons are excluded from the marine insurance (Clause 6.3), but are insured by the War and Strikes Clauses (Clause 1.3).

15.16 It thus appears that containers, including their machinery, are insured for damage done by derelict mines and other weapons by the War and Strikes insurance. For mines and other weapons, to which the appellation "derelict" cannot be applied, there is insurance under the marine clauses except possibly to their machinery. Even in this case, Clause 4.2.1 could be stretched to include an "explosion" of these weapons, because it originates externally.

15.17 The Through Transport Mutual Insurance Association Ltd. and the Through Transport Mutual Insurance Association of Europe Ltd. do not qualify their insurance by the word "derelict". "War Risks" are defined to include "mines, torpedoes, bombs, rockets, shells, explosives or other similar weapons of war".

CARGO

15.18 The "all risks" insurances, broadly the (A) Clauses, give insurance against "all risks" of loss or damage except that derelict mines etc. are excluded (Clause 6.3). These are insured by the war clauses (Clause 1.3). It can thus be said that mines and other weapons are insured by the (A) Clauses, except for derelict mines and other weapons which are insured by the war clauses.

15.19 The clauses that give more limited insurance, the (B) and (C) Clauses, are in a very similar position to ships and freight. They too give insurance for a set number of insured perils, among them "fire or explosion" (Clause 1.1.1). They too exclude derelict mines and other weapons (Clause 6.3), but are insured for derelict mines and other weapons by the war clauses (Clause 1.3).

15.20 The redrafting of the Institute Time Clauses in the early 1980s was excellent, but in the case of mines and other weapons there are a series of anomalies. It has always been the intention of the London market that mines and other weapons should be excluded from the marine clauses and insured by the war clauses. This could easily be achieved by deletion of the word "derelict" in both sets of clauses. If, as the learned authors of the Institute Clauses Handbook suggest, there is a wish to give insurance in cases such as the *Nassau Bay* case, then the addition of a sentence in brackets which included "derelict" mines and other weapons would suffice.

CHAPTER 16

Strikers, locked-out workmen or persons taking part in labour disturbances, riots or civil commotions

16.1 Riots and civil commotions are civil disturbances of a serious nature and are discussed in Chapter 17. There appears to be no case in which strikers or their counterparts, workmen who have been excluded from their workplace by their employer locking the factory gates, or persons taking part in labour disturbances, have been judicially considered in the context of a War Risks Policy.

16.2 The clause which is the heading to this chapter was taken from the S.G. Form with Institute War & Strikes Clauses attached, and was part of the "positive" cover given by the pre-1983 form of War Risks Policy as compared with the "negative" cover imported into the War Risks Policy by the F.C. & S. Clause and the Explosives and Weapons of War Clause (para. 1.19). It has never been regarded as a well-drafted or happily-worded clause and has given rise to difficulties in its interpretation. One of these difficulties is dealt with below. It is a pity that "riots and civil commotions" were not in 1983 removed to Clause 1.1 of the MAR form, leaving this clause to deal with the consequences of industrial action which are themselves serious enough to merit a clause of their own. Had this been done, then the true intentions of the War Risks Policy would have been better expressed, namely that the policy should give cover for a number of violent disturbances, as expressed in *Pan American World Airways Inc* v. *The Aetna Casualty & Surety Co.*[1] as being in descending order of seriousness whoever caused them, and a separate clause would be left to deal with loss or damage caused by industrial disputes or disturbances which can be of a violent nature.

16.3 It has been suggested that "persons" should be read *ejusdem generis* with "strikers" and "locked-out workmen". If this were so, then some very odd results would follow. Cover would only be given in riots and civil commotions if the perpetrators were strikers or locked-out workmen or something akin, and it would not be given in the case of anyone else who could not be so described. Alternatively, it could also be argued that damage done by strikers and locked-out workmen and other persons would not be covered at all unless it was a riot or civil commotion or a labour disturbance of a most violent nature which would involve considering if an insured peril had arisen simply because of the degree of violence used. If this were correct, then there would be an important gap in the insurance cover where stevedores, workmen or other persons like them caused damage to a ship, because the War Risks Policy would not pay for it and Clause 24 of the Marine Policy would be strong enough to exclude it from that policy's cover.

---

1. [1974] 1 Lloyd's Rep. 207; [1975] 1 Lloyd's Rep. 77. See paras. 6.16–6.26, 8.13, 8.30, 8.31, 17.13, 17.24–17.26.

16.4 Furthermore, if two strikers of an alarming appearance should damage a ship, there would be no cover because two people cannot form a riot; they would need to be joined by more people before there could be a riot, when cover would be given by the War Risks Policy. This would effectively frustrate the intentions of the new Institute Time Clauses, both marine and war that, like the old S.G. Forms which they were replacing, there should be no gaps in the insurance cover that was provided. A very artificial position would arise if this reading were adopted as the correct one. It is suggested that the following summary truly reflects the intention of the Institute War and Strikes Clauses and is consistent with the wording that is used in it. These clauses give insurance against loss or damage caused by (1) strikers, or (2) locked-out workmen, or (3) persons (whoever they are) taking part in labour disturbances, riots or civil commotions.

16.5 Turning now to considering the three separate insured perils, there is an enormous body of case law on "strikers", all of it arising, in the maritime field, out of charterparty and bills of lading disputes, mostly on laytime. Apart from the special cover given by the Mutual War Risks Associations (Chapter 23), where in one narrow instance "strikers" has a wider application, it must be remembered that the Institute War and Strikes Clauses are solely concerned with physical loss or damage that they cause to the insured object. This means that, unless they cause their damage by means of a weapon, which gives rise to other insured perils, their proximity to the insured object is essential. The Institute War and Strikes Clauses are not concerned with the effects on laytime of strikers far inland on the railways bringing the cargo to the port, or on the workers dealing with the goods to be shipped, or on the consequences of previous strikes which hold up the ship although they are over by the time she arrives in the port. Further, it is not necessary to go deeply into the question whether workmen, fleeing from a port for fear of cholera or plague, or engaging in ca'canny or wildcat strikes, are "strikers". There are now some accepted definitions of "strikers" from laytime cases which, it is submitted, are equally applicable to the narrower purposes of the new Institute War and Strikes Clauses.

16.6 In 1876, it was held that there was a strike if the workmen went on strike for higher wages and for this purpose alone. Unions had only recently become lawful, and the emphasis was on more money to relieve the appalling poverty of the time. This rather restrictive view was developed in further cases until Sankey J.'s famous definition which appeared in *Williams Bros. Hull Ltd.* v. *Naamlooze Vernootschap W H Berghuys Kolenhandel.*[2] The ship was chartered by her Dutch owners for a voyage from Hull to Rouen. The owner found that his crew refused to face the German submarine menace in the North Sea and no other seafarers could be induced to take their place. Sankey J. had some difficulty in deciding there was a strike which arose from fear to do a particular thing, or perform a particular contract, but he eventually held that a "grievance", not necessarily connected with wages, would be sufficient: "I think the true definition of the word 'strike', which I do not say is exhaustive, is a generally concerted refusal by workmen to work in consequence of an alleged grievance . . ."

16.7 MacKinnon J. followed this by holding in *Seeberg* v. *Russian Wood Agency*

2. (1915) 21 Com. Cas. 253.

Limited[3] that a sympathy strike was also a strike. A Latvian ship was ready to load in Leningrad. The stevedores, in pursuing a policy of refusing to handle Latvian ships in sympathy with some Latvian unions grievances, refused to load her. The rest of the port was working normally. This was still a "strike". McNair J. had to deal with a very similar case in *J. Vermaas Scheepvaartbedrijf NV* v. *Association Technique de L'Importation Charbonniere (The Laga)*.[4] The *Laga* arrived in Nantes on 12th March, 1963, to discharge coal, and by the time it was her turn to discharge, the stevedores, crane drivers, pilots and tug crews refused to unload coal ships. They had no grievance with their employers, but they wanted to assist the French coalminers who were on strike. Counsel for the shipowners contended that a sympathetic strike was not a strike, there being no grievance against the employers on the part of the strikers. McNair J. ruled against him in a judgment which made much of the General Strike (1926). Nobody could say that this was not a "strike", even though most of those taking part had no quarrel with their employers: " . . . The word 'strike' is a perfectly good, appropriate word to use to cover a sympathetic strike and a general strike and there is no need for it today to have any ingredient of grievance between those who are refusing to work and their employers."

16.8 It made no difference that only coal carriers were affected and the rest of the port was working normally. Finally, the Court of Appeal decided that there was a strike in *Tramp Shipping Corporation* v. *Greenwich Marine Inc. (The New Horizon)*.[5] The ship arrived in St. Nazaire in May, 1973, to discharge grain from Norfolk. It was usual and normal for the stevedores to work three shifts around the clock when asked, although there was no legal or contractual obligation on them to do so. At the time, they were engaged in industrial action to improve their working conditions, and were restricting their work to eight hours a day. For 10 days, during the ship's stay in the port, they refused to do any work at all. Lord Denning M.R. noted Sankey J.'s definition and added:

"If I may amplify it a little, I think a strike is a concerted stoppage of work by men done with a view to improving their wages and conditions, or giving vent to a grievance or making a protest about something or other, or supporting or sympathising with other workmen in such endeavour. It is distinct from a stoppage which is brought about by an external event such as a bomb scare or by an apprehension of danger."

Stephenson L.J. added to this:

"In my judgment, it is a species of stoppage. There cannot be a strike without a cessation of work by a number of workmen agreeing to stop work; and the question is, what kind of concerted stoppages are properly called strikes today? It must be a stoppage intended to achieve something, to call attention to something, as my Lord has said; a rise in wages, improvement of conditions, support for other workers; for political changes; an expression of sympathy or protest."

Geoffrey Lane L.J. agreed.

16.9 In this work, conclusions are attempted, and even though the courts have yet to give guidance on these three insured perils (namely, strikers, locked-out workmen, and persons taking part in labour disturbances), the guidance that does

3. (1934) 50 Ll.L.Rep. 146.
4. [1966] 1 Lloyd's Rep. 582.
5. [1975] 2 Lloyd's Rep. 314.

exist is firm enough to make the following conclusions. Although most of the above definitions are given in laytime cases, there would appear to be no reason to suppose that these very firm and comprehensive definitions should not apply to the insured perils in the War Risks Policy. Moreover, there is no reason to limit the "strikers" to those who are engaged in the business of the ship in some way, such as stevedores, tug crews, crane drivers, linesmen, pilots or customs officers, who render some services to her; strikers from other places of work or interests, even those that have no connection with the ship or even with shipping in general, can give rise to the insured peril. The miners in the miners' strike in the United Kingdom [1984–85] (para. 8.33) would seem an obvious example, and it is suggested that the insured peril would have been complete if they had destroyed or damaged some object insured on the Institute Time Clauses in addition to the other property which they destroyed. If this is accepted, then there should be no difficulty in recognising and identifying with sufficient precision "locked-out workmen"as people locked out of their place of work by their employers, usually as a means of exerting pressure in a labour dispute where some "grievance" has been expressed.

16.10 "Persons taking part in labour disturbances" are more difficult to define and here the conclusions must be offered more tentatively. It is suggested that they are not workmen with some sort of "grievance" and may be people who simply attach themselves to some labour disturbance, interpreted in its broadest sense, and may not have any justifiable or legitimate interest in its outcome.

16.11 In 1977, a union claimed the right to represent all the work-people at the Grunwick photographic processing plant in North London. Although some of the work-people belonged to the union in question, most of them did not wish to belong to any union at all and their employers refused to compel them to do so. Several other unions of a more militant nature supported the first union's demands and mounted a picket outside the plant's gates to prevent the work-people going in to work by intimidation or, if necessary, by force. This was an illegal action and the police set about removing the picket. Although successful, they were met by violent resistance and, besides injuries to people, much damage was done to the property of the hapless local residents. The difficulty here was that there was no "grievance" on the part of the factory's work-people, who were perfectly content with their terms of work, and any "disturbance" was only caused by some unions, some of which had no legitimate standing or interest in the matter, making and seeking to enforce an illegal demand. It is nonetheless suggested, although tentatively, that this was a "labour disturbance" within the terms of the insured peril.

16.12 A clearer case, where the same suggestion can be made with more confidence, concerns newspapers where the print-workers' antics had become so intolerable that they were even threatening the continued existence of the newspapers themselves. The owner dismissed them and removed his business to a plant in Wapping, East London, which was fully automated and did not require the print-workers' services. The plant itself was based in a fortress-like structure bearing a remarkable resemblance to a high security prison and heavily defended in various ways. Unable to penetrate his defences, the dismissed workers mounted a large picket to prevent lorries carrying the printed newspapers away for distribution, and were prepared to use violent means to this end. They were joined by a large number of people, whose motives must be regarded as suspect, but who had no legitimate personal interest whatever in the outcome. Several pitched battles took place with the police, with many people injured and much damage done to property. Here there was a recognisable grievance, and it could be said of the persons who joined in that they were "persons taking part in a labour disturbance". It is suggested that, had they turned their hands to destroying or damaging a ship, cargo, containers or whatever, the insured peril would have been complete.

CHAPTER 17

Riots, civil commotions

17.1 In ordinary parlance, "riot" and "civil commotion" are not easy to distinguish one from the other and the victims are not likely to appreciate fine distinctions. Moreover, when the courts are faced with only one or other term, either as an insured peril or as an excluded peril, which they must consider in the circumstances of the case, the distinctions can become further blurred. Nevertheless, there are important distinctions between them and in a work such as this, they must be explored. As a start, there are definitions of "riot" and "civil commotion" which, in the legal field, are to be preferred to the definitions given by the *Oxford English Dictionary*. These will be illustrated with cases.

17.2 Until recently, "riot" had a well-settled meaning in English common law. Various definitions have been given, but the most comprehensive were those given by the courts in *Field* v. *Receiver of Metropolitan Police*[1] and *Munday* v. *Metropolitan Police Receiver*.[2] Each element had to be present.

(a) The number of persons concerned must be at least three.
(b) They must have a common purpose.
(c) The execution or inception of that common purpose must be proved.
(d) There must also be proved an intent on the part of the persons in question to help one another, by force if necessary, against any person who may oppose them in the execution of that common purpose.
(e) There must be proved force or violence, not merely used in and about the common purpose but displayed in such a manner as to alarm at least one person of reasonable firmness and courage.

17.3 Since 1st April, 1987, when sections 1, 2 and 10 of the Public Order Act 1986 came into force, the law on "riot" has been substantially altered. The Act abolishes the common law offence of "riot", which is essentially a criminal offence with the results being insured by the insured peril of "riot". In its place is substituted section 1 of the Public Order Act 1986:

"(1) Where twelve or more persons who are present together use or threaten unlawful violence for a common purpose and the conduct of them (taken together) is such as would cause a person of reasonable firmness present at the scene to fear for his personal safety, each of the persons using unlawful violence for the common purpose is guilty of riot.

(2) It is immaterial whether or not the twelve or more use or threaten unlawful violence simultaneously.

---

1. [1907] 2 K.B. 853.
2. [1949] 1 E.R. 337.

(3) The common purpose may be inferred from conduct.

(4) No person or reasonable firmness need actually be, or be likely to be, present at the scene.

(5) Riot may be committed in private as well as in public places.

(6) A person guilty of riot is liable on conviction on indictment to imprisonment for a term not exceeding 10 years or a fine or both."

17.4 Section 10(2) of the Act provides that Rules 8 and 10 of the Marine Insurance Act 1906 shall be construed in accordance with section 1. This is an oblique reference only, saying in effect that rioters who attack the ship from the shore must be rioters within the definition of section 1, and "arrests etc. of Kings, Princes and people" (which is no longer an insured peril) shall not include rioters who come within the definition of the same section. Nevertheless, the intention seems clear that the section 1 definition should, in respect of policies taking effect on or after 1st April, 1987, apply to the insured peril of "riot". It would indeed be strange if rioters who attack the ship from the shore must be 12 or more in number, whereas for every other purpose three would be enough.

17.5 There are substantial differences, but these may be more apparent than real in practice. Comments can be made as follows:

1. There now needs to be 12 persons or more taking part in place of the previous three. As will be noted in the subsequent pages, the American courts have expressed reservations about as few people as three being enough to constitute a riot. The Criminal Law Revision Committee seems (1982) to have reached the same conclusion without, however, reference to the American views. Riot is an extremely serious matter and the Committee felt, and Parliament accepted, that the new statutory offence of "violent disorder", created by section 2 of the Public Order Act 1986, which is not an insured peril, would be enough to cover what was previously the common law offence of "riot".

2. There is now the need for unlawful violence, or at least the threat of it, whereas under the common law it was enough that the rioters were prepared to commit a tort which was not a crime. Since all violence is unlawful—except in self-defence—there is probably no substantial difference.

3. The common purpose remains but this may now be inferred from conduct. It seems that it is no longer necessary to show that the common purpose was either completed, or at least actually began.

4. The necessity to prove force or violence displayed in such a manner as to alarm a person of reasonable firmness or courage has disappeared. The threat of force or violence is enough and may be inferred from conduct on the common purpose.

5. The fear of force or violence is now related to personal safety, but the person of reasonable firmness or courage need not be present at the scene. It is enough that if he were, he would fear for his personal safety.

6. Riot, as was held in *London & Lancashire Fire Insurance Co.* v. *Bolands*,[3] can be committed in private as well as in public places.

17.6 It is suggested that, unlike the criminal courts, the insured peril of "riot" is

3. [1924] A.C. 836.

not concerned with who is guilty of "riot" because they use unlawful violence as opposed to those in the crowd who refrain from its use. It is enough to complete the insured peril that there is a crowd of 12 or more individuals, some of whom commit unlawful violence or threaten it, and have the other characteristics described above. In spite of the alterations to the law which section 1 of the Public Order Act 1986 has effected, the following cases still seem to be helpful in spite of the obvious differences, particularly in the numbers involved.

17.7 It has long been accepted that damage to some real property caused by a "riot" must be paid for by the community on the basis that the community owes a duty to each subject to keep the Queen's peace and must pay for any damage arising out of any failure to do so. In 1886 the financial aspects of this duty were transferred to the police as the representatives of the community. In the leading case of *Field* v. *Receiver of Metropolitan Police*[4] the Divisional Court of the King's Bench Division considered an appeal from the Southwark County Court which had ruled in favour of the Receiver. In a rough area of London, seven or eight youths were playing a violent game along a wall which collapsed with a loud noise. The caretaker of the timber yard appeared and the youths ran off. The caretaker's wife was greatly alarmed by the noise of the wall's collapse but there was no evidence that, whilst the play of the youths was in progress, even though they were shouting obscenities, any other person had been alarmed. The Divisional Court, applying the principles set out in the first quotation, upheld the County Court, that the cost of repairing the wall, altogether £3 10s. 0d., could not be claimed from the Receiver.

17.8 In *Ford* v. *Receiver of Metropolitan Police*[5] and in *Munday* v. *Metropolitan Police Receiver*[6] the Receiver had to pay damages on the basis that in each case there was a "riot". In the *Ford* case the crowd wished to celebrate the end of the First World War with a bonfire in the street. They were in a cheerful and happy mood when they broke into the plaintiff's derelict house in search of timber. They did a considerable amount of damage in tearing it out. The neighbour, afraid they might do the same to his house and greatly alarmed by their demeanour, begged them to spare his property, which they did. He was however too frightened to plead with them to spare Mr. Ford's property. Bailhache J. held that there was a "riot".

17.9 In the *Munday* case[7] a number of persons were debarred from a football ground where, in 1945, Chelsea was playing the Moscow Dynamos. The ground was full and there was no suggestion that they were debarred because of their behaviour. Wishing to see the match, they broke into the plaintiff's garden and climbed on to the garage roof. Their attitude was threatening and they assaulted the plaintiff's daughter, greatly alarming her, and the gardener, both of whom tried to stop them. Pritchard J. likewise held that, as all the elements quoted above were present for common law riot, there was a "riot" and awarded £175 against the Receiver for the damage done to Mr. Munday's property.

17.10 In *London and Lancashire Fire Insurance Company Limited* v. *Bolands*,[8] the House of Lords held that the commission of a crime can, in certain circum-

---

4. [1907] 2 K.B. 853.
5. [1921] 2 K.B. 344.
6. [1949] 1 E.R. 337.
7. *Ibid*.
8. [1924] A.C. 836.

stances, constitute a "riot". The City of Dublin Bakery was insured against burglary and loss of cash in a policy which contained an exclusion clause: "This insurance does not cover loss . . . caused by or happening through . . . riots, civil commotions."

17.11 Late in the evening of 25th January, 1921, the watchman, thinking that it was the stableman who was knocking at the door, opened it and four armed men burst in. He and the six cashier staff were held up at gunpoint. Two vanmen who arrived minutes later were also captured, although one managed to escape briefly and raise the alarm. Some force was used to subdue him. The robbers escaped with £1,250. The arbitrators who heard the case held that there was a "riot" and stated a case for the consideration of the courts. As in the *Cooper* case,[9] this case made its way to the House of Lords by way of a tortuous chain of appeals to the High Court of Appeal for Ireland, the Court of Appeal for Southern Ireland and the King's Bench Division of the High Court of Justice in Southern Ireland, all of whom held there was no "riot"; apparently they were following *Motor Union Insurance Co. Ltd* v. *Boggan*[10] which was only subsequently reversed by the House of Lords. Following its own decision in the *Boggan* case,[11] the House of Lords unanimously decided that there was a "riot" and that the underwriters were not liable for the loss.

17.12 The author would respectfully suggest that this case, like the *Boggan*[12] and *Cooper*[13] cases arises out of the troubled state of Ireland in the early 1920s before the establishment of the State of Eire, and that some caution is necessary before it is accepted that similar crimes can also amount to "riot". Some useful guidance is given by *Dwyer Ltd.* v. *Metropolitan Police Receiver*[14] and the recent Court of Appeal decision of *D. H. Edmonds Ltd.* v. *East Sussex Police Authority*.[15] Besides this, the soundness of the House of Lords judgment in the *Bolands*[15a] case has been judicially doubted. It was soundly denounced by the District Court in the *Pan Am* case[16] apparently with the subsequent approval of the Circuit Court of Appeals: "With all the deference we accord the ancestral authorities on the old mysteries, the opinions in the House of Lords are not impressive. Apart from that, there are aspects of the opinions that diminish their force as persuasive authority."

17.13 From what was said in the *Pan Am* case[16] the American courts would tend to favour a looser description of "riot" than that adopted by the English courts although it may be questioned if in most, if not in all, cases their tests would lead to different conclusions. Aetna had pleaded that, as an insurance term, "riot" includes a gathering of three or more persons with a common purpose to do an unlawful act and with an apparent intention to use force or violence against anyone

---

9. *Cooper* v. *The General Accident Fire & Life Assurance Corporation Ltd*. (1922) 12 Ll.L.Rep. 514; (1922) 13 Ll.L.Rep. 219 (H.L.); (1923) 128 L.T. 481. See paras. 17.30, 17.31.
   10. (1924) 130 L.T. 588. See para. 17.33.
   11. *Ibid.*
   12. *Ibid.*
   13. Footnote 9, above.
   14. [1967] 2 Q.B. 970.
   15. *The Times*, 15th July, 1988.
   15a. [1924] A.C. 836.
   16. *Pan American World Airways Inc.* v. *The Aetna Casualty & Surety Co.* [1974] 1 Lloyd's Rep. 207; [1975] 1 Lloyd's Rep. 77. See paras. 6.16–6.26, 8.13, 8.30, 8.31, 17.24–17.26.

who may oppose that purpose; moreover, in an apparent reliance on the *Cooper*[17] and *Boggan*[18] cases, no measure of uproar or tumult was necessary where an insurance contract is concerned. The District Court, after finding that "riot" is a kind of disturbance between fellow citizens, rejected this:

"These definitions [of Aetnas] . . . give serious trouble at the outset, and probably would not serve even if there were sound reasons to use them. Plaintiff's aeroplane was hijacked by two people, not three. There was to be a stop at Beirut as the improvised plan unfolded, and as many as nine others came on board temporarily, then, still meeting the minimum, a third man stayed on board to Cairo, but the notion of a flying riot in geographical instalments cannot be squeezed into the ancient formula. Among its other attributes, as the cases reflect, a riot is a local disturbance, normally by a mob, not a complex travelling conspiracy of the kind in this case."

The 2nd Circuit Court of Appeals fully approved this and added:

"The gist of the offence of riot at Common Law is the *in terroram populi* effect of the assembly. It may not be conducted by mail, by telephone or in the present case by radio. No matter how many people were involved behind the scenes, the hijacking was accomplished by only two persons."

17.14 For the immediate purposes of the case, the Circuit Court did not feel that it was necessary to go any further than this. Like the District Court before it, it felt it necessary to emphasise that tumult was a necessary ingredient. It noted with approval Appleman on *Insurance Law and Practice* (1970 edition), paragraph 3.1.1.1, page 377: "Riot is to be given its popular usual meaning as constituting a disturbance of the peace by several persons or more . . . in violent and noisy manner" and added "The criminal law in effect at the time of a putative riot is some evidence of the ordinary meaning of the term."

17.15 In emphasising the necessity for tumult and the *in terroram populi* factor, the court pointed to *Hartford Fire Insurance Company* v. *War Eagle Coal Company*.[19] In that case (which concerned "civil commotion" as well as "riot"), the 4th Circuit Court of Appeals held that there was no "riot" where five stealthy conspirators set the mine on fire at dead of night because: "There was no tumult or disturbances, not even a demonstration before the fire."

In this case there were some disturbances some distance away where miners were protesting about their conditions of work and demanding the recognition of their union. The damage done to Eagle's property was connected with these disturbances.

17.16 Finally, it should be noted that the District Court in the *Pan Am* case[20] questioned whether as few people as three could create the necessary degree of tumult for a "riot". Whilst the American courts will have close regard to the English decisions, no easy assumption should be made that they will always regard a "riot" as an established fact when so few people are involved. Neither, now, will the English courts.

17.17 Unlike "riot", "civil commotion" does not enjoy a well-defined character

17. Footnote 9, above.
18. (1924) 130 L.T. 588.
19. 295 F. 663 (1924).
20. Footnote 16, above.

in English law. In *Levy* v. *Assicurazione Generali*[21] the Privy Council approved the following definition from *Welford and Otter-Barry on Fire Insurance* (3rd edition), page 64:

"Civil Commotion. This phrase is used to indicate a stage between a riot and civil war. It has been defined to mean an insurrection of the people for general purposes, though not amounting to rebellion; but it is probably not capable of any very precise definition. The element of turbulence and tumult is essential; an organized conspiracy to commit criminal acts, where there is no tumult or disturbance until after the acts, does not amount to civil commotion. It is not, however, necessary to show the existence of any outside organization at whose instigation the acts were done."

17.18 The facts of the case are obscure, but it would appear that a claim arose out of a fire policy following a fire in Palestine during the days of the British Mandate when Jews and Arabs were attacking each other's property. As will be seen from the findings of the court in the *Spinney's* case[22] the last sentence of the definition should now be regarded as qualified at least to some extent.

17.19 In *Langdale* v. *Mason*[23] Lord Mansfield had to direct the jury on "civil commotion" which was an excluded peril. He did so in the following terms: "I think a civil commotion is this; an insurrection of the people for general purposes, although it may not amount to a rebellion, where there is usurped power."

17.20 In the event, the jury did decide that the Gordon Riots amounted to a "civil commotion", which meant the judgment had to be entered for the defendant underwriter. It will be recalled that the Gordon Riots were directed against the Catholics, which the jury thought was a general purpose and they did not have as a purpose the overthrow of the government which was, as we have seen, a treasonable purpose.

17.21 It is indeed strange to contemplate that, within living memory, women had all the obligations of citizenship including (if single) the payment of taxes, but not the right to vote for the government which should rule them. In the early years of this century, the ladies decided to do something about this and the Suffragette Movement was formed. Besides chaining themselves to the railings of Buckingham Palace and No. 10 Downing Street, and undoing the braces of policemen, whose arms were full of other struggling Suffragettes, they felt that their cause would be helped to a great if undefined degree by breaking all the shop windows in the West End of London. Armed with hammers, they set out individually, although simultaneously, for this purpose. For a short while, the calm of the West End of London was disturbed by strident shouts of "Votes for women" and the crash of splintering glass. They did not disturb unduly or frighten their fellow citizens and, when arrested, went peacefully, indeed serenely, off to jail. They were charged with causing damage to property but not with Public Order offences such as riot, unlawful assembly or affray, and in course of time were duly sentenced. There was some evidence that whilst awaiting trial they were all bailed out of the police station by the same people. Clearly there was some evidence of a central organisation.

The involvement of the law did not end with the sentencing of these Amazons.

21. (1940) 67 Ll.L.Rep. 174; [1940] A.C. 791.
22. *Spinney's (1948) Ltd. and Others* v. *Royal Insurance* [1980] 1 Lloyd's Rep. 406. See paras. 7.7–7.16, 8.17, 8.18, 17.27–17.29.
23. (1780) *Bennett's Fire Insurance Cases* 16. See para. 8.12.

The plate glass was insured for damage: "Caused directly by, or arising from, civil commotion or rioting."

17.22 When *London and Manchester Plate Glass Company Limited* v. *Heath*[24] came before Bucknill J. he removed it from the jury on the basis that, following Lord Mansfield's direction which is quoted above, there could not have been a "civil commotion". He was unanimously upheld by the Court of Appeal, Vaughan L.J. saying: "It is plain that in this case there has been no insurrection of the people for the purpose of general mischief" and Buckley L.J.: "Commotion connotes turbulence or tumult and, I think violence or intention to commit violence . . . The acts were done without causing any tumult or disturbance" and Hamilton L.J.: " . . . A civil commotion . . . must at least involve that the acts which constitute the commotion should be acts done by the agents together, and not merely acts which are done in pre-concert and simultaneously and in proximity to one another."

17.23 The South African courts also had to consider "civil commotion" and Soloman J. made the following observations in *Lindsay Pirie* v. *The General Accident Fire & Life Assurance Corporation Limited.*[25] He noted that Lord Mansfield was directing a jury in a particular case and was not giving a definition suitable for all occasions. He then added: " . . . and that the effect of his directions to the jury was that a rising of the people (by which I presume he meant a considerable number of the population) for purposes of general mischief amounting to civil commotion . . . "

The court also noted that the Gordon Riots started as a rising against Roman Catholics, eventually degenerating into destruction and plunder. There was never an "insurrection" which intended to overthrow the government.

17.24 The exclusion of "civil commotion" was pleaded by Aetna in the *Pan Am* case.[26] The main judgment, which was fully approved by the 2nd Circuit Court of Appeals, was given by the District Court. Some additional facts, set out in diary form, are necessary for an understanding of the District Court's decision. They are given here rather than in the general history of the case because they are only pertinent to the "civil commotion" point.

1970

Spring and early Summer

Particularly severe tensions exist between the Palestinians and the Jordanian Government leading to armed clashes in which the Jordanian Army is involved.

June

A portion of Amman is occupied by the Palestinians and two major hotels are also occupied, with their guests being held as hostages to put pressure on the King.

June to early September

Various incidents accompanied by sporadic gunfire take place. An attempt is made to assassinate the King. Demonstrations are held where the King is denounced as a traitor.

17th September

Immediately in the wake of the hijackings (para. 5.3) and the subsequent destruction of the aircraft, the Jordanian Army begins the operation of expelling the Palestinians. By the end of September, this operation is completed after severe fighting.

24. [1913] 3 K.B. 411.
25. [1914] S.A.R. (App. D) 574.
26. Footnote 16, above.

There was certainly some disorder in Jordan at the time, and the Palestinians were the cause of it.

17.25 The District Court made the point: "Civil commotion occurs in a locale—a city, a country or an area. It is essentially a kind of domestic disturbance . . . The authorities speak consistently of and the cases all concerned local . . . outbreaks and domestic disturbances." Applying this to the *Pan Am* case,[27] the District Court found great geographical difficulties: "It stretches the concept beyond breaking to reach for our hijacking from Dawsons Field or the rest of Jordan, or to sweep the Pan American aeroplane into a kind of globally scattered 'commotion' based upon a supposed identity of causes, motives or purposes."

17.26 Aetna pleaded the *Cooper*[28] case as authority for the proposition that a loss arising from a "civil commotion" need not take place at the scene of the commotion. The court found itself unimpressed by the reasoning of the House of Lords and felt more persuaded by the decision of the 4th Circuit Court of Appeals in the *Hartford* case.[29] Besides setting fire to the mine, a crowd of miners had caused some disturbance some distance away from the mine on the issue of whether the union should be recognised by the mine's owners. The 4th Circuit Court of Appeals decided that even if there was a "civil commotion", it was too far away to have been responsible for the damage to the mine. Bearing in mind the requirement of the American law that loss or damage arising from a "civil commotion" must be caused at the scene of the commotion itself, which is reflected in the District Court's decision, it is not surprising that the District Court in the *Pan Am* case[30] felt that it was not necessary to go into the vexed question of whether there was a "civil commotion" in Jordan as a whole (although it did decide there was no such commotion at Dawsons Field for the simple reason that there was no population to disturb there) and dismissed Aetna's plea that the loss of the 747 was due to "civil commotion" with the comment:

"Less needs to be added concerning the contention that the loss 'resulted' more generally from 'civil commotion' in Jordan. However wide the net of causation may be, it cannot in fact span this much on any sensible reading of our record, including especially the P.F.L.P.'s go-it-alone terrorist 'external operations'."

17.27 Coming now to *Spinney's* case,[31] Mustill J. described a "civil commotion" as something more serious than a mere leaderless mob and particularly noted two further points (which are not quoted above). Bucknill J. and Vaughan Williams L.J. in the *Plate Glass* case[32] found that the Gordon Riots involved: "A general rising up of the people to do terrible things" and Luxmore L.J. in the *Levy* v. *Assicurazione Generali*[33] case found that "civil commotion" was "An insurrection of the people for general purposes though not amounting to a rebellion; but it is probably not capable of any precise definition. The element of turbulance or tumult is essential."

---

27. *Ibid.*
28. *Cooper* v. *The General Accident Fire & Life Assurance Corporation Ltd.* (1922) 12 Ll.L. Rep. 514; (1922) 13 Ll.L.Rep. 219 (H.L.); (1923) 128 L.T. 481. See paras. 17.30, 17.31.
29. 295 F. 663 (1924). See para. 17.15.
30. Footnote 16, above.
31. *Spinney's (1948) Ltd. and Others* v. *Royal Insurance* [1980] 1 Lloyd's Rep. 406. See paras. 7.7–7.16, 8.17, 8.18.
32. Footnote 24, above. See paras. 17.21–17.23.
33. (1940) 67 Ll.L.Rep. 174; [1940] A.C. 791. See paras. 17.17–17.18.

17.28 The findings of the court in the *Spinney's* case[34] give some really firm guidance on "civil commotion" and enables distinctions to be drawn between "civil commotion", "insurrection" and "riot". The court said, on the difference between an "insurrection" and a "civil commotion":

"It still remains to be considered whether the 'civil commotion' assumed the proportions of or amounted to a popular rising—which is broadly to be equated to an 'insurrection'. For a popular rising, there must be some unanimity of purpose . . . and this must involve the displacement of the government. I doubt whether a violent attack by one section of the population on the other on the grounds of . . . religion or race would be described as a rising. Adopting this interpretation, I would not say that the disturbances in the Lebanon amounted to a popular rising,"

and on the dimensions of the proportion of the population involved and the degree of tumult for a "civil commotion" to exist: "All one can say is that it must involve a really substantial proportion of the populace, although obviously not all of the population need participate, and that there should be tumult and violence on a large scale."

17.29 Mustill J. concluded:

" . . . I find nothing in the authorities compelling the court to hold that a civil commotion must involve a revolt against the government, although the disturbances must have sufficient cohesion to prevent them from being the work of a mindless mob. Confusing and fragmentary as the violence in the Lebanon may appear, . . . "

a state of "civil commotion" nevertheless existed. The emphasis on size and seriousness both of the disturbances and the degree of tumult should be noted.

17.30 Two decisions of the House of Lords need to be noted in support of the proposition that "riots" and "civil commotions" (and indeed "rebellion") do not need to arise in the place where the loss or damage occurs provided that the loss or damage can be said to be a result. Both cases arise out of the troubled state of Ireland before the founding of the State of Eire in 1921. In *Cooper* v. *The General Accident Fire & Life Assurance Corporation*[35] a motor car was insured with an exclusion clause "excluding loss or damage occasioned by riot or civil commotion occurring within the land limits of Ireland".

17.31 The trial judge found as a fact that, at the scene of the theft in Ballinrea, there was no disturbance but that "civil commotion", possibly even rebellion, existed in the nearby neighbourhood of County Cork during the time in question, namely October, 1920. Police evidence was given that "Guerrilla warfare existed in parts of County Cork and Cork City." The owner of the car was forced by a man with a gun to stay indoors whilst his car was being stolen. In giving judgment for the underwriter Viscount Cave L.C. said: "On the facts, the car must have been taken by emissaries of the rebels for the purposes of the rebellion" and Lord Atkinson held it was: " . . . really absurd to hold that you must have some civil commotion at the very place that the theft is committed."

17.32 This case reached the House of Lords only after a tortuous process through the original trial, the King's Bench Division, the Court of Appeals for Southern Ireland and the High Court of Appeal for Ireland. The first three of these

34. Footnote 31, above.
35. (1923) 128 L.T. 481.

courts found for the plaintiff and the last one for the underwriter, as did the House of Lords.

17.33 The other case is *Motor Union Insurance Company Limited* v. *Boggan*.[36] A motor car was insured with the following exclusion clause: "Excluding loss or damage arising during . . . or in consequence of . . . riot, civil commotion."

In November, 1920, the chauffeur was stopped by four masked men who were armed with revolvers and was ordered out of the car. Apart from this incident, the neighbourhood appears to have been peaceful. He was blindfolded, and detained for 3–4 hours and then released. At the time of the theft, police evidence was given in a somewhat contradictory fashion that, whilst there were no serious disturbances, they had been ordered in from outlying posts because they were too exposed to attack. Martial law was not declared until the 4th January, 1921. Some sporting guns and mails had been stolen. In spite of the evidence of the police, O'Connor L.J. in one of the lower courts had declared: "I am of the opinion that the true meaning and scope of this policy is that where the area of the ordinary law is paralysed by commotion, disturbance or riot, the insurers are not liable for theft by armed men." This dictum was approved by the House of Lords who gave judgment for the underwriters.

17.34 As has already been noted[37] the American courts presently insist that it is an essential feature that the loss or damage take place at the scene of the "civil commotion", and they have so far declined to follow the House of Lords' ruling in these two judgments.

17.35 In attempting to draw conclusions, the minor differences that have become apparent between the English law and the American law will be shown.

A "civil commotion" has the following characteristics:

   (1) A substantial proportion of the population, or at least a substantial number of people, rise to engage in "general mischief" or "to do terrible things".

   (2) Such "general mischief" or "terrible things" do not envisage the overthrow of the government as a principal cause (although this may be regarded as a desirable result by at least some of the participants); if they did, the insured perils of "rebellion" or 'insurrection" would arise. There must, however, be a principal cause or causes such as arise out of differences in political views or aspirations, religious beliefs, or racial or ethnic differences.

   (3) It is not necessary that there should be leaders or factions which promote such principal cause or causes, although if there are such leaders or factions, the presumption that "civil commotion" is responsible for any violence is enhanced, particularly if they instigate it or do nothing to discourage or disown it.

   (4) Widespread tumult is a necessary ingredient and furthermore a very considerable degree of tumult. Tumult here involves violent damage to persons or property or the threat or possibility thereof or at least the intention to cause it. It also requires a considerable number of persons

36. (1924) 130 L.T. 588.
37. At para. 17.26.

acting together. A mere criminal conspiracy to do damage by individuals, perhaps even small groups of individuals, and even similar damage simultaneously over a wide area, will not constitute tumult, although in some circumstances there may be a number of simultaneous "riots". Tumult does not need to be continuous and may be sporadic over a long period.

(5) The English law recognises that if a "civil commotion" exists elsewhere, loss or damage caused in a peaceful place, always provided that the loss or damage is done in the general cause of the "civil commotion", will still be loss or damage caused by "civil commotion". The American law insists that the loss or damage should take place at the scene of the tumult. It is possible, however, that this difference, or these differences, may disappear if in future cases the American courts will accept that O'Connor L.J.'s *dictum*[38] represents a proper reason for the English decisions, which, it is respectfully suggested, is the case.

17.36 "Riot", on the other hand, now has the characteristics set out in section 1 of the Public Order Act 1986, which are noted at the start of this chapter. The following should also be noted:

1. American law pays close regard to the English definition and the English decisions but it does not regard itself as being rigidly bound to a similar degree. The American courts do, however, insist on a measure of tumult (in a more general sense than is necessary for "civil commotion") which is *in terroram populi* being present and moreover present at the scene where the "riot" takes place. The differences may be small and perhaps, in the event, insignificant, but they clearly feel that their hands should not be tied by a rigid formula.

2. It can be a once-only disturbance without a principal cause.

3. It can be the work of a "mindless mob" of the kind rejected by Mustill J. when considering "civil commotion" in the *Spinney's* case.[39]

4. Unlike "civil commotions" it can be a disorder in a very small area without the widespread tumult that "civil commotion" requires. The English courts will, unlike the American, recognise that loss or damage can arise some distance away from the scene of the "riot". It would seem that O'Connor L.J. meant his *dictum*[40] to apply to "riot" as much as it does to "civil commotion".

5. The same cause can give rise to a number of separate and individual riots in several localities, sometimes many miles apart, and possibly even simultaneous. Reference is made at para. 8.33 to the miners' strike in the United Kingdom (1984–85). The National Union of Mine Workers led their members out on strike to protest and to prevent a programme of pit closures being implemented. Pickets of considerable size, sometimes as many as 150 men, were posted outside the gates of many collieries to prevent any attempt by anyone from entering the collieries and working there. At the time, it was lawful to seek to dissuade by peaceful means anybody

38. See para. 17.33.
39. Footnote 31, above. See para. 17.27.
40. See para. 17.33.

from entering and working in the collieries, but it was illegal to attempt to do this by intimidation or by force, which the pickets made clear they were prepared to use. The police, in attempting to clear the entrances to allow those who wished to enter and work in the collieries to do so, met forcible resistance. Some pitched battles took place in many parts of the country, and there were frequent cases of injury to people and to property. Whether the situation is judged by the rules of the common law or by section 1 of the Public Order Act 1986 (which was not then in effect), it can be said that there were a number of separate and individual riots taking place, sometimes simultaneously, in many parts of the country.

CHAPTER 18

any terrorist . . .

18.1 In 1964 a limpet mine, thought to have been placed by Cuban exiles who disapproved of British ships trading with Cuba, seriously damaged the hull of a British ship and injured some of her crew whilst in Miami. Under the F.C. & S. Clause as it then stood, it was doubtful if the incident was excluded from the Marine Policy in such a way that it would fall upon the war risk cover provided by the ship's Mutual War Risks Association. In order to resolve the question, the marine hull underwriters accepted the claim, although it was at least arguable whether they need have done so, and subsequently altered the Market Marine Policy to exclude what was generally known as the Malicious Damage Clause (see para. 1.19). When fully developed, this clause read: "Warranted free from loss damage liability or expense arising from: (a) the detonation of an explosive (b) any weapon of war and caused by any person acting maliciously or from a political motive." This risk was transferred to the War Risks Policy.

18.2 In its drafting of the MAR form, Mr. Alan Jackson's Committee reduced this to: " . . . or any person acting maliciously or from a political motive." It was thought unnecessary to include "detonation of an explosive" or "any weapon of war". Other insured perils contained in the new MAR form seemed adequate to include these insured perils.

18.3 In the early 1980s the Market underwriters and the Mutual War Risks Associations became extremely concerned about the activities of terrorists whose depredations were spreading far and wide. No serious action had so far been taken against ships, but it was clear that ships could soon become their targets as aircraft already were. Even before *The Andreas Lemos*[1] in 1982, it was doubtful if they could be called "pirates" because there was then always a political motive of some sort, and there is no such thing as a political "pirate" (para. 20.20). It was true that if the terrorists employ "mines, torpedoes, bombs or other weapons of war", the damage or destruction of the ship would be covered by the war risk policy because, in the case of these insured perils, people's motives are immaterial. But these are not the only means of destroying or damaging a ship, and in case a terrorist group should set her on fire or should flood her and then sink her, what would happen then? It could be said that they were acting "maliciously" and that this was the insured peril, although an indication by Phillimore L.J. (para. 19.1) may be said, at least for the time being, to leave this in some doubt. The task of proving that they

---

1. *Athens Maritime Enterprises Corporation* v. *Hellenic Mutual War Risks Association* (*Bermuda*) *Ltd.* (*The Andreas Lemos*) [1982] 2 Lloyd's Rep. 483. See paras. 20.33–20.38.

were acting from a "political motive" would face the assured with almost unimaginable difficulties of proof where this was not explicable to the logical mind. It was also feared that these difficulties could, oddly enough, be compounded if the damage or destruction should degenerate, as it has since done in several instances, into sheer wanton destruction and murder apparently for its own sake, although justified in some strange fashion. They therefore added to their cover the new insured peril of "terrorist", being anxious that a modern danger should be described directly rather than indirectly. Now the new Institute Time Clauses and the Mutual War Risks Associations' Rules give insurance in the form of the heading to this chapter.

18.4 This insured peril, being new, has so far received little judicial interpretation, but there is one case from the U.S. District Court which is of great interest, namely the *Chilean Fruit* case. Until there are more cases in which the issue arises directly, this work can only describe the reasons for including "terrorists" as an insured peril, and deal with the ordinary meaning of the word.

18.5 Historically "terrorists" have a very political connotation. The Reign of Terror during the French Revolution was applied by people describing themselves as "terrorists" and it seems from the *Oxford English Dictionary* that the word first then appeared in a meaningful form. Terror was used in pursuit of political aims to achieve a better Government of France and ultimately to export the principles of that government abroad. Professor Schama's interesting work *Citizens* describes "the terror" as lasting from April, 1793 to July, 1794—a far shorter time than is generally supposed—and can be said to have ended when its chief proponent and terrorist, Robespierre himself, was guillotined. Whilst it lasted, it was not entirely aimed at the *ancien régime* purely out of motives of spite or revenge. Its main purpose was to eliminate political rivals—the *ancien régime* being the foremost of these—who might have engineered the failure of the Revolution. Even the Revolution's adherents were among its victims. The Montagnards purged the Herbertistes whose only offence was to counsel and attempt to pursue different methods of ensuring the Revolution's success. During the 19th century one of the extreme revolutionary societies in Russia was called, or called itself, "The Terrorists". Their aim by murdering, or attempting to murder, the Czar and his ministers was to get a Government of Russia which was more to their liking. More in line with the modern meaning of the word, the same dictionary defines "terrorists": "Anyone who attempts to further his views by a system of coercive intimidation." and dyslogistically: "One who entertains, professes or tries to awaken or spread a feeling of terror or alarm; an alarmist, a scaremonger."

18.6 Terrorism can be government by intimidation, but more particularly for the purposes of this work: "A policy intended to strike with terror those against whom it is adopted; the employment of methods of intimidation; the fact of terrorising or condition of being terrorised" and "terror": "To strike with terror, to terrify." These definitions were given in 1933 and a lot has happened since that date. They can, however, be read as embracing the more modern form of terrorist as explained below.

18.7 Obviously some limit must be placed on these definitions, and the difficulty lies in defining "terrorists" in the modern and popular sense of the word. There is now a line of decisions, beginning with Pickford J. and the Court of Appeal in the

Republic of Bolivia case (paras. 20.19–20.25), and going on with Goddard J. and Lord Greene M.R. in the *Bantham* case (paras. 6.6–6.10), with Staughton J. in the *Andreas Lemos* case (paras. 20.33–20.38), and recently with Saville J. in the *Mozambique* case (paras. 8.22–8.26), to the effect that where businessmen use a term in a commercial document, that term must be given its normal everyday meaning. Just what does "terrorists" mean in today's insurance policy? In an attempt to answer that question, a description will be given of the line of thought that led to its inclusion as an insured peril in 1982.

18.8 A terrorist is someone who kills, maims, or destroys indiscriminately for a public cause. The term can include:

   (i) Those who kill maim and destroy for the sake of doing so. The public cause which they espouse may be hazy, incoherent, and to the logical mind totally meaningless. It is still however a public cause, and this separates them from other criminals who do these things for their own gain or purposes.

  (ii) Those who are motivated by a recognisable and well defined public cause even though its achievement is most unlikely. The I.R.A. wishes to unite the Province of Northern Ireland with Eire to form a single unified State of Ireland and to see British troops leave the Province. The Red Army Faction and the Angry Brigade wished to see Germany and Italy respectively become Eastern-model socialist states rather than Western-style capitalist countries.

 (iii) Those who aim to force their countries to allow them to set up independent ethnic states of their own. The Sikhs have long sought independence from India. The E.T.A. wishes to force Spain to allow them to break away into a separate Basque State.

 (iv) Those who recognise that their aims are unlikely to be achieved, and act out of motives of revenge or protest. Various Arab groups have attacked Israel, often targeting civilians rather than the military, in revenge for their expulsion in 1948, and the continued occupation of the West Bank and the Gaza Strip. The Baader Meinhoff gang sought revenge on an affluent West German society from which they saw many (not necessarily themselves) as being excluded. The Tamils feel they are oppressed by the majority in Sri Lanka.

  (v) Those who form the various splinter groups which have split away from the main terrorist organisations, and who engage in internecine warfare among themselves, often regardless of the harm caused to others. They have been known to attack people who are totally unconnected with any Arab cause and who cannot be described as opponents.

18.9 This list is not of course exhaustive, and neither is it totally descriptive of "terrorists". Too strictly interpreted, it could include people who cannot be so described. The leaders of the National Union of Mineworkers led a strike of miners (1984–1985) in which they described their members as the "shock troops of the working class". There were instances of much disorder with pitched battles with the police, and there were many acts of mayhem and vandalism. The objective of overthrowing the elected government was openly boasted. Yet throughout this remained a trade dispute in a more than usually violent form, and it would have come to an immediate end if a settlement of the dispute over mine closures had been reached.

18.10 "Indiscriminately" and "Public Cause" need to be considered further and so does the identity of the perpetrators. This will be done separately:

"Indiscriminately"

18.11 An attack may be centred on a specific target, such as an individual, a military installation, a government office, a shop, or a private business, and it may succeed in killing or destroying its target. The terrorists of the French Revolution and the later Russian terrorists, when pursuing their political causes by means of terror, chose their targets with care and some measure of precision. For all that is said, the French revolutionaries were intent on purging particular political enemies, and were not concerned with those who, whether from fear or from conviction, supported the revolution. The modern terrorist is not concerned with the unconnected people who he may kill or maim, or whose property he may destroy in pursuit of his objective. The word can be taken further than this. The shooting of airline passengers in the terminals of Rome, Tel Aviv and Vienna, and the highjacking of an aircraft, to the great dismay of the airline, the passengers and the crew, undoubtedly need considerable care to organise; but they are still indiscriminate in the sense that they are directed against people who have no power to change things, or who cannot be described as opponents in any sense of the word. The same is true of a terrorist who places a device on board a ship or among the cargo. Some unconnected interests will suffer, whether they are the shipowners, the cargo-owners, or the crew, and in this sense the act is indiscriminate.

"Public cause"

18.12 This needs to be contrasted with a private grudge or grievance, or the attempt to make a private gain. This can best be shown by the cases of people who have poisoned food or medicines in supermarkets. If the miscreants do this to express disapproval of using animals to test various objects which are going to be used or consumed by humans, it can be said they are acting in a public cause. It would be different however where the motive was to blackmail the supermarket into paying large sums of money or to give expression to a private grudge or grievance, as in a recent case where a detective-sergeant poisoned babyfood to express disgust with the police force which employed him. These two matters concern the pursuit of private ends, and cannot be said to be public causes. Regrettably, this brings matters back to human motives, always a very difficult matter for the courts to determine, whereas the new War and Strikes Clauses, introduced in the 1980s, sought to avoid this and concentrate instead on the events of a number of insured perils.

The identity of the perpetrators

18.13 Had a case of terrorism come before the courts 100 years ago, there can be little doubt that, in the immediate wake of the French "*Terroristes*" and the 19th century Russian terrorists, it would have been judged in the historical sense. This would have meant that the perpetrators would only have been held to be terrorists if they had been acting in pursuit of a political cause. Moreover, the identity of the terrorists, and also the character of the political cause itself, would have had to be proved to the strict standards required by the courts. This would have posed great difficulties for the plaintiff which are immeasurably increased today.

18.14 The modern terrorist group has a highly organised security system with "cells" and "cut-offs" so that even its own highly placed members do not always know of their own operations, or if they do, they are ignorant of the names of the individuals who executed them. Even if their identities could be discovered, it is unrealistic in the extreme to expect individuals to turn up in court to give evidence which would justify their immediate arrest and severe punishment. In any case, with a few exceptions which relate to fraud, no man can be required to give evidence which would incriminate himself. As for the public cause itself, we have noted that in some cases it is easily recognisable. In some other cases, it is so hazy, rambling and incoherent that it would challenge even the highly developed analytical powers of the judges themselves. In any case, it is highly undesirable to turn the courts into sounding boards for the dissemination of propaganda of terrorist groups who are engaged in the commission of atrocious acts.

18.15 In order to prevent this happening, the intention was, when the insured peril was introduced in 1982, that the act should speak for itself. It is quite capable of doing this because the damage which is done and the surrounding circumstances would point to only one conclusion—or point away from it as the case may be. This would usually be enough to prove the indiscriminate nature of the attack. It should be reasonably clear who the perpetrators were, even if only on the balance of probabilities. Obviously some evidence of the public cause should be available to the courts. It was, and still is, hoped that they would be content with expert evidence of what this is from such people who make a close study of terrorist groups and the causes they espouse. If these conditions can be wholly, or at least substantially, met, then the insured peril will be complete.

18.16 Acting on these principles, the insurance market and the Mutual War Risks Associations have dealt with the following cases without dispute:

(1) In 1987, an Air-India Boeing 747 was destroyed over the North Atlantic by a bomb placed among the aircraft's navigational equipment. This was clear from the wreckage which was, with some difficulty, brought to the surface. The aircraft and her cargo were lost, and all on board were killed. The perpetrators were thought to be Sikh extremists living in Canada, although this was never proved with certainty. The public cause was the desire of the Sikhs for an independent state of their own. The indiscriminate nature of the incident needs no comment.

(2) In 1988, a Pan-American Boeing 747 was destroyed over Lockerbie in Scotland by a bomb placed among the passengers' luggage. This again was clear from the wreckage. Again, the aircraft and her cargo were lost and all on board were killed. In addition, people were killed and injured, and much property was destroyed or damaged in the town of Lockerbie onto which some of the wreckage fell. The perpetrators were originally

unknown (at least publicly), and the public cause was thought to be a revenge attack for the recent accidental shooting down of an Iranian Airbus by the *U.S.S. Vincennes*. Painstaking investigation by the Scottish police later indicated that some others may have been responsible. They have yet to be extradited and tried, so that nothing can be said whether they did or did not cause the loss of the aircraft. Likewise the public cause cannot be ascertained. It was clear from the damage that this was a terrorist attack, that it was indiscriminate, and that somebody had caused it, almost certainly for a public cause, even if that public cause was uncertain. This was sufficient to complete the insured peril.

(3) Again in 1988, the *City of Poros*, a Greek holiday ship which gave tourists day trips to the Greek Islands in the neighbourhood of Athens, sailed from Piraeus with 400 passengers. A group among the passengers threw hand grenades and opened fire with machine guns. Many passengers were killed or injured and the ship herself was seriously damaged. The outrage had been carefully planned; it cannot have been an easy task to smuggle the weapons on board, and fast motor-boats were on hand to convey the perpetrators from the scene. The perpetrators were not known with any certainty, although it is thought that Abu Nidal, a splinter group which had broken away from the P.L.O., were probably responsible. Abu Nidal's exact aims are not certain, and may not even exist, but it is known to nurse a grievance that the State of Israel continues to exist, and a grudge that the P.L.O. pursues policies which are not to its liking. In spite of these uncertainties, the Mutual War Risks Association concerned accepted that the insured peril was complete. Again the indiscriminate nature of the attack needs no comment, and nobody does this sort of thing unless they are terrorists.

18.17 Since the printing of the first edition of this work, there has been a case in the United States District Court (ED Pennsylvania), *New Market Investment Corporation* v. *Fireman's Fund Insurance Company*.[2] During March 1989, the U.S. Embassy in Chile received anonymous telephone calls that Chilean fruit shipped to the United States had been poisoned with cyanide in order to protest the plight of the Chilean poor and to bring the economic injustice in Chile to the attention of the United States and the world. Such warnings cannot be ignored, and the U.S. Government disseminated this warning through the "Terrep" system which is designed to deal with "terroristic activities". There was widespread investigation of all fruit imported from Chile which caused delay in its transmission. Delay is fatal to fruit, and much of it was ruined with great loss to the importers. Two grapes unloaded from the *Almeria Star* were found to be poisoned with cyanide causing the entire shipment to be withheld from the market. The plaintiff was insured for loss or damage caused by "acts . . . carried out for . . . terroristic purposes".

18.18 The insurers were prepared to pay for the two grapes, but disputed their liability for the loss caused by the delay. Broderick D.J. ruled against them on this point. He did not define terrorism for the benefit of the jury as a matter of law, but left it to the jury to decide as matters of fact whether "Acts of Terrorism" had

2. 774 F. Supp. 909 (1991).

taken place. The jury decided that they had, and judgment was signed in the plaintiff's favour. In one sense this is disappointing. Judicial definition of the insured peril is required, and little help is likely to be forthcoming from the criminal law, which in general prefers to use the many other shots in its locker with which it feels safer. In another sense it is gratifying, because the jury was prepared to reach its conclusions broadly on the lines which led to the inclusion of the insured peril of "Terrorists" into the War and Strikes Clauses in 1982. This is at least some confirmation of the ordinary meaning of the word as it is understood by ordinary people. It is suggested that the jury was clearly right. The poisoning of the grapes spoke for itself, and was undoubtedly indiscriminate. The public cause was clear. Only the identity of the miscreants was not known, but they can only have been "terrorists" to do such a thing.

CHAPTER 19

. . . or any person acting maliciously or from a political motive

MALICE AND MALICIOUSLY

19.1 "Malice" or "maliciously" has not received much judicial consideration in the field of civil law, and then only for very specific purposes. There is very little in the context of an insured peril in an insurance policy. It would seem that the only definitions were given in *The Mandarin Star*[1] where Lord Denning M.R. described it: "I think 'maliciously' here means spite, or ill-will, or the like" whilst Phillimore L.J. thought that acting maliciously was only intended to deal with damage arising in the course of civil disturbance. It is respectfully suggested that this puts the insured peril on too high a level, and that it is not necessary that there should be a civil disturbance before persons act "maliciously". Nevertheless this judicial pronouncement exists, at least for the time being, and it cannot be ignored. It is however the position that neither in *The Mandarin Star*,[2] where the shipowner was attempting by some unorthodox and unusual means to exercise a lien, nor in *The Salem*[3] was there in fact any malice; indeed in the latter case, the plaintiffs did not pursue this point on appeal. This alone deprived the judges of any serious opportunity to consider "persons acting maliciously". As the following examples will show, the practice of the underwriters is to follow the guidance of Lord Denning M.R. which is quoted above.

19.2 There is little help to be gained from the law of tort, because malice is not generally an essential element in a civil wrong, except in such matters as malicious prosecution. *Johnson* v. *Emerson and Sparrow*[4] concerned a case where a solicitor, actuated by malice, successfully applied to have the plaintiff adjudged bankrupt. Malice existed beyond doubt, but it was not essential to the plaintiff's case. *Allen* v. *Flood*[5] dealt with the demarcation dispute between carpenters and ironworkers on a ship where a union delegate was alleged to be malicious. Again, his malice, if it existed, was not material to the issues. Although this does not deal with damage to property, Halsbury's *Laws*, Volume 28, paragraph 145, defines malice in defamation cases as: "Express or actual malice is ill-will or spite towards the plaintiff or any indirect or improper motive in the defendant's mind."

---

1. *Nishina Trading Co. Ltd.* v. *Chiyoda Fire and Marine Insurance Co. Ltd.* (*The Mandarin Star*) [1969] 1 Lloyd's Rep. 293. See para. 12.55.
2. *Ibid.*
3. *Shell International Petroleum Co. Ltd.* v. *Caryl Antony Vaughan Gibbs* (*The Salem*) [1981] 2 Lloyd's Rep. 316; [1982] 1 Lloyd's Rep. 369; [1983] 1 Lloyd's Rep. 342. See paras. 12.54–12.63.
4. (1871) L.R. 6 Ex. 329.
5. [1898] A.C. 1.

19.3 The criminal law is more helpful, and there are a wealth of cases arising under the Malicious Damage Act 1861, the Offences against the Person Act 1861 and the Criminal Damage Act 1971. Although it must be borne in mind that the criminal law is concerned with applying "malice" and "maliciously" to criminal acts where criminal intent is always an important element, the cases demonstrate how far "recklessness" is to be taken into account in deciding whether a reckless accused is guilty of malice or has acted maliciously. Some examples are:

(1) The accused, knowing that there was a risk of causing injury, fired in the direction of another huntsman to frighten him off. This was held to be malicious. *R. v. Ward.*[6]

(2) The accused threw a stone at an opponent in a street brawl and broke a window. He would only have broken the window "maliciously" if he had intended to do so or, knowing that it was there, had been "reckless" in that he did not care whether it was broken or not. *R. v. Pembliton.*[7]

(3) The accused obstructed the exit of the theatre and turned off all the lights. There was a panic and several people were seriously injured. It was held that a man acted maliciously when he "wilfully" and without lawful excuse did something which he knew would injure another. *R. v. Martin.*[8]

(4) The accused broke open a gas meter and stole the money within it. Unknown to him, he also damaged the gas main and thus allowed gas to seep into the next door property. This endangered the life of the occupant. The trial judge directed the jury that "maliciously" merely meant "wickedly". On appeal it was held that it should have been left to the jury to decide whether, even if the accused did not intend to injure the neighbour, he foresaw that what he was doing might cause injury to another, but nevertheless carried on with his course of action. *R. v. Cunningham.*[9]

(5) The accused, believing his air-gun was unloaded but without checking that this was so, aimed the air-gun at another and fired it. If he honestly believed that it was not loaded, he did not foresee physical harm resulting from his action, and thus could not be guilty of maliciously wounding, even on the basis of "recklessness". *W. (a minor) v. Dolbey.*[10]

Subsequently a majority of the House of Lords held that "wilfully" means "recklessly" as well as "intentionally". *R. v. Sheppard.*[11]

19.4 In the *Cunningham* case, Professor Kenny's *Outlines of Criminal Law*, 16th edition was quoted with approval:

"In any statutory definition of a crime, malice must not be taken in the old vague sense of wickedness in general but as requiring either (i) actual intention to do the particular kind of harm that was in fact done; or (ii) recklessness as to whether such harm should occur or not (i.e. the accused had foreseen that the particular kind of harm might be done and yet has gone on to take the risk of it). It is neither limited nor does it indeed require any ill-will towards the person injured."

6. (1872) L.R. 1 C.C.R. 356.
7. (1874) L.R. 2 C.C.R. 119.
8. (1881) 8 Q.B.D. 254.
9. [1957] Cr. App. R. 155, C.C.A.
10. [1983] Crim. L.R. 681, D.C.
11. [1980] 3 All E.R. 899, H.L.

19.5 Professor Kenny's views have received added endorsement in the House of Lords' decisions in *R.* v. *Caldwell*[12] and *R.* v. *Lawrence*[13] which are currently regarded as leading decisions when "recklessness" should be equated with "wilfulness". Caldwell had conceived a grudge against his employer, got himself into an advanced state of intoxication, and had set fire to the residential hotel where he worked. He pleaded that he was so drunk that he never appreciated the risk to those who lived there. Fortunately, the fire was put out without difficulty and without any harm to life or limb. To Lord Diplock, Professor Kenny was at pains to indicate, by the words in brackets, the particular species within the genus "reckless states of mind" that constitute "malice" in criminal law. His Lordship thought that the Professor's views may have been suitable for the Malicious Damage Act 1861, but now that the Criminal Damage Act 1971 was law, he could go a little further:

"In my opinion, a person charged with an offence under Section 1(1) of the Criminal Justice Act 1971 is 'reckless' as to whether any such property would be destroyed or damaged if
  (1) he does an act which in fact creates an obvious risk that property will be destroyed or damaged and
  (2) when he does the act he either has not given any thought to the responsibility of there being any such risk or has recognised that there was some risk involved but has nonetheless gone on to do it."

19.6 Lord Edmund Davies felt some measure of disagreement with Lord Diplock. He drew attention to the thoughts of the Law Commission which led to the Criminal Damage Act 1971:

"A person may be reckless if (a) knowing that there is a risk that an event may result from his conduct or that a circumstance may exist, he takes that risk, and (b) it is unreasonable for him to take it, having regard to the degree and nature of the risk which he knows to be present."

19.7 There is currently some belief that the principles enunciated by these two cases have been altered by the recent cases concerning two doctors, an anaesthetist and a plumber, but it is suggested that this is not so. These cases concerned death caused by "gross negligence" when carrying out professional duties, and this is not necessarily to be equated with recklessness or malice.

19.8 The criminal law gives some help with equating "recklessness" with "malice" and "maliciously" even if it does not always do so in a clear and unambiguous way. It must be remembered, however, that the criminal law only regards a wrongful act as a crime if there is intent, and it therefore has to ask if "recklessness" in any particular circumstances is of such a nature that intent can be said to exist. In the civil field, "recklessness" can generally be described as such irresponsible conduct that a reasonable man must have foreseen that harm would result either to person or to property, and there need not be intent in the criminal sense to cause that harm in any shape or form. It will be noted from the quoted cases that for the commission of a crime, and particularly where it is to be equated with "malice" or "maliciously", "recklessness" has to be defined in a narrower and stricter sense than is necessary for the civil law.[14]

---

12. [1982] A.C. 341.
13. [1982] A.C. 510.
14. For examples of recklessness in marine insurance cases, see the *Orient* and *Isothel* cases (paras. 29.4, 29.5).

19.9 Turning now to the *Oxford English Dictionary*, it is suggested that it contains no surprises. "Malice" is: Bad quality, badness; chiefly in a moral sense wickedness. Power to harm, harmfulness; harmful action or effect. The desire to injure another person; active ill-will or hatred. Wrongful intention generally. That kind of evil intent which constitutes the aggravation of guilt distinctive of certain offences; whilst "maliciously": "In a spirit of malice or ill-will".

19.10 The field is still open to the courts to define "any person acting maliciously", and it is not for the author to forecast what the judges will decide. This work contains a warning about equating criminal offences and insured perils too readily (see paras. 5.3 and 5.4). Even so, it is respectfully suggested that this insured peril is more akin to criminal acts as indicated by the quoted cases. Moreover, "recklessness" (which is not an insured peril) will only be included within the bounds of the insured peril if it is "malice" within the sense of Professor Kenny's definition as extended by Lords Diplock and Edmund Davies. It may be helpful to describe some of the cases where the Mutual War Risks Associations have accepted claims on the basis that persons were "acting maliciously":

(1) In Haifa, fires broke out simultaneously in the ship's crew accommodation aft, in the accommodation amidships and in the paint store forward. The fire brigade found definite evidence that arsonists had been at work. The crew could have caused these fires, but it was thought more likely that the stevedores had done so, being disgruntled with the Master.

(2) In Canada, drunken youths threw inflatable life rafts over the side of ferries to see if they floated.

(3) Again in Canada, a moored ship was cut adrift.

(4) In Mombasa, three naval ratings from H.M.S. *Eagle*, well gone in drink and disgusted with their officers, their ship and East Africa in general, entered the engine room of a merchant ship and smashed all the gauge-glasses.

(5) Between Durban and Singapore, a North Korean crew expressed their disgruntled feelings with the owners and the Greek officers by throwing the navigation equipment overboard.

19.11 This does leave open the argument that a collision may be caused "maliciously" and even "recklessly" in the sense used in this chapter. Collision is a risk which is within the Marine Policy. Both the new Institute War and Strikes Clauses, like their predecessors, and the Rules of the Mutual War Risks Associations, exclude from the cover any loss, damage, liability or expense which is covered by the Marine Policy, and these provisions would seem to be sufficient to exclude any question of a claim on the War Risk Policy.

POLITICAL MOTIVE

19.12 "Political motive" so far appears to have received no judicial definition, and the *Oxford English Dictionary* defines political in a restrictive way, more in line with the actions of a civilised democratic society rather than in the sense it is obviously intended to have in War and Strikes insurance. In the early history of this insured peril, "political motive" was intended to include such actions as those of Cuban exiles in Miami in 1964. Disapproving of British ships trading to Cuba, they placed limpet mines on the hulls of British ships regardless of whether they were themselves trading with Cuba. During the early stages of its work, Mr. Alan Jackson's Committee considered "ideological motive". It was felt that this was too narrow for the purposes of the war and strikes insurance.

19.13 It will be apparent to the reader that there is a considerable degree of overlap between "terrorists", "acting maliciously" and "political motive". The underwriters are concerned to give insurance cover which is within the ambit of the War Risk Policy with limits which are reasonable having regard to the purposes of that policy. As always, this insurance is given in advance of any judicial decisions or guidance which may dictate alteration or revision to the insured perils or at least the views expressed in this work. The best that can presently be done is to describe the intentions behind the inclusion of these insured perils.

CHAPTER 20

Piracy

20.1 For many years, piracy was insured under the S.G. Form with Institute War and Strikes Clauses attached and was thus a peril insured by the war policy. In 1983, the new MAR form transferred the risk to the Marine Policy. This does have the advantage of including loss by piracy and loss by thieves under one policy, and makes unnecessary the drawing of fine distinctions between the two. On the other hand, shipowners who have marine policies on forms other than the MAR form may well find that their marine policies do not include piracy, and the new war risks policy on the MAR form does not include this insured peril either. There is thus the danger of being inadvertently uninsured for this important risk. In order to prevent this happening to their members, the Mutual War Risk Associations continue to insure the perils of "piracy and violent theft by persons from outside the ship" in the war policy, where their members traditionally expect to find them. This can lead to double insurance, and it is necessary that the Associations' Rules contain a reservation that claims so arising: " . . . will be payable subject to Section 80 of the Marine Insurance Act 1906." thus leaving open the claim for a contribution from the marine underwriters.

20.2 "Piracy" and "pirates" are elastic terms whose meanings can vary depending on the circumstances. There is:

(1) Piracy *jure gentium* by *hostes humani generis*, or piracy against the Law of Nations by the enemies of all mankind. It is a criminal offence, and any state which captures a pirate may try and punish him regardless of where his crimes were committed.

(2) Piracy which is a crime against the domestic laws of a state. These will vary from state to state.

(3) Piracy as defined by various League of Nations or United Nations Conventions. These have their own purposes.

(4) Piracy as defined by statute entitling officers and men of the Royal Navy to a bounty for dealing with pirates.

(5) Piracy for the purposes of commercial documents such as charterparties, bills of lading, and insurance policies.

20.3 This work is particularly concerned with the last aspect, but there are some common threads which run through them all, and in considering "piracy" as applied to commercial documents, the other aspects cannot be dismissed. Moreover, during the years, the public perception of pirates has changed. In days gone by, the pirate was regarded as a kind of romantic outlaw or an unmitigated and very dangerous nuisance, depending upon whether one's livelihood was totally independent of, or dependent upon, the sea. Today the emphasis is on international and uniform laws to suppress this dangerous species even if, at the time of writing, much has yet to be done to make this effective.

20.4 The early cases provide little help even in the criminal field. This is not surprising when the difficulties are remembered of bringing pirates, when caught, to trial. The Captain of an 18th or 19th century warship who captured pirates could not readily send them for trial in the nearest Admiralty Court which might be thousands of miles away. If alone, he could not leave his station. To send them in another ship meant sending with them some of his best officers and men to give evidence. It could be months, if ever, before he saw them again. To keep them on board as prisoners until his commission was finished posed dangers of an unacceptable nature to his own ship and crew. So he did what his superiors expected him to do. He hanged them from the yardarm with no more formality than an entry in the logbook. Nobody would have dreamt of suggesting that he had committed murder, but it did little to provide a body of judicial precedent. Such criminal trials as did take place are scantily reported. Pirates were pirates who had met their just deserts and there was no point in labouring the fact.

20.5 Two early cases are quoted in connection with piracy, *Jeffery* v. *Legender*[1] and *R.* v. *Dawson*.[2] In the *Jeffery* case, the ship was bound from London to Naples, and her insurance contained a warranty that she was to depart with convoy. In June (the year is uncertain) she did so. Two days later, she was separated from the convoy by a storm and sought refuge in Foy (Fowey). The rest of the convoy anchored in Tor Bay, 10 leagues away. The following March, she sailed to rejoin her convoy, but another tempest drove her 70 leagues away where she was taken by pirates. The report does not define pirates, or recite any evidence that they were in fact responsible for her loss. Possibly this was regarded as unnecessary, because the case turned on whether she had, or had not, complied with her warranty. Holt C.J. and the majority of the court held that she had complied with her warranty, and awarded judgment to the plaintiffs.

20.6 The *Dawson* case[3] was a criminal trial of Dawson and his five co-accused. All six were seamen who had not been paid. They, and others who were not before the court, decided that self-help was justified. They took the *Charles II* on which some of them were serving and, having first landed the officers and other seamen who would not go with them, "feloniously and piratically" took three English and two Danish ships besides other serious depredations before they were apprehended. All were acquitted on one charge (even Dawson, who had pleaded guilty) but were convicted on the remaining charges and disappeared from history under the inelegant procedures of the time for dealing with convicted pirates. Sir Charles Hedges directed the jury:

"Now piracy is only a sea term for robbery, piracy being a robbery committed within the jurisdiction of the Admiralty. If a man be assaulted within that jurisdiction, and his ship or goods violently taken away without a legal authority, this is robbery and piracy. If the mariners of any ship shall violently dispossess the Master, and afterwards carry away the ship

1. (1692) 3 Lev. 320.
2. (1696) St. Tr. 5.
3. *Ibid.*

itself, or any of the goods, or tackle, apparel, or furniture, with a felonious intention, in any place where the Lord Admiral hath, or pretends to have jurisdiction, this is also robbery and piracy.

Now the jurisdiction of the Admiralty is declared, and described in the statute, and commission, by virtue of which we here meet, and is extended throughout all seas, and the ports, creeks, and rivers beneath the first bridges next the sea even unto the higher water mark.''

This singularly robust direction, accompanied by a further direction on ''your duty'', probably represents the criminal law today, although the strict insistence on the Admiralty's jurisdiction is somewhat modified by the recent case of *The Andreas Lemos*,[4] at any rate so far as piracy in commercial documents is concerned.

20.7 Dr. Lushington added some further judgments which are of some limited help only. The first of these, *The Serhassan Pirates*,[5] dealt with claims for bounty by Royal Navy officers and men which the court held to be due to them by the provisions of a statute which was aimed at the suppression of piracy. On the 10th May, 1843, H.M.S. *Dido*, having received a report of a piratical act against a ship, despatched two cutters under the command of Lt. Horton to patrol a stretch of the Borneo coast. An interpreter was sent with them. When the two cutters came near to Serhassan Island, six prahns (a type of native craft) rounded a point and approached the cutters. From the beating of gongs and other signs, their intentions were clearly hostile. Even so, the two cutters covered their cannon and attempted to parley. At 150 yards range, the prahns opened fire and a brisk engagement ensued. One prahn was captured, and her surviving crew were made prisoners. The rest fled to the shore with the cutters in hot pursuit. The pirates were rounded up and treated to a firm lecture by Lt. Horton. Nobody was going to be taken off for trial but it had to be clearly understood that this sort of behaviour would not be tolerated. No doubt with the aim of making them the best policemen of the area that could be hoped for, it was made clear that any repetition, by them or by anybody else in the neighbourhood, would result in their island being laid waste. It is clear from the report that the engagement, whilst close to the land, was still at sea, whilst its ferocity can be judged by the fact that 33 pirates out of 120 were killed. The prahns were well equipped with cannon, other firearms, spears and knives. Dr. Lushington, noting that Lt. Horton had done everything possible to avoid bloodshed:

''It matters not that they may possibly have entertained no inclination to bring themselves in conflict with the British power; it is sufficient, in my view of the question, to clothe their conduct with a piratical character if they were armed and prepared to commence a piratical attack upon any other persons.

Now can it be imagined that the title of pirate attaches solely persons following an avowed piratical occupation upon the high sea(s)? In the seas where this transaction took place, there is every species of distinction to be found. There are for example, persons who carry on the sole business of pirate, and whose only occupation is piracy. There are others, again, who resort to it only at fixed and particular periods; whilst others are found, who, availing themselves of contingent circumstances, show a piratical disregard of all rights only as opportunities favourable to the attempt may arise.''

4. *Athens Maritime Enterprises Corporation* v. *Hellenic Mutual War Risks Association (Bermuda) Ltd.* (*The Andreas Lemos*) [1982] 2 Lloyd's Rep. 483. See paras. 20.33–20.38.
5. (1845) 2 Rob. 354.

20.8 This case makes an important distinction. For the purpose of claiming the bounty, the petitioners did not have to show that the pirates were the enemies of all mankind. It was sufficient that they were sea robbers. The same distinction will be noted in the insurance cases, *Republic of Bolivia* v. *Indemnity Mutual Marine Insurance Co. Ltd.*[6] and *The Andreas Lemos*.[7]

20.9 The *Eliza Cornish's* voyage was adventurous in the extreme, both at sea and subsequently in the courts. The ship was insured for £1,800 under a time policy from 22nd April, 1851, to 21st April, 1852. The insured perils included both "pirates" and "takings at sea". *Dean* v. *Hornby*[8] dealt with the claim against the underwriters, whilst the Royal Naval personnel again claimed their bounty for dealing with pirates in *The Magellan Pirates*.[9] There were yet further proceedings with which this work is not concerned. In 1851 there was some political unrest in Chile and, during the ship's voyage, some of the officers and soldiers, who were in league with the convicts of the penal settlement which they were guarding in Punta Arenas, mutinied and murdered or deposed their superiors. The ringleader was a Lt. Cambiaso.

1851

7th November

The ship sails from Valparaiso bound for Liverpool with a cargo of guano, cocoa, bark and a quantity of specie said to be worth £20,000.

1st December

The ship puts in to Punta Arenas to repair some minor storm damage. She is forcibly seized by Cambiaso and his men. The Master and Mr. Deane, a passenger and part owner, are murdered. The rest of the crew are imprisoned.

13th December

The Mate and the rest of the crew, under duress, agree to prepare the ship for sea.

31st December

The ship sails under the command of Briones, one of Cambiaso's accomplices, with nearly 200 people on board. By now she is armed with cannon and the men of the party are also armed.

1852

2nd January

The ship joins an American ship, the *Florida*, which has similarly been taken. Her owner, who was on board, has also been murdered. She is commanded by Cambiaso himself.

At some stage, a further murder is committed. A Chilean Government revenue cutter is found to be ashore on a sandbank. A musket is fired in her direction and one of the customs officers is killed.

There is a Royal Navy squadron in Valparaiso and the Chilean Government requests Admiral Thoresby for help. H.M.S. *Virago* is despatched.

28th January

The ship is sighted and chased and a shot is fired across her bows to stop her. She surrenders. One hundred and twenty-eight armed men, 24 women and 18 children are found on board. They are sent in the ship to Valparaiso with a Royal Navy party on board to guard the prisoners and to sail the ship.

6. [1909] 1 K.B. 785, 792.
7. Footnote 4, above.
8. (1854) El. & Bl. 180.
9. (1853) 1 Sp. 81.

15th February

The *Florida* is recaptured at San Carlos, Chile Island, and all the insurgents who can be captured are handed over to the Chilean authorities. The specie is found on board the *Florida* and recovered.

23rd February

The ship reaches Valparaiso and the prisoners are sent ashore. The Royal Naval party remains on board.

10th March

The ship leaves Valparaiso for Liverpool under the command of Mr. Charles Bowden. This gentleman is described as a Queen's officer and appears to be a navigation Master in H.M.S. *Daedalus*. As such, he is perfectly competent to navigate the ship with the help of a naval crew. Admiral Thoresby is sending her home for adjudication by the Admiralty Court.

24th April

The ship puts in to Montevideo to repair some heavy weather damage.

30th April

Notice of Abandonment is tendered and refused by the underwriters.

19th August

Having suffered yet further heavy weather damage, the ship puts in to Fayal for repairs. The surveyors think that she is beyond repair and, on their recommendation, Mr. Bowden sells her. This he has no right to do.

9th December

A writ is issued against the underwriters.

At some unknown time

The naval party arrives in the United Kingdom with the purchase price. They are shortly followed by the *Eliza Cornish* herself. She has been repaired by her purchaser at a "trifling cost" and has been put back into service. The shipowners and the underwriters join together to apply to the Admiralty Court for an order for possession. This is granted, and the ship is sold with the proceeds of sale being deposited to await the outcome of the proceedings.

20.10 *The Magellan Pirates*[10] was heard first and Dr. Lushington, being in no doubt that the Royal Naval personnel were entitled to bounty, dealt rather cursorily with the case: "I apprehend that, in the administration of our criminal law, generally speaking, all persons are held to be pirates who are found guilty of piratical acts; and piratical acts are robbery and murder on the high seas." He quoted with approval from *Russell on Crime*:

"The offence of piracy, at common law, consists in committing those acts of piracy and depredation on the high seas, which, if committed on land, would have amounted to a felony there . . . If robbery be committed in creeks, harbours, ports etc. in foreign countries, the Court of Admiralty indisputably has jurisdiction of it, and such an offence is consequently piracy."

20.11 It was pleaded by H.M. Treasury that the taking of the two ships and the murders were committed in port and not at sea, and therefore there was no question of piracy. The court declined to make a hard and fast ruling. The ships were carried away by those who seized them and the murders and depredations could be taken as continuing on the high seas. Moreover the court considered that there was

10. *Ibid.*

no connection with the political unrest, and that these were acts of wanton cruelty and murder of foreign nationals. In any case, an insurgent could also be a pirate.

20.12 In the *Dean* case[11] which followed, there appears to have been little inclination to question the opinion of so distinguished a judge as Dr. Lushington. The question turned on whether the shipowner had the right to claim for a total loss or whether, having had the opportunity to recover his ship, he was entitled to a partial loss only. He was held entitled to a total loss in a decision which clearly stretched many points in his favour.

20.13 Two other cases appear in connection with piracy, *Re Tivnan and Others*[12] and *Attorney General for Our Lady the Queen for the Colony of Hong Kong* v. *Kwok-a-Sing*.[13] Both were extradition cases, and as such were surrounded by the usual number of complicating issues which are to be expected in such proceedings.

20.14 During the American Civil War, Tivnan (or Tevana) and his accomplices were passengers on board a Unionist (the North) schooner, the *Joseph E. Gerity*, bound for New York with a cargo of cotton. They seized the ship and turned the Master and some others adrift. By their own exertions, they managed to save themselves. Subsequently some of the persons who seized the ship took refuge in the United Kingdom, and the United States applied for their extradition for trial as pirates on the high seas. This was refused due to the complications of the extradition treaties, but quite apart from this it may be questioned if they were even pirates at all. Their leader, Hogg, was said to be a Major in the Confederate (the South) army and if this was true, they were probably acting on the authority of a *de facto* government.

20.15 Kwok was a Chinese coolie who sailed with 309 other coolies from Macao for Peru on board a French ship, *La Nouvelle Penelope*. Under Portuguese law, the coolies could only be sent abroad if they consented to go and signed a contract to that effect. Their confinement in barracoons ashore, and the escort of Portuguese soldiers down to the ship, raised questions just how freely this consent was given. Once on board, they were confined below at night but were permitted to walk around the fore part of the ship in the daytime. They were forbidden to go aft, and a barricade with cannon athwartships prevented this. About 100 coolies complained that they had been kidnapped and Kwok, with a large body of disgruntled coolies, stormed the after part of the ship, killing the Captain and some of the crew. They threw the bodies overboard and forced the remaining mariners to return to China where they made good their escape. Kwok was arrested in Hong Kong as a suspicious character and a danger to the Queen's peace. China applied for his extradition. This was also refused, again due to the complications of the extradition treaties. The Hong Kong courts, which twice released Kwok under the Habeas Corpus Act, seemed to have taken the view that the ship was a slave ship and that Kwok was entitled to regain his liberty by whatever means were open to him, even committing murder to do so. The Attorney General appealed to the Privy Council which took the opposite view. The Council did not agree that the evidence showed that the ship was a slave ship, and considered that there was no justification for the murders. It thought that Kwok should have been prosecuted in Hong Kong for pir-

11. (1854) El. & Bl. 180.
12. (1864) 5 B. & S. 645.
13. (1873) L.R. 5 P.C. 179.

acy *jure gentium*. Lord Mellish approved Sir Charles Hedges' direction to the jury in the *Dawson* case (para. 20.6) and added: "Of course there can be no difference between mariners and passengers, and there was unquestionably evidence that Kwok-A-Sing was a party to violently dispossessing the Master, and carrying away the ship herself and the goods therein."

20.16 The views of two important 19th century writers are worth noting. Sir Robert Phillimore defined piracy in *International Law*, 3rd edition (1879): "Piracy is an assault upon vessels navigated on the high seas, committed *animo furandi* whether robbery or forcible depredation be effected or not or whether or not it be accomplished by murder or personal injury", whilst Kenny (writing at least before 1930) defined it as follows: "Piracy is any armed violence at sea which is not a lawful act of war."

20.17 At the beginning of the 20th century, the law on "piracy" and "pirates" was, for the purpose of interpreting a commercial document, not entirely clear. It could, however, be said with reasonable certainty that if people robbed at sea and employed a measure of violence in doing so, they were "pirates", and it was not necessary, for the purpose of an insurance policy, that they should also be the enemies of all mankind. It was of course necessary that there should be *animo furandi*, which can be broadly translated as "ferocious intent". In addition, they were still "pirates" if the robberies were committed within the jurisdiction of the Admiralty Court, which included ports, creeks, and rivers. Some uncertainties were being introduced to the old common law jurisdiction which Sir Charles Hedges knew in the 1690s, because there were already moves afoot to define this jurisdiction by statute and this was bound to have a distorting effect.

20.18 During the 20th century, however, there have been a number of developments which have assisted understanding, including three important insurance cases.

The first of these is the Marine Insurance Act 1906 itself. Rule 8 for the construction of policies reads: "The term 'pirates' includes passengers who mutiny and rioters who attack the ship from the shore." This seems intended to give effect to the decision of the Privy Council in the *Kwok*[14] case, in preference to the decisions in the *Kleinwort*[15] and *Naylor*[16] cases (paras. 12.40–12.42, 12.38–12.39), where passengers mutiny. Since it is almost unimaginable that mutinous passengers and rioters from the shore can ever be regarded as the enemies of all mankind, as Dawson and his accomplices unquestionably were, there must be an inference that, for insurance purposes, the culprits need not have this characteristic, even though it is an essential element of piracy *jure gentium*.

20.19 Remote areas of the world were, in the 19th century, often the subject of frontier treaties without, however, demarcation on the ground, and this was very productive of disputes if it was found that the land had something valuable to offer. In 1867 a treaty between Bolivia and Brazil ceded Colonias to Bolivia. This remote region was reached only with the greatest difficulty by sailing up the River Amazon, beyond Manaus which ocean going ships could reach, navigating a tributary of the Amazon, and a further tributary of the tributary to reach the River Acre. There was a small population of Bolivians and Brazilians who seemed to get on amicably

14. (1873) L.R. 5 P.C. 179. See para. 20.15.
15. *Kleinwort* v. *Shepard* (1859) 1 El. & El. 447.
16. *Naylor* v. *Palmer* (1853) 8 Ex. 739.

enough, and such government as there was, was provided by Brazilian magistrates. Nobody seemed concerned that some of them exercised their jurisdiction on the Bolivian side of the agreed frontier. This sleepy backwater was galvanised into activity by the rubber boom of the late 19th century, which created vast fortunes and promoted Manaus into a prosperous city. The Bolivian Government now decided to assert its rights in Colonias, and despatched an expedition for this purpose. It would take months to arrive, and as a preliminary a Customs House was set up at Puerto Alonzo. None of this suited the Brazilian section of the population. They turned out the Customs officers, killing one of them, and, getting no support from the Brazilian Government, set up the independent Republic of El Acre. The Bolivian expedition, when it arrived, suppressed the Republic. Its adherents, however, had very definite prospects of forcing the Bolivians to leave. The expedition could only be supplied from the river, and it was simple to stop the steamers which came up the river from Para at the mouth of the Amazon. Several steamers were stopped but were permitted to proceed where no Bolivian Government property was found on board. The *Labrea*, loaded with stores for the expedition, was thus stopped and her stores, being the property of the Bolivian Government, were taken. They were insured on the S.G. Form from Para to Puerto Alonzo and/or other places on the River Acre. There was an F.C. & S. Clause, but "piracy" was expressly excluded from its operation and was thus an insured peril. In *Republic of Bolivia* v. *Indemnity Mutual Marine Insurance Company Limited*,[17] the plaintiffs claimed loss by piracy.

20.20 Pickford J. signed judgment in favour of the underwriters:

"The plaintiffs . . . have referred me to several definitions of piracy, some given by writers on international law and some by writers on criminal law. I am not sure that the definitions so given are necessarily in point on the question as to the meaning of the word in a policy of insurance . . . I am not at all sure that what might be piracy in international law is necessarily piracy within the meaning of the term in a policy of insurance. One has to look at what is the natural and clear meaning of the word 'pirates' in a document used by businessmen for business purposes."

Having said this, he considered that Hall's *International Law*, 5th edition, described the business meaning of piracy as well as any:

"Besides, though the absence of competent authority is the test of piracy, its essence consists in the pursuit of private, as contrasted with public, ends. Primarily the pirate is a man who satisfies his personal greed or his personal vengeance by robbery or murder in places beyond the jurisdiction of any State. The man who acts with a public object may do like acts to a certain extent, but his moral attitude is different, and the acts themselves will be kept within well marked bounds. He is not only not the enemy of the human race, but he is the enemy solely of a particular State."

20.21 On appeal, the plaintiff urged that a policy which covered a river passage only required that a special meaning should be given to piracy, and that there should be no strict insistence on the high seas. The defendants pointed out that the captors were trying to set up a State, and that they were not at war with the whole of mankind. Vaughan-Williams L.J. particularly approved Pickford J.'s adoption of Hall as the popular and business meaning of "pirate" and: "He is not a pirate who operates against the property of a State for a public end, such as setting up a State."

17. [1909] 1 K.B. 785; [1909] 1 K.B. 792 (C.A.).

20.22 In any case it could not be piracy: "In the first place, I do not think that the place where these events happened, . . . was a place where piracy could be committed . . . Piracy is a maritime offence, and what took place on this river . . . far up country, did not take place on the oceans at all . . . ".

20.23 Farwell L.J. wondered if this was a civil commotion. If it was, the appeal must fail. Kennedy L.J. thought Pickford J. was right, and quoted with approval from Carver on *Carriage of Goods by Sea*, 4th edition: "Piracy is a forcible robbery at sea, whether committed by marauders from outside the ship or by mariners or passengers within it. The essential element is that they violently dispossess the Master, and afterwards carry away the ship herself, or any of the goods with a felonious intent."

20.24 He seemed inclined to favour the idea that there could have been piracy here. This was a voyage wholly by the river and was insured as such. He did not pursue the point, there being plenty of other factors which on their own would have prevented a finding of piracy. Pirates plunder for their own gain, and not for such purposes as setting up their own State: "They seized the goods not for their private gain, but in furtherance of a political adventure . . . "

20.25 The appeal was accordingly dismissed. The case itself represents a very considerable advance in the law of piracy in a commercial insurance policy. The judges seem to have gone out of their way to give directions on the law for the benefit of assured and insurers alike, but the facts of the case prevented them from going to the full extent that commercial men would have wished.

20.26 *Banque Monetaca & Carystuiaki* v. *Motor Union Insurance Company Ltd.*[18] was a case of some complexity. In June, 1920, the *Filia* was bound from Constantinople to Batum. She had some engine trouble and anchored off the Turkish coast, first at Samsun and then at Kerassounde. Her insurance included the insured perils of "capture, seizure, or arrest and the consequences thereof, or warlike operations, whether before or after declaration of war". Piracy was however an excluded risk.

20.27 This was the time of great political upheaval in Turkey following the First World War. The Government of Turkey, before it was taken into the firm hands of Kemal Ataturk, was weak and uncertain. There was, however, the general aim of resisting the Greek army, which was preparing to invade Turkey, and of expelling it from the Aegean coast of the country. Some military operations had already taken place. In the Kerassounde area, a local warlord, Osman Agha, held sway. He was the President of the National Defence Association, a body affiliated to the Turkish Nationalists whose main aim was resistance to the Peace Treaty. Osman was in part a nationalist leader, and in part a feudal baron. Barons good, barons bad, Osman was one of the worst, looting and robbing his fief and helping himself to whatever took his fancy. He had recently boarded and robbed a French steamer, and the Kemalists had found it necessary to apologise to the French Government. The presence of the *Filia* aroused his worst instincts, and it was not long before he had boarded and seized her, even running up the Turkish flag. She was never recovered, and it appears that the Master, the crew, and the passengers were murdered.

18. (1923) 14 Ll.L.Rep. 48.

20.28 Roche J. declined to find that the *Filia*'s losses were due to piracy. Osman may have been a brigand of the most unpleasant sort with few, if any, saving graces, but:

"I am satisfied that he did capture and seize this Greek vessel under cover of and largely upon motives of a political character. That is to say, he desired to effect a stroke against the Greeks. It may be, and I dare say it was, the case that personal gain was also a motive, but the action in my view was dominantly political and military."

This led to the conclusion:

"I am satisfied, so far as I have the evidence, that in this case there was a loss from seizure and not from piracy."

On this, judgment was signed for the plaintiff.

20.29 The evidence here showed that Osman's main motives were to attack his country's enemies wherever he could find them, and they were thus military or political by nature rather than robbery for personal gain. He had some local standing, and even became governor of the province in December, 1920. Following the *Republic of Bolivia* case, it was impossible to call him a pirate. This was a seizure case.

20.30 *Re Piracy Jure Gentium*[19] is freely quoted in piracy cases although it was entirely criminal with no commercial elements at all. On the 1st April, 1931, two Chinese junks pursued a third cargo junk and fired shots at her from a range of 200 yards. They were prevented from boarding her by the very courageous intervention of two merchant steamers, the *Hang Sang* and the *Shui Chow*, until H.M.S. *Somme*, in answer to their radio messages, could arrive. Being unwilling to face the destroyer's massive fire power, the pirates surrendered and were taken off to Hong Kong for trial as pirates *jure gentium*. The jury found them guilty but themselves posed a question of law: "whether an accused person may be convicted of piracy in circumstances where no robbery has taken place".

20.31 The full Court of Hong Kong decided that, in such circumstances, there was no piracy without robbery, which meant that the accused had to be acquitted. This was a surprising decision, because the criminal law has, for many years, regarded an unsuccessful attempt to commit a crime as equally blameworthy as a successful one. It is possible that the court was misled by the previous legal writers to whom they looked for authority. The question was posed to the Privy Council whether actual robbery is an essential element to the crime of piracy *jure gentium*, or whether an attempt to commit a piratical robbery, albeit a frustrated attempt, will make the offence complete. The Privy Council answered: "Actual robbery is not an essential element to the crime of piracy *jure gentium*. A frustrated attempt to commit a piratical robbery is equally piracy *jure gentium*."

20.32 The Privy Council thus answered the narrow question posed by its terms of reference. It included a review of the findings of the previous legal writers, which is a fascinating account.[20] The Council did however add a passage of its own, after noting Kenny's view (para. 20.16) that piracy is "any armed violence at sea which is not a lawful act of war":

" . . . Although even this would include a shooting affray between passengers on a liner

19. [1934] A.C. 586.
20. The student of history will find this in the report, [1934] A.C. at pages 589–600.

which could not be held to be piracy. It would, however, correctly include those acts which, as far as their Lordships know, have always been held to be piracy, that is, where the crew or passengers of a vessel on the high seas rise against the Captain and officers and seek by armed force to seize the ship."

20.33 The Mutual War Risks Associations were much concerned with violent thefts, which became commonplace in the 1970s and the 1980s, particularly in the Malacca Straits and the roadstead to Singapore Port, the Nigerian coast, and the Caribbean. Whilst some of the robberies took place from moving ships and were daring in the extreme, most took place from ships at anchor within a State's territorial waters and were often accompanied by distressing incidents of murder, or at the least very serious assault and injury to the crews. Feeling that a more up-to-date decision was required, particularly on the liability of insurers whose policies covered "piracy", the Board of the Hellenic (Bermuda) Association decided to fight a test case when a particularly suitable incident occurred. This appeared soon enough with a claim on the *Andreas Lemos*.[21] The amount at stake was very small, $5,754.40, and the assured shipowner was guaranteed his costs. The Captain's report was accepted by each side as the facts of the case so that no witnesses need be called.

20.34 On 22nd June, 1977, the *Andreas Lemos* was at anchor off Chittagong at a point 3.5 nautical miles east from the Patenga light beacon and 2.8 nautical miles from the coast. She was well inside the Bangladeshi 12 mile limit, and was also within the port limits of Chittagong. During the evening the deck watchman found six or seven natives on the fo'c'sle throwing the mooring lines into the sea. He gave the alarm and, armed with a variety of weapons, the crew rushed forward. The natives drew knives. The sight of the Master's revolver, and the second officer's firing of Very lights close to their heads, caused a hasty change of mind. They dived into the sea and escaped on the sampans which had brought them to the ship. The hawsehole was secured and it is thought that they got on board with grapnels. Next morning four mooring ropes were found to be missing, one mooring rope had been cut in an attempt to remove it, and a long knife was also found. Staughton J. made the following findings:

1. Six or seven men were acting in concert as a gang, band or company.
2. They were not lawfully on board.
3. They came in one or more craft.
4. For a time, they were in effective control of the fo'c'sle.
5. They were seriously armed.

20.35 Staughton J. emphasised the difference which had appeared in the *Republic of Bolivia* case[22] between piracy *jure gentium*, which is a crime having definite requirements before a pirate can be prosecuted in any State regardless of where his crimes took place and of who was injured by his activities, and "piracy" as an insured peril: "It is by no means self evident that similar considerations (such as apply to piracy *jure gentium*) point to the same definitions of piracy for domestic purposes, and in particular for the interpretation of contracts of insurance." But

---

21. *Athens Maritime Enterprises Corporation* v. *Hellenic Mutual War Risks Association (Bermuda) Ltd. (The Andreas Lemos)* [1982] 2 Lloyd's Rep. 483.
22. Footnote 17, above. See paras. 20.18–20.25.

the malefactors must still be sea robbers. Carver's *Carriage of Goods by Sea*, 12th edition (1971) Volume I, paragraph 183, was particularly approved: "Piracy is forcible robbery at sea, whether committed by marauders from outside the ship, or by mariners and passengers within it."

20.36 Where can piracy (as an insured peril) take place? Sir Charles Hedges was very clear in the *Dawson* case[23] that it must take place within the jurisdiction of the Admiralty Court. Several other writers and judges have favoured the high seas, notably Dr. Lushington in *The Sarah*[24] and Lord Herschell in *The Zeta*.[25] "High seas" seemed an elastic term meaning different things to different judges. The authorities had been helpfully reviewed by Scott L.J. in *The Tolten*.[26] In the *Republic of Bolivia* case[27] Pickford J. "was not satisfied" that the incident had occurred within the jurisdiction of the Admiralty Court. Vaughan-Williams L.J. was quite categoric that it had not. Staughton J. made a clean sweep of the most incisive nature:

"In face of that authority, I cannot accept [the plaintiffs'] submission that piracy may be committed anywhere within the Common Law jurisdiction of the Court of Admiralty 'in places where great ships go' or 'at places where the tide flows, and below all bridges'. But I can see no reason to limit piracy to acts outside territorial waters. In the context of an insurance policy, if a ship is, in the ordinary meaning of the phrase, 'at sea', or if the attack upon her can be described as a 'maritime offence', then for the business purposes of a policy of insurance she is, in my judgment, in a place where piracy can be committed."

20.37 Support for this view came from the Supreme Court of the United States in *United States* v. *Furlong*[28] which concerned robbery from a vessel at anchor in a roadstead within a maritime league of the shore. Johnson J. gave the court's opinion: " . . . A vessel in an open road may well be found by the jury to be on the high seas. It is historically known, that in prosecuting trades in many places, vessels lie at anchor in open situations . . . ".

20.38 At this point, it might be thought that the owner of the *Andreas Lemos* had won his case. There was, however, a further essential element which, being absent, meant that judgment was signed in the Association's favour. The robbery must be committed by force, or the threat of force, which must be present when it is committed. The theft of the mooring ropes had taken place clandestinely and was complete without any force. Force was used, but only to make good the culprits' escape. It has long been the law in other fields that, where a crime requires force, the crime is not complete if force is only used to escape. In Staughton J.'s words: "The very notion of piracy is inconsistent with clandestine theft . . . Piracy is not committed by stealth."

20.39 As a matter of practice, the Mutual War Risks Associations have refused to recognise as piracy a claim where a ship was invaded by marauders and damaged whilst she was tied up alongside in the port of Santos. The port is in a lagoon which is approached by a narrow channel and the ship could not be said to be "at sea" in

23. *R.* v. *Dawson* (1696) St. Tr. 5. See para. 20.6.
24. (1862) Lush. 459.
25. [1893] A.C. 468.
26. [1946] P. 135.
27. [1909] 1 K.B. 785; [1909] 1 K.B. 792 (C.A.). See paras. 20.19–20.25.
28. (1820) 5 Wheat 184.

any sense of the word; moreover the marauders came from the shore and seemed to be the normal petty criminals which are to be found in any city or port. On the other hand, the Mutual War Risks Associations would have no difficulty in recognising Lt. Cambiaso's taking of the *Eliza Cornish* as a "maritime offence"[29] and thus basically piratical. Cambiaso was interested in taking the ship, besides committing murder, and not merely in causing a vandal's petty damage or removing some minor objects from her. Another case which was accepted by one of the Mutual War Risks Associations as a case of piracy is of interest. The ship was waiting at sea to enter the port of Lagos. She was not at anchor, but was stopped in the water with her engines on stand-by. She was boarded from a small boat by several persons who attacked the crew, forced open several of the containers, and began thieving. The ship was got under way and the marauders were chased off the deck. Before they dived into the sea, they let both the bower-anchors go. The anchor chains snapped, and both anchors were lost. It seemed uncertain exactly when the anchors were let go, but the Association concerned accepted that they were let go during the course of the thieving and the assaults upon the crew, and that this was a case of piracy.

20.40 As conclusions, the following are suggested:

1. Piracy as an insured peril in an insurance policy must be distinguished from the criminal offence of piracy *jure gentium*, or a criminal offence under a local statute. The two have a number of similarities but:

   (a) the criminal offence will only exist if the accused is *hostes humani generis*—the enemy of all mankind—so that he may be tried and punished by any State which captures him, regardless of where he has committed his depredations or whom he has injured whereas,

   (b) for the purposes of the insured peril in any insurance policy, he need only be a "sea robber", and the further conclusions which follow relate to such a "sea robber" only.

2. Piracy must be committed "at sea" or "on the sea" as it is generally understood in everyday parlance, and such considerations as port limits or a State's territorial waters are immaterial.

3. Piracy may be committed in ports, harbours or inland waters immediately adjacent to the sea provided that it merits the new concept developed by Staughton J. from the *Republic of Bolivia*[30] case of "maritime offence". A ready example is *The Magellan Pirates*[31] where the ship was seized in Punta Arenas for use as a pirate ship. It is suggested that Dr. Lushington would have approved this concept had it been proposed. Again, a distinction must be made with mere opportunistic thieving in the same places which is not piracy.

4. Violence, or the threat of violence, is an essential element to piracy as it is to robbery and must be present before or at the time the offence is committed. Violence only to effect escape is not sufficient.

5. A pirate's aim must be his personal gain but this need not be material gain.

29. *Dean* v. *Hornby* (1854) E. & B. 180; *The Magellan Pirates* (1853) 1 Sp. 81. See paras. 20.9–20.12.
30. Footnote 27, above.
31. Footnote 29, above.

It will be sufficient if his depredations are committed to satisfy his desire to cause material or physical harm to others.

6. There is no piracy where the predators are pursuing political aims, however unlikely their fulfilment might be. They were undoubtedly pursuing political aims in the *Republic of Bolivia*[32] case, but it might not be so easy to distinguish whether the culprits in the *City of Poros* massacre [1988] were motivated by a political aim or a simple psychotic desire to murder, and any enquiry is unlikely to reach a definite conclusion. This might not give rise to difficulty if they can be described by the newly introduced insured peril of "terrorist", on which there is, so far, only one judicial decision.

7. There is no piracy where the predators are acting under the authority of a State or with a State's commission, however atrocious their acts may be.

8. It seems to be generally accepted that in English law both passengers and crew may commit piracy by seizing the ship and there are several indications among the judgments quoted above that this is so. It is hard to draw a distinction between an outsider who robs a seaman or a passenger, and a fellow seaman or passenger who does the same thing. It is not clearly defined in the judgments.

9. The *Greene*[33] and *Hai Hsuan*[34] cases indicate an important apparent difference between American and English law. In English law the crew can seize their own ship and thereby commit piracy, whereas two important American decisions indicate that a crew cannot seize that which is already entrusted to them and is lawfully in their possession; they can only be barrators because they abuse the trust reposed in them. It is suggested, however, that this apparent difference should be approached with caution, and in future American decisions it could disappear.

20.41 Piracy, after a long period as an insured peril of the war insurance, is now returned to the marine insurance, except for the insurance provided by the Mutual War Risks Associations. The insurance given in respect of ships, freight, containers and cargo is not always uniform one with another, and this is described in the chapters devoted to these objects.

---

32. Footnote 27, above.

33. *Greene* v. *Pacific Mutual Life Insurance Co.* (1864) 91 Mass. (9 Allan) 217. See paras. 12.43–12.45.

34. *Republic of China, China Merchants Steam Navigation Co. Ltd. and the United States of America* v. *National Union Fire Insurance Co. of Pittsburg, Pennsylvania (The Hai Hsuan)* [1957] 1 Lloyd's Rep. 428; [1958] 1 Lloyd's Rep. 351. See paras. 12.46–12.51.

CHAPTER 21

Confiscation and expropriation

THE CLAUSES

21.1 "Confiscation" and "Expropriation" are new insured perils. They first appeared in the new Institute Clauses when they were introduced with the MAR form in the early 1980s. They did not figure in the S.G. Form or the Institute Clauses attached to it. They are not insured perils of the new Cargo Clauses, which were introduced at the same time, and which do not contain the excluded risks which will be discussed in this chapter.

Ships

21.2 The Institute War and Strikes Hulls—Time 1.10.83 contain "Confiscation" and "Expropriation" as insured perils in Clause 1.6. The relevant exclusions read:

"4. Exclusions
   This insurance excludes
   4.1 Loss damage liability or expense arising from
       4.1.3 requisition or pre-emption
       4.1.4 capture seizure arrest restraint detainment confiscation or expropriation by or under the order of the Government or any public or local authority of the country in which the vessel is owned or registered."

Freight

21.3 The Institute War and Strikes Clauses Freight—Time 1.10.83 contain the same insured perils as the ships' hulls insurance, except that they are numbered Clause 1.2.3 and must be caused by "loss (total or partial) of the subject matter insured arising from loss or damage to the vessel". The exclusions are the same except that Clause 4.1 reads: "4.1 loss (total or partial) or expense arising from".

Containers insured on the London Market

21.4 The Institute War and Strikes Clauses Containers—Time 1.1.87 contain the same insured perils and exclusions as the ship's insurance, except that Clauses 4.1.3 and 4.1.4 become 5.1.3 and 5.1.4, and the government or public authority must be in the place where the assured have their principal place of business. Containers are not registered as ships are.

21.5 Containers are insured for their marine insurance by the Institute Container

Clauses—Time 1.1.87 on an "all risks" basis except for their machinery, which is effectively insured for a list of insured perils. It is necessary for them to have an additional exclusion which is not found in the marine insurance for ships or for freight. This reads:

> "6 In no case shall this insurance cover loss damage liability or expense caused by
> 6.4 confiscation nationalisation requisition or pre-emption."

Containers insured by the two Through Transport Mutual Insurance Associations

21.6 The insurance given by these two Mutual Insurance Associations is best left to Chapter 39. There are some differences; for instance, the insurance of requisitioned containers is not terminated by the requisition. It is, in effect, merely suspended.

MATTERS CONSIDERED BY THIS CHAPTER

21.7 It is thus necessary to discuss in this chapter not only the insured perils of "Confiscation" and "Expropriation", but also the excluded risks of "requisition", "pre-emption" and "nationalisation". It is also necessary to distinguish "angary".

CONFISCATION, EXPROPRIATION

21.8 So far, there has been no judicial determination of these new insured perils in the context of War and Strikes insurance. Some limited help is obtained from the *Dictionary of English Law* by Earl Jowitt, because this takes into account the mass of legal decisions which have been given in other fields. "Confiscation" is defined:

"In international law, is where a state seizes property, belonging to another state, or to its subjects, and appropriates it. Confiscation is the punishment for carrying contraband of war or for attempting to carry supplies to a place besieged or blockaded."

21.9 "Expropriation" is defined:

"Compulsorily depriving a person of a right of property belonging to him in return for compensation. The term has been introduced from its use in foreign countries to denote a compulsory purchase of land etc. for public purposes."

21.10 Neither definition seems comprehensive enough for this modern world, and it is more than likely that in a future case, the courts will give these insured perils wider meanings than this. The punishment for carrying contraband is not always strictly enforced, and there is no compulsion on a state to take this extreme measure. During the Iran/Iraq War, the Iranian navy insisted on some ships bound for Kuwait, which was the Iraqis' main supply port, going into Bandar Abbas for search. Being a belligerent, they were quite entitled to do this. Any contraband found on board was discharged in Bandar Abbas, and the ship was then permitted to sail. Furthermore, expropriation has not been confined to foreign countries. During the 19th and 20th centuries, a great deal of land has been expropriated to build railways, motorways and houses in the United Kingdom. This has invariably been done under statutory powers, and has often been given the name of "compulsory purchase".

21.11 It has been suggested that "Confiscation" and "Expropriation" have been introduced to clarify the War and Strikes insurance in the light of the *Anita* decision,[1] but the purpose must have been wider than this. These two new insured perils are particularly suitable, perhaps even designed, to deal explicitly with the regrettable propensity of certain States to seize ships and other insured objects, often under the flimsiest of pretexts and sometimes by the most dubious means. As such, these new insured perils are intended to increase the scope of the insurance which was previously provided by the insured peril of "seizure". There are some limits. As it will be seen from the quotation of Clause 4.1.4 in the ships' War and Strikes insurance (Clause 5.1.4 in the case of containers), there is no insurance for confiscation or expropriation by the authorities of the country where the ship is "owned or registered", or, in the case of containers, "where the Assured have their principal place of business". The assured is taken to have accepted the risks of doing business there. There is another exclusion which is intended to exclude insurance in case of the assured's blameworthy conduct. In the ships' War and Strikes insurance, Clause 4.1.5 reads:

"*4 Exclusions*

This insurance excludes
4.1 loss damage liability or expense arising from
    4.1.5 arrest restraint detainment confiscation or expropriation under quarantine
        regulations or by reason of infringement of any customs or trading regulations."

This clause is numbered 5.1.5 in the containers' War and Strikes insurance.

21.12 The result is that confiscation and expropriation is insured in all respects save for these two instances, and thus there is insurance for some of the outlandish things that nowadays happen in some countries.

REQUISITION

21.13 Most countries have laws requiring their subjects to assist in times of national emergency, which is not confined to wartime, and to allow the authorities, not necessarily the military or naval authorities, to use their property in the national interest. As a general, but not invariable, rule, compensation must be paid for the time that it is used and for any damage that it may suffer. An exception to this general rule will be noted in the *Robinson* case.[2] In the United Kingdom requisition has been part of the Royal Prerogative for many centuries, although since the late 18th century the acquisition of land for such purposes as building fortifications, billeting troops and providing them with training areas, has been governed by statutes whose provisions reflect the Royal Prerogative. This has not been abolished, but it is in many cases easier to proceed under the terms of a written Act of Parliament which supersedes it and the executive has taken advantage of the greater convenience which the statutes offer. Where the State needs to acquire ships it still uses

---

1. *Panamanian Oriental Steamship Corpn.* v. *Wright (The Anita)* [1970] 2 Lloyd's Rep. 371.
2. *Robinson Gold Mining Co. & Others* v. *Alliance Insurance Co.* [1901] 2 K.B. 919; [1902] 2 K.B. 489 (H.L.). See paras. 12.22–12.28.

the ancient powers of the Royal Prerogative. Swinfen Eady L.J. described this in *The Broadmayne* case (para. 21.18): "It is not disputed—indeed it is beyond dispute—that it is part of the Prerogative of the Crown in times of emergency to requisition British ships."

21.14 To give examples, the Royal Prerogative was used to acquire British ships on the 3rd August, 1914, before the First World War broke out, on the acquisition of British ships for the Anglo-French invasion of the Suez Canal area in 1956, and to support the Falkland's Task Force on the 4th April, 1982. In each case a Royal Proclamation was made which defined the requisitioning officers' powers, and recognised that compensation would be payable and terms of engagement agreed. The Royal Prerogative is very wide, and would allow ships to be acquired by transferring their title to the Crown. In practice this is not done, and the Crown can satisfy itself with leaving their title and their operations in the hands of their owners, merely contenting itself with being able to order their use. This ensures that the ships remain in the hands of skilled ship managers, who see to it that they are insured, have sufficient crews, are victualled, kept in class with the necessary dry dockings, and supplied with all the other details which a ship requires. This puts the Crown in the position of a time charterer, which is perfectly adequate for its purposes; this is requisition "for use".

21.15 It is perhaps understandable that the courts have not welcomed the opportunity to define requisition with any degree of total precision and it would appear that any such definition would not be helpful. It has been said that the Royal Prerogative can only be used in connection with British ships when they are in the territorial waters of the United Kingdom. In the *Russian Bank* case[3] where the British Admiralty requisitioned the *Wolverhampton* in Novorossijsk and placed her at the disposal of the Russian Government, Bailhache J. was in no doubt that the requisition was *ultra vires*:

"It is suggested . . . that the requisition in this case is within the Royal Prerogative . . . I was not referred to any proclamation or Order in Council and I know of no such prerogative . . . Disobedience to such an *ultra vires* order is not illegal but . . . to compel obedience is."

21.16 The practice is, however, different, although this is not to say that practice can make lawful that which is unlawful. At the same time, with something as indefinite as the boundaries of the Royal Prerogative, which can be stretched to meet obvious modern needs, and will be stretched by the Executive so long as it thinks that it will not be called to order by the Judiciary, a query will arise as to whether this forthright direction is now totally accurate, and whether or not today's conditions have brought about a measure of change. In 1956 at least one British cargo ship was requisitioned in Antwerp for the Anglo-French invasion of the Suez Canal area, in 1982 a British cruise liner was requisitioned in Naples for use as a hospital ship during the Falklands operation, and in the First World War, as the cases will show, a British ship was requisitioned in Finland. In no case was this challenged by the shipowners, although in each case there was little inducement to do so and every reason to accept what the Crown wished to do. However this may be, there are some helpful cases which indicate when there is requisition and when there is not.

3. *Russian Bank for Foreign Trade* v. *Excess Insurance Co. Ltd.* [1918] 2 K.B. 123.

21.17 *The Sarpen*[4] concerned a Norwegian ship which went aground in the far north of Scotland in the first few days of the First World War. The *Simla* was a tug which had been requisitioned and was in Kirkwall, although at that date the hire and the terms and conditions of her engagement had not been agreed. The naval officer in charge gave her permission to salvage the *Sarpen*. This she achieved. Was she a King's ship? There is an ancient rule that King's ships cannot claim salvage, although their officers and crews may do so if they have the permission of the Admiralty. At the time this rule was enshrined in section 557 of the Merchant Shipping Act 1894. In the Court of Appeal Pickford L.J. gave the following views with which the rest of the court agreed:

"I do not deny that there may be a requisition under such terms as to give the Crown the dominion as well as the control of the ship, and it may be in such a case she may be said to belong to the Crown, although not in the ordinary sense belonging to it."

and:

" . . . the word requisition . . . means that the Crown has the right to require the services of the ship without the consent of the owner, but it does not define the terms upon which the Crown may see fit to take those services."

The *Simla* was held to be entitled to salvage.

21.18 *The Broadmayne*[5] involved many similar circumstances. The *Broadmayne* herself stranded outside Harwich harbour and was salvaged by the tug *Revenger*. The tug, engaged on the same terms as the *Simla*, was likewise held not to be a King's ship. Pickford L.J. asked what requisition means, and answered the question:

"There is no particular magic in the word itself; it does not connote the same state of things in every particular case. In this case it was made under the proclamation of the 3rd August, 1914, that the [tug] was requisitioned, and that authorised the Lords Commissioners of the Admiralty to requisition and take up for the service of the Crown any British ship for certain services on condition that the owners of all ships and vessels so requisitioned should receive payment for their use . . . "

Bankes L.J. added: "It is, in my opinion, equally immaterial that the terms of payment and employment are incorporated in a charterparty or other form of agreement."

21.19 The American case of *Flota Merchante Dominicana C. Por. A, Owner of the "Santo Domingo" v. American Manufacturers Mutual Insurance Company et al*[6] also contains some useful guidance.

1965

24th April

The ship sails from New York bound for Santo Domingo. News of an uprising in the Dominican Republic reaches the ship. The crew is in a state of nervous excitement and relapses into a state of alcoholic indiscipline.

4. [1916] P. 306.
5. [1916] P. 64.
6. [1970] A.M.C. Vol. II, 1678.

27th April

The crew forces the Master to send a message sympathetic to "the new constitution". (Those seeking to establish a new constitution are variously referred to in the judgment as "the new constitutionalists" and "the rebels".)

29th April

The Master calls a meeting of the officers to decide whether or not to dock. Having received no orders to change their destination, and fearing the attitude of the crew, they decide to do so.

The ship docks in the Ozama river, two hundred metres from a fort held by 1,000 national police loyal to the existing government. The Master goes ashore to get news. He is caught up in the fighting and never returns to the ship. Before leaving he instructs the passengers and crew to remain on board. They apparently disobey him, taking their individual choice of sides.

30th April

The rebels attack the fort which is evacuated by the national police, who it seems have not eaten for three days. Four to five hundred policemen board the ship, take all the food and clothes they can find, and use two lifeboats to ferry themselves over the river.

The ship is now occupied by the rebels, who fire on troops of the U.S. 82nd Airborne Division, sent by President Johnson to guard American lives and property. The troops return the fire and shell the ship, setting her on fire. She burns out and sinks, becoming a constructive total loss.

21.20 The case was heard before Harold R. Tyler Jr. D.J. in the Southern District Court of New York. Amongst other pleas, the war risk underwriters pleaded that the ship was requisitioned by the Dominican Government, and, this being excepted from the War Risk Policy, they were not liable. The court noted that there were not many cases on requisition and turned to Oppenheim which described a requisition as: "The name for the demand for the supply of all kinds of articles necessary for an army". Furthermore various conventions laid down formalities and provided for receipts and payments. The court ruled: "Nevertheless, both these sources suggest that in requisitioning there is an aspect of formalism which flows from considered military decisions" and: "Requisition in this policy means something much closer to formal civil condemnation than a swift rummage through the ship by four hundred or more hungry, frightened policemen who made off with the food and the lifeboats . . . ". Judgment was signed for the plaintiff.

21.21 So much for indications of what is the nature of requisition. There are two other cases, which are representative of several others, which indicate that there is no requisition in circumstances where it might have been expected to arise. Lord Sterndale M.R. gave the Court of Appeal's judgment in *Bombay and Persia Steam Navigation Company* v. *The Shipping Controller*.[7] In September 1919 the *Homayum* was bound for Alexandria with a cargo of coal. A rail strike started in the United Kingdom which endangered the delivery of coal to the ports. Being anxious to maintain the supply of bunker coal in the coaling ports, the Shipping Controller ordered all British ships carrying coal to abandon their voyages and discharge their cargoes at coaling ports. In obedience to his directions the ship headed for Port Said, only to be sent away again by the Senior Naval Officer in the port. She duly discharged in Alexandria and the owners claimed for the extra expenses. Lord Sterndale M.R. refused to decide a lot of things, including what a requisition was, because:

" . . . It does contemplate employment of some sort by the government for government purposes. Here they merely directed [the ship] to go to a place to which otherwise she would not

---

7. (1921) 7 Ll.L.Rep. 226.

have gone . . . in order that, if somebody thought fit, he or they might lay their hands on the cargo."

21.22 *France Fenwick and Company Limited* v. *The King*[8] followed the same lines. In 1921 there was a miners' strike which again endangered the supply of coal. The government acted under the Emergency Powers Act 1920 and armed itself with regulations which permitted it to requisition ships, prohibit their unloading, take possession of stocks of coal and to pay compensation. On 2nd April, 1921, the *Lockwood* arrived at Rotherhithe to discharge coal from the north-east coast. While she was moored at the buoys awaiting her berth, a Customs officer, Mr. Taylor, boarded her. There was a conflict of evidence in what he told the crew to do. The crew said that Mr. Taylor had told them that the ship was requisitioned. Mr. Taylor's version, which the court accepted, was that he said: "In no circumstances is the vessel to discharge without permission." On 21st April the Board of Trade requisitioned the ship and on the following day ordered her to discharge at Erith. She completed discharge at Erith on 23rd April. It may be thought that the regulations had distorted the position, but in the High Court, Wright J. emphasised that even under the common law there was no requisition: "I think, however, that (requisition) can only apply . . . to a case where property is actually taken possession of, or used by, the government, or where by the order of a competent authority, it is placed at the disposal of the government." A mere negative prohibition, even though lawful, does not constitute requisition. In both cases the Shipping Controller and the King were awarded judgment.

21.23 It should be noted that requisition, whether for title or for use, terminates the insurance (Chapter 4). The position is different in the case of the two Through Transport Mutual Insurance Associations, where it merely suspends the insurance during the period of the requisition (para. 39.14). It is again different in the case of the British Mutual War Risks Associations. Where it is for use only, the insurance can continue (para. 23.38).

ANGARY

21.24 Akin to requisition, but in fact separate from it, is the *droit d'angarie* or angary. It is separate because "requisition" contemplates that a government can requisition only the property of its own nationals, whereas angary, a right which exists in International Law, allows a belligerent, in the words of Earl Jowitt's *Dictionary of English Law*, " . . . to use or destroy, for purposes of offence or defence, neutral property found on their own or on enemy territory or on the open sea subject to the obligation to make compensation to the owners".

21.25 The right, whilst it undoubtedly exists, does not have firmly-established boundaries. The right to take on the open sea may be questionable. Moreover the definition does not emphasise, as the Privy Council did when it was hearing *The Zamora*,[9] that urgency, perhaps extreme need, must exist. The *Zamora*, a neutral ship carrying to Stockholm a cargo of copper which was consigned to a neutral, was stopped on 8th April, 1915 by a British warship and was sent into Kirkwall for

8. [1927] 1 K.B. 458.
9. [1916] 2 A.C. 77.

search. Before the Prize Court made any findings of condemnation, and when the cargo undoubtedly still belonged to its neutral owner, the War Office requisitioned the cargo. It was a desirable commodity, but the War Office's evidence revealed no pressing need for it. A great many issues were raised in the case, but Lord Parker of Waddington, in giving the judgment of the Council (pages 99–122 of the report), stressed:

"First, the vessel or goods in question must be urgently required for the use in connection with the defence of the Realm, the prosecution of the war, or other matters involving national security."

and:

"The right of a belligerent to requisition the goods of neutrals found within its territory, or territory of which it is in military occupation, is recognised by a number of writers on International Law. It is sometimes referred to as the right of angary, and is generally recognised as involving an obligation to make full compensation."

21.26 Reference was also made to the sinking by the Prussians of British ships in the River Seine during the Franco-Prussian War (1870). The Prussians subsequently pleaded their "great necessity" which gave rise to the right of angary, and paid full compensation. Lord Parker doubted if the "necessity" was as great as they said it was and therefore it was questionable if the right of angary in fact existed. Lord Parker was not, of course, passing judgment on the Prussians' actions which had taken place 44 years before; he was merely commenting on what was bygone history and his doubts on the soundness of the Prussians' assertion.

21.27 Angary was again considered in *Commercial and Estates Company of Egypt* v. *The Board of Trade*.[10] In 1914 the *Falls of Nith*, a British ship, loaded timber in Finland for carriage to Alexandria. The First World War broke out and the ship took refuge in Frederikshamn, a port in Finland. On the 3rd August, 1917, she was requisitioned by the United Kingdom Shipping Controller. On arrival in the United Kingdom the timber, which by this time was on board this ship and several others, was requisitioned by the Controller of Timber Supplies. The Egyptian timber owners protested and then sued, and Bailhache J. held that the Controller of Timber Supplies could justify what he had done as angary which meant that full compensation was payable. In the Court of Appeal, Bankes and Atkin L.JJ. were of the view that angary had arisen, the latter saying:

" . . . there is a well ascertained right of a belligerent sovereign to take possession of the property of neutrals so found within his territory or the territory occupied by his forces for the purposes of warfare. This is the right of angary. It appears to me to be well recognised . . . the sovereign so exercising this right makes full compensation".

21.28 Scrutton L.J., the dissenting judge, felt that it was not necessary to decide on whether the right of angary came into the matter; compensation was payable under wartime legislation and regulations. It is noticeable that neither Bailhache J., Banks L.J. or Atkin L.J. stressed the urgency of the United Kingdom's need of the timber on which, in *The Zamora*,[11] Lord Parker had been so insistent.

21.29 Angary is not an exception from the cover of the War Risk Policy and, being readily distinguishable from requisition, which is, should not prevent a claim

10. [1925] 1 K.B. 271.
11. [1916] 2 A.C. 77.

for "capture" or "seizure" should a belligerent take a neutral ship and require her to perform in his service.

21.30 During the Six Day War between Israel and Egypt (1967), an American ship in Alexandria was required to carry war stores by the Egyptian navy. The Master and crew refused, and were replaced by a naval crew. The war came to an end before the Egyptian armed forces could make use of her. Presumably their need was urgent, but it did appear that they were justifiably using the right of angary to secure the ship's services.

PRE-EMPTION

21.31 Pre-emption is the right to purchase property before or in preference to others. This is sometimes contained in a contract or a statute, particularly statutes which allow the acquisition of land for certain defined purposes. In another guise, it used to be part of the Royal Prerogative to buy necessaries for the Royal household, but this right was abolished in 1660. Earl Jowitt in the *Dictionary of English Law* defines it in the sense with which this work is concerned: "In International Law, pre-emption is the right of a government to purchase, for its own use, the property of the subjects of another State *in transitu*, instead of allowing it to reach its destination."

21.32 Pre-emption has proved remarkably difficult to define, and appears to have arisen in the way described by Lord Parker in *The Zamora*.[12] The British view, formed during the Napoleonic Wars, was that naval stores were contraband and were lawful prize, even when carried in a neutral ship. Other countries took the view that such stores were only contraband if destined for use by an enemy government, and if destined for use by civilians were not contraband at all. The British view on what were naval stores was probably very wide indeed, wider perhaps than was really justified, so a compromise was reached; instead of condemning such stores they were purchased compulsorily from their neutral owners. This practice was enshrined in treaties and finally came to be recognised as fully warranted by international law. Apparently it was confined to naval stores only. Again it is an ill-defined right, and it is possible to see it being applied to ships in wartime, but such a use may be held to be unlawful.

NATIONALISATION

21.33 Nationalisation is more easily recognised than it is described. It consists of taking into public ownership, by means of a statute or decree properly and lawfully passed by the Sovereign Assembly or Sovereign Authority of the government concerned, any asset or private ownership within that government's jurisdiction. In this respect it is different to requisition, which is the use of existing powers, whether the Royal Prerogative or statutory powers, to acquire an object—a ship, a piece of land, a house—for public use in an emergency. Nationalisation does require pay-

12. [1916] 2 A.C. 77.

ment to be made to the dispossessed owners, but nationalisation may still exist if that payment is not forthcoming. It would be unrealistic to suppose that payment was made for the dispossessing of General Somoza in the *Somoza Ships* case (paras. 7.17–7.23), but the decree of the Sandinista Government of Nicaragua by which the four ships were purportedly nationalised into public ownership, was nonetheless effective as a nationalising measure of a sovereign government.

21.34 Even though ships and containers spend most of their time out of the jurisdiction, they can nevertheless become nationalised by taking over their private ownership if that is within the jurisdiction. It is sufficient if the shareholdings in the owning companies are transferred to the public corporation. Even when the private ownership is outside the jurisdiction, but the asset concerned is within it, a nationalisation statute or decree can still be effective. An example of this is the nationalisation of the Suez Canal in 1956, and the passing of the property in the Canal into the hands of the Suez Canal Authority. Most of the private ownership in the shape of the shareholders was outside Egypt; the asset however was on Egyptian soil. Less extreme examples are furnished by the nationalisation of Imperial Airways in 1939 when it became B.O.A.C., the mines in 1947 when they became the property of the National Coal Board, and the four great railway companies in 1948 when they passed into the ownership of British Railways. No doubt many foreign nationals owned shares in these undertakings. The assets or the private ownership were still within the United Kingdom, and there could be no doubt that the nationalising statutes were effective.

21.35 The presence of "nationalisation" among the exclusions of the Institute Container Clauses—Time 1.1.87, should not be seen as a complicating factor. These clauses, unlike the insurance for ships, give insurance on an "all risks" basis, and it is not the intention that they should pay for a loss caused by nationalisation. This is left, as in the case of ships and freight, to the War Risks insurance.

21.36 Nationalisation is not mentioned, either as an insured peril or as an excluded risk, in the War and Strikes insurance, either for ships or for containers. There is a good reason for this. If it is accepted that Clause 4.1.4 of the ships' War Risks Clauses (Clause 5.1.4 in the case of containers),[13] is sufficient to exclude nationalisation by the country of the ship's ownership or register, or in the case of containers, the country where the assured has his principal place of business, then it becomes easier to accept in turn that nationalisation elsewhere is either "Seizure", "Confiscation", or "Expropriation". The decrees which transferred the Onassis fishing fleet in a wholesale fashion to Peru, and the equally wholesale transfer of the K.P.M. ships to Indonesia, both during the 1950s, were probably effective decrees of nationalisation, and not simply because any attempt to remove the ships would have been met by force. So far as the War and Strikes insurance was concerned however, the incidents came within the bounds of at least one of these three insured perils.

21.37 As conclusions it is suggested:

1. Confiscation and expropriation, as insured perils, should be given their natural and ordinary meanings in the sense described by this chapter. They are probably indistinguishable from "seizure" and possibly "capture" as

13. See Appendices D and M.

well, except that both have an air of finality about them, which is not necessarily so of either "capture" or "seizure".

2. Requisition, as an exclusion to the insurance, concerns only the acquisition, by a State, of the property of its own subjects or nationals, and can be either for title or for use. It requires some formality, however brief, by a government officer or official, and must be lawful.[14]

3. Generally speaking, requisition envisages payment for the title to the property, or, when for use, payment for its use and for any damage suffered during the period of the requisition. For the purposes of the War and Strikes insurance, requisition may still be complete even if the laws of the requisitioning country do not provide for payment, or only for limited or conditional payment. The *Robinson* case (paras. 12.22—12.28), is an example.

4. Some very definite service must be required. For ships, this is what ships normally do, namely the carriage of cargo, and for containers, the loading and transportation of cargo. This service may consist of waiting, sometimes for a lengthy period, in some place until they are wanted. Where there is no formal requisition, the mere fact that ships or containers are told to wait, or to go somewhere else, does not amount to requisition, even though the orders are lawfully given.

5. Pre-emption, as an exclusion to the insurance, probably cannot arise at all, because there is authority for saying that it applies only to naval stores owned by neutrals. Any attempt to apply it to a neutral ship, or to containers owned by neutrals, is more likely to be angary.

6. Angary is the right of a belligerent to take for service or for destruction the property of a neutral within the territory of the belligerent, or the territory occupied by the belligerent's armed forces. It carries with it the obligation to compensate the neutral owner. The view has been expressed that it may be exercised on the high seas, but this appears to be doubtful. It is neither an insured peril nor an excluded risk of the War and Strikes insurance, and thus it comes within the bounds of the insured perils of "capture" or "seizure", or the new insured perils of "confiscation" or "expropriation".

7. The nature of nationalisation is described in this chapter. Where it arises in a place other than where the ship is owned or registered, or where the container owner has his principal place of business, the insured perils of "seizure", and possibly "confiscation" and "expropriation", will arise.

8. Whenever requisition, pre-emption, nationalisation, or angary arise, or are alleged to arise, most careful enquiry needs to be made on the actual facts to establish whether or not this is so. In the case of requisition and nationalisation, this will involve close examination of the local law.

14. In some cases, requisition can terminate the insurance. See Chapter 4.

CHAPTER 22

Freight

THE INSURED PERILS

22.1 The Institute War and Strikes Clauses Freight—Time 1.10.83, set out the insured perils in Clause 1:

"Loss (total or partial) of the subject matter insured caused by:–
War civil war revolution rebellion insurrection, or civil strife arising therefrom, or any hostile act by or against a belligerent power.

Capture seizure arrest restraint or detainment, and the consequences thereof or any attempt thereat.

Derelict mines torpedoes bombs or other derelict weapons of war,

Loss (total or partial) of the subject matter insured arising from loss of or damage to the vessel caused by:–
Strikers, locked-out workmen, or persons taking part in labour disputes, riots or civil commotions.

Any terrorist or any person acting maliciously or from a political motive.

Confiscation and expropriation."

The Mutual War Risks Associations also give freight cover.

22.2 The split of the first three clauses from the last three is strange but would appear to be of historical interest only. The subject matter of the insurance is the freight or the other interests insured, an intangible matter when compared to the solid nature of the hull and machinery of the ship. It is easy enough to envisage circumstances where a "war" or a "capture" would cause the loss of the freight. It is equally simple to think of a freight being lost because "strikers" or "terrorists" cause the loss of, or damage to, the insured ship. As a matter of grammar, it is less easy to think of a "derelict mine" or "torpedo" directly causing the loss of the freight, and it is tempting to think that the clause on "derelict mines" etc. should be put into the second half rather than the first. However that may be, the insured perils are the same for the freight as they are for hull and machinery insurance and need no further description to that given in Chapters 5–21. As soon as an insured peril has arisen, and the door to the underwriters' liability is therefore opened, two matters of peculiar difficulty arise.

22.3 The first of these is the nature of freight as a subject for insurance. Several definitions have been given on freight in this context and the most concise seems to that given by Lord Wright M.R. in *The Yero Carras*[1]:

"What is insured under the freight policy is not a chattel like a ship or a cargo; it is, even in

---

1. *Yero Carras (Owners)* v. *London & Scottish Assurance Corpn. Ltd.* (1935) 53 Ll.L.Rep. 131. See paras. 22.11–22.16.

the case of a chartered freight . . . merely a chose in action, a right of earning freight under the charter; *a fortiori* where there is merely an expectancy of earning freight, though enough to constitute an insurable interest."

to which Greene L.J. added: "If that right is lost through a peril of the sea the underwriters are liable . . . "

The second is the nature of the clauses relating to freight insurance. The ones to be considered are:

First group

22.4 Institute Time Clauses Freight—Time, incorporated by reference into the Institute War and Strikes Clauses Freight—Time Policy.

15.1 In the event of total loss (actual or constructive) of the vessel named herein the amount insured shall be paid in full, whether the vessel be fully or partly loaded or in ballast, chartered or unchartered.

15.2 In ascertaining whether the vessel is a constructive total loss, the insured value of the insurances on hull and machinery shall be taken as the repaired value and nothing in respect of the damaged or breakup value of the vessel or wreck shall be taken into account.

Institute Time Clauses—Hulls, included by reference into the Institute War and Strikes Clauses—Hulls, the "matching provision":

20. In the event of total or constructive total loss no claim to be made by the underwriters [i.e., the hull and machinery underwriters] for freight whether Notice of Abandonment has been given or not.

Second group

22.5 Institute War & Strikes Freight—Time.

4.4 Loss proximately caused by delay...............
4.5 Any claim based upon loss of or frustration of any voyage or adventure.

Institute Time Clauses—Freight, incorporated by reference.

14. This insurance does not cover any claim consequent on loss of time whether arising from a peril of the sea or otherwise.

22.6 At this stage, it may be remarked that the exclusions of the second group have been held to have some strange effects, and it is not going too far to say that in cases where there is every reasonable expectation that a claim will arise from an insured peril, the "small print" of the policy has arbitrarily removed the insurance cover in a way that the draftsmen cannot have intended.

22.7 This criticism is not always appropriate; the *causa proxima*, found only after an exhaustive examination of the facts, will often establish that the real cause of the casualty is not an insured peril, which may at first sight seem to be the case, but an excluded risk.

HOW FREIGHT IS INSURED

22.8 Starting with consideration of the first group, the modern tendency, although by no means universal, is to insure a ship for freight for the full amount permitted under her hull and machinery policy, namely 25%. If an owner puts a value of £10m on the hull and machinery of his ship, he can if he wishes insure her hull and machinery for £8m and her freight for £2m. If she is an actual total loss or is so badly damaged that she is a constructive total loss on the hull and machinery policy, he will recover £2m under the freight policy besides the £8m under the hull and machinery policy. At the same time he has cover for lost freight up to £2m in case the ship is damaged and, due to an insured peril, the freight is lost. He cannot, of course, have it both ways; if the ship is lost because of an insured peril and he recovers the full £2m, by now commonly regarded as part of the value of the ship herself, he will not also recover any lost freight from the freight underwriter. This modern tendency pays scant regard to history, being modern opportunism built on the provisions of the Hull and Freight policies which were aimed at correcting the harsh provisions of the common law. Whilst the Marine Insurance Act 1906 contains very little on the subject of freight insurance, section 63(2) gives continued effect to the common law rule that, where a ship is abandoned to the hull and machinery underwriter, but nonetheless her freight is subsequently earned, that freight belongs to the hull and machinery underwriter; moreover because the freight is earned, the shipowner has no claim on his freight policy. This caused great disadvantage to the shipowner and clauses 15 and 20 were inserted into the Marine Policies and made applicable to the War Risk Policies in the manner described above. They were not the complete answer so far as the shipowner was concerned as Hamilton J. pointed out in *Coker* v. *Bolton*.[2]

22.9 In 1910 the *Ivy* was engaged on a voyage carrying grain from the Baltic to Manchester. Her freight was insured for £900. In the River Mersey she stranded on the 2nd December, 1910, and was a constructive total loss. Notice of Abandonment was given on the same day and was refused. Also on that day, the Liverpool Salvage Association took charge of the wreck, refloated it, and towed it to Manchester. The cargo was discharged and the freight, altogether £630 12s 0d., was paid to the shipowner. He also claimed the right to keep the whole £900. The court considered that such a view regarded the then equivalent of Clause 15: " . . . As a separate and independent insurance which gives to the plaintiff, apart from any loss of freight, the right to receive the amount of the policy in the event of the total loss of the steamer."

The court considered that such an interpretation would make the freight policy into a gaming policy and as such unenforceable at law. The court held that, although the shipowner had the right to the whole amount insured by the freight policy and was also entitled to the freight from the owner of the goods, he still had to account to the freight underwriter for the "salvage" or recovery of the £630 12s 0d. The judge, with an eye on the then recent case of *United Kingdom Mutual Steamship Assurance Association* v. *Boulton*[3] added:

"In my opinion [Clause 15] was introduced for the purpose of meeting the hardship that has long been felt to exist that a shipowner, who has given Notice of Abandonment and has consequently lost his right to freight subsequently earned, is precluded from suing on the policy for freight."

22.10 What then happens if the shipowner loses his ship by an actual or construc-

2. [1912] 3 K.B. 315.
3. (1898) 3 Com. Cas. 330.

tive total loss, whilst in the latter event managing to show that she is a constructive total loss under the hull and machinery policy? In either case, he will recover the whole sum insured under the freight policy. If, as is so often the case, he regards the freight policy as part of the security for the ship's hull and machinery, he will have no insurance for the freight that he may have lost as a result of the casualty, because the freight policy will not pay out twice. Moreover, if, subsequent to the Notice of Abandonment, the freight is earned, he will have to account to his freight underwriter for it. Only if he insures his ship for her full value under the hull and machinery policy, and the freight at risk under a freight policy, will he be adequately secured against the financial loss of a casualty. This is, however, a matter of choice at the time that the insurance contracts are made and this lies with the shipowner. Where a war risk casualty happens, it is more likely that the insured ship will be an actual or constructive total loss. This was the case with nearly all of the ships hit by Exocet missiles during the Iran/Iraq War (1980–1988). It could happen, however, that a ship is only damaged, and cannot proceed without extensive repairs. This was usually the case where ships were damaged by the mines planted in the Red Sea (1984). What happens to the freight policy then?

TOTAL LOSS OF FREIGHT—HOW JUDGED

22.11 There is a long history of legal decisions which indicate how Clauses 15 and 20 are to be treated, the most prominent being *Moss* v. *Smith*,[4] the House of Lords decision in *Rankin* v. *Potter*,[5] where the House of Lords took the advice of the judges, and *Assicurazioni Generali and Schenker & Co.* v. *SS Bessie Morris Company and Browne (The Bessie Morris)*.[6] The law arising from these and from other cases is thoroughly described in two more recent decisions of the Court of Appeal, *Yero Carras (Owners)* v. *London & Scottish Assurance Corporation Limited*[7] and *Kulukundis and Others* v. *Norwich Union Fire Insurance Society Limited*.[8] Each case had a considerable effect on the other, both happened in the same part of the world from the same peril, and both were heard by Porter J. in the High Court with only a short period in between. Since in each case the Court of Appeal unanimously overturned both judgments, it is more fruitful to study the Court of Appeal's judgments.

22.12 The *Yero Carras* was chartered on 16th September, 1930, to Chilean Nitrate Producers to load nitrate in Chile, the cancelling date of the charterparty being 20th November, 1930. The charterparty excluded the consequences of perils of the seas. The ship's freight was insured in the amount of £9,000 for a voyage from Montevideo to the west coast of South America and thence to the United Kingdom. On 13th November, 1930, whilst approaching the loading port, the ship stranded off Cape Upright in the Straits of Magellan. On 17th November, Notice of Abandonment was given to the hull and machinery underwriters. On the 6th December, 1930, the ship was salvaged and taken to Magellanes. The estimates of

4. (1850) 9 C.B. 94.
5. (1873) L.R. 6 H.L. 83. See paras. 27.57, 27.58.
6. [1892] 1 Q.B. 571; [1892] 2 Q.B. 652.
7. (1935) 53 Ll.L.Rep. 131.
8. [1937] 1 K.B. 1. See paras. 22.18–22.24.

the costs of repair varied enormously and the court clearly found them confusing. It was clear that the ship was seriously damaged and the question arose whether, with the salvage and other charges and repairs put together, it was a worthwhile proposition for the shipowner to attempt to continue the charter whose cancelling date was, in any event, long since past. The hull and machinery underwriters paid the ship's full insured value (under a rather strange arrangement which left the ship in the hands of her owners and was not a true constructive total loss) and the shipowners invited the freight underwriters to do the same. They declined to do this. The ship was abandoned to the salvors who, interestingly, sold her to Messrs. Ragusi of Montevideo. Ragusi repaired her and put her back into service where she subsequently enjoyed a long and useful life around the coasts of South America.

22.13 Lord Wright M.R. gave the main judgment and first reminded the parties that the position under the charterparty had first to be considered before there was any question of considering any liability of the freight underwriter. The shipowner may be relieved of liability to the charterers under the terms of the charterparty: "If the vessel is so damaged or disabled as to be incapable of being repaired save at an expense exceeding her value when repaired." This was the test applied in *The Bessie Morris*[9] by Lord Esher M.R. and Bowen L.J.

22.14 The test had also been put in more general terms in *Moss v. Smith*[10] by Maule J., where he thought the ship had suffered: "Such extensive damage, that it would not be reasonably practicable to repair her—seeing that the expense of repairs would be such that no man of common-sense would incur that outlay."

22.15 In the same case, Cresswell J. had agreed that this was the correct way to examine the matter. The test had also been described that the repairs would be "so ruinously expensive that no prudent owner would undertake them". Lord Wright M.R. approved the way that Maule and Cresswell JJ. had described it. If this test can be answered in the affirmative, then the test of the freight underwriters liability is the same. To put it another way, provided there is an insured peril, which in the *Yero Carras*[11] case was perils of the seas, there is a claim on the freight policy. In Lord Wright M.R's words: "In my judgment there was here an actual total loss of freight. The freight was lost because the charterparty . . . was destroyed by the perils of the seas."

22.16 On the effect of the modern Clause 15 Lord Wright M.R. has this to say:

"I do not think that, apart from express terms, the right to claim a total or constructive total loss under this policy can depend upon whether there is a constructive total loss under the hull policies. Certainly Clause 5 (now 15.2) contains no such condition. Clause 5 can only apply where it is the constructive total loss of the ship that is an essential condition of recovery of the freight policy. The first part of Clause 4 (now 15.1) deals with the case referred to above where the shipowner, but for the clause, would lose his freight on the ground that it has been earned by the ship after it has been abandoned to the underwriters, and the clause in such an event gives an added right of recovery of the full freight . . . "

and:

"I do not think that Clause 5 can be applied to the facts of this case, because I do not think

9. Footnote 6, above.
10. (1850) 9 C.B. 94.
11. (1935) 53 Ll.L.Rep. 131.

the freight policy required that there should be a constructive total loss of the ship within the true meaning of that phrase in Clause 5 of the freight policy."

22.17 The other two judges agreed. Greene L.J., later to give the main judgment in the *Kulukundis*[12] case, simply noted his agreement. Slesser L.J. added a forthright comment: "But to say *simpliciter* that it is necessary to prove on a freight policy that the vessel is a constructive total loss is, to my mind, not correct."

22.18 The *Kulukundis* case[13] involved a ship loaded with a cargo. The *Mount Taygetus* was chartered on 2nd November, 1933, to carry a full and complete cargo of cereals from Chile to the United Kingdom for the account of Messrs. Gianoli Mustakis & Co. A lumpsum freight of £8,000 was payable on discharge, although the loading disbursements were to be paid out of it by the charterers and debited to the freight. The freight policy was expressed to cover a voyage from Liverpool—Bristol Channel—Rio—ballast via Magellan—west coast South America—via Magellan to U.K./Continent. Clauses 4 and 5 (now 15.1 and 15.2) were incorporated. After loading in Chile, the ship sailed for the United Kingdom and on 23rd December, 1933, she went aground on the Memphis Rock, English Narrows in the Straits of Magellan. On 27th December, 1933, Notice of Abandonment was given. This was refused, with the owners being put in the same position as though they had issued a writ. On 13th January, 1934, salvors refloated her, after jettisoning 100 tons of cargo, and she proceeded under her own steam to Magellanes. The shipowners and the hull and machinery underwriters agreed that the voyage should be abandoned, and the ship was subsequently abandoned to the salvors. The cargo owners were told that the voyage was being abandoned, whereupon the cargo underwriters (who were partly reinsured by the defendants) paid a total loss. Subsequently the salvors made sufficient repairs to sail the ship to Rotterdam, discharging there 4,250 tons of cargo. This seems to have been financially well worth their while, even though they subsequently sold the ship to breakers.

22.19 In the High Court, Porter J. again gave judgment for the underwriters. Before the case was heard by the Court of Appeal, that court heard *The Yero Carras*[14] which caused the plaintiffs to change their pleas. Before the Court of Appeal, they pleaded that the ship was prevented in a business sense from performing the charter by the perils of the seas, and, on the figures, no prudent man would do the repairs and continue the voyage. This time the court dealt more specifically with the figures rather than the general principle. The *Yero Carras* case can be distinguished because the perils of the seas caused a cancelling date to be missed and, with it, the loss of the freight. The *Mount Taygetus* was loaded with cargo, which the shipowner had contracted to carry to the discharging port and (in Slesser L.J.'s words): "In considering whether a prudent uninsured owner would incur (the necessary repairs)" some precision on costs was necessary.

22.20 Slesser L.J. considered that the first question to be asked was whether the shipowners were bound to do temporary or permanent repairs. Temporary repairs and discharge of the salvors' lien would cost £19,161 whilst the value of the temporarily repaired ship, the net freight and cargo's contribution to the repairs amounted

12. [1937] 1 K.B. 1.
13. *Ibid.*
14. (1935) 53 Ll.L.Rep. 131.

in all to a total to the shipowner of £18,979. On these figures, a prudent uninsured owner would not incur them. Permanent repairs would however give him a much more valuable ship and they would alter figures substantially. Lord Chelmsford seemed to have answered this question in *Rankin* v. *Potter*[15]:

"The only question is whether, by the perils of the sea, the ship was so damaged . . . as to be rendered incapable, unless sufficiently repaired, of performing the [contracted] voyage. . . . The cost of repairing the vessel . . . so as to make her seaworthy . . . would have exceeded the value of the ship when repaired."

22.21 Lord Chelmsford considered that the cost of temporary repairs to make the ship seaworthy to bring home the cargo—and so complete the contractual voyage—was the right figure. Some support for this view was obtained from the judgment of Maule J. and Wilde C.J. in *Moss* v. *Smith*.[16] Slesser L.J. concluded: "These *dicta* all indicate that, in freight insurance, the temporary expenditure necessary to earn the freight—that is to complete the voyage—is the true criteria." He allowed the appeal in the shipowner's favour.

22.22 Greene L.J. gave the main judgment. It is very long and, as will be seen from pages 60 to 69 of *Lloyd's Law Reports*, is extremely closely argued. It would be most difficult to do it justice to put it in a synopsis. Moreover, there are some minor points upon which the author would respectfully disagree. In the example of the ship which broke her back at the entrance of the discharge port, she must surely be a constructive total loss, in the absence of the most unusual circumstances, and this would entitle the shipowner to the entire sum insured by the freight policy in any event. The freight underwriter would be entitled to the net recovery of any freight earned by lightering the cargo into the discharging port, but this would not excuse him from his obligation to the insured shipowner under Clause 15.1 of the freight policy. However this may be, Greene L.J.'s calculation of figures is extremely interesting and indicates that the shipowner managed to prove that the *Mount Taygetus* was "lost in a commercial sense" by a margin of no more than £213.

22.23 Greene L.J.'s judgment reinforced the previous *dicta*:

"The rule that a shipowner is entitled to be freed from his obligations to the freighter [charterer], if the vessel is lost in a commercial sense, is now well-established, and it cannot in my judgment be treated as the same rule, or as a breach of the same rule, as that which applies between the owner and the hull underwriter. It stands on foundations of its own, and its scope and effect must be ascertained accordingly."

22.24 Scott L.J. adopted a different and a more general approach:

" . . . Preferring to rest my judgment on the actual commercial loss of the ship within the meaning of the charterparty, or alternatively on the ground that in the circumstances known to the insured at the time, their decision to treat it as an actual loss was justified under the charterparty contract and under the policy."

There was a measure of difference between his reasoning and that of the other two judges. He did not wish it to be thought that a shipowner could be released from his obligation to his charterers simply because the voyage had become unprofitable even as a result of an insured peril. On the contrary, nothing less than:

15. (1873) L.R. 6 H.L. 83. See paras. 27.57, 27.58.
16. (1850) 9 C.B. 94.

"The failure of a basic condition of this obligation such as occurs when by the [perils of the seas] either the carrying ship is lost, physically or commercially, and so rendered unavailable for performance of the contract of affreightment according to its terms, express or implied, or the whole adventure is frustrated."

will allow him to claim on his freight underwriter for his lost freight. The implication must be that a more stringent test needs to be satisfied, although on this occasion he also allowed the appeal in the shipowner's favour.

DELAY[17]

22.25 Moving on now to the second group (para. 22.5), in *The Yero Carras*[18] and the *Kulukundis*[19] cases, the proximate cause of the two losses was unquestionably perils of the seas. The position is different where the proximate cause must be regarded as delay or loss of or frustration of any voyage or adventure, because this is excluded from the cover given by the freight policy. As the following cases will show, it is not always an easy matter to decide how the cause of the loss can best be described, and the margin between what is a justified claim under the freight policy, and what is excluded by these clauses, may be a narrow one.

22.26 *Bensaude & Co.* v. *The Thames & Mersey Marine Insurance Company*[20] is a case where this is particularly shown. The *Peninsular* was chartered in 1895 to carry troops and stores from Lisbon to Lourenço Marques. Her freight policy insured her owner for £2,500 for 12 months and, in language only slightly different from the modern Clause 14, warranted the policy to be free from: "Any claims consequent on loss of time whether arising from a peril of the sea or otherwise."

On 16th April, 1895, the day after sailing from Lisbon, the ship's main shaft broke. This was admitted to be a peril of the seas. She had to be taken back to Lisbon and from thence had to go to Cadiz to carry out the repairs, taking in all 14 days. Under Portuguese law, which applied to the charterparty, the charterers were entitled to, and did, cancel the charter, and engaged another ship for the service. The underwriters refused to pay the shipowner's claim on the basis that the loss of time was the cause of the loss, not the perils of the seas.

22.27 Collins J. ruled in favour of the shipowner on the basis that the perils of the seas, which was complete before there was any loss of time, caused the loss. The Court of Appeal allowed the underwriters' appeal, Lord Esher M.R. saying: "The cause of the total loss [of the freight] was . . . the breaking of the shaft by reason of perils of the sea followed by the consequent loss of time. Is it possible to say that the claim for a total loss was not consequent on loss of time?"

22.28 To Lord Esher M.R. it was not possible to do so. Lopes L.J. agreed with him, saying that the insured perils established that the actual wording of the warranty protected the underwriters. Rigby L.J. agreed. Whilst this was not stated by the court, it is impossible to avoid the conclusion that the court was guided by the fact that the charterer was entitled to, and in fact did, cancel the charter because of

17. Delay has a wider application than just the freight insurance. Since most of the cases where delay has been considered relate to the freight, it is convenient to deal with it in this chapter.
18. (1935) 53 Ll.L.Rep. 131. See paras. 22.11–22.16.
19. [1937] 1 K.B. 1. See paras. 22.18–22.24.
20. [1897] 1 Q.B. 29.

the delays necessary to do the repairs. This, and not the insured peril, was the true cause of Bensaude's loss. This came out clearly in the further appeal to the House of Lords which upheld the decision of the Court of Appeal. Lord Halsbury L.C. on the question of whether the freight was lost:

"Not *simpliciter* because the main shaft was broken, but because the main shaft was broken under special circumstances—that is at a distance from any place where it could be repaired within such a time as would have enabled the vessel to prosecute the voyage"

and Lord Herschell:

"What is the meaning of saying that the underwriter is not to be liable for any claim consequent upon loss of time? It must mean that although the subject matter insured has been lost, and although it has been lost by a peril insured against, if the claim depends upon loss of time in the prosecution of the voyage so that the adventure cannot be completed within the time contemplated, then the underwriter is to be exempt from liability."

22.29 The *Bensaude*[21] case was followed three years later by *Turnbull Martin & Co v. Hull Underwriters Association Limited*.[22] A fire in the ship's refrigeration machinery made it impossible to load the cargo of meat and the contract for its carriage was lost. Once again the cause was held to be delay and, as such, was excluded from the cover. Then there came the decision of Bailhache J. in *Russian Bank for Foreign Trade v. Excess Insurance Company Limited*.[23] Barley was loaded on board the British ship *Wolverhampton* in Novorossijsk for carriage to Falmouth. It was insured against the usual perils of a war risk policy, but all claims for delay were excluded. At the start of the First World War, the Dardanelles were closed, and on 5th November, 1914, Turkey declared war on the United Kingdom. The barley began to heat and was discharged ashore. On 15th March, 1915, the ship was "requisitioned" by the British Admiralty and put at the disposal of the Russian authorities. Notice of Abandonment of the barley was given to the underwriters and refused. Bailhache J. considered that the closure of the Dardanelles was a "restraint of Princes" and on due Notice of Abandonment, the cargo would be a constructive total loss but for the exclusion of claims for delay. Loss of time and delay were the same thing. He quoted extensively from Lord Herschell's judgment which, in his view, said all that was necessary. For a judgment which was later regarded as determinative on the issue of delay defeating a claim under a freight policy, there is very little fresh material; most of the judgment is devoted to the act of requisition which, being outside the territory and territorial waters of the United Kingdom, Bailhache J. regarded as being *ultra vires*.[24] The case went to the Court of Appeal[25] where Bailhache J.'s judgment was generally upheld, although the court did not go into the matter in any depth. It declined to consider whether the requisition was *ultra vires*; the war being over there seemed to be little point in doing so. Scrutton L.J. ventured the opinion that even if it was *ultra vires*, it could still be called a "restraint".

22.30 By the time that *Petros M. Nomikos Ltd. v. Robertson*[26] was heard, the

21. [1897] 1 Q.B. 29.
22. [1900] 2 Q.B. 402.
23. [1918] 2 K.B. 123.
24. See para. 21.15.
25. [1919] 1 K.B. 39.
26. [1939] A.C. 371.

courts were beginning to have misgivings whether such clauses as "consequent on loss of time" were being given more effect than was intended by the original drafts-men of the freight policy, and whether the courts' decisions indicated that it was, in some circumstances, nearly impossible to make a claim on the freight policy at all. Lord Atkin and Lord Tankerton L.JJ. questioned whether the *Bensaude*[27] case, which, being a House of Lords decision, bound them, had not taken matters too far. In one sense they had every reason for their doubts. A clause put into an insur-ance policy to prevent mere delay or loss of time giving rise to a claim under the freight policy was defeating the obvious intention of the policy itself, which was to give cover in the event of certain listed insured perils arising. The *Bensaude*,[28] *Turnbull*[29] and *Russian Bank*[30] cases all concerned occasions where insured perils had undoubtedly arisen, a broken propeller shaft, a fire, and a closure by Princes of a waterway. What were undoubtedly *bona fide* claims of the kind for which the assured undoubtedly needed protection were being defeated by the "small print" of the policy, and, because all of these insured perils were to a greater or lesser extent productive of delay by their very nature, one began to wonder whether there could ever be a successful claim of any kind. Contracts, and with them the freight, would not be lost in most cases unless the insured peril itself caused the delay. Was not a clause, put in for a limited purpose, being allowed to defeat the entire object of the insurance? It began to look as if this was a case of "heads I win, tails you lose". In the *Bensaude*[31] and *Turnbull*[32] cases, if the repairs could have been done in time, the contracts would have been saved and there would have been no claims under the freight policies in any event. In the *Russian Bank* case,[33] delay was the very essence of "restraints of Princes", and there would be no loss and certainly no con-structive total loss unless it was to continue for some time; and the lapse of time itself prevented there being any claim at all!

22.31 In case the last paragraph should seem too despairing, the point made by Lord Watson in the *Bensaude* case[34] should be borne in mind, that if it had not been for the time taken to repair the broken shaft, there would not have been a claim. From reading the reports, it seems that it was not then the practice of the judges, as it more usually is nowadays, to emphasise the *causa proxima* of the casualty and the resulting claim on the insurance. Then it was treated in a more general way, and the *causa proxima* was regarded as a more or less self-evident fact. It is now the practice of the judges to summarise at length the facts which they find which lead to the establishment of the *causa proxima*, however this may be des-cribed (Chapter 30), of the casualty. This leads in a clearer fashion to its identifi-cation, and in turn this points to an insured peril or an excluded risk. This does not mean that this procedure was not followed in the earlier cases; it was simply not described in the way that now customarily it is, and this can lead to misunderstand-ing. In the *Bensaude* case for instance, the *causa proxima* for the purposes of the

27. [1897] 1 Q.B. 29.
28. *Ibid.*
29. [1900] 2 Q.B. 402.
30. [1918] 2 K.B. 123.
31. [1897] 1 Q.B. 29.
32. [1900] 2 Q.B. 402.
33. [1918] 2 K.B. 123.
34. [1897] 1 Q.B. 29.

freight insurance was not so much the breaking of the shaft, which was an insured peril, as the time taken to repair it, which was an excluded risk.

22.32 Even so, it is impossible to escape the conclusion that the earlier cases did go too far in favouring the excluded risk and discounting the insured peril. Things took a somewhat different turn in the cases of *Roura & Forgas* v. *Townsend and Others*[35] and *Petros M. Nomikos Ltd.* v. *Robertson*,[36] although in both these cases, unlike the earlier cases, both the ships were, in their own way, constructive total losses.

22.33 In the *Roura* case, events took the following course:

1917

August

The plaintiffs, jute merchants living in London, sell a quantity of jute, then in Calcutta, to merchants in Valencia. It has to be shipped by the end of January, 1918.

13th September

The Spanish ship *Igotz Mendi* is chartered to carry it on completion of her forthcoming voyage from Delagoa Bay to Colombo with coal.

17th November

The anticipated profit being £30,000, the plaintiffs effect insurance for this amount. This insures them for total or constructive total loss of the ship from Delagoa Bay to Colombo and Calcutta and until she sails loaded from the last port. This insurance gives cover for marine and war risks and includes loss caused by the enemies of the United Kingdom. The War Risks section does not insure claims arising from delay, deterioration, or loss of market.

4th November

The ship sails from Delagoa Bay with coal for Colombo. Her E.T.A. is the first week in December.

17th November

The ship is captured by the German cruiser *Wolf*. She is used as a collier by the warship and also accommodates some of the prisoners the *Wolf* has taken. Nothing of this is currently known to anyone else, and the ship is thought to have been lost.

—

The *Wolf* with the ship accompanying her sails for Germany. Bombs are placed on board the ship to scuttle her if they fall in with Allied warships. The mate throws them overboard. This greatly annoys the German officers.

1918

31st January

The buyers cancel the sale contract.

23rd February

The plaintiffs ask Lloyd's to post the ship as missing.

27th February

The ship strands on the Danish coast in fog. The Danish authorities send the prize crew home and release the prisoners. This is the first information that anyone else has of what has happened to the ship.

9th March

The ship, in a badly damaged condition, is refloated. She is not insured, so no Notice of Abandonment can be given. It takes until September, 1918, to repair her.

35. [1919] 1 K.B. 189.
36. (1937) 59 Ll.L.Rep. 182, (1938) 61 Ll.L.Rep. 105, (1939) 64 Ll.L.Rep. 45.

14th March

The plaintiffs issue a writ against the underwriters.

22.34 Both parties agreed that, since there was nothing to abandon, no Notice of Abandonment was necessary. The underwriters based their defence on three points:

(1) The ship was not a constructive total loss.
(2) If she was, she was restored before the action, and this precluded the claim.
(3) The cause of action arose from delay and this was not insured.

22.35 Roche J. held that even though the ship was not insured, she was in fact a constructive total loss, and there had been a total loss of the plaintiffs' rights and profits under the charter. He disposed of the delay point thus:

"It is said that it was the lapse of the time during which the *Igotz Mendi* was in German hands that caused the loss, and that such lapse of time was delay within the meaning of the exception . . . in this case it is, in substance, the venture itself which is insured . . . I have decided that the *Igotz Mendi* was not merely delayed but was captured and lost, although she was afterwards found and recovered . . . in consequence this venture, being the profit on the charter, was lost . . . the claim to recover for the loss is not a claim arising from delay."

On these grounds, judgment was signed for the plaintiffs. The capture of the ship was the proximate cause, not the delay.

22.36 In the *Nomikos* case, the history was as follows:

1936

20th July

The hull and machinery of the *Petrakis Nomikos*, an oil tanker, is insured for £28,000 for 12 months. There was a deductible of £1,000 for particular average claims. The key to understanding the course which the shipowner took lies in the provision that, in the case of a constructive total loss, the insurance is only to pay £14,000. The freight is also insured at the same time for one year in the amount of £4,110. The freight insurance contains the following clauses[37] which read:

"(5) In the event of the total loss, whether absolute or constructive of the steamer, the amount underwritten by this policy shall be paid in full, whether the steamer be fully or only partly loaded or in ballast, charterered or unchartered."
"(6) In ascertaining whether the vessel is a constructive total loss the insured value in the policies on the ship shall be taken as the repaired value."
"(8) Warranted free from any claim consequent on loss of time whether arising from a peril of the sea or otherwise."

23rd September

The ship is chartered to carry a full cargo from Venezuela to the United Kingdom or the Continent. The cancelling date is 10th November.

18th October

Having completed discharge of the previous cargo in Le Havre, the ship sails to Rotterdam for repairs.

31st October

As the repairs are completed, there is a violent explosion and a fire in the after-part of the ship. The cross bunker and the stern section are very badly damaged. There is now no question of being in Venezuela by 10th November.

Early November

The shipowner is now faced with a choice. The lowest tender for repairs is £37,400, which means that he can claim for a constructive total loss. To do this he must give Notice of Abandonment at once. He will only get £14,000 from the hull and machinery underwriters, and £4,110 from the freight underwriters.

---

37. The modern numbers of these clauses and their present form is shown at paras. 22.4 and 22.5.

Freight rates are rising strongly after a long period of depression, and with them the values of the ships. If he chooses to treat the casualty as a partial loss only, which section 61 of the Marine Insurance Act 1906 allows him to do, he will spend £37,400 and recover £27,000 from the hull and machinery underwriters. He will also have a much more valuable ship. He elects to repair her.

1937

31st May

The repairs are completed.

22.37 The shipowner had no trouble with his claim against the hull and machinery underwriters, but the freight underwriters refused to pay, claiming that the loss of the charter was due to delay. In the High Court, Goddard J. upheld their refusal. He agreed that delay was the course of the charterer's loss, and in any case he could not accept that there could be such a thing as a constructive total loss without a Notice of Abandonment being given—which was never done. His judgment was reversed by the Court of Appeal, Greer L.J. considering that the parties had agreed what a total loss was to be, and that Notice of Abandonment was not necessary, for very much the same reasons as the House of Lords subsequently gave. MacKinnon L.J. delivered a concurring judgment, whilst Slesser L.J. simply noted his agreement. The freight underwriters appealed to the House of Lords.

22.38 The House of Lords also decided in favour of the shipowner. Lords Wright and Porter gave the main judgments, with Lords Atkin, Thankerton and Russell noting their agreement. Lord Wright made the point that the underwriters based their defence on two main grounds:

(1) there was no constructive total loss because no Notice of Abandonment had been given; and
(2) the repairs after the explosion and fire took so long that it was impossible to perform the charter.

22.39 In his Lordship's view, they were wrong on both points. Section 61 of the Marine Insurance Act 1906 gave the shipowner the choice whether to treat the casualty as a mere partial loss, or as a total loss. If he elected to treat it as a constructive total loss, then section 62 obliged him to give Notice of Abandonment to the underwriters. The underwriters were confusing two separate concepts, a constructive total loss which the facts would establish, and the formalities that must be observed if the assured chose to claim it. Furthermore, Clauses 5 and 8 must be read together. Under Clause 5, the freight underwriters' liability to pay depends on the loss, actual or constructive, of the ship. It accrues at once, even if it takes time to ascertain the true position. Here the loss was complete at the date of the explosion and the fire, and the loss of time after the casualty was irrelevant to the question of the underwriter's liability.

22.40 That should have been enough to settle the matter in the shipowner's favour, but Lord Wright went on to deal with the underwriter's points on Clause 8, whether the claim is excluded by delay:

"So far as authority goes, such a contention has been rejected under circumstances similar in principle to the present by Roche J. in *Roura and Forgas* v. *Townend and Others* and by the Court of Appeal in the *Carras* case." (Paras. 22.33–22.35, 22.11–22.16.)

22.41 The *Bensaude* case could be distinguished. In that case, there was no total loss of the ship:

"The loss of freight was caused simply by the delay in repairing the particular average damage arising from the peril of the sea, the delay being such as to frustrate the object of the adventure . . . If the claim depends on loss of time in the prosecution of the voyage so that the adventure cannot be completed within the time contemplated, then the underwriter is to be exempted from liability . . . (in the *Bensaude* case). The loss of freight was due to loss of time and nothing else although arising from a peril of the sea."

22.42 Lord Porter was more cautious, and showed a disinclination to step outside the issues before the House. He fully agreed with Lord Wright on the existence of a constructive total loss, and that there was no necessity for a Notice of Abandonment. On Clause 8, and the *Bensaude*, *Turnbull Martin* and *Russian Bank* cases:

"In all these cases there was a total loss of the adventure by which the freight was to have been earned. Nevertheless that loss was held to be due to delay . . . In none of these cases, however, was there a total or constructive total loss of the ship."

22.43 Thus there was no opportunity in these earlier cases to study the inter-action of Clauses 5 and 8 which were so important to the *Nomikos* case. This inter-action took the following form:

"Read together it is possible to construe them in either of two ways. They may mean either (i) If loss of freight be caused by loss of time the underwriters shall not be liable, provided that if the vessel is a constructive total loss, then the underwriters will pay in full whether the cause of the loss of freight be loss of time or not, or they may mean (ii) In no case will the underwriters be liable for loss caused by loss of time, whether the vessel be a constructive total loss or not."

22.44 Of the two alternatives, the former one was to be preferred. Lord Porter found Clause 8 doubtful in its meaning, and being an exclusion clause, was to be interpreted against the underwriters.

22.45 In each instance, therefore, the assureds won their cases by showing that the insured perils had caused the casualties, and that in neither case were they caused by delay. It is true that, as a leading case on the subject of delay, the *Nomikos* case is complicated by the nature of the constructive total loss and the resultant liability of the underwriters under Clause 5. It is however suggested that there is sufficient, particularly in the judgments of Roche J. and of Lord Wright, and to some lesser extent in that of Lord Porter, to say that the courts will still make a very close examination of the facts to determine the proximate cause, and will not be deterred from a finding that the loss is due to a peril of the seas even where there is no constructive total loss. If, for instance, the *Petrakis Nomikos* had been less seriously damaged so that she was not a constructive total loss, but was still badly enough damaged so that she could not sail, it could still have been said that she had lost her charter and her freight due to a peril of the seas. Leaving Rotterdam on 31st October, to be in Venezuela by the 10th November, was pretty tight and any postponement of sailing would make it impossible. The result in court must of course remain a matter for conjecture.

22.46 *Atlantic Maritime Company Inc.* v. *Gibbon*[38] is a very firm indication that it is the proximate cause that matters, particularly in the judgment of Lord Evershed M.R.

---

38. [1954] 1 Q.B. 88.

1949

15th July

The *Atlantic Trader's* hull and machinery and freight is insured on the S.G. Form with the F.C.& S. Clause deleted. The freight is insured for $93,600. The policy includes the following exclusions clauses: "Nevertheless this policy is warranted free of any claim based upon loss of, or frustration of, any voyage or adventure caused by arrests, restraints or detainments of Kings, Princes, people . . . "

"Warranted free of loss proximately caused by delay."

"Warranted free from any claims consequent on loss of time whether arising from a peril of the sea or otherwise."

16th July

The ship is chartered to load salt at Taku Bar, Tientsin for Moji, Japan.

1st August

The ship arrives at Taku Bar and anchors. Although the Nationalists are the *de jure* government in China, the Communists are in control of the port. She is told to be ready to load on 13th August. Three other ships are at anchor a short way from her and also a Chinese patrol boat, K264.

8th August a.m.

A Nationalist destroyer arrives and the ship is boarded by a heavily-armed naval party. The boarding officer tells the Master in no uncertain terms not to communicate with the shore and to leave North Chinese ports as soon as possible, otherwise the Nationalists will take no responsibility for any damage to his ship. The boarding officer visits the other ships, presumably giving them the same message.

8th August p.m.

The destroyer sinks K264. Another Nationalist destroyer arrives and signals that the ships had better leave at once because "new activity" will start before 20.00 hrs. If a ship is damaged it is her own fault.

8th August, 19.00 hrs

The ship sails.

8th August, 20.00 hrs

Gunfire is heard from the direction of Taku Bar. It later transpires that a ship in the harbour is sunk.

9th August

The Master is ordered by the shipowners to proceed to British Columbian ports to load timber under a new charterparty. He does so, making no attempt to return to Taku Bar. Subsequently it is learnt that after the shelling, several parcels of salt are loaded as liner shipments.

22.47 Sellers J. heard the case in the High Court. He held that the ship had not voluntarily left Taku Bar but had done so under compulsion "by reason of civil war and restraint of Princes" which also prevented the loading of the cargo and the earning of the freight. The freight underwriters, however, resisted the claim on the grounds that the adventure was lost by frustration or alternatively by delay. Sellers J. remarked that the voyage had begun and that lay days had started but: "In so far as the claim has to be made on the restraint of Princes peril, underwriters are not liable."

22.48 The owners and the underwriters having expressly agreed that "restraints of Princes" were not to be covered, this is not surprising, but the judge went on to say that this was a loss of time matter: "Dealing with the question as one of fact, I find in this case . . . that the Time Clauses would defeat the claim based on restraint of Princes in the absence of the frustration clause", and the same result would have been reached if the shipowner had sought to establish, and succeeded in establishing, the insured peril of civil war. On this judgment was signed for the underwriters.

22.49 On appeal, Lord Evershed M.R. gave the main judgment. He also took the view that the Master had acted under compulsion and therefore involuntarily, but that the appeal should nevertheless fail. The proximate cause was "restraint of Princes" and not of "civil war", and the frustration clause protected the underwriters. *The Yero Carras*[39] case could be distinguished because here the proximate cause was perils of the seas. Although this disposed of the matter, he then went on to consider the loss of time clauses, where he clearly felt that the previous judgments had gone too far. He drew attention to what Lord Herschell had said in his judgment in the *Bensaude* case[40] and a further part of Lord Halsbury L.C.'s judgment in the same case: "The reason why there was loss of freight was that the repairs would have taken so long a time as would have defeated the adventure."

22.50 On the *Russian Bank* case[41] he noted: "Closure [of the Dardanelles] was of so long a time or of so indefinite a duration that the restraint, which the declaration of war involved, was treated as being conclusive." His own view was very concisely expressed[42]:

"In a case such as the *Russian Bank*,[43] and in this case, it seems to me that the time element is relevant, not as a consequence of the mishap, but to ascertain correctly the nature and quality of the accident. If, because of the length of time which is likely to subsist during which the peril lasts, it is justifiable to say 'this finally disposes of the bargain' then the freight is lost then and there immediately upon the happening of the insured peril and is attributable solely to that peril. The time element has only been essential in order to estimate correctly the extent of that peril."

22.51 He found support from MacKinnon L.J. in the *Nomikos* case[44]: "[The exception] will bar any claim whenever it is necessary for the assured to assert the lapse of time as one of the facts establishing his course of action" which Lord Evershed M.R. explained: "That is, the actual lapse of times as it in fact occurs." Morris L.J. signified his agreement with the views of Lord Evershed M.R.

22.52 *Ikerigi Compania Naviera S.A. and Others* v. *Palmer and Others (The Wondrous)*[45] is a case which really belongs to Chapter 13 as a detainment case. There was a claim on the freight insurance which involved delay, although this took the form of detainment by the Customs Authorities in Bandar Abbas because of infringement of customs regulations. The freight insurance contained an exclusion which read:

"This insurance excludes loss (total or partial) arising from . . . detainment . . . by reason of infringement of any customs . . . regulations".

This is the wording of Clause 4.1.5 of the Institute War and Strikes Clauses Freight—Time 1.10.83.

22.53 Hobhouse J. had to consider whether the plaintiffs had suffered any loss in fact or in law. They had suffered none in fact because, in spite of the lengthy delays, the ship had completed her voyage and had earned her freight. In law:

"In my judgment, the detainment was by reason of the infringement of customs regulations. It follows that the operative cause was not an insured peril. This is fatal to the shipowners case however they put it."

---

39. (1935) 53 Ll.L.Rep. 131. See paras. 22.11–22.16.
40. [1897] 1 Q.B. 29. See paras 22.26–22.28.
41. [1918] 2 K.B. 123. See paras. 21.15– 22.29.
42. [1954] 1 Q.B. at p. 127.
43. [1918] 2 K.B. 123.
44. [1939] A.C. 371. See paras. 22.36–22.44.
45. [1991] 1 Lloyd's Rep. 400, [1992] 2 Lloyd's Rep. 566.

PRESENT DAY EXCLUSIONS

Ships—freight

22.54 The Institute War and Strikes Clauses Hulls—Time 1.10.83 contain an exclusion which reads:

"*4 Exclusions*

This insurance excludes
4.4 any claim for expenses arising from delay except such expenses as would be recoverable in principle in English Law and Practice under the York–Antwerp Rules 1974."

22.55 There is no further general exclusion of delay in either the marine or war and strikes insurance for ships, although there is a particular exclusion, as Hobhouse J. noted, in the *Wondrous* case (paras. 22.52, 22.53).

22.56 The Institute War and Strikes Clauses Freight—Time 1.10.83 have a slightly different exclusion which reads:

"*4 Exclusions*

This insurance excludes
4.4 loss proximately caused by delay or any claim for expenses arising from delay except such expenses as would be recoverable in principle in English law and practice under the York–Antwerp Rules 1974."

22.57 These clauses similarly contain no further general exclusion of delay, but, like the ship's war and strikes clauses, they have the same particular exclusion which was the subject of the *Wondrous* case.

22.58 The position with freight, however, does not end there. Several freight clauses were considered in the *Nomikos* case, and they still exist. Clauses (5) and (6) are now numbered 15.1 and 15.2 respectively. Their text is set out at para. 22.4. Clause (8) is now Clause 14 which reads:

"*14 Loss of Time*

This insurance does not cover any claim consequent on loss of time whether arising from a peril of the sea or otherwise."

22.59 Clauses 14, 15.1 and 15.2 are all clauses of the Institute Time Clauses Freight 1.8.89. They are incorporated into the Freight War and Strikes Clauses by Clause 2. Clause 14 complements the Freight War and Strikes Clause 4.4.

Cargo—containers

22.60 The Institute War Clauses (Cargo) 1.1.82 contain the following exclusions of delay and frustration of the voyage or adventure. These read:

"*Exclusions*

3 In no case shall this insurance cover
3.5 loss damage or expense proximately caused by delay, even though the delay be caused by a risk insured against [except those arising in General average or as salvage charges]
3.7 any claim based upon loss of or frustration of the voyage or adventure."

22.61 The Institute Strikes Clauses (Cargo) 1.1.82 contain similar exclusions, save that the frustration exclusion is numbered 3.8. This pattern is continued throughout the clauses for special cargoes. The Institute War and Strikes Clauses Containers—Time 1.1.87 contain an exclusion of delay, numbered 5.3, in exactly similar terms. There is no exclusion relating to frustration of the voyage or adventure. All the exclusions of delay require that the loss, damage or expense shall be "proximately caused" by the delay. This produces some welcome clarity. The Through Transport Mutual Insurance Association Ltd. and the Through Transport Mutual Insurance Association of Europe Ltd. have no exclusions of delay in their Rules.

Frustration of the voyage or adventure

22.62 Frustration of the voyage or adventure is dealt with at paras. 36.42–36.52.

CONCLUSIONS

22.63 As conclusions it is suggested that:

1. The nature of freight as a subject for insurance is well defined by Lord Wright M.R. (para. 22.3) and that the same definition is relevant whether a marine or a war risk policy on freight is effected.
2. The insured perils are the same, and have the same meanings, as the insured perils of the War Risk Policy on hull and machinery.
3. Loss of freight will arise from the loss of a freight contract, either wholly or in part, which is brought about by an insured peril.
4. A total loss under a freight policy does not depend upon the same rules as does a constructive total loss under the Hull and Machinery Policy. It can arise where the ship is so badly damaged by insured perils that the repairs would be "so ruinously expensive" that no prudent shipowner would undertake them. "Ruinously expensive" is not an abstract notion but depends, in general, on proving the repaired value of the ship as against the estimated expenses of temporary repairs. Whilst there is an unavoidable margin of error in any estimates, this must be reduced to the maximum extent that it is humanly possible to do so. The *Kulukundis* case[46] is an example.
5. Some strong judicial doubts have been expressed whether or not the *Bensaude* case was correctly decided. It is a House of Lords decision and, as such, is binding on the lower courts. As long as the doctrine of "proximate cause" is followed (Chapter 30), and the courts continue to make exhaustive investigations to establish the proximate cause, called by Hobhouse J. in the *Wondrous* case "the operative cause", this should establish satisfactorily whether the casualty comes within an insured peril or an excluded risk.
6. If the insured ship should become a constructive total loss under the Hull and Machinery War Risks Policy, the full sum insured by the Freight Policy

---

46. [1937] 1 K.B. 1. See paras. 22.18–22.24.

becomes payable under Clause 15 of that policy, which is relevant to that situation alone. If freight is subsequently earned, not by any means an impossible situation, the shipowner must account to the freight under-writer for that freight.

CHAPTER 23

Special insurance given by the Mutual War Risks Associations

23.1 This work has already discussed the hull and machinery insurance and the freight insurance provided by the Lloyd's Market on the MAR form, with Institute War and Strikes Clauses attached, and the Mutual War Risks Associations. This is very similar, and attention has been drawn in earlier chapters to the differences which exist.

23.2 In the following chapter, some differences to insurance as it is normally understood must first be noted in order that the reader can follow the text, even though a fuller description of the character of the Mutual War Risks Associations is given at paras. 2.4–2.5. The shipowners who "enter" their ships in a Mutual War Risks Association become members of that Association besides being insured shipowners. They elect from their number the directors of the Association. The Association is run by managers, who are immediately responsible to the Board of Directors and through them to the members of the Association. An insured ship is referred to as "the entered ship". To these shipowner members the Mutual War Risks Associations provide additional insurance. Furthermore, there is one very special provision on "orders, prohibitions and directions" which, so far as the author is aware, appears in no other maritime insurance. For the purpose of discussing these, this chapter will be divided into six sections.

1. Detention and diversion insurance;
2. War Risks Protection and Indemnity insurance;
3. The discretionary insurance;
4. The orders, prohibitions and directions rule;
5. Constructive total loss provision;
6. Miscellaneous.

1. DETENTION AND DIVERSION INSURANCE

23.3 An entered ship which is detained or has to divert because of certain insured perils or events results in substantial loss and expense to her owners. The insured perils and other events are listed in the Rules and can be briefly summarised:

1. War, civil war, revolution, rebellion, insurrection, civil strife, or hostile acts by or against a belligerent power—or conditions resulting from any of them.

251

2. An order direction or prohibition made by the directors (paras. 23.17–23.20), by her own government, or by another government having the right to do so, which is aimed at keeping the ship out of harm's way.
3. The actions of a government or an agency thereof which in the opinion of the directors is politically motivated; the actions of a political movement maintaining an armed force; the actions of terrorists, pirates, bandits or rioters.
4. Action taken by ship owners to avoid loss or damage to the entered ship so far as the directors in their discretion determine.

23.4 These insured perils and other events are only briefly described here for the purposes of this work. There is a danger of distortion by such a brief summary. The rule of the proximate cause still applies, and it is wise to refer to the actual Rules themselves before deciding if a claim arises to see if the facts of any particular case fit within the insurance. Some examples will follow to show the claims which have been paid. There are no helpful judicial decisions in the context of the detention and diversion insurance, although the insured perils of war, civil war, and so on will be interpreted in the same way as they are in respect of hull and machinery claims.

23.5 If therefore the ship is detained because of one of these insured perils, her owner is entitled to receive his out-of-pocket expenses for the time that his ship is detained. At the date of the first edition of this work, the heads of these out-of-pocket expenses were defined in a schedule to the Rules of the Hellenic (Bermuda) Association. This list was long and very complex, and the members of the Association have found it difficult to use. They have requested something simpler which does "rough justice", but which does not require them to prove their losses down to the last cent, which posed great difficulties in some cases. As a result, new Rules are being adopted to the effect that, if a ship is detained by reason of one of these insured perils, her owner is entitled to receive 10% per annum, *pro rata* for the actual period of detention, of her insured value. The insured value will include the amounts insured for her hull and machinery and her freight. There will be a deductible of the first seven days. To this amount will be added any additional premiums which she may have to pay during the period of her detention, and the port charges. Similarly, if one of these insured perils should require diversion of the ship, her owner will receive a similar 10%, *pro rata* to the length of time the voyage is prolonged as a consequence of the diversion. Again there is a deductible of the first seven days.

23.6 The 90-day Rule, which was mentioned in the First Edition, is also being changed. A diversion is unlikely to last for 90 days, but there have been cases where detention through one of the insured perils has lasted for more than 90 days and this is a very serious matter. Under the former Rule, her owner was entitled to receive 10% of her insured values (again including the amounts insured for hull and machinery and freight), for the period of detention after 90 days. There was a drawback to this, because if the ship subsequently became a total loss, one half of this was deducted from the total loss payment. This too has been simplified; in future, her owner will receive 5% of the insured value, in addition to the 10%, for the time she is detained after 90 days have passed. The amended Rule, like its predecessor, does not apply to all the above-named insured perils. (Appendix P.).

23.7 The rights to the amounts of 10% and 5% will come to an end when the insured ship ceases to be insured; this may well come about because she becomes a constructive total loss because of the detention.

Remembering that this insurance covers the expenses caused by detention and diversion, and that the conditions and exceptions to this part of the insurance have no application to other parts of the insurance afforded by the Mutual War Risks Association, in particular the cover for hull and machinery risks, the conditions and exclusions to the detention and delay insurance can be briefly summarised. There are express exclusions in respect of the following:

1. Time lost because of strikes, lock-outs, industrial action or labour disturbances and the actions of those taking part or steps taken to avoid such events. The Mutual War Risks Associations are not ship owners' Strike Clubs which provide this insurance.
2. Time spent awaiting or undergoing repairs, even if made necessary by an insured peril.
3. If the entered ship is damaged because of an insured peril during the detention, this amount is deducted from amounts payable under the 90-day Rule unless the directors otherwise decide.
4. Hire or other sums paid on a time basis, such as demurrage, are deducted from the out-of-pocket expenses and the amounts payable under the 90-day Rule. If these amounts are due but not paid, the owner is required to assign his rights to the Association.
5. Diversion expenses are only payable if the entered ship is already on her voyage at the time any order, direction or prohibition is made.

23.8 Some examples where detention and diversion expenses have been paid are:

1. In 1956, during the Anglo-French invasion of the Suez Canal area, the fighting around the Suez Canal area made it too dangerous to go near it. Ships were directed by their Mutual War Risks Associations to stay away. Those already at sea had to sail round the Cape of Good Hope. Their diversion expenses, being the extra costs which they had to find, were paid.
2. In 1967, during the Six Day War, the same thing happened. Again the entered ships already at sea had their diversion expenses, being the extra expenses they had to find, paid.
3. In 1967, again during the Six Day War, some ships were trapped in the Suez Canal. The ships entered in the Mutual War Risks Associations had their detention expenses paid until they were accepted as constructive total losses (paras. 13.52–13.53).
4. In 1971, during the India/Pakistan War, an entered ship was due to call at Indian ports. In normal times, her Pakistani crew would simply be forbidden to leave the ship while she was in port. Now, they could expect to be interned. She diverted to Colombo to change her crew and the extra costs which she had to pay for this purpose were paid.
5. In 1973, during the Yom Kippur War, entered ships were discharging into lighters off Gaza. Everything was peaceful but it was most unlikely that it would remain so. Their Mutual War Risks Association ordered them to

leave. They did so and the extra expenses which they had to meet were paid.

6. During the Iran/Iraq War, which began in 1980, ships were detained in the Shatt-al-Arab River and at other ports in Iraq (the facts of the detention are set out in the description of *The Bamburi*).[1] In June 1981 the Hellenic (Bermuda) Association accepted that the ships were constructive total losses. Between September 1980 and June 1981 the Mutual War Risks Association paid the detention costs, being the out-of-pocket expenses and claims under the 90-day Rule.

23.9 This list is not comprehensive, being merely some examples of where detention and diversion expenses have been paid since the Second World War. There would be little point in setting out a comprehensive but repetitive list of the many occasions that this insurance has been called upon to pay for detention and diversion expenses.

2. WAR RISKS P. & I. INSURANCE

23.10 The insurance given by the Protection and Indemnity Associations is third party liability insurance, or the consequences of what a ship does to other people. The scope of protection and indemnity insurance is enormous but the Mutual P. & I. Associations exclude, from their insurance, risks arising from a war or matters similar to a war. For instance, Rule 5.E of the Rules of The United Kingdom Mutual Steam Ship Assurance Association (Bermuda) Limited reads:

"The Association shall not indemnify an Owner against any liabilities, costs or expenses (irrespective of whether a contributory cause of the same being incurred was any neglect on the part of the Owner or on the part of the Owner's servants or agents) when the loss or damage, injury, illness or death or other accident in respect of which such liability arises or cost or expense is incurred, was caused by: i. War, civil war, revolution, rebellion, insurrection or civil strife arising therefrom, or any hostile act by or against a belligerent power; ii. Capture, seizure, arrest, restraint or detainment (barratry and piracy excepted) and the consequences thereof or any attempt threat; iii. Mines, torpedoes, bombs, rockets, shells, explosives or other similar weapons of war . . ." (This exclusion is qualified to allow the P. & I. Clubs to ensure claims arising from weapons being carried as cargo.)

In spite of this, some Protection and Indemnity Associations have armed themselves with powers to give War Risks insurance in certain cases (see para. 23.13).

23.11 The Mutual War Risks Associations give insurance for the risks thus excluded from the Marine P. & I. Associations' cover by the quoted clause, the intention being that there should be full "dovetailing" between the cover provided by the Marine P. & I. Associations, and that provided by the Mutual War Risks Associations. The risks excluded from the Marine Associations' insurance are set out in the Mutual War Risks Associations' Rules word for word as insured perils with only one minor difference; the Mutual War Risks Associations' Rules include as an insured peril "other weapons of war", leaving out the word "similar".

23.12 So much for the risks clearly excluded from the Marine P. & I. Associations' cover and assumed as insured perils by the Mutual War Risks Associations

1. [1982] 1 Lloyd's Rep. 312. See paras. 13.63–13.72.

on the "dovetailing" principle. The Mutual War Risks Associations do, however, go a bit further than this, and trespass on the ground where the Marine P. & I. Associations do themselves, in part, give insurance. By doing so, problems of double insurance will undoubtedly arise which need specific mention in the Mutual War Risks Associations' double insurance rule. The recent *City of Poros* tragedy (1988) has made them concerned for their members that, irrespective of what other underwriters do and what cover they give, their members shall have cover from their Mutual War Risks Association for their liabilities arising out of the activities of:

—Strikers, locked-out workmen, or persons taking part in labour disturbances.
—Any terrorist or any person acting maliciously, or from a political motive.
—Piracy or violent theft from persons coming from outside the entered ship.

From the Mutual War Risks Associations' Rule Book, it will be seen that there are three additional and special considerations which need express inclusion into the insurance provided by the Mutual War Risks Associations:

1. Liability for collision is a special case, because three-quarters of the liability for collision damage is paid for by the Institute Time Clauses attached to the MAR form. The Mutual War Risks Associations have extended their insurance to include the collision liabilities which are excluded from the Institute Clauses by their Clauses 23 to 25 (see Appendix C).
2. Crew can be detained, indeed interned, in a war situation. A special rule is included in the Mutual War Risks Associations' Rules to include insurance for such liabilities to them.
3. If a Mutual War Risks Association should give its members an order, prohibition or direction (paras. 23.17–23.20), the contract of carriage of the goods should permit the shipowner to comply without any question of liability to the goods owners for deviation. Should this expectation be disappointed and the shipowner be held liable to pay damages to the cargo owners, the Association's insurance will pay them.

23.13 There are two other factors which need to be noted.

1. Unlike the Protection and Indemnity Associations where, with well-defined exceptions, insurance is not subject to any limit, recovery under the Protection and Indemnity Rules of the Mutual War Risks Associations is subject to limits which, under the terms of the Rules, are fixed by the directors at the start of each policy year. The War Risks Associations themselves are too small to consider the provision of unlimited insurance as do the Protection and Indemnity Associations, but the directors will see to it that the upper limits on insurance are extensive enough to cover most claims that can be expected to arise.
2. Some of the Protection and Indemnity Associations now give insurance for the risks excluded by Rule 5.E (para. 23.10) under special powers which were first introduced in 1987. These will provide protection and indemnity insurance up to a limit which is fixed by the directors every year for P. & I. type liabilities which would otherwise be excluded by Rule 5.E. Such insur-

ance is subject to a large deductible, and the shipowner is expected to effect what primary insurance he can elsewhere; it therefore follows that those who have an entry with a Mutual War Risks Association, having war risks protection and indemnity insurance from that Association, will be expected to look to their Mutual War Risks Association for the primary insurance and only to their Protection and Indemnity Association for any insurance in excess thereof.

23.14 Most of the recent examples consist of paying the amounts which, under their ships' Articles, the shipowners are obliged to pay in respect of seamen who are killed or injured because of attacks on their ships. There have been a number of such claims during the Iran/Iraq War (1980–88). These claims include hospital and medical expenses, repatriation costs and wages. Other examples include seamen murdered ashore in Beirut and a case where a ship, hurriedly leaving Beirut after being fired upon during one of the periodic bouts of fighting, damaged one of the silos which were discharging a cargo of wheat. During the India/Pakistan War (1971), an entered ship was bound for India with a Pakistani crew (para. 23.8). Normally, the Pakistani crew would merely be forbidden to leave the ship whilst she was in port but, on this occasion, they could expect internment. Their repatriation expenses from Colombo were paid. The most extreme example of all occurred during the same war where an Indian destroyer fired a Russian-made Ossa missile at the Refinery in Karachi. The missile went astray, hitting the messroom of an entered ship awaiting a berth to discharge, and killing several seamen. Compensation, which was due to their relatives under the ship's Articles was paid by the Mutual War Risks Association and it is a happy feature of this tragic incident that India, whilst refusing to pay anything for the loss of the ship, made additional *ex gratia* payments to the relatives.

23.15 Lastly it should be noted that the war risk P. & I. insurance given by the Mutual War Risks Associations is additional to the insurance which they provide for hull and machinery risks. There is thus no danger of an insured shipowner having his recovery for the loss of or the damage to the hull and machinery of his entered ship being reduced because of claims arising under the war risks P. & I. cover.

3. THE DISCRETIONARY INSURANCE

23.16 The Mutual War Risks Associations are institutions consisting of, and existing for the benefit of, their shipowner members. The insurance they provide is at the cost of the members for a number of insured perils which are set out in the Rules which, at the start of the policy year, the members agree to bear mutually for the new policy year. Theoretically it is possible to change the terms of insurance during the course of a policy year if all the members agree, but in practice this is not done. It would not be an acceptable practice to put upon a member a whole lot of additional burdens to which he had not agreed. The Rules are, from time to time, changed and new risks are added. This is only done on renewal, and with the agreement of the members obtained in General Meeting, with the changes taking effect at the start of a new policy year. A member who feels disinclined to bear the burdens of additional risks can, if he wishes, leave the Association on the expiry of the old policy year.

The application of this provision, in spite of its apparently wide and sweeping powers, is thus very limited in practice. It can only extend to such par s of war risk insurance which are not specifically provided for by the Rules, and which are sometimes required. It is there to ensure that the spirit of the insurance is not necessarily defeated by its letter.

4. THE ORDERS, PROHIBITIONS AND DIRECTIONS RULE

23.17 The directors of the Mutual War Risks Associations have power to give orders, prohibitions and directions regarding routes, trading areas, ports, stoppages, convoys, cargoes, methods of loading or discharging cargoes, modes of management or of navigation and manning and equipment. This includes the power to instruct the shipowners whose ships are entered in the Association that an entered ship shall not proceed to or remain at any port, place, country, zone (· area, or if within it then to leave it.

23.18 This is not as autocratic as it may sound. It is true that with a Mutual War Risks Association, as with all Mutual Associations, members should not be permitted to trade with areas of acute danger, usually for a much enhanced freight, and expect their fellow members who pursue more cautious trades to pay for the loss of or damage to their ship. This is a device for withdrawing the cover afforded by the Association in respect of a specified area, so that if a member nevertheless trades there, he does so without the Association's insurance. The Rule does however contain a very much greater protection for the Association's members than the bare wording of the Rule might suggest to the reader.

23.19 The courts are naturally reluctant to accord to a Master the right to leave a port, or to refuse to go there, simply because he decides that it is unsafe, unless there is a very good reason for his decision. The Master's power must be used reasonably and not arbitrarily, and what appears reasonable at the time may, in retrospect, appear unjustified. Moreover, the law on unsafe ports is not always certain enough so that a Master can decide that a port is unsafe, and be totally confident that the courts will support his decision in any subsequent proceedings. In any case, these will usually be heard years after the event, and much more information will be available to the court than was available to the Master at the time. It will seem curious to the reader that it is often more difficult to judge whether a port is unsafe because of hostilities and the liklihood of hostile attacks than it is when the factors to be considered are the weather and the sea. Some recent decisions on unsafe ports in the context of war risks are briefly set out in Chapter 31 and it is hoped that they will be of interest.

23.20 The order by a Mutual War Risks Association is a different matter. Its directors must only use it reasonably, and must be prepared to justify any decision that they might make, but provided that they are able to do this, they may instruct their members not to go to a place or area, and if within it to leave it at once or, as it is more usually expressed, "with due despatch". There have been occasions when the local authorities have wanted the cargo and have refused to let the entered ship sail. Provided that she sails as soon as she is able to, her insurance is not prejudiced. As the contract of carriage allows the entered ship to obey the dictates of her war risks underwriters, provided that such underwriters have a proper and valid power to make them, and excuses what would otherwise be a deviation, the Rule is a most valuable protection to the shipowners whose ships are entered in the Mutual War Risks Association to keep their ships, their cargoes and their crews away from dangerous areas.

23.21 Some examples will serve to illustrate this:

1. The Six Day War between Egypt and Israel broke out very suddenly in 1967. After two days, the Suez Canal was closed and it was far from clear when it would be reopened. Heavy fighting was taking place within its immediate area as the Israelis attacked the Egyptian army in the Sinai Desert. Whilst liner bills of lading were usually more liberal in that they permitted the shipowners to follow their chosen routes to their destinations, and if necessary to tranship cargo, the bulk carriers and the tankers had a much more difficult problem. The usual obligation of a shipowner is to follow the normal and customary route to his destination and in a voyage from northern Europe or North America to the Far East or vice versa, it was difficult to contend that this lay anywhere other than through the Suez Canal. Few if any charterparties had foreseen this situation, even to the extent of providing that the route lay via Suez, and the spectre of deviation always loomed. At the same time it was, with rare instances, impossible to say that the voyage was frustrated.

By 1967 the law of frustration of contract had developed to the point that a contract was only considered as frustrated if the circumstances had altered to such an extent and in a way that the parties had not foreseen or provided for, that to compel them to perform their contract would be to require them to perform different obligations to those they had voluntarily undertaken. The advice of the lawyers was that, except in rare instances where it was a physical impossibility for the ship to sail round the Cape, a voyage round the Cape of Good Hope was not so substantially a different obligation to one through the Suez Canal that frustration of contract would be said to arise. There were also grave practical difficulties. To claim that a charterparty is frustrated means that the cargo has to be disposed of. The prospect of having large quantities of grain, ore or scrap dumped on their quaysides for an indefinite time did not appeal to various harbour masters who, understandably enough, refused to allow it. The discharging costs would have to be met by the shipowners with the uncertain prospect of recovery from the charterers. Oil posed a special problem; it cannot even be dumped on a quayside and the owners of the storage tanks had better uses for what storage tanks existed. In effect, a shipowner who has a cargo on board can only discharge it at its destination, although there have been exceptions to this. In 1971, many ships were carrying coal to Chittagong in what was then East Pakistan. The India/Pakistan War broke out and, anticipating fighting in the immediate area, the Mutual War Risks Associations ordered the entered ships which were already lying off Chittagong, or were on their way there, either to leave at once or not to go there. There was no doubt that the voyages were frustrated in this instance; the Government Agency of East Pakistan to whom the cargoes were consigned ceased to exist. The Singapore Port Authorities allowed the discharge of their cargoes in their port.

2. During the India/Pakistan War in 1971, naval operations were threatened in the Arabian Sea off the Pakistani coast. An order was made that ships should avoid this area. This involved a substantial deviation to reach the port of Bombay, but at least they could do so without any fear of being in breach of contract, and still keep out of the area of possible naval engagements.

3. The Yom-Kippur War broke out very suddenly in 1973. A substantial number of ships were in the roads off the port of Gaza. The port was working normally and everything was peaceful, but an air attack by the powerful airforces of Egypt or Israel could be expected at any time. An order was made that the ships should leave. This protected them from any hostilities without any fear of breach of contract. Any attempt by the Masters to sail away without such an order could later have been held to be unjustified by the courts, as no air attack ever took place.

4. From the outset of the Iran/Iraq War, the area in the immediate neighbourhood of the Shatt-al-Arab and Bandar Khomeni was always exceedingly dangerous. It was impossible to enter the Shatt, and the Iranian port of Bandar Khomeni was constantly attacked by the Iraqi Air Force. Its approach channel, the Khor Musa, was also attacked, usually by helicopters armed with AS-12 missiles. This weapon, an obsolescent British-made missile is wire-guided on to its target. Although its range is only six kilometres, it is extremely accurate and it caused very extensive damage to any ships which it hit. The Mutual War Risks Associations therefore prohibited entered ships from entering the area. Later this prohibition was extended to include Kharg Island and ships trading to it. The Iraqi Air Force acquired the Super Etendard plane in 1983 with its French-made Exocet missile, which at that date had a range of 30 kilometres. The range of the Super Etendard is limited and it is a subsonic plane, being no faster than the latest type of Boeing 747. It was later supplemented by the latest marks of supersonic Mirage fighter bombers whose range included the entire Gulf, and a subsequent version of the Exocet with a range of nearly 70 kilometres. They used this missile to attack ships trading to Kharg Island, and whilst there were a few instances of ships being sunk and cargoes destroyed, the ships usually survived the attack and the cargoes were for the most part completely undamaged. Nevertheless, the damage caused was still considerable and the danger of attack was extreme.

The Iranians retaliated, not by the more effective means of engaging the attacking aircraft with their Phantoms, but by attacking ships bound for Arab ports. For this they used the Maverick anti-tank missile and, whilst this was not very effective, it caused some damage and some deaths and injuries as well. Whilst some precautions could be taken by the ships themselves it was still a hazardous weapon. Later mines were sown, or simply allowed to drift in the Gulf, and the welcome appearance in the Gulf of the Royal Navy, the U.S. Navy, and the navies of the U.S.S.R., France, Italy, Belgium and Holland did much to obviate this menace and also to produce some measure of stability in other directions. Nevertheless, no direction was made by the Mutual War Risks Associations in respect of parts of the Gulf other than those listed. High as the degree of danger was, it was not thought to be sufficiently serious to justify such a step.

5. During the Falklands War, the prospect of fighting between the very powerful armed forces of the United Kingdom and Argentina persuaded the Mutual War Risks Associations to prohibit entered ships from entering or remaining in a large

part of the South Atlantic besides the ports in the Falklands themselves and Argentina. The extent of this area was reduced as soon as it was felt to be justified when the fighting finished. This prohibition affected ships trading around Cape Horn because it prevented them from taking advantage of the current along the Argentine and Brazilian coasts. They had to make a considerable detour to avoid the prohibited area. Nevertheless, it ensured the safety of the ships, the cargoes and the crews and if, for any reason, the contracts of carriage were held not to permit the resultant deviation in any one case, the insured shipowners had insurance cover from the Mutual War Risks Associations (para. 23.12).

23.22 There are two other points on the orders, prohibitions and directions rule which should be noted. The directors have power to determine for the purposes of the insurance provided by the Association what is and what is not a safe port or a place of safety. An order, prohibition or direction has the status of a warranty that it will be complied with exactly (Chapter 26). The unfortunate effects of the *Good Luck* case (paras. 26.20–26.35), are now being changed; the Mutual War Risks Association can now only regard the insurance as being terminated if it gives written notice to that effect to the shipowner.

23.23 A lot of things have been said about this rule and it has frequently been criticised as a means of withdrawing cover just when it is most needed. Its use needs care and discretion, but it is hoped that the explanation in this section will emphasise its beneficial aspects to the shipowners whose ships are insured by the Mutual War Risks Associations.

5. THE CONSTRUCTIVE TOTAL LOSS PROVISION

23.24 Under a marine policy, a constructive total loss will not arise unless the ship suffers a physical casualty, when the cost of repairs, and perhaps salvage as well, need to be compared to her insured value. Likewise, physical damage can similarly lead to a constructive total loss under a war risk policy. But, in addition, a ship can suffer "capture, seizure, arrest, restraint, detainment, confiscation or expropriation" and, although not damaged in any physical sense, can become a constructive total loss as a result of these insured perils alone. Section 60 of the Marine Insurance Act 1906 governs the situation:

"(2) In particular, there is a constructive total loss—
    (i) Where the assured is deprived of the possession of his ship or goods by a peril insured against, and it is unlikely that he can recover the ship or goods . . . [within a reasonable time]".

23.25 The best and easiest examples are the decisions in *Polurrian Steamship Co. Ltd.* v. *Young*,[2] which is also the authority for adding the words "within a reasonable time", and *The Bamburi*.[3] The intention of the policy is that the insured perils, when they arise, must first be based on the passage of time in that they have operated for some time, and secondly, at the date when the constructive total loss must be judged, it is unlikely that they will cease to be operative, or that they will come to an end, within a reasonable time so that the insured ship can be recovered.

2. [1915] 1 K.B. 922. See paras. 11.32–11.36.
3. [1981] 1 Lloyd's Rep. 312. See paras. 13.63–13.72.

As already noted (paras. 11.4–11.7), "the date when the constructive total loss must be judged" is the date that the writ is issued, or the date that a Notice of Abandonment is refused by the underwriter and the insured shipowner is put in the same position as if a writ had been issued. To put it another way, it is intended to give insurance in cases where there is a lengthy detention, which is probably going to continue for some time, but it is not intended the trivial hold-ups of the kind all too common with shipping will give rise to a claim.

23.26 There must however be reason and moderation in all this, and a period of detention must not be too long or too short. The Mutual War Risks Associations do not wish to require their members to wait for years before their ships can become constructive total losses, as the underwriters pleaded in *The Bamburi*.[4] On the other hand the possibility of the period of detention too short cannot be ignored as the following, an admittedly extreme, example will show.

Monday

The ship is "seized".

Tuesday

Notice of Abandonment is tendered to the underwriter.

Wednesday

The Notice of Abandonment is refused by the underwriter.

Thursday

A writ is issued against the underwriter.

Friday

Quite unexpectedly, the ship is released.

If, on the Thursday, events are such that there is no likelihood of the ship being released within a reasonable time, a constructive total loss could arise on this date even though the ship is released on the Friday. Such a constructive total loss would, in such circumstances, be totally unjustified.

23.27 In order to balance these two requirements so that neither a too short or a too long period is required, the Mutual War Risks Associations have adopted a rule that no claim for an actual or a constructive total loss shall arise if the insured ship-owner is deprived of the free use and disposal of the insured ship by capture, seizure, arrest, restraint, detainment, confiscation or expropriation for a lesser period than 183 days. The directors can, if they see fit, reduce this period in suitable circumstances, and would do so where such circumstances indicated that there was patently no point in requiring the shipowner to wait for six months before accepting a constructive total loss. This rule does ensure that a constructive total loss based upon capture, seizure etc. does first depend upon the passage of time without, however, unreasonable insistence on too much time having to pass. It will be noted from Section 1 (para. 23.6) of this chapter, the circumstances where claims in respect of the waiting time, both for detention expenses and under the 90-day rule, can be made.

23.28 The London Market introduced the Detainment Clause when redrafting the Institute Time Clauses in the 1980s. Although this clause had been in existence for many years, it had previously scarcely been used at all. It reads:

4. *Ibid.*

"In the event that the vessel shall have been the subject of capture, seizure, arrest, restraint, detainment, confiscation or expropriation, and the assured shall thereby have lost the free use and disposal of the vessel for a continuous period of twelve months then for the purpose of ascertaining whether the vessel is a constructive total loss, the assured shall be deemed to have been deprived of the possession of the vessel without any likelihood of recovery."

23.29 This clause is contained in the Institute War and Strikes Clauses Hulls—Time dated 1.10.83 (Clause 3) and in the Institute War and Strikes Clauses Containers—Time dated 1.1.87 (Clause 4). It also appears in a modified form in the Institute War and Strikes Clauses Freight—Time 1.10.83, again as Clause 3, where it reads:

"In the event that a claim for a constructive total loss of the vessel is paid on the war risks insurance of the vessel under Clause 3 . . . (of the ship's war and strikes insurance) . . . as a result of the loss of the free use and disposal of the vessel for a continuous period of 12 months . . . the amount insured hereunder shall be paid in full . . . "

23.30 The Detainment Clause is not contained in any of the War and Strikes Clauses which insure cargo. It does however appear in a slightly modified form in the Rules of the Through Transport Mutual Insurance Association Limited and the Through Transport Mutual Association of Europe Limited where they give "War Risks" insurance to "Equipment" (for definitions, see para. 39.7). Rules 2.4.2 (a) and (b) of Part 1, Section 1, and 6.4.2 (a) and (b) of Part 1, Section 4 read:

"(a) Where you have been deprived of possession of an item of insured equipment for a continuous period of twelve months by reason of its capture, seizure, arrest, restraint, detainment, confiscation or expropriation (such item not having previously become a total loss by reason of a risk insured under this paragraph 2.4), such item shall be deemed a constructive total loss for the purposes of your insurance under this paragraph 2.4 at the date such continuous period commenced.

(b) Such item shall only be deemed a constructive total loss in accordance with paragraph 2.4.2(a) if you were insured by the Association under this paragraph 2.4 in respect of such item on the date on which such continuous period commenced."

(The wording is identical for both Rules except that in Part 1, Section 4 the references to paragraph 2.4 read 6.4.)

23.31 A different clause is required by the Mutual War Risks Associations to accommodate the 183-day Rule. For instance, the Hellenic's Rule reads:

"*3.12 Capture, seizure, arrest, restraint, detainment, confiscation or expropriation—*

If an Owner is deprived of the free use and disposal of an Entered Ship by capture, seizure, arrest, restraint, detainment, confiscation or expropriation:

3.12.1 No claim for an actual or constructive total loss shall arise if such deprivation lasts for a period of less than 183 days (or such shorter period as the Directors may, in their discretion, decide);

3.12.2 if such deprivation lasts for a continuous period of 12 months, the Owner shall be deemed to have been deprived of the possession of the ship without any likelihood of recovery."

23.32 Rule 3.12.1 of the Hellenic's Rules has existed in a different form for many years, but the Detainment Clause and Rule 3.12.2 were added as a result of the *Bamburi* case (paras. 13.63–13.72). The Rules of the British Mutual War Risks Associations contain a Rule (Rule 4F.3) which, although its wording is slightly different, has the same effect.

23.33 Undoubtedly the Detainment Clause and Rule 3.12.2 will give rise to anomalies however carefully they may be drawn, as for instance where a ship is likely to be released after detention lasting a year and a day. This is inevitable where clauses depend on the passage of time for their effect; this is still worthwhile because it introduces certainty into an otherwise uncertain position.

6. MISCELLANEOUS

The American Hull Form

23.34 The Hellenic (Bermuda) Association's insurance has been designed to the insurance given by the Institute Time Clauses Hulls 1.10.83, and it is necessary for shipowners whose ships are insured for marine risks on other forms to ensure that there are no gaps in the insurance which could leave them, in the event of certain casualties, without insurance. It is now changing its Rules so that its insurance is suitable to shipowners whose ships are insured for marine risks on the American Hull Form.

Missing vessels

23.35 As explained in Chapter 30 on The Proximate Cause, there is a presumption, now contained in section 58 of the Marine Insurance Act 1906, that a ship which is missing and is not heard of is, after the lapse of a reasonable time, presumed to be an actual total loss. An example of this which is often quoted is *The Charming Peggy*.[5] In the *Munro Brice* case[6] Bailhache J. gave some useful guidance how this presumption was to be applied. Whilst his judgment was subsequently reversed by the Court of Appeal, this was only done on the grounds that he had discounted too far the possibility that a U-boat had sunk the *Inveramsay*. The Court of Appeal did, when hearing *The Arnus*[7] approve a judgment of Roche J.[8] which also dealt with this presumption.

23.36 The Missing Vessels Clause reads:

"In the event of the vessel insured hereunder being posted as missing at Lloyd's or is announced by the Admiralty as missing, it is specially agreed that such vessel is to be treated as a war loss for the purpose of this insurance, and this policy will pay claims hereunder accordingly within thirty days of presentation of proper documents. In consideration of such payment The Hellenic Mutual War Risks Association (Bermuda) Limited are to have subrogation to any claim which the Assured may have against the Marine Underwriters with whom the vessel is insured, but this insurance is not to operate as a double insurance.

In the event of this clause becoming operative it is understood that The Hellenic Mutual War Risks (Bermuda) Limited hereon will in no circumstances pay more than the sums insured hereunder for war risks, either for hull and/or increased value of hull or protection and indemnity risks. It is further understood that the sum payable hereunder on hull and/or increased value of hull shall not exceed the total amount insured on hull and disbursements

---

5. *Green* v. *Brown* (1743) 2 Str. 1199. See para. 30.68.
6. [1918] 2 K.B. 78. See paras. 30.70–30.80.
7. *Compania Naviera Martiartu* v. *Royal Exchange Assurance Corpn. (The Arnus)* (1922) 11 Ll.L.Rep. 174; (1922) 13 Ll.L.Rep. 45, 83, 298 (C.A.); (1924) 18 Ll.L.Rep. 247; (1924) 19 Ll.L.Rep. 95; [1924] A.C. 850 (H.L.). See paras. 30.81–30.83.
8. *Compania Maritima of Barcelona* v. *Wishart* (1918) 23 Com.Cas. 264; (1918) 14 Asp.M.L.C. 298. See para. 30.79

for marine risks and that the sum payable hereunder for war protection and indemnity risks shall not exceed the amounts recoverable under the marine protection and indemnity placings unless until such time as arbitration decides the vessel is a war loss."

This provides in effect that a missing vessel is to be accepted as a war risk loss rather than a marine loss. In the late 1970s a few mortgagees required the borrowing shipowners war risk insurance to assume the burden of the presumption rather than the marine insurance, and, although there appeared to be very little advantage in this, the Mutual War Risks Associations wished to be in a position to furnish such an undertaking if they were required to do so.

Requisition

23.37 The Hellenic (Bermuda) Association's Rules exclude insurance for any loss or damage arising out of the requisition of a ship (Rule 3.4). Also the insurance comes to an end on the requisition of a ship, whether for title or for use (Rule 4.2.3). In this respect, the Association's insurance is affected in the same way as the insurance given by the Institute War and Strikes Clauses Hulls—Time 1.10.83 (Clauses 4.1.3 and 5.2.3), (Appendix D).

23.38 The Rules of the British Mutual War Risks Associations are however different in one respect, and this is because of the Queen's Enemy Risks insurance which they provide. There is still no insurance for the fact of requisition (Rule 4F.6), whether it is for title or for use. If an owner continues to have an insurable interest in a requisitioned ship, namely when she is requisitioned for use only, she remains insured for losses, liabilities, costs and expenses that may be suffered during the period of requisition. This enabled the Associations to continue the insurance of the ships which were requisitioned to support the Task Force during the South Atlantic War in its operations to repossess the Falkland Islands.

Fines and penalties

23.39 The insurance provided by the Institute War and Strikes Clauses Hulls—Time 1.10.83 exclude matters arising under quarantine regulations or for infringing customs or trading regulations (Clause 4.1.5). The penalties for doing so will usually result in fines, which concern the Protection and Indemnity Associations, but can include the confiscation of the ship. Because of the nature of these exclusions, confiscation of the ship will be excluded from the insurance.

23.40 The Rules of the Mutual War Risks Associations go a little further than this and exclude the contravention of the laws of any state, or action taken to enforce fines and penalties, which in any event are matters concerning the Protection and Indemnity Associations.[9] Like the insurance given by the London Market, these Rules exclude a claim for the confiscation of a ship which arises out of such contraventions.

23.41 The Mutual War Risks Associations do however, reserve to their directors power to accept such claims, notwithstanding the exclusionary nature of these Rules, if; in their discretion, they consider that such a course should be taken.

---

9. Rule 4F.4 of the British Mutual War Risks Associations, and Rule 3.5 of the Hellenic (Bermuda) Association.

There is a very special reason for this. It is regrettably the case that in many modern states, ships are detained, and in some cases confiscated, by totally spurious allegations that some laws have been contravened, and these allegations have been used as a cloak to conceal the true motive; the desire to do as much damage as possible to a particular owner, or to the ships of a particular flag, or even to hide the peculations of some political leaders or officials of the state concerned. The directors wish to have power to look beyond the ostensible reasons for the action taken against a ship, and to judge her owner's claim against the background of the actual reasons. This is a discretion which they are not bound to use. They may use it if they consider the circumstances justify their doing so. The discretion is very wide, and allows the directors to accept a claim in whole or in part.

Imprudent conduct

23.42 The Rules of the British Mutual War Risks Associations contain an exclusion for "Imprudent Conduct" (Rule 4E.4). This reads:

"If any act or omission shall be committed on board or in connection with the Entered Ship which ought reasonably to be anticipated as being of such nature as to render the Entered Ship liable to any loss or damage, or to capture, seizure, arrest, restraint, detainment, confiscation or expropriation, and if such act or omission shall cause or in any way contribute to such loss or damage or to such capture, seizure, arrest, restraint, detainment, confiscation or expropriation, then the Association shall not be liable for the loss or damage, to, or detention of the Entered Ship nor for any losses, liabilities, costs or expenses resulting therefrom."

23.43 This exclusion shall not apply if the conduct concerned was agreed beforehand with the managers of the Association, or if the Assured Member shall prove that it occurred without the fault or privity of himself or the Entered Ship's Managers. Again the directors have a discretion to pay a claim, in whole or in part, if in all the circumstances, they think it should be paid.

23.44 The word "imprudent" is slightly wider than the word "wilful". "Wilful Misconduct" is excluded from the insurance by section 55(2)(a) of the Marine Insurance Act 1906 (Chapter 29). The Rule itself dates from the days of the Spanish Civil War, when certain owners engaged their ships in activities which were "risky", but their conduct did not amount to the extreme degree of "wilful misconduct".

CHAPTER 24

Sue and labour

24.1 It is not the purpose of this chapter to describe at length sue and labour provisions which are contained in the Institute Time Clauses and the Rules of the Mutual War Risks Associations. These provisions are discussed meticulously by other works, notably Arnould, 16th edition, Chapter 25, and the *Institute Clauses Handbook* by Mr. N. G. Hudson and Mr. J. C. Allen. This chapter would serve the reader better, first by reminding him of certain general principles, and then discussing some recent war risk cases to demonstrate how, in practice, the sue and labour provision works. Again, it is hoped that the reader will find subheadings useful.

GENERALLY

24.2 The S.G. Form contained a centuries-old provision which read:

" . . . and in the case of any loss or misfortune it shall be lawful to the assured, their factors, servants and assigns, to sue, labour, and travel for, in and about the defence, safeguards and recovery of the said goods and merchandises, and ship, etc., or any part thereof without prejudice to this insurance; to the charges whereof we, the assurers, will contribute each one according to the rate and quantity of his sum herein assured."

24.3 This permissive wording contrasted with the more mandatory language of section 78(4) of the Marine Insurance Act 1906 which reads:

"It is the duty of the assured and his agents, in all cases, to take such measures as may be reasonable for the purpose of averting or minimising a loss."

24.4 Since section 78(4) is a part of the Act where the parties are allowed to express a contrary intention, it could be said that the S.G. Form's wording should prevail. Yet Arnould (*Marine Insurance*, 16th edition, para. 770), repeating a view which went right back to the first edition, stated very firmly that it had long been recognised, both in England and the United States, that the assured is under a duty to sue and labour. The accuracy of this assertion has been questioned in South Africa in the *Shooter* case (footnote, para. 30.65), but this would appear to be because, in South Africa, there is no statutory obligation to sue and labour, but only a general duty to minimize a loss. The last days of the long-lived S.G. Form, Eveleigh L.J. in the *Integrated Container* case (paras. 24.19–24.21) gave unequivocal support to Arnould's view. At the best, there was some confusion whether the assured was permitted to sue and labour if he so chose, or whether he was under an obligation to do so.

24.5 Some further doubts were noticeable whether section 78(4) imposed on the underwriters an obligation to pay the assured's expenses. Manning J., when considering the Australian equivalent of the Marine Insurance Act 1906, which uses identical language to section 78(4), could not accept that the assured must sue and labour except at the expense of the underwriters. Neill J., in the *Integrated Container* case (paras. 24.19–24.21) was not so sure; if a statutory obligation to sue and labour was imposed on the assured, then the statute would have gone on to say that the underwriters must meet the expenses if that was what was intended. Once again Eveleigh L.J., in the same case, was of the same view as Manning J.

24.6 It is important to appreciate these matters when examining the cases which were heard before the new Institute Clauses were introduced during the 1980s. These now provide contractual provisions as follows:

> Institute War and Strikes Clauses dated 1.10.83 (for ships)—by incorporating Clause 13 of the Institute Time Clauses—Hulls.
> Institute War Clauses (Cargo) dated 1.1.82 (for Cargo)—Clauses 11 and 12.
> Institute Strikes Clauses (Cargo) dated 1.1.82 (for Cargo)—Clauses 11 and 12.
> Institute War and Strikes Clauses Containers—Time dated 1.1.87 (for containers)—by incorporating Clauses 18 and 19 of the Institute Container Clauses—Time.

24.7 These contractual provisions state that "it is the duty of the assured" to take reasonable measures to avert or minimise a loss at the expense of the underwriters (usually in terms which are very close to section 78(4)), and that such measures are taken without prejudice. In the cargo and container clauses, there is an added obligation to ensure that rights against carriers, bailees and other third parties are properly preserved and exercised. These new provisions should resolve the previous doubts on whether the assured was or was not obliged to sue and labour, and whether the underwriters were to meet the costs of doing so.

24.8 All these clauses confirm what is already contained in section 78(1) of the Marine Insurance Act 1906, that amounts spent on sue and labour are recoverable in addition to the amount of the claim for the loss or damage to the insured object. The clauses relating to cargo and containers are straightforward enough, and the only restriction is that the amounts spent should be reasonable, but attention is drawn to what is said on taking measures promptly at paras. 34.36 and 34.37. Regarding ships, there are some additional restrictions and conditions. General average, salvage charges (paras. 34.36–34.38) and collision defence or attack costs cannot be recovered as sue and labour; they are insured elsewhere by the Institute Clauses. There is a total limit on the sue and labour costs which shall not exceed the amount insured. The terms of Clause 13.4 should also be noted (Appendix C).

24.9 The old principle, enshrined in section 78(3) of the Marine Insurance Act 1906, that there can be no recovery of expenses incurred to avert or diminish a loss which is not covered by the insurance, has very recently received a firm endorsement from Hobhouse J. in the *Wondrous* case (paras. 13.45–13.49, 22.52, 22.53): "Sue and labour expenses are not recoverable if incurred to avert or minimise a loss not covered by the policy."

24.10 The Mutual War Risks Associations also give insurance for sue and labour, and they do not seek to put a duty on the assured which is similar to the Institute Clauses. Part of their service to their members consists of handling the claims themselves, so that when a claim is notified to the managers under other provisions of the rules, the managers will become actively involved in consultation with the assured in the handling of the claim. This includes taking the necessary measures to avert or minimise a loss.

CASES ILLUSTRATING THE GENERAL PRINCIPLE

24.11 Mention should be made of some of the leading cases which contain some useful general points. *Great Indian Peninsular Railway Company* v. *Saunders*,[1] was a case heard by six judges in the Court of Exchequer Chamber on a writ of error (in modern parlance, an appeal) from the Queen's Bench Division, where judgment had been awarded to the underwriters. In November, 1858, the railway company had shipped 480 tons of iron rails, altogether 1,995 bars, on board the *Bombay* for carriage to Kurrachee and Bombay. The freight was payable in London "ship lost or not lost". It was in fact paid at the rate of 25 shillings per ton and amounted in all to £629 9s. 10d. The rails were insured with a warranty that made all the difference: "Warranted free from particular average unless the ship is stranded, sunk or burnt." There was also the usual form of sue and labour clause in the S.G. policy.

24.12 In the Channel the ship met with a very severe storm. Dismasted and severely damaged, she was towed into Plymouth by H.M.S. *Argus*. There she was judged to be a constructive total loss and was eventually broken up. The rails were handed back to the railway company, which forwarded them to Bombay on three vessels. The *Cospatrick* charged 30 shillings, and the *Lancashire Witch* and the *Poictiers* 40 shillings a ton, amounting in all to £825 11s. 7d. The railway company claimed this extra freight. Erle C.J. gave the court's judgment:

"The expenses that can be recovered under this labouring clause are expenses incurred to save an impending loss, and to prevent an impending loss . . . According to my mind, these expenses have no relation to the labouring clause, because that must be construed with reference to the peril insured against, and there has no such peril taken place."

This was a policy against total loss only, and the rails had not been lost. There was thus no insured peril to which the sue and labour clause could be attached. Judgment was signed in favour of the underwriters.

24.13 *Booth* v. *Gair*[2] demonstrated once again the inherent danger of despatching valuable cargo with reduced insurance cover. In 1862, 118 boxes of bacon, valued at £750, were shipped on board the *Plantagenet* from New York to Liverpool. It was insured on the S.G. Form with the usual sue and labour clause, but it was also warranted: "Free from average unless general, or the ship be stranded, sunk or burnt."

24.14 The ship met with severe gales and was working and straining heavily. The crew pumped continuously to contain the many leaks, and she eventually had to bear away for Bermuda. There she could only be repaired at an expense exceeding her value, and she was eventually condemned and sold. When the court came to hear the case, it accepted that she was a constructive total loss. Some of the bacon was badly damaged and was sold locally for an undefined purpose. The rest, damaged to a lesser extent, was sent to Liverpool on the *Magnet* and the *Surprise* which delivered it safely. The owner of the bacon claimed for the extra expenses of

1. (1862) 6 L.T. 297.
2. (1863) 33 (II) (N.S.) L.J.C.P. 99.

freight and transport, pleading that, if it had been left in Bermuda, it would have inevitably been a total loss. Erle C.J. was unimpressed, and found that the case did not differ from the *Great Indian*[3] case. Once again, judgment was signed in the underwriters' favour.

24.15 These two cases establish that a sue and labour claim can only be made if the insured shipowner incurred expense to ward off or avert an insured peril. At first sight, *Kidston* v. *The Empire Marine Insurance Co. Ltd.*[4] seems to point the other way. A close examination of its facts, and the reasoning of the judges, indicates that this is not so. The *Sebastopol* was the ship in question:

1863

16th March

The ship is chartered to load guano from Chincha Islands to the United Kingdom. The freight, payable on arrival, is 75 shillings per ton. Whilst this is nowhere stated as such, the cargo seems to be 1,315 tons, a plausible figure for a ship of the period, and the freight £4,930.

18th August

The freight, valued at £5,000, is insured for £2,000. It is: "Warranted free from particular average, also from jettison, unless the ship be stranded, sunk, or burnt."
  There is the usual S.G. Form's sue and labour clause.

End 1863/beginning 1864

The ship encounters a very severe storm around Cape Horn and is severely damaged.

1864

7th February

The ship reaches Rio de Janeiro. She is not worth repairing and is sold. The guano is warehoused. In Rio it attracts charges of about £100 in landing, warehousing and reloading.

12th March

The Master charters the *Caprice* to carry the guano to Bristol. At 37s. 6d. per ton the freight is £2,467 11s. 10d. which the plaintiff pays.

The *Caprice* reached Bristol safely and the shipowner received the full payment of the *Sebastopol*'s freight, about £4,930.

24.16 The plaintiff sued for the freight of the *Caprice* plus the charges incurred in Rio. Obviously the totals were irrecoverable because the freight was underinsured. Both courts dealt with principles rather than with actual figures, and the amount quoted on appeal of £1,145 5s. 6d. looks as if the plaintiff's claim had been scaled down to two-fifths of his total expenditure, this being the proportion which the amount insured bore to the freight's total value. If this is correct, it explains the confusion of the figures in the case, and aids understanding of the two judgments. The defendant underwriter simply pleaded that as the ship had not stranded, sunk or burnt, there was a particular average loss and that this was not covered by the policy.

24.17 The first court was asked to review an award in the plaintiff's favour made by a jury before Erle C.J. in late 1865. Willes J. gave the court's judgment. The argument was:

"Whether the [sue and labour] clause ought to be limited in construction to a case where the assured abandons, or may perchance abandon, so that the expense incurred is . . . upon

  3. (1862) 6 L.T. 297.
  4. (1866) L.R. 1 C.P. 535; on appeal (1867) L.R. 2 C.P. 357.

property which . . . becomes, or may become, theirs [the underwriters], or whether it extends to every case in which the subject of the insurance is exposed to loss or damage for the consequences of which the underwriters would be answerable, and in warding off which labour is expended."

The court preferred the latter construction, namely that the clause was aimed at "warding off". On the warranty:

" . . . The warranty against the particular average, does no more than limit the insurance to total loss of the freight by the perils insured against, without reference to extraordinary labour or expense which may be incurred by the assured in preserving the freight from loss, or rather from never becoming due, by reason of the operation of the perils insured against."

No part of the *Sebastopol*'s freight was due in Rio de Janeiro. It was only due on arrival in Bristol and then in total; otherwise no part of it was due at all. So in finding for the plaintiffs:

" . . . We have . . . come to the conclusion that there was a danger of the total loss of the freight by reason of the loss of the ship by perils insured against; that the measures taken by the plaintiff to avert the loss, and the expenses incurred therein, were taken and incurred for the benefit of the underwriters, in averting a loss for which they would have been liable."

This judgment was upheld on appeal. Kelly C.B.:

"We are of the opinion, therefore, that whether it be the duty or not of the Master, under circumstances like these, to forward the cargo in another ship to its destined port, that upon the facts of this case, there was a total loss of freight when the ship had become a wreck, and the goods had been landed in Rio; and that the cost incurred by the Master in shipping the goods by the *Caprice*, and causing them to be conveyed to this country, is a charge within the express terms of the sue and labouring clause . . . ".

Altogether nine judges in both courts reached unanimous conclusions.

24.18 Whilst the *Kidston*[5] case was not a war risk case, it is a guide to the position which all too frequently arises where ships become war risk casualties. During the Iran/Iraq War (1980 to 1988) ships were frequently hit and severely damaged when sailing loaded from the Gulf ports. The cargo often survived and could be transhipped in Dubai. The consideration frequently arose whether the shipowner should save his freight by transhipment at his own cost, and, as has already been noted, he had an express obligation to minimise his claim on his freight underwriters to the maximum extent that he could reasonably do so (paras. 24.14–24.7).

24.19 Turning to some modern cases, there are two of particular interest, one which concerns the old S.G. Form, and another which deals with the new clauses. *Integrated Container Service Inc.* v. *British Traders Insurance Company Ltd.*[6] concerned a claim for sue and labour where in 1972 Integrated Container Services Inc. had hired out to Omaya Shipping Company Ltd. a large number of their containers and other equipment. In August, 1975, Omaya went bankrupt leaving a large number of Integrated's containers in Singapore, Manila, Taipeh, and Penang. Integrated set about their recovery, and this involved engaging lawyers, negotiating with ship's agents and port authorities, and a certain amount of travel costs. They succeeded in recovering all but two of their containers at a cost of $136,150. The

5. Footnote 4, above.
6. [1981] 2 Lloyd's Rep. 460.

underwriters refused to pay this amount, and proceedings were started in the High Court.

24.20 The insurance was arranged on an "all risks" basis on the S.G. Form, which included the permissive provision, which is noted above, that "it shall be lawful" for the assured to sue and labour. There was however an express provision in the attached clauses that "It is the duty of the assured" to sue and labour in terms which were very similar to section 78(4), so there could be no question that in this instance the assured was obliged to sue and labour. Neill J. considered the matter on a preliminary point for the guidance of the Official Referee, whose job it was to assess the proper amount (if any) of the assured's claim. He thought that, thus far, section 78(4) imposed no duty on the underwriters to pay the costs. In this, as is noted above (para. 24.5), he differed with Manning J. in the Supreme Court of New South Wales. The matter was put beyond doubt by a further additional clause which obliged the underwriters to pay the expenses which the assured was obliged to incur, and he duly gave directions to the Official Referee that the plaintiffs' costs could be examined. The Official Referee passed most of them, and it was from his judgment that the insurers appealed.

24.21 The Court of Appeal[6a] had little sympathy for the underwriters who were giving "all risks" insurance. The plaintiffs' property had been put in some peril by Omaya's bankruptcy, and there was the risk of theft, misuse, or even loss of the containers through the enforcement of liens. Eveleigh L.J. considered that section 78(4) required the assured:

" . . . to take such measures as may be reasonable for the purpose of averting or minimising a loss . . . these words seem to me to impose a duty to act in circumstances where a reasonable man intent on preserving his property, as opposed to claiming on underwriters, would act . . . As the right to recover expenses is a corollary to the duty to act . . . the assured should be entitled to recover all extraordinary expenses incurred by him . . . "

24.22 There is also the very recent case *Noble Resources Ltd.* v. *Greenwood (The Vasso)*,[7] which was heard by the High Court on the 21st May, 1993. In April, 1991, the plaintiff's cargo of lump iron-ore had sunk with the ship in circumstances where there was a strong *prima facie* case against the shipowner for damages for breach of the contract of carriage. The insurance of the cargo contained a sue and labour clause in exactly the same terms as Clauses 11 and 12 of the Institute War Clauses (Cargo), dated 1.1.82, the Institute Strikes Clauses (Cargo), dated 1.1.82, and Clauses 18 and 19 which are imported into the Institute War and Strikes Clauses Containers—Time, dated 1.1.87. The ship was owned by a one-ship company, and it appeared likely that its only asset was its insurance claim against its hull and machinery underwriters. The underwriters of the cargo refused to pay on the grounds that the assured should have applied for a *Mareva* injunction forbidding the shipowners from removing the proceeds of the hull and machinery claim from the United Kingdom.

24.23 Hobhouse J. was in no doubt that there was a duty on the assured to sue and labour, but considered that this duty stretched no further than acting in a reasonable and proper way. The plaintiffs' solicitors had no evidence that there were any assets within the jurisdiction of the court, and considered that they

6a. [1984] 1 Lloyd's Rep. 154.
7. [1993] L.M.L.N. 355.

could not properly swear an affidavit that there were in the form required by the Rules of Court. In these circumstances, the plaintiffs were not in breach of their obligations, and judgment was signed in their favour.[8]

24.24 Before leaving the decided cases, it should be emphasised that only the assured, his servants or agents, can incur sue and labour expenses. *Uzielli* v. *Boston Marine Insurance Company*[9] explains this. An underwriter himself incurred expense to save some damaged property. He recovered this expense from his re-insuring underwriter. The reinsuring underwriter was himself further reinsured, but he could not recover this expense from the further reinsurer; he had not himself incurred the expenses and neither had his servants or agents.

SALVAGE—SALVAGE CHARGES AND PARTICULAR CHARGES

24.25 The most important of the decided cases which is mentioned in detail in this work deals with salvage in particular. *Aitchison* v. *Lohre* was heard by the Queen's Bench Division, the Court of Appeal[10] and the House of Lords.[11] The *Crimea* was valued at £2,600, and was insured for £1,200, for a voyage from the Clyde to Eastern Canada and back to the Clyde again. In January, 1873, during the last stages of her return voyage, she encountered a severe storm and was in imminent and grave danger of sinking when she was found by the steamer *Texas*. The *Texas* took the ship in tow and brought her safely into Queenstown. There was no salvage agreement—an Atlantic winter gale and imminent danger of sinking is scarcely the place to argue terms—so the *Texas* enforced her undoubted right to maritime salvage for ship, freight and cargo by exercising her equally undoubted maritime lien. She was awarded salvage, the *Crimea*'s proportion being £515. The shipowner meanwhile undertook the virtual rebuilding of an elderly and severely damaged ship, spending (excluding the metalling, the costs of which are not available) in the process £4,414. A deduction of one-third "new for old", which was then customary, produced a net sum of £3,178, which was still far above the amount for which the ship was insured. A statement made to the court, which seems to have been commonly agreed by the parties, was that all the work, except the metalling, was reasonably necessary to make the ship seaworthy, even if it made her a stronger and better ship afterwards and worth no less than £7,000. Even so, it is easy to see why the shipowner, who had long since exhausted his existing but inadequate insurance, should have wished to recover the £515 for salvage in addition to the £1,200 paid for the hull repairs. He could only do this if he could show that it was a sue and labour charge and as such payable in addition. The Queen's Bench Division, Mellor and Lush JJ., decided against him for the same reasons as did the House of Lords, and gave judgment for the underwriters.

---

8. For a case in which a time-charterer successfully sued his liability underwriter, who insured him for his liabilities to the shipowner, for the expenses of discharging and reloading a cargo of coal which was about to catch fire see *MacMillan Bloedel Ltd.* v. *Youell (The Warschau)*, a decision of the Supreme Court of British Columbia given 11th March, 1991, L.M.L.N. 311.
9. (1884) 5 Asp. M.L.C. 405.
10. (1877) 3 Q.B.D. 501; (1878) 3 Q.B.D. 558.
11. (1879) 4 Asp. M.L.C. 168.

24.26 On appeal, however, this decision was reversed. Brett L.J. indicated that the Court of Appeal took a broad view of the sue and labour clause, and looked at it at its face value:

"Now the general construction of the clause has been held to be, and we think is, that if by perils insured against the subject matter of insurance is brought into such danger that without unusual or extraordinary labour or expense a loss will very probably fall upon the underwriters, and if the insured or his agents or servants exert unusual or extraordinary labour, or if the assured is made liable to unusual or extraordinary expense in or for efforts to avert a loss . . . as a contribution independent of and even in addition to the whole sum insured . . . "

then several authorities and the *Kidston*[12] case seemed to show:

" . . . that the clause in question is a wholly independent contract in the policy from the contract to pay a certain sum in respect of damage done to the subject matter of insurance, and consequently that it applies, whatever be the amount of such damage, and whether indeed any such damage occur or not".

24.27 On this the court gave judgment for the plaintiff. The House of Lords, however, considered this to be wrong. It reversed this finding and restored the judgment of the Queen's Bench Division. Judgment was given: " . . . that general average and salvage do not come within either the words or the object of the suing and labouring clause, and that there is no authority for saying that they do".

24.28 The words of the clause say that, in case of misfortune, it:

" . . . shall be lawful for the assured, etc., to sue labour and travel for . . . The object is to encourage exertion on the part of the assured, not to provide an additional remedy for the recovery from the insurers of indemnity for a loss which is, by the maritime law, a consequence of the peril . . . The owners of the *Texas* did the labour here, not as agents of the assured, and to be paid wages for their labour, but as salvors acting on the maritime law . . . [which] gives them a claim against the property saved . . . and a lien upon it . . . irrespective of whether there is an insurance or not."

24.29 The House of Lords in the *Aitchison* case[13] approved Willes J.'s definitions of "salvage charges" and "particular charges" which now appear in the Marine Insurance Act 1906 under these descriptions. In effect, it decided that maritime salvage under the maritime law (i.e., without a contract) is part of the loss suffered from the insured peril which gave rise to it, and the necessity for salvage, and the resulting expense is "salvage charges". "Salvage charges" are not part of sue and labour, and therefore cannot be recovered under the engagement which is supplementary to the contract of insurance. Room for them has to be found within the limit set by the insured values. "Salvage charges" have to be contrasted with salvage under a contract, for instance where the insured shipowner engages a tug for payment to rescue a ship from a position of danger. This is considered to be a "particular charge", which is a particularly relevant expense for the sue and labour clause, and is therefore recoverable under the supplementary engagement. Salvage charges and particular charges are now dealt with by the following sections of the Marine Insurance Act:

"65.—(1) Subject to any express provision in the policy, salvage charges incurred in preventing a loss by perils insured against may be recovered as a loss by those perils.

12. Footnote 4, above. See paras. 24.15–24.17.
13. (1879) 4 Asp. M.L.C. 168.

(2) "Salvage charges" means the charges recoverable under maritime law by a salvor independently of contract. They do not include the expenses of services in the nature of salvage rendered by the assured or his agents, or any person employed for hire by them, for the purpose of averting a peril insured against. Such expenses, where properly incurred, may be recovered as particular charges or as a general average loss, according to the circumstances under which they were incurred.

78.—(1) Where the policy contains a suing and labouring clause, the engagement thereby entered into is deemed to be supplementary to the contract of insurance, and the insured may recover from the insurer any expenses properly incurred pursuant to the clause, notwithstanding that the insurer may have paid for a total loss . . . "

SALVAGE—THE WAR RISKS POLICY

24.30 There are two situations which are likely to arise out of a war risk casualty:

(a) A ship is hit by a missile and catches fire. She is abandoned by her crew. Later another ship discovers her still afloat, puts out the fire and tows her to a place of safety. She does this without any contract and this is maritime salvage. The entitlement to salvage can be enforced by a maritime lien. Whether or not such draconian steps are taken, the position seems clear; the payment for the salvage awarded is part of the loss suffered from the insured peril, namely the missile. This is a "salvage charge".

(b) A ship in ballast is mined and is beached to prevent her sinking. The crew is taken off. Later on the insured shipowner concludes that the ship can be rescued. He employs for hire at a reasonable rate two tugs and other necessary equipment to tow her clear and take her to a repair yard. The operation is successful. Again the position seems clear; the expense is a particular charge and is recoverable as sue and labour. (There being no other interests, general average cannot arise.)

LLOYD'S OPEN FORM

24.31 In real life the position may not be so clear cut as this. What if the salvage is effected under Lloyd's Open Form, as most salvage operations in fact are? Here there are complications which are usually resolved by practice as the matter appears not to be judicially decided. The learned editors and authors of Arnould, 16th edition, Chapter 25, paragraphs 908 to 915, and the *Institute Clauses Handbook* by Hudson and Allen (pages 116–118) give very concise descriptions of the position, the problems, and the solutions which are reached in practice. There is only one point in the *Handbook* which the author would respectfully question, and that is whether an unsuccessful attempt to rescue a ship under a contract (situation (b) above) is not "sue and labour expenditure". However that may be, the practice again provides a solution as the immediately subsequent description in the *Handbook* shows.

24.32 During a long experience with Lloyd's Open Form, the author has always considered that the old form (before Lloyd's Open Form 1980 and now Lloyd's Open Form 1990) did not in fact make any difference to the nature of the salvage or change it from being maritime salvage in every sense of the word. It is true that the document starts by reciting the names of the parties as an agreement usually does. On the other hand, its heading includes the phrase "No cure–no pay" which is the very essence of maritime salvage as opposed to salvage under a contract where the salvor gets paid whether he is successful or not. Lloyd's Open Form 1990 goes on to provide for the same position as normally exists in maritime salvage; the salvor shall use his best endeavours to bring the ship to a place of safety which may be named but frequently is not; he may use the ship's gear; but above all he does not get paid unless he succeeds. The rest of the form provides for the posting of security; for arbitration to settle the salvage award; for appeal by either party; for partial success in case some of the property is saved; for the Master's authority[14] as custodian of ship, freight and cargo. All these provisions do not change the nature of maritime salvage; they merely provide quick and easy-to-use and convenient methods of discharging the salvor's lien and settling his remuneration—if he is successful. Admittedly Lloyd's Open Form 1990 does contain a contractual provision, but this is aimed at encouraging salvors to work on a stranded ship where damage to the environment is likely. Article 14 of The International Convention on Salvage 1989 is now incorporated into Lloyd's Open Form 1990. This reads:

"1. If the salvor has carried out salvage operations in respect of a vessel which by itself or its cargo threatens damage to the environment and has failed to earn a reward under Article 13 at least equivalent to the special compensation assessable in accordance with this Article, he shall be entitled to special compensation from the owner of the vessel equivalent to his expenses as herein defined.
2. If, in the circumstances set out in paragraph 1, the salvor by his salvage operations has prevented or minimized damage to the environment . . . ",

then the special compensation may be increased to 30% of the salvor's expenses, or even to 100% if the arbitration tribunal considers this appropriate. These expenses are removed entirely from any argument whether they are salvage charges or particular charges, because the P. & I. Association in which the vessel is entered gives her insurance against them. Without such an inducement, the salvor may be reluctant even to try. But it is still considered arguable that this provision, although admittedly it weakens the argument to some extent, does not affect the essential nature of Lloyd's Open Form as dealing with maritime salvage, and that the expenses to which it gives rise are thus salvage charges.

24.33 Since there is presently no judicial decision to give guidance, it is perhaps better to apply the test which is suggested in paragraph 911, Arnould's 16th edition, until such guidance is given:

"The question, it is submitted, depends on whether, looking at the transaction as a whole, it may reasonably be inferred that the contract (if any) between the parties was intended to be the basis of their mutual rights and liabilities to the exclusion, *pro tanto*, of the maritime law."

Also the practice set out in the *Handbook*, page 117, can be followed. So far this chapter has concentrated on giving an indication of the positions which are likely to arise from war risk casualties. Some descriptions of recent practice by one of the Mutual War Risks Associations may be found to be helpful.

14. For limitations on the Master's authority, see the recent case *The Choko Star* [1989] L.M.L.N. 249; [1990] 271.

IRAN/IRAQ WAR (1980–1988)—MUTUAL WAR RISKS ASSOCIATION PRACTICE

24.34 During the Iran/Iraq War (1980 to 1988), many ships were attacked with Exocet missiles. The Exocets used by the Iraqis, being radar guided, usually but not invariably went for the biggest part of the ship, namely the superstructure above the engine room. Being sea skimming they hit in way of the engine room and exploded inside it. All that was visible from the outside was a neat round hole, but within the engine room there was a shambles of mangled machinery, usually made even worse if there was a fire. The ship usually remained afloat (very few ships were sunk by Exocets) and was brought into Dubai, sometimes into Sharjah, by the salvors. Undoubtedly salvage had arisen, and the ships were with rare exceptions constructive total losses. The shipowner was in a position simply to collect his total loss and to leave the salvor to exercise his lien on the wreck and collect his remuneration in that way. Such a solution would require a lot of time and impose a lot of problems. If the wreck was in the port for any length of time whilst the salvor was enforcing his rights, she would be an unmitigated nuisance. She would incur port charges which would be heavy. Since the Association never accepted Notice of Abandonment, these would fall on the shipowner in whose ownership the wreck remained. In the way of all unattended ships, she could break adrift and damage other ships or property; it was by no means clear where the insurance was to come from to meet the resulting liabilities. She, a badly damaged wreck, might even sink in the harbour and cause a huge bill for her removal. Since the sinking would arise from the insured peril, the missile, the Association would have to pay this under its liability insurance (para. 23.11). So whether the award to the salvors was a salvage charge or a particular charge, it made sense to dispose of the wreck immediately to a breaker on an "as is, where is" basis. This had the effect of removing the wreck to a breaker's yard without delay, where it could cause no more trouble or expense. It also established, for the purposes of the salvage award, the value of the salved property on arrival at the place of safety. The purchase price had to be deposited as security for the salvage award, otherwise the salvor would not release his lien. When the award was settled, the salvor was paid from this deposit and the Association received what remained.

24.35 In another case during the Iran/Iraq War, a tanker laden with Iranian oil was struck in way of the engine room and a fire started. Three of the crew were killed outright and the rest abandoned ship. Two independent salvors put out the fire and, under an uneasy arrangement between them, took the ship in tow for Dubai. Lloyd's Open Form was agreed by the shipowners. A few hours later, the Iranian Navy appeared and forced the two salvors to tow the ship to Lavan Island, even firing shots to enforce their demands. This completed, the salvors were peremptorily dismissed from the scene and the cargo was pumped ashore. The wreck was then taken to the anchorage where, to all intents and purposes, the Iranians simply lost interest in her. The wreck did, however, pose some very serious problems for the shipowners, the salvors, and the Association. The ship was incurring port dues, and in her badly-damaged condition could have sunk at the anchorage. Removal of the wreck could have caused huge expense to the Association and it would have been no answer to an Iranian claim that the Iranians themselves had caused all the trouble in the first place. A further explosion on board through an unidentified source added urgency to the problem. The shipowner conducted a delicate series of negotiations with the Iranians which eventually resulted in their releasing the wreck. One of the salvors could be induced to waive his claim for salvage and tow the ship to Khor Fakan. She was, of course, promptly arrested by the other salvor, but by now the problem was becoming containable. The wreck was then sold to a breaker on an "as is, where is" basis, but the expenses incurred by the owner exceeded the proceeds of sale, particularly as the second salvor had an unanswerable case. He had, after all, helped to tow the ship to Lavan Island, which was a place of safety, even though involuntarily. The shipowner's additional expenses, after deducting the sale price, were accepted by the Association as a particular charge incurred in preventing a possible wreck removal claim.

A RANSOM CASE

24.36 This is a case of a most unusual nature. In 1980, a salvage tug left Beirut for her home port of Piraeus. A few miles outside Beirut, she was stopped by some armed men in a rubber dinghy who forced her to go to Jounieh, the stronghold of the Christian Phalange. The Master met their leader, who explained that whilst the tug may have left Beirut with the usual port clearances, it had not received clearance from the Phalange. The first meeting was very affable, and it seemed that the matter could soon be resolved without substantial difficulty. The second meeting later on the same afternoon was, however, very different. The leader, obviously a man of many and changeable moods, was by now in a towering rage and, after upbraiding the Master, announced that the ship would be "fined" for neglecting her obligations to get the Phalange's clearance. Needless to say, there was no legal basis whatever for such a "fine". A good deal of abuse of a political nature was heaped on the Master's head, and he had no reason to doubt that if the fine was not paid, the leader would carry out his threat of confiscating, and possibly even destroying, the tug. He was clearly dealing with some very dangerous people, and their lack of any discipline with their firearms was demonstrated during the course of the evening, when the armed guards on board the tug used a buoy for target practice.

24.37 The excellent banking system of the Lebanon was still working, and the owner's superintendent had no difficulty in collecting the necessary money in American dollars. Transporting it from Beirut to Jounieh was another matter; a taxi driver could only be induced to undertake the dangerous journey at several times the legal fare. As expected, the demand was increased to provide "a contribution to the Christian wounded of the war". The superintendent had foreseen this, but not by a great enough margin. A second journey was required, attended by the same transport difficulties, but this time the Phalange declared itself satisfied. The tug promptly sailed, and was met in international waters by a Greek destroyer to prevent any attempt at a repetition.

24.38 The Association accepted a claim for sue and labour charges in averting a claim for the almost certain loss of the tug and the detention, if not worse, of the crew; quite apart from the obvious humanitarian considerations, such a risk was, as will be seen from paras. 23.10–23.15, also insured by the Association.

SALVAGE BY CREW

24.39 The question is often asked whether a crew can salvage their own ship, even though they are bound to use their best endeavours to bring her safely to port. This was demonstrated in a war risk case, *The San Demetrio*[15] described by counsel in court as one of the great stories of the sea. In November, 1940, the ship, loaded with petrol, was in a convoy of 38 ships from Halifax bound for the United Kingdom. On 5th November an enemy battle cruiser was sighted and the convoy's escort, H.M.S. *Jervis Bay*, an armed merchant ship, turned to engage her. An unequal contest was soon over, although *Jervis Bay's* self-sacrifice permitted the convoy more time in which to scatter. The battle cruiser then turned her attention to the merchant ships. Two were rapidly despatched and then the *San Demetrio* was shelled. She was hit by the third salvo and holed in the bow, just above the water line. The Master, Captain Waite, ordered the abandonment of the ship, and the crew, 45 men in all, took to three lifeboats. Another salvo hit the ship and set her on fire. The boats separated during the night and the weather and sea became very bad. On the afternoon of 6th November one of the boats, commanded by Mr. Hawkins the Chief Officer, and Mr. Pollard the Chief Engineer, sighted the *San Demetrio* once more. Miraculously the ship was still afloat, but there was a lot of petrol on the water and it was decided not to approach her immediately. On 7th November, the weather had moderated, so a sail was set on the lifeboat and with considerable difficulty the ship was boarded. She was still glowing hotly amidships, and the bridge and superstructure were burning fiercely. The deck was punctured in many places and petrol was spurting through the holes. By means of extreme exertion the crew of the lifeboat, in all 16 men, managed to put out the fires and get the ship under way again. The bridge and all the navigational equipment was destroyed, and the only means of navigation were a school atlas and such sight of the sun and the stars as they could get. The hand steering aft was, although badly damaged, got to work. Another storm blew up, this time from the north-west, which set the ship down in a southerly direction. This increased the steering difficulties. The holes in the deck were plugged as well as possible, but no light of any sort could be allowed. One of the seamen, who was badly hurt when getting into the lifeboat, died of his injuries, exacerbated by his personal exertions after the reboarding.

24.40 On 13th November the ship reached Blacksod Bay, which the court considered was a place of safety even though the anchors could not be dropped; there was not enough steam on deck to raise them again. On 14th November the tug *Superman* appeared and shortly afterwards H.M.S. *Arrow*. With these two ships in attendance the ship reached the Clyde on 16th November and delivered her remaining cargo, some 10,000 tons. The shipowners were so impressed that they guaranteed the crew's costs in the action before the Admiralty Court to establish both that salvage had taken place and also the proper amount of the award.

24.41 In court, counsel emphasised that the crew could have stayed in their lifeboat with every reasonable expectation of being rescued, as indeed the crew in the two remaining lifeboats was. They could not raise their lifeboat on the davits of the

15. (1941) 69 Ll.L.Rep. 5.

ship and had to let it drift away, thus abandoning the most promising means of escape should the *San Demetrio* sink; they had thus chosen the more hazardous course in attempting to bring her into port. Langton J. considered that salvage had arisen, the four conditions required by Dr. Lushington in *The Florence*[16] being satisfied in ample measure. For a crew to be able to claim salvage on their own vessel, the original abandonment must have been:

1. At sea, and not upon a coast.
2. Without hope of returning to the ship.
3. *Bona fide*, for the purpose of saving life.
4. By order of the Master, in consequence of danger because of the damage to the ship and the state of the elements.

There can be no doubt that the salvage awarded to the crew in this case was "salvage charges" in every sense of the word.

16. (1852) 16 Jur. 572.

CHAPTER 25

Ordinary judicial process

25.1 As has already been noted, "ordinary judicial process" is excluded from the insured perils of "arrests, restraints or detainments of Kings, Princes and people". When the S.G. Form was still in use, Rule 10 for the "Rules for construction of policy", which was set out in the Marine Insurance Act 1906, particularly provided that arrests etc. of Kings, Princes and people referred to political or executive acts and did not include losses caused by ordinary judicial process. In the modern Institute Time War and Strikes Clauses there are the simpler insured perils of "arrest, restraint or detainment", which means that Rule 10 no longer has any application. An express exclusion had to be inserted which reads:

"*4 Exclusions*

This insurance excludes
4.1   loss damage liability or expense arising from
      4.1.6 the operation of ordinary judicial process, failure to provide security or to pay any fine or penalty or any financial cause."

25.2 This clause appears in the ship's and the freight's war and strikes clauses as Clause 4.1.6, and the container's war and strikes clauses as Clause 5.1.6. It does not appear in either the cargo war or the cargo strikes clauses.

25.3 The purpose of excluding ordinary judicial process from the insurance given by the War Risks Policy is simply stated. Ships are frequently arrested or detained in actions for civil debts, either in actions *in rem* or because a lien arises. These being civil actions, there is no suggestion of any harmful or vindictive action being taken against the insured ship, and in any case it is customary to give guarantees to meet any judgment of the court and so effect the release of the insured ship. The rule which is expressed in Rule 10 had its origins in *Finlay* v. *The Liverpool and Great Western Steamship Company*.[1] This was a claim against a shipowner for cargo which was not delivered at the port of destination. A Mr. Thomas W. Mann shipped bales of cotton on to the *Idalio* in New York and he was given a bill of lading which named him as the shipper. He endorsed the bill of lading over to Mr. Finlay. It seems that the ownership of 165 bales forming part of the shipment was disputed, and the courts of New York ordered the Master to hand them over to a Mr. William J. Porter from whom Mr. Mann was alleged to have obtained them by deception. The Master complied. In answer to Mr. Finlay's claim for short delivery, the shipowner pleaded the provisions in the bill of lading which excused him from the consequences of "restraint of Princes and Rulers". Noting that this defence had

---

1. (1870) 22 L.T. 251.

never before been raised in connection with the orders of a court, and that the phrase itself was more relevant to a capture situation, Martin B. dealt with the matter:

"The acts and restraints of Princes and Rulers mentioned and provided against in the Bill of Lading, have reference to the forcible interference of a State or of the government of a country taking possession of the goods *manu forti*; and do not extend to the legal proceedings which . . . afterwards took place in the courts of New York . . . This was the act of court, which was not one of the exceptions, and not the act of restraint of Princes and Rulers which was excepted."

25.4 This principle was reinforced in the subsequent case *Crew Widgery & Co.* v. *Great Western Steamship Company*.[2] The report is very short but indicates that the court looked for authority to other sources than the *Finlay*[3] case which appears not to have been considered. Butter was loaded on to the *Cornwall* at New York bound for London. The bill of lading contained exceptions of "perils of the seas" and "restraints of Princes, Rulers, or people". She collided with another ship and had to return to New York, where the other shipowners arrested her. There was considerable delay and damage to the butter. The delay could be split into two periods, namely that of putting back to New York and that caused by the legal proceedings. The court held that the first period of delay was excluded by "perils of the seas". Was the second period caused by "restraints etc."? Field and Wills JJ., on the authority of Arnould, 2nd edition, page 836, who based his views on the French writer, Boulay Paty, held that it did not. "Restraints of Princes, Rulers, or people" were held to mean: "Seizure by the government of this country or some friendly power for State purposes" and the arrest of a vessel in a legal proceeding did not fall within this definition.

25.5 At first sight "ordinary judicial process" is an all-embracing phrase but it seems to be well accepted that it relates to civil proceedings only. There has never been a suggestion that it applies to proceedings in a Prize Court; if it did, the insured peril of "capture" would hardly ever arise. Equally, there has never been a suggestion that it applies to criminal or quasi-criminal cases. Mocatta J. dealt with this aspect of "ordinary judicial process" in *The Anita*[4]:

"In my opinion, the words 'ordinary judicial process' in Rule 10 refer to the employment of Courts of Law in civil proceedings. If a *rationale* be required for this, it is that in such cases the State is merely providing a service to litigants, rather than exercising its own power through the courts for its own purposes."

25.6 Mocatta J. noted that counsel for the insurers in *Miller* v. *The Law Accident Insurance Co.*[5] had relied on *Finlay's* case[6] to show that "restraints of people" did not apply to the mere operation of municipal law. Vaughan Williams L.J. made a distinction: "There seems to be no analogy between this case and that of arrest or detention of a ship to enforce the rights of a private individual." In *The Anita*,[7] the court considered that in any case the proceedings in Vietnam could not have been

2. (1887) W.N. 161.
3. (1870) 22 L.T. 251.
4. *Panamanian Oriental Steamship Corpn.* v. *Wright (The Anita)* [1970] 2 Lloyd's Rep. 371. See paras. 13.35–13.44.
5. [1902] 2 K.B. 694; [1903] 1 K.B. 712; [1904] A.C. 359. See paras. 13.11–13.15.
6. (1870) 22 L.T. 251.
7. Footnote 4, above.

"ordinary judicial process"; this was a military court operating outside the normal judicial structure of Vietnam.

25.7 It thus seems indisputable that ordinary judicial process refers to civil proceedings alone and this can be regarded as the conclusion which this work tries to reach. What, however, of criminal or quasi-criminal proceedings? The modern Institute War and Strikes Clauses specifically provide (Clause 4.1.5): "Arrest, restraint and detainment, confiscation or expropriation under quarantine regulations or by reason of infringement of any customs or trading regulations" are excluded from the insurance.

25.8 This would seem to include most criminal or quasi-criminal proceedings that are likely to be taken against a ship, although it is not impossible to imagine other types of criminal or quasi-criminal proceedings being instituted for matters which fall outside the strict terms of this clause. This is an exclusion clause and will, as always, be interpreted strictly against the underwriter.

25.9 The Rules of the Mutual War Risk Associations go a little further than this, and exclude from the cover losses arising from action taken by a State or public authority under the criminal law, or because of contravention of law, or to enforce payment of a fine or other penalty, or because of quarantine regulations. Their directors do, however, have a discretion to waive this provision, but it is most unlikely that they will do so unless they are absolutely satisfied that the proceedings instituted against the ship are an elaborate pretence for an unjustifiable seizure or restraint of her. It should be noted that some fines (although not the loss of a ship) are insured by the shipowners' Protection and Indemnity associations.

25.10 It is true that sometimes arrest in pursuit of a civil claim can take a menacing form. In 1977, one of the Mutual Associations was concerned with a claim where a ship was arrested in Saudi Arabia and an armed guard from the Coast Guard was put on board to prevent her from sailing. The report of the Major General of the Coast Guard to the Prince introduced a further flavour of military action. At the time, there were several ways of effecting an arrest for a civil claim in Saudi Arabia and applying to the Coast Guard for such an arrest was one of them. It transpired that the arrest in this case was effected at the suit of a ship's agent in respect of his claim for disbursements, and the Association's denial of liability on the grounds of "ordinary judicial process" was upheld in the subsequent arbitration.

CHAPTER 26

The Marine Insurance Act 1906

26.1 The Marine Insurance Act applies to war risks insurance policies as much as it does to marine policies and, as such, is described throughout this work in the relevant places. This chapter deals with two other separate matters, namely its construction and its effect on the common law, and its warranties.

CONSTRUCTION AND EFFECT ON THE COMMON LAW

26.2 It is not the purpose of this work to go into the chequered history of the Bill which is described in the Introduction to 1st edition of Digest (1901) in the 9th edition of Chalmers' *Marine Insurance Act 1906*. We should note that the Act begins with the following words: "An Act to codify the law relating to marine insurance".

26.3 At the time that the Bill was first introduced in 1894, moves were afoot, which have continued to the present day, to codify the common law and the law merchant which were founded upon the decisions of the judges, sometimes stretching over many years. Codifying Acts had appeared on such matters as partnership, arbitration and sale of goods. The intention was always, and remains, to produce the existing law in a code contained in an Act of Parliament with as few changes as possible, except in instances where the existing case law had ceased to represent the public perception of what the law ought to be. Two latter-day examples of this are the welcome disappearance in 1948 of the former rules that a plaintiff guilty of contributory negligence should recover no damages at all (except in Admiralty law where the rules were different), and that a workman injured by the negligence of a fellow workman should be debarred from recovering damages by the doctrine of common employment. Another feature of the codifying Acts is that it is perfectly permissible to contract out of their provisions. As a general rule this must, however, be done expressly.

26.4 The problem of a codifying Act is, however much care is used, and in the drafting of the Marine Insurance Act great care was used by a number of very eminent people, some changes in the law are made. One is dealt with in *Polurrian Steamship Co. Ltd.* v. *Young*[1] where "unlikelihood of recovery" is substituted for "uncertainty of recovery" where there is a claim for constructive total loss because the owner of the ship or goods is deprived of possession. When making this substitution Parliament may or may not have foreseen the consequences described by

---

1. [1915] 1 K.B. 922. See paras. 11.32–11.36.

Kennedy L.J. and Lord Wright.[2] More important than this, however, are the rules of construction of a codifying statute which can have consequences which the draftsmen of the Act cannot have foreseen in their entirety.

26.5 These rules came to the fore in *Sanday* v. *British & Foreign Marine Insurance Co.*[3] where Swinfen-Eady L.J. described the canon of construction which was applicable to a codifying Act in the following terms:

"The proper course is in the first instance to examine the language of the statute, and to ask what is its natural meaning, uninfluenced by any considerations derived from the previous state of the law, and not to start with enquiring how the law previously stood, and then, assuming that it was probably intended to leave it unaltered, to see if the words of the enactment will bear an interpretation in conformity with this view."

This was particularly the view of Lord Herschell in *Bank of England* v. *Vagliano Brothers*[4] which was followed in *Robinson* v. *Canadian Pacific Railway Company*[5] and *Bristol Tramways Co.* v. *Fiat Motors Limited.*[6] Here the court was concerned with a constructive total loss. It is true that section 91 of the Act[7] continued to apply the rules of the common law and the law merchant so far as they were not inconsistent with the terms of the Act. Section 56(1) does, however, state that "any loss other than a total loss, as hereinafter defined, is a partial loss" and section 60 seemed to be an exhaustive definition of a constructive total loss of the subject-matter of the insurance, which Swinfen-Eady L.J. noted did not include loss of the venture. The subject-matter of the insurance, defined as required by section 23, was linseed which had not been totally lost, and the subject-matter of the insurance did not mention the venture which it could easily have done. Therefore there could not have been a claim for constructive total loss of the venture.

26.6 Bray J., sitting in the same case in the Court of Appeal, approached the matter differently. He pointed to section 91(2) of the Marine Insurance Act which provides: "The rules of the common law, including the law merchant, save in so far as they are inconsistent with the express provisions of this Act, shall continue to apply to contracts of marine insurance." This required him to ask if, before the Act, there would have been a constructive total loss under the law as it then stood. He concluded that, on the authorities, provided that Notice of Abandonment was given in time, the loss of the voyage would have constituted a constructive total loss of the goods. The next question was, had the Act altered the previous law?

26.7 To effect an alteration, the Act must contain an express provision in clear and unambiguous terms which is inconsistent with the common law and the law merchant. Had there been any instances where this had happened? The *Polurrian* case[8] has, as has already been mentioned, furnished one, but that was a result of a clear and unambiguous term. He agreed that the definitions in the Act of actual and constructive total loss were exhaustive, but here the court had to consider what was the "subject-matter" of the insurance. There being no definition of "subject-matter" in the Act, the subject-matter of an insurance policy on goods remained as

---

2. See para. 11.36.
3. [1915] 2 K.B. 781. See paras. 13.17–13.26.
4. [1891] A.C. 107.
5. [1892] A.C. 481.
6. [1910] 2 K.B. 831 at 836.
7. See para. 26.6.
8. [1915] 1 K.B. 922. See paras. 11.32–11.36.

Lord Ellenborough had described it in *Anderson* v. *Wallis*.[9] In Bray J.'s words:
" . . . A loss of the voyage on received principles of law is considered as a total loss of the goods which were to have been transported in the course of such voyage, or as he put it, a destruction of the contemplated venture."

26.8 In *Sanday's* case[10] the contemplated venture had been destroyed. The unique rule that an insurance policy on goods, that the insurance includes loss of goods and loss of venture, is illustrated in the *Forestal* cases.[11]

In the House of Lords, Lord Loreburn, Lord Parmoor, and Lord Wrenbury put the matter even more strongly. They regarded it as self-evident that the Act codified the previous common law and that section 91 merely reinforced this view. Staughton J. took the same view in *The Bamburi*[12] where he quoted Lord Wrenbury:

"But it remains that the Act is a codifying Act. That being so, I should look more carefully in a codifying Act to see whether any existing law is altered by express words, and should not hold that the Act is going beyond codification unless it puts the matter beyond dispute."

26.9 It can be said that the judgment of Swinfen-Eady L.J. seems to be more technically correct, following as it does some very recent decisions. It is not easy to accept Lord Parmoor's somewhat brusque rejection, which does not set out his reasons to contradict or overrule the lengthy arguments which guided Swinfen-Eady L.J. to his finding.[13] On the other hand, Bray J.'s judgment, reinforced as it is by the weighty and powerful authority of the House of Lords, seems better to represent the obvious intentions of the draftsmen of the Act and seems to have guided the House of Lords in the *Forestal* cases.[14] It is respectfully suggested that in any future doubts that may arise whether the Act has altered the previous common law or not, Bray J.'s approach should be used to resolve them[15] rather than the rather curt pronouncements of the House of Lords. Certainly the practice of the London Market is to regard the Act as making no difference to the previous common law, unless it does so expressly in clear and unambiguous terms, and the process of reasoning which Bray J. adopted would have more attraction than any other judicial reasoning.

WARRANTIES

26.10 Lord Griffiths in the *Vesta* case (see paras. 26.16 and 26.17) said:

"It is one of the less attractive features of English Insurance Law that breach of a warranty in an insurance policy can be relied upon to defeat a claim under the policy even if there is no causal connection between the breach and the loss."

26.11 Warranties do not play a big part in war risks insurance. Since this is insur-

---

9. (1813) 2 M. & S. 240.
10. [1915] 2 K.B. 781.
11. *Forestal Land, Timber & Railways Co. Ltd.* v. *Rickards (The Minden)*; *Middows* v. *Robertson (The Wangoni)*; *W.W. Howard, Bros & Co.* v. *Kann (The Halle)* (1940) 67 Ll.L.Rep. 484; (1940) 68 Ll.L.Rep. 45 (C.A.); (1941) 70 Ll.L.Rep. 173; [1942] A.C. 50 (H.L.). See para. 13.28.
12. [1981] 1 Lloyd's Rep. 312.
13. See para. 26.5.
14. Footnote 11, above.
15. See paras. 26.6, 26.7.

ance against what other people do to the insured object, it is not surprising that their influence is very small on war risks insurance compared with the part that they play in the insurance against marine risks. Yet there is now a leading case on warranties in marine insurance which comes from the war risks field, *Bank of Nova Scotia* v. *Hellenic Mutual War Risks Association (Bermuda) Ltd. (The Good Luck)*.[16]

26.12 The nature of a warranty in a marine insurance policy, whether for marine or war risks, is clearly described in section 33 of the Marine Insurance Act 1906 which reads:

"33. Nature of Warranty

(1) A warranty, in the following sections[17] relating to warranties, means a promissory warranty, that is to say, a warranty by which the assured undertakes that some particular thing shall or shall not be done, or that some condition shall be fulfilled, or whereby he affirms or negatives the existence of a particular state of facts.

(2) A warranty may be express or implied.

(3) A warranty, as above defined, is a condition which must be exactly complied with, whether it be material to the risk or not. If it be not so complied with, then, subject to any express provision in the policy, the insurer is discharged from liability as from the date of the breach of warranty, but without prejudice to any liability incurred by him before that date."

26.13 A few of the recent cases will illustrate the immediate background to warranties before the *Good Luck* case was heard:

26.14 Capital Coastal Shipping Corporation and Another v. The Hartford Fire Insurance Company (United States of America Third Party)[18]

The tug *Christie* was insured against marine risks under terms that she was only insured when Captain Chism was in command. She sailed to a casualty, and herself got into trouble, under Captain Bailey. The U.S. District Court for the Eastern District of Virginia (Hoffman D.J.) found for the underwriters for a number of reasons, among them breach of this warranty.

26.15 Richard Henry Outhwaite v. Commercial Bank of Greece S.A. (The Seabreeze)[19]

The *Seabreeze* became a total loss through perils of the seas. The underwriters paid a total loss, $250,000, into the hands of the brokers. They then discovered that additional insurances over and above the limits allowed by the Institute Time Clauses had been effected, and that the warranty that these limits would be observed had been broken. They demanded the return of the money. Even though the Commercial Bank as mortgagees had nothing to do with the breach of warranty, Staughton J., in the High Court held that the warranty must be "exactly complied with" and ordered the return of the money, even though the breach of the warranty had no bearing on the loss of the ship.

16. [1988] 1 Lloyd's Rep. 514, [1989] 2 Lloyd's Rep. 238, [1991] 2 Lloyd's Rep. 191.
17. The sections relating to warranties are sections 33 to 41.
18. [1975] 2 Lloyd's Rep. 100.
19. [1987] 1 Lloyd's Rep. 372.

26.16 Forsikrings A/K Vesta v. J.N.E. Butcher and Others[20]

A Norwegian fish farm, Fjordlaks Tafjord, insured its fish farm with Vesta which reinsured its liabilities with Lloyd's underwriters represented by Mr. Butcher. Among the special conditions and warranties was one which required the maintenance of a 24-hour watch. The principal of the fish farm, when he saw these conditions, rang up Vesta's office to protest that such a watch was not possible. Vesta said that they passed this warning on, but it seems to have got lost somewhere along the chain, and was never seen by the London underwriters. There was a severe storm which caused considerable damage to the fish farm. Many of the fish made good their escape.

26.17 Under section 51 of the Norwegian Contracts Act 1930, which allows no contracting out of the section, the warranty would only defeat the assured's claim if it was material to the loss. This was not the case here, and Vesta was liable to Fjordlaks. The London underwriters pleaded that the breach of the warranty totally excused them. Hobhouse J., in the High Court, the Court of Appeal and the House of Lords seem to have been satisfied that, in a totally English situation, they would have been right; they were however reinsuring Norwegian liabilities with a "follow on" clause, and must therefore pay Vesta.

26.18 State Trading Corporation of India v. M. Golodetz Ltd.[21]

Kerr L.J. saw a breach of warranty thus:

"Thus, the correct analysis of a breach of warranty in an insurance contract may be that, upon the true construction of the contract, the consequence of the breach is that the cover ceases to be applicable unless the insurer subsequently affirms the contract, rather than to treat the occurrence as a breach of the contract by the insured which the insurer subsequently accepts as a wrongful repudiation."

26.19 This indicates that there are two ways of looking at a breach of warranty. The first is that the insurance dies at the time it was committed, but can be brought back to life if the insurer so chooses. The second is that the assured is guilty of a breach of a fundamental term of the contract which goes right to its very root, and the insurer, when he finds out about it, can repudiate the contract of insurance provided that he does so within a reasonable time after his discovery. Unless and until he does so, the insurance remains alive. Of the two alternatives, Kerr L.J. considered the first to be the proper way of looking at a breach of warranty.

Both these two alternatives which were identified by Kerr L.J., were examined in detail by the Court of Appeal and the House of Lords in the *Good Luck* case, and events took the following course.

26.20 The Good Luck

The owners of the *Good Luck*, Franicons, entered the ship for insurance in the Hellenic Association and also mortgaged her to the Bank of Nova Scotia. In accordance with normal practice, the Association, on the owners' request, gave a

20. [1989] 1 Lloyd's Rep. 331.
21. [1989] 2 Lloyd's Rep. 277.

letter of undertaking to the bank by which it undertook to tell the bank if the insurance ceased. Naturally, it was a matter of importance to the bank to know if the borrower was no longer insured for war risks. There were many facets to this case and, at first instance,[22] Hobhouse J. found the Association liable in damages for failing to observe a "duty to speak". This finding was unanimously reversed by the Court of Appeal, which entered judgment in favour of the Association, but this chapter can only be concerned with what the Court of Appeal had to say on the subject of warranties.

26.21 As will be seen at paras. 23.17–23.23, the directors of a Mutual War Risks Association have the power to give orders, prohibitions and directions that ships entered in the Association for insurance shall not go to "any port, place, country, zone or area" which has become so dangerous that the Association does not give insurance within it. The full nature of this power and the reasons for it are described in section 4 of Chapter 23. The Rules of the Association contain the following provision, which in 1982 read as follows:

"Every insurance given by the Association shall be deemed to contain or shall contain a warranty by the owner that all such orders, prohibitions, directions . . . shall be acted upon and complied with by the insured ship . . .
PROVIDED ALWAYS that:
The breach of such warranty shall not operate to invalidate the insurance if the owner shall prove that such breach occurred without any personal fault or any want of due diligence on the part of the owner or managers of the entered [insured] ship or was committed in order to avoid loss by the risks insured by the policy."

26.22 Right at the start of the Iran/Iraq War in 1980, the directors of the Association had made a direction that ships entered in the Association were not to go to Bandar Khomeini or its approaches. A fuller description of this particular direction is given at para. 23.21. On 6th June, 1982, the *Good Luck* was hit by missiles whilst within the prescribed zone and suffered such severe damage that she subsequently became a constructive total loss. The bank contended that at the date of the attack, or very shortly afterwards, the Association knew that the insurance of the ship had ceased because of the breach of warranty in being in the neighbourhood of Bandar Khomeini at all, but it did not tell the bank. The Association contended that the insurance had not ceased, (the issue of a constructive total loss only became clear much later) and that it was entitled to a reasonable time to make up its mind whether or not to regard the insurance as terminated. In the event, on 4th August, 1982, the directors of the Association decided that the claim should not be paid; they did not, however, decide that the insurance should be terminated, but that it should be left to run its normal course. The bank was advised of this decision on 5th August, 1982. Unknown to the Association, the bank, between April and mid-July 1982, advanced further money to the owner, the *Good Luck* being part of the security, and this money was the basis of the damages awarded against the Association.

26.23 Had the insurance in fact ceased when the ship entered the prohibited zone on 6th June, 1982? The Court of Appeal took as its baseline two well-established principles of law. First, in any contract, the breach of a condition, which is a term going right to its root, or the repudiation of a contract, by one party gives

22. [1988] 1 Lloyd's Rep. 514.

the other party an option. He may accept the position that the contract is at an end and sue for damages. Alternatively, he may disregard the breach or refuse to accept the repudiation, when the contract remains in full effect; in other words he can hold the first party to his bargain. Secondly, in general insurance law (excluding marine insurance) the position appeared to have been well stated by the Law Reform Committee's fifth report (1957):

"The effect of any promissory undertaking by the insured relating to the risk, in the law of insurance, contrary to general usage (always called a warranty) is perfectly clear. Ever since the time of Lord Mansfield [*De Hahn* v. *Hartley*[23]] it has been consistently held that warranties must be strictly and literally complied with, and that any breach entitles the insurer to repudiate."

Signed by Lords Jenkins, Parker, Devlin and Diplock, this statement is backed by powerful authority.

26.24 The Law Commission in 1980 had similarly reported:

"The word warranty is used in insurance law in a special sense to denote a term of the contract of insurance which must be strictly complied with and upon any breach of which, however trivial, the insurer is entitled to repudiate the policy. It follows that upon breach of a warranty the insurer has a right to repudiate the whole contract from the date of the breach, regardless of the materiality of the term, the state of mind of the insured, or of any connection between the breach and the loss."

In the Court of Appeal's words "This is not the language of automatic avoidance." The court went on to quote from *MacGillivray & Parkington on Insurance Law* (1988) and *Chitty on Contracts* (1983) which makes the point that there is required a positive declaration or other act by the insurer that he regards the insurance contract as being at an end from the date of the breach of the warranty. If, with knowledge of the breach, he acts as though the contract were still subsisting he may waive the breach, and could even be estopped from pleading it.

26.25 The Court of Appeal then went on to consider warranties in marine insurance contracts with the following prior declaration: "It by no means follows that this rule applies to the law of marine insurance which, unlike other types of insurance, is the subject of a statutory code. It is therefore necessary to examine the Marine Insurance Act 1906." This may initially puzzle the reader because in some instances, and with the warranty of *The Good Luck* case in particular, the respective rights and obligations of both insurer and insured are very much the same. In language which did nothing to displace the reasoning of Bray J.[24] the Court of Appeal indicated that two questions must arise when interpreting a warranty in a marine insurance policy. What kind of warranty is it and what are its purposes? What sections of the Marine Insurance Act apply to it? Any attempt to short circuit this process will result in a wrong conclusion.

26.26 In dealing with a voyage policy which defines the places of departure and destination, any alteration to either (without the underwriters' consent) will mean that "the risk does not attach" (sections 43 and 44). To May L.J. this was readily intelligible, because an alteration would itself alter the basis on which the insurance contract was made, and the underwriter would never be "on risk". Some sections use the language of avoidance:

23. (1786) 1 T.R. 343.
24. See paras. 26.6–26.9.

(i) Section 17. A contract of marine insurance is based on utmost good faith on the part of each party. If one party does not observe utmost good faith, the other may "avoid" the contract.

(ii) Sections 18(1) and 20(1). If the insured shipowner fails to make a proper disclosure, or misrepresents the position during the pre-contract negotiations, the underwriters may avoid the contract.

(iii) Section 36(2). If a ship is expressly warranted to be neutral, and does not carry proper and necessary papers to establish this, the underwriter may avoid the contract.

(iv) Section 42(1). Where a voyage policy insures the ship for a voyage "at or from" or "from" a particular place, and the ship is not at that place at the time the contract of insurance is made, she must start her voyage "within a reasonable time". If she does not do so, the underwriter may avoid the contract.

Until there is "avoidance" the contract remains in full force and effect. It was not so stated by the Court of Appeal but it is suggested that the act of avoidance must take place within a reasonable time after the underwriter discovers the true facts.

26.27 Yet other sections speak of discharge of liability. Where:

(v) Section 45(2). A change of voyage takes place,

(vi) Section 46(1). A deviation without lawful excuse is made,

(vii) Section 48. There is failure to prosecute with reasonable despatch a voyage covered by a voyage policy, unless there is a reasonable excuse,

the underwriter is discharged from liability, probably automatically.

26.28 Two other sections were not specifically mentioned by the Court of Appeal:

(viii) Section 39. There is an implied warranty that where a policy insures a voyage, the ship shall be seaworthy at various times. There is no specific provision as to what is to happen if she is not. In a time policy, there is no implied warranty that she is seaworthy at any stage of the adventure. Where, however, she is sent to sea in an unseaworthy state with the privity of the insured "the insurer is not liable for any loss attributable to unseaworthiness".

Here it would seem that the underwriter is not bound to do anything except to plead, if he wishes to do so, that a claim is irrecoverable because of unseaworthiness.

(ix) Section 41. There is an implied warranty that the adventure is a lawful one and will be performed in a lawful manner.

Failure by the insured shipowner to comply would appear, in general, to make the contract of insurance void for illegality.

26.29 The provisions of the "statutory code" give a very clear picture of what is to happen, and what are the rights and obligations of a party to a contract of insurance, in some very-well-defined instances which are thus not simply left to the rules of common law. May L.J. went on:

"When one asks whether a breach of warranty gives a right to avoid (as in sections 17, 18, 20,

36 and 42), or effects discharge from liability (as in sections 45, 46 and 48) the obvious answer is that it effects a discharge of liability because that is the language the Act uses and a parliamentary draftsman uses the same language to mean the same thing."

26.30 The court then considered section 33 of the Act, and noted that section 34(3) enacts the common law rule that "A breach of warranty may be waived by the insurer." It is interesting to note that during its chequered passage to the statute book, the second sentence of section 33(3) of the Bill at one stage read: "If it be not so complied with, the insurer may avoid the contract . . . " This wording disappeared during the consideration of the Bill. Even so, the Court of Appeal found themselves much impressed by the views of Sir MacKenzie Chalmers (who was one of the main draftsmen of the Bill):

"The use of the term 'warranty' as signifying a condition precedent is inveterate in marine insurance, but it is unfortunate, because, in other branches of the law of contract the term has a different meaning. It there signifies a collateral stipulation, the breach of which gives rise merely to a claim for damages and not to a right to avoid the contract . . .

But it is often said that breach of a warranty makes a policy void. But this is not so. A void contract cannot be ratified, but a breach of warranty in insurance law appears to stand on the same footing as the breach of a condition in any other branch of contract. When a breach of warranty is proved, the insurer is discharged from further liability unless the insured proves that the breach has been waived."

The Court of Appeal then concluded:

"We have for these reasons concluded that section 33(3) is to be read as enacting the same rule as that which applies, in the absence of contrary agreement, to breach of express promissory warranties in the law of non-marine insurance."

and in another part of the judgment, it dealt specifically with the point at issue:

"We do not agree that the entry of a vessel into a PZ [prohibited zone] . . . in breach of warranty . . . has the effect automatically and without more of bringing the contract of insurance to an end. It entitles the insurer to treat the contract as at an end if he so chooses, but the matter is one for his choice."

26.31 Since on the facts there was not unreasonable delay on the part of the Association in making its decision, the Association would have been entitled, if it so chose, to wait until 4th August to decide whether it treated the contract as being at an end; had it done so, notification would then have had to be given to the Bank without delay.

26.32 The House of Lords[25] reversed the judgment of the Court of Appeal and restored that of Hobhouse J. Before explaining the House's judgment, three points need to be explained, because they clearly coloured the House's view of the whole matter. In the Court of First Instance, the Association was found to have knowledge before the casualty occurred on 6th June, 1982, that a number of its member shipowners were entering the additional premium area of the Arabian Gulf, and even the prohibited zone, without giving the Association notice. This is correct. The court further found that the Association did nothing about this situation. This is incorrect; in late 1981, the Association remonstrated strongly with its errant members in a series of personal interviews, and successfully persuaded most of them to mend their ways. In addition, the trial judge seems to have had difficulty

25. [1991] 2 Lloyd's Rep. 191.

in accepting that when the casualty happened, the Association felt the need to be absolutely certain of the position of the ship when she was attacked. Was she, or was she not, within the prohibited zone? So far as the court was concerned, the Association had all the information it needed on 6th June, and should have acted on, or very shortly after, that date. It was critical of the Association for not doing so. The Association, however, did not feel totally convinced by the owner's description of the ship's position at the time of the attack, and was not impressed by the loudly voiced opinions of an anonymous Iranian Lieutenant-Commander, who was totally unknown to it and was likely to remain so. It felt the need to interview the crew, who were the only people likely to answer the question of the ship's position when she was attacked determinatively, but they were detained in Iran. Only three weeks later, a substantial delay in a case like this, was it possible to see them when they had returned to Athens. In a sense, the case got off on the wrong foot so far as the Association was concerned.

26.33 Lord Goff gave the unanimous judgment of the House:

"So it is laid down in Section 33(3) that, subject to any express provision in the policy, the insurer is discharged from liability as from the date of the breach of warranty. These words are clear. They show that discharge of the insurer from liability is automatic and is not dependent upon any decision by the insurer to treat the contract or the insurance as at an end; even though . . . the insurer may waive the breach."

26.34 Lord Goff explained this further:

" . . . if a promissory warranty is not complied with, the insurer is discharged from liability as from the date of the breach of warranty, for the simple reason that fulfilment of the warranty is a condition precedent to the liability or further liability of the insurer."

26.35 As for the Court of Appeal:

"I cannot help feeling that the Court of Appeal in the present case were to some extent led astray by passages in certain books and other texts which refer to the insurer being entitled to avoid the policy of insurance, or to repudiate, when the Assured has committed a breach of a promissory warranty . . . in truth the insurer, as the Act provides, is simply discharged from liability as from the date of the breach."

26.36 It is possible to read too much into this judgment and to be too dismayed about its effects on the insurance market. It is indeed very difficult to accept with equanimity the dismissive reference to some of the most eminent jurists in the land, including the draftsman of the Marine Insurance Act himself. The questions have often been asked, Is this judgment too blinkered? Does it concentrate too much on the narrow interpretation of section 33 without having regard to the effects it will have on the marine insurance market? Is this yet another judgment which is right simply because it is intellectually perfect? Does the doctrine of precedence give too much opportunity for intellectualism and allow it to defeat the ends of justice? Are we getting too far away from the old tradition of the English Bench, so noticeable in the judgments of 100 and 200 years ago, where the judges were patently concerned with the effects their judgments had on the community?

26.37 It is suggested that, to the further question which is never asked, whether these criticisms posed as questions are fair and just, the answer is that they are neither fair nor just, and, with one particular exception where the position is left in some doubt, the practice of the insurance market is quite unaffected. Where an underwriter discovers that a breach has taken place without any claim arising, he must say so at once (or run the risk of waiving the breach), and add that he is minded to regard himself as discharged from liability. This gives an opportunity, particularly to the mortgagees whose interests will be most affected, to discuss things with him and to try to persuade him to continue with the insurance. If persuasion fails, then there is still the chance to arrange other insurance. This will not change. Where an underwriter, faced with a claim to pay as in the case of *The Seabreeze* (para. 26.15), suddenly discovers a previous breach and refuses to pay, he will be justified in his refusal. This too will not change, even though Lord Griffiths may, quite rightly, deplore the situation. The position is not quite so clear in a case such as the *Good Luck* case where the breach and the claim are simultaneous and are related to one another. Is the underwriter still to be allowed a reasonable time to investigate the facts so that he is absolutely certain what they are, and then to make up his mind whether or not he will raise the breach as a defence to the claim or to waive it? Here the position is rather more doubtful; whilst it was dealt with at some length by the Court of Appeal, it was totally ignored by the House of Lords, and, since it was a point of the case, it is respectfully suggested it should have been considered. Perhaps however, this is a matter for the draftsman of the insurance terms; the Hellenic (Bermuda) Association is currently considering a rule change to the effect that a breach of warranty of this nature shall not discharge the Association from liability as from the date of the breach unless it so elects by notice in writing to its assured. The choice is thus one for the underwriter to make—not a choice to be imposed on him whether he wants it or not.

MISCELLANEOUS POINTS

26.38 Two other facts on warranties need to be noted. First, before the passing of the Marine Insurance Act 1906, a warranty had to be "literally" complied with and attention is drawn to what Lord Mansfield had to say in the *De Hahn* case (para. 26.23). During its consideration of the Bill, the House of Lords Committee changed section 33 to provide that a warranty had to be "exactly" complied with. It was thought that this expression was a more compelling description of the insured shipowners' obligations.

26.39 Secondly, there is a practice in the London Market that exclusions from the cover given by the policy are prefaced by the words "warranted free of" or "from" followed by a number of instances where the policy does not give insurance cover. The marine policy on the S.G. Form was warranted free of the perils listed in the Free of Capture and Seizure Clause. Many instances will be noted in the cases referred to in this work that certain insurances are "warranted free of particular average" or of other matters which are not included in the insurance cover. These are not warranties at all and the statement that they are could be misleading. They are express exclusions from the insurance cover given by the policy. They cannot in any event fit the definition of a warranty given by section 33(1), not being promissory in character. It seems, however, from what Mocatta J. said in *The Anita* case[26] that their true nature and the intentions that lie behind them are well under-

26. See paras. 1.15–1.16.

stood by the courts, and that it is unlikely that the inaccurate description will lead to unforeseen results. Reference has also been made to the custom of the London Market in referring to visits to dangerous areas as "breaches of warranty" and the additional premiums charged for such visits as "breach of warranty premiums". References are made to this practice in greater detail in Chapter 4.

CHAPTER 27

Total loss and partial loss—Notice of Abandonment

INTRODUCTORY

27.1 In the first edition, there was no chapter devoted to these subjects, and they were left to the very comprehensive descriptions given in Arnould's *Law of Marine Insurance and Average* (16th edition, Chapters 28, 29, and 30, paragraphs 1134–1297) and the Chalmers' *Marine Insurance Act 1906* (9th edition). Since most of the cases on which the law was formulated concerned marine insurance casualties, it seemed that matters could be left on this basis. On the other hand, total loss, partial loss, and Notice of Abandonment frequently pose questions of the most difficult nature and of a character all of their own where there are casualties which concern the War and Strikes insurance. It is hoped that this chapter will be of assistance to those who have to deal with the almost unimaginable difficulties which they pose.

27.2 The sections of the Marine Insurance Act 1906 which are specifically devoted to "Loss and Abandonment" are sections 55 to 78.

SECTION 56

27.3 Section 56 provides that a loss may be either total or partial, and that any loss other than a total loss is to be a partial loss. Total loss is further divided into actual total loss and constructive total loss, and the court has power to reduce a claim for a total loss to only a partial loss where the evidence indicates that this is appropriate. The section does contain a specific provision in addition to these general provisions; where goods reach their destination in specie but cannot be identified because their marks are obliterated, then any loss is to be treated as a partial loss and not a total loss. There are special rules applied by sections 71, 72 and 76(1) where a part only of a consignment of goods is totally lost, and the remainder retain their specie when they reach their destination.

TOTAL LOSS

27.4 When the texts of sections 57 (actual total loss) and 60 (constructive total loss) are placed side by side, the difference in character of the two types of total loss immediately becomes apparent. Actual total loss is a loss which arises from an insured peril and which leads to the physical destruction of the subject-matter of the insurance so that it is no longer a thing of the kind insured, or the destruction of the assured's ownership thereof. It is to be contrasted with constructive total loss which arises from an insured peril and which leads to the subject-matter of the insurance being abandoned rather than destroyed, or to the cost of its restoration exceeding its value or, more usually nowadays, the value for which it is insured. It also includes total loss which arises from deprivation of ownership of the subject-matter of the insurance rather than its destruction in the senses mentioned above.

27.5 Actual total loss is defined by section 57 which reads:

"(1) Where the subject-matter insured is destroyed, or so damaged as to cease to be a thing of the kind insured, or where the Assured is irretrievably deprived thereof, there is an actual total loss.
(2) In the case of an actual total loss no notice of abandonment need be given."

27.6 Notice of Abandonment is not required in the case of an actual total loss.

27.7 Constructive total loss is defined by section 60 which reads:

"(1) Subject to any express provision in the policy, there is a constructive total loss where the subject-matter insured is reasonably abandoned on account of its actual total loss appearing to be unavoidable, or because it could not be preserved from actual total loss without an expenditure which would exceed its value when the expenditure had been incurred.
(2) In particular, there is a constructive total loss:
    (i) Where the Assured is deprived of the possession of his ship or goods by a peril insured against, and (a) it is unlikely that he can recover the ship or goods as the case may be,* or (b) the cost of recovering the ship or goods, as the case may be, would exceed their value when recovered; or
    (ii) In the case of damage to a ship, where she is so damaged by a peril insured against, that the cost of repairing the damage would exceed the value of the ship when repaired.
        In estimating the cost of repairs, no deduction is to be made in respect of general average contributions to those repairs payable by other interests, but account is to be taken of the expense of future salvage operations and of any future general average contributions to which the ship would be liable if repaired; or
    (iii) In the case of damage to goods, where the cost of repairing the damage and forwarding the goods to their destination would exceed their value on arrival."

27.8 Notice of Abandonment, which is dealt with in subsequent sections of this chapter, is a very definite requirement for a claim for a constructive total loss.

THE ASSURED'S OPTION

27.9 The assured is not compelled to treat a casualty as a constructive total loss. He has an option, as the terms of section 61 make clear. It reads:

"Where there is a constructive total loss the assured may either treat the loss as a partial loss, or abandon the subject-matter insured to the insurer and treat the loss as if it were an actual total loss."

---

* The *Polurrian* case is authority for adding the words "within a reasonable time" to the statutory provision (paras. 11.32–11.36). The test of "unlikely" as opposed to "uncertainty" was described by Lord Wright in the *Forestal* cases (paras. 13.27–13.34).

27.10 At first sight, this section appears to confuse an actual total loss and a constructive total loss, but Cotton L.J. made it clear:

"A constructive total loss is when the damage is of such a character that the Assured is entitled, if he thinks fit, to treat it as a total loss."[1]

27.11 Lord Wright confirmed this in the *Nomikos* case (paras. 22.36–22.44), when giving his judgment in the House of Lords. The assured has a choice under section 61 to regard the loss as a mere partial loss or to treat it as a total loss. If he chooses the latter course, section 62 tells him what he has to do and the formalities he has to observe:

"In my opinion Notice of Abandonment is not an essential ingredient of a constructive total loss. The appellants argument confuses two different concepts, because it confuses a constructive total loss with the right to claim for a constructive total loss. The right to claim except in certain cases depends on due Notice of Abandonment under Section 62 of the Act."

MISSING SHIPS

27.12 Sometimes ships go missing and are never heard of again. Although the miracle of modern communications and the modern "Mayday" procedure have made this much rarer than it once was, there are still instances where this happens as the recent disappearances without trace of large bulk carriers will testify. Section 58 reads:

"Where the ship concerned in the adventure is missing, and after the lapse of a reasonable time no news of her has been received, an Actual Total Loss may be presumed."

27.13 There have been instances of insistence, usually at the behest of mortgagees, that a provision should be inserted in the war insurance that a missing ship should be treated as a war rather than a marine loss. Whilst it is more likely that a missing ship will, in these times, be a victim of a war rather than a marine peril, no absolute assumption that this is invariably the case is justified. Apart from the instances mentioned above, pirates have often been responsible for disappearances, and they are now, in general, a marine peril (Appendix C).

22.14 What is a "reasonable time" is defined by section 88 as a question of fact. Good examples are given by the *Charming Peggy* case[2] and the *Munroe Brice* cases.[3] It should be noted that the actual total loss "may be presumed"; it is not conclusive, and a presumption may always be rebutted by evidence to the contrary. The section makes no specific mention of cargo, but since it speaks of "the ship concerned in the adventure", the presumption equally applies to the cargo and the containers which were on board.

ABANDONMENT COMES IN TWO TYPES

27.15 Much confusion is caused by the habit of equating "abandonment" with abandonment to the underwriters to the exclusion of every other sense. Confusion

---

1. *Kaltenbach* v. *Mackenzie* (1878) 3 C.P.D. at 479.
2. *Green* v. *Brown* (1743) 2 Str. 1199, para. 30.68.
3. [1918] 2 K.B. 78, paras. 30.70–30.80.

can, however, be avoided if it is remembered that the Marine Insurance Act 1906 uses the word in two different senses:

(1) Section 60 defines a constructive total loss and describes how it can arise. "Abandonment" for the purposes of this section means reasonable abandonment by the Master or those in charge of the ship or goods because their actual total loss appears to be unavoidable, or because they cannot be preserved from actual total loss without an expenditure which would exceed their value when it had been incurred.

(2) If a constructive total loss arises under section 60, section 61 requires the assured to make up his mind if he wishes to treat the matter as a constructive total loss or as a partial loss. If he decides to treat it as a constructive total loss, then section 62 tells him what he has to do, namely to give prompt Notice of Abandonment to the underwriters (paras. 27.39–27.41). Both sections 61 and 62(1) speak of "abandon the subject-matter insured to the insurer", and in this sense "abandon" clearly means, and can only mean, that the assured elects to abandon the subject-matter of the insurance to the underwriters. Section 63(1) continues in this sense, and provides that the underwriters may, if they wish, take over the assured's interest in the wreckage. They are not however compelled to do this.

27.16 Some examples will help to emphasise the difference, particularly on reasonable abandonment by the Master or those in charge of the goods:

27.17 Roura & Forgas v. Townend and Others[4]

The adventurous story of the *Igotz Mendi*'s voyage is given at paras. 22.33–22.35. Roche J., when giving judgment for the plaintiffs, did not make a clear declaration that abandonment by the Master under section 60 is one thing, and abandonment to the underwriters is quite another, but his treatment of the case indicates that he was following this line. The underwriters pleaded that there was no constructive total loss of the ship, or if there was, restoration before the commencement of proceedings precluded any claim, and in any case the claim arose from delay which was excluded from the insurance cover. The judge answered them thus:

"(Underwriters) Counsel . . . did not shrink . . . from the conclusion that here, since the Shipowners were uninsured, and since in that state of facts no notice of abandonment by them was possible, there could never be a constructive total loss of this ship and the risk never attached. I do not find myself in agreement with the defendants' reasoning or their conclusions, and I accordingly decide against their contention . . . "

27.18 Regarding unlikelihood of recovery, Roche J. went on to say (although expressing himself in the sense of uncertainty), having regard to the bombs placed on board:

" . . . not merely uncertain whether her Owners would recover her within a reasonable time, but probably they would never recover her."

Finally, if delay was alleged to have caused the plaintiffs' loss, he was prepared to hold that it had arisen through the insured peril of capture.

4. [1919] 1 K.B. 189.

27.19 Bradley v. H. Newsom Sons & Co.[5]

On 7th October, 1916, the *Jupiter* was crossing the Firth of Forth on the final stage of a voyage from Archangel to Hull with a cargo of timber. At 1540 hours, a U-boat surfaced and fired shots to force her to stop. The Master and crew were ordered to leave the ship and took to the boats. German officers boarded the ship in search of her papers and placed bombs on board to scuttle her. The U-boat took the two boats in tow and eventually cast them off five miles out to sea. Explosions were heard from the ship and it was assumed she had sunk. It was too dark to see that this was not so. The crew was rescued by a trawler and landed early next morning at Aberdeen. The Master reported the loss of his ship to the Royal Navy and to Mr. Bradley in Hull. On 9th October, 1916, Mr. Bradley wrote to Newsoms saying the ship had been sunk. Early in the morning of the 11th, however, the Royal Navy, having found her still afloat and scarcely damaged by the bombs, beached her near to Leith. The charterers promptly elected to take delivery of the cargo at that port. Since the shipowner had abandoned the voyage by saying the ship had been sunk, they declined to pay the freight. The ship was able to continue the voyage, and the cargo was delivered in Hull without prejudice to the charterers' contentions.

    27.20 The House of Lords decided that the shipowner was entitled to the freight (Lord Sumner only dissenting), and Lord Finlay L.C. had this to say about abandonment:

"For this purpose there must be abandonment without any intention to retake possession, and it must be the act of the Master and Crew . . . The crucial question is this. Was this vessel, when she was picked up by the salvors, a derelict in the legal sense of the term; or in other words, had the Master and crew abandoned her without any intention of returning to her, and without any hope of recovery?"

    The answer to this question had to be no, as Viscount Haldane pointed out: "The Master and crew really left the steamer not of their own volition but under duress, being forced to do so."

27.21 Court Line Ltd. v. The King[6]

On 18th July, 1942, the *Lavington Court* was on a voyage in convoy from the United Kingdom to the Middle East via the Cape of Good Hope with a cargo of military stores. Late that night whilst in the same latitude as Gibraltar, she was struck by two torpedoes fired from a U-boat. She fell astern of the convoy and, fearing that she was going to be torpedoed again, the Master ordered the crew to take to the two lifeboats. H.M.S. *Wellington* rescued the survivors, including the Master, from one lifeboat, and promised to return for the other in the morning. The Master expressed the view to the warship's Captain, Commander Segrave, that, failing another attack, the ship would float for a considerable time and could be saved. She was still afloat when the warship returned, and the Master and some of his officers made an inspection. They concluded that provided the weather stayed fair, she could be towed to safety. Commander Segrave, on the Master's

---

5. [1919] A.C. 16.
6. (1945) 78 Ll.L.Rep. 390.

urging, requested tugs from Gibraltar, but pointed out that he could not stay on the scene. His ship had duties to the convoy, and in any case it was most unsafe to stay in the vicinity. To do so would invite an attack on his own ship. He therefore sailed, taking the Master and crew with him.

27.22 The Master's judgement proved to be sound. Tugs found the ship and took her in tow. Only when the weather turned bad did she sink on 1st August, 1942. The action by the shipowners was for hire between 18th July and the 1st August, 1942. The hire clause in the charterparty read:

"Should the vessel become a constructive total loss such loss shall be deemed to have occurred and the hire under this contract shall cease as from the day of the casualty resulting in such loss."

27.23 Although this was not a claim against underwriters, this clause did require that sections 57, 60, 61, 62 and 63 had to be considered. In the Court of First Instance, Tucker J. gave judgment for the shipowners. The Crown appealed to the Court of Appeal which affirmed Tucker J.'s judgment. Scott L.J. thought:

"Section 60(1) deals with events which take place before any abandonment to the Underwriters, and before any passing of the insured property to them. Neither can happen until a constructive total loss as defined by Section 60 has first occurred; its occurrence is a condition precedent to any abandonment and passing of property to Underwriters."

27.24 The Master had had to leave the scene of the casualty because naval needs were of paramount importance. He had nevertheless done all that could be expected of him to save his ship, and therefore it could not be said of him that he was taking:

" . . . any such independent action as is predicated by 'abandonment' in Section 60—and the Court must give due weight to that consideration."

27.25 Petros M. Nomikos Ltd. v. Robertson

The facts of *Petros M. Nomikos Ltd.* v. *Robertson*[7] are given at paras. 22.36–22.44. This is one of the rare cases where the assured decided to repair the ship, and by so doing he chose under section 61 to treat his claim as a partial loss only so far as the hull and machinery policy was concerned. Even so, she was still a constructive total loss by the terms of section 60, and therefore his claim on his freight insurance succeeded in full.

27.26 Another case in which the author was involved did not reach the courts, and concerned a Greek ship which caught fire in 1970 whilst 250 miles south-west of Bermuda. The Master sent out a distress call and the crew took to the boats. A German ship was first on the scene and rescued the crew. The German Captain declined to fight the fire and salve the ship, saying that he had to reach Freeport in time so that his shipowners would not have to pay stand-by time to the stevedores who were awaiting his arrival. The Greek Master protested, but to no avail. Next to arrive were two other Greek ships whose crews put out the fire, and decided that the ship was derelict, and was now their property. They duly renamed her and painted her new name along the sides. Having done this, they engaged a Dutch tug

7. [1939] A.C. 371.

on a daily rate of hire to tow the ship into Bermuda. The shipowner engaged another crew which was flying out to take over the ship when a noisy and at times angry, meeting was taking place in Bermuda. Eventually the lawyers for the two salvage ships could be persuaded that the Master and the shipowners had not abandoned the ship; the Master had been taken from the scene protesting volubly, and the shipowner was even then providing another crew. Even so, it proved very difficult to persuade them to leave the ship in a peaceable fashion, and to rely on their undoubted rights of salvage.

27.27 As a conclusion, it is suggested that the definition given by Lord Finlay L.C. (para. 27.20), gives the best and clearest definition of "abandonment" for the purposes of section 60. It is abandonment, for good and compelling reason, of the ship, the goods, or the containers as the case may be, by the Master or those in whose charge they lie, without the intention of returning to them or reasserting possession of them.

NATURE OF ABANDONMENT TO UNDERWRITERS

27.28 The original and ancient concept of abandonment to the underwriters first appeared on the Continent, and only began to be adopted in England in the mid 18th century by Lord Mansfield. Lord Abinger C.B., suggested in 1836 that such abandonment was a necessary doctrine to prevent marine insurance from becoming equated to a wager, which, then as now, was illegal.[8] By that date, it was well accepted that where a ship or goods were totally destroyed, as for instance sinking by the enemy in deep water without any hope of salvage, or capture and condemnation by a Prize Court so that the ownership was changed, there was nothing to be saved and therefore nothing to be abandoned to the underwriters. Where some residue of the subject-matter of the insurance remained however, it was only fair and equitable that the underwriters should be given the opportunity, if they wished to take it, to step in themselves and save something from the disaster. Such salvage did rightfully belong to them in any case, and Notice of Abandonment, which had to be given promptly, was the formality which advised them that the time had now come to exercise their rights if they so wished. In any case, there was something abhorrent in allowing the assured to collect a total loss payment and keep the sale proceeds of the wreckage for himself. Some reflection of the ancient rules remains in section 62(7) which provides that Notice of Abandonment is not necessary where, at the time the assured receives information of the loss, there would be no possibility of benefit to the underwriters if such notice was given to them.

27.29 *Roux* v. *Salvador* is in itself an interesting case. On 31st May 1831, 1,000 salted hides of a value of £1,117 were loaded onto the *Roxalane* at Valparaiso for carriage to Bordeaux. The ship suffered heavy weather damage, and put into Rio de Janeiro to repair a leak. The hides were landed on 7th July, 1831, and were found to be damaged by seawater. If they had been reloaded, they would have become completely putrescent by the time they reached Bordeaux and would have been worthless. They were, therefore, sold locally by the Master for £273. The ship eventually reached Bordeaux (after grounding in the mouth of the River Garonne),

8. *Roux* v. *Salvador* (1836) 3 Bing. N.C. 266, at 282 to 286.

and on 29th December, 1831, the plaintiff learnt for the first time of the damage and the sale of his goods. In 1835 the Court of Common Pleas held, rather harshly, that Notice of Abandonment should have been given to the underwriters more promptly than it was, and signed judgment in their favour.[9] The Court of Exchequer heard the case on a writ of error, in modern parlance an appeal, and held that the hides were an actual total loss; there was no way in which they could have been carried to Bordeaux without becoming totally worthless, and there would have been nothing to abandon to the underwriters and equally no need for a Notice of Abandonment. In signing judgment in the plaintiff's favour, Lord Abinger C.B., described Notice of Abandonment in a way which is still good today:

" . . . a party insured may, for his own benefit, as well as that of the Underwriter, treat the case as one of a total loss, and demand the full sum insured. But if he elects to do this, as the thing insured, or a portion of it still exists, and is vested in him, the very principle of indemnity requires that he shall make a cession of his right to the recovery of it, and that too within a reasonable time after he receives the intelligence of the accident, that the Underwriters may be entitled to all the benefit of what may still be of any value; and that he may, if he pleases, take measures at his own cost, for realising or increasing the value."

27.30 Today however, abandonment to the underwriters is useless formality, because underwriters dare not assume ownership, particularly of a ship. They are not shipowners, and have no facilities for coping with the myriad obligations which are imposed on the modern shipowner, even of a wreck. An underwriter who accepts a Notice of Abandonment takes over the entire interest in the ship, the goods or the containers, and with it all the liabilities which flow from his ownership. He is not compelled to accept it however, and he has a choice. Section 63(1) reads:

"Where there is a valid abandonment, the insurer is entitled to take over the interest of the assured in whatever may remain of the subject-matter insured, and all proprietary rights incidental thereto."

This choice is repeated in the wording of section 79(1) which deals with salvage and subrogation.

REASONS WHY NOTICE OF ABANDONMENT IS OUT-OF-DATE

27.31 For the reasons which follow, it is suggested that Notice of Abandonment is an out-of-date procedure which had some use in days gone by, but which has no useful function in today's world. It is to be hoped that in any revision of the Marine Insurance Act, it will be dispensed with. Until that happens, it remains a statutory requirement and an essential step to be taken by the assured who wishes to prove a constructive total loss. It cannot be ignored by the assured, the underwriters, or the courts. There is however, precious little incentive for an underwriter to accept Notice of Abandonment, and so become the owner of the wreck, and every reason for him to refuse to do so. In the author's own experience, underwriters who accepted Notice of Abandonment in a marine case found themselves served with a wreck-removal order, and were thus obliged to pay for its removal without the help

9. (1834) 1 Bing. N.C. 526.

of the owners' Protection and Indemnity Association, which would otherwise have had to respond had the wreck remained in the shipowner's possession.

27.32 In a War or Strikes casualty which leaves the ship in the owner's control, experience shows that when the ship is hit by a missile or other weapon and is so badly damaged that she is a constructive total loss, the only hope of any salvage is to sell her to breakers, even though the proceeds of any sale are likely to be minimal. The main breakers of the world live in Spain, India, Pakistan, Bangladesh, Taiwan, and latterly, The People's Republic of China. A lengthy ocean towage is an expensive proposition, particularly if some work has to be done on the wreck to make it fit for the voyage. The breaker's market is notoriously fickle, and can be relied on to take advantage of a sale where there is no choice but to sell, and they do not have to induce a shipowner to sell them a ship for breaking whilst he still has the choice of trading her. A better price cannot be obtained by selling the wreck on an "as is, where is" basis, because the cost of the towage will be reflected in the price which the breaker is willing to pay.

27.33 On the other hand, keeping the wreck at an anchorage or in a port whilst a buyer is found or a better price is sought poses huge problems. Port or other dues have to be paid, and these will be heavy. A ship without a full crew and without power is liable to break adrift and cause much damage for which there will be liability. If she sinks, the cost of removing the wreck will be astronomical. There is thus small inducement to the modern underwriter to accept Notice of Abandonment and take on huge responsibilities in the chance of a return which is likely to be so small that it is out of all proportion to the risks involved.[10]

The same considerations apply to a lesser extent to goods and containers. Whilst they are unlikely to sink in the harbour or collide with other ships, yet even they will incur warehouse and storage charges. All in all, it makes better sense for the underwriter to refuse to accept the Notice of Abandonment and simply to rely on his general right to receive any salvage that may be obtained. This is an ancient right, now enshrined in section 79(1), and described by Gibbs C.J., in the case of a missing ship thus: "The underwriters, on payment of a total loss, would of course be entitled to the ship, if she afterwards turned up, as salvage."[11]

COURSES NORMALLY TAKEN

27.34 Unless there are the most unusual circumstances, the underwriter will generally retreat onto the much used formula of refusing to accept Notice of Abandonment and put "the Assured in the same position as though a Writ had been issued". At first sight this is an anomaly, because the issue of a writ requires the delivery of a statement of claim and a defence within certain strict and specified time limits. There being no writ, there cannot be any statements of claim or any defences. The formula is however a device, well understood by the assured, the underwriters, and the courts for refusing to accept the Notice of Abandonment and thus becoming the ship's owner, but agreeing to treat the assured as though he had issued a writ on the day of the underwriter's refusal. This, particularly in cases of

10. The Mutual War Risks treatment of casualties of the Iran/Iraq War is described at paras. 24.34, 24.35.
11. *Houstman* v. *Thornton* (1816) Holt N.P. 242.

capture, seizure, arrest, restraint, detainment, confiscation, or expropriation, is of some importance to him (paras. 11.5–11.7). It does not prevent the assured from issuing a real writ if he eventually wishes to bring the matter before the courts, but gives him an incentive not to proceed with litigation immediately with all that litigation entails, and to remain, at least for the time being, within the field of negotiation and persuasion. The underwriter is protected from all the liabilities attendant on ownership, but still has his rights to any proceeds that can be saved from the calamity.

27.35 If the underwriter has thus ample means to protect himself from being saddled with the ownership of a wreck with all that it entails, and at the same time to ensure his rights to any salvage, what of the assured himself? Is he free of all the potential risks and liabilities attendant on the legal ownership of the wreckage? Attempts have been made to show that the wreckage is *res nullius*, or an object in which nobody has any property. If this was not already a most doubtful doctrine and one which is very difficult to establish, the elaborate provisions of sections 62 and 63(1), which allow ownership to be shifted to and fro, would seem to nullify any assertion that nobody owned the wreckage. It is true that Bailhache J. seemed inclined to this view on the grounds that the Notice of Abandonment had divested the shipowners of their property and the underwriters, having refused to accept the Notice, had not assumed it.[12] This view did not commend itself to Greer L.J., who considered that abandonment was not to "all the world".[13] Cohen L.J. found these two *dicta* inconsistent one with another, and expressed a preference for that of Greer L.J.[14] Plowman J. had great difficulty in a tax case in accepting that a person could rid himself of his ownership in an object simply by saying that he no longer wanted it.[15] The point does not seem to have been definitively decided, but the better, and probably safer, view seems to be that if the underwriter refuses to accept the Notice of Abandonment, and thus will not accept the property in the subject-matter of the insurance, it remains in the assured, who retains all the attendent liabilities and potential risks which accompany ownership.

27.36 Moreover, a shipowner's Protection and Indemnity cover ceases when the underwriter accepts a constructive total loss (excepting only liabilities resulting from the casualty), and it is unlikely in the extreme that he can replace it with any fresh insurance to meet further liabilities that may arise. There are certain liabilities such as port dues and warehouse or storage costs against which he cannot insure. The solution lies elsewhere.

ONE-SHIP COMPANIES

27.37 Where the ship is owned by a one-ship company, the shipowner should be adequately protected, because, in theory at least, any further liability can only be enforced against the company's property, and that itself is a wreck for which he has already been paid. Attempts to pierce the corporate veil have met with varying suc-

12. *Boston Corporation* v. *France Fenwick & Co.* (1923) 28 Com. Cas. 367.
13. *Oceanic Company* v. *Evans* (1934) 40 Com. Cas. 111.
14. *Blane Steamships Ltd.* v. *Minister of Transport* [1951] 2 K.B. 965.
15. *Vandervell* v. *I.R.C.* [1966] Ch. 261, [1964] T.R. 93.

cess, so it cannot be regarded as a certain shield. Nevertheless, where the ship or the goods are not at the immediate disposal of the assured, it probably represents all that can be done to protect him. As it happened, all the ships which were trapped in Iraqi ports during the Iran/Iraq War with which the Mutual War Risks Associations were concerned, were owned by one-ship companies, so that no special precautions were necessary. The British ships trapped in the Great Bitter Lake following the Six Day War in 1967 were all owned by large companies, so they had to be sold to a shell company so that their owners were similarly protected.

THE BEST SOLUTION

27.38 A description of the methods which the Mutual War Risks Associations advised their members to use where, in the Iran/Iraq War, ships were hit by Exocet missiles and became constructive total losses, is set out at paras. 24.34, 24.35. The assured is only prudent if, when the wreckage remains in his control, he disposes of it immediately and without delay to a purchaser. Whilst he should always attempt to get the best price he can obtain, he is not required to expose himself to exaggerated risks simply to help his underwriter. He must act reasonably in all the circumstances, and what is reasonable in any given circumstances is always a question of fact. Attention is drawn to what the House of Lords had to say regarding the *Wangoni*'s cargo in the *Forestal* cases (para. 13.33). The same is true where the subject-matter of the insurance is goods or containers; whilst these are unlikely to sink in the harbour or break adrift, their storage charges will have an adverse impact on the proceeds of sale, and will reduce it substantially with the passage of time. There were cases (not concerning the Mutual War Risks Associations) where ships damaged by Exocets in the Iran/Iraq War were left for months in Dubai or Sharjah whilst their fates were decided. In the author's submission, their owners were, unnecessarily and unjustifiably, running huge and possibly uncontainable risks when there was no valid reason for them to do so.

TIME FOR GIVING NOTICE OF ABANDONMENT

27.39 This is governed by section 62 which reads:

"(1) Subject to the provisions of this section, where the assured elects to abandon the subject-matter insured to the insurer he must give notice of abandonment. If he fails to do so the loss can only be treated as a partial loss.

(2) Notice of abandonment may be given in writing, or by word of mouth, or partly in writing and partly by word of mouth, and may be given in any terms which indicate the intention of the assured to abandon his insured interest in the subject-matter insured unconditionally to the insurer.

(3) Notice of abandonment must be given with reasonable diligence after receipt of reliable information of the loss, but where the information is of a doubtful character the assured is entitled to a reasonable time to make enquiry.

(4) Where notice of abandonment is properly given, the rights of the assured are not prejudiced by the fact that the insurer refuses to accept the abandonment.

(5) The acceptance of an abandonment may be either express or implied from the conduct of the insurer. The mere silence of the insurer after notice is not acceptance.

(6) Where notice of abandonment is accepted the abandonment is irrevocable. The acceptance of the notice conclusively admits liability for the loss and the sufficiency of the notice.

(7) Notice of abandonment is unnecessary where at the time when the assured receives information of the loss there would be no possibility of benefit to the insurer if notice were given to him.

(8) Notice of abandonment may be waived by the insurer.

(9) Where an insurer has reinsured his risk, no notice of abandonment need be given by him."

27.40 The terms of the section tend to indicate that a degree of latitude and informality in giving Notice of Abandonment is permissible, but this is deceptive. The most important part of the section is sub-section (3), and this provides in mandatory language that the notice "must be given with reasonable diligence" when the assured has reliable information. The courts have interpreted this requirement strictly, because if an underwriter is to have the chance of taking steps himself to effect some recovery, he must be given this chance promptly. Where the initial information of a casualty is vague or uncertain, some latitude is allowed, but as soon as it becomes certain and reliable, Notice of Abandonment should not be further delayed. In the words of Lord Kenyon the assured must:

"make his election speedily whether he will abandon or not, and so put the Underwriters in a situation to do all that is necessary for the preservation of the property, whether sold or unsold."[16]

It is respectfully suggested that he could have put it wider than this, and stated "their interests" in place of "the property".

27.41 Two cases will show how strict the courts have been in the past on the election being a speedy one, and the Notice of Abandonment being as prompt as the circumstances will allow, and there is no reason to think that they would be any less insistent today:

27.42 Kaltenbach v. MacKenzie[17]

On 4th October, 1870, the *Admiral Protet* was insured for £4,000 for a voyage from Saigon to Hong Kong. She grounded on the Britts Shoal and was badly damaged. She was brought back to Saigon on 24th January, 1871, where she was surveyed. The surveyor recommended that she be sold, as condemnation seemed very possible. The shipowners had an office in Singapore, which, once they had read the reports from Saigon, instructed the Master to sell the ship on 7th February, 1871. He did so, and managed to obtain $1,600 for her on 23rd February, 1871. On 27th February, 1871, a report was sent to the owner's head office in Switzerland suggesting that the underwriters should be informed. The underwriters declined to pay a total loss because Notice of Abandonment had not been given.

27.43 In the subsequent action before the Court of Common Pleas, Coleridge J. gave judgment for the underwriters. The shipowners applied for an order for a new trial, and this was granted. The case was heard afresh by Brett, Cotton and Thesiger L.JJ., when Coleridge J.'s judgment was upheld. Brett L.J. considered

16. *Allwood v. Henckell* (1795) 1 Park 399.
17. (1878) 3 C.P.D. 467 C.A., (1878) 4 Asp. M.C. 39.

that the ship was undoubtedly a constructive total loss, but held that the shipowners had not given Notice of Abandonment in good time. Thesiger L.J. agreed, saying:

" . . . the Assured had to prove either that he gave notice of abandonment as soon as he received full information as to the state of the vessel; that is to say, as soon as he had all the materials to enable him to elect what course he would pursue, or to prove that the state of the circumstances was such as to make a notice of abandonment unnecessary . . . did the Plaintiff in fact elect to abandon in reasonable time, and give notice of abandonment in reasonable time?"

27.44 In his Lordship's view, he did neither of these things. There was a telegraph line between Singapore and London, and he should have used it on 7th February, 1871, to give Notice of Abandonment. Even if the 27th February letter could have been regarded as a suitable Notice of Abandonment, it was far too late.

27.45 Fleming v. Smith[18]

On 18th August, 1841, the *William Nicol* was insured for 12 months for £6,000. On 12th April, 1842, she sailed from Port Adelaide for Bombay hoping to find a cargo there. On 18th May, 1842, she was badly damaged in a storm and took refuge in Mauritius. Some repairs were done, and these were covered by a bottomry bond for £4,356. There was much correspondence to the owners in London from their agents in Mauritius and the Master, in which the agents emphasised that only very poor freight-rates could be obtained in India at the time. In their view, the ship would be better employed carrying a cargo of sugar to the United Kingdom, and the Master accordingly loaded one. The Master reported the full extent of the damage to the ship, and the steps he had taken to make the ship seaworthy enough to carry the sugar, in a letter despatched in July, 1842. Such was the speed in communications in those days that this letter was not received by the shipowners until November, 1842. The ship arrived in the United Kingdom on 27th March, 1843, and in her still partly damaged condition only realised £2,780 on sale. This amount, even when the freight had been added, did not equal the bottomry bond. On 30th March, 1843, the ship was abandoned to the underwriters.

27.46 The jury found in favour of the shipowner, but left open the question whether Notice of Abandonment had been given in time or not. The court of first instance found that the notice had not been given in time. When the appeal reached the House of Lords, Lord Cottenham L.C. and Lord Brougham held that the shipowners had long since had all the information necessary to decide whether to abandon or not. They only decided to do so after a voyage to England, and this was too late. Lord Campbell was equally emphatic, pointing out that the shipowners had all the information to make their decision in November, 1842, and should have given Notice of Abandonment then. They had left it too late.

27.47 This strictness poses particular difficulties where casualties concern the War and Strikes insurance. Admittedly there is no special difficulty where a ship is hit by an Exocet missile and is brought to a place which can easily be reached. It if is desired not to rely on local surveyors, and many are very skilled, a surveyor can be flown to anywhere in the world and can telephone, telex, or telefax his findings with

18. (1848) 1 H.L. Cas. 513.

great expedition. Difficulties do arise in parts of the world where the local authorities will not permit easy entry through their frontiers, or which are dangerous in a military or a political sense. It is often a difficult decision whether reliance should be placed on local surveyors, whose reports can be subjected to local pressure of a misleading nature, and which may be long delayed. Other difficulties arise when ships are detained, and it is not immediately clear whether they have been seized or have otherwise suffered an insured peril of the War or Strikes insurance. Strange as it may seem, it is often very difficult indeed to get a clear explanation for a ship's detention, particularly in some countries with despotic regimes. Much time-consuming enquiry is needed to establish what the actual position is, and prompt Notice of Abandonment which is also valid can become an impossibility.

27.48 As examples from recent events of the difficulties in obtaining reliable information on a War or Strikes casualty, the *Good Luck* (paras. 26.20–26.35), the *Angolan* cases (para. 13.57), and the ships detained in Iraqi ports during the Iran/Iraq War may be quoted. In *The Good Luck*, the ship was struck in the way of the engine-room in June, 1982, by AS–12 missiles fired by Iraqi helicopters whilst in the Khor Musa Channel leading to Bandar Khomeini. At the time, the AS–12 missile was an obsolescent British-made missile which had a range of six kilometres and was wire-guided onto its target. It had been used in the Falklands War with varying success; sometimes it destroyed its target, at other times it caused only trivial damage. The hits were said to have caused a fire, but it was not at all clear whether the damage was only slight, or was so serious that it would have led to the ship becoming a constructive total loss. The channel and the port lay in a closed military area, and foreign surveyors were not allowed to enter it. An Iranian Lieutenant-Commander, whose name was never known and whose qualifications for giving an opinion were never revealed, was reported to be giving views very freely, although never to the shipowners to whom he was not allowed to talk. After some delay, a rather sketchy report was received from a surveyor of the nationalised Iranian Survey Service, who was quite unknown to the shipowners, which did not contain any information on which any reliance could be put. The only people who could give definite information were the Master and the crew, but they were detained in Iran in conditions where they were virtually incommunicado, and were certainly unable to speak freely. At the trial, the trial judge showed the greatest reluctance to accept these facts, and that it was not known with certainty until the crew returned to Athens that the fire was no trivial matter; it had completely gutted the engine room, the accommodation, and the bridge structure. Fortunately, the issue of whether the Notice of Abandonment had or had not been given in time did not arise, but if it had done, a notice based on the crew's information might have been found to be too late.

27.49 The facts of the *Angolan* cases are given at para. 13.57. The civil proceedings against the ships were initially very puzzling, and it was not clear for a long time that they were not *bona fide* in nature. Not surprisingly, Angolan officials were not prepared to admit this, and it was only gradually, and by degrees, that further indications could be obtained that they had as their object, not the hearing and determination of a civil dispute, for which the ships could have been released by guarantees to meet the judgments of the courts, but the actual confiscation of the ships. Strictly speaking, Notice of Abandonment should have been given as soon as the ships were detained. As a practical proposition however, it was not at all clear that, at that date, there was any reason to involve the War and Strikes cover at all.

27.50 Some very difficult questions arose in *The Anita* (paras. 13.35–13.44) and *Bamburi* cases (paras. 13.63–13.72), just when Notice of Abandonment should be given so that it was not too early so that it had no meaning, and not too late so that it was ineffective. In both cases, the shipowners had to prove that their ships were constructive total losses because they had been deprived of their possession and it was unlikely that they would recover them within a reasonable time (section 60(2)(i) Marine Insurance Act 1906). The *Anita*'s detention began shortly after her arrival on 7th March, 1966, but Mocatta J. thought that the first Notice of Abandonment, which was given on 29th September, 1966, was too early; at that date it was not unlikely that the shipowner would recover his ship within a reasonable time. At the dates of the two subsequent Notices of Abandonment, 12th May and 29th August, 1967, it was "unlikely" and the unlikelihood increased as time went on. The *Bamburi*'s detention began on 23rd September, 1980, but Notice of Abandonment was not given until 30th September, 1981, although it was repeated on 14th October, 1981. Staughton J. was quite prepared to treat these two notices as valid and given in time. The shipowners had to show that it was unlikley they could recover their ship within a reasonable time at the date of the Notice of Abandonment, and this they succeeded in doing. It was of course still open to the underwriters to show such unlikelihood arose at a very much earlier date than September or October, 1981, and had they succeeded in doing this, then these notices may have been too late.

27.51 All that can be said that, in cases similar to the quoted examples, it needs the exercise of very fine judgement by the assured just when Notice of Abandonment must be given. It may be advisable to give successive Notices of Abandonment, unsatisfactory as this course is, when new facts can be dragged forth into the light of day. There does not seem to be any objection to this, as Atkinson J. said in the *Pesquerias* case (paras. 6.11–6.15) on a point on which he was not overruled by the Court of Appeal or the House of Lords:

"By a Notice of Abandonment the Assured merely make an offer, which remains executory unless and until it is accepted. Until it is accepted the Assured has the right to look at intervening events which may restore in whole or in part his former situation, and may limit his claim accordingly if it suits him better to claim as for a partial loss . . . Indeed if it were not so, section 62(6) . . . would have been otherwise expressed."

This must work both ways. If the Notice of Abandonment is an offer which is refused, then it can be repeated.

THE 12-MONTH CLAUSE

27.52 This clause, which was previously an optional and rarely used addition to the War and Strikes insurance, now appears in permanent form as Clause 3 (Appendix D) of the ships Institute War and Strikes Clauses dated 1.10.83, and as Clause 4 in the Institute War and Strikes Clauses Containers—Time dated 1.1.87. Its text is given at para. 23.28. Where there are cases of capture, seizure, arrest, restraint, detainment, confiscation, or expropriation, it is likely to be of considerable help to both underwriter and assured alike. It does not appear in the new Cargo War Clauses or the new Cargo Strikes Clauses, so cargo derives no benefit from it.

27.53 The Mutual War Risks Associations use a clause in a different form. The Hellenic Association's Rule 3.12 will serve as an example. It reads:

"If an Owner is deprived of the free use and disposal of an Entered Ship by capture, seizure, arrest, restraint, detainment, confiscation or expropriation:

    3.12.1 No claim for an actual or constructive total loss shall arise if such deprivation lasts
        for a period of less than 183 days (or such shorter period as the Directors may, in
        their discretion, decide):

    3.12.2 If such deprivation lasts for a continuous period of 12 months, the owner shall be
        deemed to have been deprived of the possession of the ship without any likelihood
        of recovery."

27.54 This clause must be seen in its proper context. It does no more than excuse the assured, where the capture etc., has lasted for an unbroken period of 12 months or more, from having to prove that it is unlikely that he can recover the ship or the containers within a reasonable time. It does not excuse him from proving that he was "deprived of possession" in the first place, and neither, it is suggested, does it excuse him from giving Notice of Abandonment within the proper time. Since the clause does not contain an express provision dispensing with Notice of Abandonment, it is only a reasonable precaution that it should be given as though the clause did not exist.

27.55 It has however yet to be decided by the courts if the clause operates in such a way that, by virtue of section 62(7), Notice of Abandonment is not necessary. In a case where a Mutual War Risks Association was concerned, a tanker was detained in Nigeria because, it was asserted, she had loaded more cargo than she was authorised to do and was engaged in smuggling cargo out of the country. There was no truth in this assertion, and the Master was acquitted on a criminal charge of attempting to do so. It became clear that the real motives of the Nigerian authorities were the confiscation of the ship, and, after the detention had lasted for more than 12 months, the directors of the Association accepted a claim for a constructive total loss. It was open to them to contend that Notice of Abandonment had not been given in time. They decided not to do so, because it appeared unlikely that there would have been any benefit to the Association if the notice had been given in a timely manner.

CASES WHERE NOTICE OF ABANDONMENT IS NOT NECESSARY

27.56 Section 62(7) provides for circumstances where Notice of Abandonment in the strict form which has been described may be dispensed with. It follows, from what has already been said, that it must be very clear that the underwriter would obtain no benefit from a chance to take over the wreckage and dispose of it himself and so reduce his loss. A leading case on the point will help to explain what is meant:

27.57 Rankin v. Potter[19]

In February, 1863, the plaintiffs, who were the mortgagees in possession, chartered the *Sir William Eyre* to De Mattos. The ship was to proceed from the Clyde to New Zealand with a cargo for the plaintiff's account, and was then to sail to Calcutta to load a homeward-bound cargo from De Mattos's factors for Liverpool or London. The homeward freight was insured against perils of the seas occurring on the outward voyage from the Clyde to Otago in New Zealand and for 30 days after arrival there. In April 1863, she arrived in Otago, having suffered heavy weather damage and a grounding during the period of the policy. The damage could not be fully examined in Otago, and there was an acute shortage of funds. It was not until some money arrived in April, 1864, that some repairs could be completed, and the ship could sail for Calcutta. There she found that De Mattos had failed the previous December, and the factors would not supply a cargo. The damage was now fully examined and was found to be much more serious than was first thought. She was a constructive total loss, and in August, 1874, Notice of Abandonment was given to both the ship and the freight underwriters. Both notices were declined.

27.58 In the action on the freight policy, the House of Lords consulted the judges, including Brett J., and considered that the plaintiffs were entitled to recover. The ship had undoubtedly suffered the damage during the period of the policy, and this damage, which came within the bounds of the insured perils, prevented her from performing the voyage and earning the freight. De Mattos's insolvency was immaterial. Lord Chelmsford made clear: "No prejudice can possibly arise to the Underwriters from withholding a notice where it is wholly out of their power to take any steps to improve or alter their position."

27.59 Where, as is more usual, Notice of Abandonment is required, such notice may be inferred from dealings between the parties, and may, under section 62(2), be sufficient. Two examples will illustrate this:

27.60 George Cohen Sons & Co. v. Standard Marine Insurance Company Ltd.[20]

On 19th December, 1921, an obsolete battleship, *Prince George*, began her last journey from Chatham to breakers in Germany. She was insured on total loss only terms for £23,000. She had no power on board, and was being towed by two tugs, *Joffre* and *Plover*. The whole expedition was under the command of a Mr. Hayter who was on board the battleship with a small riggers crew. Relations between Mr. Hayter and the tug captains were strained. After two days at sea, both tugs said they needed provisions, and, leaving the battleship anchored, went off to Yarmouth where they remained over Christmas. The battleship drifted onto the Dutch coast at Kamperdun. She finished up lying on her port side on top of the groynes which were an essential part of the sea defences of Holland. She could have been salvaged with some difficulty, and even if the groynes' owners, the Dyke Reeve Board, had objected as they probably would, it was reasonable to suppose that they would eventually have been overruled by higher authority in the Dutch

19. (1873) L.R. 6 H.L. 83, (1873) 2 Asp. 65.
20. (1925) 30 Com. Cas. 139.

Government or even by the Dutch courts. Even so, the cost of the salvage was likely to be well in excess of £23,000.

27.61 Roche J. declined to find that the battleship was an actual total loss. Cohens were not "irretrievably deprived" of her, and neither was she destroyed to the extent that she was no longer a thing of the kind insured. He was however, willing to find that she was a constructive total loss. Was the formal Notice of Abandonment, which was only given in April, 1922, given in time? He was sympathetic to the delay, pointing out that it would have taken much time to get the necessary consents from the Dutch authorities, and it would only have been reasonable for Cohens to have explored the matter with them at length to be fully sure of their ground. The owner's solicitors however, had written on 23rd February, 1922, to the underwriters:

"Will you kindly note that our clients have written claiming what has already been indicated—namely a total loss—and we are asked to collect the sum insured on their behalf. We shall be glad if you will, therefore, kindly arrange to let us have remittance accordingly for £23,000."

27.62 Even though this could be criticised as being too early, his Lordship considered that this was tantamount to a Notice of Abandonment, which was made in the realistic expectation of the troubles which could be expected with the Dutch authorities. Judgment was therefore signed for a constructive total loss in Cohen's favour.

27.63 Currie v. Bombay and Native Insurance Company[21]

On 2nd June, 1867, the *Northland*, loaded with a cargo of timber from Moulmein bound for Madras, was anchored at Halfway Creek in the River Irrawaddy to wait for a change of tide. The timber was insured on total loss only terms. The ship drifted onto a sandbank and was seriously damaged. She may well have broken in two, because when she was seen shortly afterwards, she had a hog of four feet. The Captain was obstructive and objected to the deck being opened up to salve the cargo. It was nonetheless salved, virtually unharmed, and the ship and the cargo were sold together for the sum of Rupees 13,300.

27.64 On the 10th June, 1867, Currie wrote to the underwriters thus:

"With regard to the *Northland*, we regret to say that she is a total wreck, and we have hereby to give you notice that we shall claim payment of the policies we hold against her cargo and disbursements."

27.65 Was this sufficient to constitute a Notice of Abandonment? The Court of the Recorder of Rangoon held that it was not. Doubtless he felt bound by the decision of Lord Ellenborough in *Parmeter* v. *Todhunter*[22] that the word "abandon" should always be used. Before the Privy Council, underwriter's counsel, with Lord Chelmsford's full approval, conceded that it was. Lord Chelmsford went on to say:

21. (1866) L.R. 1 C.P. 535.
22. (1808) 11 Camp. 541.

"But whatever strictures of construction may have been applied to notice of abandonment in former times, it could never have been absolutely necessary to use the technical word 'abandon'; any equivalent expressions which informed the underwriters that it was the intention of the assured to give up to them the property insured upon the grounds of its having been totally lost, must always have been sufficient."

27.66 In spite of these reassuring indications, abandonment is a very serious matter, and it suggested that it is always wise to put the position beyond all doubt by adopting Lord Ellenborough's guidance.

AMOUNT OF RECOVERY

27.67 This depends upon whether the policy of insurance is valued or unvalued. This subject is dealt with very comprehensively in Arnould's *Law of Marine Insurance and Average*, 16th edition, paragraphs 421 to 453. The only addition the author would suggest is to paragraph 428, where ostensibly excessive valuations are discussed and the decisions are quoted that, in the absence of fraud, this is frequently justified. Nowadays many ships are mortgaged, and it is quite common for mortgagees to require insurance to be effected for an amount of 120% or even 130% of the outstanding loan. This in itself may be as much as 80% of the original purchase price. In times when the freight markets are poor, the shipowners may have difficulty in paying the interest, and loans are then "rescheduled", meaning that the unpaid interest, or part of it, is added to the outstanding loan. During the Iran/Iraq War, when the freight markets were generally depressed, and the sale values of ships were correspondingly low, it was not uncommon for a ship with a sale value of $2 million to $3 million to have an insured value of $8 million; when the freight insurance was added, the insured value reached $10 million. On occasions, this difference became even more extreme. A V.L.C.C., which had been purchased with the aid of a loan when the freight markets were high, had an insured value of $30 million and a sale value of no more than $4 million. There was nothing strange or reprehensible about this, and it is not going too far to say that if a mortgagee cannot be certain of recovering his loan in full, and of holding an undertaking from the underwriter or broker that if the ship is lost the insurance moneys will be paid to him, financing of shipping by means of loans will become impossible.

27.68 The sections of the Marine Insurance Act 1906 which have a bearing on valuation of the subject-matter of the insurance are 16, 27, 28, and 68. For the purposes of this work, it is sufficient to quote this last, which reads:

"Subject to the provisions of this Act, and to any express provision in the policy, where there is a total loss of the subject-matter insured,—

   (1) If the policy be a valued policy, the measure of indemnity is the sum fixed by the policy;
   (2) If the policy be an unvalued policy, the measure of indemnity is the insurable value of the subject-matter insured."

27.69 Unvalued policies, once quite common, are now extremely rare, and can be excluded from consideration. The words "Agreed Value (if any)" in the modern

MAR form will, if the value of the subject-matter of the insurance is inserted, serve at least two purposes. Since most insurance premiums are calculated as a percentage of the value of the subject-matter of the insurance, the figure inserted will form the basis for the calculation of the premiums. This figure will also show that a value has been agreed between the underwriters and the assured, and that the insurance is a valued policy. In the words of Cockburn C.J.:

"Where the value is stated in the policy in a manner to be conclusive between the two parties, the insurer and the insured, as regards the value, then in respect of all rights and obligations which arise upon the policy of insurance, the parties are estopped . . ."

from disputing the value stated.[23]

27.70 In the case of ships, assurance is made doubly sure by Clause 2 of the Institute War and Strikes Clauses which incorporates by reference Clause 19 of the Institute Time Clauses—Hulls dated 1.10.83, the marine policy for ships. This states that in case of a constructive total loss, the insured value shall be taken as the repaired value, and this in turn means that the insured value shall be paid to the assured. The same provision appears in the Institute Container Clauses—Time dated 1.1.87 as Clause 16.1, which is similarly incorporated into the Institute War and Strikes Clauses Containers—Time dated 1.1.87.

27.71 Cargo does not have the benefit of this provision in either the new cargo War Clauses or the new cargo Strikes Clauses; this does not however prevent them from being valued policies where the "Agreed Value (if any)" section in the MAR form contains the value of the cargo. The Rules on whether cargo is or is not an actual or a constructive total loss, and whether or not Notice of Abandonment has to be given, are not materially different from those applying to ships. Many cases concerning cargo are quoted in this work, but two which will serve as examples are the *Rodocanachi* case (para. 11.21) and the *Mullett* case (para. 30.37), particularly as in the latter case it might have been expected that Notice of Abandonment would have been required. Although it was given, it was held not to be necessary because the cargo had been "destroyed" by the sale which had put it out of reach of any recovery. Another case where the Notice of Abandonment received some interesting treatment by the courts is the *Stringer* case (paras. 30.47–30.50).

27.72 Freight is in a class on its own being, as Lord Wright M.R. noted in the *Yero Carras* case (paras. 22.11–22.16), an intangible matter, and questions may arise whether it is an actual total loss or a constructive total loss.[24] The question did not arise, as it might have been expected to, in the Iran/Iraq War where tankers were hit by Exocet missiles. Mostly they stayed afloat (very few tankers were sunk by the Exocets), were salved, and were taken into Dubai, Sharjah, or Khor Fakkam. They were usually hit in way of the engine room, and whilst the cargo tanks and with them the cargo were usually, although not invariably, completely untouched, the damage to the ships was so serious that they were constructive total losses. This being so, the shipowners could, under Clause 2 of the Institute War and Strikes Clauses Freight dated 1.10.83, which incorporated Clause 15 from the Freight Marine Clauses, require payment of the whole amount insured by the

23. *North of England Insurance* v. *Armstrong* (1870) L.R. 5 Q.B. 248.
24. The question is very fully discussed in Arnould's *Law of Marine Insurance and Average*, 16th edition, paragraphs 1164 to 1165 and 1233 to 1258.

freight insurance.[25] The shipowner, being amply protected by the charterparty for his failure to carry the cargo to its destination, thereupon called upon the cargo owners to arrange for the transhipment of the cargo. The cargo owner could do this, and had a claim upon the new cargo War Clauses for the expenses involved.[26]

27.73 Freight may easily become an actual total loss independently of what happens to the ship as the *Yero Carras* and *Kulukundis* cases will demonstrate (paras. 22.11–22.16, 22.18–22.24). These cases will also show the special considerations which apply to the judgment of freight as a total loss. In *Rankin* v. *Potter*,[27] the homeward freight may well have been regarded as an actual rather than a constructive total loss. In this case, as it has already been remarked, the House of Lords consulted the judges, and Brett J. gave his opinion that he doubted if freight could ever be a constructive total loss, although he refused to rule out the possibility entirely:

"This conclusion does not go to the length of determining that there never can be a constructive total loss of freight. If, for instance, the ship should be damaged as described, but cargo which was on board has been saved under circumstances which leave it doubtful whether such cargo might or might not be forwarded in a substituted ship, or if the original cargo should be lost and the ship may or may not probably earn some freight by carrying other goods on the voyage insured, it may be, and I think the rule is, that in order to make certain his right to recover as for total loss on the policy on freight, the assured should give notice of abandonment of the chance of earning such substituted freight".

27.74 Casualties which concern the ship's War and Strikes insurance are likely to lead to situations where a ship is:

(1) So badly damaged that under her War and Strikes Hull insurance she is a constructive total loss, and the shipowner treats her as such; or

(2) So badly damaged that she is a constructive total loss, but the shipowner elects to repair her and treat his claims as a partial loss; or

(3) Is damaged but not to the extent of being a constructive total loss. It will take months to repair her.

27.75 In situation (1) there is no problem. As it has already been remarked (para. 22.8) the freight insurance is payable in full in any event, and this will exhaust the liability of the freight underwriters. In situations (2) and (3), anxious thought needs to be given to the freight, and to its insurance. Is the freight an actual total loss, or is it realistic to expect that something can be saved from it? If the latter appears to be the position, then a constructive total loss may, in spite of Brett J.'s doubts, arise, and, as the law presently stands, Notice of Abandonment must be given. Finally, consideration will have to be given to Clause 13.1 of the Institute Time Clauses Freight, which is incorporated into the Institute War and Strikes Freight—Time by Clause 2. This reads:

"The amount recoverable under this insurance for any claim for loss of freight shall not exceed the gross freight actually lost."

25. Clause 2 incorporates terms from the Institute Time Clauses Freight dated 1.10.83, whereas these clauses were amended on 1.8.89. The failure to amend Clause 2 to reflect this is probably an oversight.
26. Attention is drawn to the new cargo War Clauses' Duration provisions (paras. 34.16–34.21, 34.26, 34.27). A cargo owner engaged in such a transhipment operation needs to make sure that his cover under the new cargo War Clauses remains continuous throughout, and that any necessary additional, or further premiums, are paid.
27. (1873) L.R. 6 H.L. 83 (paras. 27.57, 27.58).

PARTIAL LOSS

27.76 The main difference between a total loss, whether actual or constructive, and a partial loss is that the expenses involved in a partial loss have to be proved by means of surveyors' reports and vouchers. Sections 69 (ships), 70 (freight), 71 (cargo), 72 (apportionment of valuation), and 77 (successive losses), and Clause 8 of both the new cargo War Clauses and of the new cargo Strikes Clauses, are particularly relevant.

CHAPTER 28

Held covered

28.1 This is a provision contained in many types of insurance policy. In war risks insurance, it frequently appears in connection with entry to an area for which an additional premium is chargeable by the underwriter. Generally, prior notice of entry is required in order that the premium may be agreed, the underwriter may be put on notice when the extra risk of greater danger arises and there may be certainty in the relationship between the shipowner and the underwriter. There has long been the danger that the insured ship may enter such an area without the shipowner's knowledge; in the past this has happened because there has been an accident on board and repairs are urgent, or because sick or injured seamen have to be landed for medical treatment ashore, or because the charterer requires the Master to load or discharge at a different port. News of this may not reach the shipowner in time for prior notice to be given. To guard against the shipowner losing his insurance cover inadvertently, an extra clause is added to ensure that his insurance will continue and a typical provision is: "Or held covered at a premium to be arranged".

28.2 This can lead to abuse because sometimes there is the temptation, to which some succumb, to enter an additional area and hope to slip in and out unobserved. If there is a casualty whilst within the area, the commonly held belief is that one is "held covered" and all that one has to do is to produce the premium to get the resulting claim paid. For the reasons which appear below, this belief is profoundly mistaken, unless it can be shown that there is a reason for the failure to give notice, which is so *bona fide* and genuine that it will convince the underwriters, or on occasion, the courts, who by this time will both be very sceptical, that the failure should be excused. The courts have many times had to deal with this problem and there exists a large body of case law. A few cases only will serve to illustrate what the law is. The first of these is *Hood* v. *West End Motor Car Packing Company*[1] where a motor car, in breach of the policy requirements that it should be loaded below deck, was shipped on deck. There was a "held covered" provision, and in the Court of Appeal Swinfen-Eady L.J. described the assured's duty: " . . . Notice must be given to the underwriters within a reasonable time after the facts have come to the knowledge of the assured if he wishes to rely on this clause" to which Scrutton L.J. added: "It is an implied term of the contract that the insured shall give notice to the underwriters within a reasonable time after he knows of the omission or error."

28.3 Subsequently the assured's duty was put more strongly by McNair J. in

---

1. [1917] 2 K.B. 38.

Overseas Commodities Limited v. *Style.*[2] The insured goods were tins and their marks were queried by the underwriters. The French suppliers gave two separate and mutually contradictory explanations. Only the more favourable explanation was shown to the underwriters: "To obtain the protection of the 'held covered' clause, the assured must act with the utmost good faith towards the underwriters, this being an obligation which rests on them throughout the currency of the policy."

28.4 Donaldson J. followed this in *Liberian Insurance Agency Inc.* v. *Mosse.*[3] There was a "held covered" clause in the policy which described the insured goods as "enamelware cups and plates" shipped in cases. Many of the goods were not cups and plates; some were touched up by overpainting; some were "seconds" bought at a cheap price; most seriously of all, a substantial part of the consignment was not even loaded in cases, but in cartons which gave less protection to their contents:

"If the assured is to take advantage of the 'held covered' clause, he must give notice to underwriters expressly or impliedly seeking cover in accordance with the clause within a reasonable time of learning of the change of voyage or of the omission or error in the description. What time is reasonable will depend on the circumstances."

28.5 No guidance on the length of time which is reasonable to suit every situation is possible and could be seriously misleading, but Donaldson J. went as far as it is possible to go:

"Thus if the assured learns the true facts whilst the risk is still current, a reasonable time will usually be a shorter period than if this occurs when the adventure is already ended. If the assured learns the true facts when the assured property is in the grip of a peril, which is likely to cause loss or damage, a reasonable time will be short indeed."

28.6 Following the lead given by McNair J., Donaldson J. made it clear that the obligations contained in section 17 of the Marine Insurance Act 1906 were not simply obligations to be observed at the time that the insurance contract was made; they arose every time the "held covered" provision operated. In *The Litsion Pride*[4] Hurst J. explained the reason for this and whilst he did not say so in so many words, it is clearly a matter within the contemplation of each party that: " . . . From a commercial point of view it seems to be most important that the underwriter should have available all the material facts which affect the fixing of an additional premium."

28.7 The courts have clearly strengthened the utmost good faith obligation by indicating that the sections of the Act immediately following section 17 instance the overriding duty of utmost good faith for which section 17 provides.

28.8 Two recent cases, although they do not concern War and Strikes insurance, will serve to demonstrate how very strictly the courts interpret "utmost good faith". The plaintiffs in *Container Transport International Inc. and Reliance Group Inc.* v. *Oceanus Mutual Underwriting Association (Bermuda) Ltd.*,[5] had previously insured the small damages to the containers which they leased to others with two sets of underwriters, first Crum & Foster and then Lloyd's underwriters. It was a

---

2. [1958] 1 Lloyd's Rep. 546.
3. [1977] 2 Lloyd's Rep. 560.
4. *Black King Shipping Corporation and Wayang (Panama) S.A.* v. *Mark Ranald Massie (The Litsion Pride)* [1985] 1 Lloyd's Rep. 437.
5. [1982] 2 Lloyd's Rep. 178, [1984] 1 Lloyd's Rep. 476.

very difficult risk with a bad claims record, and it is the sort of insurance where the claims records are difficult to keep. Their third underwriters were Oceanus, who complained that the assured had (a) put forward inaccurate, incomplete, and misleading claims records, (b) failed to disclose that the Lloyd's underwriters had declined to renew, and (c) had failed to make a full disclosure to Lloyd's when obtaining their insurance there. Lloyd J., when considering section 18, said:

"In general, I would say that underwriters ought only to succeed on a defence of nondisclosure if they can satisfy the Court by evidence or otherwise that a prudent insurer, if he had known the fact in question, would have declined the risk altogether or charged a higher premium."

28.9 He signed judgment in favour of the plaintiffs, and Oceanus appealed. The Court of Appeal took a much sterner view. Kerr L.J. delivered the main judgment:

"The duty of disclosure, as defined or circumscribed by Sections 18 and 19, is one aspect of the overriding duty of the utmost good faith mentioned in Section 17. The actual insurer is thereby entitled to the disclosure to him of every fact which would influence the judgment of a prudent insurer in fixing the premium or determining whether he will take the risk . . . that the judgement in this sense, of a prudent insurer would have been influenced the circumstances in question had been disclosed. The word 'influenced' means that the disclosure is one which would have had an impact on the formation of his opinion and on his decision making process in relation to the matters covered by Section 18(2)."

Parker L.J. agreed, but added that the emphasis was on a prudent underwriter rather than a particular underwriter. Stephenson L.J. recorded his agreement with both views.

28.10 It is impossible not to feel some sympathy for the plaintiff in *Inversiones Manria S.A.* v. *Sphere Drake Insurance Company Plc and Others (The Dora)*[6] and Phillips J. said as much when dealing with the case of non-disclosure which surrounded the placing of her insurance. The principal of the plaintiff company only wanted to buy a yacht for use in the Adriatic, and was obviously quite unaware of the trickery which, in some cases, surrounds the yacht building and selling processes. The yacht was to be built in Taiwan, and imported into Italy. The underwriters raised many points on which there had been non-disclosure when the insurance was proposed, the most important being that the hull only was built in Taiwan, and the fitting out was to be done in Italy; the yacht was not produced by established and satisfactory procedures; the yacht was a prototype, and was to be used for demonstrations; the yacht skipper and even the plaintiff's own representative had, unknown to the plaintiff, criminal records. When she was discharged from the ocean vessel in Trieste, the skipper, who had attended her building in Taiwan, was found by the Italian customs to have loaded her before her shipment with a mass of dutiable goods which could not have been intended for her fitting out. He put off the customs officers in Trieste with a story that the goods were in transit for Yugoslavia, and he and the plaintiff's representative later on the same day had great difficulty in explaining why they were being unloaded into the skipper's own boatyard in Italy. There was a mass of matters which had not been disclosed which should have been, mostly because the unfortunate owner had no knowledge of them, and the miscreants had no interest in drawing attention to them. When a few

6. [1989] 1 Lloyd's Rep. 69.

weeks later the yacht caught fire and sank off Dubrovnik, the underwriters refused to pay for her total loss, and Phillips J. held that they were justified.

28.11 The obligations of the assured arose once again in the recent case of *Black King Shipping Corporation and Wayang Panama S.A.* v. *Mark Ranald Massie (The Litsion Pride)*.[7] Black King were the ship's owners, Wayang were the ship's mortgagees and Mr. Massie was a representative underwriter of the War Risks Policy. There is no purpose in describing in detail the mass of contradictory evidence before the High Court with which Hurst J. had to contend. The report itself covers 70 two-column pages. Various important points of law will be dealt with in this work where they are appropriate. The basic facts were fairly simple. Black King was a one-ship company among a group of similar companies forming the Macedonia Group. All the ships were mortgaged to S.H.L. of Lubeck except for Black King's ship, the *Litsion Pride*, which was mortgaged to Wayang. She was insured on the S.G. Form with Institute War and Strikes Clauses attached. Additional premiums were to be paid for visits to various areas, one of them the Arabian (Persian) Gulf north of latitude 24° north. Notice was to be given of visits to these areas by a special clause which was also a "held covered" clause: "Information on such voyage . . . shall be given to insurers as soon as practicable, and in the absence of prior advice shall not affect the cover hereon."

28.12 The clause went on to provide that the insured could choose not to insure his ship, but in this event he had to advise the underwriters "before the commencement of the voyage". The underwriters would then decide whether to reinstate the insurance after the ship left the additional premium area. This last provision seems to be based on a provision of the Mutual War Risks Associations' Rules, which allow an insured shipowner to suspend his insurance (with the mortgagee's consent) during the time that the ship is within the additional premium area. The insurance in that case automatically takes effect once again as soon as the ship leaves the additional premium area. There are thus two very important differences between the *Litsion Pride's* clause and the provisions of the Mutual War Risks Associations' Rules which, whilst they should be noted, are not material to this case. During the material time, the Iran/Iraq War was in its second year. Events took the following course:

1982

2nd July

The ship sails from Dunkirk with sugar for Iran. This means that she must enter the additional premium area, and at this stage, this fact is amply apparent to her owners.

4th July

E.T.A. Bandar Abbas is notified for 26th July. During the war, ships bound for Iranian ports always called at Bandar Abbas either for discharge, or for orders and convoy to northern ports.

8th July

Wayang raises the point that the ship is going to Iran and seeks confirmation that she is fully covered. They do not wish their name to be connected with the enquiry and they do not address their query to the owners.

7. [1985] 1 Lloyd's Rep. 437.

14th July

The enquiry is now addressed to the owners in Cyprus saying that the insurers had raised it, which is not so. The owners could infer that the underwriters already knew of the voyage.

21st July

The charterers nominate Bandar Khomeini as the discharging port. This is presently the most dangerous port in Iran, being well within the range of the Iraqi helicopters and airforce bombers. Several ships have already been attacked.

27th July

The ship reaches Djibouti.

2nd August

The ship crosses latitude 24° north.
   A letter bearing this date is prepared in the owner's London office. Addressed to the brokers, it gives formal notice of the ship's proposed visit to Persian Gulf. It is not despatched and a junior employee is subsequently blamed for an oversight.

11th August

The ship is hit by missiles launched from Iranian helicopters in the Khor Musa Channel, which is the entrance to Bandar Khomeini port. Her cargo of sugar catches fire, she grounds and is lost. Notice is given to the underwriters of the casualty. This is their first intimation that the ship is within the additional premium area.

12th August

The 2nd August letter is now given to the underwriters who see it for the first time.

26th August

A writ is issued.

28.13 The court took immense pains to analyse the "held covered" clause and the obligations of utmost good faith and it would be doing it an injustice to attempt to summarise its very careful findings, which stretch over pages 462 to 471 and pages 507 to 512 of *Lloyd's Law Reports*, because of the danger of distortion. The findings include a review of the law which is only briefly, but hopefully effectively, given in this chapter. The underwriters pleaded that it was a condition precedent that notice of the entry of the additional premium area should be given as soon as practicable, and the shipowners had plenty of notice of the ship's impending entry. Hurst J. felt that he could not so hold. It would have been a very simple matter to have made an express provision in the contract that the giving of notice was a condition precedent to the cover, and there had lately been a general move by the courts away from holding that a condition precedent could be implied where none was expressed. His attention was drawn to the Rules of the Hellenic (Bermuda) Mutual War Risks Association which, at the time of the casualty, read: "It is a condition of the insurance [given by the Association] . . . that the owner shall give prompt written notice . . . of the fact that the entered [insured] ship will enter, has entered or is in the additional premium area as soon as the owner knows of such fact." This was suggested to be a good example of an express provision which was totally lacking in the *Litsion Pride's* "held covered" clause. On this point he ruled against the underwriters although they won the case on other grounds.

28.14 It should be noted that at the time of the drafting of the above-mentioned Hellenic clause (1976), there was anxiety to ensure that notice was given in proper time and also to protect the shipowner in case, through no fault of his own, and some instances are given earlier in this chapter, an entry to an additional premium area was made without notice first being given to the Association. At that time there was still the possibility of this happening. The earlier cases were concerned with ships which were very often out of contact with their owners. The miracle of modern communications had not then been achieved and some latitude had to be given by the courts based on an understanding that the owner could not always be expected to know just where his ship was or what she was doing. In the *Hood* case (para. 28.2) there was also a possible problem of communications in wartime. Nowadays it is possible to communicate with the ship by telephone and often by the ubiquitous telex as well, besides even more sophisticated means such as Sattel. There is now every reason for the shipowner to know just where his ship is and what she is currently doing. The Hellenic (Bermuda) Mutual War Risks Association felt justified in strengthening the clause mentioned above to its present form to provide: "The owner of an Entered [insured] ship shall give written notice to the Association . . . before the ship enters any Additional Premium area."

28.15 As conclusions the following are suggested:

1. In the absence of an express provision, the giving of notice under the "held covered" clause is not a condition precedent, either to the continued insurance cover of the insured ship, or to the insurance cover whilst she is in the additional premium area. It needs an express provision to make it so.

2. In the absence of an express provision, notice must be given within time which is reasonable in all the circumstances after the insured shipowner becomes aware, or ought to have become aware, of the position of his ship.

3. The earlier cases allowed considerable latitude to the insured in giving notice, because of the greater difficulty of communications at the time. With the increasingly greater efficiency of modern communications, this latitude will be reduced—always provided, of course, that some event such as a war does not intervene to hinder communications.

4. Irrespective of whether there is a condition precedent, the giving of notice is one of the utmost good faith between the insured shipowner and the underwriter. Section 17 of the Marine Insurance Act 1906 does not apply merely to the time the insurance contract is made; it applies throughout the contract and in particular on every occasion that the necessity to give notice arises.

5. The obligations of utmost good faith can be modified by the policy. This can be achieved either by its express terms, or by the manner in which its other terms are intended to work; but it can be foreseen that the courts would be loth to excuse either party from this obligation unless there is a very clear provision that the parties intend this.

CHAPTER 29

Wilful misconduct

29.1 Section 55 of the Marine Insurance Act 1906 begins by providing what is perhaps a truism, that the insurer is liable to pay for any loss which is proximately caused by a peril insured against, but is not liable for any loss which is not so proximately caused. It goes on to say, in subsection 2(*a*):

"The insurer is not liable for any loss attributable to the wilful misconduct of the assured but, unless the policy otherwise provides, he is liable for any loss proximately caused by a peril insured against, even though the loss would not have happened but for the misconduct or negligence of the Master and crew."

29.2 There have been a considerable number of cases where shipowners have claimed on their insurers for ships which have been scuttled, with their connivance, to obtain the insurance money. It is undoubtedly fraudulent, and indeed criminal, for a shipowner to arrange to sink his own ship, and then to represent to his underwriters that she was lost through an insured peril, and the underwriter needs no help from section 55 when he refuses to pay such a claim. The ordinary common law of fraud will, if the facts justify such a finding, prevent the assured profiting from his own criminal wrongdoing. This is so well established that no legal argument is going to change the position, and the scuttling cases are mostly concerned with the factual evidence which each party produces to establish guilt or innocence. The common law does not require an underwriter to prove conclusively that a claim is fraudulent; he only has to show a high degree of probability that this is so, and once he has succeeded in doing this the burden of proof shifts to the shipowner to prove his innocence. *Slattery* v. *Mance*,[1] although a first instance decision, is generally regarded as determinative on this point. There is a further provision of the common law that, even where there is no fraud, the assured must not cause his own claim. In the field of non-marine insurance, to which the Marine Insurance Act 1906 has no application, this is usually enough to defeat a claim where the assured has caused his own accident.

29.3 Inversely, however, this may be the key to the understanding of section 55. In the marine insurance field, the shipowner's carelessness or negligence, or "the misconduct or negligence of the Master and crew" will not defeat a claim on the underwriters. To do this, the shipowner's own misdeeds must reach higher degrees of guilt than those provided by the common law, and amount to "wilful misconduct", an expression which is wide enough to include "purposeful" misconduct. The two words must be read disjunctively and not conjunctively. For instance, it

1. [1962] 1 Lloyd's Rep. 60.

may be "wilful" to send a well-founded ship to sea in a North Atlantic winter gale, but it is scarcely misconduct.

29.4 Curiously, section 55 has received very little judicial consideration but there are two cases of interest which will serve as examples of "wilful misconduct", particularly because they demonstrate that actual intention to cause the loss is not a necessary element. They also indicate that "recklessness" may be sufficient to amount to "wilful misconduct". The first is the American case of *Orient Insurance Company* v. *Adams*,[2] where a ship was sent to sea knowing that she was not in a condition to counter its perils. This was held to be "wilful misconduct". The second is a decision of the Supreme Court of Queensland, *Wood* v. *Associated National Insurance Company Ltd. (The Isothel)*.[3] The *Isothel* was a fishing vessel which left port in May, 1981, with a crew of four, the skipper who was part owner and the only person on board qualified to manage the boat, and three fishermen, none of whom could navigate her or even use the radio. Shortly after sailing, the bilge pump was found not to be working, and the boat was anchored in a position which was unsafe in any winds blowing from north of east. There was no danger at the time because the wind was in the south-east although it was rising. The skipper went ashore to get help, and together with his father, another part-owner, repaired the bilge pump and also did some repairs to the main engine which needed attention. Both men then returned ashore leaving the boat anchored and in the charge of an unskilled crew.

29.5 During the next two days the skipper visited the beach opposite the position where the boat was anchored. On the second day, it was raining and he could not even see the boat. Although well aware from the weather forecasts that the wind was backing to the north-east and a storm was expected from that quarter, he made no attempt to return to the boat but spent the night at home. In the subsequent storm, the anchor line parted, the crew abandoned the boat, and she was driven onto the rocks and became a total loss. The trial judge found that there was no intention to cause her loss, but that the plaintiffs had recklessly disregarded the consequences of their conduct to such an extent that they were guilty of "wilful misconduct". This finding, which was based upon section 61(2)(*a*) of the Marine Insurance Act 1909 (Commonwealth), which is in the same terms as section 55(2)(*a*) of the Marine Insurance Act 1906, was upheld on appeal.

29.6 Much of this is of only academic interest to War and Strikes insurance. Any shipowner intending to cause the loss of, or damage to, his ship cannot necessarily depend on the actions of other people to achieve this, however vindictive they may be. There is, however, the possibility, as the *Orient* and *Isothel* cases seem to indicate (paras. 29.4–29.5), of there being "wilful misconduct" through "recklessness". In the War and Strikes context, this could arise through deliberately sending the ship into a situation where danger exists well knowing that something is certain, or very nearly certain, to happen to her. It is suggested that the danger is one of degree. It is not "recklessness" amounting to "wilful misconduct" to require the ship to trade in an area of some danger such as an additional premium area. To require her to trade to an area where it is certain, or very nearly certain, that she

2. 123 U.S. 67 (1887).
3. 1984.

will become a War Risks casualty probably is such "recklessness", and the *dicta* of Goddard J., in the *Papadimitriou* case should be noted. See paras. 29.8–29.10.

29.7 Before moving on from subsection 2(*a*), however, two points need to be noted. There is no provision that the parties may contract out of the first part of the subsection's provisions (down to the word "but") and any attempt to do so would fly in the face of every canon of the doctrine of public policy. There is a long line of cases which have established that the negligence of the Master in the loss of or damage to the insured ship is a peril of the sea and will not rob the shipowner of his claim against the underwriters. This was illustrated by *Trinder Anderson & Co.* v. *Thames and Mersey Marine Insurance and Others*[4] where the Master was also a part-owner. The *Gainsborough's* freight was insured on a voyage from Australia to San Francisco with coal. The ship ran short of water and intended to put into Honolulu to replenish her supply. Due to negligence she ran aground. A.L. Smith L.J. in the Court of Appeal made a clear distinction between negligence, even of an extreme degree, and the wilful act of the assured:

"I believe that there cannot be found in the insurance law of England a single case to support the proposition now contended for by the underwriters, which is that, assuming the loss has not been occasioned by the wilful act or default of the insured but is immediately caused by a peril of the sea, the remote and not the proximate cause is to be looked at."

29.8 There is only one reported case where "wilful misconduct" was raised as a defence to a claim in a War Risks Policy, namely *Papadimitriou* v. *Henderson*.[5] The *Ellenico Vouno* was insured for a voyage on the S.G. Form with Institute War and Strikes Clauses attached. There was a warranty in the policy that the ship was not to go to a Spanish port or a Spanish possession in the Mediterranean and was not to carry arms, ammunition, or instruments of war, but this was not to exclude cars, trucks, benzine, coal, coke "or similar". From the outset, it was appreciated by all concerned, including the underwriters, that this was a risky venture, because the goods were to be carried from the U.S.S.R. the principal supporter of the Republican Government of Spain, for that government's use. The Spanish Navy had mostly declared for General Franco, and the Nationalists in the Spanish Civil War always had a strong naval force at their disposal. The impression is gained from reading the report that the defendants had intended to prove more than they succeeded in doing, a litigation hazard which will be readily recognised by the lawyers. Moreover, some of the facts are not entirely clear from the judgment, and the High Court had difficulty in establishing them. Even supposing that they were more unfavourable to the insured than appears from the report, there is no reason to suppose that the court's judgment would have been different.

1938

Early

The ship is chartered to load lorries and spare parts in Odessa for the Republican Government of Spain. The contemplated discharge port is Marseilles. The charterers later express a wish to discharge in Oran, but the negotiations in London take a lot of time.

4. [1898] A.C. 114.See also para. 29.17.
5. (1939) 64 Ll.L.Rep. 345.

29th April

Whilst in Pireaus and before sailing to Odessa, the Master is given a letter by the owner advising him of the possibility that he will be discharging in Oran, which is still not arranged.

12th May

The ship sails from Odessa. The shippers' agents, Inflot, tell the Master he will discharge in Oran, this having been agreed with a suitable addendum to the charterparty. The discharging port is left blank in the bill of lading, although this is later filled in, presumably by the Master during the voyage. This seems to indicate other messages reaching the ship during the voyage which did not appear before the court.

Probably 14th–15th May

On passing Istanbul the owner's agent, Dabcovich, attempts to reach the ship but fails to do so.

17th May

The owner telegraphs the Captain "but it is now agreed to go to Malta for orders" but it seems doubtful if the Captain ever received this message or a subsequent message telling him to stand by for a message.

18th May

The owners inform the Captain that they have agreed terms for a recall to Piraeus and tell him to return there. There is a vague indication of trouble off Cap Bon, which it seems is all the information that the owners have. The ship is "160 miles east of Malta" and the Captain confirms he is obeying this instruction. He telegraphs his position which is picked up by the Franco cruiser *Canarias*.

19th May

The *Canarias* overhauls the ship and boards her. On seeing in the bill of lading that the buying organisation is a Spanish Government company, the *Canarias* sends the ship to Palma with a prize crew on board. She is later escorted by another Franco warship. the *Mar Cantabrico*. Judging by the massive force which they have assembled, it seems that the Nationalists were lying in wait for the ship. The court finds that she is a total loss at this date.

Later

In Palma the ship is appropriated by the Nationalists and the crew is sent home. It is not clear if she is condemned by the Prize Court, but Goddard J. holds that this does not matter:
  "I have no doubt, if it was considered by a Prize Court, that no court would have any difficulty in applying the doctrine of continuous voyage. So it is at least likely—I do not say more than that—that if this ship was brought into a Prize Court, she was condemned because she was carrying a cargo of contraband."

29.9 The owner claimed for the loss of his ship and freight and it is now difficult to see why the underwriters chose to fight this case, particularly on the grounds of "wilful misconduct". The owners had been perfectly open about their intentions and had made no secret of their proposal to carry lorries and other goods from the U.S.S.R., one of the Spanish Republican Government's main supporters, to ports in neutral countries conveniently situated from the point of view of the Spanish Government. Even if the underwriters did not actually know who the receivers were, the nature of the voyage which they insured from Odessa to the Western Mediterranean ports was itself indicative of the cargo's ultimate destination. Any of the goods specifically allowed by the insurance policy could have been regarded as contraband by the Spanish Nationalists. They must have appreciated that this voyage, whilst perfectly lawful (as Goddard J. found), entailed a measure of risk of capture and subsequent confiscation. The court made the points that the owner, when asked to send the ship to Malta, made arrangements to do so, although it seems his messages failed to reach the Master. When asked to arrange for her return to Piraeus, he again did so, and neither he nor the Master was to know of the presence or position of the *Canarias*. To say that there was "wilful misconduct" here would be tantamount to saying that there was also "wilful misconduct" during the First World War, when ships were sent into the area where German U-boats were operating and ran the risk of being torpedoed. Goddard J. went on:

"I think it would be a very dangerous doctrine to lay down in the courts of this country that the Captain of a neutral ship or the owner of a ship belonging to a country not at war, is guilty of wilful misconduct if he tries to proceed with his contract voyage, simply because there is a risk of capture, as there must always be a risk of capture during a war, which is the reason why shipowners and merchants insure against war risks."

29.10 The judge made an important distinction:

"Of course, if it was a case in which the shipowners got warning that the blockade had been established at a particular port or that a ship was lying waiting at a particular point, and the shipowner deliberately sent his ship forward to that point to run the blockade, it may be that there would be, in certain cases, an inference to be drawn that he was not endeavouring to carry out the voyage, but what he was endeavouring to do was to get his ship captured, and that, of course, would be wilful misconduct."

Since in this case the ship was engaged on a lawful voyage which she continued to carry out, and the shipowners endeavoured to avoid danger, there could be no question of "wilful misconduct" here. Judgment was signed for the owners.

29.11 It may questioned that if the policy had contained a warranty that the ship was not to carry contraband, this may have changed the position. Again it is arguable that this was not so. The ship was engaged on carrying goods that were specifically permitted by the policy, and the knowledge that the underwriters had of the voyage and the goods which she was due to carry, coupled with the facts set out above, could have been held to render the contraband warranty ineffectual.

29.12 During the Iran/Iraq War, many attacks were made on ships by both sides. The Iranians attacked ships by launching Maverick missiles from helicopters. These are basically anti-tank missiles and depend upon a television eye in the nose to find their target. At night, they cannot form a picture of the target and are therefore useless. Although not designed for use against ships, there were several instances of very severe damage, sometimes amounting to total loss, particularly to tankers which were not in a gas-free condition. The normal route for ships going to load in the Arabian Gulf is the rhumb-line course between the entrance, the Straits of Hormuz, and the loading ports in the central and northern parts of the Gulf, taking advantage of the only deep water in it. The distances are, however, too great to complete this voyage under the cover of night, and the danger of attack, particularly in the neighbourhood of the Shah Allum Shoal, was extreme. The practice therefore grew up of entering the Gulf at dusk and sailing along the southern shore to Dubai, Jebel Ali light vessel or Jaz Niat Island, anchoring there during the day, and the next night sailing north to pass the helicopter bases on the oil platforms to reach a point 60 miles (the maximum helicopter range) north of the nearest helicopter base by dawn. The outward loaded passage was followed in reverse.

29.13 This has several objectionable features. As a start it took extra time and time is money. Some of the slower ships needed a daytime stop at Das Island to complete the dangerous part of the passage. Even for the faster ships, which could do it in two nights, it was a hair-raising business. The ships needed to go flat-out to have any chance to complete the night-time sailing during the hours of darkness, and the task of navigating a fully laden V.L.C.C. hrough the shallow waters in the western part of the Gulf put an immense strain on the shipmasters. It says much for their competence that no ship went aground. In spite of these hazards this was a safer course to follow and one used by the prudent majority. Nevertheless, if some continued to take the rhumb-line course, what would be the result if they were attacked? Were they guilty of "wilful misconduct" in doing so? According to the *Papadimitriou* case[6] they were not. Would this conduct have been "reckless"? If, however, the *Orient* and *Isothel* cases were followed, it could have been "reckless". This was not tested in the courts and now, happily, the war is at an end and the danger of an attack no longer exists. Had it been tested, however, it is equally possible that the courts would have been prepared to find that it was "reckless" to follow the rhumb-line course, and that such would be "wilful misconduct".

29.14 The author would prefer that this last statement, even though it has some support from the *Orient* and *Isothel* cases (paras. 29.4, 29.5), should be regarded as tentative, because the law is not entirely clear just how much "recklessness" there has to be before there is "wilful misconduct". Perhaps it will never be entirely clear, because there is a strong case for saying that "recklessness" which amounts, or does not amount, to "wilful misconduct" will always depend on questions of fact and these are always individual to each case. Thus all we can hope to do is to note the cases as they arise. There are a number of definitions of "recklessness" in connection with "malice" and "maliciously" (paras. 19.1–19.11), but none of these are very satisfactory. Most of the cases relate to criminal, or quasi-criminal, actions, and it is not necessary that "recklessness" or "wilful misconduct" should reach a criminal dimension before they defeat an assured's claim under a marine insurance policy, although of course they may well do so. "Recklessness" appears to be of a higher degree of blameworthiness than negligence or carelessness which will not deprive an assured of his claim, and it may, in extreme cases, even reach the degree of "wilful misconduct" which does. The student of the subject of "recklessness" can turn to *Forder* v. *Great Western Railway Company*,[7] *Horabin* v. *B.O.A.C.*[8] and *Rustenburg Platinum Mines Ltd.* v. *South African Airways and Pan-American World Airways Inc.*[9] There is little point in discussing these in any detail in this work because, not being marine cases, they will not be concerned with "recklessness" reaching the degree of "wilful misconduct".

29.15 There are however two additional cases in the field of marine insurance where consideration was given to recklessness, even though the first of these, which was decided in the early 19th century, is more concerned with "gross negligence" and is not regarded as strong authority today. *Pipon* v. *Cope*[10] concerned the greater than usual difficulties encountered by a shipowner whose crews insist upon trading for their own account. The *General Doyle* was a Post Office packet ship carrying mail and passengers between Weymouth and the Channel Islands. She was insured on terms that the cover was warranted "free from captures and seizures and the consequences of any attempt thereof". In 1806 and 1807 the crew smuggled spirits and tobacco without the owner's knowledge. The Customs seized the ship, but freed her when convinced of the owner's innocence. A fresh crew was signed

6. (1939) 64 Ll.L.Rep. 345.
7. [1905] K.B. 532.
8. [1951] 2 Lloyd's Rep. 450.
9. [1977] 1 Lloyd's Rep. 564.
10. (1808) 1 Camp. 434.

on, and exactly the same thing happened, except this time the smuggled commodity was salt. Again she was seized and released. A third time was too much even for the patience of the Customs, and this time she could only be released on payment of a fine when the Customs authorities could be convinced of the shipowner's innocence.

29.16 Whilst seized and awaiting release, another ship drifted down upon her and damaged her. The shipowner's action for the fine which he had to pay to the Customs and the collision damage was heard by Lord Ellenborough L.C. Having held against the underwriters that captures could only be hostile, and therefore, in this context, "seizures", when interpreted *ejusdem generis*, could only be hostile as well:

"But this is a clear case of *crassa neglentia* on the part of the assured. It was the plaintiff's duty to have prevented these repeated acts of smuggling by the crew. By his neglecting to do so, and allowing the risk to be so monstrously enhanced, the underwriters are discharged."

It is interesting to note that the shipowner lost his collision damage claim as well on the strange, and not well explained grounds that, whilst she was seized, he ceased to have any interest in her.

29.17 The case on the *Gainsborough*'s freight is described at para. 29.7 where the story of the casualty is set out. *Trinder Anderson & Co.* v. *North Queensland Insurance Company*[11] dealt with the hull claim when the shipowner was again awarded judgment. Kennedy L.J. in the Court of Appeal held that the shipowner would have no claim for acts done knowingly and wilfully: " . . . or at least with reckless disregard of possible risk to the safety of the subject matter of the insurance".

29.18 Finally, it should be noted that some (but not all) of the Mutual War Risks Associations have an "imprudent conduct" rule. The British Mutual War Risks Association's Rule 4.E.4 presently reads:

"If any act or omission shall be committed on board or in connection with the entered ship which ought reasonably to be anticipated as being of such a nature as to render the entered ship liable to any loss or damage, or to capture, seizure, arrest, restraint, detainment, confiscation or expropriation, and if such act or omission shall cause or in any way contribute to such loss or damage or to such capture, seizure, arrest, restraint, detainment, confiscation or expropriation, then the Association shall not be liable for the loss of or damage to, or detention of the entered ship, nor for any losses, liabilities, costs or expenses resulting therefrom."

This provision applies to all parts of the insurance except the Queen's Enemy Risk.

29.19 This Rule, which is in addition to, but not in substitution of, the provisions of section 55 of the Marine Insurance Act 1906, has not been invoked since the days of the Spanish Civil War. It is the general intention that the continuation of the shipowner's insurance shall not be prejudiced but that there would be no claim for loss or damage arising out of any "imprudent conduct". "Imprudent conduct", from the wording of the Rule, clearly embraces "recklessness". Further provisions have the effect that it needs to be the "imprudent conduct" of the insured owner or the managers of the ship and not that of the crew in spite of the Rule's opening words. In addition, the Mutual War Risks Associations have the power to waive the Rule by prior agreement with the Association's managers in special circumstances,

11. (1897) L.J.Q.B. 802.

such as a ship going into a dangerous area to rescue refugees where her charitable mission might not be respected. The directors have power to allow payment of a claim, either in whole or in part, if in all the circumstances they consider it is the proper thing to do. There may be mitigating circumstances where it is inappropriate to apply the full rigour of such a Rule.

CHAPTER 30

The proximate cause

30.1 The courts will give effect to the intention of the parties as expressed when they make their contract, and in a written contract, the courts will interpret the parties' intentions from the words which they use. The courts are always concerned to avoid inadvertently changing the parties' intentions, which they express in their contract. Such intentions should be expressed with precision, both in respect of insured and excluded perils, bearing in mind that these are now for the most part defined by previous decisions to which the courts will look for authority and for guidance, and the courts will assume that they are so expressed. It is a fundamental principle of English law that the assured who seeks to establish a claim, or the underwriter who seeks to contest it, must first establish the facts of the casualty, and then show that the facts bring the casualty within the bounds of an insured peril, or in the case of the underwriter, within the bounds of an exclusion. These principles are too well known to need emphasis here, and a reader who desires to look into this aspect of the matter more closely will find the principles admirably explained by the learned authors of Arnould, 16th edition, paragraphs 761–763 and 1133–1142, particularly with regard to marine insurance. It would be more helpful if this work concentrated on the aspects of proof which are most likely to be of concern to the assured or to the underwriter concerned with a war risk casualty. We shall therefore consider four particular aspects:

1. Proximate cause generally.
2. Several things happen more or less at once. What caused the casualty? Is it an insured peril or is it an exclusion?
3. A casualty happens and then develops into something worse. Is it insured in its worse aspect?
4. A casualty happens but its cause cannot be established with any certainty.

30.2 Under these subheadings it would be desirable if this chapter could be confined to consideration of decisions on the war risk policy only, and the author has made every effort to include such leading decisions. The law on the proximate cause does, however, depend heavily on marine cases, and even cases where there is no maritime element at all. Whilst such cases are kept to a minimum in this chapter, there would be a danger of distortion if they were excluded.

PROXIMATE CAUSE GENERALLY

30.3 The Marine Insurance Act 1906 contains in section 55(1) a somewhat neutral provision which shows that Parliament cannot legislate on what is and what is not an insured peril or an excluded risk in any particular instance. This must be left to the judges. Section 55(1) reads:

"Subject to the provisions of this Act, and unless the policy otherwise provides, the insurer is liable for any loss proximately caused by a peril insured against, but subject as aforesaid, he is not liable for any loss which is not proximately caused by a peril insured against."

30.4 In describing the test of the proximate cause of the casualty, judges have used different expressions (and have given some warnings) how the proximate cause or the excluded risk is to be established. A list of some of the recent decisions will be helpful in demonstrating the principles on which they have acted, and also the modern tendency of the judges to insist upon precision in establishing the proximate cause, thus leading them to the insured peril or the excluded risk.

30.5 Rhesa Shipping Company S.A. v. Herbert David Edmunds (The Popi M)[1]

When presented with several possible causes, judges must not feel bound to choose the least unlikely explanation for the casualty. In the words of Lord Brandon: "The Judge needs to be satisfied on the evidence that it is more likely to have occurred than not."

30.6 In other words, if the judge is not satisfied that any of the possible causes is more likely to have occurred than not occurred, he must say so. Such a finding will result in the plaintiff being held to fail in his primary task of proving that the loss or damage occurred through an insured peril.

30.7 C.C.R. Fishing Ltd. and Others v. Tomenson Inc. and Others (The La Pointe)[2]

The *La Pointe* was built as a tug in 1906 and was converted to a trawler in 1979 and 1980. In 1981 she was laid up in Vancouver Harbour. In July, 1982, she sank without warning. There were two possible causes, wear and tear as alleged by the underwriters, or failure of the carbon steel cap screws used to secure the flanges on the sea suction line, which formed the basis of the plaintiff's case. These screws were negligently fitted by the repairers as they were apt to corrode; copper, brass, or stainless steel cap screws should have been used because they do not corrode. Was this a case where the proximate cause was "fortuitous"? asked Mme. Justice McLachlin. The evidence pointed in the direction of the repairer's negligence and judgment was signed for the owners.

30.8 Century Insurance Company of Canada and Others v. Case Existological Laboratories Ltd. and Others (The Bramcell)[3]

The *Bramcell* was a specialist craft used in oceanography. Her trim was adjusted by air in compartments. A valve was negligently left open and she sank. Mr. Justice Ritchie decided that the "proximate cause" of the loss was a peril of the seas.

1. [1985] 2 Lloyd's Rep. 1 (H.L.) (paras. 30.90, 30.91).
2. [1986] 2 Lloyd's Rep. 513—Sup.Ct. of Canada.
3. [1986] 2 Lloyd's Rep. 524—Sup.Ct. of Canada.

30.9 J.J. Lloyd Instruments Ltd. v. Northern Star Insurance Company Ltd. (The Miss Jay Jay)[4]

The *Miss Jay Jay* was a fast motor pleasure craft of a type which has an appeal to a certain type of sailor because of its high performance and speed. Its construction has to be light, and invariably it is driven at full-tilt regardless of weather or sea conditions. On this occasion, part of its outer hull was found to be missing after a boisterous channel crossing. Mustill J., having to consider whether it was unseaworthiness or bad weather which had caused the damage, considered there was a clear chain of causation in initial unseaworthiness, adverse weather, and loss of water-tight integrity all adding up to a loss by a peril of the seas. Judgment was signed in favour of the plaintiff. The Court of Appeal upheld his judgment, Lawton L.J. seeking the "dominant cause" whilst Slade L.J. applied the "commonsense view".

30.10 OPE Shipping Ltd. and El Porvenir Shipping Company Inc. v. Allstate Insurance Company Inc.[5]

In assessing the reasons for the loss of the plaintiffs' ships, which were seized by the Sandinista rebels, the courts sought "the real underlying cause of the loss of the Somoza ships" which they thought was "the civil war in Nicaragua". Also sought were the causes which were "predominant and determining" and "real efficient" as was done in *Standard Oil of New Jersey* v. *United States*.[6] The Court of Appeals went on to say:

"Determination of the proximate cause in these cases is thus a matter of applying commonsense and reasonable judgement as to the source of the loss alleged."

30.11 Commodities Reserve Company v. St. Pauls Fire and Marine Insurance Company[7]

The plaintiff's cargo of chickpeas became infested because the carrying ship was carrying ammunition contrary to Greek law and she was detained by the Greek authorities. Farris C.J. sought the cause "which is most nearly and essentially connected with the loss as its effectual cause". He was following *Standard Oil Company* v. *United States*[8] and *Blaine Richards & Company* v. *Marine Indemnity Insurance Company*.[9] In this case: " . . . the dominant cause for the transhipment costs was the detention . . . "

30.12 Farris C.J. also added a comment which, it is suggested, nowadays represents a better view than that taken by Hilbery J. in the *Forestal* case (para. 13.31):

" . . . where the loss results from a combination of causes, one of which is excluded from the coverage, Courts generally isolate a single peril as the dominant or efficient one."

4. [1985] 1 Lloyd's Rep. 264, [1987] 1 Lloyd's Rep. 32—Q.B. (Com.Ct.) and the C.A.
5. [1983] A.M.C. 22 and 30—Dist.Ct., Southern District of New York, U.S. Court of Appeals 2nd Circuit (paras. 7.17–7.23).
6. [1951] A.M.C. 1, 4–5.
7. [1989] A.M.C. 2409—Dist.Ct., North District of California, U.S. Court of Appeals 9th Circuit.
8. [1951] A.M.C. 1–4.
9. [1981] A.M.C. 1–7.

30.13 It will be noted that some judges have felt that the words "proximate cause" are descriptive of themselves and no further explanation is needed, whilst others have considered it necessary to go further than this. "Commonsense and intelligence of the ordinary man", "commonsense and reasonable judgement", "in substance the cause", "to be determined by commonsense principles", "the dominant cause", "a clear chain of causation", "the real underlying cause", "predominant and determining", "real efficient", "which is most nearly and essentially connected with the loss as its effectual cause", appear in the reports, and, it is suggested, all point to the modern tendency prevailing in the courts. The judges will require firm evidence which points in a clear direction to establish what actually caused the loss, and where the cause can only be surmised, the evidence must still be firm enough to satisfy the court "that it is more likely to have occurred than not". Only then will they move on to considering whether the proximate cause points to an insured peril or to an exclusion from the insurance. Such insistence on precision on what caused the casualty, which is most clearly demonstrated by Farris C.J. in the *Commodities Reserve* case (para. 30.11), will do much to alter the somewhat unsatisfactory position described by Hilbery J. in the *Forestal* cases (para. 13.31); nowadays the casualty is either an insured peril or an exclusion from the insurance. Only in the rarest cases will it have both characteristics. It can also be said that Lord Esher M.R.'s test in the *Pink* case (paras. 14.11, 14.12) can no longer be regarded as a proper statement of the law.

30.14 Many people find it difficult to accept that a War Risks case presents more than usual problems in determining what was the proximate cause. There will of course be no difficulty where a missile strikes the ship or a shell hits her. The surrounding circumstances and the damage speak for themselves. But it is not always so easy where there is a fire in the cargo. Was this caused by spontaneous combustion, or was it caused by sabotage? The difficulties are exacerbated when the ship is sunk in deep water and cannot readily be examined. Especial difficulties will be found with oil cargoes, where the risk of explosion in the tanks is always a high one. Was the proximate cause inherent in the cargo or the gases which it gives off, or was there some incendiary device in the tanks? Mines are, curiously enough, difficult to blame with absolute certainty for some casualties as will be seen in other parts of this work. They are rarely seen, and the modern type of mine lies on the bottom of the sea where it is well out of sight. Although the new type of War Risks insurance tries to name the event itself as the insured peril, and concentrates less than before on the motives of people, these will inevitably arise where there are cases of detention. Lastly, evidence depends on that most imponderable of elements in all litigation, the witness, and in a superlative degree the expert witness, and the effect they create on the court. The tests to be applied to establish the proximate cause are clear enough, but the results in court can never be regarded as a foregone conclusion.

SEVERAL THINGS HAPPEN MORE OR LESS AT ONCE

This is well illustrated with cases:

30.15 Green v. Elmslie[10]

The *Fly* was bound from Exeter to London. She was insured only against "capture". She was driven by a high wind over to the French coast where a French privateer captured her. The underwriters contended her loss was due to perils of the seas which was not insured. Lord Kenyon C.J. found the case too clear to admit of argument. On any other coastline she would have been perfectly safe. She had suffered "capture" and the underwriters had to pay.

30.16 Livie v. Jansen[11]

The *Liberty* was bound from New York to London. A letter, saying that she would sail in spite of the American embargo, was seen by the underwriters when the insurance was placed and this led to the insurance being given but "warranted free from American condemnation". In December 1808, laden with valuable cargo, she was waiting in New York for a suitable opportunity to elude the embargo. This opportunity was thought to occur on the night of 15th January, 1809, and, with a pilot on board, she took a proper course for the open sea. Ice drove her ashore on Governors Island where she was badly damaged. Next day, the U.S. Customs seized her and managed to refloat her. Lord Ellenborough C.J.: "It all depends on what was the proximate cause. If partially damaged before, and later totally lost, prior damage does not give rise to a claim against the underwriters. The total loss was the event which gives rise to a claim but it was an excepted peril." The proximate cause was held to be the American seizure and judgment was signed for the underwriters.

30.17 Hahn v. Corbett[12]

In July 1822 Manchester cotton goods were loaded on to the *Mary* for carriage from London to Maracaibo. They were insured against perils of the seas, but the insurance was "warranted free of capture and seizure". The cotton was consigned to those who had espoused the revolutionary cause during the South American Wars of Independence. On 17th September, 1822, the ship arrived off the Gulf of Maracaibo and the next day, being unable to get a pilot, she anchored near the bar. She drifted into shoal water, ran aground and was lost. The Master asked Fort San Carlos for help only to find that, unbeknown to him, the Royal Forces of the King of Spain had recently recaptured it from the rebels. He and the crew were put in jail and the Spanish authorities treated the ship and cargo as prize. All the cargo, both the damaged and undamaged cargo, was removed and seized by the Spanish authorities.

Burrough J. gave judgment for the plaintiff, subject to a case being stated; under the procedure of the time, this meant review by a higher court. Best C.J. distinguished this case from the *Livie*[13] case. There the ship and the goods were only damaged by perils of the seas. In the *Green*[14] case, the ship was driven,

10. (1784) 1 Peake 278.
11. (1810) 12 East 648.
12. (1824) 2 Bing. 205.
13. (1810) 12 East 648.
14. (1784) 1 Peake 278.

undamaged, over to the French coast and there captured. In the *Hahn*[15] case, however, the ship was destroyed by the grounding, nine miles off the coast, and the goods were as good as lost before the Spaniards took them, not to save them but to appropriate them. Judgment was rightly given for the owners of the goods.

30.18 Boudrett v. Hentigg[16]

The ship carrying the insured goods was wrecked on the Île de France. Some of the goods were saved but, before they could be taken away, they were stolen by the local inhabitants. They were held to be a total loss by perils of the seas and judgment was signed in favour of the plaintiff.

30.19 The Ionides case[17]

The facts of this case are set out at paras. 14.5–14.10. From there it will be seen that error in navigation was held to be the proximate cause of the loss of the majority of the coffee, and not the extinguishing of the lighthouse's light.

30.20 The Cory case[18]

The facts of this case are set out at paras. 12.12, 12.13, 12.16–12.19. It will be seen that the barratrous agreement made by the Master led to the ship being seized by the Spanish revenue authorities. The seizure was held to be the cause of the loss, not the misdeeds of the Master.

30.21 The facts in *Leyland Shipping Company Limited* v. *Norwich Union Fire Insurance Society Ltd.*[19] were easily established, so that altogether nine judges in the High Court, the Court of Appeal and the House of Lords could agree that the torpedo and not the subsequent foundering was the proximate cause of her total loss. Those that expressed an opinion on proximate cause did so in different terms which are interesting to note.

30.22 In January, 1915, the *Ikaria* was on the last stages of a voyage from South America to Le Havre. She was insured for marine risks on the normal S.G. Form with the F.C. & S. Clause attached which warranted that the policy was free from: "The consequences of hostilities or warlike operations."

1915

30th January

The ship, 25 miles north-west of Le Havre, stops to pick up a pilot. A U-boat torpedoes her in way of number 1 hold on the port side. A large hold is torn in her plates 4 ft. below the water line and the hold fills with water. The explosion is very violent and clearly weakens the ship's structure in the neighbourhood. She settles by the head. She is brought into Le Havre and berthed at the Quai d'Escale.

It seems to be common ground that if she can remain at the quay, she can be saved. The Quai d'Escale is most important, because soldiers bound for the western front disembark there from the United King-

15. (1824) 2 Bing. 205.
16. (1816) Holt's Rep. 149.
17. *Ionides* v. *The Universal Marine Insurance Co.* (1863) 14 C.B. (N.S.) 259.
18. *Cory & Son* v. *Burr* (1881) 8 Q.B.D. 313; (1882) 9 Q.B.D. 463; (1883) 8 App. Cas. 393.
19. [1918] A.C. 350.

dom and it is extensively used by the Red Cross. Apparently her forward draught is too deep to permit her to enter the inner harbour.

31st January

A gale gets up and the ship ranges heavily in the swell against the quayside. Fearing that she will sink at the quay with serious results for other traffic, the authorities order her to leave. She does so and anchors in the outer harbour, the Batadeau where there is also considerable swell.

Her position is very serious. In place of the 23 ft. draught on a nearly even keel before the torpedoing, she is now drawing 32 ft. forward and 15 ft. aft. The bow goes aground at low tide, and at other times pounds heavily against the bottom. Nothing can be done to prevent this.

2nd February

The bulkhead between numbers 1 and 2 holds, already weakened by the explosion, can take no more and crumples. The ship breaks her back, sinks and is a total loss.

30.23 On these facts, the shipowners sued for a total loss caused by perils of the seas, pleading that there was a *novus actus interveniens*. The underwriters defended the suit, pleading that the loss was caused by hostilities and that there was an unbroken chain between the torpedoing and the total loss. This being a marine and not a war risk policy, these were the respective positions they could be expected to take. In the High Court, Rowlatt J. signed judgment in favour of the underwriters and the shipowners appealed.

30.24 On the subject of proximate cause Rowlatt J. held: " . . . All the efforts she made, before she became a total loss, were merely efforts to escape from the casualty in the grip of which she was throughout." In the Court of Appeal, Swinfen-Eady L.J. thought: "She was in imminent risk of sinking from the moment of being injured . . . The train of causation from the act of hostility to the loss was unbroken."

30.25 Bankes L.J. agreed, but Scrutton L.J. had his doubts:

"I agree with these findings [of the casualty], but I think it also follows, whatever the legal effect might be, that the sinking did not necessarily follow from the explosion; that is to say, that with fine weather, and a stay in the first berth, the ship would have been saved; with the weather she in fact met, and in the berth to which in consequence of that weather she was ordered, she was lost."

Scrutton L.J. was much influenced by *Reischer* v. *Borwick*[20] and appeared to be on the brink of holding that there was a *novus actus interveniens*. In the event, he joined the other two Lords Justices in a unanimous dismissal of the shipowner's appeal.

30.26 The shipowner appealed further to the House of Lords. Lord Finlay L.C. did not share these doubts and agreed with the majority of the Court of Appeal. The ship undoubtedly sustained further damage by the grounding, but of her injuries: "Indeed they appear to me to establish that the loss was a direct consequence of hostilities."

30.27 Viscount Haldane was satisfied that if the ship had remained at sea, she would have sunk. He clearly felt that Scrutton L.J. was not justified in his doubts, and that *Reischer* v. *Borwick*[21] pointed the other way. The ship had struck "a snag" and was holed. She anchored and the hole was plugged. Whilst under tow, the plug gave way, the ship ran aground and was abandoned. The Court of Appeal held that the proximate cause was the hitting of "the snag", Davey L.J. saying: "My Lords,

20. [1894] 2 Q.B. 548.
21. *Ibid.*

these words express what the commonsense of mankind would assert in such a case" whilst on the *Leyland* case, Viscount Haldane held: "The fact that attempts were made to obviate the natural consequences of the injury inflicted by the torpedo does not introduce any break in the direct relation between the cause and its effect which culminated in the damage sustained."

30.28 Lord Dunedin gave firm guidance:

"Yet I think the case turns on a pure question of fact to be determined on commonsense principles. What was the cause of the loss of the ship? I do not think that the ordinary man would have any difficulty in answering she was lost because she was torpedoed"

and:

"The solution will always lie in settling as a question of fact which of the two causes was what I would venture to call (though I shrink from the multiplication of epithets) the dominant cause of the two. In other words, you seek for the *causa proxima*, if it is well understood that the question of what is *proxima* is not solved by the mere point of order in time."

30.29 Lord Atkinson agreed with the other judgments but did not add anything himself to proximate cause. Lord Shaw of Dunfermline reinforced Lord Dunedin:

"The cause which is truly proximate is that which is proximate in efficiency. That efficiency may have been preserved although other causes may meantime have sprung up which have yet not destroyed it, or truly impaired it and may culminate in a result of which it still remains the real efficient cause to which the event can be ascribed.
    Where various factors or causes are concurrent, and one has to be selected, the matter is determined as one of fact, and the choice falls upon the one to which may be variously ascribed the qualities of reality, predominance, efficiency."

30.30 *P. Samuel & Company Limited* v. *Dumas*[22] is often quoted in relation to the problems of proximate cause. Samuels were insurance brokers who effected a marine insurance policy on behalf of P. Samuel & Co., the mortgagee who advanced money on the purchase of the ship. The ship herself was found by Bailhache J. to have been scuttled with the shipowner's connivance. He held that an innocent mortgagee was entitled to recover a loss caused by perils of the seas. Apparently the ship had been sunk by letting in seawater through the bilge lines and when the seamen not involved in the plot had left her, by an explosion as well. The incursion of seawater had caused her to sink, a process that required 13 hours. This judgment was reversed by the Court of Appeal and later by the House of Lords. No purpose would be served by going into the extremely complicated facts of the case or the equally complex reasons of the two higher courts for reversing the High Court's judgment, and this work will simply concentrate on what their Lordships had to say on proximate cause. Eve J. sitting in the Court of Appeal:

"It has been strenuously contended that *Small's* case[23] . . . ought not to be treated as finally deciding . . . that a loss due to the incursion of seawater is a peril insured against in a case where a proximate or dominant cause is really the felonious act of the owner and not the incursion of the seawater. Put in this way the argument would seem to be the question, which I take to be, which is the proximate or dominant cause—the felonious act of the owner or the incursion of the seawater?"

22. [1923] 1 K.B. 592 (C.A.); [1924] A.C. 431 (H.L.).
23. *Small* v. *United Kingdom Marine Mutual Insurance Association* [1897] 2 Q.B.D. 42 and 311.

30.31 Bankes L.J. did not express an opinion but Scrutton L.J. still had some doubts:

"Recent decisions of the House of Lords and the Privy Council have elucidated the effect of the maximum *causa proxima non remota spectatur*, which used to be considered as directed to the proximate cause in time, but is now taken as referring to the 'dominant' or 'effective' cause, even though it may not be the nearest in time."

He had to accept the position but clearly thought it was not correct. He added by way of explanation: "Damage by negligence of the crew of the ship insured, though a dominant cause, may still be an accident incidental to navigating a ship at sea . . ." For various reasons, which it is not necessary for this work to go into, he joined the other two Lords Justices in setting aside the judgment of Bailhache, J., and finding in favour of the underwriters.

30.32 A further appeal to the House of Lords again ended in the underwriters' favour, but on the point of proximate cause, Viscount Cave considered:

"There appears to me to be something absurd in saying that, when a ship is scuttled by her crew, the loss is not caused by the act of scuttling, but by the incursion of water which results from it. No doubt both are part of the chain of events which result in the loss of the ship, but the scuttling is the real and operative cause—the nearest antecedent which can be called 'a cause'."

30.33 Lord Parmoor agreed with Viscount Cave, particularly that the scuttling was the proximate cause. Viscount Finlay added, apparently referring to the reluctant conversion of Scrutton L.J.: "As pointed out by Scrutton L.J., in his judgment, the question as to proximate cause is really as to what is the dominant or effective cause;" (On a note of caution, the reader must bear in mind that this is a chapter on proximate cause. Since the *Samuel* case, there have been a number of decisions, many of them recent, on scuttling and the onus of proof that is required in such cases. This chapter is not concerned with them, and the reader who has to contend with a scuttling case must not rely upon the *Samuel* case alone.)

30.34 Finally, two very weighty authorities have made their presence felt to the same effect. The judgment of the Privy Council was given by Lord Wright in *Canada Rice Mills Limited* v. *Union Marine and General Insurance Company Limited*.[24] A cargo of rice was loaded on to the *Segundo* in Rangoon for carriage to Fraser River in British Columbia. It was insured on a normal cargo policy. When it arrived it was found to be damaged by heating caused by moisture migration. Was this heating caused by the inherent vice of the rice, namely the moisture content of the rice itself, or was it caused by the condensation resulting from the closing of ventilation during the voyage? In the former case, it would not have been insured by the policy, in the latter case it would have been so insured. The holds were ventilated through the Samson posts and cowl ventilators on deck and when the weather permitted, the hatches were also opened. Only for a brief period of altogether 50 hours was the ventilation closed entirely because of bad weather.

30.35 In the court of first instance in British Columbia, the special jury found that the closing of ventilation was the cause of the damage, and that the weather and the sea at the time were bad enough to constitute a peril of the seas. Robertson J. signed judgment for the plaintiff. This was reversed on appeal because the jury

---

24. [1941] A.C. 55.

were not specifically asked to, and therefore did not, find as a fact that perils of the seas were the proximate cause. On a further appeal to the Privy Council, the original judgment was considered to be right and that the judgment of the Appeal Court should be set aside. It could be inferred from the evidence, a process permitted by the rules of court, that perils of the seas were the proximate cause of the damage. On the point on which we are most interested, Lord Wright had this to say: "But it is now established by [many authorities] . . . that *causa proxima* in insurance law does not necessarily mean the cause last in time, but what is 'in substance' the cause, *per* Lord Finlay, or the cause 'to be determined by common-sense principles' *per* Lord Dunedin."

30.36 *Athel Line Limited* v. *Liverpool & London War Risks Insurance Association Limited*[25] is not a case which, strictly speaking, should appear in this part of the chapter. There was only one possible cause to the accident but Lord Greene M.R. gave such firm directions on the establishment of what was the proximate cause that it should be noted here. In 1940 the *Atheltemplar*, a tanker, carried fuel for the Royal Navy from Trinidad to Lochalsh. She was insured by the Mutual War Risks Association against "the consequences of hostilities or warlike operations by or against the King's enemies". Lochalsh was a temporary wartime naval base with all the hazards of such establishments. On arrival, the ship anchored in the place designated by the naval authorities. As always around the British coast, there was a considerable movement of water besides the normal flow and ebb of the tides. A proper anchor watch was kept and there was no question of the ship dragging her anchors or drifting. She grounded on a rock in way of number 8 tank and slightly to starboard of the centre line of the ship and remained aground during the whole of the ebb tide. It appears that nobody knew that the rock was there, and in the hurried circumstances of wartime, it may be assumed that the harbour was not properly surveyed. The ship refloated on the next flood tide and subsequently discharged her cargo successfully at Lochalsh and Scapa Flow. The arbitrator found that the damage to her bottom was the consequence of a warlike operation, and Atkinson J. upheld his award in the High Court. The judgment and the award were further upheld by the Court of Appeal where Lord Greene M.R. gave the main judgment:

"The other question is that of consequence. The legal theory of causation has, in the course of years, had a remarkable history, but the point at which it appears to have come to rest at the moment, is that which lays it down that this type of question of causation is really a matter for the commonsense and intelligence of the ordinary man."

A CASUALTY HAPPENS AND THEN DEVELOPS INTO SOMETHING WORSE—"BAD BECOMES WORSE"

30.37 The third aspect is where a casualty happens and then develops over a period of time into something worse. Is it insured in its worse aspect? This can be an acute problem if the insurance comes to an end, either by expiry of time or otherwise, before the worse aspect makes itself apparent. As is often the case (and this is demonstrated in earlier chapters, particularly on "seizure"), the modern common

25. [1946] 1 K.B. 117.

law is based upon older decisions which are still quoted, although their relevance is now somewhat obscure. When bearing in mind how the common law has developed, there is no reason for surprise at this. As the older decisions are still quoted as authority by counsel, some mention should be made of them here. *Mullett* v. *Shedden*[26] concerned a cargo of 300 tons of saltpetre shipped from Calcutta to the United States. Its owner, Mr. Boyd, had been given a licence by the East India Company to despatch this cargo. It was insured for £500 but was warranted "F.P.A. under £10%". The carrying ship was the *Martha*.

1807

November

The ship loads in Calcutta and sails.

1808

10th January

H.M.S. *Sceptre* intercepts the ship and orders her into Capetown so that the Vice-Admiralty Court can consider the saltpetre. Proceedings are commenced to condemn it.

19th March

The Captain writes to the cargo owner from Capetown advising him of the proceedings.

25th April

The saltpetre is condemned, unloaded and sold for the benefit of the captors. The ship, with the remaining cargo on board, is free to sail.

11th May

The Captain writes from Capetown to the cargo owner to report the condemnation.

28th June

The plaintiff receives the Captain's letter dated 19th March.

19th August

The plaintiff receives the Captain's letter dated 11th May, and immediately gives Notice of Abandonment.

1810

1st March

The sentence of condemnation is reversed on appeal and a decree is made ordering restoration of the property or payment of its value, less the expenses of capture.

30.38 This is a case, rather akin to the *Rodocanachi*[27] and *Doelwyck*[28] cases where the position has improved with the passage of time rather than worsened. Lord Ellenborough C.J. held that the cargo was "destroyed" by the sale, and Notice of Abandonment was not required; there was an actual total loss. If the goods had been detained and subsequently restored after the seizure had

26. (1811) 13 East 304.
27. *Rodocanachi* v. *Elliott* (1873) L.R. 8 C.P. 649. See para. 11.21.
28. *Ruys* v. *Royal Exchange Assurance Corporation* [1897] 2 Q.B. 135. See paras. 11.25, 11.26.

been found to be unjustified, a Notice of Abandonment would have been required before there was any question of a total loss. Bayley J. approached the matter differently. The original condemnation was proper until overruled, and there was a total loss by the sale. The successful appeal had not changed things. The plaintiff was awarded judgment.

30.39 The relevance of *Mellish* v. *Andrews*[29] with the matter which is currently being considered, namely "The bad to worse situation", may be questioned, although it is frequently quoted in this context. In August, 1810, the *Minerva* sailed from London to Gothenburg. She was insured under terms which warranted that the insurance was "free from capture in her port of discharge". In October, 1810, she sailed in convoy from Gothenburg and arrived off Karlshamn in November, 1810. An attempt to call at Schwenemunde resulted in her being ordered out of the port. She returned to Karlshamn where she undertook bad weather repairs. On 7th December, 1810, the civil authorities took away her papers. On hearing of this, the owner gave Notice of Abandonment to the underwriters on 8th January, 1811. This seems to have been a leisurely process, since the notice did not reach the underwriters until 17th January. On 30th April, 1811, the military authorities seized the cargo. The action started during the Trinity Term 1811. Lord Ellenborough L.C. held that the Notice of Abandonment was not given in reasonable time, and the judgment was given for the defendant. This case has an interesting subsequent history. Ellenborough L.C., after review with his brother judges, concluded that the Notice of Abandonment was not necessary after all, and this reversed his first decision into the plaintiff's favour. The underwriters then pleaded that a deviation had arisen, but the court ruled against them on this point. On appeal to the Court of Exchequer Chamber, that court upheld this decision.

30.40 Cases which give a far firmer indication of "bad to worse" are *Stringer and Others* v. *The English & Scottish Marine Insurance Company Limited*[30]; *Levy & Co.* v. *The Merchants Marine Insurance Company*[31]; *Crossman* v. *West; Crossman* v. *British American Insurance Company*[32]; and *Fooks* v. *Smith*.[33] It can be said that the modern law depends upon these cases.

30.41 Although it was a marine case with no war risk character to it, *Thornely* v. *Hebson*[34] should first be described, as it is frequently mentioned in the decided cases. The *William* was insured under a marine policy for £1,200 for a voyage from Hull to New York. Mr. Thornely, the plaintiff, was the agent for Mr. Townsend and Mr. White, merchants of the City of New York, who owned the ship.

30.42 From the start, the *William's* voyage was adventurous even by the standards of the time. Shortly after sailing from Hull, she grounded on a sandbank and had to put into Dover for repairs. There is no indication in the report how serious the damage was.

29. (1812) 15 East 13.
30. (1870) 22 L.T. 802.
31. (1885) 5 Asp. M.L.C. 407.
32. (1887) 13 App. Cas. 160.
33. [1924] 2 K.B. 508.
34. (1819) 2 B. & Ald. 513.

1816

19th December

The ship sails from Dover. There is a succession of westerly gales.

1817

14th February

There is a very severe gale from the south-west. The main mast is badly sprung.

15th February

The foreyard and foresail are carried away. The foretopsail is torn to pieces and the bowsprit is badly sprung. Constant pumping on the one pump available takes place round the clock.

16th February

By this time the crew is totally exhausted. A consultation between the Master, the officers and the crew reaches the conclusion that they must save their lives. A distress call is made to two ships, the *Hyder Ali* and the *Navigator*, both of which bear down on the ship. They stand by all night but the *Navigator* gets separated by the storm.

17th February

The crew go on board the *Hyder Ali*. Eight fresh men from the *Hyder Ali* go on board the ship. The two ships are later separated.

4th March

The *Hyder Ali* arrives in New York, and Mr. Townsend and Mr. White are informed what has happened. The ship's fate at this stage is unknown.

8th March

The shipowners take the first opportunity to write to Mr. Thornely who is directed to give Notice of Abandonment.

10th March

The ship arrives in Newport, Rhode Island.

17th April

Mr. Thornely receives the 8th March letter.

18th April

Mr. Thornely gives Notice of Abandonment to the underwriters who refuse to accept it. The underwriters know that the ship has reached Newport which is only 200 miles from New York.

   The ship is refitted and repaired by the salvors who are awarded salvage which is assessed at one-half of the ship's value. They obtain a court order for sale which fetches £315. After payment of the salvors' award, £112 10s. remains in court.

19th November

The action is started against the underwriters.

30.43 The owners claimed for a total loss. The underwriters were only willing to concede a partial loss. Before Lord Ellenborough L.C., a verdict was given for the plaintiff subject to the opinion of the court. The court, however, overturned the verdict. Abbot C.J. held that there was no total loss at any time. The assured had allowed the ship to be sold by the Admiralty Court's decree when they might have prevented this from happening. He distinguished the *Goss* case.[35] There the salvage was such that the assured had no reasonable means of paying it. Here, however: "If in this case, it had appeared that the owners had used all the means in their power, and were still unable to have paid this salvage, it would have been different."

---

35. *Goss* v. *Withers* (1758) 2 Burr. 683. See paras. 11.8–11.11.

30.44 Bayley J. agreed. There was no total loss on the crew leaving the ship. To be a total loss on sale it: "must have been found to have been necessary, and wholly without the fault of the owners" and: "It is a very beneficial rule, and consistent with the meaning of the policy, for the court to say that the assured cannot abandon so as to make it a total loss, unless they have exerted the utmost of their power to prevent the necessity for it."

30.45 These two judgments set stringent, perhaps extreme, standards that the shipowners should use "all the means in their power" and exert "the utmost of their power". Later cases have now softened this requirement so that the shipowner must act as a reasonable, prudent and uninsured owner. Perhaps, however, this less extreme standard of behaviour would have made no difference. The shipowners were after all in the immediate neighbourhood—not the other side of the world with insuperable communication difficulties—and, considering all that the salvors did, the salvage award seems to have been very moderate. Payment of the salvage award would have released the ship from the salvors' lien. Purchase of the ship could have been achieved at a fraction of her value. Holroyd J., with whom Best J. seems to have concurred, put the matter less severely:

"I am of the same opinion. The desertion of the ship by the crew does not of itself constitute a total loss; and the subsequent taking possession by the salvors was not adverse, but an act done for the benefit of the owners, and therefore did not dispossess them. The custody of the vessel was in the salvors until the salvage was paid; but the legal possession was still with the owners. I think, also, that the sale will not amount to a total loss, so as to entitle the insured to recover, if it was in their power to prevent it; and it lies upon them to show that they could not do so."

30.46 Judgment was given for the underwriters. The report does not deal with the possibility that the repairs for hitting the sandbank, the sprung mainmast, the lost yard, the torn sails, and sprung bowsprit and the salvage award, when added together, brought the ship within the range of a constructive total loss. No doubt there were good reasons for the plaintiffs not pleading their case in this way, but it is still tempting to wonder what the result would have been.

30.47 The Exchequer Chamber heard *Stringer*'s case[36] on a writ of error from the Court of Queen's Bench, in modern parlance an appeal. Goods were shipped on board *Dashing Wave* from Liverpool to Matamoras in Mexico. They were insured on the S.G. Form without an F.C. & S. Clause so that the insurance included: "Takings at sea, arrest, restraints, and detainments of all Kings, Princes and people." There was also a sue and labour clause.

30.48 It was the time of the American Civil War and a large part of the *Dashing Wave*'s troubles appear to have been due to the proximity of Matamoras to American ports which were being blockaded by the Unionists, although Matamoras itself, as a neutral port, was not blockaded. To approach the port, however, deep laden ships had to anchor in the mouth of the river where they were exposed to the attentions of Unionist warships.

---

36. *Stringer and Others* v. *The English & Scottish Marine Insurance Co. Ltd.* (1870) 22 L.T. 802.

1863

July

The ship sails from Liverpool.

2nd November

The ship is about three miles from Mexican territory. The weather is bad and there is no communication with the shore.

5th November

The ship is boarded and searched by Unionist officers from the warships. They have every right to do this (para. 11.54). Suspecting contraband, they send the ship into New Orleans.

23rd November

The ship arrives in New Orleans. Prize Court proceedings are started.

29th November

The plaintiff's agent, Mr. Walsh, notifies the brokers, Stavert Zigomala & Co. There is later some doubt if Notice of Abandonment is given at this time, and at the hearing in the Exchequer Chamber, it is assumed that none is in fact given.

1864

24th March

The hearing starts in New Orleans.

22nd June

Judgment is given against the captors and, by decree, restitution is ordered. The captors immediately appeal to the Supreme Court of the United States. Detention of the goods is to continue, pending the outcome of the appeal.

12th September

The plaintiffs write to the defendants giving a history of the claim to date. There is some indication of previous correspondence. This letter is treated as Notice of Abandonment which is refused.

7th December

The plaintiffs ask if the underwriters would join in a bid to prevent sale of the cargo. They refuse.

1865

9th February

Urged on by their New Orleans representative, the plaintiffs make another unsuccessful attempt to get the underwriters to co-operate.

24th April

The Prize Commissioner, Mr. Thorpe, asks permission of the court to sell the cargo which is in a "ruinous condition". The Prize Court gives him a decree authorising sale.

26th May

The ship and the goods are now sold.

30.49 The Court of Queen's Bench held that the sale, and therefore the total loss, were occasioned by the seizure. It is true that the plaintiff could have secured the release of his goods by giving a bond. In the circumstances, it would not be reasonable to expect the plaintiff, as a prudent uninsured, to give a bond in the paper currency of the United States, which, at the time, was very weak and subject to wild fluctuations. During the Civil War, the United States' dollar did not have the pre-eminence it has since attained. Judgment was given for the plaintiff.

30.50 At the Exchequer Court hearing, Kelly C.B. considered the Notice of Abandonment and the possible provision of security. He held that the Notice of

347

Abandonment was given within a reasonable time. The goods' owner was only required to act prudently in giving security, and not to expose himself to further risk. He was therefore not in default in not giving security. Was the plaintiff justified in treating the whole case together as a case of total loss? In the circumstances, the decree of sale, and the sale of the goods, arose out of capture "Arising through a series of circumstances . . . " and:

"The loss of goods arises, though not directly, out of the original capture (which was of itself, if so treated, a total loss) through a series of consequences, *viz.*, the institution, the different steps, and the continuance of the suit until the decree was pronounced. The sale was the completion, if I may use the expression, of a total loss itself originating and commencing with the capture of the ship and goods in the month of November 1863 which entitled the plaintiff to treat the case altogether as a case of total loss, with or without abandonment of the goods."

The rest of the court agreed, and the judgment of the Court of Queen's Bench was affirmed. Some of Blackburn J. and Martin B.'s *dicta* particularly figured in later cases and it would be convenient to set them out here.

30.51 Blackburn J. considered that the goods' owners had not given Notice of Abandonment in time, but the sale put the matter on a very different footing. This deprived the owner of his property. On provision of security, the plaintiff was only bound to act reasonably, and was not required to go to unreasonable lengths to prevent a sale. Moreover:

"If the steps necessary to prevent the sale were such as a prudent uninsured owner would not have adopted, we think that they were not in default, and the sale was then a total loss occasioned by the seizure"

and:

"We come, therefore, to the conclusion of fact that the assured could not, by any means which they would reasonably be called upon to adopt, have prevented the sale by the American Prize Court, which at once put an end to all possibility of having the goods restored in specie, and consequently entitled the assured to come upon their insurer for a total loss."

30.52 Martin B. distinguished the *Thornely* case[37]:

"Holroyd J. pointed out, as indeed did all the judges, that to hold that to be total loss would be holding that which was really a partial loss to be a total loss, because the assured had not taken a step to prevent the sale which he ought to have taken."

In other words, Thornely had such an opportunity, whereas Stringer did not, or not one which he could reasonably have been expected to take. The obligations of the assured to act reasonably were described in the *Forestal* cases (para. 13.33), and have also been the subject of the very recent *Vasso* case (paras. 24.22, 24.23).

30.53 In *Levy & Co.* v. *The Merchants Marine Insurance Co.*,[38] Levy's were the mortgagees of the *Ardenlea* which was chartered to sail from Greenock to Cardiff and thence to Gibraltar loaded with coals. Thereafter she was to be sold as a coalhulk. Levy's instructed their broker to arrange insurance cover for the ship for £1,000 for "absolute total loss only". It seems that there was some hitch about the actual placing, and the otherwise dull correspondence was enlivened by the owners,

---

37. *Thornely* v. *Hebson* (1819) 2 B. & Ald. 513. See paras. 30.41–30.46.
38. (1885) 5 Asp. M.L.C. 407.

who said that they only sent their ship to sea on being assured by Levy's (albeit in good faith) that she was insured, telling Levy's in no uncertain terms "you are now our underwriters". It would appear, however, that this little contretemps was, in some way, satisfactorily resolved.

1881

19th November

The ship sails from Greenock. She runs into a gale and collides with a steamer, shortly afterwards going ashore. The defendants arrange a survey and it is clear that immediately after the stranding, she is a constructive total loss. Notice of Abandonment is given.

November to

1882

January

The vessel lies stranded and the damage worsens during the winter gales.

17th January

The ship is sold. During the subsequent months the purchaser strips all the gear off her. The hull is of no value and is left where it is.

30.54 Mathew J. heard the case in the High Court. He first of all had to consider the scope of the insurance. He seems to have been unimpressed with the expert witnesses who attempted to explain what was meant by an absolute total loss, and he ended by rejecting their evidence and holding that the words meant: "The total annihilation of the subject of the insurance" and:

"It seems to me that in the policy in question the phrase 'absolute total loss' is meant to be contrasted with 'constructive total loss' and that the underwriters intended to be exempt from losses which were not actually, but only technically, total . . . Accordingly it seems to me that the underwriters meant to restrict their liability to a destruction of the ship so complete as would entitle the owners to recover whether a Notice of Abandonment had been given or not."

30.55 In November, 1881, she was a constructive total loss and if the policy had been in the normal form, Notice of Abandonment would have been required. She was still exposed to the insured perils on 17th January, 1882, when she was sold. By that time: "She was in the condition to entitle the owner to claim for a total loss without abandonment."

30.56 The underwriters had pleaded that when she was a constructive total loss, their liability ended, and therefore the policy came to an end before the subsequent "absolute" loss was complete. Mathew J. rejected this: "I think that the vessel became a wreck from perils which were continuous, or, at any rate recurrent in their operation from the time she stranded, and the effects of which could not be averted by any means which the plaintiffs could reasonably have adopted." He therefore held that the loss ultimately became an absolute total loss within the policy's meaning and signed judgment for the plaintiff.

30.57 *Crossman* v. *West, Crossman* v. *British American Insurance Co.*[39] was a decision of the Privy Council on consolidated appeals from the Supreme Court of Nova Scotia. The *L.E. CAN* was insured with Mr. West, who was no doubt a

39. (1887) 13 App. Cas. 160.

representative underwriter for hull risks from noon on 28th November, 1881, to noon 28th November, 1882, and with British American for freight, the freight policy covering the voyage from Mexico to New York. The ship was chartered by the Master, Captain Brooks, to Antonio Granes to carry associated produce from Vera Cruz and Tucolota to New York at a lumpsum freight of $6,000. It would seem that Brooks was in league with Granes and the agent, Campos, to destroy the vessel and divide between them the insurance proceeds. There is a reference in the report that the cargo was "a sham", although some cargo, altogether 40% of that mentioned in the bill of lading, was in fact loaded.

1882

January and February

The ship is at Vera Cruz and Tucolota.

30th March

The ship sails for New York.

27th April

Captain Brooks signals the *George W. Lockner* that the ship is sinking, and goes on board her with his entire crew. The ship is abandoned.

4th May

The crew arrives in Philadelphia.

24th May

The ship is found by the *Resolute* and the *North America*. She has not sunk even though holes have been bored in the hull below the water line with an auger. She is salvaged and taken to Lynnhaven Bay, Norfolk.

August

The salvors are awarded $5,000 for salvage, although it seems that there was no division between ship and cargo. She is hauled out of the water at Graves Shipyard and found to be basically sound. Even though she is repaired and subsequently put back into service, she fetches on sale only $3,183.

30.58 At the hearing in first instance, the Chief Justice found that there was an actual total loss of the ship and freight and therefore that no Notice of Abandonment was necessary. The proof of the loss was quite satisfactory, and the shipowner was totally unconnected with Brooks' misdeeds. He did not give his reasons for his judgment in the plaintiff's favour. Appeal was made to the Supreme Court which ruled in the defendant's favour by a majority of 3 to 1 (the 1 being the Chief Justice himself!) that:

—It was a constructive total loss only.
—Notice of Abandonment had not been given (which was indeed the case).
—No sufficient proof of loss had been given.

30.59 The judgment of the Privy Council was given by Sir Barnes Peacock. No doubt after hearing that the ship was in a hopeless condition, the owner had decided that there was no point in incurring further expense. This was a reasonable decision as no prudent uninsured owner would have done this. The owner might, if he had wished, have tried to establish a C.T.L. but this would have required a Notice of Abandonment which had not been given. But:

"Their Lordships are of the opinion that after the sale under the decree of the Court of

Admiralty there was an actual total loss. By that sale, the property and the vessel and cargo were transferred to the purchaser, and the vessel and cargo ceased to be the property of and were wholly lost to the original owners thereof. To constitute a total loss within the policy of marine insurance, it is not necessary that a ship should be actually annihilated or destroyed."

The ship could have been captured and condemned. She could have been damaged and repaired: "It [the ship] is lost to the owners by an adverse valid and legal transfer of this right of property . . . by . . . a Court of Competent Jurisdiction in consequence of a peril insured against, it is as much a total loss as if it had been totally annihilated."

30.60 The judgments of Blackburn J. and Kelly C.B. in the *Stringer* case[40] were quoted with much approval and the *Thornely*[41] case was distinguished on the basis that Thornely had the opportunity, which he should have taken, to prevent things going from "bad to worse" and had not taken it.

30.61 Sir Barnes concluded the case by remarking that, even if possession by the salvors could be regarded as a constructive total loss, because there was still a chance she would be saved, the court order of sale concluded it and entitled the plaintiff to claim for an actual total loss without abandonment. This would seem to be a reason why this case should be considered as one of the cases where a "bad to worse" situation had arisen.

30.62 *Fooks* v. *Smith*[42] is a very clear case of a "bad to worse" situation. Mr. Fooks was a merchant dealing in hides and Mr. Smith was the war risk underwriter. The hides were valued at £790. The War Risks Policy, when it came to be written, was on the S.G. Form and included the insured peril "restraints of Princes".

1914

22nd April

Mr. Fooks sells hides to Mr. Moscona, a Bulgarian importer. They are to be shipped from Calcutta to Varna and Mr. Fooks is to insure them.

May

The hides are loaded on to an Austrian Lloyd steamer for carriage to Trieste, where they are to be shipped to Varna by coaster. At this stage they are insured against marine risks only.

13th July

The goods arrive in Trieste and are transhipped on to an Austrian ship, the *Stanbul*.

30th July

The ship sails from Trieste.

31st July

In view of the imminence of hostilities, the goods are now insured against war risks.

3rd August

The ship is at Valona. The Master receives notice from the shipowners of the Austrian Government's order that Austrian ships shall seek safe ports in view of the possible outbreak of war. He is ordered to return to Trieste and does so.

40. *Stringer and Others* v. *The English & Scottish Marine Insurance Co. Ltd.* (1870) 22 L.T. 802. See paras. 30.47–30.52.
41. *Thornely* v. *Hebson* (1819) 2 B.& Ald. 513. See paras. 30.41–30.46.
42. [1924] 2 K.B. 508.

13th August

Austria and the United Kingdom go to war.

Late September

The hides are discharged and taken "up country".

1916

The hides are requisitioned by the Austrian Government and sold.

1921

The plaintiff finds out for the first time what has happened to the hides. No Notice of Abandonment has ever been given.

30.63 Bailhache J. doubted in an earlier trial whether the underwriter was liable for either an actual total loss or a constructive total loss and adjourned the trial for argument to be advanced on the possibility of a partial loss. When the trial resumed, he held that there was a "restraint of Princes" which required the ship to return to Trieste. A loss of adventure could still be a total loss even though the goods were in sound condition (paras. 36.42–36.57). A constructive total loss could have been claimed if Notice of Abandonment had been given promptly after the expiry of a reasonable period of time to ascertain the facts: "I have come to the conclusion that with due diligence sufficient facts might well have been ascertained before in fact they were."

30.64 It is suggested that there can be no criticism of this finding even allowing for the wartime difficulties of communication. The presence of Mr. Fooks in the proceedings indicates that he was not paid by Mr. Moscona, and he must have been aware of the loss of the adventure at a very early stage. It seems that it took him no less than three years between 1918 when the war ended and 1921 to discover what had happened to his hides.

30.65 The goods had remained in specie and were not requisitioned and sold by the Austrian Government for nearly two years after they were returned to Trieste. The plaintiff pleaded that, because of "restraints of Princes", a constructive total loss had originally arisen and had since become an actual total loss. The *Mellish*[43] and the *Stringer*[44] cases were quoted, but judgment was given:

"As I understand the law, it stands in this way. Whereby a peril insured against there is a constructive total loss and no Notice of Abandonment is given, then in the ordinary course of an unbroken sequence of events following upon the peril insured against the constructive total loss becomes an actual total loss—as for instance, if there is a capture followed by confiscation—the underwriter is liable in respect of the total loss. If, however, the ultimate loss is not the result of a sequence of events following in the ordinary course upon the peril insured against, but is the result of a supervening cause, the underwriter is not liable. That is the illustration of the doctrine *proxima causa non remota spectatur*."

Here the subsequent sale was *nova causa superveniens* long after the policy had finished and was: "Not the necessary and direct result of the restraint of Princes". The plaintiffs were in considerable difficulty. Undoubtedly the goods had suffered "capture" by the requisition and the sale, but if the War Risks Policy had indeed come

---

43. *Mellish* v. *Andrews* (1812) 15 East 13. See para. 30.39.
44. Footnote 40, above.

to an end by 1916, the insured peril only arose when the policy had already expired. This would seem to be the explanation why the plaintiff had seen his only chance of raising a claim against the underwriters by establishing a constructive total loss through "restraints of Princes" which later became an actual total loss because "bad becomes worse". But on one view on the case, there never could be a constructive total loss because for no very good reason, there never was a Notice of Abandonment, and therefore "bad" which was not established could not become "worse". Even so, Bailhache J. was clearly prepared to take a more open view of the failure to give Notice of Abandonment (as the previous cases had indicated he could justifiably do), if there had been "an unbroken sequence of events" between the constructive total loss and the requisition and sale, or the actual total loss. On his findings of fact, there was no such unbroken sequence and judgment had therefore to be signed for the underwriter.

30.66 It is suggested that the case could have gone either way, because the Austrian Government only had the goods in its possession as a result of their return to Trieste and their discharge there, and was in no position to "capture" them if it had not already exercised a "restraint of Princes". If, on the other han , the intention to requisition was only later formed when the leather was requ.red for the Austrian war effort (leather to make boots is an essential military commodity) the break in the chain between the constructive total loss through loss of adventure and the requisition, which would change irrevocably and for all time the character of the goods, becomes very clear. In the absence of any indication of a clear and definite "unbroken sequence of events" which satisfied the court on the facts, Bailhache J.'s judgment does not appear to be out of line with the earlier cases as a first examination of the report tends to indicate.

A CASUALTY HAPPENS BUT ITS CAUSE CANNOT BE ESTABLISHED

30.67 This chapter has so far dealt with the problems of two possible insured perils both of which are known, and one insured peril where "bad becomes worse". This last part will deal with a situation which is all too common with war risk insurance, where the cause of the casualty is not known for certain and has to be deduced from what facts can be established, or at any rate inferred as the probable cause. Where there are two policies covering different insured perils, and the possible cause of the loss is likely to fall on one or other of the two policies, a serious problem can arise for the assured. If he sues each underwriter separately, the views formed by two different judges of what actually happened might well be opposed, and might each separately decide that the proximate cause was not insured by the one policy which was presently before the court. His only safe course is to sue both underwriters in the same proceedings, so that one judge can form a view on what the facts were on the balance of probabilities, and then proceed to decide which policy (or neither policy) should respond. This involves the risk of paying the costs of the successful underwriter, which could be very substantial, and it can only be hoped that, in the case of a shipowner, his Freight, Demurrage and Defence Association will stand behind him and meet the resulting bill.

30.68 Given the nature of seafaring, it is scarcely surprising that this problem has arisen on scores of occasions. An early case is *Green* v. *Brown*.[45] The *Charming Peggy* sailed from North Carolina bound for London. She was insured with a warranty in the policy against captures and seizures. She disappeared without trace. The underwriters insisted that because of the capture and seizure clause the owners must prove that the loss was due to other causes. Lea C.J. instructed the jury, however: "All that is required is the best proof that the nature of the case admits of which plaintiff has given."

30.69 The jury found for the plaintiff. It is to be noted that the underwriters did not produce a plausible account of the loss which might have excused them. The only other possible cause was loss by perils of the seas. Subsequently, there were many other cases but for modern purposes it is only necessary to note section 58 of the Marine Insurance Act 1906: "Where the ship concerned in the adventure is missing, and after the lapse of a reasonable time no news of her has been received, an actual total loss may be presumed."

30.70 To move to more recent history, *Munro Brice & Co.* v. *War Risks Association Limited and Others*[46] is a typical case where the loss of the ship may have been due to perils of the seas and was equally likely to have been caused by a war risk. The War Risks Association in this case was the war risk underwriter, and the others were the marine underwriters, Anchor Marine Mutual Underwriting Association Limited. The *Inveramsay* was a steel-hulled sailing ship. The shipowners would obviously have preferred to win against the war risks underwriters, who gave insurance for £5,460 for: "Risks of capture, seizure and detention of King's enemies, or consequences of hostilities and warlike operations by or against the King's enemies" whereas the marine underwriters gave insurance for £1,500 for perils of the seas. Their policy contained the F.C. & S. Clause. The cargo of timber, which also belonged to Munro Brice, was insured against war risks by the Crown. Under the procedures of the time, the plaintiffs had to proceed separately by way of Petition of Right, and these proceedings at first instance seem not to have been reported. Enough can, however, be deduced of their nature from the judgment of the Court of Appeal.

30.71 The ship left a Mexican Gulf port on 21st March, 1917. She was fully loaded with timber and had the usual deck cargo, but there was no suggestion that she was overloaded, or was unsafely loaded in any way or was not well-found. She was never heard of again. The normal length of her voyage to Fleetwood was 40–60 days, and expert evidence was given that in the weather encountered en route there was no reason for a well-found ship such as this to founder. The actual evidence of the weather was that it was no more than force 9, a strong gale, on a few occasions and for brief periods only. The evidence on the weather was throughout contradictory even making allowance for the fact that, in these proceedings, no evidence of the probable course of the sailing ship was available. Evidence from two other ships was given. The *Olivebank's* (in the Court of Appeal referred to as the *Olive Branch*) log book showed that she had left a Mexican Gulf port on 17th March and had met with strong gales with squalls on 9th April and freshening gales, whole

45. (1743) 2 Str. 1199.
46. [1918] 2 K.B. 78.

gales, and strong gales (between 8 and 10 on the Beaufort scale) with heavy squalls on 12th, 13th and 14th April. By this time she would have been well out into the Atlantic. The *Ancenis* left Mobile on 18th March, 1917, and met with a storm (force 10) on 30th March to 5th April and "heavy weather" with a very high sea on 6th to 10th April. She too would have then been well out into the Atlantic. There was ample evidence of very bad weather on any probable route of the ship during her voyage. The war risk was posed by U-boats off the Irish coast, about 250 to 300 miles out into the Atlantic. Their range was limited, but at this stage of the First World War they attacked anything they saw and the danger was very considerable. In the High Court, Bailhache J. found as a fact that the sinkings of timber ships were "definitely known" although of course some had disappeared without trace after being attacked. He remarked that to succeed on the War Risks Policy the court would have to be satisfied "beyond reasonable doubt" that the ship had been torpedoed: "The difficulty in the case is to get the [ship] within the danger area. If that difficulty were overcome I would have no hesitation in finding that she was sunk there by a war peril although nothing is definitely known."

30.72 Bailhache J. was later overruled by the Court of Appeal, but only on the inferences to be drawn from what was known of the circumstances. His judgment on the application of the law was left untouched and makes interesting reading, coming as it does from a very experienced commercial judge. He stated the "base line" position of section 58 thus: "The assured having proved that his vessel foundered at sea has proved a loss by perils of the sea, for in the last resort every vessel that sinks at sea is lost by a peril of the sea."

30.73 This was the effect of *The Charming Peggy*.[47] If the question had to be decided on the form of pleading, the F.C. & S. Clause did not need to be set out in full and each element of it "negatived" by the plaintiff. That may have been the practice 100 years before, but not now. He particularly noted two cases, which he considered put the F.C. & S. Clause in its proper perspective, an Irish case, *Gorman v. Hand-in-Hand Insurance Company*[48] and a recent case of *Hirst v. Evans*,[49] which at first sight seemed to conflict. In the *Gorman* case, a house was insured against fire but there was an exception if the fire was caused by an incendiary. Palles C.B. held that the insured only had to prove a *prima facie* case that the house had burnt down (it had) and it was then open to the underwriter to discharge the burden of proof which now rested upon him, if he could do so, that it was the work of an incendiary or an arsonist. In the *Hirst* case, jewellery was insured against theft with the exclusion of theft by a servant. Lush J. held that the assured had to satisfy the court that the theft had been committed by somebody who was not a servant. Bailhache J. preferred Palles C.B.'s view. It is suggested that later in his judgment, the judge went a long way to answering the apparent conflict when the individual natures of the two insurance contracts are considered. Regrettably, houses do burn down all too often, and it is only rarely that an arsonist is responsible. In the *Hirst* case, the underwriters in effect qualified the whole insurance that they gave because the house was full of servants and equally regrettably servants do steal jewellery; the evidence that it was an "inside job" must be a very strong

47. *Green* v. *Brown* (1743) 2 Str. 1199. See para. 30.68.
48. (1877) I.R. 11 C.L. 224, 230.
49. [1917] 1 K.B. 352.

pointer to one of the servants as the thief, and the burden of proof shifted back to the plaintiff to prove otherwise. It is submitted that if Lush J. had had before him Bailhache J.'s three Classes, which are given below, he would have had strong justification for choosing Class 2(a) or 3 as a proper description of the contract which he was considering.

30.74 Bailhache J. gave some very useful guidance how the problem of proof must be approached:

1. As a start, the plaintiff must prove the facts which bring his claim *prima facie* within the terms of the "promise" (i.e., the policy's insurance).
2. Assuming that he successfully does this, the next question is whether the "promise" is qualified by exceptions. If so,
   (a) is the exception as wide as the "promise" thus qualifying the whole? or,
   (b) does it merely exclude from the operation of the promise particular classes of causes which, but for the exception, would come within it, leaving the rest of the promise unqualified?
3. Is the promise qualified by a provision: "which covers the whole of the promise".

If the exception falls into Class 2(b), the plaintiff must prove a *prima facie* case leaving it to the underwriters to discharge the burden of proof that, nonetheless, the exception applies. His Lordship quoted from other fields such as a vendor being obliged to deliver "Strikes excepted" or a charterer undertaking to load a ship within the laydays "specific exceptions" excluded. If the exception is better described by Classes 2(a) or 3, which are to some extent co-extensive, then the plaintiff cannot make out a *prima facie* case without bringing himself within the "promise" as a whole: "There is *ex hypothesi* no unqualified part of the promise for the sole of his foot to stand upon."

30.75 An example is the particular average franchise of the marine policy: "It is a promise to pay particular average exceeding 3%. To bring himself within that promise a plaintiff must show more than particular average loss; he must show a particular average loss of more than 3%."

30.76 Bailhache J. held that the free of capture and seizure clause came within Class 2(b), and that the underwriters had failed to discharge the burden of proof, or at least raise a very strong inference, that the ship had reached the danger zone where U-boats were operating so as to justify a finding that a U-boat had sunk her. That being so, the normal presumption applied that a ship which disappears without trace is lost by perils of the seas. Judgment was signed in the plaintiff's favour against the marine underwriters and the war risk underwriters were excused.

30.77 The proceedings by the cargo owners against the Crown reached a similar result and judgment was signed in the Crown's favour. The exact reasons are not known, but since the case was also heard by Bailhache J., it can be assumed that he followed the same line. In these proceedings, Captain Richards, an expert witness of considerable experience, produced a chart upon which he had marked out the putative course of the ship.

30.78 The Court of Appeal adopted a radically different approach when reversing Bailhache J.'s judgments and ordering the war risk underwriters to pay for the loss of both ship and cargo. The cases reached the court under the names of *Munro*

Brice & Co. v. *F. W. Marten* (the hull claimant) and *Munro Brice & Co.* v. *The Crown* (the cargo claim)[50] and were heard together. Bankes L.J. gave the unanimous judgment of the court, Scrutton and Atkin L.JJ. simply concurring. He began:

"[Counsel] says, of course, as in every case of circumstantial evidence, that it is a question of weighing the probabilities; but it is not enough to say (when you find on one side a bare possibility not amounting even to a probability and on the other side you find a series of probabilities which ought to carry conviction to a reasonable mind) that there is a bare possibility which has not been excluded, and therefore no definite conclusion ought to be arrived at."

This does seem to be a rather harsh view of Bailhache J.'s judgment but Bankes L.J. went on to explain what he meant. The trial judge found that the ship might have reached the U-boat danger area. She met with bad weather but she ought to have coped with that. There was "just the possibility" that something may have happened. "Now I ask myself, is that a sufficient justification for refusing on the balance of probabilities to arrive at a conviction that the real cause of this vessel foundering was that she did reach the submarine area and was torpedoed?"

30.79 The Court of Appeal quoted with strong approval the judgment of Roche J. in *Compania Maritima of Barcelona* v. *Wishart*[51] which Bailhache J. had doubted. This is another case of doubt whether the *Pelayo* was lost by perils of the sea or enemy action:

"At all events, my own conclusion upon the facts is that the *Pelayo* was not torpedoed, was not mined, and that the facts and probabilities strongly point to her loss being a loss by foundering through the action of wind and sea. The line between surmise and legitimate inference is not easy to draw. But although in this case demonstration and certainty are not unobtainable, the law allows, and ever demands, that an inference shall be drawn from such facts as point to a conclusion."

30.80 On the strong authority of the Court of Appeal, it would seem that the clearest explanation of how to proceed in such matters comes from Roche J., that every known fact should be considered and a conclusion reached in a commonsense way. It is tempting to think that the technical approach adopted by Bailhache J. in the *Munro Brice*[52] case must be correct. Technically it is, and would answer questions posed by such cases as *The Charming Peggy*.[53] As the Court of Appeal subsequently showed, it is not safe to take too literally Bailhache J.'s guidance where the defendant underwriter produces a plausible explanation for the loss of the ship.

30.81 The problem was taken one stage further when the Court of Appeal had to consider the loss of the *Arnus* in *Compania Naviera Martiartu* v. *The Royal Exchange Assurance Corporation*.[54] The ship left Vivero on 26th April, 1921. A proper course would have taken her clear of the Armen Rock Light, Ushant and Penmarsh Point. On the night of 27th April, the 2nd Officer, who was on watch, saw what he described as floating wreckage about 75 yards long and 24 yards wide about two feet above the water. It looked like a hull or a large raft and seemed to

50. (1920) 2 Ll.L.Rep. 2.
51. (1918) 23 Com.Cas. 264; (1918) 14 Asp.M.L.C. 298.
52. *Munro Brice & Co.* v. *F. W. Marten, Munro Brice & Co.* v. *The Crown* (1920) 2 Ll.L.Rep. 2.
53. *Green* v. *Brown* (1743) 2 Str. 1199. See para. 30.68.
54. [1923] 1 K.B. 651.

pass clear of the ship down the port side. He heard no noise and felt no shock. The night was fine and clear with a smooth sea. The ship subsequently sank in deep water, settling down by the head. The crew abandoned the ship three hours before she finally sank, and were all picked up by fishing boats. The plaintiffs' case was that she hit this wreckage, stripping off the bilge-keel causing damage to the plates of the ship's side. The defendant's case was that the Chief Engineer had admitted seawater deliberately by opening a valve in the valve box in the boiler room, and further opening a sea inlet. This admitted water to a ballast tank whose port man-hole cover was loose or open. The watertight doors failed to stop the water from passing to the cross bunker and from thence into the fore part of the ship, which accounted for her sinking by the head. Moreover, the owners had connived in all of this.

30.82 In the High Court, Bailhache J. found for the shipowner. The judge formed an unfavourable impression of the Chief Engineer but a favourable opinion of the 2nd Officer. This was an error, because the 2nd Officer gave his evidence on commission and was never before the court. The judgment concluded:

"I agree that in a case of this kind when a ship goes to the bottom of the sea in calm weather on a fine night, although it is enough to make a *prima facie* case against the underwriter to say she is at the bottom of the sea, yet very little evidence shifts the burden on to those claim-ing against the underwriters and imposes upon them the obligation of showing what the par-ticular peril was that sent her to the bottom of the sea, apart of course from the seawater."

The underwriters appealed. The Court of Appeal asked shipowner's counsel what would be the result if the court was left in doubt whether or not the shipowners had made out their case. He answered that the court must then fall back on the pre-sumption that, the ship being a seaworthy and properly-found ship, she was lost by an unascertained peril and that the peril was covered. This answer did not find favour with the court. Bankes L.J., on the facts of the case, was not willing to rest his judgment entirely on counsel's point:

"This contention is, in my opinion, quite untenable having regard to the facts of this case. If the assured makes out a *prima facie* case, as the (shipowner) in the present case did, then unless the underwriters displace their *prima facie* case the assured is no doubt entitled to rely upon the presumption. On the other hand, if the *prima facie* case, which was the foundation on which the presumption was rested, fails because the underwriters put forward a reason-able explanation of the loss, the superstructure falls with it. If both the assured and the underwriters put forward an explanation of the loss, the loss is not unexplained in a sense which would admit of the presumption, merely because the court is unable to say which of the two explanations is the correct one."

30.83 Bankes L.J., as were the other judges, was quite certain that the ship had been scuttled and he felt that the trial judge had been influenced by the unfortunate misapprehension of the 2nd Officer's evidence. The shipowners may have estab-lished that the loss of the vessel was due to a peril covered by the policy; on the other hand, the underwriters had advanced a perfectly reasonable and tenable defence which, on the evidence, he preferred. Scrutton L.J. did not wish to discuss the burden of proof but:

" . . . In my present view, if there are circumstances suggesting another cause than a peril insured against was the dominant or effective cause of the entry of the sea water into the ship . . . and an examination of all the evidence and probabilities leaves the court doubtful what is the real cause of the loss, the assured has failed to prove his case" and, when distinguishing *The Charming Peggy*[55]:

" . . . When there is evidence on each side suggesting the real cause the court must determine on a balance of probabilities, as in every case of circumstantial evidence, and not be deterred from finding in favour of the stronger probabilities by the fact that some remote possibility exists the other way."

Eve J., sitting in the Court of Appeal, agreed, and the court allowed the appeal. Subsequently Scrutton L.J.'s *dictum* was unanimously approved by the House of Lords in *Rhesa Shipping Co. S.A.* v. *Fenton Insurance Co. Ltd., Rhesa Shipping Co. S.A.* v. *Herbert David Edmunds (The Popi M)*.[56]

30.84 Three other cases must be mentioned; in one, the ship and her cargo and crew disappeared without trace and proceedings were instituted against the marine and war risks underwriters separately; in another, the actual sinking, but not the reason for it, was well witnessed; in the third, it was held that the *dictum* of Mr. Sherlock Holmes was not considered to be a reliable guide in assessing evidence in a civil case which turns on the balance of probabilities.

30.85 *Mitrovich Bros. & Co.* v. *Merchants Marine Insurance Company Ltd.*[57] was a case very similar to the *Munro Brice* cases (para. 30.70), except that the plaintiffs sued the marine and the war risks underwriters in separate actions. On 14th January, 1917, the French iron sailing ship *General de Boisdeffre* sailed from Mejillones in Chile with a cargo of nitrate for Brest. She was never heard of again. The voyage should have taken five months, which does seem a long time, and the question arose whether she had been lost by perils of the seas or had been torpedoed by a U-boat almost within sight of her destination. Either was perfectly possible. First, it was necessary to round Cape Horn. No evidence was given to the court of the weather conditions round the Cape at the time. Most of the gales come out of the west or south-west, and these would have been favourable to her; there is the world of difference between running before a gale and beating up into it. In August, 1917, some fishermen found a barrel off Penmarsh, which was way off her course for Brest, of the type which was used in lifeboats. It did not have the name of the ship to which it belonged upon it, as all lifeboat equipment is supposed to have, and 30 hours later, in the same area, a coat was found with a seaman's book in the pocket. The coat was identified by the seaman's parents as belonging to their son, a seaman on the ship. Rowlatt J., when invited to decide that the ship had been lost by perils of the seas in the approaches to the English Channel, was deeply sceptical and declined to do so. He found it particularly difficult to accept that the coat could have remained afloat for a minimum of 30 hours, and considered that if the ship had been in the area at all, then it was more likely that she had been torpedoed by a U-boat. The war risks insurance was placed in France, and it appears from the scanty details in the report that the French war risks underwriters had successfully denied liability.

30.86 *United Scottish Insurance Company Ltd.* v. *British Fishing Vessels Mutual War Risks Association Ltd. (The Braconbush)*[58] was a case between two insurance companies, because the plaintiff had issued an "all risks" insurance policy to the

55. *Green* v. *Brown* (1743) 2 Str. 1199. See para. 30.68.
56. [1985] 2 Lloyd's Rep. 1; [1985] 1 W.L.R. 948; [1985] 2 All E.R. 712. See paras. 30.5, 30.90, 30.91.
57. (1922) 12 Ll.L.Rep. 451, (1923) 14 Ll.L.Rep. 25.
58. (1945) 78 Ll.L.Rep. 70.

owners of the *Braconbush* and had reinsured its war and strikes liabilities with the defendant. On 29th January, 1942, the *Braconbush*, whilst one mile off Duncansby Head suffered a casualty which was variously described as an underwater explosion or an underwater noise. This ripped open her hull, and in spite of efforts made to beach her with the assistance of another fishing boat, she sank in deep water. The crew all survived. There were two possibilities, and both were considered as likely to have caused her loss. Did she hit some underwater wreckage, or did she hit a drifting float which had broken adrift from the German minefields in the North Sea? These floats were laid around the peripheries of the German minefields, and, with a small explosive charge, seem to have been intended to give warning to any German ship off her proper course that she was straying into a minefield. Against a strong hulled ship, they would have done no damage. Against a ship with a frailer hull such as a fishing boat, they could prove fatal. They were always breaking adrift, and during the Second World War, they were a considerable nuisance in the North Sea.

30.87 Atkinson J. reviewed the law on burden of proof, clearly feeling it was well described in the *Munro Brice* case (paras. 30.70–30.80). He quoted with approval the *dictum* of Bankes L.J. on probabilities and possibilities (para. 30.78) and that of Roche J. in the *Wishart* case (para. 30.79), and added further that of Atkin L.J. in the *Munro Brice* case:

"The plaintiffs had to establish that the claim which they made was made out by the facts. To do so it was not necessary that they should produce witnesses who saw the war risk operating . . . what you want is to weigh probabilities, if there be proof of facts sufficient to enable you to have some foothold or ground for comparing and balancing probabilities at their respective value, the one against the other."

30.88 He also noted what Scrutton L.J., in the same case, had to say on how individual judges will react when quoting another case:

" . . . two learned Law Lords in the minority were of the opinion that the three in the majority were guessing, and the three learned Law Lords in the majority were of the opinion that they were drawing a reasonable inference from the facts proved . . . "

30.89 In the *Braconbush* case, Atkinson J., having reviewed all the evidence that was available at great length, came to the conclusion that the most likely explanation for the loss of the ship was an explosive float and gave judgment for the plaintiffs.

30.90 The *dictum* of Mr. Sherlock Holmes is taken from *The Sign of Four* and is "When you have eliminated the impossible, whatever remains, however improbable, must be the truth." However sound this may or may not be for criminal investigation, it cannot be acceptable in a civil case which turns on the balance of probabilities. Lord Brandon, who gave the unanimous judgment of the House of Lords, made this very clear in *Rhesa Shipping Company S.A.* v. *Herbert David Edmunds and Others (The Popi M)*[59] when he actually quoted this *dictum*. On 5th August, 1978, the *Popi M* was in the Mediterranean bound on an easterly course and off the coast of Algeria. The weather was fine and the sea was calm. There was a sudden inrush of water into the engine room and the ship sank. There were two plausible reasons advanced for this, that she had suffered a failure of her hull

59. [1985] 2 Lloyd's Rep. 1.

plating, or that she had had a collision with a submarine. In the High Court, Bingham J. rejected the evidence that the hull plating had failed, even though she was an elderly ship, and was scarcely convinced that she had been in collision with a submarine, although such collisions were not unknown during the days of the Cold War. This led him to accept, that on the balance of probabilities, the collision with the submarine was the more likely and this justified a finding that the ship was lost by perils of the seas. The Court of Appeal, although it ventured the opinion that the collision with the submarine was most unlikely, upheld the judgment. The House of Lords, however, reversed the judgments of the lower courts, and gave judgment in favour of the underwriters. Too close attention to the two theories had led them away from the third possibility, that neither theory was right. In this case, the shipowners had failed to discharge the burden of proof of explaining what was the actual peril of the sea which had caused the loss of the ship, and in such a case they were not entitled to judgment. Scrutton L.J. had explained it in the *Martiartu* case (paras. 30.81–30.83) in the following terms:

" . . . if there are circumstances suggesting that another cause than a peril insured against was the dominant and effective cause of the entry of the seawater into the ship . . . and an examination of all the evidence leaves the Court doubtful what is the real cause, . . . the assured has failed to prove his case."

30.91 Lord Brandon added: "The Judge needs to be satisfied on the evidence that it is more likely to have occurred than not."

SOME RECENT CASES

30.92 To demonstrate the practice of underwriters, three cases can be shown where no dispute was taken to the courts, but where the underwriters, in this case a Mutual War Risks Association, have had to deal with cases where no certain cause of the loss could ever be established.

30.93 In 1968, a ship carrying ammonium nitrate to India reached a point in her voyage off the southernmost point of Malagasy. During the late afternoon, a loud explosion was heard accompanied by a high column of water in way of number 4 hold on the portside and just aft of the superstructure. Dead fish were noticed in the water. The Captain and the Chief Officer entered the hold but could not examine the damage which was below the top level of the cargo. There was an inrush of water which the pumps were unable to control. The only way of saving the ship seemed to be to beach her on Malagasy, and a suitable course was set with the Captain steering and the Chief Engineer remaining in the engine room. The bulkhead between the engine room and number 4 hold bulged ominously inwards so that the remaining engine room crew were evacuated. They succeeded in beaching the ship but unfortunately they beached her on quicksand and she very rapidly sank up to the weather deck. There was no possibility of examining the damage which, no doubt, could have told its own story.

30.94 Several possibilities were explored. Was there an explosion in the cargo, a commodity given to explosions? The cargo was calcified with 26% chalk mixed in with it to prevent this happening. Moreover, any fumes from an explosion of ammonium nitrate would have made it impossible for the two officers to have entered the hold. They would have been suffocated if they had tried. Was this a case of static electricity in the fuel tanks igniting the explosive vapour given off by the fuel? At the time, there had been a number of crashes of the new Boeing 727 which were ascribed to this cause. Nothing like this had ever happened before and the possibility, after close examination, could be ruled out. During the Second World War, the Japanese Navy, whilst it had the use of the Singapore Base, laid mines in this area to catch the allied convoys bound for India. The presence of the minefield during the war was never suspected, and it was only after the recapture of the Singapore Base, when an examination could be made of the Japanese records, that the presence of the minefield was discovered. It was promptly swept, but by the standards of the time, a sweep was only 75% successful and a special sweep 95% successful; a 100% success was never possible and neither was it guaranteed. Was it possible that a mine, which had remained in the water undisturbed for 25 years, could have exploded against the hull of the ship? Mines are supposed to disarm themselves after a certain period, and natural deterioration should have rendered it ineffective. On the other hand, of all the improbabilities, this seemed the least improbable. No other explanation seemed possible, and the Mutual War Risks Association accepted a claim for an actual total loss.

   30.95 In 1984, a ship was navigating in the southern part of the Red Sea. A loud explosion was heard under the ship and again there was a column of water. The ship proceeded to her discharging port and an examination showed considerable damage to her plates amidships and large hog. Several other ships were damaged in the Red Sea at about this time, and it was thought that mines, sown mischievously from a ro-ro ship were responsible, although this was never proved conclusively. There was no war in the Red Sea and the nearest conflict taking place at the time was in the Persian Gulf which never spilt over into the Red Sea. There had never been any information of mines being sown in this part of the Red Sea during the recurrent Arab/Israeli wars. During sweeping operations conducted by several navies, the Royal Navy discovered at least one bottom-lying mine of recent Soviet manufacture. It had quite clearly been in the water for only a short time. The nature of the damage to the ship indicated that a mine was the only possible cause and again the case had to be accepted as a partial loss by the Mutual War Risks Association.

   30.96 A case of much greater difficulty was the sinking in 1985 of a dry cargo engines-aft ship at the southern entrance to the Gulf of Suez. During the early morning, a muffled explosion was heard underneath the ship without, however, the usual tell-tale column of water. In spite of pumping to maximum effort, the engine room flooded. The Master and the crew made extreme efforts over three hours to save their vessel and were eventually rescued by another ship in a dishevelled and exhausted condition. Was this or was this not a scuttling case? At first sight this seemed very likely, but a close and painstaking analysis of the evidence indicated that, very probably, this was not the case, and the underwriters, in this case a Mutual War Risks Association, had to think again.

   30.97 The crew consisted of Greek officers and eastern European ratings. Although there had been the usual crew changes, they had served together for a long time. Employment on board a ship offered a source of escape from the difficult conditions of home life in eastern Europe, and it seemed unlikely that the crew was anxious to cause the loss of the ship. A bomb of sufficient power put into the engine room would have had to be of considerable size and would have caused a large explosion, probably killing all the engine room watch. In the event, nobody was injured. There was no opportunity for the owner to plant the bomb in north European ports or in Crete, where there were changes in three of the crew, with sufficient precision to cause her to sink in deep water. It had to be an explosion from outside the ship, and this in itself would tend to obviate any question of the owner's involvement. But there was no violent explosion and no column of water, so how could this have been caused by a normal naval mine which has enormous destructive power?

30.98 From the accounts of the engine room watch, the inrush of water took place in way of a grating on the underside of the ship, and for the first time the possibility of a limpet mine was raised. Limpet mines are small in size and easily handled, requiring as they do only a small charge. Limpet mines are manufactured as weapons, but they are easy enough to make from materials which can be purchased in normal shops without arousing suspicion. The explosive cannot, of course, be so obtained but there was at the time plenty of explosive in the Middle East; anybody knowing where to look could get hold of it. A small device with a 5 lb. charge would be easily handled, particularly as all objects lose weight when under water, and it would pose no problem to an amateur underwater aqualung or scuba diver. Water, and particularly sea water, is the best tamping agent there is. If a charge is placed against a wall and exploded, there is the possibility that only a small dent will be made in the wall. If, however, a plastic bag full of water is placed against it, it will readily punch a hole through the wall. In sea water, care must be taken that the bubble caused by the explosion of the charge shall not break the surface—if it does it will exhaust its force into the open air and lose its effect. If, however, it is placed sufficiently far below the surface, it will not do this; its full force will be directed on to the hull and will punch a hole right through it, and even through the deck plates of the engine room, even though this is above a double-bottom tank. Depth charge explosions at sea work on this principle, and at the moment of the explosion the "doming" of the surface can be seen. Only later will there be a large column of water caused by the escaping gases when the lethal cavity caused by the explosion has filled again and, having lost their force, they make their way to the surface to escape. The escaping gases from a small charge of 5 lbs or so would not create any noticeable surface disturbance comparable with a depth charge with its huge force. Expert advice indicated that of all the improbabilities, a limpet mine fixed to the engine room gratings whilst the ship was waiting at Port Said to go through the Suez Canal was the least unlikely. It was thought that it was placed by a terrorist group anxious to improve its skills, even though no responsibility was ever claimed for the explosion and the loss of the ship. Again the Mutual War Risks Association accepted an actual total loss.

30.99 As will be noted in these three cases, the balance of probabilities was weighed and the most probable (or least unlikely) cause was accepted as the proximate cause of the loss or the damage to the ships concerned. To put it another way, and one which is more descriptive of the law on burden of proof, the owners in each case were in a position to produce a plausible explanation for their loss. The Association on the other hand could not have countered it in any realistic way.

30.100 As a conclusion, it must be said that whether or not a particular casualty comes within the terms of an insured peril, or an excluded peril, must turn upon the facts of any case, upon the evidence which is available, and the conclusions that can be drawn from them. Strangely, war risk cases usually pose extremely difficult questions in all these fields. The facts do not always present themselves in an understandable form, and considerable extra investigation is necessary. Even when this is done, an analysis of the result does not always point to a definite conclusion. Regarding evidence, there is frequently far too much of it which is not to the point, and far too little which is. All too often accounts are volunteered which on closer inspection turn out to be opinions given by those far from the scene masquerading as actual facts at the scene itself. Again all too often, the people who really know what happened and why cannot be induced to recount their knowledge or their motives. It therefore frequently happens that inferences have to be drawn to supplement that which is definitely known and can be established. To attempt to draw definite conclusions with the intention that they should give guidance would probably only succeed in making things even more difficult to comprehend. It does seem that the most that can be done is to take the situations which are most likely to arise where there is a question of a war risk casualty, and discuss the situations against the background of the decided cases. This is what this chapter has attempted to do.

CHAPTER 31

Unsafe ports and places—some recent cases concerning war or hostilities

31.1 Whilst they are, strictly speaking, outside the scope of a work on war risks insurance, there have recently been a number of cases on ports which have become unsafe because of war or some form of hostilities. It is hoped that this chapter will be of general interest to the reader.

31.2 Gem Shipping Company of Monrovia v. Babanaft Lebanon S.A.R.L. (The Fortevivo)[1]

In March 1972, the *Fortevivo*, a Somali flag ship, carried high-grade gasoline from Turkey for discharge in Lattakia. It was a time of great tension betweeen Syria and Israel, and shortly before the ship's arrival, the crew saw an unidentified aircraft on fire. She berthed during the morning, and shortly afterwards the anti-aircraft guns began firing at what were alleged to be Israeli aircraft. The firing continued for about an hour, but the attacking aircraft—if indeed there were any—made no attempt to attack the port or the tank farm. During the evening, the anti-aircraft guns began firing again, and splinters from their shells fell around the ship. Potentially these are lethal to a gasoline carrier, and the crew were much alarmed. The Master ascribed this to an air-raid, but this was not noted in the log-books of other ships in the port at the time. It later seemed that the gunners were engaged in practice firing only. The port authorities ordered the ship to be blacked out with no lights showing. This was the final straw for the crew, and they persuaded the Master to leave the port. For three days, the ship remained in Syrian territorial waters whilst receiving steadily more insistent demands that she should return and complete discharge of her cargo. During these three days, and after her eventual return, Lattakia enjoyed sunny and peaceful days without any visits from the Israeli airforce. The owners claimed they were entitled to demurrage for the three days, but the arbitrator, and subsequently Donaldson J., held that the Master was not justified in leaving the port. In the judge's words, it was a case of cold feet in a warm climate.

31.3 Kodros Shipping Corporation v. Empresa Cubana de Fletes (The Evia) (No. 2)[2]

The ship was chartered on the Baltime form, which contained the usual provision

1. [1975] 1 Lloyd's Rep. 339.
2. [1982] 2 Lloyd's Rep. 307.

that "The vessel was to be employed . . . between good and safe ports." Besides this, there was another provision which read:

"The vessel unless the consent of the owners be first obtained not to be ordered nor continue to any place or on any voyage nor to be used on any service which will bring her within a zone which is dangerous as a result of any actual or threatened act of war, war hostilities, warlike operations . . . "

31.4 In 1980 the ship, whilst on time-charter to Empresa Cubana, loaded cement for carriage to Basrah. At the time the orders were given, Basrah was a peaceful port and was expected to remain so. The ship entered the port and completed discharge on 22nd September, the day that war broke out between Iraq and Iran. She was unable to leave because of the fighting across the river. No mention is made in the report of the Iraqi prohibition (para. 13.59), and it would appear that the courts made their decisions on the grounds of physical danger only.

31.5 The parties had varying fortunes before the arbitrator, the High Court and the Court of Appeal, but it is suggested that this work should concern itself only with the unanimous decision of the House of Lords. This was given by Lord Roskill, Lord Brandon having assisted him to draw it up, with Lords Diplock, Elwyn-Jones and Keith concurring.

31.6 Lord Roskill noted that in the High Court, Goff J. had used the famous definition of unsafe ports given by Sellers L.J. in *Leeds Shipping Company Ltd.* v. *Société Française Bunge (The Eastern City)*[3]:

"If it were said that a port will not be safe unless, in the relevant period of time, the particular ship can reach it, use it and return from it without, in the absence of some abnormal occurrence, being exposed to danger which cannot be avoided by good navigation and seamanship, it would probably meet all the circumstances as a broad statement of the law."

31.7 Goff J. therefore concluded:

" . . . I have to give these words their natural and ordinary meaning, unless the context otherwise requires; and I am bound to say that on their natural and ordinary meaning they comprise a warranty of any port or place to which the vessel is ordered shall be safe for the vessel throughout the period of the vessel's contractual service there."

31.8 Lord Roskill did not approve of this interpretation of Sellers L.J.'s judgment. He considered:

"The charterers contractual promise must, I think, relate to the characteristics of the port or place in question, and in my view, means that when the order is given that port or place is prosectively safe for the ship to get to, stay at, so far as necessary, and in due course, leave."

31.9 Sellers L.J. was considering a case where wind and weather could make a port unsafe, whereas Lord Roskill was dealing with "some abnormal occurrence" such as the possibility that a port could be shut by ice, or blocked by a wreck, or made unsafe because of a war, but with the reasonable expectation that when the ship reached the port, the obstacle would have been removed or the war situation would have been resolved so that the port was once again safe. If, however, this expectation was not fulfilled then the charterer had: " . . . a further secondary obligation to cancel his original order and . . . to order her to go to another port . . . [which] is prospectively safe . . . ".

3. [1958] 2 Lloyd's Rep. 127.

31.10 The charterer is only obliged to give orders with which the ship can comply. Here there was no question that the ship could leave Basrah, and therefore there was no liability on the charterer.

31.11 The House of Lords intended this to be general guidance on time-charter cases only, and declined to give any general guidance on voyage-charters. It is respectfully suggested that the principle which the House expounded is suitable to apply to voyage-charters as well, particularly where the ship is to load or to discharge within a range of ports. The case deals with a situation where the Master had no opportunity to leave the port. An example of a case where he did have such a chance occurred during the Yom Kippur War in 1973. The ship was discharging into lighters in the roads of a small port to the west of Port Suez. Israeli tanks suddenly appeared on the beach and began firing at the ships. The Master sailed in a hurry. The charterers, initially most annoyed, could be persuaded not to pursue the matter.

31.12 D/S A/S Idaho v. Colossus Maritime S.A. (The Concordia Fjord)[4]

The ship was chartered for two years on the New York Produce Exchange form to work in a liner service from the United States to the Eastern Mediterranean. On 10th June, 1978, the charterers ordered her to discharge in Beirut, which was then a safe port. According to Lord Roskill's *dictum*, this was a perfectly proper order. By the end of June, fighting had broken out again, and it could no longer be considered safe. Following *The Evia (No 2)*, the charterers were obliged to order her to another port. They did not do so. The ship entered Beirut, and was hit by a napalm rocket which set her on fire. The charterers acknowledged that they should have subsequently ordered her to another port, but pleaded that since they had reimbursed the owners for the additional premiums which the underwriters had demanded, they should not be held liable.

31.13 The arbitrator found against them. Whilst it does depend on the actual terms of the charterparty, the general rule is that, by paying the owners the additional premiums, the charterers do not buy themselves immunity from damages for sending the ship to a port which is unsafe because of war risks. Bingham J. subsequently upheld the arbitrator's award, finding that it contained nothing which was inconsistent with the House of Lords judgment in the *Evia (No. 2)* case.

31.14 Motor Oil Hellas (Corinth) Refineries S.A. v. Shipping Corporation of India (The Kanchenjunga)[5]

The following was the sequence of events:

1978
8th August

The *Kanchenjunga* is fixed to load four consecutive cargoes from Arabian Gulf ports excluding Fao and Abadan. The ship is subchartered, and then sub-subchartered, but the charterparty which concerned the courts contains the usual provision ("the first provision") that the ship is only to trade between good and

---

4. [1984] 1 Lloyd's Rep. 385.
5. [1989] 1 Lloyd's Rep. 354, [1990] 1 Lloyd's Rep. 391.

safe ports. It also contains another clause ("the second provision") which is typical of many charters which reads:

> "20(vi)(*b*). If owing to any war, hostilities, warlike operations . . . entry into any such port of loading . . . or the loading . . . of cargo at any such port is considered by the Master or owners in his or their discretion dangerous or prohibited . . . the charterers shall have the right to order the cargo . . . to be loaded . . . at any other safe port."

22nd September

The Iran/Iraq War breaks out.

20th November

The ship is ordered to load at Kharg Island.

21st November

The order is repeated and the owners instruct the Master to proceed. He protests but complies.

23rd November

The ship arrives at Kharg Island and gives Notice of Readiness. She waits in the roads.

25th November

The owners request priority berthing. There is anti-aircraft firing. The owners protest to the charterers that the port is unsafe.

30th November

A berth becomes available, but the ship is unable to reach it because of fog.

1st December

The Iraqi air-force raids Kharg Island and drops free-fall bombs. At this stage of the war, the Iraqis lack the advanced equipment they later acquire. The Master promptly sails the ship away to a distance of 25 miles.

2nd December

The owners tell the charterers what has happened and ask for the nomination of another port. The charterers insist the ship loads at Kharg Island. The Master refuses to return.

31.15 In the subsequent arbitration, the arbitrators found that the Master was justified, and that the charterers had committed a repudiatory breach of contract which entitled the owners to treat the charter as being at an end. The case came before the courts, and Hobhouse J., the Court of Appeal, and the House of Lords all considered that the award was incorrect. The owners had waived their right to refuse to go to Kharg Island (the first provision), but this did not mean that they had also waived their rights to leave a dangerous place (the second provision). In the House of Lords, Lord Goff summed up the views of the judges as follows:

31.16 On the first provision—

"The trial Judge and the Court of Appeal . . . both held the owners had elected to waive their right to reject the nomination. In my opinion they were right to reach this conclusion."

31.17 And on the second provision—

"Both the [trial] Judge and the Court of Appeal held this clause was effective to protect the owners from liability in damages, although it did not render the charterers liable in damages in the events which had happened."

31.18 These two provisions, or something similar to them, are found in nearly every charterparty, and the courts have firmly distinguished them as being separate from one another. The case is of great importance in war risks cases, because this situation arises on countless occasions. It should be noted that neither side could claim damages. Clause 20(vi)(*b*) provided the shipowners with a shield with which to protect themselves; it was not a sword with which they could attack the charterers. Lord Brandon did, however, venture the opinion that if the owners had pleaded a claim for loss of freight, they would probably have won it.

31.19 Abu Dhabi National Tanker Company v. Product Star Shipping Ltd.[6]

Events took the following course:

1987

6th April

The *Product Star* is chartered for a six months period, with an option for a further six months, to carry successive oil cargoes from United Arab Emirates (U.A.E.) ports to Bangladesh. The charterparty provides—

> "40(2) If [A] any port of loading or discharge named in this charterparty . . . be blockaded or [B] owing to any war . . . (a) entry to any such port . . . or the loading or discharging of cargo at any such port be considered by the Master or owners in his or their absolute discretion dangerous . . . , or (b) it is considered by the Master and owners in his or their discretion dangerous or impossible for the vessel to reach any such port of loading or discharge, then charterers shall have the right to order the cargo . . . to be loaded or discharged at any other port of loading or discharge within the range of loading or discharging ports . . ."

There is also a provision (Clause 50) whereby the owners should pay the annual war risks premium, and the charterers should reimburse the owners for a part of the additional premiums demanded by the underwriters for the time that the ship spends in the Arabian Gulf.

27th April

The ship is delivered at Fujairah.

28th August

The ship discharges the fourth cargo at Chittagong.

The four cargoes have been loaded at Ruweis, and there has been no mishap. Ships in the northern and middle parts of the Gulf have been attacked, particularly ships bound to and from Kuwaiti ports by the Iranians, and to and from ports in the northern part of Iran by the Iraqis. More lately, there have been attacks in the southern part of the Gulf by the Iranians, but it is a noticeable feature that ships bound to and from U.A.E. ports have rarely been attacked, and then probably as the result of the mistakes which are all too common in wartime.

31st August

The charterers order the next cargo to be loaded at Ruweis, and follow up by giving details of the cargo.

7th September

The Master advises E.T.A. Ruweis on 12th September.

9th September

The owners telex the charterers:

> " . . . owing to recent developments in waters adjacent to Ruweis . . . owners and Master* consider the entry there to be dangerous . . . therefore in accordance with Clause 40 . . . owners and Master* request (Charterers) to nominate another load port . . . vessel has been instructed not to proceed north of Latitude 24 degrees north . . ."

10th September

The Master advises the charterers that the ship is lying stopped just south of Latitude 24 degrees North. He is instructed not to cross this latitude.

15th September

The charterers insist that the area around Ruweis is safe and they exercise their six-month option.

25th September

The charterers finally accept the owners' conduct as a repudiation.

---

6. [1991] 2 Lloyd's Rep. 469, [1993] 1 Lloyd's Rep. 397.
* It later turns out that the Master was not consulted.

29th September

The owners accept the charterers' orders to go to Ruweis as a repudiation.

31.20 There was a lot to be said for the owners' case. There had been a partial truce between 20th July and 29th August following a United Nations resolution on the Iran/Iraq War. Nonetheless, there had been several incidents during this period notably the mining of the *Texaco Caribbean* and the *Anita* off Fujairah. The Iraqis had broken the truce on 27th August by attacking the Iranian tanker *Alwind* in the northern part of the Gulf. Naval convoys by the U.S. Navy and the Royal Navy had been introduced, even though a ship in the very first convoy had struck a mine. The warships of several other nations were hurrying to the scene, and there had been some "re-flagging" of Kuwaiti ships. On 9th September, the Iranians had attacked the *Haven*, which was sailing without convoy, although she had loaded at a Saudi port. Between 30th August and 2nd September, there were altogether 14 attacks on ships.

31.21 On the other hand, during the previous loadings at Ruweis, the Grand Mosque in Mecca had been attacked and many Iranian pilgrims had been killed. A ship bound from a U.A.E. port had been attacked from a small boat, fortunately with only minor damage. This was thought to have been a mistake. Neither of these two incidents had drawn any protests from the owners that Ruweis was now unsafe. There was a dispute about some deductions from the hire which was becoming increasingly bitter. No evidence was given to the trial judge on the state of the freight market, and the judge therefore did not comment upon it. The charterers' exercise of their six-month option seems to indicate that it was rising, and they would want to keep a ship on a lower rate. This would be matched by a similar, if opposing, wish on the part of the owners to find more lucrative employment.

31.22 Judge Diamond, sitting as a High Court judge, considered that some limitation had to be placed upon Clause 40, and if the owners were to take advantage of it, they must be able to show:

(a) they were acting *bona fide*, and had an honest belief that the port was now dangerous; and,

(b) they must demonstrate that there was such a degree of danger that a reasonable owner would consider that reaching the port was dangerous.

31.23 Judge Diamond went on:

"In Clause 40, I would construe the word 'dangerous' as meaning dangerous by reference to the standards and circumstances which existed at the date of the charterparty . . . in the present case the charterparty entitled the charterers to order the vessel to ports, which at the date of the charter, were situated in a war zone and therefore gave rise to a certain degree of risk to the vessel and her crew. It seems to me that it is in that context that it has to be considered whether a reasonable owner, informed of the relevant facts, would reasonably consider the port to be dangerous."

31.24 There was also the matter of Clause 50 which obliged the charterers to reimburse the owners for some part of the additional premiums which the underwriters demanded because the ship was trading within the Arabian Gulf. Judge Diamond continued:

"In my judgment therefore, as a matter of the proper construction of the charterparty the word 'dangerous' in clause 40 has to be read in the context of the contract as a whole and, in particular, in the light of Clause 50."

31.25 The owners' evidence was inadequate, and could scarcely be called convincing, that there was in fact a substantially higher degree of danger on 9th September, 1987, than there was on 6th April, 1987, or that the owners sincerely believed that there was. Judgment was signed in favour of the charterers.

31.26 Judge Diamond was subsequently upheld by the Court of Appeal, although its judgment was given in slightly different terms. Leggatt L.J. gave the court's unanimous judgment:

"Although at the time when the charterparty was made the whole of the Gulf, including U.A.E. waters constituted a war risks zone, the owners were, by the combination of Clauses 10, 40(2), and 50, accepting that in the circumstances prevailing at the date of the charterparty the risks of proceeding to U.A.E. ports and loading there were not such as they would consider 'dangerous' so as to render the discretion under Clause 40(2) exercisable."

31.27 Leggatt L.J. went on:

"They were only entitled to object in the event that the risks had so far increased that in their discretion they considered such voyages to have become dangerous."

31.28 There was a mass of authority which says that such a discretion must be exercised honestly and in good faith and not in an arbitrary, capricious or unreasonable way. The owners' evidence had failed to convince the court that the discretion had been properly exercised. They had placed too much reliance upon the attack on the *Nissan Maru*, which had been trading with Iran and was carrying an Iranian cargo. There was also no explanation why they had permitted another ship under their management, the *East Star*, to trade in the Gulf at the same time.

CONCLUSIONS

31.29 Whilst the rights and obligations of the parties must depend on the terms of their charterparty, the following general points can be seen from these cases:

   (i) There must be very good and compelling reasons to disobey the orders of the charterer. The owner, on whom the burden of proof rests, will have to be prepared to justify to some sceptical arbitrators and judges that their discretion and that of the Master was properly, honestly, and reasonably exercised; not only were they acting in a *bona fide* way, but the facts themselves would have justified their decision in the eyes of reasonable people.

  (ii) The two provisions which are usually found in every charterparty, the charterer's right to nominate a good and safe port, and the owner's right to avoid or leave a dangerous place, are separate one from another. If the owner waives, or does not object, to a faulty nomination by the charterer, this does not prejudice his right to avoid or leave a dangerous area.

 (iii) Where the charterer properly nominates a port which is prospectively safe when he names it, but which later becomes unsafe, he has an obligation to nominate another safe port.

(iv) Where a charterparty requires performance in an area where there is already a degree of danger, the degree of danger which exists at the date of the charterparty is the point from which any "increase" in the danger must be judged.

CHAPTER 32

Ships and freight

INTRODUCTORY

32.1 Ships may be insured for War and Strikes Risks by the London Market or, in certain cases, by the Mutual War Risks Associations. The Mutual War Risks Associations exist to give insurance to ships of certain flags or ownership, and these are described in Chapter 2. Besides giving all the insurance which is given by the clauses used by the London Market, the Mutual War Risks Associations (or Clubs as they are known) give in addition some very special insurance such as (in some cases) Queen's Enemy Risks insurance (Chapter 41) and insurance against other perils (Chapter 23). It is considered more helpful to give here a description of the London Market's insurance, which is available to all who want it, and to refer the reader who is interested in the Mutual War Risks Associations' insurance to Appendix N, which sets out the British Mutual War Risks Associations' Rules which give their insurance, and to Chapters 41 and 23. It will be noted that the Mutual War Risks Associations insure both hull and machinery risks and freight in one insurance, and do not separate them as does the London Market.

32.2 The insurance of ships by the London Market, both for Marine and War and Strikes risks, requires consideration of two different forms of insurance, the hull and machinery insurance and the insurance for freight. The reason for this is described more fully at para. 22.8. Briefly, if an owner puts a value of £10 million on his ship, he can if he wishes insure the hull and machinery for £8 million and the freight for £2 million. If the ship is lost, he will recover the full £10 million. The freight insurance thus fulfils two different functions; it gives insurance against loss of freight, and it also acts as part of the insurance against the actual corpus of the ship herself.

32.3 A list of the main Hull and Machinery and Freight Clauses, both for Marine and War and Strikes insurance, which are considered in this chapter and, together with the abbreviations which are used, reads:

32.4 In use before 1st October, 1983

    (1) Institute Time Clauses Hulls—dated 1.10.70: "the old Marine Hull Clauses".

    (2) Institute Time Clauses Freight—dated 1.10.70: "the old Marine Freight Clauses".

    (3) Institute War and Strikes Clauses Hulls—Time—dated 1.10.70: "the old War Hull Clauses".

(4) Institute War and Strikes Clauses Freight—Time—dated 1.10.70: "the old War Freight Clauses".

32.5 In use after 1st October, 1983

(5) Institute Time Clauses Hulls—dated 1.10.83: "the new Marine Hull Clauses".

(6) Institute Time Clauses Freight—dated 1.8.89: "the new Marine Freight Clauses".

(7) Institute War and Strikes Clauses Hulls—Time—dated 1.10.83: "the new War Hull Clauses".

(8) Institute War and Strikes Clauses Freight—Time—dated 1.10.83: "the new War Freight Clauses".

32.6 Some minor changes were made to the new Marine Freight Clauses which were introduced in 1983, and the new version is dated 1.8.89. The most important of these reflect the entry into force of the Limitation Convention 1976. Unlike cargo, War and Strikes insurance for ships is insured under one and not two sets of clauses (Chapters 33 and 34).

MARINE CLAUSES IN USE BEFORE 1ST OCTOBER, 1983

Institute Time Clauses Hulls—dated 1.10.70: ("the old Marine Hull Clauses")

32.7 Before 1st October, 1983, ships were insured for hull and machinery risks on the S.G. Form with the old Marine Hull Clauses attached. The history of the S.G. Form from the 17th century until the 1980s is dealt with in Chapter 1.

The insured perils

32.8 The courts have commented on several occasions, notably in the *Salem* case (paras. 12.54–12.63) that the old Marine Hull Clauses did not give insurance on an "all risks" basis as do some of the Cargo Clauses (Chapter 33). They gave insurance for a specified number of insured perils, some of which were to be found on the face of the S.G. Form itself in the magnificent language redolent of a bygone age. This reads:

"Touching the adventures and perils which we the assurers are contented to bear and do take upon us in this voyage: they are of the seas, men of war, fire, enemies, pirates, rovers, thieves, jettisons, letters of mart and countermart, surprisals, takings at sea, arrests, restraints, and detainments of all kings, princes, and people, of what nation, condition, or quality soever, barratry of the master and mariners, and of all other perils, losses, and misfortunes, that have or shall come to the hurt, detriment, or damage of the said goods and merchandises, and ship etc, or any part thereof."

32.9 There was a further provision of somewhat uncertain effect which reads:

"And it is agreed by us, the insurers, that this writing or policy of assurance shall be of as much force and effect as the surest writing or policy of assurance heretofore made in Lombard Street, or in the Royal Exchange, or elsewhere in London."

32.10 Further insured perils were added by Clause 7 of the old Marine Hull

Clauses, known as the *Inchmaree* Clause, and this dealt with machinery break-downs, explosions, negligence of the Master and crew, and contact with other objects. The most important insured peril by far was "perils of the seas", which included collision liability, salvage, and general average, although the two latter matters are the subjects of sections 65 and 66 of the Marine Insurance Act 1906. The sue and labour clause, which appeared on the face of the S.G. Form itself, was a rather permissive provision, which contained none of the compulsion that pertains nowadays (paras. 24.4, 24.5).[1]

The exclusions

32.11 A comparison with the Free of Capture and Seizure Clause ("the F.C. & S. Clause) (para. 1.15), and the Malicious Damage Clause (para. 1.19), which appeared as Clauses 23 and 24 of the old Marine Hull Clauses, will show that these exclusions removed the great majority of the insured perils which are listed on the face of the S.G. Form itself. It is true that the most important and most inclusive perils, the true marine risks, such as "perils of the seas" and "fire" remained, as did barratry and jettison. Everything else, set out as insured perils, was not after all insured; these exclusions effectively removed them. When nuclear weapons appeared, a further exclusion was added. Clause 25 of the old Marine Hulls Clauses reads:

"Warranted free from loss damage liability or expense arising from any weapon of war employing atomic or nuclear fission and/or fusion or other like reaction or radioactive force or matter."

Institute Time Clauses Freight—dated 1.10.70: ("the old Marine Freight Clauses")

32.12 Before 1.10.83, freight was also insured on the S.G. Form with the old Marine Freight Clauses attached. These too did not give insurance on an "all risks" basis. The insured perils and the exclusions were the same as those of the old Marine Hull Clauses except that there was an additional exclusion which reads:

"16. Warranted free of any claim based upon loss of, or frustration of, the insured voyage or adventure caused by arrests restraints or detainments of Kings Princes Peoples Usurpers or persons attempting to usurp power."

Frustration of the voyage or adventure is dealt with at paras. 36.42–36.52.

WAR AND STRIKES CLAUSES IN USE BEFORE 1ST OCTOBER, 1983

Institute War and Strikes Clauses Hulls—Time—dated 1.10.70: ("the old War Hull Clauses")

32.13 Before 1.10.83, ships were insured on the S.G. Form with the old War Hull Clauses attached. Likewise this was not insurance on an "all risks" basis, but for a restricted number of insured perils.

---

1. In spite of its permissive language, the courts have nonetheless held that the assured was under an obligation to sue and labour—paras. 24.19–24.21.

The insured perils

32.14 To the strict legal analyst, the position was confusing. All of the insured perils set out in the S.G. Form, with the exception of "perils of the seas", "fire", "jettisons", and "barratry", were by nature War Risks. The F.C. & S. Clause then removed them from the insurance. It should have been deleted and generally was, but this was sometimes overlooked. The old War Hull Clauses then restored them.

32.15 However this may have been, it was generally accepted by the courts that the definitive list of the insured perils of the old War Hull Clauses was set out in their Clause 1. Clause 1(1)(a) incorporated word for word the F.C. & S. Clause, this time as part of the list of the perils which they insured. Clause 1(1)(b) did the same with the Malicious Damage Clause, and it too became part of the list of insured perils. Clause 25 of the old Marine Hulls Clauses, the Nuclear Exclusion Clause, was not similarly treated, and Nuclear Risks were similarly excluded from the insurance of the old War Hull Clauses. Even so, the process of "dovetailing" whereby the exclusions of the F.C. & S. Clause and the Malicious Damage Clause of the old Marine Hull Clauses (Clauses 23 and 24) became insured perils of the old War Hull Clauses [Clauses 1(1)(a) and 1(1)(b)] was complete. The results were not always happy (paras. 1.15–1.18). In addition, there were some further insured perils set out in Clause 1(2), (3), and (4) which read:

"1. Subject always to the exclusions hereinafter referred to, this insurance covers only . . .
(2) loss of or damage to the property hereby insured caused by:
    (a) hostilities, warlike operations, civil war, revolution, rebellion, insurrection, or civil strife arising therefrom;
    (b) mines, torpedoes, bombs or other engines of war;
(3) loss of or damage to the property hereby insured caused by strikers, locked-out workmen, or persons taking part in labour disturbances, riots or civil commotions;
(4) destruction of or damage to the property hereby insured caused by persons acting maliciously."

32.16 These clauses gave rise to a certain amount of duplication with Clauses 1(i)(a) and (b), and with the insured perils set out on the face of the S.G. Form itself, which is never a desirable feature of any insurance.

The exclusions

32.17 The exclusions were the same as those of the new War Hull Clauses and will be considered there.

Cancellation and automatic termination

32.18 Clause 5 contained the Notice of Cancellation and Automatic Termination of Cover Clause. This is the subject of Chapter 4.

Institute War and Strikes Clauses Freight—Time—dated 1.10.70 ("the old War Freight Clauses")

32.19 The insured perils and the exclusions were the same as those of the old War Hull Clauses, save only that there was an additional exclusion of any claim based on loss of or frustration of the voyage or adventure when this was caused by the arrests, restraints or detainments of Kings, Princes, Peoples, Usurpers or persons attempting to usurp power. This is considered further at paras. 36.42–36.52.

MARINE CLAUSES IN USE AFTER 1ST OCTOBER, 1983

Institute Time Clauses Hulls—dated 1.10.83 ("the new Marine Hull Clauses")

32.20 As is described in Chapter 1, the new MAR form is now used with the new Marine Hull Clauses attached. The MAR form itself (Appendix B) only sets out the details of the subject-matter of the insurance, and does not set out any of the insured perils or exclusions. This is left to the attached clauses.

The insured perils

32.21 Again the new Marine Hull Clauses do not provide insurance on an "all risks" basis, and the insured perils are set out in list form by Clause 6 (Appendix C). If the list looks somewhat restrictive, it must be remembered that the insured perils themselves are very wide in their scope, particularly "perils of the seas", which embrace just about everything that the dangers of the deep and the shallow can do to a ship. There are added provisions to deal with the negligence (or worse) of those in charge of the ship. It will be noted that "piracy", which between 1937 and 1983 was an insured peril of the War and Strikes insurance, is now returned to being an insured peril of the marine insurance. In one sense this is to be welcomed: pirates may not always be violent thieves from outside the ship (Clause 6.1.3), and where "violent theft" is concerned, whether by pirates or by those who do not fall within this very technical description, it avoids consideration of more than one insurance. In another sense, it is less welcome; it cuts across the clear division that the marine clauses insure against the perils of nature and the misdeeds of the crew, whilst the war and strikes clauses insure against "what other people do to the ship".[2]

The exclusions

32.22 The exclusions which are important for the purposes of this work are headed, and will doubtless become known as, the "War Exclusion", the "Strikes Exclusion", the "Malicious Acts Exclusion" and the "Nuclear Exclusion". They are numbered 23, 24, 25 and 26 respectively. They read:

"*23 War Exclusion*

In no case shall this insurance cover loss damage liability or expense caused by
23.1 war civil war revolution rebellion insurrection, or civil strife arising therefrom, or any hostile act by or against a belligerent power
23.2 capture seizure arrest restraint or detainment (barratry and piracy excepted), and the consequences thereof or any attempt thereat
23.3 derelict mines torpedoes bombs or other derelict weapons of war.

2. Piracy remains an insured peril of the Mutual War Risks Associations (para. 20.1).

24 Strikes Exclusion

In no case shall this insurance cover loss damage liability or expense caused by
24.1 strikes, locked-out workmen, or persons taking part in labour disturbances, riots or civil commotions
24.2 any terrorist or any person acting from a political motive.

25 Malicious Acts Exclusion

In no case shall this insurance cover loss damage liability or expense arising from
25.1 the detonation of an explosive
25.2 any weapon of war
and caused by any person acting maliciously or from a political motive.

25 Nuclear Exclusion

In no case shall this insurance cover loss damage liability or expense arising from any weapon of war employing atomic or nuclear fission and/or fusion or other like reaction or radioactive force or matter."

Institute Time Clauses Freight—dated 1.8.89 ("the new Marine Freight Clauses")

32.23 The insured perils are the same as those of the new Marine Hull Clauses, and the differences lie in the exclusions. The only one which is important for the purposes of this work is "Loss of Time" which is dealt with in Chapter 22. The exclusions headed "War Exclusion", "Strikes Exclusion", "Malicious Acts Exclusion" and "Nuclear Exclusion" are the same, and are numbered Clauses 17, 18, 19 and 20 respectively. These clauses were originally introduced on the same date as the other clauses on 1st October, 1983, and have since been altered in some minor respects to reflect the coming into force of the Limitation Convention 1976; hence the different date.

WAR AND STRIKES CLAUSES IN USE AFTER 1ST OCTOBER, 1983

Institute War and Strikes Clauses Hulls—Time dated 1.10.83 ("the new War Hull Clauses")

32.24 The clear division of the War and Strikes Clauses from the Marine Clauses for which Mocatta J. begged and UNCTAD insisted has been achieved (paras. 1.15–1.18). The new War Hull Clauses stand on their own without any dependence on other sets of clauses, and they have their own insured perils and exclusions. There is a measure of incorporation of some of the Marine Clauses, but this does not affect this new characteristic.

The insured perils

32.25 These are contained in Clause 1 which reads:

"*1 Perils*

Subject always to the exclusions hereinafter referred to, this insurance covers loss or damage to the Vessel caused by
1.1 war civil war revolution rebellion insurrection, or civil strife arising therefrom, or any hostile act by or against a belligerent power

1.2 capture seizure arrest restraint or detainment, and the consequences thereof or any attempt thereat

1.3 derelict mines torpedoes bombs or other derelict weapons of war

1.4 strikers, locked-out workmen, or persons taking part in labour disturbances, riots or civil commotions

1.5 any terrorist or any person acting maliciously or from a political motive

1.6 confiscation or expropriation."

32.26 It will be noted that Clauses 1.1 to 1.3 are in exactly similar terms to the War Exclusion Clause of the new Marine Hull Clauses, and this time they are insured perils. The only exception is the omission of the words "(barratry and piracy excepted)". These are insured perils of the new Marine Hull Clauses, and the clear intention is that those clauses should insure barratry, as they have always done, and piracy.

32.27 Similarly, Clauses 1.4 and 1.5 are in exactly the same terms as the Strikes Exclusion Clause of the new Marine Hull Clauses, and again they are this time insured perils.

32.28 There is, however, no specific word for word mention of the perils excluded from the new Marine Hull Clauses by the Malicious Acts exclusion, but it would appear that Clause 1.5 of the new War Hull Clauses is sufficient to include the depredations of these people.

32.29 "Confiscation" and "Expropriation" are added to the list of insured perils (Clause 1.6). There seems to have been some doubt in the minds of the draftsmen whether the insured peril of "seizure" is an adequate term to include appropriation of the ship by legal, or perhaps only semi-legal, means (Chapter 21).

32.30 The Nuclear Exclusion risks which are excluded by Clause 26 of the new Marine Hull Clauses are not included in the list of insured perils of the new War Hull Clauses; indeed they are again specifically excluded, with the result that these risks are not insured by either set of clauses.

Detainment

32.31 Clause 3 contains the 12-month Clause (para. 23.28).

The exclusions

32.32 The passages within the quotation marks are part of Clause 4, whilst those outside the quotation marks are comments on their effects. Clause 4 reads:

"*4 Exclusions*

This insurance excludes

4.1 loss damage liability or expense arising from

4.1.1 any detonation of any weapon of war employing atomic or nuclear fission and/or fusion or other like reaction or radioactive force or matter, hereinafter called a nuclear weapon of war."

32.33 This exclusion is the same as the Nuclear Exclusion of the new Marine Hull Clauses. Unlike some of the Cargo Clauses, this provision is very clear and incisive, and serves to exclude the consequences of such a detonation whether it be purposeful and therefore hostile, in practice, or accidental; neither the new Marine

Hull Clauses nor the new War Hull Clauses give insurance for the loss or damage caused by such a detonation.

32.34 If the detonation is hostile, then it will also cause the automatic termination of the ship's War and Strikes insurance (Chapter 4).

"4.1.2 the outbreak of war (whether there be a declaration of war or not) between any of the following countries:
United Kingdom, United States of America, France, the Union of Soviet Socialist Republics, the People's Republic of China."

32.35 In the context of Clause 4, this exclusion operates to exclude from the War and Strikes insurance the loss or damage which arises out of such a war. Under Clause 5, the insurance will also terminate automatically on its outbreak.

32.36 The U.S.S.R. is now defunct, and the clause is under consideration. It is thought that "U.S.S.R." will be replaced by "the Russian Federation". A simpler provision would be one which provides for the outbreak of war between the Permanent Members of the Security Council of the United Nations Organisation.

32.37 *"4.1.3 requisition or pre-emption."* Requisition and pre-emption are considered by Chapter 21. Nationalisation is not specifically mentioned, but it is arguably excluded from the War and Strikes insurance by Clause 4.1.4.

32.38 Requisition will cause the Automatic Termination of the War and Strikes insurance under Clause 5 (Chapter 4). In this case, the insurance will terminate in respect of the requisitioned ship only; there will be no general termination in respect of the other ships insured if the insurance is a "fleet policy".

"4.1.4 capture seizure arrest restraint detainment confiscation or expropriation by or under the order of the Government or any public or local authority of the country in which the vessel is owned or registered."

32.39 The line of thought that lies behind this exclusion is that the assured is taken to accept the risks of doing business in any particular country, and should look to the government of that country for any compensation. It is suggested that "expropriation" is wide enough to include nationalisation.

"4.1.5 arrest restraint detainment confiscation or expropriation under quarantine regulations or by reason of infringement of any customs or trading regulations."

32.40 The *Anita* and the *Wondrous* cases will serve as a demonstration of this exclusion (paras. 13.35–13.44 and 22.52, 22.53).

"4.1.6 the operation of ordinary judicial process, failure to provide security or to pay any fine or penalty or any financial cause."

32.41 Ordinary judicial process is considered by Chapter 25. Fines are a matter for the ship's Protection and Indemnity insurance.

"4.1.7 piracy (but this exclusion shall not affect cover under Clause 1.4)."

32.42 Far from being an insured peril of the new War Hull Clauses, piracy is an exclusion from the insurance except in one limited aspect—the exclusion is not to affect the piratical acts of strikers, locked-out workmen etc. Since the *Andreas Lemos* case (paras. 20.33–20.38), it can be regarded as settled that piracy can only take place "on the seas", and it is difficult to see how these activities, which essentially take place on the shore, can ever become piracy. It is true that stevedores working on a ship in the roads may go on strike and then forcibly take over the ship. If they do so, they could be said to be pirates pure and simple, and as such concern the marine insurance (para. 20.1). At first sight the words in brackets present an unwelcome complication with the possibility of double insurance between the marine and the War and Strikes insurance. It is suggested, in advance of any judicial determination of the words, that their proper reading is to the effect that if the malefactors start off as strikers etc., they remain "Strikers" whatever they subsequently do, and the War and Strikes insurance should respond for what they do to the ship, irrespective of what characteristic they later acquire. The point is not free of doubt however, and the possibility that they start off as strikers etc., and later by their actions become pirates, should be borne in mind.

"4.4 any claim for expenses arising from delay except such expenses as would be recoverable in principle in English Law and practice under the York–Antwerp Rules 1974."

32.43 "Delay" is a matter which is considered in Chapter 22.

32.44 Clauses 4.2 and 4.3 have not been quoted in the list: they are respectively exclusions of matters which come within the ambit of the Marine Clauses, and a double insurance clause.

Cancellation and termination

32.45 Clause 5 consists of the Cancellation and Automatic Termination of Cover Clause. This is the subject of Chapter 4.

Incorporation

32.46 Clause 2 of the new War Hull Clauses incorporates by reference several provisions of the new Marine Hull Clauses, and the most important for the purposes of this work are:

32.47 (1) Clause 7 reads:

"7. Pollution Hazard
This insurance covers loss of or damage to the vessel caused by any governmental authority acting under the powers vested in it to prevent or mitigate a pollution hazard, or threat thereof, resulting directly from damage to the vessel for which the Underwriters are liable under this insurance . . . "

32.48 In the wake of the *Torrey Canyon* disaster in 1967, some governments armed themselves with legal powers to take steps to mitigate a pollution hazard following a casualty at sea. In doing so, they have power to damage or destroy the ship. The *Torrey Canyon* for instance was bombed by the Fleet Air Arm to try to burn up the remaining oil. At first sight, the damage or destruction may seem closer to the War and Strikes insurance rather than the Marine insurance, but at the time the desire was that the damage or destruction would follow the insured peril of the original casualty. If this was a casualty concerning the Marine insurance, then that insurance would respond for the damage or destruction, and likewise the War and Strikes insurance would respond if the original casualty arose out of a War and Strikes risk.

32.49 The author would respectfully agree with the learned writers of Hudson and Allen's *The Institute Clauses Handbook* (1986 edition) that this result has been achieved. The important point is that the pollution hazard, or its threat, must result directly from an insured peril of the respective insurance. That will determine which insurance should respond for the subsequent damage or destruction of the ship.

32.50 (2) Clause 8, the 3/4 liability collision clause (page 334).

32.51 (3) Clause 13, the Duty of Assured (sue and labour) Clause. Sue and Labour is considered in Chapter 24.

32.52 (4) Clause 19, the Constructive Total Loss Clause. Constructive total loss is considered in Chapter 27.

Institute War and Strikes Clauses Freight—Time—dated 1.10.83 ("the new War Freight Clauses")

The insured perils

32.53 Clause 1 reads:

"*1 Perils*

Subject always to the exclusions hereinafter referred to, this insurance covers
1.1   loss (total or partial) of the subject-matter insured caused by
1.1.1 war civil war revolution rebellion insurrection, or civil strife arising therefrom, or any hostile act by or against a belligerent power
1.1.2 capture seizure arrest restraint or detainment, and the consequences thereof or any attempt thereat
1.1.3 derelict mines torpedoes bombs or other derelict weapons of war,
1.2   loss (total or partial) of the subject-matter insured arising from loss of or damage to the vessel caused by
1.2.1 strikers, locked-out workmen, or persons taking part in labour disturbances, riots or civil commotions
1.2.2 any terrorist or any person acting maliciously or from a political motive
1.2.3 confiscation or expropriation."

32.54 The insured perils are word for word the same as those of the new War Hull Clauses, but the difference lies in Clauses 1.1 and 1.2, and this affects the operation of the new War Freight Clauses. The new War Hull Clauses need only the happening of an insured peril to the ship to begin to operate. The same is true of Clause 1.1 of the new War Freight Clauses, but Clause 1.2 will only begin to operate if there is firstly loss or damage to the ship. This could result in loss of freight not being insured in circumstances where it could be assumed that insurance would exist. The reason for this is not immediately clear, and seems to be historical; Clause 1.2 is a virtual repeat of Clause 1(3) of the old War Freight Clauses.

32.55 It will be noted that Clauses 1.1.1 to 1.1.3 include all the risks set out in the War Exclusion Clause of the new Marine Freight Clauses, and this time they are insured perils. The only exception is the omission of the words "(barratry and piracy excepted)". These are insured perils of the new Marine Freight Clauses, and the clear intention is that those clauses should give insurance for barratry and piracy. Similarly Clauses 1.2.1 and 1.2.2 include all the risks set out in the Strikes Exclusion Clauses of the new Marine Freight Clauses.

32.56 There is no specific word for word mention of the risks set out in the Malicious Acts Exclusion of the new Freight Marine Clauses, but it would appear that Clause 1.2.2 is sufficient to include the depredations of these people.

32.57 "Confiscation" and "Expropriation" are added to the list of insured perils (Clause 1.2.3). There seems to have been some doubt in the minds of the draftsmen whether the insured peril of "seizure" is an adequate term to include appropriation by legal, or perhaps only semi-legal, means (Chapter 21).

32.58 The Nuclear Exclusion risks which are excluded by Clause 20 of the new Marine Freight Clauses are not included in the list of insured perils of the new War Freight Clauses; indeed they are specifically excluded, with the result that these risks are not insured by either set of clauses.

Detainment

32.59 Detainment is considered at para. 23.28, and it will be seen that the 12-month Clause of the new War Freight Clauses is slightly different. The reason for this is that if the ship is a constructive total loss, it is well established that the freight insurance will pay the amount insured in full. The 12-month Clause in the new War Freight Clauses follows this line of thought.

The exclusions

32.60 These are the same as those of the new War Hull Clauses except that there is an additional exclusion. Clause 4.5 reads:

"4 This insurance excludes
  4.5 any claim based upon loss of or frustration of any voyage or adventure."

Frustration of the voyage or adventure is considered at paras. 36.42–36.52.

Termination

32.61 Clause 5 consists of the Cancellation and Automatic Termination Clause. This is the subject of Chapter 4.

Incorporation

32.62 Clause 2 of the new War Freight Clauses incorporates several clauses of the new Marine Freight Clauses. At first sight, Clause 7 of the new Marine Freight Clauses, which is their insured perils clause, is also incorporated; this must be a mistake, particularly as Clause 4.2 excludes anything insured by the new Marine Freight Clauses. Clause 2 further incorporates the new Marine Freight Clauses dated 1.10.83, whereas these were changed on 1.8.89 to include a reference to the Limitation Convention 1976. It seems that when the new marine clauses were introduced in 1989, the necessity to make a small alteration to Clause 2 was overlooked. The clear intention is to incorporate clauses from the new Marine Freight Clauses dated 1.8.89 (without their insured perils clause), and the following description will proceed on this basis.

32.63 The most important for the purposes of this work are:

(1) Clause 8, the Pollution Hazard Clause. This is the same as the similar clause in the new War Hulls Clauses (para. 32.47).
(2) Clause 9, the Freight Collision Clause.
(3) Clause 14, the Loss of Time Clause. This is considered in Chapter 22.
(4) Clause 15, the Total Loss Clause. This clause provides that if the ship becomes a total loss, whether actual or constructive, the amount insured by the new War Freight Clauses will be paid in full. This also is considered in Chapter 22.

There is no sue and labour provision in the freight insurance clauses.

English law and pracitce

32.64 All the new clauses which were introduced in 1983, whether for Marine or War and Strikes insurance, contain at the head of the respective clauses, a provision which reads: "This insurance is subject to English Law and Practice."

32.65 At the time that it first took effect in 1983, this provision would have been fully effective to give the English courts sole and exclusive jurisdiction. Since that date however, the parts of the Civil Jurisdiction and Judgments Act 1982, which give effect to the Civil Jurisdiction Convention, have been brought into force in 1987. It is still too early to say what effect the Convention will have on this provision, but it can be said that its impact in other directions, particularly in the field of jurisdiction provisions in bills of lading which are also contractual by nature, has already been considerable.

CHAPTER 33

Cargo

INTRODUCTORY

33.1 The insurance of cargo is considered in this chapter and in Chapters 34, 35 and 36, and in each the abbreviations which immediately follow will be used. This chapter gives a brief history of the way in which cargo was insured before 1st January, 1982, and goes on to describe how cargo is insured today. This bein a work on marine war risks, Chapter 34 describes how cargo is presently insured against War and Strikes risks. Chapter 36 considers the insured perils and the exclusions, whilst Chapter 35 deals with the insurance of special cargoes.

33.2 A list of the main cargo clauses which are considered by this chapter and by Chapters 34, 35 and 36, together with any abbreviations that are used, is as follows:

33.3 In use before 1982

(1) Institute Cargo Clauses (All Risks)—1.1.63.
(2) Institute Cargo Clauses (F.P.A.)—1.1.63.
(3) Institute Cargo Clauses (W.A.)—1.1.63.
(4) Institute War Clauses (Cargo)—11.3.80—"the old cargo War Clauses".
(5) Institute Strikes Riots & Civil Commotions Clauses—1.1.63—"the old cargo Strikes Clauses".

33.4 In use after 1st January, 1982

(6) Institute Cargo Clauses (A)—1.1.82—"the (A) Clauses".
(7) Institute Cargo Clauses (B)—1.1.82—"the (B) Clauses".
(8) Institute Cargo Clauses (C)—1.1.82—"the (C) Clauses".
(9) Institute War Clauses (Cargo)—1.1.82—"the new cargo War Clauses".
(10) Institute Strikes Clauses (Cargo)—1.1.82—"the new cargo Strikes Clauses".

CARGO MARINE CLAUSES—PRE-1982

33.5 Before 1982, cargo was insured on the S.G. Form with the relevant Institute Cargo Clauses attached. There were three main types of Institute Cargo Clauses for insurance of cargo against marine risks:

385

The clauses and the insured perils

(1) Institute Cargo Clauses (All Risks)—1.1.63

33.6 These clauses were first introduced in this format on 1st January, 1951, and set out to give cover against all risk of loss and damage during the transit of the goods insured with however, express exclusions for delay and for damage caused by inherent vice.[1]

(2) Institute Cargo Clauses (F.P.A.)—1.1.63

33.7 These clauses gave cover on a "Warranted free from Particular Average" basis, and thus for total loss only, unless the carrying ship was stranded, sunk or burnt, when the full measure of the assured's loss, even for partial damage, would be insured.

(3) Institute Cargo Clauses (W.A.)—1.1.63

33.8 These clauses gave cover on the same basis as the Institute Cargo Clauses (F.P.A.) except that partial loss was covered in excess of the minimum percentage or franchise stipulated in the individual policy.

33.9 All these clauses gave insurance cover from the time that the insured goods left the warehouse or storage place at the commencement of their journey until they reached their destination. Although mainly insurance cover for a voyage by sea, some insurance cover was given for carriage overland. They were all in the same terms except for Clause 5 in each case, and this clause can be regarded as the clause defining the insurance cover and describing the insured perils in each separate instance.

The exclusions

33.10 Each set of clauses contained exclusions of War Risks in identical terms:

33.11 *Clause 12.* This contained the Free of Capture and Seizure (F.C. & S.) Clause which provided that the cargo marine policy was not to pay for loss or damage which arose from the risks included in this clause.[2] Some bold print provided however, that it could be deleted, and this was a departure from the practice of marine policies for ships; if it was deleted, then the current cargo Institute War Clauses, the old Cargo War Clauses, would be included in the marine insurance.

33.12 *Clause 13.* This provided that the cargo marine policy was not to pay for loss or damage caused by strikers, locked-out workmen, or persons taking part in labour disturbances, riots or civil commotions, or resulting from strikes, lock-outs, labour disturbances, riots or civil commotions. It too contained a similar provision

1. For comments on "all risks", see paras. 33.41, 33.42.
2. The text of the clause is set out at para. 1.15.

for its deletion; if it was deleted, then the current cargo Institute Strikes Riots and Civil Commotions Clauses, the old Cargo Strikes Clauses, would be included in the marine insurance.

33.13 It should be noted that there was no similar provision in the cargo marine clauses to that contained in the Institute Time Clauses (Hulls)—1.10.70, whose Clause 25 read:

"Warranted free from loss damage liability or expense arising from any weapon of war employing atomic or nuclear fission &/or fusion or other like reaction or radioactive force or matter."

33.14 Whilst it may be said, albeit with some doubts, that the F.C. & S. Clause may have excluded the loss or damage resulting from a hostile nuclear explosion from the cargo marine insurance cover, it would seem, particularly in the case of the Institute Cargo Clauses (All Risks) Clauses, that insurance cover for a practice or an accidental explosion of an atomic weapon was not excluded (paras. 36.11–36.25).

Open Cover and Floating Policies

33.15 Before leaving the description of the cargo marine clauses before the fundamental changes which took effect on 1st January, 1982, a brief mention should be made of the Institute Standard Conditions for Open Covers and the Institute Standard Conditions for Floating Policies, both of which date from 1st January, 1930. These were incorporated into the Institute Standard Conditions for Cargo Contracts, whose latest version which was in use before 1982 was dated 26th March, 1980. Fundamentally, this was a form of open cover allowing for periodic declarations to be made whenever the necessity arose. It contained no explicit conditions or exclusions such as the F.C. & S. or the Institute Strikes Riots and Civil Commotions Clauses, although its Clause 7 read:

"Should the risks of war, strikes, riots and civil commotions be included in the cover granted by this contract the relevant Institute War Clauses and Institute Strikes Riots and Civil Commotions Clauses shall apply."

33.16 There was a degree of imprecision here, beginning with the clarity of the intentions of the parties whether War and Strikes insurance cover was or was not to be given, and if a dispute arose, there might have been some uncertainty. In the Institute Cargo Clauses, whether All Risks, F.P.A., or W.A., Clauses 12 and 13 provided that such insurance cover was not to be given unless these clauses were deleted. Deletion was a deliberate and also an affirmative act, and if Clauses 12 and 13 were deleted, then War and Strikes insurance cover was given by the cargo Marine Clauses (paras. 33.11, 33.12). It seems curious that the modest degree of precision attained by the Institute Cargo Clauses was not adopted for the open cover.

CARGO WAR AND STRIKES CLAUSES—PRE-1982

33.17 Cargo was insured for War Risks by two separate sets of clauses:

The clauses and the insured perils

(1) Institute War Clauses (Cargo)—11.3.80 ("the old cargo War Clauses")

33.18 These gave insurance for risks excluded from the Standard Form of English Marine Policy by the F.C. & S. Clause, and thus gave insurance cover for the risks which were excluded from the cargo marine policy by its Clause 12. Further insured perils were specifically added thus:

"1.2 Loss of or damage to the interest insured caused by
   1.2.1 hostilities, warlike operations, civil war, revolution, rebellion, insurrection or civil strife arising therefrom
   1.2.2. mines, torpedoes, bombs or other engines of war."

and in a separate paragraph:

"1.3 general average and salvage charges incurred for the purpose of avoiding, or in connection with the avoidance of, loss by a peril insured against by these clauses . . . ."

33.19 Again, as in the case of the war policies for ships, there was a measure of duplication, never a desirable feature of any insurance policy, with the insured perils imported into the old cargo War Clauses by the F.C. & S. Clause.

(2) Institute Strikes Riots and Civil Commotions Clauses 1.1.63 ("the old cargo Strikes Clauses")

33.20 These clauses gave insurance cover for some, but not all, of the risks excluded from the cargo marine policy by Clause 13. This excluded from the cargo marine insurance cover not only loss or damage caused by strikers, locked-out workmen, or persons taking part in labour disturbances, riots or civil commotions, but also loss or damage resulting from strikes, lockouts, labour disturbances, riots or civil commotions. The point can be made clearer by quoting the insured perils of the old cargo Strikes Clauses thus:

"1. This insurance covers loss of or damage to the property hereby insured caused by
   (a) Strikers, locked-out workmen, or persons taking part in labour disturbances, riots or civil commotions;
   (b) persons acting maliciously."

33.21 The old cargo Strikes Clauses were intended to give insurance cover only for physical loss or damage which arose out of these insured perils; they were not intended to insure delay, particularly delay resulting from a strike, so they were:

"2. Warranted free of
   (1) Loss or damage proximately caused by
     (a) delay, inherent vice or nature of the property hereby insured
     (b) the absence, shortage or withholding of labour of any description whatsoever during any strike, lock-out, labour disturbance, riot or civil commotion."

33.22 Some expenses for delay were insured if they arose in general average, but the clauses were further warranted free of:

"2. (iii) loss or damage caused by hostilities warlike operations, civil war, or by revolution rebellion insurrection or civil strife arising therefrom."

Thus there was to be no duplication with the insurance given by the old cargo War Clauses.

GENERAL COMMENTS ON CARGO CLAUSES IN USE BEFORE 1982

33.23 Before leaving the insurance of cargo as it was effected before 1982, there are some general points that should be noted:

1 The old cargo War Clauses contained an exclusion of loss damage or expense arising from any hostile use of a nuclear weapon. This was not to be found in the old cargo Strikes Clauses.

2 The old cargo Strikes Clauses gave insurance cover to the goods during the whole period of their journey from the time that they left their starting point until the time that they arrived at their destination in terms which were similar to those of the cargo Marine Clauses. They gave insurance cover whilst the goods were ashore. The Waterborne Agreement, which provided that certain war risks could only be insured whilst the insured goods were afloat, prevented the old cargo War Clauses from doing the same. Thus the old cargo War Clauses could only give insurance cover between loading and discharge, or in other words whilst the insured goods were afloat. The provisions are complicated, and are better considered in the context of the new cargo War Clauses.

3 The old cargo War Clauses excluded any claim based on loss of, or frustration of, the insured voyage or adventure caused by arrest restraints or detentions of Kings Princes Peoples Usurpers or persons attempting to usurp power. This too will be considered in the context of the post–1982 clauses (paras. 36.42–36.52). There was no similar provision in the old cargo Strikes Clauses.

4 Neither the old cargo War Clauses nor the old cargo Strikes Clauses contained the Notice of Cancellation and Automatic Termination of Cover Clause (Chapter 4). There were not therefore the problems with additional premiums or automatic termination on the detonation of a nuclear weapon or the outbreak of war between the great powers which were (and still are) of concern to ships.

5 Undoubtedly the draftsmen of the pre–1982 clauses did, in general, achieve their object to insure the cargo War Risks by insurance which was separate from that which insured the cargo marine risks in the same way as they had done for ships (para. 1.15), and that the marine, old cargo War Clauses and old cargo Strikes Clauses complimented one another by means of similar "dovetailing". On the other hand, the same strictures which Mocatta J. and UNCTAD have made (paras. 1.15, 1.17, 1.18), applied with equal force. In the case of cargo insurance, there was at least one further criticism. Revolution, rebellion and insurrection or the civil strife arising therefrom were insured perils of the old cargo War Clauses, whereas civil commotions was an insured peril of the old cargo Strikes Clauses. A study of Chapters 8 and 17 will show how wafer-thin the

distinctions between these insured perils can be. There would thus have been some unwelcome doubt which of the two clauses was concerned with any particular incident. Nevertheless, it is all too easy to be critical, and the difficulties facing the draftsmen are explained in Chapter 1.

CARGO MARINE CLAUSES—POST 1ST JANUARY, 1982

Introductory

33.24 The welcome rationalisation, indeed metamorphosis, of the marine and war clauses for ships is described in Chapter 1. It was preceded by the same process for the Institute Cargo Clauses, both marine and war, which took effect on 1st January, 1982. They are now in a very different form to the Cargo Institute Clauses in use before that date. Again, all are intended for use as attachments to the MAR form (Appendix B) which has the same characteristics as that which is used for ships. Again, the MAR form contains none of the insured perils; they, together with the exclusions, are all set out in the respective Institute Cargo Clauses in an easy-to-read format. Cargo is now insured for marine risks:

The clauses and the insured perils

(1) Institute Cargo Clause (A)—1.1.82 ("the (A) Clauses")

33.25 These give insurance cover against "all risks" except as provided in Clauses 4, 5, 6 and 7.[3]

(2) Institute Cargo Clause (B)—1.1.82 ("the (B) Clauses")

33.26 These give insurance cover only in respect of a specific list of insured perils which reads:

"*1 Risks Covered*:

This insurance covers, except as provided in Clauses 4, 5, 6 and 7 below,
  1.1 loss or damage to the subject matter insured reasonably attributable to
1.1.1 fire or explosion
1.1.2 vessel or craft being stranded grounded sunk or capsized
1.1.3 overturning or derailment of land conveyance
1.1.4 collision or contact of vessel craft or conveyance with any external object other than water
1.1.5 discharge of cargo at port of distress
1.1.6 earthquake volcanic eruption or lightning,
  1.2 loss of or damage to the subject-matter insured caused by
1.2.1 general average sacrifice
1.2.2 jettison or washing overboard
1.2.3 entry of sea lake or riverwater into vessel craft hold conveyance container liftvan or place of storage,
  1.3 total loss of any package lost overboard or dropped whilst loading on to, or unloading from, vessel or craft."

---

3. The nature of "all risks" is described at paras. 33.41, 33.42.

(3) Institute Cargo Clauses (C)—1.1.82 ("the (C) Clauses")

33.27 These give insurance cover only in respect of a specific list of insured perils except as provided by Clauses 4, 5, 6 and 7. The list of insured perils is the same as in the (B) Clauses except:

1.1.6 is omitted

1.2.2 jettison only is an insured peril

1.2.3 is omitted

   1.3 is omitted

The exclusions

33.28 Clauses 4, 5, 6 and 7 are in very similar, but not totally identical terms. This work will deal with exceptions of peculiar interest to War and Strikes Risks.

Nuclear exclusion

33.29 All three sets of clauses contain the nuclear exclusion clause which reads:

"4. In no case shall this insurance cover
4.7 loss damage or expense arising from the use of any weapon of war employing atomic or nuclear fission &/or fusion or other like reaction or radioactive force or matter."

In the (B) and (C) Clauses this clause is numbered 4.8.

Deliberate damage

33.30 The (B) and (C) Clauses contain an exclusion of deliberate damage or destruction thus:

"4. In no case shall this insurance cover
4.7 deliberate damage to or deliberate destruction of the subject matter insured or any part thereof by the wrongful act of any person or persons."

33.31 This clause does not appear in the (A) Clauses, but then the (A) Clauses are on an "all risks" basis, whereas the (B) and (C) Clauses give insurance cover only for a limited number of insured perils. This Clause 4.7 is of particular interest to piracy (para. 36.6).

War exclusion

33.32 All three sets of clauses contain the War Exclusion Clause. This reads:

"6. *War Exclusion Clause*

In no case shall this insurance cover loss damage or expense caused by
6.1 war civil war revolution rebellion insurrection, or civil strife arising therefrom, or any hostile act by or against a belligerent power
6.2 capture seizure arrest restraint or detainment (piracy excepted)*, and the consequences thereof or any attempt threat

---

* The (A) Clauses give insurance on an "all risks" basis, and this includes piracy. Hence it is necessary to include the words "(piracy excepted)" in order not to prejudice this insurance. The (B) and (C) Clauses only give insurance against a listed number of insured perils which do not include piracy, and the bracketed words are therefore unnecessary; they are therefore omitted from their version of Clause 6.

6.3 derelict mines torpedoes bombs or other derelict weapons of war."

Strikes exclusion

33.33 All three sets of clauses contain the Strikes Exclusion Clause. This reads:

"7. Strikes Exclusion Clause
In no case shall this insurance cover loss damage or expense
7.1 caused by strikers, locked-out workmen, or persons taking part in labour disturb-ances, riots or civil commotions
7.2 resulting from strikes, lock-outs, labour disturbances, riots or civil commotions
7.3 caused by any terrorist or any person acting from a political motive."

It should be noted that, unlike Clauses 12 and 13 of the Institute Clauses which where in use before 1982, there is no "bold print" allowing for the deletion of Clauses 6 and 7.

GENERAL COMMENTS ON THE MARINE CARGO CLAUSES IN USE POST 1ST JANUARY, 1982

33.34 (1) It is a most welcome development that in the case of cargo insurance, as in the case of insurance for ships, the cargo Marine Clauses have concentrated on the insurance of, and the exclusion of, easily recognisable perils with a minimum emphasis on the motives of the people who cause the damage. As will be seen from a study of the *Pan-Am* and the *Spinney's* cases,[3a] the courts have found immense difficulties in defining the motives of people which might make all the difference whether a peril is an insured peril or an excluded risk in any particular instance.

33.35 (2) No mention is made here of a large number of the exceptions to the insurance cover given by the (A), (B) and (C) Clauses because they are not, or are not likely to be, of interest in the war risks context.

33.36 (3) Clauses 8, 9 and 10 deal with the period of the cargo marine insurance cover. They are all in common form, and provide for the insurance cover to start at the time the insured goods leave the warehouse or place of storage until the time they reach their destination. Even though this is insurance cover for a voyage by sea, insurance cover is provided whilst the goods are travelling overland. The pro-visions are complicated even if they are comprehensive. Special considerations apply to the war risks insurance cover, and the period that the insurance cover is in effect is, in a work devoted to the study of war risks, best left to a study of the duration provisions of the new cargo War Clauses and the new cargo Strikes Clauses (paras. 34.15–34.32).

33.37 (4) Clause 13 is the Constructive Total Loss Clause, and is in common form in the (A), (B) and (C) Clauses. It reads:

"No claim for Constructive Total Loss shall be recoverable hereunder unless the subject-matter insured is reasonably abandoned either on account of its actual total loss appearing to be unavoidable or because the cost of recovering, reconditioning and forwarding the subject-matter to the destination to which it is insured would exceed its value on arrival."

33.38 This clause is not new, appearing as it does as Clause 6 of the Institute Cargo Clauses in use before 1982. Its wording follows and expands upon the text of

---

3a. Paras. 6.16–6.26, 8.13, 8.30, 8.31, 17.13, 17.24–17.26 and 7.7–7.16, 8.17, 8.18, 17.27–17.29.

section 60(1) and (2)(iii) of the Marine Insurance Act 1906. By its opening words, it excludes the application of section (2)(i) and (ii) which are of much greater import-ance in the context of War and Strikes insurance for ships.

33.39 (5) Under the headings of Minimising Losses and Avoidance of Delay there are Clauses 16, 17 and 18 as sue and labour provisions. These are in a much simpler form than those contained in the marine insurance cover for ships (Appen-dix C), and are a welcome extension of the sue and labour provisions of the Insti-tute Cargo Clauses in use before 1982. They are all in common form in the (A), (B) and (C) Clauses, and also in the new cargo War Clauses and the new cargo Strikes Clauses. They will be considered in this latter context (paras. 34.33–34.35).

33.40 (6) Clause 19 is common to the (A), (B) and (C) Clauses, and provides that the insurance is subject to English Law and Practice. This Clause is also com-mon to the new cargo War Clauses and the new cargo Strikes Clauses, and will be considered in this latter context (paras. 34.39).

33.41 (7) In the days of the S.G. Form, it could be said that there was some doubt whether the term "all risks", which was contained in the Institute Cargo Clauses which were attached to it, conflicted with the limited list of insured perils which were set out on its face. These doubts were, however, set at rest in the light of the judgment of Lord Birkenhead L.C., in *British and Foreign Marine Insurance Co. Ltd.* v. *Gaunt*[4] that "all risks" means some event "due to some fortuitous cir-cumstances or casualty". Lord Birkenhead drew heavily on the judgment of Wal-ton J., in *Schloss Bros.* v. *Stevens*[5] where some bales only reached their destination in Columbia 18 months after their dispatch from the coastal port. They were much damaged by atmospheric damp, rain water and vermin. Their "all risks" insurance entitled their owners to recover. This line of reasoning was followed by Croom-Johnson J., in *Theodorou* v. *Chester*[6] where some sponges were carried across the Atlantic twice and were damaged by water, dirt, paint and other substances. Again their "all risks" insurance allowed recovery, although there was much to be said for the underwriter's contentions that they had only suffered from the normal hazards of their two voyages. Sellers J. also followed it in *F.W. Berk & Co. Ltd.* v. *Style*[7] when dealing with an "all risks" case, even though he found in favour of the under-writers because the goods had been inadequately packed and this had caused the damage. Goddard L.J. took the same course in *London and Provincial Leather Processes Ltd.* v. *Hudson.*[8] Some skins, which were insured against "all and every risks howsoever arising", were being treated in Germany when the firm treating them went bankrupt. They were seized by the German Administrator in Bank-ruptcy. Even though there was some doubt about his right to do so, the owners were held entitled to recover. In a more recent case, the *Integrated Container* case (paras. 24.19–24.21), neither Neill J., nor any of the judges of the Court of Appeal had any doubts that the assured was entitled to recover where his containers had become scattered and stranded all over the Far East due to the bankruptcy of the lessee. Dillon L.J. expressed the view:

4. [1921] 2 A.C. 41, H.L.
5. [1906] 2 K.B. 665.
6. [1951] 1 Lloyd's Rep. 204.
7. [1955] 3 All E.R. 625, Q.B.
8. [1939] 2 K.B. 724.

"I can see no reason why the risk of lawful sale by a third party should be excluded. The plaintiffs effectively lose their containers whether the sale is lawful under a lien—port regulations, or the process of judicial execution—or unlawful."

33.42 Nowadays the MAR form, by introducing no insured perils of its own, avoids this complication of the S.G. Form, but it is worth noting that even when it was in use, the courts were prepared to hold that "all risks" was a wide and all inclusive term.

OPEN INSURANCE COVER

33.43 Before leaving this description of the cargo Marine Clauses, the (A), (B) and (C) Clauses, it should be noted that the Institute Standard Conditions for Cargo Contracts (paras. 33.15, 33.16) has also been updated and now bears the date 1st April, 1982. They retain the same character as a form of open cover allowing for periodic declarations as the necessity arises. Clause 7 has only been changed to reflect the new names for the new cargo War Clauses and the new cargo Strikes Clauses. It now reads:

"Should the risks of war, strikes, riots and civil commotions be included in the cover granted by this contract the relevant Institute War Clauses and Institute Strikes Clauses shall apply."

33.44 This seems curious, because Clauses 6 and 7 of the (A), (B) and (C) Clauses no longer have any similar "bold print", which is to be found in Clauses 12 and 13 of the Institute Cargo Clauses in use before 1982, that they could be deleted with the effects that are noted at paras. 33.11, 33.12. This is one instance where rather haphazard wording has survived the alterations which took effect on 1st January, 1982.

CARGO WAR AND STRIKES CLAUSES—POST 1ST JANUARY, 1982

33.45 These too have been extensively revised in a most welcome fashion. Since this is a work on war risks, consideration of the relevant clauses is given in a chapter of their own (Chapter 34).

CHAPTER 34

Cargo War and Strikes Clauses—post 1st January, 1982

INTRODUCTORY

34.1 Unlike ships, cargo is insured for War and Strikes under two separate sets of clauses. These also are clauses attached to the MAR form, and again they contain all their insured perils, together with their relevant exclusions, set out in an easy-to-read format.

Institute War Clauses (Cargo)—dated 1.1.82 ("the new cargo War Clauses")

The insured perils

34.2 The list of insured perils reads:

"Risks covered

1. This insurance covers, except as provided in clauses 3 and 4 below, loss of or damage to the subject-matter insured caused by
1.1 war civil war revolution rebellion insurrection, or civil strife arising therefrom, or any hostile act by or against a belligerent power
1.2 capture seizure arrest restraint or detainment, arising from risks covered under 1.1 above, and the consequences thereof or any attempt thereat
1.3 derelict mines torpedoes bombs or other derelict weapons of war.
2. This insurance covers general average and salvage charges, adjusted or determined according to the contract of affreightment and/or the governing law and practice, incurred to avoid or in connection with the avoidance of loss from a risk covered under these clauses."

34.3 All the risks excluded by Clause 6 of the (A), (B) and (C) Clauses are included, this time as insured perils. There is, however, one important difference between these insured perils and those of Clause 1.2 of the War and Strikes insurance for ships (Appendix D). In the latter, capture, seizure etc., are insured perils in their own right, and are not dependent on other insured perils first arising. In the case of cargo, Clause 1.2 of the new cargo War Clauses is qualified by the words "arising from risks covered under 1.1 above". An insured peril of Clause 1.1 has first to arise before there can be any insurance under Clause 1.2 (paras. 36.26–36.29).

Institute Strikes Clauses (Cargo)—dated 1.1.82 ("the new cargo Strikes Clauses")

The insured perils

34.4 The list of insured perils reads:

395

"Risks covered

1. This insurance covers, except as provided in clauses 3 and 4 below, loss of or damage to the subject matter insured caused by

1.1 strikers, locked-out workmen, or persons taking part in labour disturbances, riots or civil commotions

1.2 any terrorist or any person acting from a political motive.

2. This insurance covers general average and salvage charges, adjusted or determined according to the contract of affreightment and/or the governing law and practice, incurred to avoid or in connection with the avoidance of loss from a risk covered under these clauses."

34.5 All the risks excluded by Clauses 7.1 and 7.3 of the (A), (B) and (C) Clauses are included, this time as insured perils, but not the risks excluded by Clause 7.2. The new cargo Strikes Clauses will therefore give insurance for the loss or damage which these people do to the cargo, but neither the new cargo Marine Clauses nor the new cargo Strikes Clauses insure the economic loss which they cause by going on strike or otherwise delaying the dispatch of the cargo (paras. 36.31–36.34). This principle is reinforced by the Exclusion Clause 3.7 of the new cargo Strikes Clauses (paras. 36.31–36.34).

THE EXCLUSIONS—INTRODUCTORY

34.6 Clauses 3 and 4 are very similar to one another in both the new cargo War Clauses and the new cargo Strikes Clauses. Some can be dealt with very briefly because they are unlikely to arise in the context of insurance against what other people do to the insured object which is the very essence of war risks insurance. Others need fuller treatment. Some of the provisions of Clause 3 provide in each case that there is to be no claim for ordinary leakage or ordinary wear and tear, for insufficiency of packaging or for inherent vice. Other exclusions are of greater interest to insurance against what other people do to the insured object.

Exclusion clauses which are common to both the new cargo War Clauses and the new cargo Strikes Clauses

34.7 In each case Clause 3 reads:

"3. In no case shall this insurance cover

3.1 loss damage or expense attributable to the wilful misconduct of the Assured (paras. 36.60, 36.61, Chapter 29.)

3.5 loss damage or expense caused by delay, even though the delay be caused by a risk insured against (except expenses payable under Clause 2 above) (paras. 22.25–22.59.)

3.6 loss damage or expense arising from insolvency or financial default of the owners managers charterers or operators of the vessel (paras. 35.35, 36.36.)

3.7 any claim based upon loss of or frustration of the voyage or adventure." (Paras. 36.42–36.52.)

(Clause 3.7 is numbered 3.8 in the new cargo Strikes Clauses.)

34.8 Whilst Clause 4 reads:

"4.—4.1 In no case shall this insurance cover loss damage or expense arising from
   unseaworthiness of vessel or craft
   unfitness of vessel craft conveyance container or liftvan for the safe carriage of the subject-matter insured
   where the Assured or their servants are privy to such unseaworthiness or unfitness, at the time the subject-matter insured is loaded therein.

4.2 The Underwriters waive any breach of the implied warranties of seaworthiness of the ship and fitness of the ship to carry the subject-matter insured to destination, unless the Assured or their servants are privy to such unseaworthiness or unfitness." (Para. 36.41.)

Exceptions clauses which are individual to either the new cargo War Clauses or to the new cargo Strikes Clauses

34.9 Other exclusions clauses are individual to one or other of the two sets of clauses.

(1) The same exclusion in different forms—the nuclear exclusion

34.10 Nuclear weapons are excluded from the new cargo War Clauses thus:

"3. In no case shall this insurance cover
3.8 loss damage or expense arising from any hostile use of any weapon of war employing atomic or nuclear fission and/or fusion or other like reaction or radioactive force or matter."

34.11 Whilst in the new cargo Strikes Clauses the equivalent provision is slightly different; there is no mention of "hostile":

"3.9 loss damage or expense arising from the use of any weapon of war employing atomic or nuclear fission and/or fusion or other like reaction or radioactive force or matter." (Paras. 36.11–36.25.)

(2) Exclusions from the new cargo Strikes Clauses

34.12 The new cargo Strikes Clauses contain two extra exclusions of their own which are not to be found in the new cargo War Clauses. They read:

"3. In no case shall this insurance cover
3.7 loss damage or expense arising from the absence shortage or withholding of labour of any description whatsoever resulting from any strike, lockout, labour disturbance, riot or civil commotion."

34.13 This clause is a similar exclusion to Clause 7.2 of the new cargo Marine Clauses, and its effect is described in paras. 36.31–36.34.

"3.10 loss damage or expense caused by war civil war revolution rebellion insurrection, or civil strife arising therefrom, or any hostile act by or against a belligerent power."

34.14 This clause prevents any duplication of the insurance given by the new cargo War Clauses.

DURATION—INTRODUCTORY

34.15 Duration of the insurance cover is different between the new cargo War Clauses and the new cargo Strikes Clauses, and this is explained by the Waterborne

Agreement which provides that certain types of war risks can only be covered whilst the insured object is afloat. Brief summaries can be given as follows, although it is necessary to refer in any particular instance to the actual terms of Clauses 5, 6 and 7 in each set of clauses (Appendices H & J).

DURATION—THE NEW CARGO WAR CLAUSES

34.16 The new cargo War Clauses give insurance cover only from the time that the insured goods are loaded onto "an oversea vessel" and continues only until they are discharged from "an oversea vessel" at the port of discharge or until the expiry of 15 days, counted from midnight of the day of "arrival", whichever shall first occur. If only part of the goods are loaded, or remain on board, then only that part is insured. An "oversea vessel" is defined as a vessel carrying the insured goods between ports on a sea-passage. "Arrival" is defined as "anchored moored or otherwise secured" at a berth or place within the harbour area; if however that is not available, "arrival" is complete, and the 15 days begin to run, when the vessel reaches the waiting area. That is the general principle, which is contained in Clause 5.1. To this general principle there are a number of exceptions to take into account to allow for the character of a sea voyage and the necessities that arise from any disruption of it so far as the Waterborne Agreement will allow.

34.17 The first of these exceptions (Clauses 5.1.3 and 5.1.4) provides that the insurance reattaches, or beings to run again, when the vessel sails from the port of discharge without having discharged the insured goods and continues until the insured goods are discharged at the final or substituted port of discharge, or 15 days after the vessel's arrival (as defined above) thereat, whichever shall first occur. It is important to note that this reattachment requires that prompt notice is given to the underwriters and that an additional, or further, premium is paid if this is required.

34.18 The second exception, contained in Clauses 5.2 and 5.3, provides what is to happen in case the oversea vessel discharges the insured goods for transhipment at an intermediate port, or discharges them there as a port of refuge. The insurance continues only for 15 days after arrival (as defined above), but will reattach when the insured goods are loaded onto an on-carrying oversea vessel or an aircraft. If they are carried onwards by sea, the insurance continues on the conditions of the new cargo War Clauses. If however they are carried onwards by aircraft, then the current Institute War Clauses (Air Cargo) will apply. Here there is an exception to the rule that the insured goods will only be insured whilst afloat; during the 15 days, the insurance remains in force whilst the insured goods are at the discharge port. If the contract voyage is terminated at another place other than the contracted destination, then the insurance cover terminates on discharge, but can reattach again on shipment onto an on-carrying vessel, and can also reattach if the original vessel continues her voyage. Again it is important to note that such reattachment requires that prompt notice is given to the underwriters and that an additional, or further, premium is paid if this is required.

34.19 The third exception, contained in Clause 5.4, provides that the insurance against the risks of "mines and derelict torpedoes" is extended to any period whilst the insured goods are on board craft in transit to or from the oversea vessel, but this is limited to a period not exceeding 60 days following discharge from the oversea vessel. This period can, however, be extended by agreement. It is curious to note that here insurance is given for "mines", unqualified by the word "derelict" as is the insurance for mines in Clause 1 (para. 34.2), whereas "torpedoes" are so qualified. The difficulties posed by the word "derelict" are discussed in Chapter 15.

34.20 The fourth, and last, exception, contained in Clause 5.5, provides that the insurance cover remains in force during a deviation by the oversea vessel from the contract of carriage, or the exercise by her of any liberty granted by its terms. Yet again it is important to note that prompt notice must be given to the underwriters and that an additional, or further, premium is paid if this is required.

34.21 Clause 6 provides that, where the assured changes the destination of the insured goods, they will be "held covered at a premium and on conditions to be arranged subject to prompt notice being given to the underwriters". Clause 7 contains the somewhat commanding text in bold print: "Anything contained in this contract which is inconsistent with Clauses 3, 7, 3.8 or 5 shall, to the extent of such inconsistency, be null and void."

DURATION—THE NEW CARGO STRIKES CLAUSES

34.22 The new Strikes Clauses however, follow a very different and very much clearer pattern. Their Clauses 5, 6 and 7 are drawn up in the same terms as Clauses 8, 9 and 10 of the (A), (B) and (C) Clauses, and, being free of the complications of the Waterborne Agreement, are more straightforward.

34.23 Clause 5 provides the general rule that the insurance commences from the time that the goods begin their journey, which may be inland, and continues until they reach their destination, which may also be inland. There is a maximum time limit of 60 days after discharge. If after discharge they are to be sent to a different destination, then the insurance ceases at the time that the journey to that other destination begins. It does however, remain in force during delay beyond the control of the assured, and this includes any deviation or other action by the shipowner exercising the liberties given to him by the contract of carriage. It does not remain in force indefinitely. The maximum time limit and other termination provisions still apply, and there is a further condition contained in Clause 6.

34.24 Clause 6 provides that if the contract of carriage is terminated, or the journey of the goods is otherwise terminated short of their destination, then the insurance will also terminate "unless prompt notice is given to the underwriters and continuation of cover is requested when the insurance shall remain in force, subject to an Additional premium if required by the Underwriters", until the insured goods are delivered to their destination, or are otherwise disposed of as may be agreed. There is again a limit of 60 days from the time the insured goods reach their original, or other, destination.

34.25 Clause 7 simply provides that when the agreed destination is changed by the assured, he is to be "held covered" at a premium and on conditions to be arranged subject to prompt notice being given to the underwriters.

DURATION—COMMENTS

34.26 What is said above on the subject of duration must be treated as general guidance only and not as determinative in any particular instance. It is impossible to foresee any particular misfortune that may befall cargo, and to give clear answers regarding whether the cargo remains insured or not, and whether any declarations need to be made to the underwriters or any additional premiums need to be paid. Whilst the new cargo Strikes Clauses seem to be fairly clear and straightforward, and are co-extensive with the cargo Marine Clauses, the duration provisions of the new cargo War Clauses are very complex and are difficult to read and to comprehend as fully as to be ideal. The only safe thing to do if some unlooked-for misfortune should befall cargo whilst it is in transit, and thus necessitate some handling or disposal which is not provided for by the contract of insurance, is to keep in close touch with the underwriters and to obtain confirmation that the insurance cover is still alive in the given circumstances. To proceed without taking this precaution is to risk finding that the tortuous and tangled nature of the duration provisions deprives the assured of insurance cover just when it is most needed.

34.27 To begin with, the cargo marine and the new cargo Strikes Clauses provide for periods of 60 days, whereas the new cargo War Clauses provide for only 15 days. This is a trap for the unwary cargo owner who may well find that a gap is opening up in the mosaic of his insurance. In Clause 5.2 of the new cargo War Clauses, there is an exception to the general rule that the cargo is insured only whilst afloat; insurance is still given whilst the goods are "at such port or place" where they are discharged. In the circumstances that are provided for by Clause 5.2, and they will invariably be confused circumstances, it is contemplated that the cargo may be carried on by air. If, for instance, the insured cargo is discharged at Suez and it is decided to carry it on by air, the long journey from Suez to Cairo airport would be without insurance by the new cargo War Clauses unless a special arrangement was made, and in the flurry of the moment this may easily be overlooked.

34.28 Clause 5.4 of the new cargo War Clauses is inexact. If there was no qualification of torpedoes being "derelict", the inference would be that insurance would only be given for "derelict mines and torpedoes" (similarly derelict) as is provided for by Clause 1.3. Clause 5.4 does not do this; it provides that the insurance is extended "against the risks of mines and derelict torpedoes" and thus builds an unwelcome measure of imprecision into the insurance provided.

34.29 There is also a bewildering array of notice and additional premiums provisions in both the new cargo War Clauses and the new cargo Strikes Clauses. They vary between:

" 'subject to prompt notice to the underwriters and to an additional premium'
'provided notice is given to the underwriters before the commencement of such further transit and subject to an additional premium'
'subject to prompt notice to the underwriters, and to an additional premium if required'
'held covered at a premium and on conditions to be arranged subject to prompt notice being given to the underwriters'
'unless prompt notice is given to the underwriters and continuation of cover is requested when the insurance will remain in force, subject to an additional premium if required by the underwriters'."

34.30 There can be no reasonable objection to the desire of the underwriters to know as soon as possible of a change in the risk which they initially agreed to bear, and to charge an additional premium to reflect any increase in that risk. But these provisions could have been standardised to a greater extent in the redrafting of the clauses which took effect on 1st January, 1982. What is their precise characteristic? Are they, or are they not, "conditions precedent" to the insurance, thus requiring the assured to take some action before the insurance can continue to run? They do not describe themselves as "conditions precedent", and, as noted in Chapter 28, there has been a general move by the courts away from an inference that a particular contractual provision is a condition precedent unless it clearly and expressly states that it is to have that characteristic. Yet the possibility that the quoted clauses are in fact conditions precedent cannot be lightly dismissed. There are the provisions of Clause 13 which are discussed below under the sub-heading "Reasonable despatch". There is also the "Note" right at the end of the Clauses which reads:

"It is necessary for the Assured when they become aware of any event which is 'held covered' under this insurance to give prompt notice to the Underwriters and the right to such cover is dependent upon compliance with this obligation."

34.31 Whilst it is clearly the intention that the quoted clauses should have the characteristic of "conditions precedent", it is difficult indeed to say that they have effectively acquired it beyond any question. It would surely have been clearer to have described them within their own wording as conditions precedent, and not just to rely upon Clause 13 and the Note to give them this characteristic in an indirect way. What can be said is they are all in the nature of "held covered" clauses, and Chapter 28 further emphasises the necessity for the "utmost good faith" between the parties, not only when the contract of insurance is made, but subsequently during its currency. Until the courts have had the opportunity to consider the quoted clauses, it can only be a wise precaution to regard them as conditions precedent and to give the prompt notice, and if necessary to pay the additional premiums, of which they speak.

34.32 Lastly, Clause 7 of the new cargo War Clauses would not appear to be necessary; Clauses 3.7, 3.8 and 5 should be able to stand on their own without any aid from a provision in the nature of a paramount clause.

MINIMISING LOSSES AND WAIVER

34.33 Clauses 11 and 12 are in the same form in both the new cargo War Clauses and the new cargo Strikes Clauses. There is a somewhat commanding air about the opening words: "It is the duty of the assured . . . .".

34.34 The terms of the Sue and Labour Clause in the S.G. Form were permissive, but this was deceptive. The courts have held (para. 24.4), that the assured was obliged to sue and labour however permissive the provision appeared to be. This modern provision removes all doubt whether the assured has a choice in the matter by saying that it is his "duty" to sue and labour. Thus the assured is obliged to take reasonable measures to avert or minimise a loss and to keep open any rights for recourse against any carrier, bailee or third party so that the underwriters may pursue them under their subrogation rights if they wish to do so. This should be read in conjunction with the deceptively mild provisions of Clause 13, which is discussed below under the heading "Reasonable Despatch". If such measures are taken, then they are not to be considered as a waiver or an acceptance of Notice of Abandonment, neither shall they prejudice the rights of either the assured or the underwriters. Any reasonable and proper expenses incurred by the assured shall be reimbursed in addition to any loss recoverable under the terms of the clauses.

34.35 Taken together, Clauses 11 and 12 form an easy-to-read and clear sue and labour provision without any of the complications attendant upon Clause 13 of the Institute Time Clauses—Hulls, the marine insurance cover for ships (Appendix C), or the Institute War and Strikes Clauses—Hulls into which this Clause 13 is incorporated.[1] It should be noted that Clause 11 of the new cargo War Clauses and the new cargo Strikes Clauses effectively expresses, with some additions, the terms of section 78(1) of the Marine Insurance Act 1906. It goes on to add that amounts spent on sue and labour are recoverable in addition to amounts recoverable for the loss, even a total loss, of the insured goods.[2]

REASONABLE DESPATCH

34.36 Clause 13 of both the new cargo War Clauses and the new cargo Strikes Clauses reads: "It is a condition of this insurance that the Assured shall act with reasonable despatch in all circumstances within their control."

34.37 This is a somewhat general provision, and at first sight might simply be regarded as a statement of the obvious. It has aleady been remarked that the courts are hesitant to infer a "condition precedent" to any rights of recovery under an insurance policy, unless it is expressly provided by the terms of the insurance contract that the insured must have done something, or refrained from following a certain course of action, before he can make any recovery. Yet it would seem from the *Litsion Pride* case (paras. 28.11–28.13), that Hurst J. would have been prepared to hold that similar wording in the Rules of the Hellenic (Bermuda) Mutual War Risks Association constituted an express "condition precedent" with all that this entails (para. 28.13), and Clause 13 should be regarded as a "condition precedent". This in turn indicates that Clause 13's impact, particularly on the Minimising Losses and Waiver provisions and on the provisions for notifying the underwriters and paying additional, or further, premiums, which are set out under the sub-heading "Duration", should be carefully borne in mind.[3]

34.38 If therefore it should be necessary to take "such measures as may be reasonable for the purpose of averting or minimising a loss" under the Minimising Losses and Waiver provisions, these must be taken promptly, particularly as Clause 11 provides that it is the duty of the assured to take them. If anything untoward should happen during the transit, which should require notice to be given to the underwriters under the Duration provisions, then this too must be given promptly

1. Sue and Labour, see Chapter 24.
2. For doubts on this point under the old S.G. Form, see para. 24.5.
3. In view of the very recent judgment of Hobhouse J., which was given on 21st May, 1993, in *Noble Resources Ltd.* v. *Greenwood* [1993] L.M.L.N. 355, it may now be doubted whether the Minimising and Waiver provisions do have the status of a condition precedent or a contractual warranty.

and without delay as soon as the circumstances come to the attention of the assured. This is further discussed above under the sub-heading Duration—Comments. See paras. 34.26–34.31.

LAW AND PRACTICE

34.39 Clause 14 of both the new cargo War Clauses and the new Strikes Clauses provides that the insurance given by both is subject to English Law and Practice. At the time that both sets of clauses took effect on 1st January, 1982, this would have been fully effective to give the English courts sole and exclusive jurisdiction. Since that date however, the parts of the Civil Jurisdiction and Judgments Act 1982, which give effect to the Civil Jurisdiction Convention, have been brought into force in 1987. It is still too early to say what effect the Convention will have upon Clause 14, but it can be said that its impact in other directions, particularly in the field of jurisdiction provisions in bills of lading which are also contractual by nature, has already been considerable.

OPEN INSURANCE COVER—CARGO STORED AFLOAT

34.40 Comments are made on the open insurance cover at paras. 33.43 and 33.44. For cargo stored afloat, there are the Institute War & Strikes Clauses—cargo stored afloat in mechanically self-propelled vessels dated 1.6.82. These clauses have the following characteristics:

1. The insured perils, contained in Clauses 1 and 2, are the same as those contained in the new cargo War Clauses and the new cargo Strikes Clauses (paras. 34.2–34.5). They are all put into the same set of clauses without any distinction between war and strikes.
2. The exclusions, contained in Clauses 3 and 4, are the same as those which apply to the new cargo War Clauses and the new cargo Strikes Clauses except—
   (i) The exclusion relating to a nuclear weapon speaks of "any hostile use" and not "the use of any weapon" with the consequences noted at paras. 36.11–36.25.
   (ii) There is an additional exclusion of:
   "3.9 loss damage or expense arising from the outbreak of war (whether there be a declaration of war or not) between any of the following countries:
   United Kingdom, United States of America, France, the Union of Soviet Socialist Republics, the People's Republic of China."[4]
   (iii) There is an additional exclusion in the nature of a double insurance clause:
   "3.11 any claim for any sum recoverable under any other insurance on the subject matter insured or which would be recoverable under this insurance but for the existence of this insurance."

4. This exclusion is presently being reconsidered as is described at paras. 4.44–4.47.

3. Duration, which is provided for by Clauses 5 and 6, contains provisions that the insurance is to last from the time that the ship enters the storage area until the time that she discharges the cargo. Unlike the Duration provisions of the new cargo War Clauses, Clause 5 is not complex or difficult to comprehend, and should be examined in any particular circumstances of change to see whether the insurance remains in force, and whether the 15-day extensions apply. It is important to note that Clause 5.4 puts a maximum duration of 12 months on the currency of the insurance from the time it commences. Clause 6 contains a "held covered" provision, subject to prompt notice and a premium to be arranged, if the vessel should leave the storage area.

4. The Minimising of Loss and the Waiver provisions (Clauses 11 and 12), are the same as those in the new cargo War Clauses and the new cargo Strikes Clauses with the effects noted at paras. 34.33–34.35.

5. Reasonable Despatch is provided for in Clause 13 and this is in the same terms as the equivalent provisions of the new cargo War Clauses and the new cargo Strikes Clauses with the effects noted at paras. 34.36–34.38.

6. This insurance is in the nature of a time policy and is not, as is most cargo insurance, a voyage policy. It is therefore not surprising to find the Notice of Cancellation and Automatic Termination of Cover Clause contained in Clause 14. This characteristic of the insurance cover also accounts for the presence of Clause 3.9. Unlike other cargo insurance, it is possible to require the payment of additional premiums. (Chapter 4).

7. English Law and Practice is provided for by Clause 14, and this is in the same terms as the equivalent provision in the new cargo War Clauses and the new cargo Strikes Clauses with the effects described at paras. 34.36–34.38.

8. There is a space for entries of the storage area, the period of the insurance, the quality and description of the subject matter insured, the insured value and for sea and territorial limits. These are all conditions of the insurance contract.

SUMMARY

34.41 It is a most welcome development that, as in the case of the Marine and War Risks insurance cover for ships (Chapter 1), the criticisms of the High Court and of UNCTAD should have led to a similar radical overhaul of the cargo insurance cover, both for marine, war and strikes risks. Each of the separate (A), (B) and (C) Clauses, the new cargo War Clauses, and the new cargo Strikes Clauses stand on their own, and division is made on the basis of clearly defined insured perils with a minimum of emphasis on the motives of people. It is no longer necessary to refer to another policy before dealing with any claim on the relevant policy in the way which drew such stringent criticism from Mr. Justice Mocatta and from UNCTAD (paras 1.15, 1.17 and 1.18). There are, however, still a number of uncertainties which remain, and these are discussed in greater detail in Chapter 36.

34.42 The excellent redrafting of the new cargo War Clauses and the new cargo Strikes Clauses does not seem to have been extended to the provisions in each set of clauses on Duration, and there is still the problem, which has already been noted, with "civil commotions". An attempt has been made earlier in this chapter to show in what respects the Duration provisions of the new cargo War Clauses are confusing to read and are thus unclear. It is particularly unsatisfactory that it should not be made clear in the wording of the Duration Clauses whether or not the notice and "held covered" provisions are to have the status of conditions precedent. It would have been preferable for "civil commotions" to be included as one of the insured perils of the new cargo War Clauses rather than of the new cargo Strikes Clauses. A study of Chapters 8 and 17 will show how wafer-thin the distinction can be between "civil commotions" and "revolution, rebellion, insurrection". In cases of doubt, and the circumstances will be confused, it is not satisfactory to have two different policies involved, particularly if they are written by different underwriters.

33.43 In the (A), (B) and (C) Clauses there is a special provision (Clause 13) which deals with constructive total loss. This is not repeated in either the new cargo War Clauses or the new cargo Strikes Clauses. Consequently, the position in respect of constructive total losses under both these latter sets of clauses is governed by section 60 of the Marine Insurance Act 1906. The workings of this section, and the rules which lie behind the establishment of a constructive total loss are described in Chapter 27 (paras. 27.7, 27.15–27.30).

34.44 Neither the new cargo War Clauses nor the new cargo Strikes Clauses contain within their text the Notice of Cancellation and Automatic Termination of Cover Clause. Thus in cargo insurance there are not the problems with additional premiums and automatic termination of the insurance cover which exist in the case of ships (Chapter 4). There is, however, a separate clause, which can if desired be added to the new cargo War Clauses, the Institute War Cancellation Clause (Cargo) dated 1.12.82 which reads:

"The cover against war risks (as defined in the relevant Institute War Clauses) may be cancelled by either the Underwriters or the Assured except in respect of any insurance which shall have attached in accordance with the conditions of the Institute War Clauses before the cancellation becomes effective. Such cancellation shall however only become effective on the expiry of 7 days from midnight of the day on which notice of the cancellation is issued by or to the Underwriters."

34.45 Unlike the insurance cover for ships, which can be cancelled during the currency of the policy (Chapter 4), the insurance cover under the new cargo War Clauses can only be cancelled before it attaches. It can of course be restored by agreement, doubtless on payment of an increased premium. It should be noted that the wording of the clause contemplates that it will apply to the new cargo War Clauses only, and not to the new cargo Strikes Clauses.

CHAPTER 35

Special cargo insurances

INTRODUCTORY

35.1 Chapters 33 and 34, describe the patterns of the Marine, War and Strikes Clauses which are used to insure cargo, whilst Chapter 36 deals with the insured perils and the exclusions. Some types of cargo have special insurance which meets their specific needs and this is the subject of this chapter. Often these special insurances are agreed with trade Associations, and the most prominent are described in this chapter. Such special cargo insurances follow closely the patterns of the (A), (B) and (C) Clauses, the new cargo War Clauses (where there is special cargo war insurance), and the new cargo Strikes Clauses.[1]

There are, however, some differences, and as these differences themselves follow a pattern, it is more helpful to draw attention to some of the more important ones in note form, and to explain their effects in Chapter 36.

The insured perils

35.2 Brief descriptions of the insured perils of the Marine Clauses are given (in addition to the insured perils of the new cargo War Clauses and the new cargo Strikes Clauses) to draw attention to any differences to the insured perils of the (A), (B) and (C) Clauses. In one case, namely the marine insurance for timber cargoes, "malicious act", an insured peril normally found in War and Strikes insurance, is included among the marine insured perils.

The exclusions

35.3 The exclusions follow closely the pattern established by the new cargo War Clauses and the new cargo Strikes Clauses. There is some measure of difference which needs to be explained.

Financial default of the shipowning interests and unseaworthiness

35.4 On some occasions the Exclusions Clauses dealing with the financial default of the shipowning interests, and unseaworthiness or unfitness of the vessel or craft (or the container, liftvan, or land conveyance) to which the assured is privy have been extended beyond the equivalent provisions, Clauses 3.6 and 4, of the new

---

1. For definitions, see paras. 33.3 and 33.4.

cargo War Clauses and the new cargo Strikes Clauses. In the notes which follow, these will be referred to as "Clauses 3.6 and 4 extended" or "not extended" as the case may be. The effect of the differences is explained at paras. 36.35 and 36.36.

Duration

35.5 Duration in the War Clauses for special cargo insurances always follows that of the new cargo War Clauses and has the same attendant difficulties of comprehension (paras. 34.15–34.32). Duration in the Strikes Clauses for special cargo insurances always follows the pattern of the relevant Marine Clauses for the goods concerned; it is thus different in nearly every case from Duration in the new cargo Strikes Clauses. These latter Duration Clauses are however always in an easy-to-read format, and it could be misleading to attempt to summarise each one. It is more helpful to describe each Duration Clause's main characteristic, and to refer the reader to its actual wording where questions arise.

Piracy

35.6 The Marine Clauses for Special cargo insurances often contain another important difference which has particular relevance to the Piracy risk. The (B) and (C) Clauses (paras. 33.26–33.30) contain in their exclusions clauses: "4.7 deliberate damage or deliberate destruction of the subject matter insured or any part thereof by the wrongful act of any person or persons," and: "6.2 capture seizure arrest restraint or detainment, and the consequences thereof or any attempt thereat."

35.7 The (A) Clauses (para. 33.25), however, are different. They do not contain Clause 4.7 and there is a marked difference to their Clause 6.2 which lies within the brackets as follows: "6.2 capture seizure arrest restraint or detainment (piracy excepted) and the consequences thereof or any attempt thereat."

35.8 The general pattern emerges that the (A) Clauses give insurance for piracy whereas the (B) and (C) Clauses do not, but this pattern is not invariably followed. Where the Marine Clauses for special cargo insurances follow the (B) or (C) patterns, it is sometimes the case that there is no Clause 4.7 and exclusion Clause 6.2 excludes piracy from its operation. In the text which follows, it will be noted either "No Clause 4.7 (piracy excepted), from Clause 6.2", or "Clause 4.7 present, no (piracy excepted) from Clause 6.2", as the case may be. The consequences of this, and the insurance of piracy, are more fully explained at paras. 36.3–36.10.

Nuclear weapons

35.9 The exclusion of "the use" or "any hostile use" of nuclear weapons will be noted in each case. The effect of the difference is explained at paras. 36.11–36.25.

THE CLAUSES

1. Commodity goods

35.10 The Institute Commodity Trades Clauses have been agreed with The Federation of Commodity Associations for insurance of shipments of cocoa, coffee, cotton, fats and oils not in bulk, hides, skins and leather, metals, oil seeds, sugar (raw and refined) and tea.

35.11 The Marine insurance is provided by the Institute Commodity Trades Clauses (A), (B) and (C), all dated 5.9.83.

35.12 *The Institute Commodity Trades Clauses (A):*

Insured Perils—same as the (A) Clauses.
Clauses 3.6 and 4 (numbered 4.6 and 5) extended.
Duration—warehouse to warehouse, maximum 60 days after discharge.
No Clause 4.7 (piracy excepted), from Clause 6.2.
"the use of" nuclear weapons excluded.

35.13 *The Institute Commodity Trade Clauses (B):*

Insured Perils—same as the (B) Clauses.
Clauses 3.6 and 4 (numbered 4.6 and 5) extended.
Duration—warehouse to warehouse, maximum 60 days after discharge.
Clause 4.7 present, no (piracy excepted) from Clause 6.2.
"the use of" nuclear weapons excluded.

35.14 *The Institute Commodity Trade Clauses (C):*

Insured Perils—same as the (C) Clauses.
Clauses 3.6 and 4 (numbered 4.6 and 5) extended.
Duration—warehouse to warehouse, maximum 60 days after discharge.
Clause 4.7 present, no (piracy excepted) from Clause 6.2.
"the use of" nuclear weapons excluded.

The War insurance is provided by the Institute War Clauses (Commodity Trades) dated 5.9.83.

35.15 *The Institute War Clauses (Commodity Trades):*

Insured Perils—same as the new cargo War Clauses.
Clauses 3.6 and 4 extended.
Duration—same as the new cargo War Clauses.
"any hostile use" of nuclear weapons excluded.

The Strikes insurance is provided by the Institute Strikes Clauses (Commodity Trades) dated 5.9.83.

35.16 *The Institute Strikes Clauses (Commodity Trades):*

Insured Perils—same as the new cargo Strikes Clauses.
Clauses 3.6 and 4 extended.
Duration—warehouse to warehouse, maximum of 60 days after discharge.
"the use of" nuclear weapons excluded.

2. Bulk Oil

35.17 The Marine insurance is provided by the Institute Bulk Oil Clauses dated 1.2.83.

35.18 *The Institute Bulk Oil Clauses:*

>Insured Perils—same as the (B) Clauses except:
>>omitted—overturning or derailment of land conveyance; washing overboard; entry of sea lake or river water; package overboard or dropped whilst loading or discharging.
>>additional—leakage (subject to Clause 15) whilst loading transhipping or discharging; negligence of crew when pumping; contamination from stress of weather.
>
>Clauses 3.6 and 4 (numbered 4.5 and 5) not extended.
>Duration—shore tank to shore tank, maximum 30 days after vessels arrival.
>No Clause 4.7 (piracy excepted) from Clause 6.2.
>"the use of" nuclear weapons excluded.

35.19 There are no War Clauses which are specially tailored to bulk oil cargoes. The new cargo War Clauses can therefore be used.

The Strikes insurance is provided by the Institute Strikes Clauses (Bulk Oil) dated 1.2.83.

35.20 *The Institute Strikes Clauses (Bulk Oil):*

>Insured Perils—same as the new cargo Strikes Clauses.
>Clauses 3.6 (numbered 3.5) and 4 not extended.
>Duration—shore tank to shore tank with a maximum of 30 days after the arrival of the vessel.
>"the use of" nuclear weapons excluded.

3. Coal

35.21 The Marine insurance is provided by the Institute Coal Clauses dated 1.10.82.

35.22 *The Institute Coal Clauses:*

>Insured Perils—same as the (B) Clauses except:
>>omitted—overturning and derailment of land conveyance; total loss of a package lost overboard or dropped whilst loading or discharging.
>>additional—"fire or explosion" is extended to include spontaneous combustion, inherent vice or nature of cargo.
>
>Clauses 3.6 and 4 (numbered 4.4 and 5) not extended.
>Duration—loading to discharge, no maximum.
>Clause 4.7 (numbered 4.5) present, no (piracy excepted) from Clause 6.2.
>"the use of" nuclear weapons excluded.

There are no War Clauses specially tailored to coal cargoes. The new cargo War Clauses can therefore be used.

The Strikes insurance is provided by the Institute Strikes Clauses (Coal) dated 1.10.82.

35.23 *The Institute Strikes Clauses (Coal):*

Insured Perils—same as the new cargo Strikes Clauses.
Clauses 3.6 (numbered 3.5) and 4 not extended.
Duration—loading to discharge, no maximum.
"the use of" nuclear weapons excluded.

4. Oils Seeds and Fats

35.24 The Institute FOSFA Trades Clauses have been agreed with the Federation of Oils, Seeds, and Fats Associations.

The Marine insurance is provided by the Institute FOSFA Trades Clauses (A), (B) and (C) dated 1.7.85.

35.25 *The Institute FOSFA Trades Clauses (A):*

Insured Perils—same as the (A) Clauses.
Clauses 3.6 and 4 (numbered 4.6 and 5) extended.
Duration—warehouse to warehouse, maximum 60 days after discharge.
No Clause 4.7 (piracy excepted) from Clause 6.2.
"the use of" nuclear weapons excluded.

35.26 *The Institute FOSFA Trades Clauses (B):*

Insured Perils—same as the (B) Clauses.
Clauses 3.6 and 4 (numbered 4.6 and 5) extended.
Duration—warehouse to warehouse, maximum 60 days after discharge.
Clause 4.7 present, no (piracy excepted) from Clause 6.2.
"the use of" nuclear weapons excluded.

35.27 *The Institute Trades Clauses (C):*

Insured Perils—same as the (C) Clauses.
Clauses 3.6 and 4 (numbered 4.6 and 5) extended.
Duration—warehouse to warehouse, maximum 60 days after discharge.
Clause 4.7 present, no (piracy excepted) from Clause 6.2.
"the use of" nuclear weapons excluded.

The War insurance is provided by the Institute War Clauses (FOSFA Trades) dated 1.7.85.

35.28 *The Institute War Clauses (FOSFA Trades):*

Insured Perils—same as the new cargo War Clauses.
Clauses 3.6 and 4 extended.
Duration—same as the new cargo War Clauses.
"any hostile use" of nuclear weapons excluded.

The Strikes insurance is provided by the Institute Strikes Clauses (FOSFA Trades) dated 1.7.85.

35.29 *The Institute Strikes Clauses (FOSFA Trades):*

Insured Perils—same as the new cargo Strikes Clauses.
Clauses 3.6 and 4 extended.
Duration—warehouse to warehouse, maximum 60 days after discharge.
"the use of" nuclear weapons excluded.

5. Frozen Food (excluding Frozen Meat)

35.30 The Marine insurance is provided by the Institute Frozen Food Clauses (Excluding Frozen Meat) (A) and (C) dated 1.1.86.

35.31 *The Institute Frozen Food Clauses (A):*

Insured Perils—same as the (A) Clauses except:
　　omitted—variation in temperature only covered in case of mishaps listed in Clauses 1.2.1 to 1.2.6.
Clauses 3.6 and 4 (numbered 4.6 and 5) not extended.
Duration—cold store to cold store, maximum five days after discharge.
No Clause 4.7 (piracy excepted) from Clause 6.2.
"the use of" nuclear weapons excluded.
Additional exclusions—Clauses 4.8 (failure of assured or servants to keep goods in cool space) and 4.9 (prompt notice of claims, no more than 30 days after termination).

35.32 *The Institute Frozen Food Clauses (C):*

Insured Perils—same as the (C) Clauses.
Clauses 3.6 and 4 (numbered 4.6 and 5) not extended.
Duration—cold store to cold store, maximum five days after discharge.
Clause 4.7 present, no (piracy excepted) from Clause 6.2.
"the use of" nuclear weapons excluded.
Additional exclusions—same as the Frozen Food (A) Clauses (numbered 4.9 and 4.10).

There are no War Clauses specially tailored to frozen food. The new cargo War Clauses can therefore be used.

The Strikes insurance is provided by the Institute Strikes Clauses (Frozen Food) (excluding Frozen Meat) dated 1.1.86.

35.33 *The Institute Strikes Clause (Frozen Food):*

> Insured Perils—same as the new cargo Strikes Clauses.
> Clauses 3.6 and 4 not extended.
> Duration—cold store to cold store, maximum five days after discharge.
> "the use of" nuclear weapons excluded.
> Additional exclusions—Clause 3.7 extended to include equipment, power,
> fuel, coolant, refrigerant besides labour; Clause 3.11
> (prompt notice of claims, no more than 30 days after
> termination).

6. Frozen Meat (not chilled, cooled or fresh meat)

35.34 The Marine insurance is provided by the Institute Frozen Meat Clauses (A), the Institute Frozen Meat Clauses (A)—24 hours Breakdown, and the Institute Frozen Meat Clauses (C) and 24 hours Breakdown, all dated 1.1.86.

35.35 *The Institute Frozen Meat Clauses (A):*

> Insured Perils—same as the (A) Clauses.
> Clauses 3.6 and 4 (numbered 4.6 and 5) extended.
> Duration—cold store (with options at loading port) to cold store, maximum 30
> days (Europe inc. U.K. and Eire, U.S.A., Canada), five days
> (elsewhere).
> No Clause 4.7 (piracy excepted) from Clause 6.2.
> "the use of" nuclear weapons excluded.
> Additional exclusions—Clauses 4.8 (onshore earthquake, volcanic eruption
> and/or resulting fire) and 4.9 (failure of assured or ser-
> vants to keep goods in cool space).

35.36 *The Institute Frozen Meat Clauses (A)—24 hours Breakdown:*

> Insured Perils—same as (A) Clauses except:
> omitted—variations in temperature only covered in case of mishaps listed in
> Clauses 1.2.1 to 1.2.6.
> Clauses 3.6 and 4 (numbered 4.6 and 5) extended.
> Duration—cold store (with options at loading port) to cold store, maximum 30
> days (Europe inc. U.K. and Eire, U.S.A., Canada), five days
> (elsewhere).
> No Clause 4.7 (piracy excepted) from Clause 6.2.
> "the use of" nuclear weapons excluded.
> Additional exclusions—same as Frozen Meat (A) Clauses.

35.37 *The Institute Frozen Meat Clauses (C) and 24 hours Breakdown:*

> Insured Perils—same as (C) Clauses except:
> additional—breakdown of refrigerating machinery for 24 hours.
> Clauses 3.6 and 4 (numbered 4.6 and 5) extended.
> Duration—cold store (with options at loading port) to cold store, maximum

30 days (Europe inc. U.K. and Eire, U.S.A., Canada), five days (elsewhere).
Clause 4.7 present, no (piracy excepted) from Clause 6.2.
"the use of" nuclear weapons excluded.
Additional exclusions—same as Frozen Meat (A) Clauses.

There are no War Clauses specially tailored to frozen meat. The new cargo War Clauses can therefore be used.

The Strikes insurance is provided by the Institute Strikes Clauses (Frozen Meat) dated 1.1.86.

35.38 *The Institute Strikes Clauses (Frozen Meat):*

Insured Perils—same as the new cargo Strikes Clauses.
Clauses 3.6 and 4 extended.
Duration—cold store (with options at the loading port) to cold store, maximum 30 days (Europe, inc. U.K. and Eire, U.S.A., Canada) five days (elsewhere).
"the use of" nuclear weapons excluded.
Additional exclusions—Clauses 3.7 (extended to include equipment, power, fuel, coolant, refrigerant besides labour), and 3.11 (onshore earthquake, volcanic eruption and/or resulting fire).

7. Jute

35.39 The Marine insurance is provided by the Institute Jute Clauses 1.1.84.

35.40 *The Institute Jute Clauses:*

Insured Perils—same as (C) Clauses except:
additional—washing overboard is added to jettison; entry of sea lake or river water; total loss of package lost overboard or dropped whilst loading or discharging.
Clauses 3.6 and 4 (numbered 4.6 and 5) extended.
    Duration—loading to warehouse ashore, maximum 30 days.
No Clause 4.7 (piracy excepted) from Clause 6.2.
"the use of" nuclear weapons excluded.

There are no War Clauses specially tailored to jute. The new cargo War Clauses can therefore be used.

The Strikes insurance is provided by the Institute Strikes Clauses (Jute) dated 1.1.84.

35.41 *The Institute Strikes Clauses (Jute):*

Insured Perils—same as the new cargo Strikes Clauses.
Clauses 3.6 and 4 extended.

Duration—loading to warehouse ashore, maximum 30 days.
"the use of" nuclear weapons excluded.

8. Rubber (excluding liquid latex)

35.42 The Marine insurance is provided by the Institute Natural Rubber Clauses (excluding liquid latex) dated 1.1.84.

35.43 *The Institute Natural Rubber Clauses:*

> Insured Perils—same as the (C) Clauses except:
>> additional—earthquake; volcanic eruption; lightning; washing over-board added to jettison; water; condensation; hooks; spill-ings or leakage of liquid; other cargo; moisture from wet or damp dunnage; theft; pilferage; non-delivery.
> Clauses 3.6 and 4 (numbered 4.6 and 5) extended.
> Duration—warehouse to warehouse, maximum 30 days.
> No Clause 4.7 (piracy excepted) from Clause 6.2.
> "the use of" nuclear weapons excluded.

There are no War Clauses specially tailored to rubber. The new cargo War Clauses can therefore be used.

The Strikes insurance is provided by the Institute Strikes Clauses (Natural Rubber) (excluding liquid latex) dated 1.1.84.

35.44 *The Strikes Clauses (Natural Rubber):*

> Insured Perils—same as the new cargo Strikes Clauses.
> Clauses 3.6 and 4 extended.
> Duration—warehouse to warehouse, maximum 30 days.
> "the use of" nuclear weapons excluded.

9. Timber

35.45 The Institute Timber Trade Federation Clauses have been agreed with the Timber Trade Federation.

The Marine insurance is provided by the Institute Timber Trade Federation Clauses dated 1.4.86.

35.46 *The Institute Timber Trade Federation Clauses:*

> Insured Perils—These are divided into two parts, Cargo whilst stowed on deck, and Cargo whilst not stowed on deck.
> Cargo on deck—same as the (C) Clauses except:
>> omitted—overturning or derailment of land conveyance.
>> additional—washing overboard added to jettison; theft; non-delivery; malicious act.
> Cargo below deck—same as the (A) Clauses.

Clauses 3.6 and 4 (numbered 4.6 and 5) extended.

Duration—start of journey to loading port to warehouse, maximum 60 days after discharge.

No Clause 4.7 (piracy excepted) from Clause 6.2.

"the use of" nuclear weapons excluded.

There are no War Clauses specially tailored to timber. The new cargo War Clauses can therefore be used.

The Strikes insurance is provided by the Institute Strikes Clauses (Timber Trade Federation) agreed with the Timber Trade Federation dated 1.4.86.

35.47 *The Institute Strikes Clauses (Timber Trade Federation):*

Insured Perils—same as the new cargo Strikes Clauses.

Clause 3.6 and 4 extended.

Duration—start of journey to loading port to warehouse, maximum 60 days after discharge.

"the use of" nuclear weapons excluded.

CHAPTER 36

Cargo—comments on the insured perils and the exclusions

INTRODUCTORY

36.1 Clauses 1 of both the new cargo War Clauses and the new cargo Strikes Clauses contain lists of their insured perils. All these insured perils have individual chapters devoted to them in this work, and the law formulated by the decided cases applies as much to cargo as it does to ships. Indeed, many of the cases referred to in this work have been concerned with cargo. This chapter will therefore concentrate on the points which have particular application to cargo insurance, or which give rise to particular difficulty in connection with it.

36.2 It will be noted that in several instances the insurance of ships is commented upon. This is done in this chapter in order to contrast the respective provisions of the cargo and the ship insurance.

PIRACY

36.3 Piracy as an insured peril is described in Chapter 20. Before 1937, it was an insured peril of the marine policies for ships. Between 1937 and 1983, it was transferred to the War Risks policies for ships. During this period, it was excluded from the marine insurance, the Institute Time Clauses—Hulls by Clause 23 (the Free of Capture and Seizure Clause), and became an insured peril of the War Risks insurance, the Institute War and Strikes Clauses—Hulls. During the same period and by the same means it was excluded from the Institute Cargo Clauses (All Risks), (W.A.), and (F.P.A.) (paras. 33.5–33.14), by Clause 12 (again the Free of Capture and Seizure Clause), and became an insured peril of the Institute War Clauses (Cargo). It is suggested that between 1937 and 1983 (1982 for cargo) it was rightly regarded as an insured peril of the War Risks insurance, because piracy is something that other people do to ships or to cargo, and this is the essence of War Risks insurance. It is still so regarded by the Mutual War Risks Associations, and they include it in their Rules as an insured peril for ships.

36.4 During the redrafting in the early 1980s which led to the Institute Time Clauses—Hulls and the Institute War and Strikes Clauses—Hulls, both of which took effect on 1st October, 1983 (only shortly after the new clauses for cargo insurance which took effect on 1.1.82), there was a wish that piracy should revert to the marine insurance. The Institute Time Clauses—Hulls therefore includes in its list of

417

insured perils Clause 6: "6.1.5 Piracy", whilst the Institute War and Strikes exclude piracy (with only minor qualifications) by their Clause 4.1.7.

36.5 From the format of the (A), (B) and (C) Clauses,[1] the new cargo War Clauses, and the new cargo Strikes Clauses, all of which took effect on 1st January, 1982, the same wish is clear, although piracy is not named as an insured peril. Moreover, piracy is not insured by all the forms of marine insurance for cargo. Its inclusion within, or exclusion from, the marine insurance depends on whether Clause 4.7 is or is not written into the respective clauses, and whether or not Clause 6.2 is amended. In Chapter 35, where there are notes on the various Institute marine, war, and strikes clauses for special cargo insurance, the abbreviations appear: "No Clause 4.7 (piracy excepted) from Clause 6.2", or, "Clause 4.7 present, no (piracy excepted) from Clause 6.2."

36.6 These must now be explained. Clause 4.7 reads:

"4. In no case shall this insurance cover . . .
4.7 deliberate damage or deliberate destruction of the subject-matter insured or any part thereof by the wrongful act of any person or persons."

Whilst Clause 6.2 reads either:

"6. In no case shall this insurance cover loss damage or expense caused by . . .
6.2 capture seizure arrest restraint or detainment (piracy excepted) and the consequence thereof or any attempt thereat."

or,

"6.2 capture seizure arrest restraint or detainment and the consequences thereof or any attempt thereat."

36.7 Deliberate damage, deliberate destruction, and seizure represents just about everything which a pirate can do to a cargo. Therefore when the marine clauses do not include exclusion Clause 4.7, and piracy is excepted from the operation of exclusion Clause 6.2, piracy is insured by the marine clauses. The converse applies; where Clause 4.7 is present, and piracy is not excluded from the operation of Clause 6.2, then the clauses cannot insure piracy.

36.8 Turning to the individual clauses:

1. The (A) Clauses provide "all risks" insurance. They do not contain Clause 4.7 and piracy is excepted from the operation of Clause 6.2. Consequently they give unrestricted insurance against piracy.
2. The (B) and (C) Clauses, which give insurance only for a list of specified insured perils (which do not include piracy), each contain Clause 4.7 and piracy is not excluded from the operation of Clause 6.2. Consequently they give no insurance against piracy.
3. The new cargo War Clauses and the new cargo Strikes Clauses give insurance only against lists of specific insured perils, and do not include piracy. Consequently they too give no insurance against piracy.

36.9 Thus the general rule emerges that the (A) Clauses give unrestricted insur-

1. For definitions, see paras. 33.3 and 33.4.

ance against piracy whilst the (B) and (C) Clauses, the new cargo War Clauses, and the new cargo Strikes Clauses, give no insurance against this risk. This principle is not however followed in all cases by the clauses for Special Cargoes (Chapter 35). It is nonetheless possible to make lists which show:

(a) Clauses which give unrestricted insurance against piracy (besides the (A) Clauses):

The Institute:
Commodity Trades Clauses (A) dated 5.9.83.
FOSFA Trades Clauses (A) dated 1.7.85.
Frozen Food Clauses (A) (except variation in temperature) dated 1.1.86.
Frozen Meat Clauses (A) dated 1.1.86.
Timber Trade Federation Clauses (for underdeck cargo only) dated 1.4.86.

(b) Clauses which give no insurance against piracy (besides the (B) and (C) Clauses):

The Institute:
Commodity Trades Clauses (B) dated 5.9.83.
Commodity Trades Clauses (C) dated 5.9.83.
Coal Clauses dated 1.10.82.
FOSFA Trades Clauses (B) dated 1.7.85.
FOSFA Trades Clauses (C) dated 1.7.85.
Frozen Food Clauses (C) dated 1.1.86.
Frozen Meat Clauses (C) and 24 hours Breakdown dated 1.1.86.

(c) Clauses which give restricted insurance against piracy. It is described as restricted because the casualty must come within the terms of the insured perils (Clause 1 in each case):

The Institute:
Bulk Oil Clauses dated 1.2.83.
Frozen Food Clauses (A) (variation in temperature) dated 1.1.86.
Frozen Meat Clauses (A)—24 hours Breakdown dated 1.1.86.
Jute Clauses dated 1.1.84.
Natural Rubber Clauses dated 1.1.84.
Timber Trade Federation Clauses (for on-deck cargo only) dated 1.4.86.

36.10 It must be borne in mind that the structure of the clauses listed in (c) provides for a specific list of insured perils only, and that any loss or damage caused by pirates must come within the terms of at least one of those insured perils to be insured against the depredations of pirates. The Timber Clauses appear in both lists (a) and (c) because timber is insured against all risks whilst stowed below deck, and for a specific list only of insured perils whilst stowed on deck. In the case of timber therefore, it is possible for an act of piracy to give rise to a claim for the under-deck cargo, but not for the on-deck cargo. So too, the Frozen Food Clauses (A) also appear in both lists (a) and (c); they are "all risks" clauses except for one instance; they only insure a specific list of insured perils for variation in temperature.

NUCLEAR WEAPONS

36.11 The marine and war insurance for ships excludes loss or damage caused by the explosion of a nuclear weapon in a comprehensive way. The Institute Time Clauses—Hulls dated 1.10.83, excludes from the marine insurance:

"26 NUCLEAR EXCLUSION

In no case shall this insurance cover loss damage liability or expense arising from any weapon of war employing atomic or nuclear fission and/or fusion or other like reaction or radioactive force or matter."

36.12 The Institute War and Strikes Clauses Hulls—Time dated 1.10.83 contain a similar exclusion from the War Risks insurance:

"This insurance excludes
4.1 loss damage liability or expense arising from
4.1.1 any detonation of any weapon of war employing atomic or nuclear fission and/or fusion or other like reaction or radioactive force or matter, hereinafter called a nuclear weapon of war."

36.13 The wording is slightly different in each case, but it is suggested that this is immaterial. The conclusion must be that neither the Marine Clauses nor the War Clauses for ships give insurance cover for ships against the consequences of the explosion of nuclear weapons however they may be caused (Appendix D).

36.14 The position in respect of cargo is very different, and very much more uncertain. It must first be remembered that nuclear weapons can explode or be exploded in three separate ways; they can be used in war by a belligerent as hostile explosions, they can be exploded in practice, and they can explode accidentally. Since 1945 there have been examples of the first two ways which are publicly known. There have been reports of accidental explosions in Russia and possibly in Iraq as well. This work must consider all three.[2]

36.15 It is only necessary to consider the (A), (B) and (C) Clauses, the new cargo War Clauses, and the new cargo Strikes Clauses. Chapter 35 shows a list of which clauses for special cargo insurances exclude from their insurance "the use of", and which exclude "any hostile use" of, nuclear weapons. In fact they follow a pattern. The Marine Clauses for Special Cargo insurance, like the (A), (B) and (C) Clauses, and the Strikes Clauses, like the new cargo Strikes Clauses, exclude "the use of" nuclear weapons, whereas the War Clauses (where there are any), adopt the wording of the new cargo War Clauses and exclude "any hostile use" of nuclear weapons.[3] Whether or not insurance is given is nothing like so clear-cut as it should be, and lacks the certainty of the insurance relating to ships.

36.16 The (A) Clauses provide insurance on an "all-risks" basis, but contain exclusions:

"4. In no case shall this insurance cover . . .

2. Hostile explosions can include explosions caused by persons who are not Governments but who have acquired nuclear weapons in some way, such as terrorists. It can also be stretched to include "derelict weapons". (Para. 36.23).
3. "Any hostile use" was exc uded from the old cargo War Clauses which were in use before 1982. The cargo Marine Clauses and the old cargo Strikes Clauses in use before that date had no exclusions relating to nuclear weapons, so that "the use of" exclusion is new.

4.7 loss damage or expense arising from the use of any weapon of war employing atomic or nuclear fission and/or fusion or other like reaction or radioactive force or matter."[4]

and also:

"6. In no case shall this insurance cover loss damage or expense caused by . . .
6.1 war civil war revolution rebellion insurrection . . . "

The (B) and (C) Clauses contain the same exclusion clauses, except that 4.7 becomes 4.8.

36.17 A hostile detonation is therefore excluded from the (A), (B) and (C) Clauses. So also is a practice detonation, because "the use of" indicates a purposeful and deliberate use. An accidental detonation does not come within the bounds of the word "use", and neither can it be hostile. The conclusion must be that the (A) Clauses insure such accidental detonations without restriction, and the (B) and (C) Clauses do the same provided only that the casualty comes within the boundaries of one of their insured perils.

36.18 Turning now to the new cargo War Clauses and the new cargo Strikes Clauses, these also pose some anomalies.

36.19 The new cargo Strikes Clauses provide in Clause 1 insurance cover against a specific list of insured perils only, namely, strikers, locked-out workmen, persons taking part in labour disturbances, riots or civil commotions, terrorists or persons acting from a political motive. These clauses exclude "the use of" nuclear weapons by Clause 3.9, so that both hostile and practice explosions (unlikely as these are) can be said to be excluded from the insurance.

36.20 This leaves accidental detonations. Among the people included within the insured perils, terrorists are, realistically, the only ones who could get their hands on a nuclear weapon. If they should do so and detonate it by accident, the consequences would not be excluded by Clause 3.9; this likewise is not "use".

36.21 The new cargo War Clauses again provide insurance against a specific list only of insured perils. There is a restriction in Clause 1.2 which requires that capture seizure arrest restraint or detainment (unlike the similar cover for ships) must arise from war civil war revolution rebellion insurrection, civil strife arising therefrom or any hostile act by or against a belligerent power. Thus the insurance given by these two clauses effectively includes war, civil war, or situations which stop short of such calamities by only a narrow margin. The exclusion clause reads:

"3. In no case shall this insurance cover . . .
3.8 loss damage or expense arising from any hostile use of any weapon of war employing atomic or nuclear fission and/or fusion or other like reaction or radioactive force or matter."

36.22 Hostile detonations are thus expressly excluded by Clause 3.8. In the situations contemplated by Clauses 1.1 and 1.2, practice detonations are unlikely although accidental explosions cannot be entirely ruled out, and it would appear that, because they are not expressly excluded, they are insured provided that the casualty comes within the terms of one of the insured perils.

36.23 There is a marked anomaly in the insured perils of Clause 1.3, which include "derelict" mines, torpedoes, bombs or other "derelict" weapons of war.

---

4. The numbering of this clause must not cause confusion with the clause, also numbered 4.7 which deals with deliberate destruction and deliberate damage and which is quoted above in connection with piracy.

These can be nuclear by nature.[5] Loss or damage caused by the explosion of one of these weapons, almost certainly after it has failed to destroy the target at which it was originally aimed, and possibly long after the conflict itself has ceased, can hardly be described as "any hostile use"; this expression indicates purposeful use against a target rather than the explosion of a weapon whose hostile use has long since ceased and which is "derelict" in the sense that this word is normally used.[6] The probability, which must await judicial interpretation, is that loss or damage caused by such an explosion is insured by the new cargo War Clauses.

36.24 The intention lying behind the drafting of the (A), (B) and (C) Clauses, the new cargo War Clauses, the new cargo Strikes Clauses, and the Special Cargo Insurances was to give effect to the insurance market's long expressed wish to exclude entirely from its insurance any claims caused by the detonations of nuclear weapons. In the case of cargo insurance, this has not been done as effectively as it has been done for the insurance of ships. Unlike ships, there are some doubts whether or not the consequences of such catastrophes are effectively excluded *in toto* from the insurance for cargo. Moreover, there could be problems with double insurance.

36.25 Containers are insured by the London Market on an "all risks" basis (except for their machinery), but both the marine and war and strikes insurance exclude loss or damage arising from any weapon of war employing atomic or nuclear fission and/or fusion or other like radioactive force or matter. It therefore seems that they both exclude all such detonations, whether they be hostile, in practice, or accidental.

CAPTURE, SEIZURE, ARREST, RESTRAINT OR DETAINMENT

36.26 Insurance for these insured perils is given to ships in an unrestricted form by Clause 1.2 of the Institute War and Strikes Clauses—Hulls dated 1.10.83 (Appendix D). The position with cargo is again very different, and there is now a restriction on the insurance which did not exist in the old cargo War Clauses. The new cargo War Clauses read:

"1. This insurance covers . . . loss or damage to the subject matter insured caused by . . .
    1.2 capture seizure arrest restraint or detainment, arising from risks covered under 1.1 above, and the consequences thereof or any attempt thereat"

36.27 From the position of the first comma, it is clear that capture, seizure, arrest, restraint or detainment are only insured in the case of war, civil war, revolution, rebellion, insurrection, or civil strife arising therefrom, or any hostile act by or against a belligerent power.

36.28 In the case of "capture", this restriction is not important. "Capture" will only arise if the cargo is taken by a belligerent government, and this indicates that war, or at least civil war, exists (Chapter 11). The cases quoted elsewhere in this work (Chapters 12 and 13) will show that seizure, arrest, restraint and detainment

5. "Derelict" is considered in Chapter 15.
6. Chapter 15.

can arise even without the momentous events set out in Clause 1.1 arising. If this is the case, then cargo, unlike ships, will have no insurance.

36.29 The new cargo War Clauses contain no exclusion of "ordinary judicial process" (Chapter 25). In the case of ships, which have unrestricted insurance for capture, seizure, arrest, restraint or detainment, such an exclusion is required to exclude from the insurance the normal workings of the civil courts when hearing and determining civil disputes. The restriction contained in Clause 1.2 of the new cargo War Clauses makes such an exclusion unnecessary for cargo insurance.

SALVAGE CHARGES

36.30 Clauses 2 of the new cargo War Clauses and the new cargo Strikes Clauses give insurance for general average and salvage charges. The nature of "salvage charges", and the reasons why they do not qualify as sue and labour is described in Chapter 24, paras. 24.25–24.35.

STRIKERS

36.31 The (A), (B) and (C) Clauses exclude from their insurance not only loss damage or expense caused by strikers (and others), but also loss, damage or expense resulting from strikes, lock-outs, labour disturbances, riots and civil commotions. Part, but not all, of the risks so excluded are insured by the new cargo Strikes Clauses as follows:

"1. This insurance covers . . . loss of or damage to the subject matter insured caused by
1.1 strikers, locked-out workmen, or persons taking part in labour disturbances, riots or civil commotions."

To this there is an exception:

"3. In no case shall this insurance cover . . .
3.7 loss damage or expense arising from the absence shortage or withholding of labour of any description whatsoever resulting from any strike, lockout, labour disturbance, riot or civil commotion."

36.32 In some of the Special Cargo Insurances, namely the Strikes Clauses relating to Frozen Food and Frozen Meat, Clause 3.7 is extended to read:

"3.7 loss damage or expense arising from the absence shortage or withholding of equipment, power, fuel, coolant, refrigerant or labour of any description whatsoever resulting from any strike, lock-out, labour disturbance, riot or civil commotion."

36.33 Clause 3.7 is reinforced by another exclusion:

"3.5 loss damage or expense proximately caused by delay, even though the delay be caused by a risk insured against . . . "

36.34 Loss caused by the violent action of, or destruction by, strikers and other people listed in Clause 1.1 is insured, but not the loss which arises from the "absence, shortage or withholding of labour" (in the case of two sets of clauses other things as well) which results from "any strike, lockout, labour disturbance, riot or civil commotion". Thus a sensitive cargo such as meat or fruit which is simply left to rot because of a strike will not give rise to a claim on the insurance. There is of course the possibility that the "absence shortage or withholding of labour" has as its purpose the destruction or the damage of the cargo. If so, it is suggested that this is not "resulting from a strike", which is normally a concerted refusal by workmen to work in consequence of an alleged grievance.[7] The possibility of raising such a plea must depend on the facts of any case and the evidence which can be adduced.

FINANCIAL DEFAULT OF THE SHIPOWNING INTERESTS

36.35 Both the new cargo War Clauses and the new cargo Strikes Clauses contain a new provision which was first introduced in 1982. It reads:

"3. In no case shall this insurance cover . . .
   3.6 loss damage or expense arising from insolvency or financial default of the owners managers charterers or operators of the vessel."

36.36 This version of the clause is described in Chapter 35 as being "not extended". It is an absolute provision, and does not depend upon the knowledge or fault of the insured cargo owners. It caused much alarm among the Associations which negotiated the Special Cargo Insurances, and thus the "extended" clause was included in the War and Strikes insurance relating to commodity goods, oils seeds and fats, frozen meat, jute, rubber and timber. In its "extended" version, the exclusion only takes effect where, at the time of loading the cargo, the assured was aware, or in the ordinary course of business should have been aware, that such insolvency or financial default could prevent the normal prosecution of the voyage. Even then, it will not take effect against a party to whom the insurance has been assigned provided that he has bought or agreed to buy the cargo in good faith. This can only mean that the purchaser was not, or had no reason to be, aware of the financial instability of the shipowning interests when he purchased the cargo.

UNSEAWORTHINESS

36.37 Both the new cargo War Clauses and the new cargo Strikes Clauses contain a seaworthiness provision. It reads:

"4.—4.1 In no case shall this insurance cover loss damage or expense arising from unseaworthiness of vessel or craft,
unfitness of vessel craft conveyance container or liftvan for the safe carriage of the subject-matter insured,
where the Assured or their servants are privy to such unseaworthiness or unfitness, at the time the subject-matter is loaded therein.
   4.2 The underwriters waive any breach of the implied warranties of seaworthiness of the ship and fitness of the ship to carry the subject-matter insured to destination, unless the Assured or their servants are privy to such unseaworthiness or unfitness."

This version of Clause 4 is described in Chapter 35 as "not extended".

7. Chapter 16.

36.38 Section 40(2) of the Marine Insurance Act 1906 provides in a somewhat sweeping fashion that, in the insurance of goods or moveables, there is an implied warranty given by the assured goods owner to the cargo underwriter that the ship is seaworthy as a ship and reasonably fit to carry the goods to their destination at the time that the voyage commences. This is an onerous provision on the assured, who may have no knowledge of any failings on the ship's part.[8]

36.39 It was usual in the cargo marine clauses in use before 1982 to nullify the provisions of this section by admitting seaworthiness. No such admission was contained in the old cargo War Clauses or the old cargo Strikes Clauses, and consequently the section applied in its full rigour. Clause 4 is thus a new provision, and it does ameliorate the effects of the section to a great extent.

36.40 Clause 4.1 provides that the assured cannot recover if, at the time of loading, he is privy to the unseaworthiness or unfitness of the vessel, craft, conveyance, container or liftvan. Clause 4.2 is aimed directly at softening the provisions of the section so that it applies only if the assured is privy to the unseaworthiness or unfitness of the ship. It should be noted here that the underwriter does not have to depend on the more onerous requirement of wilful misconduct (Chapter 29); the privity of the assured is sufficient.

36.41 Like the insolvency exclusion (Clause 3.6), (paras. 36.35 and 36.36), the seaworthiness clause, even though it did reduce to a great extent the rigours of section 40(2), was still viewed with some alarm. The Associations which negotiated the Special Cargo Insurances obtained a version, described in Chapter 35 as the "extended" version, in respect of the War and Strikes insurances for commodity goods, oils seeds and fats, frozen meat, jute, natural rubber and timber. The "extended" version has two main differences to that which is "not extended". Unseaworthiness or unfitness at the time of loading cannot be pleaded to defeat the claim of the party who has bought or agreed to buy the cargo in good faith and to whom the insurance has been assigned. The warranties contained in section 40(2) of the Marine Insurance Act 1906 are waived entirely by the underwriters.

FRUSTRATION OF THE VOYAGE OR ADVENTURE

36.42 The new cargo War Clauses contain the following exclusion which reads:

"3. In no case shall this insurance cover . . .
3.7 any claim based upon loss of or frustration of the voyage or adventure."

36.43 The new cargo Strikes Clauses contain a similar exclusion save that it is numbered 3.8. This pattern is repeated throughout the Special Cargo Insurances (Chapter 35), except that, in the case of the strikes insurance relating to oil and coal, the exclusion is numbered 3.7.

36.44 In its original concept, insurance against War and Strikes Risks, whether for ships or for cargo, provided insurance against two distinct types of loss, always provided of course that the casualty came within at least one of the insured perils; physical loss or damage to the subject-matter insured, and loss caused by the frus-

---

8. Moveables are defined by section 90 of the Act as any tangible property other than the ship, and includes money, valuable securities and documents.

tration of the voyage or adventure. The *Rotch* case (paras. 13.7–13.10) and the *Rodocanachi* case (para. 11.21), will serve to illustrate how loss caused by the frustration of the voyage or adventure was held to be insured in the case of ships and cargo respectively. Staughton J., when making his award in *The Bamburi* case in 1981 (paras. 13.63–13.72), reviewed the history of the insurance for loss caused by the frustration of the voyage or adventure so far as it related to ships, and came to the conclusion that, by 1857 at the latest, it had disappeared. From the middle of the 19th century, ships were insured by the War and Strikes insurances for physical loss or damage only.

36.45 In the case of cargo however, the insurance of physical loss or damage on the one hand, and frustration of the voyage or adventure on the other, continued as it always had been, and in 1915 the *Sanday* case (paras. 13.17–13.26) was decided in the plaintiff's favour on the grounds that the voyage or adventure had been frustrated. This result came as a surprise to the underwriters, so in 1919 an exclusion was introduced into the War insurance relating to cargo with the aim of removing such frustration from the insurance and to bring the cargo War insurance into line with that provided for ships. By the time that the old cargo War Clauses were introduced in 1980, the last version in use before the new cargo War Clauses took effect in 1982, this had been refined to read:

"2 This insurance excludes
  2.1 any claim based upon loss of, or frustration of, the insured voyage or adventure caused by arrests restraints or detainments of Kings Princes Peoples Usurpers or persons attempting to usurp power."

36.46 There was no similar provision in the old cargo Strikes Clauses, and the provision on frustration of the voyage or adventure which now appears in the new cargo Strikes Clauses was first introduced in 1982.

36.47 There is a considerable difference between the old and the new. The old cargo War Clauses provided unrestricted insurance for the insured perils most likely to give rise to frustration of the voyage or adventure, namely capture, seizure, arrest, restraint or detainment, and only excluded claims based upon loss of or frustration of the voyage or adventure caused by arrests, restraints or detainments of Kings Princes Peoples or Usurpers. The exclusion did not expressly stretch to capture, seizure, arrest, restraint or detainment by others. In the case of capture, this is probably unimportant, since capture can only be effected by belligerent rulers, who can be usurpers who have succeeded in seizing power.[9] A study of the chapters on Seizure (Chapter 12) and Arrest Restraint or Detainment (Chapter 13) will indicate that these insured perils can arise through the actions of those who are not Kings Princes Peoples or Usurpers. In the 63 years of the exclusion's life from 1919 to 1981, it appears that the point was never judicially determined, but it is suggested that it is a reasonable conclusion that loss caused by frustration of the voyage or adventure continued to be insured by the cargo War insurance long after it had disappeared entirely for the similar insurance for ships; only if it arose from the actions of Kings Princes Peoples or Usurpers was it excluded from the insurance.

36.48 In 1982 however, when the new cargo War Clauses took effect, the position was changed dramatically by the wording which appears at the beginning of

---

9. Capture is described in Chapter 11. Usurpers are described at paras. 8.6–8.8 *et seq.*

this section of this chapter. It is first of all tacitly recognised that seizure, arrest, restraint and detainment can be effected by persons other than Kings Princes Peoples or Usurpers, and mention of these people disappears from the clauses. The clauses exclude "any claim" based on frustration of the voyage or adventure, and this probably reflects with greater precision the intentions of the original draftsmen in 1919. Moreover, as has already been remarked in another section to this chapter, cargo is no longer insured for capture, seizure, arrest, restraint or detainment without restriction; these insured perils have also to come within the insured perils of Clauses 1.1 to be insured at all. Finally, in 1982, the frustration exclusion was inserted into the cargo Strikes insurance for the first time.

36.49 Between 1919 and 1981, there are only two reported cases in which the frustration exclusion was reviewed, and since 1982 there have been no such cases. In the *Forestal* cases (paras. 13.27–13.34), Hilbery J. regarded the insurance of goods against physical loss and damage and the frustration of the voyage or adventure as indivisible. He was later overruled on this point by the Court of Appeal and the House of Lords, and Viscount Maugham explained at some length why he was wrong; they are totally separate one from another:

"The contract is an insurance against loss of two different kinds in relation to goods. The first involves loss or damage to the goods themselves; the second involves merely that they have not reached their destination, though they be perfectly safe."[10]

36.50 His Lordship went on to point out that the Frustration Clause relieved the underwriters of at least some liability under the second head; it had no effect on their liability under the first head.

36.51 Hilbery J., on the basis that his line of thinking was correct, made an interesting finding that where there are two causes of one loss, one of which is insured and the other is excluded, the assured cannot recover (para. 13.30). However sound this may be as a general principle, it is as well that he was overruled in this particular instance. The concept of frustration of the voyage or adventure has not disappeared from the law; it is, quite simply, not insured any longer. Had his finding been allowed to stand, many proper claims for capture, seizure, arrest, restraint or detainment, which may well involve such frustration besides physical loss, would be held to be uninsured.[11]

36.52 Even though any claims based on loss or frustration of the voyage or adventure are not insured by the new cargo War Clauses and the new cargo Strikes Clauses, it must be borne in mind that the law of constructive total loss, when the subject-matter if the insurance has been captured, seized, arrested, restrained or detained, had made very considerable advances during the last 30 years. It will be seen from paras. 13.51–13.72 why and how it has advanced, and that it now seems well settled that where the subject-matter of the insurance suffers from one of these insured perils, it can, even though it is not harmed in any way, become a constructive total loss and therefore a physical loss. It is going too far to say that the modern law on constructive total loss has, amongst other things, completely replaced frustration of the voyage or adventure. It can be said that the circumstances in which each arise are likely to be so similar that it is indeed difficult to draw a distinction.

10. (1941) 70 Ll.L.Rep. 173.
11. The other case is the *Atlantic Maritime* case, paras. 22.46–22.51.

FRUSTRATION OF THE VOYAGE OR ADVENTURE—
ADDITIONAL EXPENSES INSURANCE

36.53 The exclusion of any insurance in respect of loss of or frustration of the voyage or adventure can be ameliorated to some degree by the Institute Additional Expenses Clauses (Cargo War Risks) dated 1.7.85. These replace the Additional Expenses Clause (War Risks) dated 1.1.71. The only substantial alteration to the earlier clauses is an additional clause providing that the insurance is subject to English Law and Practice. Thus they do not enjoy the clearer drafting of the new cargo War Clauses or the new cargo Strikes Clauses which took effect in 1982. It is hoped that their main characteristics can usefully be shown briefly in note form:

> The insurance is "only to cover additional expenses", incurred through "War Risks". This somewhat imprecise expression is clarified by Clause 1, which is the insured perils clause.

36.54 The insured perils are:

> In the event of interruption or frustration of the voyage or adventure by arrests, restraints detainments or acts of Kings Princes and Peoples in prosecution of hostilities, or
> by blockades or other warlike operations, whether war is or is not declared, whether by belligerent or non belligerent, or
> by the carrier exercising a liberty in the contract of carriage, then

36.55 If any one or more of these things happen and the goods are discharged elsewhere than their destination, the underwriters will pay:

> landing and warehousing charges, and/or
> transhipment to original destination, or
> return of goods to point of origin, or
> transhipment to a substituted destination.

36.56 There are several conditions set out in Clauses 2 to 10 which are in an easy-to-read form, and two of them should be noted; there is no insurance for "any hostile use" of a nuclear weapon, and Clause 8 puts time limits on the underwriter's liability.

36.57 This brief description is not determinative, and in case of any casualty the exact wording of the clauses must be examined (Appendix K). It is hoped, however, that it gives a general idea of these clauses, and also demonstrates that they do not provide a total substitute for the insurance which was formerly given for loss or frustration of the voyage or adventure.

CONSTRUCTIVE TOTAL LOSS

36.58 The (A), (B) and (C) Clauses contain a provision on constructive total loss which follows and expands upon the text of sections 60(1) and (2)(iii) of the Marine Insurance Act 1906, but which, by the open words of the clause, excludes section (2)(i) and (ii) (paras. 33.37–33.38). The new cargo War Clauses and the new cargo

Strikes Clauses have no provision on constructive total loss. This has the appropriate consequence that the whole of section 60 in its original wording applies to these two sets of clauses with the exception of section 60(2)(ii), which is stated to apply to ships alone.

36.59 The law on the constructive total loss of cargo is the same as that pertaining to ships (Chapter 27). The reader is reminded of such matters as the importance of the tendering of the Notice of Abandonment, the importance of the date of the issue of the writ, or the importance of the date where the more modern practice is followed of the underwriter refusing to accept the Notice of Abandonment and placing the assured in the same position as though a writ had been issued. It is equally important to remember that where a cargo suffers an insured peril such as capture, but is restored to its owner before a Notice of Abandonment is given, it is possible that the claim will be for a partial loss only. If on the other hand it is only restored after the date of the giving of the Notice of Abandonment (or the issue of the writ), then the definite possibility of a constructive total loss will still arise. A last point is the question of "delay", particularly if the passage of time has any relevance to the loss. "Delay" is dealt with in a separate section of this chapter.

WILFUL MISCONDUCT

36.60 Both the new War Clauses and the new Strikes Clauses contain the exception:

"3. In no case shall this insurance cover
3.1 loss damage or expense attributable to wilful misconduct of the Assured."

36.61 Wilful Misconduct is described in Chapter 29, and this clause does no more than reiterate the essential provisions of section 55(2)(a) of the Marine Insurance Act 1906. It will be noted from the sections of this chapter which deal with "Unseaworthiness" and "Financial default of the Shipowning interests" that lesser standards of blame on the part of the assured are sufficient in certain limited instances to excuse the underwriters. In unseaworthiness, it is sufficient if the assured is "privy" to it. Where financial default is concerned, there are some clauses among the Special Cargo Insurances, which are noted in the relevant section of this chapter, where the underwriters are only excused if "the Assured are aware" or "should be aware" of the shipowning interests financial instability. "Privy" and "aware" represent much lower degrees of guilt than does "wilful misconduct".

DELAY

36.62 Both the new cargo War Clauses and the new cargo Strikes Clauses contain an exceptions clause which reads:

"3. In no case shall this insurance cover
3.5 loss damage or expense proximately caused by delay, even though the delay be caused by a risk insured against (except expenses payable under Clause 2 above)."

36.63 This provision is in virtually the same terms as section 55(2)(b) of the Marine Insurance Act 1906. The section does allow contrary intentions to be expressed in the policy, and here there is an express provision that the exclusion is not to apply to a claim for expenses for delay where these arise in general average.

36.64 "Delay" is discussed in detail in Chapter 22 because it has mostly been an issue in freight cases. *Pink* v. *Fleming*[12] (paras. 14.11, 14.12) is a case where freight was not concerned, but the judgment of Lord Esher M.R. has since been much criticised. Nowadays the emphasis is placed on the "proximate cause" of the loss, and the judges will only be satisfied when they have established it. It therefore follows that, even in a case where there has been a measure, perhaps a great deal, of delay, the exclusion will only operate where "delay", and not an insured peril, is the proximate cause of the loss.

12. (1890) 25 Q.B.D. 396.

CHAPTER 37

Containers—insurance by London Market

INTRODUCTORY

37.1 Containers have been used for many years to transport goods, but until the containers revolution in the mid-1960s, their use was on a very small scale among a limited number of trades. Where there was a sea voyage, it was usually of short duration. A typical example was the trade between the Baltic States, where the container was usually a truck which was loaded by the consignor before proceeding to its destination, where it was unloaded by the consignee. Between these two points the goods were not touched at all, and the truck crossed the frequent stretches of water onboard ferries like the modern ro-ro ships onto which it could be driven, and from which it could be discharged, always as a single unit. By 1966 and 1967, however, the great increase in the prosperity of the Western world in the 20 years since the Second World War meant that shippers wanted to move, and consignees wanted to receive, goods in much greater bulk than ever before, and the drive began to reduce the costs of doing so. The amount of handling that was necessary to move individual piece-goods, such as cartons containing television sets, cases of liquor, carcasses of meat, or bags of coffee from where they were produced to where they were required was enormous, and its cost was continually escalating and threatening to spin out of control. Individual handling of each carton, case, carcass or bag onto and off railcars, roadtrucks and ships was perceived as being extremely wasteful, particularly as individual shippers were by now well able to fill one (or more) T.E.U., or 20-foot equivalent unit, for the use of one buyer overseas. How much more economical it would be to load the goods into containers at the point of production, often many miles inland, and to despatch them as one single unit to the buyer, also frequently many miles inland, on the other side of the world. Between seller and buyer the goods would not be touched at all, and the handling of the containers themselves onto specially adapted ships, railflats, and roadtrucks would be by means of purpose-built loading and discharging bridges and cranes. The opportunities for loss or damage to the goods and for pilferage would be much reduced, and the whole process would be much quicker.[1]

37.2 And so it has proved in the years since 1967 when the container revolution began to gather pace. Containers are now the universal workhorses for the carriage

---

1. Whilst the pilferage of goods is now much less of a problem than it once was, there have been cases where the entire container has disappeared. One was discovered in Texas with people living in it. Another was found a short way outside Southampton being used to house chickens. The contents in each case were never found.

of piece-goods and have amply fulfilled the high hopes placed in them, and have repaid in full measure the huge investment that they required. It does mean that containers have a comparatively short insurance history. On the other hand, their insurance was not immediately revised in wholesale fashion as it was for cargo in 1982 and for ships in 1983. This was only done on 1st January, 1987.

37.3 A list of the main Container Clauses which are considered by this chapter and by Chapter 38 together with any abbreviations that are used, is as follows:

37.4 In use before 1987

(1) Institute Container Clauses Time (All Risks) dated 1.10.69.
(2) Institute Container Clauses Time (Total Loss, General Average, Salvage, Salvage Charges, Sue and Labour) dated 1.10.69.
(3) Institute War and Strikes Clauses Containers—Time dated 1.10.69 ("the old Container War and Strikes Clauses").

37.5 In use after 1st January, 1987

(4) Institute Container Clauses—Time dated 1.1.87 ("the new Container 'all risks' Clauses").
(5) Institute Container Clauses—Time (Total Loss, General Average, Salvage, Salvage Charges, Sue and Labour) dated 1.1.87 ("the new Container T.L.O. Clauses").
(6) Institute War and Strikes Clauses Containers—Time dated 1.1.87 ("the new Container War and Strikes Clauses").

37.6 This list shows the clauses in use by the London insurance market. Containers are also insured on mutual terms by the Through Transport Mutual Insurance Association (Bermuda) Limited, which is one of the largest underwriters in this field. The insurance which it provides is described in Chapter 39.

THE ASSURED CONTAINER OWNERS

37.7 Containers are owned by:

1. The owners of the container ships.
2. The owners of the goods being transported.
3. The owners of the containers who do not own either ships or cargo, but who lease them out for use by others.
4. The Non Vessel Owning Carriers (N.V.O.C.s) using either their own or leased containers.

37.8 Commonly containers are loaded ("stuffed") at depots ashore, often far inland, and are unloaded ("unstuffed") at similar depots at their destination. These depots may belong to the shipowners, to the owners of the goods themselves, to a contractor owning a depot, or to an inland transport company such as a railway company.

THE SCHEDULE

37.9 All the Container Clauses, both those in use before 1st January, 1987, and those in use after that date, have one thing in common—a schedule. In the clauses in use before 1987 this schedule appeared at the very top of the clauses, whereas in the clauses in use since that date it appears at the end. The schedule itself consists of a series of boxes in which are entered some details of obvious importance to the insurance such as the type and size of the containers which are insured, their identification marks, their value, and the agreed Deductible. What does seem to be beyond doubt however, is that the details entered in the box "Sea and Territorial Limits (which are deemed to include normal flying routes between these Sea and Territorial Limits)" describe the geographical area within which the containers are to have insurance and thus go to the very root of the insurance contract. As such they are "warranties" with all that warranties in a marine insurance contract entail. It is possible that the details entered in the box "Overseas Vessels" also have this characteristic, although shipment on other ships than those named is less likely to pose acute problems for the assured; in all but the most unusual circumstances, it should be possible for the assured to draw the underwriter's attention to what has happened if containers are shipped on ships other than the named vessels and to make sure that the insurance is not compromised before there is a casualty.[2]

37.10 There will not of course be a problem where the words "worldwide" and "all Overseas Vessels" are entered in these boxes. If, however, some geographical limits are inserted, then the possibility that the assured is in breach of warranty if the containers are taken outside these limits cannot be lightly dismissed. The effect of the recent judgment of the House of Lords in *Bank of Nova Scotia* v. *Hellenic Mutual War Risks Association (Bermuda) Limited (The Good Luck)*[3] might well be that the insurance becomes void, and simply ceases to exist, as from the moment of the breach irrespective of the state of anybody's knowledge.

37.11 Some amelioration of the effects of a breach of warranty is offered in the case of the two sets of marine clauses. Clause 9 of the new Container "all risks" Clauses (Clause 8 of the new Container T.L.O. Clauses), repeating a provision of the marine clauses in use before 1987, reads:

"9. Each Container is covered, including whilst on deck, within the sea and territorial limits specified in the Schedule below. Breach of these limits held covered at a premium to be agreed, subject to prompt notice being given to the Underwriters."

37.12 It will be seen from Chapter 28 that the "held covered" provision does pose problems of its own. Nevertheless, it is suggested that it does offer a reasonable chance for the assured to save his insurance for marine risks if he notifies the underwriters as soon as he becomes aware of the facts and is willing to pay any extra premium that is required. No such facility is offered by either the old or the new Container War and Strikes Clauses. In the confused circumstances which invariably surround a War and Strikes casualty, the containers may well be removed from the agreed geographical limits without the assured being able to prevent this happening, and possibly even without his knowledge. From the *Bank of*

2. Chapter 26, paras. 26.10–26.37.
3. [1991] 2 Lloyd's Rep. 191, see paras. 26.32–26.35.

Nova Scotia judgment, it must be concluded that the insurance will come to an end from the date of such removal without the possibility of saving it.

CONTAINER MARINE POLICIES—PRE-1987

37.13 Before 1987, containers were insured on the S.G. Form with the relevant Institute Container Clauses attached. From what has already been said, it will be seen that there was no lengthy insurance history for containers as there was for ships and for cargo. Nevertheless, the methods of insurance for containers were the same as for ships and for cargo, and these are described in Chapter 1.

37.14 The two sets of marine clauses in use were the:

(1) Institute Container Clauses Time (All Risks)—1.10.69.

These provided insurance on an "all risks" basis, except that loss and damage to the container's machinery, if there was any, was only insured in the case of the incidents listed by Clause 3. With this qualification, the judicial decisions quoted in paras. 33.41 and 33.42, are as relevant to containers as they are to cargo.

(2) Institute Container Clauses Time (Total Loss, General Average, Salvage, Salvage Charges, Sue and Labour)—1.10.69.

These provided insurance on a total loss only basis, although as their name implies, some other types of casualty were also insured.

37.15 Apart from Clauses 3, 5 and 6, which are especially relevant to "all risks" but not to total loss only insurance, both sets of clauses were identical. Thus the War and Strikes risks were excluded from the insurance for marine risks in the same terms. Using the numbering of the "all risks" clauses:

37.16 Clause 17 contained the Free of Capture and Seizure (F.C. & S.) Clause in identical terms to that used for the insurance of marine risks for ships and for cargo. It is quoted in para. 1.15. There was also Clause 18 which read:

"18. Warranted free of loss or damage or expense directly or indirectly caused by or contributed to by or arising from
(a) ionising radiations from or contamination by radio activity from any nuclear fuel or from any nuclear waste from the combustion of nuclear fuel;
(b) the radioactive, toxic, explosive or other hazardous properties of any explosive nuclear assembly or nuclear component thereof."

37.17 These two clauses are far from clear. Clause 18(a) would seem to exclude nuclear fuel and nuclear waste from the insurance, but the purposes of Clause 18(b) are not readily apparent. It would certainly exclude the unpleasant properties of an assembled nuclear weapon being carried as cargo, and its very proximity to Clause 18(a) could lead to the conclusion this was its sole purpose. If, as was probable, the intention was to exclude loss, damage, or contamination resulting from the detonation of a nuclear weapon, then the clause could have been worded at least as clearly as Clause 26 of the marine clauses for ships (Appendix C). It is however, possible, and it is suggested permissible, to give it a wider reading, and to say that Clause 18(b) excludes from the insurance for marine risks the consequences of the explosion of a nuclear weapon, whether it be hostile, in practice, or accidental.

"19. Warranted free of loss or damage or expense arising from confiscation or nationalisation or requisition or pre-emption."

Confiscation, Requisition, Pre-emption, and Nationalisation are described in Chapter 21.

"20. Warranted free of loss or damage or expense caused by strikers, locked-out workmen, or persons taking part in labour disturbances, riots or civil commotions."

Whilst the exclusions of the activities of these people does vary, depending on whether the insurance for marine risks is for ship, for cargo, or for containers, this clause did effectively remove them from the scope of the insurance for marine risks for containers.

CONTAINER WAR AND STRIKES POLICIES—PRE–1987 ("THE OLD CONTAINER WAR AND STRIKES CLAUSES)

37.18 Like the War and Strikes Clauses for ships, but in contrast to those for cargo, the old Container War and Strikes Clauses insured both War and Strikes in one set of clauses. Clause 1, which can be described as the Insured Perils Clause, stated that the risks excluded from the "all risks" insurance for marine risks by the F.C. & S. Clause and by Clause 20 (although it was not named as such), would be insured by the old Container War and Strikes Clauses, this time as insured perils. Thus far, the strictures of Mocatta J. and UNCTAD apart (paras. 1.15, 1.17, 1.18), the position was reasonably clear. From then on an element of complexity, beloved by lawyers and universally detested by everyone else, was included into the last four lines of Clause 1. Setting out each element separately, and for the sole purpose of making them clearer, they read:

"The Institute Container Clauses Time (All Risks) 1.10.69.
    except lines 7 and 8 in Clause 1,
    Clause 16,
    and the words 'confiscation or' in Clause 19,
are deemed to be incorporated in this insurance in so far as they do not conflict with the provisions of these Clauses."

37.19 The intention was clear enough, to include clauses from the "all risks" insurance for marine risks which were also relevant to the old Container War and Strikes Clauses, but the method chosen was puzzling in the extreme. To begin with, there was no mention of Clause 20 which had now become a set of insured perils; their presence in the old Container War and Strikes Clauses in this guise depended on the rather loose wording of the last 14 words "in so far as they do not conflict with the provisions of these Clauses". The meaning of the remainder could, with persistence, be disentangled:

Lines 7 and 8

37.20 In the marine "all risks" clauses, containers which left the geographical areas of the agreed sea and territorial limits were held covered at a premium to be arranged. As is mentioned under the sub-heading of "The Schedule" (paras. 37.9–37.12), such a facility was not available to the old Container War and Strikes Clauses.

Clause 16

37.21 The insurance given by the marine "all risks" clauses could be cancelled by either side on 30 days' notice. This did not apply to the old Container War and Strikes Clauses.

"Confiscation or" in Clause 19

37.22 Clause 19 is quoted at para. 37.17, and excludes from the marine "all risks" insurance confiscation, nationalisation, requisition, and pre-emption. So far as the old Container War and Strikes insurance was concerned, "confiscation" was not excluded from the insurance (although it was not specifically named as an insured peril), whereas nationalisation, requisition, and pre-emption were—unless they could be said to come within the terms of the F.C. & S. Clause, which was hardly a model of precision, by virtue of the same 14 words "in so far as they do not conflict with the provisions of these Clauses". Complexity did not end there, because "confiscation" was not insured if the containers were confiscated by the government of the country in which they were owned.

37.23 The old Container War and Strikes Clauses included the Notice of Cancellation and Automatic Termination of Cover Clause (Chapter 4). Apart from noting this, it appears that there is no point in describing their complexities further, apart from saying that they probably deserved even greater denunciation than they in fact received from UNCTAD, (paras. 1.17, 1.18) and this work would be better employed in moving onto the new clauses, both marine and War and Strikes, which were introduced on 1st January, 1987.

CONTAINER MARINE POLICIES—POST 1st JANUARY, 1987— INTRODUCTORY

37.24 If the rationalisation, indeed metamorphosis, of the insurance for containers, both marine and War and Strikes, came late in time, it was nonetheless welcome. The Container Clauses, like the clauses for ships and for cargo, are intended to be used as attachments to the MAR form (Appendix B). Its characteristics are described at para. 1.24. Again the MAR form sets out no insured perils or exclusions; these are left to the relevant clauses where they are set out in an easy-to-read format. Containers are now insured for marine risks by the London Market as follows.

INSURED PERILS

37.25 1. Institute Container Clauses—Time 1.1.87 ("the new Container 'all risks' Clauses"). These give insurance on an "all risks" basis except that loss or damage to the container's machinery (if there is any) is only insured in a number of specific instances which are set out in Clause 4. With this qualification, the decisions quoted at paras. 33.41, 33.42 apply as much to containers as they do to cargo.

37.26 2. Institute Container Clauses—Time (Total Loss, General Average, Salvage, Salvage Charges, Sue and Labour) 1.1.87 ("the new Container T.L.O. Clauses"). These give insurance on a total loss only basis, whether the total loss is actual or constructive, although, as their name implies, they give insurance for some further types of casualty as well.

EXCLUSIONS TO THE INSURED PERILS

37.27 The exclusions in both sets of clauses which give insurance for marine risks are identical, save that in the new Container "all risks" Clauses they are numbered 5, 6, 7 and 8, whilst in the new Container T.L.O. Clauses they are numbered 4, 5, 6 and 7. In the commentary which follows, the numbering of the "all risks" Clauses will be used.

37.28 *Clause 5.* None of the provisions of Clause 5 are incorporated in the new Container War and Strikes Clauses, and therefore no mention of them will be made here. Clauses 6, 7 and 8 are of greater interest.

37.29 *Clause 6* reads:

"6. In no case shall this insurance cover loss damage liability or expense caused by
    6.1 war civil war revolution rebellion insurrection, or civil strife arising therefrom, or any hostile act by or against a belligerent power
    6.2 capture seizure arrest restraint or detainment (barratry and piracy excepted) and the consequences thereof or any attempt thereat
    6.3 derelict mines torpedoes bombs or other derelict weapons of war
    6.4 confiscation nationalisation requisition or pre-emption."

37.30 It should be noted that Clause 6 is in identical terms with its equivalent clause, Clause 23 of the Institute Time Clauses Hulls—1.10.83, the clauses which provide the insurance for marine risks for ships (Appendix C) with one exception only; in the ships clauses, Clause 6.4 does not appear. "Confiscation" (together with "Expropriaton") is an insured peril of the new Container War and Strikes Clauses (Clause 1.6), although "requisition" and "pre-emption" are again excluded from those clauses by Clause 5.1.3. All these matters, including nationalisation, are dealt with in Chapter 21.

37.31 It will be seen that, like the Clause 23 which is mentioned above, "barratry" and "piracy" are excluded from the operation of Clause 6, and therefore in clauses which give insurance on an "all risks" basis, even for total loss only, they are included in the insurance against marine risks. Regarding piracy, (Chapter 20), the same considerations apply to containers as they do to ships and to cargo (paras. 36.3 *et seq.*). So far as barratry is concerned, attention is drawn to *The Salem* case (paras. 12.54–12.63) and to the American cases, the *Greene* and *Hai Hsuan* cases (paras. 12.43–12.45 and 12.46–12.51).

37.32 *Clause 7* reads:

"7 In no case shall this insurance cover loss damage liability or expense
    7.1 caused by strikers, locked-out workmen, or persons taking part in labour distrubances, riots or civil commotions
    7.2 resulting from strikes, lock-outs, labour disturbances, riots or civil commotions
    7.3 caused by any terrorist or any person acting from a political motive."

37.33 Again Clause 7 bears a remarkable resemblance to its equivalent clause, Clause 24 of the Institute Time Clauses Hulls 1.10.83, which provide the insurance against marine risks for ships. Again there is an exception; in the ship's clauses, Clause 7.2 does not appear. Its presence in the Container Clauses is necessary because they give insurance on an "all risks" basis, whereas the insurance for ships only gives insurance for a specific list of insured perils. Between them Clauses 7.1 and 7.2 operate to exclude from the new Container "all risks" and T.L.O. Clauses everything that the named people can do to containers. Its matching provision in the new Container War and Strikes Clauses, Clause 5.2, is more narrowly drawn, and will be considered when dealing with these latter clauses.

37.34 *Clause 8* reads:

"8 In no case shall this insurance cover loss damage liability or expense arising from any weapon of war employing atomic or nuclear fission and/or fusion or other like reaction or radioactive force or matter."

37.35 Unlike the insurance of cargo (paras. 36.11–36.25) there can be no doubt that the consequences of a detonation of a nuclear weapon, whether hostile, in practice, or accidental, is excluded from both the new Container "all risks" and T.L.O. Clauses. The matching clause in the new Container War and Strikes Clauses, Clause 5.1.1, whilst not entirely similar in its wording, will have the same effect so far as such detonations are concerned, and will be considered in Chapter 38.

Container War and Strikes Clauses—post 1st January, 1987

INTRODUCTORY

38.1 These are also clauses attached to the MAR form, and again they contain all their insured perils, together with their relevant exclusions, once more in an easy-to-read format.

INSURED PERILS

38.2 Institute War and Strikes Clauses Containers—Time 1.1.87. These give insurance for the following insured perils. Clause 1 reads:

"1. This insurance covers, except as provided in Clause 5 below, loss of or damage to the subject matter insured caused by
1.1 war civil war revolution rebellion insurrection, or civil strife arising therefrom, or any hostile act by or against a belligerent power
1.2 capture seizure arrest restraint or detainment, and the consequences thereof or any attempt thereat
1.3 derelict mines torpedoes bombs or other derelict engines of war
1.4 strikers, locked-out workmen, or persons taking part in labour disturbances, riots or civil commotions
1.5 any terrorist or any person acting from a political motive
1.6 confiscation or expropriation.
2. This insurance covers general average salvage and salvage charges, adjusted or determined according to the contract of affreightment and/or the governing law and practice, incurred to avoid or in connection with the avoidance of loss from a risk covered under these Clauses.
For the purpose of claims for general average contribution salvage and salvage charges recoverable hereunder the subject matter insured shall be deemed to be insured for its full contributory value."

EXCLUSIONS

38.3 Clause 5 sets out the exclusions which, with some differences which are noted below, are identical to the exclusions Clause 4 (Appendix D) of the Institute War and Strikes Clauses Hulls—Time 1.10.83, which provide the War and Strikes insurance for ships. The differences are:
38.4 (1) *Clause 5.1.4.* Capture, seizure, arrest, restraint, detainment, confiscation or expropriation is excluded from the insurance in the case of ships if it is done

by some governmental authority of the country "in which the Vessel is owned or registered". Containers are not registered in the way that ships are with all the legal consequences that registration involves. In the case of containers, the following is substituted for the quoted words " . . . where the Assured have their principal place of business". The difference seems immaterial, and follows the concept that the assured accepts the risk for himself of doing business in a particular place, and should look to the seizing authority for any compensation.

38.5 (2) *Clause 5.2.* reads:

"5 This insurance excludes
5.2 loss damage or expense arising from the absence shortage or witholding of labour of any description whatsoever resulting from any strike, lockout, labour disturbance, riot or civil commotion."

38.6 This clause does not appear in the ship's War and Strikes insurance, although it figures prominently as Clause 3.7 in the Institute Strikes Clauses (Cargo)—1.1.82, and also in the Strikes Clauses for Special Cargoes (Chapter 36). In the latter, it is sometimes in an extended form.

38.7 Clauses 7.1 and 7.2 of the new Container "all risks" Clauses (Clauses 6.1 and 6.2 of the new Container T.L.O. Clauses) remove the total consequences of what strikers and others do from the insurance for marine risks. Arguably, the exclusion from the insurance given by the new Container War and Strikes Clauses is somewhat narrower; it is only the "absence shortage or withholding of labour" which is excluded. The difference may be more apparent than real, because the physical damage or destruction which these people do is insured, whereas only the absence of labour is not. It is difficult to see what else these people can do to a container otherwise than damage or destroy it or hold it up by going on strike, but nevertheless the difference in wording results in a narrower exclusion which, in a dispute, will be construed strictly against the underwriter.

38.8 *Clause 5.4* reads:

"This insurance excludes
5.4 loss damage or expense arising from insolvency or financial default."

38.9 Clause 5.4 does not appear in the ships War and Strikes insurance, and is wider than the similar clauses for the cargo insurance (Chapter 36). This time it includes the "insolvency or financial default" of anyone, not just the shipowning interests, and there is no provision as there is for cargo, that this exclusion will only apply if there is some fault or privity on the part of the assured. In short, it is an exclusion of an absolute nature.

38.10 Another exclusion of particular importance, this time similar to the ship's War and Strikes insurance, needs to be noted.

38.11 *Clause 5.1.1* reads:

"5 This insurance excludes
5.1 loss damage liability or expense arising from
5.1.1 any detonation of any weapon of war employing atomic or nuclear fission and/or fusion or other like reaction or radioactive force or matter . . . "

38.12 As stated above (para. 37.35), Clause 8 of the new Container "all risks" Clauses (Clause 7 of the new Container T.L.O. Clauses) excludes all the losses and damage which can be laid at the door of a nuclear weapon. Clause 5.1.1 is drawn a little more narrowly, and only excludes the consequences of "a detonation". Again the difference may be more apparent than real, but nuclear weapons are known to leak a certain amount of radioactivity within their immediate vicinity, and it is at least arguable that, in the case of the new Container War and Strikes clauses, such leakage is not excluded.

38.13 The remaining exclusions can be dealt with quite briefly here.

38.14 *Clause 5.1.2* excludes the outbreak of war between the U.K., the U.S.A., France, the U.S.S.R., and the People's Republic of China. This comes as a related matter within the scope of the Notice of Cancellation and Automatic Termination of Cover Clause under that sub-heading below.

38.15 *Clause 5.1.3* excludes requisition or pre-emption. These are described by Chapter 21.

38.16 *Clause 5.1.5* excludes the consequences of breaches of quarantine, customs, or trading regulations. The *Anita* and *Wondrous* cases (paras. 13.35–13.44 and 22.52, 22.53) provide the best examples.

38.17 *Clause 5.1.6* excludes the operation of ordinary judicial process. This is explored in Chapter 25.

38.18 *Clause 5.1.7* excludes piracy. This is an Insured Peril of the new Container "all risks" and T.L.O. Clauses and is insured by the marine clauses (para. 37.31). There is, however, an exception to this exclusion, which prevents it affecting the insurance given by Clause 1.4. It is difficult indeed to see how piracy can arise under Clause 1.4, since these are all shore-based activities, and piracy can only happen "at sea". (Chapter 20).

38.19 *Clause 5.3* excludes loss, damage or expense proximately caused by delay. The word "proximately" is helpful to resolve doubts whether a casualty is caused by an insured peril or by delay. This is dealt with in Chapter 22, paras. 22.25–22.61.

38.20 *Clauses 5.5 and 5.6*. These are double insurance clauses.

SCOPE OF INSURANCE

38.21 This is the heading which is used to describe what is known as "Duration" in the insurance of cargo, and again the Waterborne Agreement has a complicating influence. The "Scope of Insurance" Clause in both the new Container "all risks" and T.L.O. Clauses which give insurance for marine risks, is straightforward; the containers are insured, including whilst they are stowed on deck, within the agreed sea and territorial limits (which can include times when they are ashore), and if these limits are breached, they are held covered subject only to a prompt notice being given to the underwriters and an extra premium, if this is required, being paid. There is an additional provision that if the containers are "sold, leased or hired" to a party who is not the assured, then the insurance shall terminate unless the underwriters agree to continue it.

38.22 In the new Container War and Strikes Clauses however, the "Scope of Insurance" is much more narrowly drawn even if it is without the tangled nature of the wording of the Duration provisions of the clauses which give war insurance to cargo (paras. 34.15–34.32). Clause 6.1 provides that the containers are insured only whilst on board an "Oversea Vessel", defined as a vessel carrying the containers from one port to another on a sea passage, or on board an aircraft. Clause 6.4 emphasises this by a negative provision that the containers are not insured whilst they are not on board an oversea vessel or an aircraft, and is reinforced by a clause in heavy print that anything inconsistent with Clause 6.4 is to be null and void. To the general rule provided by these two clauses there are two exceptions:

1. The insurance for the risks of "mines and derelict torpedoes, floating and submerged" is extended by Clause 6.2 whilst the containers are on board any vessel or craft. This must mean whilst they are on board a lighter or a barge which is not an "Oversea Vessel". The wording "mines and derelict torpedoes" poses the same difficulties with containers as it does with cargo (Chapter 15).

2. The insurance for the risks insured by Clauses 1.4 and 1.5 is extended by Clause 6.3 whilst the containers are on board any vessel or craft (other than an oversea vessel) or whilst ashore. This includes whilst loading and unloading. To this extension, there is an exclusion which is relevant to this extension alone; the loss or damage must not arise out of war, civil war, revolution, rebellion, insurrection, or civil strife arising therefrom, or any hostile act by or against a belligerent power. This could cause problems because, as a study of Chapters 8 and 17 will show, the difference between "Revolution, Rebellion and Insurrection" on the one hand, and "Civil Commotion" on the other, can be wafer thin. Whether or not insurance exists can turn on very fine points of fact which will not be immediately apparent.

38.23 As is described under the sub-heading "The Schedule" above, there is no provision, as there is in the two sets of clauses which give containers insurance for marine risks, for the containers to be "held covered" should they leave the agreed sea and territorial limits for any reason. Because the sea and territorial limits amount to a warranty, leaving these limits will be a breach of that warranty whatever the reason, and this could result in the entire insurance for War and Strikes becoming void as from the date of the breach without any means of saving it.[1]

38.24 As in the case of the War and Strikes insurance for cargo (paras. 34.15–34.21 and 34.26, 34.27), the unwary container owner might well find that a gap is opening up in the mosaic of his insurance cover if a war or strikes situation should develop, particularly if the containers should be landed from the oversea vessel. This might be difficult for him to cope with, particularly as the circumstances are likely to be confused, and it may take some time to establish the true facts.

AUTOMATIC TERMINATION

38.25 The new Container War and Strikes Clauses contain the Notice of Cancellation and Automatic Termination of Cover Clause as Clause 7. This is described in Chapter 4.

38.26 Where war breaks out between the U.K., the U.S.A., France, the U.S.S.R., and the People's Republic of China, this clause operates to bring the insurance to an immediate and automatic end. It is complemented by Clause 5.1.2,

---

1. This matter is discussed further under "The Schedule" (para. 37.10) and in Chapter 26.

which provides that loss damage liability or expense arising from the outbreak of war between these five major powers is excluded from the insurance. Thus this latter clause operates to exclude any loss or damage that may be suffered by the containers on the outbreak of war immediately before the insurance is terminated.

38.27 Similarly Clause 7 operates to bring the insurance to an immediate and automatic end if "the Container' is requisitioned either for title or for use (Chapter 21). It has been said that if only one container (and there may be hundreds insured by the same policy) is requisitioned, then the clause operates to bring the Container War and Strikes insurance to an end for all the containers, but it suggested that this cannot be so.

38.28 It is true that the new Container "all risks" and T.L.O. Clauses do not contain Clause 4 of the Institute Container Clauses Time (All Risks) 1.10.69 which was incorporated into the old Container War and Strikes Clauses which were in use before 1987. This Clause 4 provided that each container should be deemed to be a separate insurance, so that if one container was requisitioned, it was only the insurance for that container which came to an end. Even so, it appears unarguable that, to give business efficacy to the insurance, each container must still be insured as a separate unit. Not all the containers insured by the policy are likely to be lost or damaged at the same time. This view is reinforced by the wording of some of the clauses. Clauses 10, 15 and 16 of the new Container "all risks" Clauses are all incorporated into the new Container War and Strikes insurance. Clause 10 speaks of "a Container" which is sold leased or hired, whilst Clause 15 deals with "a Container" which is damaged, and Clause 16 describes the position where "a Container" is a constructive total loss. The letter of Clause 4 may not have survived the redrafting in 1987, but it is suggested that it certainly lives on in spirit.

INCORPORATION

38.29 The new Container War and Strikes Clauses incorporate several clauses from the new Container "all risks" Clauses. The most important of these are Clauses 16 (Constructive Total Loss) and 18 and 19 (Minimising Losses).

38.30 Regarding constructive total loss of a container, Clause 16 of the new Container "all risks" Clauses is the same as Clause 19 of the Institute Time Clauses Hulls 1.10.83, which provide the insurance for marine risks for ships, which is similarly incorporated into the ship's War and Strikes Clauses. The only changes that are made to the wording are minor, and such as are necessary for container insurance. There is no specially tailored clause, as is sometimes found in cargo insurance. The provisions of the Marine Insurance Act 1906 which govern constructive total loss are described in Chapter 27.

38.31 So far as "Minimising Losses" is concerned, Clauses 18 and 19 of the new Container "all risks" Clauses do not follow the lengthy and rather laboured provisions of Clause 13 of the Institute Time Clauses Hulls 1.10.83 (Appendix C), which are similarly incorporated into the ship's War and Strikes insurance. Instead, they are exactly the same as Clauses 16 and 17 of the Institute Cargo Clauses (A) 1.1.82 and Clauses 11 and 12 of the Institute War Clauses (Cargo) 1.1.82 and the Institute Strikes Clauses (Cargo) 1.1.82. In this simplified form they are commented upon at paras. 34.33–34.35. It should be remembered however, that the old and rather permissively worded Sue and Labour provision of the S.G. Form no longer applies; there is now an expressed duty to sue and labour. Nevertheless section 78 of the Marine Insurance Act 1906 still operates to make these clauses, as sue and labour provisions, supplementary engagements to the contract of insurance, with the effect that expenses incurred in pursuing the assured's obligations under these clauses are recoverable even in addition to total loss payments.

DETAINMENT

38.32 The 12-month Detainment Clause (para. 23.28) is contained in the new Container War and Strikes Clauses as Clause 4.

JURISDICTION

38.33 All the Container Clauses, whether they give insurance against marine risks or War and Strikes, contain a clause immediately under the heading which reads: "This insurance is subject to English Law and Practice."

This provision is considered at para. 34.39.

MISCELLANEOUS

38.34 The new Container War and Strikes Clauses are, as has been said, more similar to the War and Strikes Clauses for ships, and are thus free of many of the complications that attend the War and Strikes insurance for cargo. There are no express exclusions similar to those in the cargo insurance (paras. 36.60–36.61) which deal with the assured's wilful misconduct which is left to section 55 of the Marine Insurance Act 1906 (Chapter 29); with unseaworthiness of the vessel or craft; or with frustration of the voyage or adventure. It is suggested that frustration of the voyage or adventure, because it is not expressly excluded, is in fact insured by the new Container War and Strikes Clauses. This matter is gone into more fully at paras. 36.42–36.52.

CONDITIONS AND WARRANTIES

38.35 In Chapter 34 (paras. 34.29–34.32), the somewhat confusing situation with the cargo War and Strikes Clauses conditions and warranties is discussed. In the case of cargo, the position is not totally clear. So far as containers are concerned, the position is very much clearer, and it is very much less likely that an assured or an underwriter will be misled by tangled wording. The new Container War and Strikes Clauses contain one condition which amounts to a warranty as noted under the sub-heading "The Schedule" above. There is one other, right at the end of the clauses, which makes it absolutely clear that it is a condition, and indeed a warranty. It reads: "It is a condition of this insurance that each Container bears clear marks of identification."

CHAPTER 39

Containers, trailers and handling equipment—insurance on mutual terms

INTRODUCTORY

39.1 Containers, trailers, and "Handling Equipment" may be insured on mutual terms, the principal underwriters of such insurance being the Through Transport Mutual Insurance Association Ltd., which is incorporated in Bermuda, and its subsidiary, the Through Transport Mutual Insurance Association of Europe Ltd., which is incorporated in the United Kingdom. It is not the purpose of this work to explore the relationship between these two bodies, which are separate concerns with separate boards of directors and separate managers. They have similarity in that they give insurance on identical terms. In a work devoted to the study of War and Strikes insurance, the expression "T.T. Club" may therefore be used to describe the insurance given by both.

39.2 The progenitor of the T.T. Club began underwriting in 1968 when the container revolution began to gather pace. As is usual with Mutual Insurance Associations, the assured are also members of the Association and will be referred to as the "Assured Members". Again it is usual for a Mutual Association to include its insured perils and the terms and conditions on which its insurance is given in a book of rules which will be referred to as "the Rules". The T.T. Club aims to give very comprehensive insurance to those engaged in the "package" or "unit" transportation of goods, and to include all the insurance that they require into one insurance so far as it is possible to do so. This is not always permissible; for instance the third party insurance which road vehicles are required to maintain can only be given by insurers which are specially licensed to do so under the laws of the various countries, and is thus forbidden to the T.T. Club. Nevertheless, the insurance includes many other objects than just containers.

39.3 It is inevitable that insurance given over such a wide range of assureds and objects insured should be complex. In order to reduce this complexity as far as possible, the Rules are written in an easy-to-read and comprehensible style which is foreign to most types of insurance, and reliance is placed on a large number of definitions which are grouped together in Part III of the Rules, and which themselves indicate the comprehensive nature of the T.T. Club's insurance. These definitions must be borne in mind at all times, and Part III consulted whenever the Rules are examined.

39.4 The structures of the two Associations follow the normal structure of a Mutual Association. The Board of Directors is elected in General Meeting by the Assured Members of the Association, the directors themselves being, with only a

445

very few exceptions, Assured Members in their own right. They are answerable to the Assured Members in the same way as the directors of a limited company are answerable to the shareholders. The Assured Members in General Meeting also appoint the managers, who are named in the bye-laws, to attend to the day-to-day work of running the Association. The managers report to the Board of Directors at their regular meetings, and through them are also answerable to the Assured Members.

STRUCTURE OF THE RULES

39.5 The Rules are divided into parts which are further sub-divided into sections. Although the T.T. Club insures a great number of risks which are likely to arise in connection with the "unit" or "package" transportation of goods, "War Risks" insurance is only given by Sections 1 and 4, although it may be given by Section 5. "Strikes, Riots and Terrorist Risks" are insured by Sections 1 to 4, and may also be given by Section 5. These remarks do not refer to War Risks on Land, which is a special case (paras. 39.79–39.102). (Definitions, see para. 39.7.)

NOMENCLATURE—OTHER THAN DEFINITIONS USED BY THE RULES

39.6 Throughout the text which follows, certain expressions are used which are not part of the T.T. Club's Rules. They are used by the author simply to describe parts of the insurance in a way which is used in other parts of this work. They are:

1. In some places, the expressions "Non-War and Strikes type insurance" and "War and Strikes type insurance" appear. Since many of the risks are land based, it is not always appropriate to use the expression "Marine Insurance", which is commonly used in other parts of this work to describe the insurance against Risks other than War and Strikes Risks. .
2. In many parts of the T.T. Club's Rules, individual Rules are described as "paragraph". Where there are quotations from the Rules it is important that the actual wording is reproduced, but the explanatory text will follow the normal practice of the Mutual Shipowner's Associations and refer to them as "Rules".

NOMENCLATURE—DEFINITIONS USED BY THE RULES

39.7 The T.T. Club relies heavily on Definitions, and these are set out in Part III of the Rules. In spite of the complexity of its insurance, there is a considerable degree of uniformity in meanings, and the Definitions which are common throughout for the purposes of this work are:

Word	Defined Meaning
"Accident"	An accident or occurrence or a series of accidents or occurrences arising from one event.

"Equipment"	Container, trailer or handling equipment.
"Container"	(1) a container, flat, pallet or other unit load device;
	(2) a part, including spares and accessories, of a container; and
	(3) plants, tools or materials for the maintenance or repair of a container.
"Trailer"	(1) A trailer, semi-trailer or chassis of any description, towed or intended to be towed on private or public roads;
	(2) a railway wagon;
	(3) a part, including spares and accessories, of a trailer; and
	(4) plant, tools or materials for the maintenance or repair of a trailer.
"Handling Equipment"	(1) An item of machinery or other apparatus (not being an aircraft, container, ship or trailer) used for the handling, movement or storage of cargo, containers and trailers, and operations incidental to such activities;
	(2) a part, including spares and accessories, of such machinery or apparatus; and
	(3) plant, tools and materials for the maintenance or repair of such machinery or apparatus or of any customer's equipment.
"War Risks"	Risks caused by the following:
	(1) war, civil war, revolution, rebellion, insurrection, or civil strife arising therefrom, or any hostile act by or against a belligerent power;
	(2) capture, seizure, arrest, restraint, detainment (piracy excepted), confiscation or expropriation and the consequences thereof or any attempt threat;
	(3) mines, torpedoes, bombs, rockets, missiles, shells, explosives or other similar weapons of war.
"Strikes, Riots and Terrorist Risks"	Risks caused by the following persons:
	(1) strikers, locked-out workmen or persons taking part in labour disturbances, riots or civil commotions;
	(2) any terrorist or person acting from a political motive.
"Ship"	Includes boat, hovercraft and any other description of vessel or structure for use in navigation on, under, over or in water.
"Aircraft"	Includes aeroplane, airship and helicopter.
"Pre-emption"	Compulsory purchase by a belligerent of such goods of neutrals as are doubtfully or conditionally contraband.
"Contraband"	Anything forbidden to be supplied by neutrals to belligerents in time of war.

COMMON PROVISIONS THROUGHOUT THE INSURANCE

39.8 Some provisions, particularly relating to "War Risks" and "Strikes, Riots and Terrorist Risks", are common to each section of Part I. In order to avoid repetition, they are set out here, and attention is drawn to their Rule numbers in each section. For ease of identification, the Rule number will be followed by one of the following headings.

Notice of Cancellation and Automatic Termination of insurance

39.9 The Notice of Cancellation and Automatic Termination of Cover Clause is described in Chapter 4. The T.T. Club has a similar provision in each of the first four sections of Part I of the Rules which reads:

"(a) At any time the Managers may terminate the insurance under this paragraph . . . by giving the Assured 7 days' notice, termination taking effect at midnight Greenwich Mean Time of the seventh day after that on which such notice is issued.

(b) Insurance under this paragraph . . . shall in any event terminate automatically upon:
(1) the occurrence of any hostile detonation of any nuclear weapon of war wheresover such detonation may occur and regardless of whether the insured equipment is involved;
(2) the outbreak of war (whether there be a declaration of war or not) between any of the following countries—France, the People's Republic of China, the Union of Soviet Socialist Republics, the United Kingdom, the United States to America."

39.10 The main difference between this provision and the similar terms of other War and Strikes type insurance is that the Notice of Cancellation Rule is a contractual provision of the simplest nature, which is accompanied by a note to the effect that it is usually a means of charging higher permiums for particular areas where the risk of claims appears to have increased significantly. On expiry of the seven days, the insurance for all other areas is usually restored without amendment. It does not rely for its effect on such inappropriate terms as breaches of warranty or breach of warranty premiums. Chapter 4 demonstrates that these are not really breaches of warranty at all. Termination of cover on the detonation of a nuclear weapon or the outbreak of war between any two of the five Permanent Members of the Security Council aims to be as descriptive as possible.

39.11 Attention is drawn to Part II, Section 10, Rule 3 of the Rules which deems the Notice of Cancellation to be issued on the day it was posted (if sent by post), or transmitted (if sent by telex or facsimile), or handed in to the telegram or cable office (if sent by telegram or cable).

39.12 Finally, it should be noted that the insurance does not terminate on requisition as is the case with War and Strikes insurance of ships.

Destruction or damage by order of Authority, Nationalisation, Requisition, Pre-emption, loss or damage after requisition

39.13 The following provisions of Part I, Sections 1 and 4 relate to "Equipment" ("Container, trailer or handling equipment"), and in Sections 2 and 3 to the more limited expression "Handling equipment." (See definitions, para. 39.7.) They do vary slightly in their wording from section to section, but without altering their effect. They read:

"You are not insured for . . .
   destruction or damage by or under the order of any authority
physical loss arising from nationalisation,
   requisition or pre-emption."

and,

"You are not insured for any risks incurred in respect of an item . . .
after it has been requisitioned."

39.14 Any loss resulting from the act of nationalisation, requisition, or pre-emption (Chapter 21) is not insured, and the Assured Member is expected to look to the authority which does these things for any compensation. As it has been noted, requisition does not end the insurance. Although loss or damage suffered during the period of requisition is not insured (again the Assured Member is expected to look to the requisitioning authority), the insurance will return to its full force and effect once the insured object is freed from the requisition, always provided of course that this happens during the currency of the insurance.

The 12-month Clause

39.15 Insurance against "War Risks" is given by Part I, Sections 1 and 4 (although not by Sections 2 and 3), and these two sections contain a 12-month Rule. It reads:

"(a) Where you have been deprived of an item of insured equipment for a continuous period of twelve months by reason of its capture, seizure, arrest, restraint, detainment, confiscation or expropriation (such item not having previously become a total loss by reason of a risk insured under this paragraph . . .), such item shall be deemed a construcüive total loss for the purposes of your insurance under this paragraph . . . at the date such continuous period commenced.

(b) Such item shall only be deemed a constructive total loss in accordance with paragraph (a) if you were insured by the Association under this paragraph . . . in respect of such item on the date on which such continuous period commenced."

39.16 The paragraphs referred to are those which give insurance against "War Risks".

39.17 The 12-month Clause is quoted at para. 23.28. Its equivalent in the T.T. Club's Rules is very much more direct and to the point. The item c ncerned is "deemed to be a constructive total loss", not merely that the assured shall be "deemed to have been deprived of the possession of the insured object without any likelihood of recovery". Moreover, the constructive total loss arises at the date the continuous period commenced, not at some indeterminate time during the period that it has been detained.

"Strikes, Riots and Terrorist Risks"—modification

39.18 Part I, Sections 2 and 3 do not give insurance against "War Risks", so the "Strikes, Riots and Terrorist Risks" (definitions, see para. 39.7) have to be qualified by a provision which reads:

"You are not insured for any Strikes, Riots and Terrorist Risks arising from war, civil war, revolution, rebellion, insurrection, or civil strife arising therefrom, or any hostile act by or against a belligerent power."

39.19 The excluded perils are basically part of the "War Risks" insurance, and the provision's purpose is to make sure that no such insurance is given unless "War Risks" themselves are insured.

Agreement necessary to insure ["War Risks" and] "Strikes, Riots and Terrorist Risks"

39.20 "War Risks" and "Strikes, Riots and Terrorist Risks" will only be insured if there is agreement between the Assured Member and the T.T. Club that they shall be insured. To make the position absolutely clear the Rules contain a provision which reads:

"If paragraph . . . is excluded from your insurance, you are not insured for [War Risks or] Strikes, Riots and Terrorist Risks."

39.21 The words in square brackets will only be found in Part I, Sections 1 and 4, because these sections alone give insurance for "War Risks".

Piracy

39.22 It will be noted from the definition of "War Risks" (para. 39.7) that piracy is excluded from the risks of capture, seizure, arrest, restraint, detainment, confiscation or expropriation, which (apart from actual destruction) is just about everything a pirate can do, where the insurance of "Equipment" is concerned. The Non-War and Strikes type insurance in each of Part I, Sections 1 and 4, does however give insurance on an "all risks" basis subject to some exclusions which do not include piracy. It therefore follows that piracy is insured by the Non-War and Strikes type insurance in each Section, and this is in line with the thought in other kinds of insurance that piracy is now a marine risk.

39.23 Part I, Sections 2 and 3 give insurance for the more limited term "Handling Equipment" which specifically excludes containers and trailers. "Handling Equipment" is essentially shore-based and, this being so, piracy cannot arise. (Chapter 20).

Mines, torpedoes, bombs, rockets, missiles, shells, explosives or other similar weapons of war

39.24 It will be noted that, in the definition of "War Risks", these weapons are not qualified by the word "derelict", the effects of this word being discussed in Chapter 15. Consequently the loss or damage done by these weapons is insured irrespective of their condition at the time of the casualty. It should be noted however, that nuclear weapons are excluded from the insurance by a separate exclusion (See "Specified exclusions from the 'War Risks' insurance only", at paras. 39.25–39.28.)

Specified exclusions from the "War Risks" insurance only

39.25 In Part I, Sections 1 and 4 where insurance is given for "War Risks", there is an exclusion which reads:

"You are not insured for any War Risks arising from:
    (a) the hostile detonation of any nuclear weapon of war:
    (b) the outbreak of war (whether there be a declaration of war or not) between any of the following countries:
        France, the People's Republic of China, the Union of Soviet Socialist Republics, the United Kingdom, the United States of America:
    (c) capture, seizure, arrest, restraint, detainment, confiscation or expropriation by or under the order of any authority of your country:
    (d) seizure, arrest, restraint, detainment, confiscation or expropriation under quarantine regulations or by reason of infringement of any customs regulations:
    (e) ordinary judicial process, failure to provide security or to pay any fine or penalty or any financial cause:"

39.26 This exclusion applies to "War Risks" only, and not to "Strikes, Riots and Terrorist Risks" (para. 39.7), and here there is a difference to the War and Strikes insurance for ships (Appendix D) where the exclusion applies to the whole insurance.

39.27 For the purposes of the "War Risks" insurance the exclusion of nuclear weapons is direct and all inclusive. Not only does the insurance terminate on the detonation, but the damage it does when the explosion takes place is excluded from the insurance. The position is different so far as the "Strikes, Riots and Terrorist

Risks" are concerned. It is unlikely in the extreme that strikers, locked-out work-men or rioters would be able to lay their hands on a nuclear weapon, but terrorists or those inspired by a political motive may succeed in doing so. It is true that the detonation they cause will terminate the insurance for all other purposes, but the damage it does to the insured objects will still be insured.

39.28 Some other points need to be noted. Some partial relief from the effects of (c) and (d) is provided in that other Rules give insurance where the confiscation results from the breach of any regulation relating to the import or export of any cargo, conveyance and equipment, immigration, and the safety of working con-ditions. Ordinary judicial process is considered in Chapter 25.

"War Risks"—only insured if on board ship or aircraft

39.29 "War Risks" insurance is provided by Part I, Sections 1 and 4, and each section contains a Rule which reads:

"You are not insured for any War Risks unless, at the time the risk occurs, the item of equip-ment concerned is on board an oversea ship or aircraft."

39.30 The T.T. Club is concerned with the Waterborne Agreement, but has managed to shake itself free of the shackles imposed by this agreement to the extent that it can give insurance in Part I, Section 1 for War Risks on Land. This provision will be discussed in the description which follows on Part I, Section 1. (See paras. 39.79–39.102.)

THE ASSURED MEMBERS AND THE STRUCTURE OF THE RULES

39.31 The T.T. Club has five distinct types of Assured Members:

1. Ship Operators (Part I, Section 1 of the Rules).
2. Terminal Operators, Stevedores, and Depot Operators (Part I, Section 2 of the Rules).
3. Port Authorities, including port operators, harbour boards, harbour auth-orities, and harbour operators (Part I, Section 3 of the Rules).
4. Freight Forwarders and Transport Operators (Part I, Section 4 of the Rules).
5. Container Lessors (Part I, Section 5 of the Rules).

The remaining Parts and Sections of the Rules are:

6. General Exclusions and Qualifications (Part I, Section 6 of the Rules).
7. General Terms and Conditions (Part II of the Rules).
8. Definitions (Part III of the Rules).
9. Appendix A—Re-insurance by the Association.
10. Appendix B—Business Interruption (Relating to Part I, Section 2 of the Rules).
11. Appendix C—Business Interruption (Relating to Part I, Section 3 of the Rules).

39.32 The T.T. Club is thus in a position to give insurance for their containers to the four kinds of container owners which are described at para. 37.7 and which are repeated here:

1. The owners of the container ships.
2. The owners of the goods being transported.
3. The owners of the containers who do not own either ships or cargo, but who lease them out for use by others.
4. The Non-Vessel Owning Carriers (N.V.O.C.'s) using either their own or leased containers.

39.33 In addition, the T.T. Club can give insurance for many ancilliary items which are required for the "unit" or "package" transportation of goods, and many other risks which arise in such activities as well.

THE INSURANCE GIVEN BY THE T.T. CLUB

39.34 In the case of ships, cargo, and containers insured by Lloyd's, it is necessary to study the Marine insurance as well as the War and Strikes insurance, because, as will be seen in Chapters 32–36, insurance is given in two, and sometimes three, separate insurances. Some of the insured perils, which come within the general description of what other people do to the insured object, are not insured by the War and Strikes insurance as might be expected, but by the Marine insurance. Barratry, piracy, and in some cases mines, are the obvious examples. The T.T. Club makes no such distinctions, and the Insured Perils, be they Marine, or in the context of this work, Non-War and Strikes type insurance, or War and Strikes type insurance, are insured by the Rules. In order to understand the War and Strikes type insurance given by the Rules to each type of Assured Member, an examination of the Non-War and Strikes type insurance given by each section of Part I of the Rules is required. This examination will be very brief, and it must be borne in mind that each piece of the Non-War and Strikes type insurance is subject to its own exclusions and exceptions. The text that follows must not, therefore, be relied upon as a fully definitive description of this insurance.

39.35 The general picture that will emerge from the description that follows is that Part I, Sections 1 and 4 give insurance against "War Risks" and "Strikes, Riots and Terrorist Risks" to "Equipment", whilst Sections 2 and 3 give insurance against "Strikes, Riots and Terrorist Risks" in a modified form to "Handling Equipment". In addition, Part I, Section 1 gives "War Risks" insurance on land. Part I, Section 5 contemplates that the insurance given to container lessors will be negotiated with the managers. It can, if necessary, include insurance against "War Risks" and "Strikes, Riots and Terrorist Risks" as may be appropriate.

SHIP OPERATORS

39.36 ("Ship Operator" is defined as "the owner, part owner, operator, charterer or manager of a ship".)

39.37 The insurance provided by Part I, Section 1 is, as the words "Ship Operators" imply, mostly for carriage by sea, and this applies particularly to containers. Insurance is, however, given for land-based risks, including the insurance of containers, and there is a provision, which is unique to this section, for the insurance of "War Risks" on land.

The Non-War and Strikes type insurance for "Equipment" (Part I, Section 1, of the Rules)

39.38 Rule 2.2 reads:

"2.2 Risks Insured

You are insured for
2.2.1 physical loss of or damage to your insured equipment arising from any accidental cause;
2.2.2 any general average or salvage contribution due in respect of your insured equipment."

39.39 Rule 2.5 contains special provisions for the Non-War and Strikes type insurance of valuable handling equipment. Such equipment is described by Rule 2.5.1 as handling equipment whose insured value exceeds U.S.$50,000, a comparatively small sum in the field of "unit" or "package" transportation of goods. Valuable handling equipment ("Handling Equipment" is defined at para. 39.7) is excluded from the insurance provided by Rule 2.2.1. Instead, Rule 2.5.2 provides insurance for valuable handling equipment to the same extent, and on the same terms and conditions, as those pertaining to handling equipment which is insured by terminal operators, stevedores and depot owners, the relevant provision being Rule 8 of Part I, Section 2 (paras. 39.48 *et seq.*).

39.40 How far does this affect the War and Strikes type insurance for valuable handling equipment? This Rule 8 has its own provision for insurance of "Strikes, Riots and Terrorist Risks" which is similar to, but not totally identical with, the same insurance which is provided by Part I, Section 1. "War Risks" are not however affected; Rule 2.5.3 provides that valuable handling equipment may still be insured by Part I, Section 1, irrespective of its insured value.

39.41 Rule 2.3 provides for the exclusions to the insurance given by Rule 2.2. There is no insurance for defects in design or manufacture, for wear and tear, for mechanical breakdown or malfunction, for mysterious disappearance, or for equipment leased or transferred to others. For the purposes of this work, the most important exclusions of Rule 2.3 are:

2.3.2(b) Destruction or damage by order of Authority. (See at paras. 39.13, 39.14.)
2.3.2(c) Nationalisation, requisition, pre-emption. (See at paras. 39.13, 39.14.)
2.3.3(b) Loss or damage after requisition. (See at paras. 39.13, 39.14.)
2.3.4   Agreement necessary to insure "War Risks" and "Strikes, Riots and Terrorist" Risks. (See at paras. 39.29, 39.30.)

39.42 Part I, Section 1 also gives further Non-War and Strikes type insurance to ship operators. This further insurance is subject to conditions and exclusions which will be found within the terms of each Rule:

Rule Number	*General description of the insurance*
3	Third Party liabilities.
3.1.1	Non-contractual liabilities—loss of or damage to the property of, and death and bodily injury to, third parties.
3.1.2	Contractual liabilities—compensation to another person for breach of contract in the circumstances prescribed by the Rule.
4	Fines—import or export of any cargo, conveyance or equipment, immigration, and the safety of working conditions.
5	Costs—investigation, defence and mitigation of any claim, disposal of damaged cargo or a damaged item of equipment, and quarantine, fumigation or disinfection, provided that the managers have agreed that they should be incurred or the directors decide they were properly incurred.
6	Discretionary insurance where the directors decide that the Assured Member should be reimbursed in instances which are incidental to the insured services, where there is unwarranted interference by an international organisation or an authority, or where the Assured Member follows a special direction of the T.T. Club.

The War and Strikes type insurance for "Equipment" (Part I, Section 1, of the Rules)

39.43 Part I, Section 1, also gives War and Strikes type insurance to Ship Operators under Rules 2.4 for their "Equipment" (definition, see para. 39.7). Rule 7 also gives insurance whilst the "Equipment" is on land. Each Rule needs to be considered separately.

39.44 Rule 2.4 reads:

"*2.4 War Risks and Strikes, Riots and Terrorist Risks*

2.4.1 You are insured, subject to paragraphs 2.4.2 to 2.4.6, for the following caused by War Risks and Strikes, Riots and Terrorist Risks:
(a) physical loss of or damage to your insured equipment;
(b) any general average or salvage contribution due in respect of your insured equipment."

39.45 *Conditions and qualifications*

> Rule 2.4.2 The 12-month Clause. (See at para. 39.15.)
> Rule 2.4.3 "War Risks" only insured if on board ship or aircraft. (See at paras. 39.29, 39.30.)
> Rule 2.4.4 Specific exclusions from the "War Risks" insurance only. (See at paras. 39.25–39.28.)
> Rule 2.4.5 Notice of Cancellation and Automatic Termination of insurance. (See at paras. 39.9–39.12.)
> Rule 2.4.6 Insurance under Rule 2.4.1 is limited if there are agreements that it is for total loss only or if there are agreed deductibles etc.

39.46 Turning now to Rule 7 of Part I, Section 1, this Rules is intended to close a gap in the insurance provided by Rule 2.4. Originally, because of the Waterborne Agreement, "War Risks" could only be insured if the "Equipment" was on board an oversea ship or an aircraft and this is reflected in Rule 2.4.3. (This qualification did not apply to insurance for the "Strikes, Riots and Terrorist Risks", which were, and still are, insured on both sea and land.) As it has already been noted, Rule 7 was later added to make it possible, if the Assured Member desires it and the T.T. Club is willing to provide such insurance, to insure "Equipment" for "War Risks" on land as well. Like the insurance under Rule 2.4 for "War Risks" and "Strikes, Riots and Terrorist Risks", it requires a specific (and separate) request by the Assured Member and agreement on the part of the T.T. Club's managers before such insurance can be given. The terms of the insurance for "War Risks" on land are complicated, and will be described under the heading "War Risks on land" (paras. 39.79–39.102). Here the terms of Rule 7 must be considered, and this reads:

"7. War Risks on Land
   You may insure your equipment against War Risks on land upon such terms and conditions as may be agreed by the Managers, provided that:
   7.1 at the time such War Risks on Land insurance commences, you are insured by the Association for War Risks and Strikes, Riots and Terrorist Risks in accordance with paragraph 2.4 or other similar provisions approved by the Managers; and
   7.2 you maintain such insurance in full force and effect throughout the entire period you are insured for War Risks on Land."

39.47 The T.T. club has therefore managed to free itself of some of the restrictions imposed by the Waterborne Agreement so that it can give insurance for "War Risks" to containers, trailers and handling equipment which is used by ship operators whilst they are ashore as well as when they are afloat.

TERMINAL OPERATORS, STEVEDORES, DEPOT OWNERS

39.48 (These terms are not defined.)
39.49 The land-based nature of the insurance will be seen from a list of the Assured Members. Rule 2.1 reads:

"*2.1 Services*

   You may be insured for providing services as the following:
   2.1.1 a Stevedore
   2.1.2 an Operator of:
       (a) an Airfreight Terminal or Depot;
       (b) a Container or Trailer Freight Station;
       (c) a Container or Trailer Repair or Storage Depot;
       (d) an Inland Clearance Depot;
       (e) a Marine Terminal;
       (f) a Rail Freight Intermodal Transfer Depot;
       (g) a Warehouse;
       (h) Handling Equipment.
   2.1.3 an Operator of a local Collection and Delivery Service
   2.1.4 a Supplier of Advice or Information relating to the above services."

39.50 There are some general exclusions which apply to all the insurance given by Part I, Section 2, including the War and Strikes type insurance under Rule 8. Rule 2.2 reads:

"*2.2 General Exclusions*

   2.2.1 Ships and Aircraft
       (a) You are not insured for any risks that you incur in respect of your interest in any ship or aircraft that arises out of its management, navigation or operation.

(b) You are not insured for any risk that you incur arising out of your management or operation of any area or building upon which aircraft land or manoeuvre, or in which they are housed, maintained or repaired.

2.2.2 Dredging Operations

You are not insured for any risk that you incur arising out of:

(a) dredging operations, while such operations are being performed;

(b) the dumping of spoil."

39.51 There is a note appended to Rule 2.2.1(a) which explains that its purpose is to prevent the transfer of Hull Risks and Protection and Indemnity Risks (both of which should be insured elsewhere) to the T.T. Club where the shipowner is operating his own terminal to service his own ships. In certain limited circumstances which are set out in the note, the managers may agree to waive the Rule.

39.52 The Non-War and Strikes type insurance—other than Rule 8 (Part I, Section 2 of the Rules)

Rule	General description of the insurance
3	Liability for cargo and Customer's ships and other property—cargo, customer's ships, aircraft or other property, misdirection, delay, wrongful delivery.
4	Third party liabilities—loss of or damage to third party property, death or bodily injury, indemnities.
5	Infringement of personal rights—false arrest, detention or imprisonment, malicious prosecution, libel or slander, wrongful entry or eviction.
6	Advice and information
7	Fines—import or export of cargo or customer's equipment, immigration, safety of working conditions, pollution.
9	Costs—investigation, defence and mitigation of proceedings, disposal of damaged property, quarantine and disinfection.
10	Business interruption and increase in cost of working—set out in Appendix B to the Rules.
11	Property—fire damage to property leased under contract or port statute.
12	Discretionary—on similar terms as in Part I, Section 1 (para. 39.42).

Rule 8—the Non-War and Strikes type insurance for "Handling Equipment" (Part I, Section 2 of the Rules)

39.53 Rule 8 provides for the insurance of "Handling Equipment" (definition, see para. 39.7) used in the insured services by the persons listed in Rule 2. Rule 8 gives both Non-War and Strikes type insurance and also War and Strikes type insurance, but the latter is limited to "Strikes, Riots and Terrorist Risks" in a qualified form. This is the only War and Strikes type insurance given by Part I, Section 2 of the Rules.

39.54 The Non-War and Strikes type insurance is provided by Rule 8.2 which reads:

"8.2 Risks insured

8.2.1 You are insured for physical loss of or damage to the insured handling equipment arising from any accidental cause.

8.2.2 You are also insured for your liability for *per diem* lease charges in respect of an item of insured handling equipment leased to you where such charges are incurred by you in consequence of an insured risk which:

(a) by rendering the item an actual or constructive total loss, prevents its redelivery to the lessor by the original intended redelivery date; or

(b) by reason of your obligation to effect repairs, delays such redelivery."

39.55 Rule 8.3 provides for the exclusions and qualifications to this insurance. There is no insurance for defects in design or manufacture, wear and tear, mechanical or electrical breakdown of any communications equipment or alarm system or any external computer, an expendable or replaceable part (unless the damage was independent of such part), experiments such as overloading, modifications (unless approved by the manufacturers), erection, dismantling or re-erection (unless in course of normal maintenance), mysterious disappearance, whilst the equipment is being used by another, or after it has been transferred to another. For the purposes of this work the most important exclusions of Rule 8.3 are:

8.3.3(c) Destruction or damage by order of Authority. (See at paras. 39.13, 39.14.)

8.3.3(d) Nationalisation, requisition, pre-emption. (See at paras. 39.13, 39.14.)

8.3.4 Loss or damage after requisition. (See at paras. 39.13, 39.14.)

8.3.6 Agreement necessary to insure "Strikes, Riots and Terrorist Risks". (See at paras. 39.20, 39.21.)

Rule 8—the War and Strikes type insurance for "Handling Equipment"

39.56 As has been remarked, the only War and Strikes type insurance provided by Part I, Section 2 is given in a qualified form. Rules 8.4 and 8.5 read:

"8.4 War Risks

You are not insured for War Risks.

8.5. Strikes, Riots and Terrorist Risks

8.5.1 You are insured subject to paragraphs 8.5.2 to 8.5.4 for physical loss of or damage to your insured equipment caused by Strikes, Riots and Terrorist Risks."

39.57 *Conditions and qualifications*

8.5.2 "Strikes, Riots and Terrorist Risks"—modification. (See at paras. 39.18, 39.19.)

8.5.3 Notice of Cancellation and Automatic Termination of insurance. (See at paras. 39.9–39.12.)

8.5.4 Insurance under Rule 8.5 is limited if there is agreement that the insurance is for total loss only or if there are agreed deductibles etc.

PORT AUTHORITIES

39.58 ("Port Authorities" are defined as "includes port operator, harbour board, harbour authority and harbour operator".)

39.59 Most of the services which are insured are land-based, but some of them are of an off-shore nature. The services themselves may be summarised by a description of the headings of Rule 2, and further explained by a very brief description of the services which come under each heading. The quoted parts are shown within quotation marks, and the unquoted parts are summaries only:

"2 Insured Services
    2.1 Services
         You may be insured for the following port services"
"2.1.1 Cargo and Equipment Handling"—provision of stevedoring, terminal or depot services, storage, equipment repair, local collection and delivery of cargo, containers and trailers.
"2.1.2 Navigational Aids, Information and Control"—Marine navigational aids, charted and advertised water depths, buoyage and lighting, navigational information and warnings, pilots and pilotage, control of movement, berthing and anchoring.
"2.1.3 Shoreside Facilities"—Provision of wharves, quays, docks, slipways, moorings, passenger terminals, buildings, structures, equipment, road and rail systems within port area, security services.
"2.1.4 Emergency"—Provision of port emergency services, firefighting, rescue, ambulance, first aid.
"2.1.5 Advice and Information"
"2.1.6 Lease to or use by others of Port Facilities or Equipment".

39.60 There are some general exclusions which apply to all the insurance given by Part I, Section 3, including the War and Strikes type insurance under Rule 9. Rule 2.2 reads:

"2.2 General Exclusions and Qualifications

2.2.1 You are not insured for any risk that you incur in respect of your interest in any ship or aircraft and that arises out of its management, navigation or operation.
2.2.2 You are not insured for any risk that you incur arising out of:
    (a) dredging operations, while such operations are being performed;
    (b) the dumping of spoil."

39.61 There is a note appended to Rule 2.2.1 which explains that its purpose is to prevent the transfer of Hull Risks and Protection and Indemnity Risks (both of which should be insured elsewhere) to the T.T. Club. This exclusion may however be modified if insurance under Rule 14 for the port authority's ships is required.

39.62 The Non-War and Strikes type insurance—apart from Rule 9 (Part I, Section 3, of the Rules)

Rule	General description of the insurance
3	Liabilities for Cargo and Customer's Ships or Other Property—loss or damage to cargo, loss or damage to customer's ships or other property, misdirection of cargo, delay, wrongful delivery.
4	Third Party Liabilities—loss or damage to third party property, death or bodily injury, indemnities.
5	Infringement of Personal Rights—false arrest, detention or imprisonment, malicious prosecution, libel and slander, wrongful entry or eviction.
6	Removal of Wreck.
7	Advice or Information.
8	Fines—breach of regulations of import or export of cargo or customer's equipment, immigration, safety of working conditions, pollution, or various port services.
10	Costs—investigating and protecting interests, disposal of damaged cargo or other property, quarantine and disinfection.

Rule	*General description of the insurance*
11	Business Interruption and Increase in Cost of Working—set out in Appendix C to the Rules.
12	Property—fire damage to leased property.
13	Dry Dock and Ship Repair.
14	Port Authority's Ships—passenger ferries, pilot boats, tugs, mooring launches, dredgers, hoppers, barges etc.
15	Other Port Authority Risks.
16	Discretionary Insurance—on similar terms as in Part I, Section 1 (para. 39.42).

Rule 9—the Non-War and Strikes Insurance for "Handling Equipment" (Part I, Section 3 of the Rules)

39.63 Rule 9 provides for the insurance of "Handling Equipment" (definition, see para. 39.7) used in the insured services by port authorities. Rule 9 gives both Non-War and Strikes type insurance and also War and Strikes type insurance but the latter is limited to "Strikes, Riots and Terrorist Risks" in a qualified form. This is the only War and Strikes type insurance given by Part I, Section 3 of the Rules.

39.64 The Non-War and Strikes types insurance is provided by Rule 9.2 which reads:

"9.2 Risks insured

9.2.1 You are insured for physical loss of or damage to the insured handling equipment arising from any accidental cause.

9.2.2 You are also insured for your liability for *per diem* lease charges in respect of an item of insured handling equipment leased to you where such charges are incurred by you in consequence of an insured risk which:

(a) by rendering the item an actual or constructive total loss, prevents its redelivery to the lessor by the original intended redelivery date; or

(b) by reason of your obligation to effect repairs, delays such redelivery."

39.65 Rule 9.3 provides for the exclusions and qualifications to this insurance. There is no insurance for defects in design or manufacture, wear and tear, external mechanical or electrical breakdown of any communications equipment or alarm system or any external computer, an expendable or replaceable part (unless the damage was independent of such part), experiments such as overloading, modifications (unless approved by the manufacturer), erection, dismantling or re-erection (unless in the course of normal maintenance), mysterious disappearance, or whilst the equipment is being used by another, or after its transfer to another. For the purposes of this work the most important parts of Rule 9.3 read:

9.3.3(c) Destruction or damage by order of Authority. (See at paras. 39.13, 39.14.)

9.3.3(d) Nationalisation, Requisition, Pre-emption. (See at paras. 39.13, 39.14.)

9.3.5(a) Loss or damage after requisition. (See at paras. 39.13, 39.14.)

9.3.7 Agreement necessary to insure "Strikes, Riots and Terrorist Risks". (See at paras. 39.20, 39.21.)

Rule 9—the War and Strikes type insurance for "Handling Equipment"

39.66 As it has been remarked, the only War and Strikes type insurance given by Part I, Section 3, is given in a qualified form. Rules 9.4 and 9.5 read:

"9.4 War Risks

You are not insured for War Risks.
9.5   Strikes, Riots and Terrorist Risks
9.5.1   You are insured subject to paragraphs 9.5.2 to 9.5.4 for physical loss of or damage to your insured equipment caused by Strikes, Riots and Terrorist Risks."

39.67 *Conditions and qualifications*

9.5.2   "Strikes, Riots and Terrorist Risks"—modification. (See at paras. 39.18, 39.19.)
9.5.3   Notice of Cancellation and Automatic Termination of insurance. (See at paras. 39.9–39.12.)
9.5.4   Insurance under Rule 9.5 is limited if there is agreement that the insurance is for total loss only or if there are agreed deductibles etc.

FREIGHT FORWARDERS AND TRANSPORT OPERATORS

39.68 The insurance provided by Part I, Section 4 is partly land-based but also includes risks that arise at sea as will be seen from Rule 2. It reads:

"2.1 Insured Services

You may be insured for providing services as the following:
2.1.1 a Freight Forwarder;
2.1.2 an N.V.O.C. (Non-Vessel Owning Carrier);
2.1.3 a Trailer Operator;
2.1.4 a Tank Container or Trailer Operator;
2.1.5 a Road Haulier;
2.1.6 a Railway or Stack Train Operator;
2.1.7 an Inland Waterway Operator;
2.1.8 a Parcel Carrier;
2.1.9 an Air Carrier;
2.1.10 a Warehouse or Depot Operator.
2.2 a Ship's Agent or Shipbroker.

39.69 There is a general exclusion which applies to all insurance, including the War and Strikes type insurance under Rule 6, which is given by Part I, Section 4. Rule 2.3 reads:

"2.3 General Exclusion—Ship or Aircraft Operator

You are not insured for any risk that you incur in respect of your interest in any ship or aircraft and that arises out of its management, navigation or operation."

39.70 There is a note appended to Rule 2.3 which explains that its purpose is to prevent the transfer of a Ship Operators Protection and Indemnity Risks and an Aircraft Operators liability insurance (both of which should be insured elsewhere) to the T.T. Club. Even so, the T.T. Club can insure an Aircraft Operators Cargo liability.

39.71 The Non-War and Strikes type insurance—apart from Rule 6 (Part I, Section 4 of the Rules)

Rule	General description of the insurance
3	Customer Liabilities—Loss of or damage to cargo, financial loss errors and omissions.
4	Customs Liabilities—Fines, customs duty etc., for breach of import or export regulations.
5	Third Party Liabilities—Loss of or damage to third party property, death or bodily injury, contractual liabilities, indemnification of others for third party liabilities that they may incur.
7	Costs—Investigation, defence and mitigation regarding misdirection, disposal of damaged property, quarantine and disinfection, general average and salvage guarantees.
8	Discretionary—on similar terms as in Part I, Section 1 (para. 39.42).

Rule 6—the Non-War and Strikes type insurance for "Equipment" (Part I, Section 4, of the Rules)

39.72 Rule 6 provides for the insurance of "Equipment" (definition, para. 39.7) used in the insured services by transport operators and freight forwarders. Rule 6 gives both Non-War and Strikes type insurance, and also War and Strikes type insurance. This is the only War and Strikes type insurance given by Part I, Section 4, of the Rules.

39.73 The Non-War and Strikes type insurance is provided by Rule 6.2 which reads:

"6.2 Risks Insured
  You are insured for:
  6.2.1 physical loss of or damage to your insured equipment arising from any accidental cause;
  6.2.2 any general average or salvage contribution due in respect of your insured equipment."

39.74 Rule 6.3 provides for the exclusions and qualifications to this insurance. There is no insurance for defects in design or manufacture, wear and tear, external mechanical or electrical breakdown, mysterious disappearance, or whilst the equipment is being used by another, or after its transfer to another. For the purposes of this work the most important exclusions of Rule 6.3 are:

6.3.2(b) Destruction or damage by order of Authority. (See at paras. 39.13, 39.14.)

6.3.2(c) Nationalisation, Requisition, Pre-emption. (See at paras. 39.13, 39.14.)

6.3.3(b) Loss or damage after requisition. (See at paras. 39.13, 39.14.)

6.3.4 Agreement necessary to insure "War Risks" and "Strikes, Riots and Terrorist Risks". (See at paras. 39.20, 39.21.)

39.75 Rule 6.5 contains a provision relating to valuable handling equipment which is similar—including the provision for the insurance of "War Risks"—to Rule 2.5 of Part I, Section 1 (para. 39.39).

Rule 6—the War and Strikes type insurance for "Equipment" (Part I, Section 4 of the Rules)

39.76 Rule 6 also gives War and Strikes type insurance to transport operators and freight forwarders under Rule 6.4 which reads:

"6.4 War Risks and Strikes, Riots and Terrorist Risks

6.4.1 You are insured, subject to paragraphs 6.4.2 to 6.4.6, for the following caused by War Risks and Strikes, Riots and Terrorist Risks:
   (a) physical loss of or damage to your insured equipment;
   (b) any general average or salvage contribution due in respect of your insured equipment."

   6.4.2 The 12-month Clause.

   6.4.3 "War Risks"—only insured if on board ship or aircraft. (See at paras. 39.29, 39.30.)

   6.4.4 Specified exclusions from the "War Risks" insurance only. (See at paras. 39.25, 39.28.)

   6.4.5 Notice of Cancellation and Automatic Termination of insurance. (See at paras. 39.9–39.12.)

   6.4.6 Insurance under Rule 6.4 is limited if there are agreements that it is for total loss only or if there are agreed deductibles etc.

CONTAINER LESSORS

39.77 The insurance of container lessors is best described by setting out the provisions in full of Part I, Section 5. These read:

"If you are a container lessor, you may be insured in accordance with such terms and conditions as may be agreed by the Managers against the risks that you incur."

39.78 A note is appended to this provision that the usual terms and conditions on which the T.T. Club is willing to give such insurance may be obtained from the managers. It may, if appropriate, include insurance against "War Risks" and "Strikes, Riots and Terrorist Risks".

"War Risks" on Land ["WROL"] for "Equipment" (Part I, Section 1 of the Rules)

Introductory

39.79 "War Risks" insurance is intended by the Waterborne Agreement to be given only when the insured object is afloat, and this is reflected by the Rule which reads:

"You are not insured for any war risks unless, at the time the risk occurs, the item of equipment concerned is on board an oversea ship or aircraft."[1]

39.80 In spite of this the T.T. Club has been able since 1982 to give "Ship Operators" insurance for "War Risks" whilst their insured "Equipment" is on land ("WROL"). This is effected by Rule 7 of Part I, Section 1 of the Rules (para. 39.46). As it has been noted, such insurance is only given where there is express

---

1. Rule 2.4.3 of Part I, Section 1, and also Rule 6.4.3 Part I, Section 4.

agreement that it should be given between the Assured Member and the T.T. Club. Where there is such agreement, a separate certificate of entry, which is additional to the certificate of entry described at para. 39.109, is issued, and this records the terms and conditions of "WROL" which are supplementary to those of Rule 7.

39.81 A study of Part I, Section 1 of the Rules will reveal that the insurance is given to those who fall within the definition of "Ship Operators" which reads: "The owner, part-owner, operator, charterer or manager of a ship." and that it gives them insurance for their "Equipment", namely "Containers", "Trailers" and "Handling Equipment" (definitions, see para. 39.7). Containers and trailers especially, and to a lesser extent handling equipment, can be employed far inland, and whilst there may be exposed to "War Risks".

The insurance

39.82 The special certificate of entry which is referred to above is known as the "Certificate of Entry (War Risks on Land)" which may be abbreviated here to "CoE(WROL)". All numbering which follows relates, unless otherwise indicated, to the CoE(WROL). The risks insured are set out under the heading "Insurance for Ship Operators—War Risks on Land". Rule 2.2 reads:

"*2.2 Risks Insured*

You are insured for
  2.2.1 loss of or damage to your insured equipment arising from:
    (a) War Risks;
    (b) nationalisation, requisition and pre-emption.
  2.2.2 Costs incurred by you after any accident that gives rise to, or may give rise to, a claim under this insurance, in:
    (a) investigating the accident and protecting your interests in relation to it, for example the fees of a lawyer, surveyor or expert;
    (b) avoiding or minimising the claim."

39.83 Such costs are not recoverable unless they are approved by the managers beforehand, or the directors decide they were properly incurred—Rule 2.3.6. There is no insurance for physical loss or damage if the insured equipment last entered the country where it happened before the commencement of the insurance—Rule 2.3.3.

39.84 It is noteworthy that nationalisation, requisition and pre-emption is insured under the WROL insurance, whereas it is excluded from the normal "War Risks" insurance given by Part I, Section 1 Rule 2.4. It therefore follows that these risks are only insured by the WROL insurance, or whilst the "Equipment" is on land. As it will be seen below, there are a number of exclusions to the WROL insurance.

39.85 The list of exclusions and qualifications is lengthy, but they are very clear. It is best to set them out in full between quotation marks followed by comments which are outside these marks. It will be noted that many of them exclude hostilities, sanctions, and disputes involving "your country" which is defined as:

"Any country in which:
  1. you are incorporated;
  2. the management of your business is conducted; or
  3. your principal place of business is situated."

39.86 Rule 2.3 reads:

"2.3 Exclusions and Qualifications

    2.3.1 You are only insured for physical loss of or damage to your insured equipment whilst such equipment is not on board an oversea ship or aircraft."

39.87 This contrasts with Rule 2.4.3 of Part I, Section 1 of the Rules (para. 39.79), and ensures that the WROL insurance is only effective whilst the insured "Equipment" is on land.

    "2.3.2 You are not insured for physical loss of or damage to your insured equipment:
      (a) arising from capture, seizure, arrest, restraint, detainment or confiscation, and the consequences thereof or any attempt thereat, by or under the order of any authority of your country;
      (b) arising from nationalisation, requisition, or pre-emption by or under the order of any authority of:
        (1) your country;
        (2) any other country, but only in cases where compensation is paid or payable to you, or for your benefit in respect of such loss or damage."

39.88 This follows the usual line of thought that the Assured Member is taken to have assumed the risks of these events in his own country, and should look to the government of that country for compensation. If they happen in another country, the exclusion will only operate if compensation is payable by the government of that country.

    " '(c) arising from capture, seizure, arrest, restraint, detainment or confiscation, and the consequences thereof or any attempt thereat, by the government or any authority of a country in furtherance or consequence of any dispute or difference between that country and your country;'
    '(d) arising from war involving your country or any hostile act by or against that country as a belligerent power;'
    '(e) arising from the outbreak of war, whether there be a declaration of war or not, between any of the countries which are the Permanent Members of the Security Council . . . ;'."

(e) has the same effect as Rule 2.4.4(b) of Part I, Section 1 of the Rules. The Permanent Members of the Security Council of the United Nations Organisation are France, the People's Republic of China, the Russian Federation, the United Kingdom, and the United States of America. Here the Russian Federation can be substituted for the now defunct Union of Soviet Socialist Republics.

    " '(f) arising from the imposition of sanctions by the government of any country against your country.'
    '(g) arising out of any contract or other agreement to which you are a party;'
    '(h) arising by reason of the insured equipment being repossessed by any titleholder'
    '(i) arising under quarantine regulations or by reason of infringement of any customs regulations;'
    '(j) arising as a consequence of ordinary judicial process or of failure to provide security or to pay any fine or penalty or of any financial cause'."

39.89 Ordinary Judicial Process is discussed in Chapter 25.

    " '(k) whilst it is leased to another person;'
    '(1) after your interest in it has been transferred to another person.' "

The 270-days Rule

39.90 This is the equivalent of the 12-month Clause in Part I, Sections 1 and 4 of the Rules, and its text in those two sections is set out at para. 39.15. For the purposes of the WROL insurance, 270 days, approximately 75% of a year, are sufficient. Rule 2.3.5 reads:

"2.3.5 (a) Where you have been deprived of possession of an item of insured equipment for a continuous period of 270 days by a risk insured under this insurance (such item not having previously become a total loss under this insurance) such item shall, for the purposes of this insurance, be deemed a constructive total loss under this insurance at the date such period commenced.

(b) Such item shall only be deemed a constructive total loss in accordance with (a) above, if you were insured under this insurance on the date on which such continuous period commenced."

39.91 The same points apply to this Rule as those which apply to the 12-month Clause in other parts of the Rules, save only that the period is 270 days and not 12 months (para. 39.15).

Insured trading areas—restriction and exclusion

39.92 The insured trading area for each individual Assured Member is a matter for agreement between the Assured Member and the T.T. Club. It can be worldwide, or it can be a geographically restricted area which is described in the Certificate of Entry. The directors have two special powers under Rule 3 to restrict the exposure of the Association where the risk increases significantly in any given area.

39.93 Firstly, they can exclude from the insurance any insured equipment which enters a specified country, or any part thereof, seven days after notice of their decision is given to the Assured Members. This does not affect insured equipment which is already within the specified country, or the specified part of the country, or any insured equipment which enters it before the seven days have expired—Rule 3.2.

39.94 Secondly, they can with immediate effect impose restrictions on the insurance in respect of claims arising in any specified country, or any part of a country, to a maximum for each Assured Member of the value of his insured equipment within the specified country or area at the time the restriction takes effect—Rule 3.1.

39.95 At present the WROL insurance for the 1993 policy year allows the assured to choose a Worldwide insurance, excluding Iran or Lebanon only, or a more restricted insurance which excludes the Middle-Eastern countries of Bahrain, Egypt, Iraq, Israel, Jordan, Kuwait, Lebanon, Oman, Republic of Yemen, Saudi-Arabia, Syria, Turkey and the United Arab Emirates.

Automatic cesser of insurance

39.96 This is provided by Rule 6.1. It reads:

"*6.1 Automatic Cesser of Insurance*

This insurance shall cease automatically:

6.1.1 Upon the occurrence of any hostile detonation of any weapon of war employing atomic or nuclear fission or fusion or other like reaction or radioactive force or matter, whensoever and wheresoever such detonation may occur and whether or not the insured equipment may be involved.

6.1.2 Upon the outbreak of war (whether there be a declaration of war or not) between any of the countries which are the Permanent Members of the Security Council of the United Nations."

39.97 This Rule is similar to, but not totally identical with, Rule 2.4.5 of Part I, Section 1 of the Rules. Although there are minor differences in the wording, it is suggested that the effect is the same. Rule 6 has no provision to allow the charge of additional premiums for trading to areas which have become dangerous, but Rules 3.1 and 3.2 should be noted (paras. 39.93, 39.94).

39.98 The Permanent Members of the Security Council of the United Nations Organisation are presently France, the People's Republic of China, the Russian Federation, the United Kingdom, and the United States of America.

General comments on the WROL insurance

39.99 The WROL insurance is an adjunct to the T.T. Club's insurance, and has its own terms, conditions, and Rules, although these are frequently the same as those of the main body of the T.T. Club's insurance.

39.100 Although the WROL insurance has existed since 1982, it is still a very young form of insurance in which few underwriters are willing to participate. A number, perhaps many, underwriters may be willing to participate in an insurance of a particular nature. If they do, they provide both competition and support; competition because the assured will have a choice which his brokers will help him to exercise to his best advantage, and support because a number of underwriters are willing to take part of its burden. Thus it is not left to just one underwriter. Support goes further than this, because the underwriters who are willing to insure the risk will also give reinsurance, and thus relieve the primary underwriter of some of the burden of a disastrous loss by any one of his assured. Support can take yet another form, and the War and Strikes insurance provided for merchant ships is a typical example (para. 2.1). There are only a few underwriters who are willing to act as "leaders" in the London Market; there are however, a greater number who are willing to "follow" them, either by taking a share in the primary risk or by re-insurance which, by means of an excess, makes them more remote from the primary risks and confines their participation to the higher amounts of any loss. All these underwriters give support to the "leaders", and thus allow them to underwrite a much greater quantity of business than would be the case if this support did not exist.

39.101 The WROL insurance does not yet enjoy such substantial support, and until it does the T.T. Club has to act on the principle that no underwriter is in a position to make a monopoly of one particular kind of insurance and do so with financial security to himself and to his assureds. The T.T. Club has therefore to limit its overall liability for WROL insurance until such a time as this support is forthcoming. This is done by the directors who determine the "WROL maximum" for any account year before its commencement, and the total WROL claims will be limited to this maximum—Rule 4.1.1. The T.T. Club's policy year begins on 1st January and continues until 31st December. The directors then have the task, in which they are assisted by the managers, of determining on the following 30th September whether or not the total of the WROL claims for the previous policy year exceeds the WROL maximum—Rule 4.2.1. If they do not, then the claims are paid in full—Rule 4.2.2. If however they do, the WROL claims are reduced by the same proportion for each Assured Member who has a claim so that they do not exceed the predetermined maximum and are then paid in these reduced amounts—Rule 4.2.3. This incidentally is one of the reasons for the 270-day Rule (para. 39.90) rather than the full year which is found elsewhere; "Equipment" which is first detained on the 1st January will have been detained for more than 270 days by the 30th September and will thus be a constructive total loss as at 1st January. The directors have power, if they consider such a course is appropriate, to review and if necessary revise any first determination of the amounts of the claims—Rules 4.3.1 and 4.3.2.

39.102 The WROL maximum is unique to the WROL insurance, and has no bearing on any of the other insurances given by the T.T. Club.

GENERAL EXCLUSIONS AND QUALIFICATIONS (PART I, SECTION 6 OF THE RULES)

39.103 This section contains the list of general exclusions and qualifications which apply to Sections 1 to 5 of Part I of the Rules. It is also specifically incorporated by reference into the WROL insurance. The most noteworthy of these exclusions and qualifications for the purposes of this work are listed below.

39.104 Rule 5 of Part I, Section 6 of the Rules provides for a general limit of the T.T. Club's liability in the case of each "Accident"—Rule 5.2.1 (definition, see para. 39.7). This general limit will not take effect where individual Rules provide for their own limits of liability in respect of the insurance which they give, and some of these take the form of aggregate limits for any one account year. The general limit for the 1993 year is U.S.$1 million, although higher or lower limits may be agreed to suit the requirements of any particular Assured Member.

39.105 Rule 7 of the Part I, Section 6 deals with radioactive and nuclear risks. It reads:

"7 Radioactive and Nuclear Risks

You are not insured for any risk incurred by you which is caused or contributed to, directly or indirectly, by:
  7.1 ionising radiations from or contamination by radioactivity from any nuclear fuel or from any nuclear waste from the combustion of nuclear fuel;
  7.2 the radioactive, toxic, explosive or other hazardous properties of any explosive nuclear assembly or nuclear component thereof;
  7.3 the radioactive, toxic, explosive or other hazardous properties of radioactive products carried as cargo other than 'excepted matter' (as defined by section 26(1) of the Nuclear Installations Act 1965 of the United Kingdom or any regulations made thereunder), for example, most radio isotopes for industrial, commercial, agricultural, medical or scientific use."

39.106 Rule 8 puts restrictions on the pollution insurance which is given by a number of Rules of Part I, Sections 1 to 5. Pollution is only insured if it is caused by an accident arising during the period of insurance, the claim is made within 12 months of the date of the accident which caused it, the pollution is sudden, unintended, and unexpected, and the Assured Member is aware of it within seven days of its happening.

39.107 Rule 14 excludes the consequences of "deliberate or reckless conduct". This is a wider exclusion than "wilful misconduct" which are the words of section 55 of the Marine Insurance Act 1906, and, under Rule 14, "reckless conduct" is specifically excluded from the insurance. The reader will note from Chapter 29 that there have been cases where "recklessness" has amounted to "wilful misconduct".

GENERAL TERMS AND CONDITIONS (PART II OF THE RULES)

39.108 This Part contains the provisions which regulate the relations between the T.T. Club and the Assured Member. They apply to all sections of Part I of the Rules, and to the WROL insurance into which they are specifically incorporated by reference. The most noteworthy for the purposes of this work are listed below. This part is divided into sections, and further sub-divided into Rules.

Certificate of Entry (Section 1, Rules 3 and 5)

39.109 As in the case of the Mutual Shipowners' Insurance Associations, the contractual document between the T.T. Club and the Assured Member is the Certificate of Entry. It is quite short, and incorporates by reference the Book of Rules and the Bye-laws, which govern the conduct of the T.T. Club and take the place of the Articles of Association of a joint stock company. It also states whether or not the assured is a Member of the Association.

39.110 The Certificate of Entry also sets out the terms of insurance which are relevant to each Assured Member. If these are changed in any way, then an endorsement is issued, or if this is desired, a new Certificate of Entry.

The assured and joint assureds (Section 2, Rules 2 to 5)

39.111 No person or corporation can be insured by the T.T. Club unless they are so named as the assured in the Certificate of Entry. Joint assured are permitted, but they must likewise be so named. All joint assured are jointly and severally liable to the T.T. Club for any amounts of money which are due to it for the insurance, are similarly bound by the Rules, and are likewise entitled to its insurance.

Period of insurance (Section 4, Rules 1 to 3)

39.112 Most forms of insurance will expire at the end of the period, usually one year, for which they are to run. The T.T. Club, however, follows the normal practice of the Shipowners' Mutual Insurance Associations, and its insurance is a continuous contract which runs from one year to another on the same terms and conditions unless specified formalities are followed either to change it or to bring it to an end. These are usually one month's notice by either the T.T. Club or the Assured Member before the end of the account year. The insurance will also come to an end if the Assured Member's insured services come to an end, or he is overtaken by some misfortune such as bankruptcy, or he fails to pay a premium which is due in spite of a final warning, or fails to make a declaration which he is bound to make—Section 6.

Premiums (Section 5, Rules 1 and 2)

39.114 Premiums are mutual premiums, and as such, are subject to supplementary premiums as provided for by Part E (Funds of the Association) of the Bye-laws. Fixed premiums may however be agreed by the managers.

Law (Part 11, Section 11, Rules 1 and 2)

39.115 These are provisions that all insurances provided by the T.T. Club are subject to and shall be construed in accordance with English law, and any dispute is to be referred to arbitration in London. This is incorporated into the WROL insurance by reference to the General Terms and Conditions in that insurance.

AMOUNTS RECOVERABLE—MINIMISING LOSSES—SUE AND LABOUR

39.116 The amounts recoverable by the Assured Members are governed by Rules which differ slightly between the sections of Part I. These can be summarised thus:

Part I, Section 1 (Rule 2.6)
Part I, Section 4 (Rule 6.6)

39.117 Where "Equipment" is owned by the Assured Member, a claim for its "loss" shall not exceed its insured value, or, if there is none, its market value. A claim for a constructive total loss requires that the estimates of the repair costs which are used to justify it must relate to damage suffered in one accident. Where such "Equipment" is damaged, the claim is for the reasonable cost of repair which shall not exceed the insured value, or, if there is none, the market value. Where "Equipment" is leased by the Assured Member from another, the claim for a "loss" is the amount specified by the lease, or, where the lease specifies no amount, the market value. Where such leased "Equipment" is damaged, the claim is based on the reasonable cost of repairs which do not exceed any amount specified by the lease as payable in respect of that damage.

Part I, Section 2 (Rule 8.6)
Part I, Section 3 (Rule 9.6)

39.118 Where "Handling Equipment" is damaged, the reasonable costs of repair form the basis of the claim, but the T.T. Club has the option to replace what is damaged. If the "Handling Equipment" is insured for less than its replacement value, the claim can be reduced proportionately. Deductions from the claim are made for the value of any part that can be used again, and for the costs of alterations, improvements, or overhauls carried out at the same time as the repairs. The costs of temporary repairs can only be claimed if the managers approve them, but the permanent repairs can begin at once as soon as the managers are notified of the claim. There is an overall limit of the insured value, or, if there is none, the market value, on the amount of any claim.

39.119 In these two Rules, there is specific provision for actual total loss and constructive total loss. Where there is an actual total loss, the insured value of the

"Handling Equipment" is paid, or if there is none, the market value. A constructive total loss arises where the reasonable costs of repair from any one accident exceed the insured value, or if there is none, the market value.

39.120 Where "Handling Equipment" is leased by the Assured Member from another, the claim is for the lesser amount of either the amount specified in the lease or the insured value, or if there is none, the market value.

Sue and labour

39.121 None of the sections of Part I of the Rules contains a sue and labour clause. This is left to Part II, Section 7, Rule 2, of the General Terms and Conditions and it thus has universal application to all the insurances given by the T.T. Club. This includes the WROL insurance which incorporates these General Terms and Conditions by reference. Rule 2, which follows a provision requiring prompt notice to the managers as soon as an accident which involves or is likely to involve the T.T. Club's insurance has happened (this includes notice of a third party claim on the Assured Member), reads:

"*2 Mitigation and Recourse against Third Parties*

2.1   If such an accident occurs or such a claim is made, you must:
2.1.1 take all reasonable measures to avoid or minimise any risks for which you may be insured;
2.1.2 give prompt notice of claim to any third party who is, or may be, responsible for the accident or the claim made against you;
2.1.3 take all reasonable steps to prevent the claim against such party from becoming time-barred and to obtain maximum recovery from him."

39.122 A note is appended to the Rule to the effect that the costs of taking such measures are insured provided that the Assured Member is insured for the risk in question. To determine this, the Certificate of Entry must be examined.

39.123 Since the S.G. Form ceased to be used in 1982 and 1983, the rather permissively worded sue and labour[2] clause in that form has been replaced by a much firmer obligation that it is "the duty" of the assured to take reasonable steps to avert or minimise any claim. The Marine Policy form for ships follows this line, as do the forms of insurance for cargo, both marine and war, which also use simpler and easier-to-read wording. Rule 2.1.1 tends to follow the cargo forms, except that it does not state that it is a duty to take "such measures as may be reasonable"; the words "you must" are equally mandatory and have the same effect.

APPLICATION OF THE MARINE INSURANCE ACT 1906 TO THE T.T. CLUB'S RULES

39.124 The Marine Insurance Act 1906 is not excluded from the Rules, and in fact the Act is not mentioned throughout. The General Terms and Conditions (Part II, Section 11, Rule 1) provide that the Rules and every insurance given by the T.T. Club are subject to and shall be construed in accordance with English law. Thus it is necessary to consider how far the Act does apply to the insurance given by the Rules. This is not always an easy question. Whilst the Act does not apply to land-

---

2. Sue and labour is discussed in Chapter 24.

based risks, it can apply to risks which are sea-based, but have some element of land carriage as well. In 1906, when the Act became law, some carriage by land was quite usual in what was primarily a sea voyage, although it could not then be foreseen how the massive extension of this characteristic would be brought about by the modern "unit" or "package" transportation of goods. The draftsmen of the Act were anxious to continue what the Common Law had previously achieved in preventing a false position arising where the Act applied to one part of the carriage and not to another. The *Rodocanachi* case (para. 11.21) will serve as an example.

39.125 The application of the Marine Insurance Act 1906 is determined by the Act's sections 1, 2 and 3, the material parts of which read:

Section 1

"A contract of marine insurance is . . . [insurance] . . . against marine losses, that is to say the losses incident to marine adventure."

Section 2(1)

"A contract of marine insurance may, by its express terms, or by usage of trade, be extended so as to protect the assured against losses on inland waters or on any land risk which is incidental to any sea voyage."

Section 3(2)

"In particular there is a marine adventure where—
    (a) Any ship, goods, or other moveables are exposed to maritime perils . . .
    (c) Any liability to a third party . . . " (arises)

39.126 The views expressed hereafter must be regarded as tentative because there is so far no judicial authority to support them. They are put forward with some hesitation. Subject to this proviso, it is suggested that:

Ship operators (Part I, Section 1, of the Rules)

39.127 The Act does apply to the whole of this section (except Section 7 which leads into the WROL insurance), which does insure mainly "Containers", and to a lesser extent only, "Trailers" and "Handling Equipment" in through transport, most of which is likely to be by sea.

39.128 The sole exception is the separate WROL insurance which, by its own express provision, does not insure "Equipment" whilst it is on board an oversea ship or aircraft. This cannot be a "marine adventure".

Terminal operators, stevedores, depot owners (Part I, Section 2 of the Rules)

39.129 The Act does not apply to any part of this section. Rule 2 describes the Insured Services, and these are all land-based. As such, they cannot be a "marine adventure".

Port authorities (Part I, Section 3 of the Rules)

39.130 Most of the insurance provided by this section is land-based and, as such, cannot be described as a "marine adventure" so that the Act applies. Some Rules however, notably Rule 2.1.2 (Navigational Aids, Information and Control) and Rule 6 (Wreck Removal), do have a flavour of the sea about them, and could just be described as "marine adventures". It is not necessary for the purposes of this work to go deeply into this matter, since the War and Strikes type insurance is only given to "Handling Equipment", and this is land-based. As such, this cannot be described as a "marine adventure".

Freight forwarders and transport operators (Part I, Section 4 of the Rules)

39.131 The insurance given by this section is not so clearly divided into land-based insurance and insurance for carriage by sea as is the previous section, and it is very difficult to distinguish the insurance to which the Act applies, and where it has no application. The only part of the section which has to be considered for the purposes of this work is Rule 6, which gives insurance for "Equipment". For the most part, this section gives insurance for "Containers" and, to a lesser extent only, "Trailers" and "Handling Equipment" which are sent by sea. As such, this could be described as a "marine adventure".

Container lessors (Part I, Section 5 of the Rules)

39.132 It can be said with more confidence that the "Containers", although there will be some measure of land carriage, will be sent by sea, and therefore the insurance is a "marine adventure" to which the Act applies.

Points which are important

39.133 The points on which it is important to a greater or lesser extent whether or not the Marine Insurance Act 1906 applies to the insurance given are:

> Partial Loss;
> Actual Total Loss;
> Constructive Total Loss;
> Notice of Abandonment;
> Warranties;
> Sue and Labour;
> Insured Values.

39.134 *"Partial Loss"* is defined by section 56(1) of the Act as any loss other than a total loss. Each section of the Rules makes it clear that it has a similar meaning.

39.135 Section 71 of the Act has some complicated provisions on the calculation of a partial loss of "goods, merchandise etc.". These are displaced by the fairer and less complex provisions of the Rules that the T.T. Club shall pay the reasonable costs of the repairs.

39.136 *"Actual Total Loss"* is defined by section 57(1) of the Act as destruction of the subject matter of the insurance, or its damage being such that it is no longer a thing of the kind insured, or the owner is irretrievably deprived thereof. Where the Act applies, so will section 57(1). Actual total loss is not defined by the Rules, but even where the Act does not apply, the wording of the Rules tends to indicate that they should have the same meaning.

39.137 Section 68 of the Act provides that, in the case of an actual total loss, the assured shall receive the insured value. The Rules have similar provisions.

39.138 *"Constructive Total Loss"* is defined in an extensive definition by section 60 of the Act (para. 27.7). Broadly speaking, it arises when the cost of repairing the insured object would cost more than the insured value, or the owner is deprived of possession without the likelihood of recovery within a reasonable time. Where the Act applies, so will section 60. Constructive total loss is not defined by the Rules, but their provisions make it clear that where the cost of repair exceeds the insured value, a constructive total loss arises. The position is not so clear where there is deprivation.

39.139 Section 68 of the Act provides that, in the case of a constructive total loss, the assured shall receive the insured value. The Rules have similar provisions.

39.140 *"Notice of Abandonment"* is required by section 62 of the Act (para. 27.40). The Rules make no provision whether or not it is required. Where the Act applies, failure to give it in time can lead to disastrous consequences for the assured. Where the Act does not apply, it is not necessary. It can only be suggested that the Assured Member should always act upon the golden rule; where there is doubt it should be given promptly. If it is not necessary after all, it does not affect the position.

39.141 *"Warranties"* are discussed in Chapter 26 (paras. 26.10–26.37). Where the Act applies, breaches of warranty can have drastic consequences for the assured. These consequences are not so severe where the Act does not apply. The Rules contain very few warranties and, where there are any, the Rules mostly provide what is to happen in case of a breach.

39.142 *"Sue and Labour"*. Section 78 of the Act provides that where a policy contains a sue and labour clause, the engagement which it contains is deemed to be supplemental to the contract of insurance. There is now a new form of sue and labour clause, and a provision with similar effect to section 78 of the Act is specifically incorporated into the Marine Policy Form for ships (Clause 13.6, Appendix C), the War Risks Policy Form for ships (Clause 2, Appendix D), and the cargo policies, both for marine and war risks, under the heading "Minimising Losses".

39.143 There is no similar provision to section 78 of the Act in the relevant part of the Rules (Part II, Section 7 Rule 2). Where the Act applies, so will section 78 of the Act, and this Rule 2 will be a supplemental engagement. Where it does not apply, this Rule 2 will not form a supplemental engagement as do other sue and labour clauses.

39.144 *"Insured Values"*. The Act contains several provisions (section 68 of the Act being an example) that where there are no agreed insured values, which is rare nowadays, the "Insurable Value" is to be taken into account. This expression is not readily understandable, and can be said to be out-of-date in today's world. The T.T. Club Rules provide that where there is no agreed insured value against which a loss can be calculated, then the "market value" is to be used. This is much easier to ascertain, and will, in general, be less productive of disputes.

CHAPTER 40

Consequences of hostilities and warlike operations

THE COXWOLD

40.1 This insured peril was included in the S.G. Form but, for the reasons set out at para. 1.18, it has not been included by Mr. Alan Jackson's Committee in the new Institute War and Strikes Clauses Hulls—Time 1.10.83, to be attached to the MAR form when it appeared in 1983. It still appears in war risks cases and it is not impossible that it will be included in the War Risks Policy by special endorsement, although it is earnestly hoped that this will not happen. It was so imprecise in its wording that, as the following cases will show, it led to a great number of decisions which are virtually irreconcilable one with another. The new Institute War and Strikes Clauses now contain far more precisely worded insured perils, and it is hoped that the chaotic situation to which "warlike operations" in particular gave rise will never again be repeated; indeed, the cases give a tacit warning that never again should such an indeterminate position be allowed to arise.

40.2 The cases culminated in *Yorkshire Dale S.S. Co Ltd.* v. *Ministry of Transport (The Coxwold).*[1] Each case turned on very fine considerations of the facts surrounding each casualty and the way that they struck the judges. Thus:

40.3 Ionides v. Universal Marine Insurance Company Ltd.[2]

(1) During the American Civil War 1861–1865, the light on Cape Hatteras was extinguished. The *Linwood* altered course, stranded and was lost. The Captain's calculation of the ship's position was incorrect by 50 miles. It was held that incorrect navigation was the cause of the loss and that there was no claim against the war risk underwriters. The extinction of the light was not a cause although if it had been alight, as it was in peacetime, there was a remote chance that the casualty would not have happened.

40.4 Green v. British India Steam Navigation Co. Ltd. (The Matiana)[3]

(2) In April 1918 the *Matiana* was bound from Alexandria to British ports with cotton. She was sailing in convoy and, on the Commodore's orders, no lights were shown. Again on the Commodore's orders the course was more northerly than

---

1. (1942) 73 Ll.L.Rep. 1; [1942] A.C. 691; [1942] 2 All E.R. 6.
2. (1863) 14 C.B. (N.S.) 259. See paras. 14.5–14.10.
3. (1920) 3 Ll.L.Rep. 205; (1920) 4 Ll.L.Rep. 245; [1921] 1 A.C. 99 (H.L.).

normal to avoid the considerable danger of submarines. She stranded on the Keith Rock, a known hazard, and was lost. Subsequently, she was torpedoed by a submarine but the loss throughout was attributed to the stranding only. Bailhache J. held that her loss was a consequence of a warlike operation. The Court of Appeal unanimously reversed this decision and the House of Lords, by a majority of three to two, agreed with the Court of Appeal that the loss was a marine loss.

(In *The Coxwold*, Lord Wright found some distinction on the grounds that the *Coxwold* was carrying war material and the *Matiana* was loaded with cotton.)

40.5 Britain S.S. Co. v. The King (The Petersham)[4]

(3) On 6th May, 1918, the *Petersham*, on charter to the British Government, was carrying iron ore for that government from Bilbao to Glasgow. She collided at night with a neutral ship and sank. Both ships were sailing without lights in accordance with Admiralty instructions and neither was held to be negligent. In an action against the Crown, which under the charterparty had assumed the position of the war risk underwriters, it was pleaded that sailing without lights involved an extra peril which should be considered to be a consequence of hostilities or warlike operations. It was held, however, by Bailhache J., the Court of Appeal unanimously and the House of Lords, again unanimously, that the loss of the *Petersham* was due to a marine risk.

40.6 Commonwealth Shipping Representative v. P. & O. Branch Service[5]

(4) In January 1916 during the Gallipoli campaign, the *Geelong*, under requisition to the Government of Australia, was bound with general cargo from Port Said to Gibraltar. She collided with the *Bonvilston* bound from Mudros, the chief British base during the campaign, to Alexandria with ambulance wagons and other military stores and subsequently sank. Both ships were sailing without lights in accordance with Admiralty orders and neither was held to be negligent. The arbitrator found that the *Geelong* was lost by a marine peril and not a war peril. Bailhache J., however, considered that the loss was due to a war peril and, again unanimously, both the Court of Appeal and the House of Lords agreed with him.

40.7 It seems that the ambulance wagons were regarded as war material and this justified a finding that the loss of the *Geelong* was a consequence of warlike operations. There is some question that if the findings of the arbitrator had been more thorough and more extensive (they drew much criticism from Viscount Cave in the House of Lords), the results might possibly have been different.

40.8 Attorney General v. Ard Coasters Limited[6]

(5) In February 1918 the *Ardgantok* was in the North Sea sailing in a northerly direction between Tees and Whitby. She collided with H.M.S. *Tartar* which was on

4. (1920) 3 Ll.L.Rep. 163, 205; (1920) 4 Ll.L.Rep. 245; [1921] 1 A.C. 99.
5. [1923] A.C. 191.
6. [1921] 2 A.C. 141. Also reported under the names of *Ard Coasters Ltd.* v. *Attorney General* (1921) 7 Ll.L.Rep. 150 and *Ard Coasters Ltd.* v. *The King* (1920) 36 T.L.R. 555.

patrol searching for submarines. *Tartar* was turning at the time through 180° to resail her course on a reciprocal bearing. Both ships were sailing without lights in accordance with Admiralty instructions. Bailhache J., the Court of Appeal and the House of Lords (both unanimously) considered that the collision was the consequence of a warlike operation.

40.9 S.S. Richard de Larrinaga v. Admiralty Commissioners[7]

(6) In July 1917, the *Richard de Larrinaga* was sailing in convoy from the United States bound for Europe when she came into collision with H.M.S. *Devonshire* which was bound from Halifax to U.S. ports to escort another convoy. Both ships, in accordance with their instructions, were sailing without lights. Again, Bailhache J., the Court of Appeal and the House of Lords (both unanimously) considered that the collision was the consequence of a warlike operation particularly because of the character of *Devonshire's* employment.

40.10 As has already been stated, the culminating case was the House of Lords decision in *Yorkshire Dale S.S. Co. Ltd.* v. *Ministry of Transport (The Coxwold)*.[8] A close examination of the facts is necessary.

40.11 The Ministry of Transport had engaged the *Coxwold* under a charterparty which stated that it would assume the position of the war risk underwriter by the following clause:

"Those risks which would be excluded from an ordinary English policy of marine insurance by the following, or similar, but not more extensive clause:
> Warranted free of capture, seizure, arrest, restraint or detainment and the consequences thereof or any attempt thereat, also from the consequences of hostilities or warlike operations, whether there be a declaration of war or not, civil war, revolution, rebellion, insurrection or civil strife arising therefrom or piracy.
> Loss or damage to the ship hereby chartered caused by:
> (i) Hostilities, warlike operations, civil war, revolution, rebellion, insurrection or civil strife arising therefrom;
> (ii) Mines, torpedoes, bombs or other engines of war."

The *Coxwold* was ordered to load petrol in drums for discharge at Narvik. The petrol was intended for the use of the British armed forces which were assisting the Norwegian armed forces in resisting the German invasion of Norway. On the evening of 6th May, 1940, the *Coxwold* was in a convoy with three other merchant vessels escorted by four destroyers. As night fell, the convoy was in the Little Minch Channel with the Island of Skye to starboard. The course, presumably the mean course because the convoy was zigzagging, was north-east by north magnetic. The visibility was very poor with heavy rain squalls. The two leading ships were showing dimmed stern lights but otherwise no lights were being shown. The speed of the convoy was nine knots. At 19.15 hours, the convoy altered course four points to starboard and immediately afterwards another four points, making 90° in all, to avoid an enemy submarine which was reported to be in the area. At 19.45 hours, the convoy resumed its mean course of north-east by north continuing to zigzag. At 01.25 hours on 7th May, the *Coxwold* lost sight of the light of the leading ship. At

7. [1920] 1 K.B. 700; [1920] 3 K.B. 65.
8. (1942) 73 Ll.L.Rep. 1; [1942] A.C. 691; [1942] 2 All E.R. 6.

02.30 hours, she gave up zigzagging in an attempt to regain the convoy, clearly feeling that she had been left behind. At about this time, she is recorded as altering course one quarter of a point to starboard to pass through the lights of approaching ships without realising that they were the leading and escorting ships of the convoy retracing their course; they had turned through 180° and were now sailing on their reciprocal bearing. On passing through the lights, the *Coxwold* resumed her course of north-east by north and at 02.45 hours she ran hard aground on the Damsel Rocks and was lost. The arbitrator, Sir Robert Ask, K.C., a most experienced arbitrator in such matters, found as facts:

   (i) There was no improper navigation.
  (ii) The convoy was on a safe course which was being accurately followed.
 (iii) There was an unexpected and unexplained tidal set to eastwards.
 (iv) The Leist Light was not being shown at full brilliance.
  (v) There was nothing to show the watch on board the *Coxwold* that the course was improper.

He therefore made an interim award that the "loss . . . was a direct consequence of a warlike operation".

    40.12 On a purely navigational point, it can be questioned whether findings (i) and (v) in the above-mentioned list were tenable. There can be every sympathy with the watch on board and navigation on a dark and squally night without proper navigation lights and with shore lights dimmed or extinguished must be a nightmare situation. On the other hand, it was readily ascertainable from the chart that the Channel between North Uist and the Island of Skye was only 13 miles wide measured in a north-westerly direction from the Leist Light. The manoeuvre between 19.15 and 19.45 hours would bring the ship some four miles to the eastward and thus nearer to the Island of Skye. A change of course by one-quarter of a point, a little less than 3°, seems an improbable manoeuvre to avoid other ships in a close-quarter situation, particularly with a merchant ship which can, at the best, be steered to within half a degree of the desired course. The probability is that this manoeuvre was a full point, about 11°, to starboard, which brought the *Coxwold* still nearer to Skye. A comparison with the last reliable daylight fix must have led the watch to conclude that, by 02.30 hours, the Island of Skye was very close indeed and far too close for safety. Currents and eddies in a narrow channel around rocky islands are very uncertain factors and depend upon the wind and the tide at the time. As such they are not, indeed cannot, be shown on a tidal chart. They are, however, well-known hazards and, as such, are avoided by keeping well out to sea unless a man with local knowledge, such as a pilot, is available. The watch was probably seeking desperately for the Leist Light to get a fix upon it but for some reason, either because it was dimmed or extinguished or was obscured by the weather, it was never seen. It is not known whether these points were urged before the arbitrator or whether he considered them and rejected them, but it was open to him to find that the loss of the ship was due to a navigational error and had he come to such a conclusion he would probably have found that her loss was a marine risk. This deviation from the account of the case is only made as a further illustration of the different views that can be formed from the facts of the case and the totally opposite results that they could lead to.

40.13 On a case stated to the High Court, Viscount Caldecot L.C.J. upheld the arbitrator's award. The Court of Appeal[9] unanimously reversed his judgment and, in doing so, Scott L.J. said:

"I think the fallacy of [the shipowners'] seemingly logical argument is that in the present case, the war character of the vessel's adventure was nothing more than an irrelevant circumstance, and that there is no chain—much less a direct link—of causation between that character and the stranding."

MacKinnon L.J. said:

"When damage manifestly caused by perils of the seas has been sustained, I can see no logic in the contention that, because the vessel was on a voyage which was itself a warlike operation, this damage by sea perils must be deemed to be a consequence of a warlike operation."

Luxmoore L.J. said:

"The only warlike operation on the part of the *Coxwold* was the carrying of material (i.e., petrol) for war purposes to a destination in the seat of war, but neither the fact that the material was required for war purposes nor the fact that its destination was a war base can have any effect on the influence of the unexpected and unexplained set of the tide on the *Coxwold*. The tidal set would have carried the *Coxwold* on to the Damsel Rocks whatever her cargo and whatever her destination, and it is for this reason I think the stranding of the *Coxwold* was the direct consequence of a marine peril, for the warlike operation had no greater part in causing it than it would have had if the stranding had been caused by a storm of sufficient force to drive the *Coxwold* on to the rocks."

40.14 On appeal to the House of Lords, the House unanimously reversed the judgment of the Court of Appeal and restored that of the Lord Chief Justice. The main speeches were delivered by Viscount Simon L.C., Lord Porter and Lord Wright. Viscount Simon L.C. so described the test to be applied to the facts:

"We thus have to steer our way between two propositions, neither of which is itself correct. It is not correct to say that, because the vessel is engaged in a warlike operation, therefore everything that happens to her during her voyage is proximately caused by a warlike operation or is a proximate consequence of a warlike operation. Neither is it correct to say that, because the accident is of a kind which arises from a marine risk (e.g., stranding or collision), therefore the particular accident can in no circumstances be regarded as a consequence of a warlike operation. The truth lies between these two extremes. It seems to me that there is no abstract proposition, the application of which will provide the answer in every case, except this—one has to ask oneself what is the effective and predominant cause of the accident that happened, whatever the nature of that accident might be."

He noted, with approval, the speech of Lord Wrenbury in *The Matiana*[10] (Lord Wrenbury was one of the majority of the House of Lords in that case):

"If the operation relied on a warlike operation as one which creates no new risk, but only aggravates or increases an existing maritime risk by removing something which, but for the war, would have been a safeguard against that risk, then the risk is not a war risk."

Viscount Simon also noted that Lord Wrenbury made a contrast, also in *The Matiana*:

"If here submarines had been sighted and the escorting vessel had ordered a notoriously

---

9. (C.A.) 70 Ll.L.Rep. 236; [1942] 1 K.B. 35, 48.
10. *Green* v. *British India Steam Navigation Co. Ltd. (The Matiana)* (1920) 3 Ll.L.Rep. 205; (1920) 4 Ll.L.Rep. 245; [1921] 1 A.C. 99. See para. 40.4

dangerous course in order to avoid a peril of war—namely submarine attack—and in consequence the vessel had gone on the rocks, the case would I think have been different."

40.15 Applying these tests to the facts, Viscount Simon considered that the
right-angled turn between 19.15 and 19.45 hours to the normal course, and the
reasons for that manoeuvre, was enough to support the arbitrator's conclusion that
the loss of the *Coxwold* was the consequence of warlike operations.

Lord Porter said:

"One must, I think, take the whole story—a ship sailing on a warlike operation at speed in
dangerous waters where unexpected currents might be found, in convoy without lights, following an ordered course and deviating from it again under orders to avoid actual or
imagined submarine attack. I do not think any one of these factors can be neglected in arriv-
ing at the cause of the loss."

He too considered the loss of the ship as a consequence of warlike operations.

40.16 Lord MacMillan agreed with Viscount Simon L.C. Lord Wright delivered
a long and analytical judgment which, like Lord Porter's, gives an overall view of
the previous cases.[11] He concurred in the motion that the appeal should be
allowed. Lord Atkin agreed with Lord Wright and Lord Porter.

40.17 There is a multitude of other cases immediately following the First World
War but enough has been said to indicate on what very fine points any decision
would turn. Now that the insured peril "consequences of hostilities or warlike
operations" has disappeared from the War Risk Policy, these cases are not of
further concern except for the possibility that the new insured peril of "war"
could also turn upon very fine considerations of facts as has been noted in
Chapter 6. If the reader should wish to have a more detailed analysis of the cases
than is attempted here, it will be found in the speeches of Lords Wright and
Porter in *The Coxwold*.[12]

40.18 As noted in Chapter 1, the F.C. & S. Clause was amended in 1943 with the
object of ensuring that only the consequences of hostilities or warlike operations
caused directly by a hostile act by or against a belligerent power would concern the
War Risk Policy. The nature of the voyage or service which the insured vessel was
performing or, where there was a collision, any other vessel was performing, was
immaterial. Whether or not this amendment would have had the desired effect in
any proceedings is difficult to say, but it did have the effect of persuading the marine underwriters, the war risk underwriters and the mutual war risks associations
not to take narrow points one way or the other and only to consider claims against
the War Risk Policy where there was clear evidence that the casualty was directly
caused "by a hostile act by or against a belligerent power". This had the effect of
reducing the great multitude of cases arising from the First World War to a mere
trickle following the Second. Possibly this is bad news for the lawyers, but the
underwriters and their insured shipowners must always have clarity and not chance
in the risks which their policy covers. If this is not achieved, at least to a reasonable
degree, it becomes impossible to rate risks properly and accurately with all the
mutual inconvenience that this involves.

11. [1942] A.C. 691 at 703.
12. Footnote 8, above.

CHAPTER 41

War risk insurance in time of war

41.1 Under the Notice of Cancellation and Automatic Termination of Cover Clause, war risk insurance provided by the Institute War and Strikes Clauses attached to the MAR form and most of the Mutual War Risks Associations terminates upon the hostile detonation of a nuclear weapon of war, or the outbreak of war between the United Kingdom, the United States of America, France, the Union of Soviet Socialist Republics and the People's Republic of China (Chapter 4). The reasons why this happens are given in Chapter 3 on "The Premiums". This does of course open a yawning gap in the insured shipowners' insurance cover, and the purpose of this chapter is to discuss how it is to be filled to the extent that it is possible to do so.

41.2 At para. 3.2, the point is made that the risk is so huge that only governments, or combinations of governments, have the necessary capacity to provide such insurance. The schemes of individual governments vary enormously in the scope or range of the insurance which they offer. The United States has a scheme, referred to generally as "The Binder" which gives ships insurance when they are taken into the service of the State during wartime. Norway, Denmark and France have similar schemes, whilst ships put into NATO's service will be insured by the Interallied Insurance Organization. A discussion in depth will concentrate upon the British scheme, which Canada has copied in most of its essential details.

41.3 Governments have different priorities than do commercial underwriters. The exercise of the Royal Prerogative of Her Majesty to requisition British ships (para. 21.13) carries with it the obligation to pay for their use, and to make good or pay for damage which they suffer whilst they are compulsorily in her service. The requisitioning laws of various countries are not necessarily the same in every respect, and, as an example, a difference can readily be seen in *Robinson Gold Mining Co. and Others* v. *Alliance Insurance Co.*[1] There the Republic of South Africa, as it existed on the outbreak of the Boer War, was obliged to pay for requisitioned cattle and wagons only; the owners of all other requisitioned property had the right to share in any booty which the Republic, if victorious, might have captured from its enemies during the course of the war. If there was no booty, then there would be no compensation. In addition, a government has a natural desire to make sure that merchant ships, if lost, should be replaced, or if damaged repaired, in the national interest so that they can continue to carry the sinews of war and the country's seaborne trade. If a government is unable to ensure that this is possible, then it probably cannot prosecute the war.

---

1. [1901] 2 K.B. 919; [1902] 2 K.B. 489. See paras. 12.22–12.28.

41.4 Immediately before the First World War, His Majesty's Government desired that the loss of or damage to merchant ships should be dealt with on insurance principles. This had several advantages. Marine insurance principles were already well developed, the compensation for lost merchant ships would be limited to their insured values, which were readily ascertained, or if the government desired, controlled, and the scheme could be virtually self-financing by charging premiums.

41.5 The resources of the State were behind the scheme, but it was always intended that the necessary funds should be raised from premiums without calling for a subvention from the taxpayer. Another vital consideration was that money to replace a lost ship or to repair a damaged one would be available immediately, and thus make possible the prompt replacement or the repair in the national interest. The government asked the London Group of War Risks Associations (The London Group) (see para. 2.5) to prepare a scheme. Out of this, the concept of insurance of King's (Queen's) Enemy Risks (in Canada referred to as the Canada Engaged Risks) was born. The London Group added the necessary extra insured perils to its insurance, known as the King's Enemy Risk, and His Majesty's Government reinsured them. These are insured perils to be contrasted with the other insured perils which the London Group covers which are discussed earlier in this work; these are not reinsured by Her Majesty's Government, there being no element of the Sovereign's enemies being involved, and they are therefore known as the Non-Queen's Enemy Risks.

41.6 From that date to this, the London Group has insured King's (Queen's) Enemy Risks and His (Her) Majesty's Government has given them reinsurance in proportions which have varied between 75% and 100%. Loss or damage suffered by merchant ships in both World Wars was paid for by this arrangement, primarily by the London Group which was reinsured by His Majesty's Government. Whilst, as we shall see, this insurance arrangement is continually operative, there have been three occasions since the Second World War when it has had real meaning; the Korean War (1950–53), the Anglo-French invasion of Egypt (1956) and the Falklands War, sometimes referred to as the South Atlantic War (1982). On all occasions, merchant ships were requisitioned or chartered to support the military to carry troops and all that troops need to fight a war. On each occasion, His, or latterly Her, Majesty had "enemies".

41.7 The complaint has often been raised, with more eloquence than reason, that shipowners have been unduly favoured by this scheme. During the First World War, the damage to civilian property in the United Kingdom was trivial, mostly resulting from some ineffectual Zeppelin raids, which nevertheless caused great alarm, and a bombardment by the German High Seas Fleet on coastal towns in the early days of the war. There was one very important exception to this general statement—the loss of and damage to merchant ships was very substantial. Those whose property was damaged by the exercise of the Royal Prerogative were compensated under the Indemnity Act 1920, some of whose workings are described at para. 11.56. In World War II when a considerable amount of damage was done to civilian property, particularly by bombing, there was a war damage scheme which also operated on insurance lines, and householders paid premiums for the cover which it afforded.

41.8 There have, during the course of the years, been several updatings of the enabling Act, which gives the Secretary of State (formerly the Minister) for Transport the statutory powers which he needs to enter into a Reinsurance Agreement, and of the Reinsurance Agreement itself. The current enabling Act is the Marine and Aviation Insurance (War Risks) Act 1952. This Act is now well out of date, and moves are afoot for a further updating so that Her Majesty's Government can give reinsurance for the latest forms that war risk insurance has taken in the past 40 years since 1952. Nevertheless, the Act does give the Secretary of State a great number of the powers which he needs for the basic essentials of the Reinsurance Agreement. The Act deals with cargo and aircraft as well as ships, but so far as merchant ships are concerned, the following characteristics are the most interesting.

41.9 The Secretary of State may give reinsurance for war risks at any time in respect of a British ship, but for a ship other than a British ship he may afford such reinsurance only "during the continuance of any war or other hostilities in which Her Majesty is engaged or arise after any such war or hostilities in consequence of things done or omitted during the continuance thereof". (section 1(1)).

41.10 There is a definition of "war risk" (section 10) but no definition of a "British ship" for the purposes of the Act. This expression, strange as it may seem, is one of the most elusive terms known to the law. It is true that the Act allows ships of India and the Republic of Ireland to be considered as "British ships" (section 10(2)) but this is not of much help nowadays. In 1952 it did not matter particularly, because British-owned ships were, with few exceptions, registered in the United Kingdom and could be described as "British ships", loose as the term is. Nowadays many British-owned ships are registered for a variety of reasons under other flags. But from a practical proposition, Her Majesty's Government will depend upon their availability in time of war. They cannot be described as "British ships" in any sense of the expression. Even registration in the United Kingdom cannot be regarded as a totally reliable guide when the very odd case of *The Polzeath*[2] is considered. There the Registrar of British ships in King's Lynn raised the question whether the ship was entitled to be registered as a British ship. She was owned by a British company with some British and some German directors, but the main shareholder was a German living in Hamburg. He was in the habit of sending instructions in the most peremptory form on the minutest details to the British directors, and, after the First World War broke out, continued doing so through neutral Dutch intermediaries. It was held by Bargrave Deane J. that the ship was not entitled to be registered as a British ship and she was accordingly struck off the register. Bearing in mind the great variety of shareholdings from all over the world which make up the ownership of British companies owning British-registered ships, the question raises itself just how far registration by itself is, in the absence of an express provision, a reliable guide as to what is or what is not a "British ship" for the purposes of an Act which gives no definition for its own purposes.

41.11 Until the Act can be amended, the Secretary of State and the London Group have done what it is possible to do to resolve the position with the following definition: "British ship—A ship registered in the United Kingdom, the Isle of

2. [1916] P. 117.

Man, any of the Channel Islands or any British Colony." This seeks to make registration alone the test; once a ship is accepted for registration in any one of these places, she can, for the purposes of the Queen's Enemy Risks Rules and Her Majesty's Government Reinsurance Agreement, be considered as a British ship, at least as long as this registration lasts. The Rules also contain a warranty that she shall remain so registered, so that if she is removed from the register for any reason, the insurance position is clear to all concerned.

41.12 This position is not entirely satisfactory and will not be so until this definition, or something similar, can be incorporated into a new enabling Act. For the present, so long as Bermuda, Gibraltar and Hong Kong remain colonies, ships registered in these territories can be considered as "British ships". Ships registered in places which were once colonies, but now no longer are, such as Singapore and the Bahamas, cannot be regarded as British ships. Their problems are dealt with by the Reinsurance Agreement (see para. 41.23).

War risks are defined by the Act (section 10(1)) as:

"War Risks means risks arising from any of the following events that is to say, hostilities, rebellion, revolution and civil war, from civil strife consequent on the happening of any of those events, or from action taken (whether before or after the outbreak of any hostilities, rebellion, revolution or civil war) for repelling an imagined attack or preventing or hindering the carrying out of any attack, and includes piracy."

41.13 As will be seen from Chapters 6 to 26, this definition falls well short of the commercial war risk cover as it has now developed. In 1952 it was quite adequate to describe the war risk cover which was excluded from the marine policy by the Free of Capture and Seizure Clause, and which was insured by the War Risk Policy. At the time of writing, over 40 years later, it no longer serves this purpose. The development of the commercial war risk cover has far outstripped it, and in any case war risks insurance is no longer given on the basis of the Free of Capture and Seizure Clause (Chapter 1). It does, however, define the insured perils for which the Secretary of State can presently give reinsurance cover, and he is not permitted to step beyond the defined boundaries, fixed as they are by statute.

41.14 Nevertheless, a considerable amount of important insurance cover can be given by the London Group and reinsured by the Secretary of State. The insured perils are set out in Rule 2.A of the London Group's Rules, and begin with a condition precedent that they: " . . . must have arisen out of war or other hostilities involving the United Kingdom."

41.15 In respect of the entered ship's hull and machinery, the insured perils are:

"War or any hostile act by or against a belligerent power;
   Capture, seizure, arrest, restraint or detainment and the consequences thereof or any attempt threat;
   Mines, torpedoes, bombs or other weapons of war, including derelict mines, torpedoes, bombs or other derelict weapons of war."

These insured perils have all been discussed in earlier chapters and they bear the same meaning for Queen's Enemy Risks as they do for the non-Queen's Enemy Risks; there is no difference.

41.16 If the entered ship is captured, seized, arrested, restrained or detained then:

(i) Her running expenses are recoverable except for the first seven days.

(ii) Likewise the expenses attending her capture etc. and her release and restoration are recoverable. Included under this head is damage to property which she may have caused during her capture, etc. for which her owner may be legally liable.

(iii) There is also a 90-day rule, similar to the rule described at para. 23.31 which applies to insured perils under the non-Queen's Enemy Risk cover.

This detention cover is subject to the same limitations as the cover which applies to insured perils for non-Queen's Enemy Risk cover.

41.17 Third party liability (Protection and Indemnity) cover is given for:

(i) Collision damage to another ship.

(ii) Removal of wreck, including the lighting or marking of a wreck, provided that the entered ship was wrecked by one of the insured perils for which the hull and machinery are insured.

The Queen's Enemy Risk cover has its own sue and labour provision.

41.18 These are the same insured perils which have been insured for many years by the Queen's Enemy Risk cover, and they have been found in two world wars to represent the most immediate risks to a merchant ship in wartime. As has been remarked already, they do not include all the risks which are now included in the commercial war risk cover but the Secretary of State does not have power to reinsure the insured perils which have made their way into war risk insurance since 1952. This gave rise to problems concerning the ships which accompanied the Task Force to the Falkland Islands (1982). The shipowners, who had obligations to their shareholders, and sometimes to their mortgagees as well, to maintain their insurance to the fullest extent that was possible, would have had to take out extra cover to insure these extra insured perils at a very heavy additional premium. In the event, Her Majesty's Government had extra powers which were pertinent to the Falklands War alone, so that it could by a separate agreement give reinsurance cover for the insured perils which fell outside the description of "war risks" contained in section 10(1) of the enabling Act. Since Her Majesty's Government was also able to give reinsurance for 100%, a satisfactory position could be reached that the ships could be insured by the London Group, and reinsured by Her Majesty's Government, without any premium at all. Nevertheless the whole matter emphasised the need for an extension of the Secretary of State's powers under the enabling Act.

41.19 There is a further rule which is intended to permit the Secretary of State to give reinsurance for ships that are "requisitioned and chartered ships" for periods outside hostilities in which Her Majesty is engaged. Ships, for instance, required to rescue British subjects from Aden or Beirut could be insured under the Rules which insure non-Queen's Enemy Risks, but this would entail a sizeable, perhaps huge, additional premium which the Secretary of State would have to pay. He might prefer to give reinsurance himself and so avoid this substantial cost. The Rule itself is presently not of much help because of the limitations which the current enabling Act put upon the Secretary of State, both as to the amount of insurance he is able to give and the ships he is able to insure during a period when Her Majesty is not engaged in hostilities. It is hoped that with a new enabling Act, this Rule can be extended to a meaningful extent, so that the Secretary of State can fulfil a natural desire when such occasions arise.

THE REINSURANCE AGREEMENT[3]

41.20 Turning now to the Reinsurance Agreement itself, the agreement between Her Majesty's Government and the London Group at the time of the Falklands War was dated 18th February, 1954. It followed the same format as the two Reinsurance Agreements used during the two world wars, and it was for such a similar conflict that it was framed. Drawn up in 1913 in haste, and starting from nothing, it was a notable achievement in its time. During both world wars, there was a strong element of practice which grew up in its interpretation and use. This expertise had all disappeared by 1982, both within Her Majesty's Government and the London Group, and the obscure drafting of the Agreement led to arguments, invariably inconclusive, on its meaning. In a matter as important and as far reaching as this, it was scarcely satisfactory that its meaning should not be readily apparent. Work on clarifying the Agreement was already projected by the London Group in 1980, but no substantial progress had been made before the Falklands War. Immediately afterwards, there was common agreement between Her Majesty's Government and the London Group that a more easily comprehensible Agreement should be used. Another feature which was regarded as being impractical was the necessity to issue special policies to all ships in wartime, which would have led to huge administrative difficulties and all the inconvenience which would have resulted. In addition, the existing Agreement was entirely unsuitable for the modern type of "war" (see paras. 6.29–6.33). Now that the London Group uses Certificates of Entry and Rule Books, which unlike the previous annual policies last throughout the time each ship is entered for insurance in one of the Associations of the London Group, surely a better way could be found. The Queen's Enemy Risks could be identified in a special section of the Rule Book so there could be no doubt as to what the insured perils were and equally no doubt that they were wholly separate from the non-Queen's Enemy Risks for which the Secretary of State gives no reinsurance. Once this was done, then they could be reinsured by quite a short Reinsurance Agreement which simply stated that it reinsured them, and contained the necessary ancillary details for this purpose.

41.21 This sensible suggestion found ready acceptance and was fairly simple of achievement. As has already been remarked, the Queen's Enemy Risks are in a special section of the Rules and a new Reinsurance Agreement, which took effect on 18th February, 1988, was drafted. Known as "Agreements concluded under section 1(1) of the Marine and Aviation Insurance (War Risks) Act 1952, between certain shipowners' Mutual Insurance Associations and the Secretary of State for the Reinsurance of British and other Ships against War Risks", it is a public document which is obtainable from Her Majesty's Stationery Office. Its most important provisions include:

---

3. See Appendix O.

The reinsurance: Clauses 1 to 3

41.22 The Secretary of State reinsures the London Group for 95% in respect of Queen's Enemy Risks, and the Group makes no changes to its Rules which affect his interest without his consent.

The reinsured ships: Clauses 4 to 5

41.23 The Secretary of State gives reinsurance for British ships (as described above) and such other ships as he is prepared to accept for reinsurance in wartime only, when Her Majesty is engaged in hostilities. Primarily this is intended for British-owned flagged-out ships where the Governments of those flags will permit them to take part in any hostilities, and whose owners will sign a letter of commitment that they will be made available to Her Majesty. On these two conditions being fulfilled, Her Majesty's Government will give the shipowner a certificate of acceptability which will enable the Mutual War Risk Association of his choice to give Queen's Enemy Risk cover in wartime when Her Majesty is engaged in hostilities. This certificate may be withdrawn by the Secretary of State if later these conditions cease to be fulfilled.

Insured Values: Clauses 6 to 8

41.24 The old method of assessing the insured values on building costs, and making allowances for depreciation, no longer pertains. Since 1972, there has been an agreement with Her Majesty's Government, now enshrined in these clauses, that marine insurance values for which each ship is insured for total loss under the marine policies shall be the insured values for the purposes of the Reinsurance Agreement. There are elaborate arrangements in the Reinsurance Agreement, and also in the Rules, for querying the insured value of any individual ship, and if necessary taking disputes to arbitration. Also there are arrangements to keep under review, and if necessary to control, insured values which may rise in times of crisis.

Conversion into sterling: Clauses 9 to 11

41.25 For non-Queen's Enemy Risks the Associations accept ships for reinsurance in a variety of currencies. In wartime, the ships are only insured in sterling, so after a General Premium Notice all values have to be converted into sterling and any further entries accepted by the London Group have to be accepted in the same currency.

The reinsurance premiums: Clauses 12 to 14

41.26 No reinsurance premiums are payable until a General Premium Notice (where ships are exposed to Queen's Enemy Risks generally) or a Special Premium Notice (where ships are exposed to Queen's Enemy Risks in a limited area only) is issued by the Secretary of State. 95% of Queen's Enemy Risks premiums are payable to the Secretary of State who determines what the premiums are to be after consultation with the London Group.

General premium notices: Clause 15

41.27 The Secretary of State determines:

—The premium period and any subsequent premium period after its expiry.
—The advance and supplementary Queen's Enemy Risk premiums.

The Queen's Enemy Risk premiums only become payable when each ship's "Get you Home" insurance cover comes to an end. The Queen's Enemy Risk premiums may be payable *pro rata* for broken periods. The London Group may, with the Secretary of State's consent, make a separate charge for other expenses which are primarily administrative charges.

Special premium notices: Clause 16

41.28 The former method, where Queen's Enemy Risks were likely to arise in a limited area, and where that area was to be subject to Queen's Enemy Risk premiums for any visiting ship, is no longer used. The Secretary of State may require additional premiums to be payable to such visits in the same way as additional premiums are charged for non-Queen's Enemy Risks cover.

Consultation: Clause 17

41.29 The Secretary of State and the London Group will consult each other throughout and seek the other's guidance on matters pertaining to General Premium Notices and to Special Premium Notices.

Settlement of claims: Clauses 18 to 21

41.30 The Secretary of State's consent is needed before acceptance of any claims for Queen's Enemy Risks. Where the directors have a discretion whether or not to accept a claim, they must first have the Secretary of State's consent to accept it.

Disputes: Clause 31

41.31 Formerly all disputes had to be submitted to arbitration. Since the Arbitration Act 1979, it is nearly impossible to appeal from an Arbitrator's Award. Since any disputes are likely to be of the most complex nature, and concern highly complicated matters of law, it seems that the highly skilled and experienced judges of the High Court are better able to resolve them. Furthermore, there is a well-settled chain of appeals to the Court of Appeal, and if necessary to the House of Lords, which never presents a substantial difficulty. Disputes under the Reinsurance Agreement between the Secretary of State and the London Group are therefore to be dealt with by the courts. Likewise disputes between the London Group and the insured shipowners on the terms of the Rules are to be dealt with similarly.

41.32 To this general rule there is but one exception. Disputes over the insured values of individual ships are to be dealt with by arbitrators. In court, a judge could only form a view on such matters with the help of expert witnesses. It is considered far better that such expert witnesses should themselves deal with the matter in a judicial capacity.

Commencement and Termination: Clauses 33 to 35

41.33 The Reinsurance Agreement commenced on 20th February, 1988. It can be terminated on 20th February in any year on three months' notice by either side.

41.34 The remaining clauses deal with the administrative arrangements which are necessary between the parties to such a Reinsurance Agreement and, in a brief synopsis of a complex Agreement, need not be mentioned here.

41.35 A brief description of the effects of this Reinsurance Agreement and the Rules must be given. The Queen's Enemy Risk insurance and its reinsurance are continuous even in time of peace. No Queen's Enemy Risk premium is charged for the insurance in peacetime, and indeed there is no reason for this as long as Her Majesty has no enemies. It lies where it is, dormant but able to take effect immediately that it is required. A war then starts involving Her Majesty. The London Group's war risk insurance does not include the Notice of Cancellation and Automatic Termination of Cover Clause, so that, unlike the London Market, the insurance given by the Rules continues unless or until the Secretary of State, considering that the time has now arrived to start charging premiums for the reinsurance, issues a General Premium Notice. This is a document, stating that from a future date (which may be no more than the next few hours) Queen's Enemy Risk premiums will be charged for reinsurance provided between certain specific dates, known as a Premium Period. This is a decision which rests with the Secretary of State alone, although it is contemplated that he would consult with the London Group before taking such a step (paras. 41.27 and 41.29).

41.36 A General Premium Notice has a much greater effect than simply stating that premiums have now got to be paid to the Secretary of State by the London Group, and charged by them to their shipowner members. It has the additional effect of bringing to an end all the non-Queen's Enemy Risk insurance given by the London Group, leaving only the Queen's Enemy Risk insurance. This termination of non-Queen's Enemy Risks insurance does not take effect immediately. The non-Queen's Enemy Risk insurance continues in respect of each individual entered (insured) ship until she has reached a safe and friendly port and for three days thereafter. Some ships, of course, may never achieve this if they are trapped in hostile ports which they never succeed in leaving; they would become the first casualties of war. The modern war being what it is (paras. 6.29–6.33), it is quite possible that the directors may wish to give non-Queen's Enemy Risk insurance, which is outside the scope of the Reinsurance Agreement with Her Majesty's Government, once more, either in whole or in part and if necessary upon special terms. They have the power to do this for what periods and for what areas of the world they see fit, on the basis of mutual contributions or fixed premiums. The reinsurance with His Majesty's Government during both world wars was given on the basis that His Majesty would probably be engaged in a global conflict. As has already been stated, the four wars in which the U.K. has been involved since the Second World War[4] have all been very local in nature and have not been "wars" in the previous and traditional sense. Local and limited in extent they may have been, but they have also been very savage in nature with plenty of opportunity for sinking or

4. Korean War (1950–53); Anglo-French invasion of Egypt (1956); Falklands (South Atlantic) War (1982); Gulf War (1990–1991).

damaging merchant ships within a limited area. On none of the four occasions did the Secretary of State, or his predecessor, the Minister, consider it necessary to issue a General Premium Notice. Had he done so, the provision of non-Queen's Enemy Risk insurance for the rest of the world which was not affected by the fighting would have been necessary.

41.37 A recent example comes readily to mind with the Falklands War (1982). The Secretary of State might have found it necessary to issue a General Premium Notice. If he had done so, the non-Queen's Enemy Risk insurance would have come to an end in the manner described at para. 41.36, a procedure which is more appropriate to a global conflict rather than the more limited war that it was always expected to be. War risks could arise in other parts of the world quite independently of the Falklands War. The directors of the London Group have power, if they see fit, to restore the non-Queen's Enemy Risk insurance subject to special conditions if these are appropriate. Had this step been necessary during the Falklands War, one obvious special condition would have been the exclusion of the area of the fighting of the war, which would have had to be geographically and precisely defined, so that the insurance would be given world wide except for this area. The necessary powers are contained in Rule 5.B of the Rule Book and provide a quick and easy method of restoring insurance. It may be necessary to restore non-Queen's Enemy Risk insurance even in the event of a global conflict, but again Rule 5.B contains the necessary powers for this purpose should the directors wish to use them.

41.38 In the previous pages, the author has attempted to give a concise description of an immensely complex agreement, and it can only be hoped that the reader will regard it as a general guide only, and use it to assist understanding of the insurance arrangement that is provided, and of the documents that give it effect. (Appendices N & O.)

THE NATO WAR RISKS INSURANCE SCHEME

Introductory

41.39 The Cold War lasted from the Berlin Blockade in June, 1948, until it effectively came to an end with the tearing down of the Berlin Wall and the Reunification of Germany in October, 1990. During the period of the Cold War, the North Atlantic Treaty Organisation was dedicated to one purpose only—to deter, and if deterrence failed, to repel, an attack by the Eastern Powers of the Warsaw Pact. Its constitution forbade it from undertaking any offensive operations, and, during the whole period of the Cold War, it was purely defensive in its nature. The 16 Member Nations who formed the Alliance are:

Belgium	Luxembourg
Canada	Netherlands
Denmark	Norway
Federal Republic of Germany	Portugal
France	Spain
Greece	Turkey
Iceland	United Kingdom
Italy	United States of America

41.40 The Treaty of Ottawa 1951 required that if any Member Nation of this Alliance should be attacked, then the other Member Nations would come to her aid.

41.41 At first the threat was seen as that of a land invasion by the numerically vastly superior armed forces of the East, but by the late 1960s the nature of the threat had changed considerably. By this time, thanks to the genius of Admiral Gorckov, the Soviet Union had built up a huge ocean-going fleet to which could be added the contingents of its allies. The submarine force was very strong, and those with memories of the Battle of the Atlantic, when the U-boats very nearly won the Second World War for Germany, could be under no illusions what this portended. If this was not enough, Admiral Kidd, CINCLANT (C.-in-C., North Atlantic) himself proclaimed in a television programme that the initial losses in ships would be "A hell of a lot". NATO's armed forces in Europe, and Europe's civilian population, depended on re-supply from North America and, to a lesser extent only, from the rest of the world. This meant huge numbers of ships, and if the ships were now in danger of attack or destruction, any war between NATO and the Warsaw Pact could be lost at sea. It is not generally realised how acute was the danger to the West during the late 1970s and early 1980s. Besides the political and military chiefs and some journalists, there were few people who appreciated how great it was. Among these were the author, and then only because he was privileged to render some services to NATO. It was only the firm resolve shown by the West, such as the stationing of cruise missiles in Western Europe in 1982 and 1983, which persuaded the West's potential opponents that NATO was too tough a nut to crack. Even then, the danger only decreased by slow degrees, and NATO could not afford to drop its guard.

41.42 If then the danger to the ships was so extreme, and NATO could not hope to win a war without them, insurance bacame an important question. As will be seen from Chapters 3 and 4, the commercial war risks insurance would come to an end on the outbreak of a war such as a war between NATO and the Warsaw Pact, and it was most questionable if the commercial market was in any position to give war risks insurance during such a conflict. Damaged ships would need to be repaired and lost ships replaced, and this meant money. Some members of the Alliance had comprehensive insurance arrangements with their shipowners such as the United States, the United Kingdom, and Canada; other Member States had less comprehensive schemes, whilst some had none at all. Some states had large fleets and only a small population. With such a small tax base, they had no hope of financing a scheme such as the British. And yet their ships were vital to the Alliance.

41.43 Out of these considerations was born the concept of a NATO insurance scheme which would be financed on the mutual principle. It was very probably the first time in history that a military and defensive alliance has undertaken marine insurance. The decision was taken, with the approval of the Council of Ministers, that such insurance should be given by a body formed specially for the purpose, the Interallied Insurance Organisation (I.I.O.); the I.I.O. should be a NATO Civil Wartime Agency (N.C.W.A.); the United Kingdom should be the host country and should provide the Secretariat; the Planning Board for Ocean Shipping (P.B.O.S.) should delegate the task of the necessary planning in peacetime to its subordinate body, the Shipping War Losses Working Group (S.W.L.W.G.); the S.W.L.W.G. should report to the Planning Board, and could look for assistance to the Senior

Civil Emergency Planning Committee (S.C.E.P.C.). It should liaise with other planning groups and departments of NATO, both civil and military. This may sound all very bureaucratic, but in an organisation as large as NATO, it is essential to establish firm lines of communication. Anyway, NATO was full of very friendly people from all the Member Nations of the Alliance who were always anxious to help. It was never difficult to have dealings with them.

First stage—1970 to 1982

41.44 After a false start in the late 1960s, the S.W.L.W.G. began its deliberations in May 1970. It was attended by delegations from most of the Member Nations of the Alliance under a Chairman provided by Greece. Admiral Pagonis was a Coastguard Admiral (the Greek Coastguard, like the U.S. Coastguard, uses naval ranks), and his civil service experience was invaluable. The delegates themselves were either senior civil servants or senior military or naval officers with a few commercial people. The Secretariat, provided by the United Kingdom, was in attendance. To this gathering was added two Technical Advisers, Mr. N. F. Ledwith and the author, to give advice on the management and organisation of a mutual insurance organisation. Later Mr. W. A. Wilson joined the Group, and remained with it until his death in 1986.

41.45 This was the pattern of meetings throughout. Over a long period of time, people came and went, Mr. G. P. Bisbas, also of Greece, took over the Chairmanship on the Admiral's sudden and untimely death in 1976, and remained until his retirement in 1987. Then Mr. P. Michelet of Norway took the Chair, and held it until the Group's meetings came to an end in 1992.

41.46 To those coming fresh from commerce, the early meetings, although always friendly and courteous, were strange affairs. They naturally took on a civil service character on an international plane. Civil service is a profession of its own, and it had its own rules of conduct, methods, courtesies, and etiquette, and if these were strange to commercial eyes, they were at least consistent, and (eventually) productive of positive and well thought-out results. It was the way that they reached their goals that was unnerving. The Council Chamber rang with denunciations on some point or another, and even now, nearly 25 years later, the Summary Record (the minutes) contains some ferocious reading. The natural conclusion was that agreement was not possible, and that it would never be possible to get an insurance scheme on its feet. Then the Admiral would disappear for a few days, and quite suddenly ring up to say that all was now arranged; the dissenters to the proposal had agreed with it all along! He had been to the various capitals, and spoken with people in the privacy of their own offices, and now he came back with agreement. At the next meeting, an issue which had previously raised so much heat was not even mentioned, or if it was, it was simply to record a formal reservation, which would, in the course of time, be equally formally removed.

41.47 It must not be thought from all this that the proceedings of the S.W.L.W.G.'s meetings were disorderly, unbusinesslike, or lacking in method. Such things were simply not in the nature of the delegates, and in any event, an experienced Chairman and an immensely professional Secretariat kept things going properly and smoothly. It needs to be stressed that the delegates were engaged on a huge and unfamiliar task which, even if it puzzled them, they attacked with resolution and gusto. They were engaged in putting together the biggest marine insurance organisation which the world had ever seen, which would have to function without any experience of its own workings (apart from a few training exercises) right from the start of any conflict. One day it would be a paper plan, and the next day it could be operational. This was a daunting enough proposition in itself. Added to that, it would be a huge marine underwriter without even any capital, reinsurance, or any of the other factors on which marine insurers usually rely.

41.48 Agreements in NATO can only be reached unanimously, and this was productive of much delay. It meant that any proposal of the S.W.L.W.G. had to be agreed unanimously before it could be submitted to the Planning Board for formal adoption. Unanimity was a drawback, but in a body such as NATO it was a very necessary safeguard without which NATO could not function at all. Some amelioration was found in the "silence" procedure; a proposal, usually after some discussion, would be circulated with a note attached saying that if there were no objections by set date, then unanimous agreement would be presumed. This worked very well, because if there were objections, they would be clearly identified and were thus open for discussion and persuasion one way or the other. In course of time the Chairman, the delegates, the Secretariat, and the Technical Advisers all came to know each other well, and with acquaintance came respect, and with respect came trust. The earlier dramas became a thing of the past, and much consultation took place between various individuals, the only proviso being that the Secretariat and the Chairman were kept informed of what was happening.

41.49 The following problems were identified as being matters of prime interest:

1. The terms and conditions on which insurance should be given, or, in other words, the Policy of Insurance. This was a major priority.
2. The charge of premiums and the method of underwriting. This too was a major priority.
3. The legal standing of the I.I.O. It had to have a corporate existence within the host country, the United Kingdom, which meant incorporation which was complete to the standards required by English law.
4. The Terms of Reference of the I.I.O. These took the place of the Memorandum in an English company, and set out the powers which were *intra vires*.
5. The Basic Principles of the I.I.O. These were its Articles of Association, and governed its internal workings.
6. The valuations of the ships, or their insured values (I.V.). On these depended the charge of premiums and the measure of compensation for any loss through an insured peril.
7. The structure of the I.I.O. It needed a board, a Chief Executive, and departments.

41.50 The form of policy was settled quickly, being based on the S.G. Form with the additions necessary for wartime. At least if a war started suddenly, the insured perils and the excluded risks were clearly identified. Likewise the charge of premiums was soon settled, although on a basis which nobody was entirely happy with. The legal standing, which should have been easily resolved, turned out to be a thorny subject and one which initially defied easy resolution. It was eventually resolved in a way which seemed strange to the eyes of an English lawyer. First of all, the Terms of Reference had to be drawn up and approved by the Council of Ministers. Since the Council had many better things to do than plough through pages of turgid wording, the Terms had to be brief. It was no easy matter for an international body to draw up a document which covered no more than two and a half sides of A4 notepaper on such complex matters, but it was eventually done, and the great day arrived when it was returned, signed by the Secretary-General to signify the approval of the Council of Ministers. Armed with this, it was then possible to get the I.I.O. incorporated by Statutory Instrument under the powers given by Parliament in the Act which ratified the Treaty of Ottawa 1951. It was all very strange, but it worked.

41.51 Of all the other matters mentioned in the above list, the most intractable was that of valuation. No reliance could be placed on the Marine Insurance Values which were sufficient for the British War Risks scheme. These values, on an international plane, varied enormously even between similar ships. This is not surprising, because Marine Insurance Values reflect what a ship is worth to her owner, and such variable factors as taxation need to be considered. Equity between the Member Nations of the Alliance was vital, and thus a uniform method had to be devised. The only way that this could be achieved was by means of a set tariff which took into account a vessel's age, type, equipment, and a host of other details. This, with great difficulty, was agreed.

41.52 Besides the matters set out in the list, the S.W.L.W.G. was called upon to consider a mass of other things, all of which needed to be thought about. Some of these were not, strictly speaking, within its remit. It was, however, one of the many think-tanks of NATO, and we all were dedicated to helping each other. In one way and another, we were all engaged in the business of deterrence, and if the S.W.L.W.G. had a big and puzzling remit of its own, then so did many of the other think-tanks whose aims and tasks were similarly dedicated. The basis of the insurance scheme, like all good ideas, was a simple one. As always, the devil lay in the detail.

41.53 Finally, all was ready, and in 1982 the S.W.L.W.G. was able to report that it had fulfilled its remit. It had to report however, that it was already out of date. The form of commercial war risks policy had changed as had the method of underwriting among the mutual insurance associations. The Group felt that NATO should have the advantages which each offered. It therefore recommended that the existing scheme should be adopted so that there was something in existence should a war suddenly begin, but that the Group should bring it up to date. This recommendation was accepted. The whole process had to begin again.

Second stage—1982 to 1992

41.54 An important thing happened in 1980. Up to that time, the considerations of the Group were, with rare exceptions, classified. This posed problems in a commercial office; even the secretaries who typed out and handled the mass of paper that was involved had to be cleared for security, and this involved prying into private lives which was not always welcome. There was a lighter side, and there are some amusing stories of Customs Officers determined to pry into briefcases which contained classified documents, and delegates and others being equally determined that they should do no such thing. In 1980, General Hackett, who had himself been a Major NATO Commander (M.N.C.), published his book, *The Third World War*. It contained much classified material, some of which could be recognised, but it was obvious from the forewords, and the acknowledgements from many senior civil servants and military officers from every Member Nation of the Alliance, that he not only had permission to write the book, but encouragement as well. From this time on, the perception of NATO was that not everything should remain behind closed doors. The doings of the military had of course to remain secret, but if the vast preparation of NATO to repel an attack could become known in general terms, this would add greatly to the primary aim of deterrence. Here the considerations of the S.W.L.W.G. and its sister groups had a part to play. If on their humble level such detail was being considered, then the potential opponents had so much more to fear from NATO's military teeth. Details of their planning could not of course be published to all and sundry, but there was no objection to their existence and their remits being matters of general knowledge.

41.55 During the second stage, there was a mass of subordinate matters which needed a lot of time and very close attention, but the main priorities were:

1. An up-to-date form of policy, which reflected the form used by the commercial market.
2. Methods of underwriting which reflected the new methods used by the Mutual Associations.
3. The structure of the I.I.O. and the responsibilities of its executives and its departments.
4. An improved valuation scheme.
5. Improved Basic Principles.

The policy

41.56 This was agreed on a format which bore a close resemblance to the Institute War and Strikes Clauses Hulls—Time 1.10.83 to which were added clauses suitable for a NATO conflict. Again it set out the insured perils and the excluded risks in an easy-to-read format. Ships would come on risk when their Member Nations had requisitioned them and placed them at the disposal of the Defence Shipping Authority (D.S.A.). They would come off risk when they were removed from the D.S.A. for any reason, or were lost.

Methods of underwriting

41.57 It was thought necessary to keep the premium periods very short—no longer than a month to keep a close eye on the scale of losses, which in the early part of any conflict were likely to fulfil Admiral Kidd's worst expectations in ample measure. Premiums, fixed by the Chief Executive, would be surcharged onto the freight and would thus be payable by the users. If, as was more likely to be the case than otherwise, particularly in the early part of the conflict, there was a deficit for the premium period, then there would be a supplementary premium. This would not be charged to the Member Nations, but would be carried forward to the next, or a subsequent premium period. The later premium periods were more likely to be properly in balance, but this depended on the Alliance's naval forces gaining the upper hand at sea; if they failed to do this, then the war would be lost in any event.

Structure

41.58 At the top, there was the Board of Directors, presided over by a Chairman who was to be elected by the Board. Each Member Nation had the right to appoint one director, and, if it wished, an alternate director as well.

41.59 Next came the Chief Executive and his Deputy. Their responsibilities included fixing the length of the premium periods and assessing the rates of premium for each. They were also responsible to the Board for the smooth running of the I.I.O.

41.60 Under them would come the Departments:

> *The Valuation Department* to assess the insured values of the ships in accordance with the tariff.
>
> *The Claims Department* to handle the claims and to keep records, premium period by premium period, of the losses which had been paid, and the estimated losses which had been suffered but which were not yet paid. They were required to make an allowance for claims Incurred But Not Reported (I.B.N.R.), the bane of any underwriter's life.
>
> *The Financial Department* to handle the huge amounts of money coming into the I.I.O.'s hands.
>
> *The General Service Department* to service the organisation, keep its data, and look after its security.
>
> *The Legal Staff* to handle the disputes involving the I.I.O. and the myriad legal problems which such an organisation could be expected to attract.
>
> *The Regional Offices* to act as agents in all parts of the world.

41.61 Whilst the I.I.O. was a Mutual Association, its members were the Member nations of the Alliance. They were not the individual shipowners; the Member Nations would be responsible to them, having requisitioned their ships for service with the D.S.A. As such, it was highly desirable that the I.I.O. should follow the normal practice of NATO and divide up the various offices and posts between the Member Nations who would nominate suitable persons to fill them. These would be the International Staff, or the "Chiefs". The "Indians" would be supplied by the host country, the United Kingdom. They too, like office staffs everywhere, had a vital role to play, but they would look to their respective International Staff of their Departments for the necessary guidance and control that is always required.

The improved valuation scheme

41.62 This was by far the most difficult problem. The valuation was to be on the basis of replacement cost less depreciation for age. Ship building prices could be expected to fluctuate considerably, particularly in wartime, and frequent adjustments would be necessary. A tariff system would result in similar ships having insured values which were very similar to each other, but even so it was inevitable that there would be anomalies which would have to be adjusted. Some ships were so specialised that they had to have their own insured values, and this gave rise to considerable problems. In general, the depreciation rate was to be calculated at a rate of 7% per annum over 18 years for ships of 20,000 grt or more, and over 20 years for ships of lesser size. After 18 (or 20) years, no further depreciation would take place of the residual values.

The improved basic principles

41.63 These needed immense care to work out, and the initial proposals worked out by the French Delegations went to no less than 10 revises.

41.64 When the welcome order to stand down was given in 1991, the second scheme was ready in all respects except for some details of the valuation scheme which needed some further time to resolve. But now it was only ready to put on the shelf, where it currently is, "just in case". There was no point in continuing, because NATO had fulfilled its primary role of deterrence. No NATO soldier had ever found it necessary to fire a shot in anger. It is not going too far to say, that even on its lowly level, the S.W.L.W.G. had played its tiny part in the vast web of deterrence.

41.65 Would the I.I.O. have worked? The answer has to be it would have worked because it would have to have worked. No doubt many of the details of its planning in peacetime would have had to be changed, and many short-cuts would have been made, to meet the exigencies of wartime. As has been remarked earlier in this work, it is much easier to change something which is planned and structured than something which has no recognisable form. Was all this vast labour necessary? Thankfully, it was never put to the test. Do those engaged in this labour resent that it was, in the event, all wasted labour? This cannot be, because those who, like the author, had experience of the Red Army after the Second World War, could never share the comfortable thesis of remote and ineffectual dons who wrote, lectured, and taught, that it was better to be "red than dead". All armies of occupation behave badly, but in this respect the Red Army was in a class of its own. It was a loathsome organisation.

41.66 It was heartening to see that deterrence was in fact working. At the "Shipping Under Fire" Seminar in Athens in 1987, Admiral Shea of the United States Navy roundly declared "The Soviets must understand that the West is resolute." Perhaps this was going a little far where some people were concerned. Unknown to the Admiral, the first two rows were occupied by Soviet journalists. The effect was gratifyingly electric.

THE SOUTH ATLANTIC WAR 1982—THE GULF WAR 1991

41.67 During the early stages of the Falklands Conflict, when the Task Force was being assembled, the question arose of the War Risks insurance for the ships which had been requisitioned and chartered to support the Task Force. Whilst the United Kingdom was engaged in the hostilities, there was no question of the Cancellation and Automatic Termination of Cover Clause operating because Argentina was not one of the nations named within it (Chapter 4). Thus insurance was still available from the commercial market. There was another reason why this clause would not have operated; the merchant ships all flew the British Flag, and were thus entered in the British Mutual War Risks Associations. These Associations do not include the clause within their Rules (para. 4.41)

41.68 Her Majesty's Government was much disturbed to find that the Additional Premiums charged by the commercial market were initially quoted at 8% per month. If the war had continued for a year, as seemed not impossible at the time, then the Crown would, after the year had passed, have paid the full insured value of the ships without having purchased them and acquired ownership of them. The Mutual War Risks Associations therefore offered the Queen's Enemy Risks insurance which was given by their Rules, and reinsured by the Crown. If the Crown would increase the amount of reinsurance which it gave to the Associations to 100%, the Associations were prepared to give the Queen's Enemy Risks insurance to the shipowners without premium provided that no premium was charged to the Associations. The Crown, having a faith that it could afford the merchant ships substantial naval and military protection, which was borne out by the event, accepted the offer, being particularly insistent that the Associations would handle the claims. This gave the Associations no problems, and they were able to give advice whether the War Risks insurance or the respective ship's Protection and Indemnity insurance should bear any particular claims. There were some of both.

41.69 Only one merchant ship was lost, the *Atlantic Conveyor* which was struck by an Exocet missile. Unlike the ships which were struck by similar missiles in the Iran/Iraq War, the *Atlantic Conveyor* sank. Her insured value, which was paid by her Mutual War Risks Association and reimbursed by the Crown, was sufficient to pay for a replacement built in a Korean yard. For political reasons, the Government supplemented the insurance monies so that the replacement could be built in a British yard. The *Monsunen* was also reported to have been scuttled by the Argentines. In fact, they had immobilised her by winding a wire around her propeller and beaching her in Choisel Sound. She was refloated by the Royal Navy, and was pressed into service; television reports showed her carrying Gurkha troops. The author saw her in 1991 in Port Stanley proudly wearing a smart new coat of green paint. Some ships were damaged, notably a tanker which was hit by a bomb dropped onto her foredeck from an Argentine aircraft. It went over the side without exploding. There were also some near misses; the *Canberra*, discharging troops and equipment in San Carlos Water, was nearly hit by a missile.

41.70 There were some cases of death and injury to merchant seamen. The most distressing cases involved the Chinese seamen on the *Sir Lancelot* and the *Sir Galahad*; these being Royal Fleet Auxiliary ships, they employed merchant seamen. The death and injury claims concerned the War Risks insurance, because they were suffered from the bombing of the two ships whilst they were engaged in landing the Welsh Guards. Difficult questions were posed by the merchant seamen who suffered trauma from their experiences, and needed long periods of medical treatment. These were not young highly trained naval seamen, trained to face war and all that war involves. They were middle-aged merchant seamen who normally pursued a peaceful calling. These claims were settled by the War Risks insurance and by the Protection and Indemnity Associations as the circumstances of each individual case indicated without any proceedings being necessary. There was one case where there could be no doubt that the Protection and Indemnity insurance should respond, and it duly did. After the hostilities were over, the Royal Artillery wanted to take home a captured Argentine artillery piece to add to their collection at their Headquarters in Woolwich. The ship's Master agreed to carry it on deck, and it was delivered alongside by two Royal Artillery bombardiers. It was then for the first time found to be loaded. The bombardiers, unhelpfully, disappeared, and the Third Engineer undertook to unload it. There are various safe ways of unloading an artillery piece, and they do not include the blowlamp which he took to the task. The inevitable happened, and he lost three fingers.

41.71 When in August 1990, the Iraqis invaded Kuwait, a huge land force was assembled in Saudi Arabia, and a considerable armada was gathered together with a correspondingly large air force. At first, the purpose of these armed forces was defensive, to prevent the invasion of Saudi Arabia, which seemed an imminent possibility. In November 1990, when it became clear that the Iraqis intended to defy the Security Council's resolutions to leave Kuwait peaceably, the purpose of this force became offensive with the aim of ejecting them and of freeing Kuwait by military means. This involved enormous preparation, and the assembly of yet more armed forces to make sure this offensive purpose could be achieved. Whilst these armed forces came from a great number of nations, the main burden of finding them, and of transporting them to Saudi Arabia, and of keeping them supplied with all that they needed, fell upon the United States of America. This meant a great number of merchant ships had to be acquired by charter.

41.72 The United States Government was neither surprised nor dismayed that the freight market rose when it started to charter the ships it required; it did not object to a 15% rise in freight rates which it regarded as reasonable. It was greatly incensed by the rise, as its officials put it, of 500% in the war risks insurance rates. The Gulf was an Additional Premium area from the time of the Iran/Iraq War, and with the vast amount of tonnage in the Gulf to meet these military requirements, the underwriters were fully justified in taking a pessimistic view, particularly as Iraq was known to be amply supplied with weapons of the latest patterns. The United States therefore decided to take the burden of the War Risks insurance itself, which it could do by using "The Binder". This only needed the President's signature to become operative, and since it was reasonable to conclude that the armed forces of the United States and its Allies were in a position to supply a very substantial degree of protection to the merchant ships, President Bush duly signed it. From then on, the United States gave war risks insurance to the merchant ships which she chartered to carry her troops and all their equipment to the scene of operations.

41.73 Things did not go entirely smoothly. The Binder had last been used in the Korean War some 40 years before. War Risks insurance had progressed considerably in the meantime, and the amount of the insurance which it provided was woefully inadequate by modern standards. Representations were made to the U.S. Department of Commerce, and it says much for the open-minded way in which the Department responded to these pleas that their insurance should be brought up to date. Once this was done, the insurance which was given by The Binder was satisfactory. In fact, the War Risks casualties during the entire war were confined to ships which were in Kuwait Harbour at the time of the Iraqi invasion.

41.74 There are lessons to be learnt from these two wars, and to some extent they are contradictory. The commercial underwriters have to take a pessimistic view of a great deal of loss and damage being suffered by the ships to whom they give insurance in such events as the South Atlantic and the Gulf wars. They would be failing in their duty to their members or their shareholders if they did otherwise. Their insurance and their premium structures are really geared to isolated war risks casualties, although they will allow this to be stretched to include events such as the Iran/Iraq War. The line should really be drawn where large numbers of merchant ships are supporting military and naval operations; whilst they are willing to give insurance in such cases, they have to charge substantial premiums for it. This tends, quite unfairly, to show them up in a bad light. Where governments are engaged in such operations, and have reason to be confident that they can protect the merchant ships, at least to a very substantial degree, then they are justified in taking themselves the burden of the War Risks insurance of the ships, whether this is done by way of reinsurance, as in the British case, or directly as the Americans did. No figures are available to show how much money was saved to the British taxpayer, but it must have been considerably more than the amounts paid for the casualties. The U.S. Department of Commerce's figure is $500 million. Whatever the figure, it must be very substantial.

APPENDIX A

The S.G. Form*

(No.   )

S.G.

Printed at Lloyd's, London, England.

Be it known that

as well in *their* own name as for and in the name and names of all and every other person or persons *themselves* to whom the same doth, may, or shall appertain, in part or in all, doth make assurance and cause and them, and every of them, to be insured, lost or not lost, at and from

Upon any kind of goods and merchandises, and also upon the body, tackle, apparel, ordnance, munition, artillery, boat, and other furniture, of and in the good ship or vessel called the

whereof is master under God, for this present voyage, or whosoever else shall go for master in the said ship, or by whatsoever other name or names the same ship, or the master thereof, is or shall be named or called ; beginning the adventure upon the said goods and merchandises from the loading thereof aboard the said ship, *as above* upon the said ship, &c., *as above* and so shall continue and endure, during her abode there, upon the said ship, &c. And further, until the said ship, with all her ordnance, tackle, apparel, &c., and goods and merchandises whatsoever shall be arrived at *as above* upon the said ship, &c., until she hath moored at anchor twenty-four hours in good safety ; and upon the goods and merchandises, until the same be there discharged and safely landed. And it shall be lawful for the said ship, &c., in this voyage, to proceed and sail to and touch and stay at any ports or places whatsoever *and wheresoever for all purposes* without prejudice to this insurance. The said ship, &c., goods and merchandises, &c., for so much as concerns the assured by agreement between the assured and assurers in this policy, are and shall be valued at

Touching the adventures and perils which we the assurers are contented to bear and do take upon us in this voyage : they are of the seas, men of war, fire, enemies, pirates, rovers, thieves, jettisons, letters of mart and countermart, surprisals, takings at sea, arrests, restraints, and detainments of all kings, princes, and people, of what nation, condition, or quality soever, barratry of the master and mariners, and of all other perils, losses, and misfortunes, that have or shall come to the hurt, detriment, or damage of the said goods and merchandises, and ship, &c., or any part thereof. And in case of any loss or misfortune it shall be lawful to the assured, their factors, servants and assigns, to sue, labour, and travel for, in and about the defence, safeguard, and recovery of the said goods and merchandises, and ship, &c., or any part thereof, without prejudice to this insurance ; to the charges whereof we, the assurers, will contribute each one according to the rate and quantity of his sum herein assured. And it is especially declared and agreed that no acts of the insurer or insured in recovering, saving, or preserving the property insured shall be considered as a waiver, or acceptance of abandonment. And it is agreed by us, the insurers, that this writing or policy of assurance shall be of as much force and effect as the surest writing or policy of assurance heretofore made in Lombard Street, or in the Royal Exchange, or elsewhere in London.

Warranted free of capture, seizure, arrest, restraint or detainment, and the consequences thereof or of any attempt thereat; also from the consequences of hostilities or warlike operations, whether there be a declaration of war or not ; but this warranty shall not exclude collision, contact with any fixed or floating object (other than a mine or torpedo), stranding, heavy weather or fire unless caused directly (and independently of the nature of the voyage or service which the vessel concerned or, in the case of a collision, any other vessel involved therein, is performing) by a hostile act by or against a belligerent power ; and for the purpose of this warranty "power" includes any authority maintaining naval, military or air forces in association with a power.

Further warranted free from the consequences of civil war, revolution, rebellion, insurrection, or civil strife arising therefrom, or piracy.

And so we, the assurers, are contented, and do hereby promise and bind ourselves, each one for his own part, our heirs, executors, and goods to the assured, their executors, administrators, and assigns, for the true performance of the premises, confessing ourselves paid the consideration due unto us for this assurance by the assured, at and after the rate of

IN WITNESS whereof we, the assurers, have subscribed our names and sums assured in *LONDON, as hereinafter appears.*

N.B.—Corn, fish, salt, fruit, flour, and seed are warranted free from average, unless general, or the ship be stranded ; sugar, tobacco, hemp, flax, hides and skins are warranted free from average under five pounds per cent., and all other goods, also the ship and freight, are warranted free from average under three pounds per cent. unless general, or the ship be stranded.

How know ye that We the Assurers, Members of the Syndicates whose definitive numbers in the after-mentioned List of Underwriting Members of Lloyd's are set out in the attached Table, hereby bind ourselves each for his own part and not one for another and in respect of his due proportion only, to pay or make good to the Assured all such Loss and/or Damage which he or they may sustain by any one or more of the aforesaid perils and the due proportion for which each of us, the Assurers, is liable shall be ascertained by reference to his share, as shown in the said List, of the Amount, Percentage or Proportion of the total sum assured hereunder which is in the Table set opposite the definitive number of the Syndicate of which such Assurer is a Member AND FURTHER THAT the List of Underwriting Members of Lloyd's referred to above shows their respective Syndicates and Shares therein, is deemed to be incorporated in and to form part of this Policy, bears the number specified in the attached Table and is available for inspection at Lloyd's Policy Signing Office by the Assured or his or their representatives and a true copy of the material parts of the said List certified by the General Manager of Lloyd's Policy Signing Office will be furnished to the Assured on application.

In Witness whereof the General Manager of Lloyd's Policy Signing Office has subscribed his name on behalf of each of us.

LLOYD'S POLICY SIGNING OFFICE,

GENERAL MANAGER.

Dated in London, the

(In the event of accident whereby loss or damage may result in a claim under this Policy, the

L.P.O. 62 settlement will be much facilitated if immediate notice be given to the nearest Lloyd's Agent.)

(12-11-39)
(15-4-43)
(25-3-64)

FOR EMBOSSMENT BY ● LLOYD'S POLICY SIGNING OFFICE ●

Definitive Numbers of Syndicates and Amount, Percentage or Proportion of the Total Sum Assured hereunder shared between the Members of those Syndicates.

In all communications please quote
the following reference

LLOYD'S LONDON

(In the event of accident whereby loss or damage may result in a claim under this Policy, the settlement will be much facilitated if immediate notice be given to the nearest Lloyd's Agent.)

APPENDIX B

The MAR Form*

* Printed by permission of the Corporation of Lloyd's.

Lloyd's
Marine Policy

We, The Underwriters, hereby agree, in consideration of the payment to us by or on behalf of the Assured of the premium specified in the Schedule, to insure against loss damage liability or expense in the proportions and manner hereinafter provided. Each Underwriting Member of a Syndicate whose definitive number and proportion is set out in the following Table shall be liable only for his own share of his respective Syndicate's proportion.

This insurance shall be subject to the exclusive jurisdiction of the English Courts, except as may be expressly provided herein to the contrary.

In Witness whereof the General Manager of Lloyd's Policy Signing Office has subscribed his Name on behalf of each of Us

LLOYD'S POLICY SIGNING OFFICE
General Manager

MAR 91
LPO 62A (1.11.91) Printed by CBC City Print Limited. 071-353 1000.

SCHEDULE

POLICY NUMBER

NAME OF ASSURED

VESSEL

VOYAGE OR PERIOD OF INSURANCE

SUBJECT-MATTER INSURED

AGREED VALUE
   (if any)

AMOUNT INSURED HEREUNDER

PREMIUM

CLAUSES, ENDORSEMENTS, SPECIAL CONDITIONS AND WARRANTIES

THE ATTACHED CLAUSES AND ENDORSEMENTS FORM PART OF THIS POLICY

Definitive numbers of the Syndicates and proportions

The List of Underwriting Members of Lloyd's mentioned in the above Table shows their respective Syndicates and Shares therein, and is deemed to be incorporated in and to form part of this Policy. It is available for inspection at Lloyd's Policy Signing Office by the Assured or his or their representatives and a true copy of the material parts of it certified by the General Manager of Lloyd's Policy Signing Office will be furnished to the Assured on application.

In all communications please quote the following reference	

Lloyd's Marine Policy

The Assured is requested to **read this Policy** and, if it is incorrect, return it immediately for alteration to:

FOR CARGO INSURANCES ONLY
In the event of loss or damage which may result in a claim under this Insurance, immediate notice must be given to the Lloyd's Agent at the port or place where the loss or damage is discovered in order that he may examine the goods and issue a survey report.

APPENDIX C

The Marine Policy Form for Ships [*]

Institute Time Clauses Hulls 1/10/83

[*] Available from Witherby & Co., London.

1/10/83   (FOR USE ONLY WITH THE NEW MARINE POLICY FORM)

INSTITUTE TIME CLAUSES
HULLS

This insurance is subject to English law and practice

1 NAVIGATION

1.1 The Vessel is covered subject to the provisions of this insurance at all times and has leave to sail or   1
navigate with or without pilots, to go on trial trips and to assist and tow vessels or craft in distress, but it   2
is warranted that the Vessel shall not be towed, except as is customary or to the first safe port or place   3
when in need of assistance, or undertake towage or salvage services under a contract previously arranged   4
by the Assured and/or Owners and/or Managers and/or Charterers. This Clause 1.1 shall not exclude   5
customary towage in connection with loading and discharging.   6
  7

1.2 In the event of the Vessel being employed in trading operations which entail cargo loading or discharging   8
at sea from or into another vessel (not being a harbour or inshore craft) no claim shall be recoverable   9
under this insurance for loss of or damage to the Vessel or liability to any other vessel arising from such   10
loading or discharging operations, including whilst approaching, lying alongside and leaving, unless   11
previous notice that the Vessel is to be employed in such operations has been given to the Underwriters   12
and any amended terms of cover and any additional premium required by them have been agreed.   13

1.3 In the event of the Vessel sailing (with or without cargo) with an intention of being (a) broken up, or (b)   14
sold for breaking up, any claim for loss of or damage to the Vessel occurring subsequent to such sailing   15
shall be limited to the market value of the Vessel as scrap at the time when the loss or damage is sustained,   16
unless previous notice has been given to the Underwriters and any amendments to the terms of cover,   17
insured value and premium required by them have been agreed. Nothing in this Clause 1.3 shall affect   18
claims under Clauses 8 and/or 11.   19

2 CONTINUATION

Should the Vessel at the expiration of this insurance be at sea or in distress or at a port of refuge or of call, she   20
shall, provided previous notice be given to the Underwriters, be held covered at a pro rata monthly premium to her   21
port of destination.   22
  23

3 BREACH OF WARRANTY

Held covered in case of any breach of warranty as to cargo, trade, locality, towage, salvage services or date of   24
sailing, provided notice be given to the Underwriters immediately after receipt of advices and any amended terms   25
of cover and any additional premium required by them be agreed.   26
  27

4 TERMINATION

This Clause 4 shall prevail notwithstanding any provision whether written typed or printed in this insurance inconsistent therewith. 28 29 30

Unless the Underwriters agree to the contrary in writing, this insurance shall terminate automatically at the time of 31

4.1 change of the Classification Society of the Vessel, or change, suspension, discontinuance, withdrawal or expiry of her Class therein, provided that if the Vessel is at sea such automatic termination shall be deferred until arrival at her next port. However where such change, suspension, discontinuance or withdrawal of her Class has resulted from loss or damage covered by Clause 6 of this insurance or which would be covered by an insurance of the Vessel subject to current Institute War and Strikes Clauses Hulls-Time such automatic termination shall only operate should the Vessel sail from her next port without the prior approval of the Classification Society, 32 33 34 35 36 37 38

4.2 any change, voluntary or otherwise, in the ownership or flag, transfer to new management, or charter on a bareboat basis, or requisition for title or use of the Vessel, provided that, if the Vessel has cargo on board and has already sailed from her loading port or is at sea in ballast, such automatic termination shall if required be deferred, whilst the Vessel continues her planned voyage, until arrival at final port of discharge if with cargo or at port of destination if in ballast. However, in the event of requisition for title or use without the prior execution of a written agreement by the Assured, such automatic termination shall occur fifteen days after such requisition whether the Vessel is at sea or in port. 39 40 41 42 43 44 45

A pro rata daily net return of premium shall be made. 46

5 ASSIGNMENT 47

No assignment of or interest in this insurance or in any moneys which may be or become payable thereunder is to be binding on or recognised by the Underwriters unless a dated notice of such assignment or interest signed by the Assured, and by the assignor in the case of subsequent assignment, is endorsed on the Policy and the Policy with such endorsement is produced before payment of any claim or return of premium thereunder. 48 49 50 51

6 PERILS 52

6.1 This insurance covers loss of or damage to the subject-matter insured caused by 53

6.1.1 perils of the seas rivers lakes or other navigable waters 54

6.1.2 fire, explosion 55

6.1.3 violent theft by persons from outside the Vessel 56

6.1.4 jettison 57

6.1.5 piracy 58

6.1.6 breakdown of or accident to nuclear installations or reactors 59

6.1.7 contact with aircraft or similar objects, or objects falling therefrom, land conveyance, dock or harbour equipment or installation 60 61

6.1.8 earthquake volcanic eruption or lightning. 62

(Continued)

515

8.3   The Underwriters will also pay three-fourths of the legal costs incurred by the Assured or which the Assured may be compelled to pay in contesting liability or taking proceedings to limit liability, with the prior written consent of the Underwriters.

EXCLUSIONS

8.4   Provided always that this Clause 8 shall in no case extend to any sum which the Assured shall pay for or in respect of

8.4.1   removal or disposal of obstructions, wrecks, cargoes or any other thing whatsoever

8.4.2   any real or personal property or thing whatsoever except other vessels or property on other vessels

8.4.3   the cargo or other property on, or the engagements of, the insured Vessel

8.4.4   loss of life, personal injury or illness

8.4.5   pollution or contamination of any real or personal property or thing whatsoever (except other vessels with which the insured Vessel is in collision or property on such other vessels).

9   SISTERSHIP

Should the Vessel hereby insured come into collision with or receive salvage services from another vessel belonging wholly or in part to the same Owners or under the same management, the Assured shall have the same rights under this insurance as they would have were the other vessel entirely the property of Owners not interested in the Vessel hereby insured; but in such cases the liability for the collision or the amount payable for the services rendered shall be referred to a sole arbitrator to be agreed upon between the Underwriters and the Assured.

10   NOTICE OF CLAIM AND TENDERS

10.1   In the event of accident whereby loss or damage may result in a claim under this insurance, notice shall be given to the Underwriters prior to survey and also, if the Vessel is abroad, to the nearest Lloyd's Agent so that a surveyor may be appointed to represent the Underwriters should they so desire.

10.2   The Underwriters shall be entitled to decide the port to which the Vessel shall proceed for docking or repair (the actual additional expense of the voyage arising from compliance with the Underwriters' requirements being refunded to the Assured) and shall have a right of veto concerning a place of repair or a repairing firm.

10.3   The Underwriters may also take tenders or may require further tenders to be taken for the repair of the Vessel. Where such a tender has been taken and a tender is accepted with the approval of the Underwriters, an allowance shall be made at the rate of 30% per annum on the insured value for time lost between the despatch of the invitations to tender required by Underwriters and the acceptance of a tender to the extent that such time is lost solely as the result of tenders having been taken and provided that the tender is accepted without delay after receipt of the Underwriters' approval.

Due credit shall be given against the allowance as above for any amounts recovered in respect of fuel and stores and wages and maintenance of the Master Officers and Crew or any member thereof, including amounts allowed in general average, and for any amounts recovered from third parties in respect of damages for detention and/or loss of profit and/or running expenses, for the period covered by the tender allowance or any part thereof.

Where a part of the cost of the repair of damage other than a fixed deductible is not recoverable from the Underwriters the allowance shall be reduced by a similar proportion.

10.4   In the event of failure to comply with the conditions of this Clause 10 a deduction of 15% shall be made from the amount of the ascertained claim.

99
100
101

102
103
104

105

106

107

108

109
110

111
112
113
114
115
116

117
118
119
120

121
122
123
124

125
126
127
128
129
130

131
132
133
134
135

136
137

138
139

(Continued)

11 GENERAL AVERAGE AND SALVAGE

11.1 This insurance covers the Vessel's proportion of salvage, salvage charges and/or general average, reduced in respect of any under-insurance, but in case of general average sacrifice of the Vessel the Assured may recover in respect of the whole loss without first enforcing their right of contribution from other parties.

11.2 Adjustment to be according to the law and practice obtaining at the place where the adventure ends, as if the contract of affreightment contained no special terms upon the subject; but where the contract of affreightment so provides the adjustment shall be according to the York-Antwerp Rules.

11.3 When the Vessel sails in ballast, not under charter, the provisions of the York-Antwerp Rules, 1974 (excluding Rules XX and XXI) shall be applicable, and the voyage for this purpose shall be deemed to continue from the port or place of departure until the arrival of the Vessel at the first port or place thereafter other than a port or place of refuge or a port or place of call for bunkering only. If at any such intermediate port or place there is an abandonment of the adventure originally contemplated the voyage shall thereupon be deemed to be terminated.

11.4 No claim under this Clause 11 shall in any case be allowed where the loss was not incurred to avoid or in connection with the avoidance of a peril insured against.

12 DEDUCTIBLE

12.1 No claim arising from a peril insured against shall be payable under this insurance unless the aggregate of all such claims arising out of each separate accident or occurrence (including claims under Clauses 8, 11 and 13) exceeds ....in which case this sum shall be deducted. Nevertheless the expense of sighting the bottom after stranding, if reasonably incurred specially for that purpose, shall be paid even if no damage be found. This Clause 12.1 shall not apply to a claim for total or constructive total loss of the Vessel or, in the event of such a claim, to any associated claim under Clause 13 arising from the same accident or occurrence.

12.2 Claims for damage by heavy weather occurring during a single sea passage between two successive ports shall be treated as being due to one accident. In the case of such heavy weather extending over a period not wholly covered by this insurance the deductible to be applied to the claim recoverable hereunder shall be the proportion of the above deductible that the number of days of such heavy weather falling within the period of this insurance bears to the number of days of heavy weather during the single sea passage. The expression "heavy weather" in this Clause 12.2 shall be deemed to include contact with floating ice.

12.3 Excluding any interest comprised therein, recoveries against any claim which is subject to the above deductible shall be credited to the Underwriters in full to the extent of the sum by which the aggregate of the claim unreduced by any recoveries exceeds the above deductible.

12.4 Interest comprised in recoveries shall be apportioned between the Assured and the Underwriters, taking into account the sums paid by the Underwriters and the dates when such payments were made, notwithstanding that by the addition of interest the Underwriters may receive a larger sum than they have paid.

13 DUTY OF ASSURED (SUE AND LABOUR)

13.1 In case of any loss or misfortune it is the duty of the Assured and their servants and agents to take such measures as may be reasonable for the purpose of averting or minimising a loss which would be recoverable under this insurance.

13.2 Subject to the provisions below and to Clause 12 the Underwriters will contribute to charges properly and reasonably incurred by the Assured their servants or agents for such measures. General average, salvage charges (except as provided for in Clause 13.5) and collision defence or attack costs are not recoverable under this Clause 13.

13.3 Measures taken by the Assured or the Underwriters with the object of saving, protecting or recovering the subject-matter insured shall not be considered as a waiver or acceptance of abandonment or otherwise prejudice the rights of either party.

13.4 When expenses are incurred pursuant to this Clause 13 the liability under this insurance shall not exceed the proportion of such expenses that the amount insured hereunder bears to the value of the Vessel as stated herein, or to the sound value of the Vessel at the time of the occurrence giving rise to the expenditure if the sound value exceeds that value. Where the Underwriters have admitted a claim for total loss and property insured by this insurance is saved, the foregoing provisions shall not apply unless the expenses of suing and labouring exceed the value of such property saved and then shall apply only to the amount of the expenses which is in excess of such value.

13.5 When a claim for total loss of the Vessel is admitted under this insurance and expenses have been reasonably incurred in saving or attempting to save the Vessel and other property and there are no proceeds, or the expenses exceed the proceeds, then this insurance shall bear its pro rata share of such proportion of the expenses, or of the expenses in excess of the proceeds, as the case may be, as may reasonably be regarded as having been incurred in respect of the Vessel; but if the Vessel be insured for less than its sound value at the time of the occurrence giving rise to the expenditure, the amount recoverable under this clause shall be reduced in proportion to the under-insurance.

13.6 The sum recoverable under this Clause 13 shall be in addition to the loss otherwise recoverable under this insurance but shall in no circumstances exceed the amount insured under this insurance in respect of the Vessel.

14 NEW FOR OLD
Claims payable without deduction new for old.

(Continued)

519

15 BOTTOM TREATMENT

In no case shall a claim be allowed in respect of scraping gritblasting and/or other surface preparation or painting of the Vessel's bottom except that [206][207][208]

15.1 gritblasting and/or other surface preparation of new bottom plates ashore and supplying and applying any "shop" primer thereto, [209][210]

15.2 gritblasting and/or other surface preparation of: [211]

the butts or area of plating immediately adjacent to any renewed or refitted plating damaged during the course of welding and/or repairs, [212][213]

areas of plating damaged during the course of fairing, either in place or ashore, [214]

15.3 supplying and applying the first coat of primer/anti-corrosive to those particular areas mentioned in 15.1 and 15.2 above, [215][216]

shall be allowed as part of the reasonable cost of repairs in respect of bottom plating damaged by an insured peril. [217]

16 WAGES AND MAINTENANCE

No claim shall be allowed, other than in general average, for wages and maintenance of the Master, Officers and Crew, or any member thereof, except when incurred solely for the necessary removal of the Vessel from one port to another for the repair of damage covered by the Underwriters, or for trial trips for such repairs, and then only for such wages and maintenance as are incurred whilst the Vessel is under way. [218][219][220][221][222]

17 AGENCY COMMISSION

In no case shall any sum be allowed under this insurance either by way of remuneration of the Assured for time and trouble taken to obtain and supply information or documents or in respect of the commission or charges of any manager, agent, managing or agency company or the like, appointed by or on behalf of the Assured to perform such services. [223][224][225][226][227]

18 UNREPAIRED DAMAGE

18.1 The measure of indemnity in respect of claims for unrepaired damage shall be the reasonable depreciation in the market value of the Vessel at the time this insurance terminates arising from such unrepaired damage, but not exceeding the reasonable cost of repairs. [228][229][230][231]

18.2 In no case shall the Underwriters be liable for unrepaired damage in the event of a subsequent total loss (whether or not covered under this insurance) sustained during the period covered by this insurance or any extension thereof. [232][233][234]

18.3 The Underwriters shall not be liable in respect of unrepaired damage for more than the insured value at the time this insurance terminates. [235][236]

19 CONSTRUCTIVE TOTAL LOSS

19.1 In ascertaining whether the Vessel is a constructive total loss, the insured value shall be taken as the repaired value and nothing in respect of the damaged or break-up value of the Vessel or wreck shall be taken into account. [237][238][239][240]

19.2 No claim for constructive total loss based upon the cost of recovery and/or repair of the Vessel shall be recoverable hereunder unless such cost would exceed the insured value. In making this determination, only the cost relating to a single accident or sequence of damages arising from the same accident shall be taken into account. [241][242][243][244]

20 FREIGHT WAIVER

In the event of total or constructive total loss no claim to be made by the Underwriters for freight whether notice of abandonment has been given or not.

21 DISBURSEMENTS WARRANTY

21.1 Additional insurances as follows are permitted:

21.1.1 *Disbursements, Managers' Commissions, Profits or Excess or Increased Value of Hull and Machinery.* A sum not exceeding 25% of the value stated herein.

21.1.2 *Freight, Chartered Freight or Anticipated Freight, insured for time.* A sum not exceeding 25% of the value as stated herein less any sum insured, however described, under 21.1.1.

21.1.3 *Freight or Hire, under contracts for voyage.* A sum not exceeding the gross freight or hire for the current cargo passage and next succeeding cargo passage (such insurance to include, if required, a preliminary and an intermediate ballast passage) plus the charges of insurance. In the case of a voyage charter where payment is made on a time basis, the sum permitted for insurance shall be calculated on the estimated duration of the voyage, subject to the limitation of two cargo passages as laid down herein. Any sum insured under 21.1.2 to be taken into account and only the excess thereof may be insured, which excess shall be reduced as the freight or hire is advanced or earned by the gross amount so advanced or earned.

21.1.4 *Anticipated Freight if the Vessel sails in ballast and not under Charter.* A sum not exceeding the anticipated gross freight on next cargo passage, such sum to be reasonably estimated on the basis of the current rate of freight at time of insurance plus the charges of insurance. Any sum insured under 21.1.2 to be taken into account and only the excess thereof may be insured.

21.1.5 *Time Charter Hire or Charter Hire for Series of Voyages.* A sum not exceeding 50% of the gross hire which is to be earned under the charter in a period not exceeding 18 months. Any sum insured under 21.1.2 to be taken into account and only the excess thereof may be insured, which excess shall be reduced as the hire is advanced or earned under the charter by 50% of the gross amount so advanced or earned but the sum insured need not be reduced while the total of the sums insured under 21.1.2 and 21.1.5 does not exceed 50% of the gross hire still to be earned under the charter. An insurance under this Section may begin on the signing of the charter.

21.1.6 *Premiums.* A sum not exceeding the actual premiums of all interests insured for a period not exceeding 12 months (excluding premiums insured under the foregoing sections but including, if required, the premium or estimated calls on any Club or War etc. Risk insurance) reducing pro rata monthly.

21.1.7 *Returns of Premium.* A sum not exceeding the actual returns which are allowable under any insurance but which would not be recoverable thereunder in the event of a total loss of the Vessel whether by insured perils or otherwise.

21.1.8 *Insurance irrespective of amount against:* Any risks excluded by Clauses 23, 24, 25 and 26 below.

21.2 Warranted that no insurance on any interests enumerated in the foregoing 21.1.1 to 21.1.7 in excess of the amounts permitted therein and no other insurance which includes total loss of the Vessel P.P.I., F.I.A., or subject to any other like term, is or shall be effected during the currency of this insurance by or for account of the Assured, Owners, Managers or Mortgagees. Provided always that a breach of this warranty shall not afford the Underwriters any defence to a claim by a Mortgagee who has accepted this insurance without knowledge of such breach.

(Continued)

245
246
247
248
249
250
251
252
253
254
255
256
257
258
259
260
261
262
263
264
265
266
267
268
269
270
271
272
273
274
275
276
277
278
279
280
281
282
283
284
285
286
287

22 RETURNS FOR LAY-UP AND CANCELLATION

22.1   To return as follows:

22.1.1   Pro rata monthly net for each uncommenced month if this insurance be cancelled by agreement.

22.1.2   For each period of 30 consecutive days the Vessel may be laid up in a port or in a lay-up area provided such port or lay-up area is approved by the Underwriters (with special liberties as hereinafter allowed)

    (a)................................per cent net not under repair

    (b)................................per cent net under repair.

If the Vessel is under repair during part only of a period for which a return is claimable, the return shall be calculated pro rata to the number of days under (a) and (b) respectively.

22.2   PROVIDED ALWAYS THAT

22.2.1   a total loss of the Vessel, whether by insured perils or otherwise, has not occurred during the period covered by this insurance or any extension thereof

22.2.2   in no case shall a return be allowed when the Vessel is lying in exposed or unprotected waters, or in a port or lay-up area not approved by the Underwriters but, provided the Underwriters agree that such non-approved lay-up area is deemed to be within the vicinity of the approved port or lay-up area, days during which the Vessel is laid up in such non-approved lay-up area may be added to days in the approved port or lay-up area to calculate a period of 30 consecutive days and a return shall be allowed for the proportion of such period during which the Vessel is actually laid up in the approved port or lay-up area

22.2.3   loading or discharging operations or the presence of cargo on board shall not debar returns but no return shall be allowed for any period during which the Vessel is being used for the storage of cargo or for lightering purposes

22.2.4   in the event of any amendment of the annual rate, the above rates of return shall be adjusted accordingly

22.2.5   in the event of any return recoverable under this Clause 22 being based on 30 consecutive days which fall on successive insurances effected for the same Assured, this insurance shall only be liable for an amount calculated at pro rata of the period rates 22.1.2(a) and/or (b) above for the number of days which come within the period of this insurance and to which a return is actually applicable. Such overlapping period shall run, at the option of the Assured, either from the first day on which the Vessel is laid up or the first day of a period of 30 consecutive days as provided under 22.1.2(a) or (b), or 22.2.2 above.

The following clauses shall be paramount and shall override anything contained in this insurance inconsistent therewith.

23 WAR EXCLUSION

In no case shall this insurance cover loss damage liability or expense caused by

23.1   war civil war revolution rebellion insurrection, or civil strife arising therefrom, or any hostile act by or against a belligerent power

23.2   capture seizure arrest restraint or detainment (barratry and piracy excepted), and the consequences thereof or any attempt thereat   326
327

23.3   derelict mines torpedoes bombs or other derelict weapons of war.   328

24   STRIKES EXCLUSION   329

In no case shall this insurance cover loss damage liability or expense caused by   330

24.1   strikers, locked-out workmen, or persons taking part in labour disturbances, riots or civil commotions   331
332

24.2   any terrorist or any person acting from a political motive.   333

25   MALICIOUS ACTS EXCLUSION   334

In no case shall this insurance cover loss damage liability or expense arising from   335

25.1   the detonation of an explosive   336

25.2   any weapon of war   337

and caused by any person acting maliciously or from a political motive.   338

26   NUCLEAR EXCLUSION   339

In no case shall this insurance cover loss damage liability or expense arising from any weapon of war employing atomic or nuclear fission and/or fusion or other like reaction or radioactive force or matter.   340
341

523

CL. 280 *Sold by Witherby & Co. Ltd., London.*

APPENDIX D

The War and Strikes Policy Form for Ships*

Institute War and Strikes Clauses Hulls 1/10/83

* Available from Witherby & Co., London.

1/10/83

(FOR USE ONLY WITH THE NEW MARINE POLICY FORM)

INSTITUTE WAR AND STRIKES CLAUSES

Hulls—Time

This insurance is subject to English law and practice

1 PERILS

Subject always to the exclusions hereinafter referred to, this insurance covers loss of or damage to the Vessel caused by

1.1   war civil war revolution rebellion insurrection, or civil strife arising therefrom, or any hostile act by or against a belligerent power

1.2   capture seizure arrest restraint or detainment, and the consequences thereof or any attempt threat

1.3   derelict mines torpedoes bombs or other derelict weapons of war

1.4   strikers, locked-out workmen, or persons taking part in labour disturbances, riots or civil commotions

1.5   any terrorist or any person acting maliciously or from a political motive

1.6   confiscation or expropriation.

2 INCORPORATION

The Institute Time Clauses—Hulls 1/10/83 (including 4/4ths Collision Clause) except Clauses 1.2, 2, 3, 4, 6, 12, 21.1.8, 22, 23, 24, 25 and 26 are deemed to be incorporated in this insurance in so far as they do not conflict with the provisions of these clauses.

Held covered in case of breach of warranty as to towage or salvage services provided notice be given to the Underwriters immediately after receipt of advices and any additional premium required by them be agreed.

3 DETAINMENT

In the event that the Vessel shall have been the subject of capture seizure arrest restraint detainment confiscation or expropriation, and the Assured shall thereby have lost the free use and disposal of the Vessel for a continuous period of 12 months then for the purpose of ascertaining whether the Vessel is a constructive total loss the Assured shall be deemed to have been deprived of the possession of the Vessel without any likelihood of recovery.

4 EXCLUSIONS

This insurance excludes

4.1   loss damage liability or expense arising from

4.1.1   any detonation of any weapon of war employing atomic or nuclear fission and/or fusion or other like reaction or radioactive force or matter, hereinafter called a nuclear weapon of war

4.1.2   the outbreak of war (whether there be a declaration of war or not) between any of the following countries:

United Kingdom, United States of America, France, the Union of Soviet Socialist Republics, the People's Republic of China

4.1.3   requisition or pre-emption

4.1.4	capture seizure arrest restraint detainment confiscation or expropriation by or under the order of the government or any public or local authority of the country in which the Vessel is owned or registered	33 34
4.1.5	arrest restraint detainment confiscation or expropriation under quarantine regulations or by reason of infringement of any customs or trading regulations	35 36
4.1.6	the operation of ordinary judicial process, failure to provide security or to pay any fine or penalty or any financial cause	37 38
4.1.7	piracy (but this exclusion shall not affect cover under Clause 1.4),	39
4.2	loss damage liability or expense covered by the Institute Time Clauses—Hulls 1/10/83 (including 4/4ths Collision Clause) or which would be recoverable thereunder but for Clause 12 thereof,	40 41
4.3	any claim for any sum recoverable under any other insurance on the Vessel or which would be recoverable under such insurance but for the existence of this insurance,	42 43
4.4	any claim for expenses arising from delay except such expenses as would be recoverable in principle in English law and practice under the York-Antwerp Rules 1974.	44 45
5	**TERMINATION**	46
5.1	This insurance may be cancelled by either the Underwriters or the Assured giving 7 days notice (such cancellation becoming effective on the expiry of 7 days from midnight of the day on which notice of cancellation is issued by or to the Underwriters). The Underwriters agree however to reinstate this insurance subject to agreement between the Underwriters and the Assured prior to the expiry of such notice of cancellation as to new rate of premium and/or conditions and/or warranties.	47 48 49 50 51
5.2	Whether or not such notice of cancellation has been given this insurance shall TERMINATE AUTOMATICALLY	52 53
5.2.1	upon the occurrence of any hostile detonation of any nuclear weapon of war as defined in Clause 4.1.1 wheresoever or whensoever such detonation may occur and whether or not the Vessel may be involved	54 55 56
5.2.2	upon the outbreak of war (whether there be a declaration of war or not) between any of the following countries: United Kingdom, United States of America, France, the Union of Soviet Socialist Republics, the People's Republic of China	57 58 59 60 61
5.2.3	in the event of the Vessel being requisitioned, either for title or use.	62
5.3	In the event either of cancellation by notice or of automatic termination of this insurance by reason of the operation of this Clause 5, or of the sale of the Vessel, pro rata net return of premium shall be payable to the Assured.	63 64 65

This insurance shall not become effective if, subsequent to its acceptance by the Underwriters and prior to the intended time of its attachment, there has occurred any event which would have automatically terminated this insurance under the provisions of Clause 5 above.

CL. 281 *Sold by Witherby & Co. Ltd., London.*

APPENDIX E

The Marine Policy Form for Freight*

Institute Time Clauses Freight 1/8/89

* Available from Witherby & Co., London.

1/8/89   (FOR USE ONLY WITH THE NEW MARINE POLICY FORM)

INSTITUTE TIME CLAUSES
FREIGHT

This insurance is subject to English law and practice

1 NAVIGATION	1
The Vessel has leave to dock and undock, to go into graving dock, to sail or navigate with or without pilots, to go	2
on trial trips and to assist and tow vessels or craft in distress, but it is warranted that the Vessel shall not be towed,	3
except as is customary or when in need of assistance, or undertake towage or salvage services under a contract	4
previously arranged by the Assured and/or Owners and/or Managers and/or Charterers. This Clause 1 shall not	5
exclude customary towage in connection with loading and discharging.	6
2 CRAFT RISK	7
Including risk of craft and/or lighter to and from the Vessel.	8
3 CONTINUATION	9
Should the Vessel at the expiration of this insurance be at sea or in distress or at a port of refuge or of call, the	10
subject-matter insured shall, provided previous notice be given to the Underwriters, be held covered at a pro rata	11
monthly premium to her port of destination.	12
4 BREACH OF WARRANTY	13
Held covered in case of any breach of warranty as to cargo, trade, locality, towage, salvage services or date of	14
sailing, provided notice be given to the Underwriters immediately after receipt of advices and any amended terms	15
of cover and any additional premium required by them be agreed.	16
5 TERMINATION	17
This Clause 5 shall prevail notwithstanding any provision whether written typed or printed in this insurance	18
inconsistent therewith.	19
Unless the Underwriters agree to the contrary in writing, this insurance shall terminate automatically at the time of	20
5.1 change of the Classification Society of the Vessel, or change, suspension, discontinuance, withdrawal or	21
expiry of her Class therein, provided that if the Vessel is at sea such automatic termination shall be	22
deferred until arrival at her next port. However where such change, suspension, discontinuance or	23
withdrawal of her Class has resulted from loss or damage covered by Clause 7 of this insurance or which	24
would be covered by an insurance of the Vessel subject to current Institute War and Strikes Clauses Hulls-	25
Time such automatic termination shall only operate should the Vessel sail from her next port without the	26
prior approval of the Classification Society,	27

5.2   any change, voluntary or otherwise, in the ownership or flag, transfer to new management, or charter on a bareboat basis, or requisition for title or use of the Vessel, provided that, if the Vessel has cargo on board and has already sailed from her loading port or is at sea in ballast, such automatic termination shall if required be deferred, whilst the Vessel continues her planned voyage, until arrival at final port of discharge if with cargo or at port of destination if in ballast. However, in the event of requisition for title or use without the prior execution of a written agreement by the Assured, such automatic termination shall occur fifteen days after such requisition whether the Vessel is at sea or in port.

A pro rata daily net return of premium shall be made.

6   **ASSIGNMENT**

No assignment of or interest in this insurance or in any moneys which may be or become payable thereunder is to be binding on or recognised by the Underwriters unless a dated notice of such assignment or interest signed by the Assured, and by the assignor in the case of subsequent assignment, is endorsed on the Policy and the Policy with such endorsement is produced before payment of any claim or return of premium thereunder.

7   **PERILS**

7.1   This insurance covers loss of the subject-matter insured caused by

7.1.1   perils of the seas rivers lakes or other navigable waters

7.1.2   fire, explosion

7.1.3   violent theft by persons from outside the Vessel

7.1.4   jettison

7.1.5   piracy

7.1.6   breakdown of or accident to nuclear installations or reactors

7.1.7   contact with aircraft or similar objects, or objects falling therefrom, land conveyance, dock or harbour equipment or installation

7.1.8   earthquake volcanic eruption or lightning.

7.2   This insurance covers loss of the subject-matter insured caused by

7.2.1   accidents in loading discharging or shifting cargo or fuel

7.2.2   bursting of boilers breakage of shafts or any latent defect in the machinery or hull

7.2.3   negligence of Master Officers Crew or Pilots

7.2.4   negligence of repairers or charterers provided such repairers or charterers are not an Assured hereunder

7.2.5   barratry of Master Officers or Crew,

provided such loss has not resulted from want of due diligence by the Assured, Owners or Managers.

7.3   Master Officers Crew or Pilots not to be considered Owners within the meaning of this Clause 7 should they hold shares in the Vessel.

(Continued)

531

8   POLLUTION HAZARD   62

This insurance covers loss of the subject-matter insured caused by any governmental authority acting under the   63
powers vested in it to prevent or mitigate a pollution hazard, or threat thereof, resulting directly from a peril   64
covered by this insurance, provided such act of governmental authority has not resulted from want of due   65
diligence by the Assured, the Owners, or Managers of the Vessel or any of them to prevent or mitigate such hazard   66
or threat. Master, Officers, Crew or Pilots not to be considered Owners within the meaning of this Clause 8   67
should they hold shares in the Vessel.   68

9   FREIGHT COLLISION   69

9.1   It is further agreed that if the Vessel shall come into collision with any other vessel and the Assured shall   70
in consequence thereof become liable to pay and shall pay by way of damages to any other person or   71
persons any sum or sums in respect of the amount of freight taken into account in calculating the measure   72
of the liability of the Assured for   73

9.1.1   loss of or damage to any other vessel or property on any other vessel   74

9.1.2   delay to or loss of use of any such other vessel or property thereon   75

9.1.3   general average of, salvage or of salvage under contract of, any such other vessel or property   76
thereon,   77

the Underwriters will pay the Assured such proportion of three-fourths of such sum or sums so paid   78
applying to freight as their respective subscriptions hereto bear to the total amount insured on freight,   79
or to the gross freight earned on the voyage during which the collision occurred if this be greater.   80

9.2   Provided always that: 81

9.2.1   liability of the Underwriters in respect of any one such collision shall not exceed their proportionate   82
part of three-fourths of the total amount insured hereon on freight, and in cases in which, with the   83
prior consent in writing of the Underwriters, the liability of the Vessel has been contested or   84
proceedings have been taken to limit liability, they will also pay a like proportion of three-fourths of   85
the costs, appertaining proportionately to the freight portion of damages, which the Assured shall   86
thereby incur or be compelled to pay;   87

9.2.2   no claim shall attach to this insurance: 88

9.2.2.1   which attaches to any other insurances covering collision liabilities   89

9.2.2.2   which is, or would be, recoverable in the terms of the Institute 3/4ths Collision Liability Clause   90
if the Vessel were insured in the terms of such Institute 3/4ths Collision Liability Clause for   91
a value per ton of her gross tonnage (calculated in accordance with the tonnage measurement   92
rules contained in Annex 1 of the International Convention of Tonnage Measurement of Ships   93
1969) not less than the equivalent in pounds sterling, at the time of commencement of this   94
insurance, of the Vessel's limit of liability calculated in accordance with Article 6.1(b) of the   95
1976 Limitation Convention.   96

9.2.3   this Clause 9 shall in no case extend or be deemed to extend to any sum which the Assured may   97
become liable to pay or shall pay for or in respect of: 98

9.2.3.1   removal or disposal, under statutory powers or otherwise, of obstructions, wrecks, cargoes or   99
any other thing whatsoever   100

9.2.3.2   any real or personal property or thing whatsoever except other vessels or property on other   101
vessels   102

9.2.3.3	pollution or contamination of any real or personal property or thing whatsoever (except other vessels with which the insured Vessel is in collision or property on such other vessels)	103 104
9.2.3.4	the cargo or other property on or the engagements of the Vessel	105
9.2.3.5	loss of life, personal injury or illness.	106

10 SISTERSHIP — 107

Should the Vessel named herein come into collision with or receive salvage services from another vessel belonging wholly or in part to the same Owners, or under the same management, the Assured shall have the same rights under this insurance as they would have were the other vessel entirely the property of Owners not interested in the Vessel named herein; but in such cases the liability for the collision or the amount payable for the services rendered shall be referred to a sole arbitrator to be agreed upon between the Underwriters and the Assured. — 108 109 110 111 112

11 GENERAL AVERAGE AND SALVAGE — 113

11.1 This insurance covers the proportion of general average salvage and/or salvage charges attaching to freight at risk of the Assured, reduced in respect of any under-insurance. — 114 115

11.2 Adjustment to be according to the law and practice obtaining at the place where the adventure ends, as if the contract of affreightment contained no special terms upon the subject; but where the contract of affreightment so provides the adjustment shall be according to the York-Antwerp Rules. — 116 117 118

11.3 No claim under this Clause 11 shall in any case be allowed where the loss was not incurred to avoid or in connection with the avoidance of a peril insured against. — 119 120

12 FRANCHISE — 121

This insurance does not cover partial loss, other than general average loss, under 3% unless caused by fire, sinking, stranding or collision with another vessel. Each craft and/or lighter to be deemed a separate insurance if required by the Assured. — 122 123 124

13 MEASURE OF INDEMNITY — 125

13.1 The amount recoverable under this insurance for any claim for loss of freight shall not exceed the gross freight actually lost. — 126 127

13.2 Where insurances on freight other than this insurance are current at the time of the loss, all such insurances shall be taken into consideration in calculating the liability under this insurance and the amount recoverable hereunder shall not exceed the rateable proportion of the gross freight lost, notwithstanding any valuation in this or any other insurance. — 128 129 130 131

13.3 In calculating the liability under Clause 11 all insurances on freight shall likewise be taken into consideration. — 132 133

13.4 Nothing in this Clause 13 shall apply to any claim arising under Clause 15. — 134

14 LOSS OF TIME — 135

This insurance does not cover any claim consequent on loss of time whether arising from a peril of the sea or otherwise. — 136 137

533

15 TOTAL LOSS

15.1 In the event of the total loss (actual or constructive) of the Vessel named herein the amount insured shall be paid in full, whether the Vessel be fully or partly loaded or in ballast, chartered or unchartered.

15.2 In ascertaining whether the Vessel is a constructive total loss, the insured value in the insurances on hull and machinery shall be taken as the repaired value and nothing in respect of the damaged or break-up value of the Vessel or wreck shall be taken into account.

15.3 Should the Vessel be a constructive total loss but the claim on the insurances on hull and machinery be settled as a claim for partial loss, no payment shall be due under this Clause 15.

16 RETURNS FOR LAY-UP AND CANCELLATION

16.1 To return as follows:

16.1.1 Pro rata monthly net for each uncommenced month if this insurance be cancelled by agreement.

16.1.2 For each period of 30 consecutive days the Vessel may be laid up in a port or in a lay-up area provided such port or lay-up area is approved by the Underwriters (with special liberties as hereinafter allowed)

(a)........................per cent net not under repair

(b)........................per cent net under repair.

If the Vessel is under repair during part only of a period of which a return is claimable, the return shall be calculated pro rata to the number of days under (a) and (b) respectively.

16.2 PROVIDED ALWAYS THAT

16.2.1 a total loss of the Vessel, whether by insured perils or otherwise, has not occurred during the period covered by this insurance or any extension thereof

16.2.2 in no case shall a return be allowed when the Vessel is lying in exposed or unprotected waters, or in a port or lay-up area not approved by the Underwriters but, provided the Underwriters agree that such non-approved lay-up area is deemed to be within the vicinity of the approved port or lay-up area, days during which the Vessel is laid up in such non-approved lay-up area may be added to days in the approved port or lay-up area to calculate a period of 30 consecutive days and a return shall be allowed for the proportion of such period during which the Vessel is actually laid up in the approved port or lay-up area

16.2.3 loading or discharging operations or the presence of cargo on board shall not debar returns but no return shall be allowed for any period during which the Vessel is being used for the storage of cargo or for lightering purposes

16.2.4 in the event of any amendment of the annual rate, the above rates of return shall be adjusted accordingly

16.2.5 in the event of any return recoverable under this Clause 16 being based on 30 consecutive days which fall on successive insurances effected for the same Assured, this insurance shall only be liable for an amount calculated at pro rata of the period rates 16.1.2 (a) and/or (b) above for the number of days which come within the period of this insurance and to which a return is actually applicable. Such overlapping period shall run, at the option of the Assured, either from the first day on which the Vessel is laid up or the first day of a period of 30 consecutive days as provided under 16.1.2 (a) or (b), or 16.2.2 above.

138
139
140
141
142
143
144
145
146
147
148
149
150
151
152
153
154
155
156
157
158
159
160
161
162
163
164
165
166
167
168
169
170
171
172
173
174
175
176
177

534

The following clauses shall be paramount and shall override anything contained in this insurance inconsistent therewith. 178 179

17 WAR EXCLUSION 180

In no case shall this insurance cover loss damage liability or expense caused by 181

17.1 war civil war revolution rebellion insurrection, or civil strife arising therefrom, or any hostile act by or against a belligerent power 182 183

17.2 capture seizure arrest restraint or detainment (barratry and piracy excepted), and the consequences thereof or any attempt thereat 184 185

17.3 derelict mines torpedoes bombs or other derelict weapons of war. 186

18 STRIKES EXCLUSION 187

In no case shall this insurance cover loss damage liability or expense caused by 188

18.1 strikers, locked-out workmen, or persons taking part in labour disturbances, riots or civil commotions 189

18.2 any terrorist or any person acting from a political motive. 190

19 MALICIOUS ACTS EXCLUSION 191

In no case shall this insurance cover loss damage liability or expense arising from 192

19.1 the detonation of an explosive 193

19.2 any weapon of war 194

and caused by any person acting maliciously or from a political motive. 195

20 NUCLEAR EXCLUSION 196

In no case shall this insurance cover loss damage liability or expense arising from any weapon of war employing atomic or nuclear fission and/or fusion or other like reaction or radioactive force or matter. 197 198

CL. 287 *Sold by Witherby & Co. Ltd., London*

535

APPENDIX F

The War and Strikes Policy Form for Freight*

Institute War and Strikes Clauses Freight—Time 1/10/83

---

* Available from Witherby & Co., London.

1/10/83   (FOR USE ONLY WITH THE NEW MARINE POLICY FORM)

INSTITUTE WAR AND STRIKES CLAUSES

Freight — Time

This insurance is subject to English law and practice

1 PERILS

Subject always to the exclusions hereinafter referred to this insurance covers

1.1   loss (total or partial) of the subject-matter insured caused by

1.1.1   war civil war revolution rebellion insurrection, or civil strife arising therefrom, or any hostile act by or against a belligerent power

1.1.2   capture seizure arrest restraint or detainment, and the consequences thereof or any attempt thereat

1.1.3   derelict mines torpedoes bombs or other derelict weapons of war,

1.2   loss (total or partial) of the subject-matter insured arising from loss of or damage to the Vessel caused by

1.2.1   strikers, locked-out workmen, or persons taking part in labour disturbances, riots or civil commotions

1.2.2   any terrorist or any person acting maliciously or from a political motive

1.2.3   confiscation or expropriation.

2 INCORPORATION

The Institute Time Clauses—Freight 1/10/83 except Clauses 2, 3, 4, 5, 12, 16, 17, 18, 19 and 20 are deemed to be incorporated in this insurance in so far as they do not conflict with the provisions of these clauses.

Held covered in case of breach of warranty as to towage or salvage services provided notice be given to the Underwriters immediately after receipt of advices and any additional premium required by them be agreed.

3 DETAINMENT

In the event that a claim for a constructive total loss of the Vessel is paid on the war risks insurance of the Vessel under Clause 3 (Detainment) of the Institute War and Strikes Clauses — Hulls—Time 1/10/83 or the Institute War and Strikes Clauses — Hulls—Voyage 1/10/83 as a result of the loss of the free use and disposal of the Vessel

```
 1
 2
 3
 4
 5
 6
 7
 8
 9
10
11
12
13
14
15
16
17
18
19
20
21
```

for a continuous period of 12 months due to capture, seizure, arrest, restraint, detainment, confiscation or expropriation whilst this insurance is in force, the amount insured hereunder shall be paid in full less any claims otherwise arising during the said period of 12 months which have been paid or are recoverable hereunder or under insurances subject to the Institute Time Clauses—Freight 1/10/83 and/or the Institute Voyage Clauses—Freight 1/10/83 and any recoveries made in respect of the said period.

4 EXCLUSIONS

This insurance excludes

4.1   loss (total or partial) or expense arising from

4.1.1   any detonation of any weapon of war employing atomic or nuclear fission and/or fusion or other like reaction or radioactive force or matter, hereinafter called a nuclear weapon of war

4.1.2   the outbreak of war (whether there be a declaration of war or not) between any of the following countries:

United Kingdom, United States of America, France,
the Union of Soviet Socialist Republics,
the People's Republic of China

4.1.3   requisition or pre-emption

4.1.4   capture seizure arrest restraint detainment confiscation or expropriation by or under the order of the government or any public or local authority of the country in which the Vessel is owned or registered

4.1.5   arrest restraint detainment confiscation or expropriation under quarantine regulations or by reason of infringement of any customs or trading regulations

4.1.6   the operation of ordinary judicial process, failure to provide security or to pay any fine or penalty or any financial cause

4.1.7   piracy (but this exclusion shall not affect cover under Clause 1.2.1),

4.2   loss (total or partial) or expense covered by the Institute Time Clauses—Freight 1/10/83 or which would be recoverable thereunder but for Clause 12 thereof,

4.3   any claim (not being a claim recoverable under the Institute War and Strikes Clauses Freight—Voyage 1/10/83) for any sum recoverable under any other insurance on the subject-matter insured or which would be recoverable under such insurance but for the existence of this insurance,

4.4   loss proximately caused by delay or any claim for expenses arising from delay except such expenses as would be recoverable in principle in English law and practice under the York-Antwerp Rules 1974,

4.5   any claim based upon loss of or frustration of any voyage or adventure.

(Continued)

5 TERMINATION

5.1   This insurance may be cancelled by either the Underwriters or the Assured giving 7 days notice (such cancellation becoming effective on the expiry of 7 days from midnight of the day on which notice of cancellation is issued by or to the Underwriters). The Underwriters agree however to reinstate this insurance subject to agreement between the Underwriters and the Assured prior to the expiry of such notice of cancellation as to new rate of premium and/or conditions and/or warranties.

5.2   Whether or not such notice of cancellation has been given this insurance shall TERMINATE AUTOMATICALLY

5.2.1   upon the occurrence of any hostile detonation of any nuclear weapon of war as defined in Clause 4.1.1 wheresoever or whensoever such detonation may occur and whether or not the Vessel may be involved

5.2.2   upon the outbreak of war (whether there be a declaration of war or not) between any of the following countries:

      United Kingdom, United States of America, France,
      the Union of Soviet Socialist Republics,
      the People's Republic of China

5.2.3   in the event of the Vessel being requisitioned, either for title or use.

5.3   In the event either of cancellation by notice or of automatic termination of this insurance by reason of the operation of this Clause 5, or of the sale of the Vessel, pro rata net return of premium shall be payable to the Assured.

This insurance shall not become effective if, subsequent to its acceptance by the Underwriters and prior to the intended time of its attachment, there has occurred any event which would have automatically terminated this insurance under the provisions of Clause 5 above.

53
54
55
56
57
58
59
60
61
62
63
64
65
66
67
68
69
70
71
72

CL.296.   *Sold by Witherby & Co. Ltd., London.*

540

The Marine Policy Forms for Cargo*

Institute Cargo Clauses (A) 1/1/82
Institute Cargo Clauses (B) 1/1/82
Institute Cargo Clauses (C) 1/1/82

---

* Available from Witherby & Co., London.

1/1/82　　　　(FOR USE ONLY WITH THE NEW MARINE POLICY FORM)

INSTITUTE CARGO CLAUSES (A)

RISKS COVERED

1 This insurance covers all risks of loss of or damage to the subject-matter insured except as provided in Clauses 4, 5, 6 and 7 below. *(Risks Clause)*

2 This insurance covers general average and salvage charges, adjusted or determined according to the contract of affreightment and/or the governing law and practice, incurred to avoid or in connection with the avoidance of loss from any cause except those excluded in Clauses 4, 5, 6 and 7 or elsewhere in this insurance. *(General Average Clause)*

3 This insurance is extended to indemnify the Assured against such proportion of liability under the contract of affreightment "Both to Blame Collision" Clause as is in respect of a loss recoverable hereunder. In the event of any claim by shipowners under the said Clause the Assured agree to notify the Underwriters who shall have the right, at their own cost and expense, to defend the Assured against such claim. *("Both to Blame Collision" Clause)*

EXCLUSIONS

4 In no case shall this insurance cover *(General Exclusions Clause)*

4.1 loss damage or expense attributable to wilful misconduct of the Assured

4.2 ordinary leakage, ordinary loss in weight or volume, or ordinary wear and tear of the subject-matter insured

4.3 loss damage or expense caused by insufficiency or unsuitability of packing or preparation of the subject-matter insured (for the purpose of this Clause 4.3 "packing" shall be deemed to include stowage in a container or liftvan but only when such stowage is carried out prior to attachment of this insurance or by the Assured or their servants)

4.4 loss damage or expense caused by inherent vice or nature of the subject-matter insured

4.5 loss damage or expense proximately caused by delay, even though the delay be caused by a risk insured against (except expenses payable under Clause 2 above)

4.6 loss damage or expense arising from insolvency or financial default of the owners managers charterers or operators of the vessel

4.7 loss damage or expense arising from the use of any weapon of war employing atomic or nuclear fission and/or fusion or other like reaction or radioactive force or matter.

5 In no case shall this insurance cover loss damage or expense arising from *(Unseaworthiness and Unfitness Exclusion Clause)*

5.1

　unseaworthiness of vessel or craft,

　unfitness of vessel craft conveyance container or liftvan for the safe carriage of the subject-matter insured,

　where the Assured or their servants are privy to such unseaworthiness or unfitness, at the time the subject-matter insured is loaded therein.

5.2 The Underwriters waive any breach of the implied warranties of seaworthiness of the ship and fitness of the ship to carry the subject-matter insured to destination, unless the Assured or their servants are privy to such unseaworthiness or unfitness.

542

6   In no case shall this insurance cover loss damage or expense caused by

> *War Exclusion Clause*

6.1   war civil war revolution rebellion insurrection, or civil strife arising therefrom, or any hostile act by or against a belligerent power

6.2   capture seizure arrest restraint or detainment (piracy excepted), and the consequences thereof or any attempt thereat

6.3   derelict mines torpedoes bombs or other derelict weapons of war.

7   In no case shall this insurance cover loss damage or expense

> *Strikes Exclusion Clause*

7.1   caused by strikers, locked-out workmen, or persons taking part in labour disturbances, riots or civil commotions

7.2   resulting from strikes, lock-outs, labour disturbances, riots or civil commotions

7.3   caused by any terrorist or any person acting from a political motive.

DURATION

> *Transit Clause*

8   8.1   This insurance attaches from the time the goods leave the warehouse or place of storage at the place named herein for the commencement of the transit, continues during the ordinary course of transit and terminates either

8.1.1   on delivery to the Consignees' or other final warehouse or place of storage at the destination named herein,

8.1.2   on delivery to any other warehouse or place of storage, whether prior to or at the destination named herein, which the Assured elect to use either

8.1.2.1   for storage other than in the ordinary course of transit or

8.1.2.2   for allocation or distribution,

or

8.1.3   on the expiry of 60 days after completion of discharge overside of the goods hereby insured from the oversea vessel at the final port of discharge,

whichever shall first occur.

8.2   If, after discharge overside from the oversea vessel at the final port of discharge, but prior to termination of this insurance, the goods are to be forwarded to a destination other than that to which they are insured hereunder, this insurance, whilst remaining subject to termination as provided for above, shall not extend beyond the commencement of transit to such other destination.

8.3   This insurance shall remain in force (subject to termination as provided for above and to the provisions of Clause 9 below) during delay beyond the control of the Assured, any deviation, forced discharge, reshipment or transhipment and during any variation of the adventure arising from the exercise of a liberty granted to shipowners or charterers under the contract of affreightment.

(Continued)

9   If owing to circumstances beyond the control of the Assured either the contract of carriage is terminated at a port or place other than the destination named therein or the transit is otherwise terminated before delivery of the goods as provided for in Clause 8 above, then this insurance shall also terminate *unless prompt notice is given to the Underwriters and continuation of cover is requested when the insurance shall remain in force, subject to an additional premium if required by the Underwriters*, either   **Termination of Contract of Carriage Clause**

9.1   until the goods are sold and delivered at such port or place, or, unless otherwise specially agreed, until the expiry of 60 days after arrival of the goods hereby insured at such port or place, whichever shall first occur,

or

9.2   if the goods are forwarded within the said period of 60 days (or any agreed extension thereof) to the destination named herein or to any other destination, until terminated in accordance with the provisions of Clause 8 above.

10   Where, after attachment of this insurance, the destination is changed by the Assured, *held covered at a premium and on conditions to be arranged subject to prompt notice being given to the Underwriters*.   **Change of Voyage Clause**

CLAIMS

11   11.1   In order to recover under this insurance the Assured must have an insurable interest in the subject-matter insured at the time of the loss.   **Insurable Interest Clause**

11.2   Subject to 11.1 above, the Assured shall be entitled to recover for insured loss occurring during the period covered by this insurance, notwithstanding that the loss occurred before the contract of insurance was concluded, unless the Assured were aware of the loss and the Underwriters were not.

12   Where, as a result of the operation of a risk covered by this insurance, the insured transit is terminated at a port or place other than that to which the subject-matter is covered under this insurance, the Underwriters will reimburse the Assured for any extra charges properly and reasonably incurred in unloading storing and forwarding the subject-matter to the destination to which it is insured hereunder.   **Forwarding Charges Clause**

This Clause 12, which does not apply to general average or salvage charges, shall be subject to the exclusions contained in Clauses 4, 5, 6 and 7 above, and shall not include charges arising from the fault negligence insolvency or financial default of the Assured or their servants.

13   No claim for Constructive Total Loss shall be recoverable hereunder unless the subject-matter insured is reasonably abandoned either on account of its actual total loss appearing to be unavoidable or because the cost of recovering, reconditioning and forwarding the subject-matter to the destination to which it is insured would exceed its value on arrival.   **Constructive Total Loss Clause**

14   14.1   If any Increased Value insurance is effected by the Assured on the cargo insured herein the agreed value of the cargo shall be deemed to be increased to the total amount insured under this insurance and all Increased Value insurances covering the loss, and liability under this insurance shall be in such proportion as the sum insured herein bears to such total amount insured.   **Increased Value Clause**

In the event of claim the Assured shall provide the Underwriters with evidence of the amounts insured under all other insurances.

14.2   **Where this insurance is on Increased Value the following clause shall apply:**

The agreed value of the cargo shall be deemed to be equal to the total amount insured under the primary insurance and all Increased Value insurances covering the loss and effected on the cargo by the Assured, and liability under this insurance shall be in such proportion as the sum insured herein bears to such total amount insured.

In the event of claim the Assured shall provide the Underwriters with evidence of the amounts insured under all other insurances.

BENEFIT OF INSURANCE

15   This insurance shall not inure to the benefit of the carrier or other bailee.   *Not to Inure Clause*

MINIMISING LOSSES

16   It is the duty of the Assured and their servants and agents in respect of loss recoverable hereunder   *Duty of Assured Clause*

16.1   to take such measures as may be reasonable for the purpose of averting or minimising such loss,

and

16.2   to ensure that all rights against carriers, bailees or other third parties are properly preserved and exercised

and the Underwriters will, in addition to any loss recoverable hereunder, reimburse the Assured for any charges properly and reasonably incurred in pursuance of these duties.

17   Measures taken by the Assured or the Underwriters with the object of saving, protecting or recovering the subject-matter insured shall not be considered as a waiver or acceptance of abandonment or otherwise prejudice the rights of either party.   *Waiver Clause*

AVOIDANCE OF DELAY

18   It is a condition of this insurance that the Assured shall act with reasonable despatch in all circumstances within their control.   *Reasonable Despatch Clause*

LAW AND PRACTICE

19   This insurance is subject to English law and practice.   *English Law and Practice Clause*

NOTE:— It is necessary for the Assured when they become aware of an event which is "held covered" under this insurance to give prompt notice to the Underwriters and the right to such cover is dependent upon compliance with this obligation.

CL. 252.   *Sold by Witherby & Co. Ltd., London.*

545

1/1/82   (FOR USE ONLY WITH THE NEW MARINE POLICY FORM)

INSTITUTE CARGO CLAUSES (B)

RISKS COVERED

1   This insurance covers, except as provided in Clauses 4, 5, 6 and 7 below,   *Risks Clause*

1.1   loss of or damage to the subject-matter insured reasonably attributable to

1.1.1   fire or explosion

1.1.2   vessel or craft being stranded grounded sunk or capsized

1.1.3   overturning or derailment of land conveyance

1.1.4   collision or contact of vessel craft or conveyance with any external object other than water

1.1.5   discharge of cargo at a port of distress

1.1.6   earthquake volcanic eruption or lightning,

1.2   loss of or damage to the subject-matter insured caused by

1.2.1   general average sacrifice

1.2.2   jettison or washing overboard

1.2.3   entry of sea lake or river water into vessel craft hold conveyance container liftvan or place of storage,

1.3   total loss of any package lost overboard or dropped whilst loading on to, or unloading from, vessel or craft.

2   This insurance covers general average and salvage charges, adjusted or determined according to the contract of affreightment and/or the governing law and practice, incurred to avoid or in connection with the avoidance of loss from any cause except those excluded in Clauses 4, 5, 6 and 7 or elsewhere in this insurance.   *General Average Clause*

3   This insurance is extended to indemnify the Assured against such proportion of liability under the contract of affreightment "Both to Blame Collision" Clause as is in respect of a loss recoverable hereunder. In the event of any claim by shipowners under the said Clause the Assured agree to notify the Underwriters who shall have the right, at their own cost and expense, to defend the Assured against such claim.   *"Both to Blame Collision" Clause*

EXCLUSIONS

4   In no case shall this insurance cover   *General Exclusions Clause*

4.1   loss damage or expense attributable to wilful misconduct of the Assured

4.2   ordinary leakage, ordinary loss in weight or volume, or ordinary wear and tear of the subject-matter insured

4.3   loss damage or expense caused by insufficiency or unsuitability of packing or preparation of the subject-matter insured (for the purpose of this Clause 4.3 "packing" shall be deemed to include stowage in a container or liftvan but only when such stowage is carried out prior to attachment of this insurance or by the Assured or their servants)

4.4   loss damage or expense caused by inherent vice or nature of the subject-matter insured

4.5   loss damage or expense proximately caused by delay, even though the delay be caused by a risk insured

4.6   loss damage or expense arising from insolvency or financial default of the owners managers charterers or operators of the vessel

4.7   deliberate damage to or deliberate destruction of the subject-matter insured or any part thereof by the wrongful act of any person or persons

4.8   loss damage or expense arising from the use of any weapon of war employing atomic or nuclear fission and/or fusion or other like reaction or radioactive force or matter.

5   5.1   In no case shall this insurance cover loss damage or expense arising from

     unseaworthiness of vessel or craft,

     unfitness of vessel craft conveyance container or liftvan for the safe carriage of the subject-matter insured,

     where the Assured or their servants are privy to such unseaworthiness or unfitness, at the time the subject-matter insured is loaded therein.

5.2   The Underwriters waive any breach of the implied warranties of seaworthiness of the ship and fitness of the ship to carry the subject-matter insured to destination, unless the Assured or their servants are privy to such unseaworthiness or unfitness.

Unseaworthiness and Unfitness Exclusion Clause

6   In no case shall this insurance cover loss damage or expense caused by

6.1   war civil war revolution rebellion insurrection, or civil strife arising therefrom, or any hostile act by or against a belligerent power

6.2   capture seizure arrest restraint or detainment, and the consequences thereof or any attempt thereat

6.3   derelict mines torpedoes bombs or other derelict weapons of war.

War Exclusion Clause

7   In no case shall this insurance cover loss damage or expense

7.1   caused by strikers, locked-out workmen, or persons taking part in labour disturbances, riots or civil commotions

7.2   resulting from strikes, lock-outs, labour disturbances, riots or civil commotions

7.3   caused by any terrorist or any person acting from a political motive.

Strikes Exclusion Clause

DURATION

8   8.1   This insurance attaches from the time the goods leave the warehouse or place of storage at the place named herein for the commencement of the transit, continues during the ordinary course of transit and terminates either

8.1.1   on delivery to the Consignees' or other final warehouse or place of storage at the destination named herein,

8.1.2   on delivery to any other warehouse or place of storage, whether prior to or at the destination named herein, which the Assured elect to use either

8.1.2.1   for storage other than in the ordinary course of transit or

8.1.2.2   for allocation or distribution,

     or

8.1.3   on the expiry of 60 days after completion of discharge overside of the goods hereby insured from the oversea vessel at the final port of discharge,

     whichever shall first occur.

Transit Clause

Continued

547

8.2 If, after discharge overside from the oversea vessel at the final port of discharge, but prior to termination of this insurance, the goods are to be forwarded to a destination other than that to which they are insured hereunder, this insurance, whilst remaining subject to termination as provided for above, shall not extend beyond the commencement of transit to such other destination.

8.3 This insurance shall remain in force (subject to termination as provided for above and to the provisions of Clause 9 below) during delay beyond the control of the Assured, any deviation, forced discharge, reshipment or transhipment and during any variation of the adventure arising from the exercise of a liberty granted to shipowners or charterers under the contract of affreightment.

9 If owing to circumstances beyond the control of the Assured either the contract of carriage is terminated at a port or place other than the destination named therein or the transit is otherwise terminated before delivery of the goods as provided for in Clause 8 above, then this insurance shall also terminate *unless prompt notice is given to the Underwriters and continuation of cover is requested when the insurance shall remain in force, subject to an additional premium if required by the Underwriters,* either

9.1 until the goods are sold and delivered at such port or place, or, unless otherwise specially agreed, until the expiry of 60 days after arrival of the goods hereby insured at such port or place, whichever shall first occur,

or

9.2 if the goods are forwarded within the said period of 60 days (or any agreed extension thereof) to the destination named herein or to any other destination, until terminated in accordance with the provisions of Clause 8 above.

10 Where, after attachment of this insurance, the destination is changed by the Assured, *held covered at a premium and on conditions to be arranged subject to prompt notice being given to the Underwriters.*

CLAIMS

11 **11.1** In order to recover under this insurance the Assured must have an insurable interest in the subject-matter insured at the time of the loss.

11.2 Subject to 11.1 above, the Assured shall be entitled to recover for insured loss occurring during the period covered by this insurance, notwithstanding that the loss occurred before the contract of insurance was concluded, unless the Assured were aware of the loss and the Underwriters were not.

12 Where, as a result of the operation of a risk covered by this insurance, the insured transit is terminated at a port or place other than that to which the subject-matter is covered under this insurance, the Underwriters will reimburse the Assured for any extra charges properly and reasonably incurred in unloading storing and forwarding the subject-matter to the destination to which it is insured hereunder.

This Clause 12, which does not apply to general average or salvage charges, shall be subject to the exclusions contained in Clauses 4, 5, 6 and 7 above, and shall not include charges arising from the fault negligence insolvency or financial default of the Assured or their servants.

13 No claim for Constructive Total Loss shall be recoverable hereunder unless the subject-matter insured is reasonably abandoned either on account of its actual total loss appearing to be unavoidable or because the cost of recovering, reconditioning and forwarding the subject-matter to the destination to which it is insured would exceed its value on arrival.

Termination of Contract of Carriage Clause

Change of Voyage Clause

Insurable Interest Clause

Forwarding Charges Clause

Constructive Total Loss Clause

14   **14.1**   If any Increased Value insurance is effected by the Assured on the cargo insured herein the agreed value of the cargo shall be deemed to be increased to the total amount insured under this insurance and all Increased Value insurances covering the loss, and liability under this insurance shall be in such proportion as the sum insured herein bears to such total amount insured.

In the event of claim the Assured shall provide the Underwriters with evidence of the amounts insured under all other insurances.

    14.2   **Where this insurance is on Increased Value the following clause shall apply:**

The agreed value of the cargo shall be deemed to be equal to the total amount insured under the primary insurance and all Increased Value insurances covering the loss and effected on the cargo by the Assured, and liability under this insurance shall be in such proportion as the sum insured herein bears to such total amount insured.

In the event of claim the Assured shall provide the Underwriters with evidence of the amounts insured under all other insurances.

(margin: Increased Value Clause)

BENEFIT OF INSURANCE

15   This insurance shall not inure to the benefit of the carrier or other bailee.

(margin: Not to Inure Clause)

MINIMISING LOSSES

16   It is the duty of the Assured and their servants and agents in respect of loss recoverable hereunder

    16.1   to take such measures as may be reasonable for the purpose of averting or minimising such loss,

and

    16.2   to ensure that all rights against carriers, bailees or other third parties are properly preserved and exercised

and the Underwriters will, in addition to any loss recoverable hereunder, reimburse the Assured for any charges properly and reasonably incurred in pursuance of these duties.

(margin: Duty of Assured Clause)

17   Measures taken by the Assured or the Underwriters with the object of saving, protecting or recovering the subject-matter insured shall not be considered as a waiver or acceptance of abandonment or otherwise prejudice the rights of either party.

(margin: Waiver Clause)

AVOIDANCE OF DELAY

18   It is a condition of this insurance that the Assured shall act with reasonable despatch in all circumstances within their control.

(margin: Reasonable Despatch Clause)

LAW AND PRACTICE

19   This insurance is subject to English law and practice.

(margin: English Law and Practice Clause)

NOTE:— It is necessary for the Assured when they become aware of an event which is "held covered" under this insurance to give prompt notice to the Underwriters and the right to such cover is dependent upon compliance with this obligation.

CL. 253.   *Sold by Witherby & Co. Ltd., London.*

1/1/82

(FOR USE ONLY WITH THE NEW MARINE POLICY FORM)

INSTITUTE CARGO CLAUSES (C)

RISKS COVERED

1   This insurance covers, except as provided in Clauses 4, 5, 6 and 7 below,   **Risks Clause**

   1.1   loss of or damage to the subject-matter insured reasonably attributable to

     1.1.1   fire or explosion

     1.1.2   vessel or craft being stranded grounded sunk or capsized

     1.1.3   overturning or derailment of land conveyance

     1.1.4   collision or contact of vessel craft or conveyance with any external object other than water

     1.1.5   discharge of cargo at a port of distress,

   1.2   loss of or damage to the subject-matter insured caused by

     1.2.1   general average sacrifice

     1.2.2   jettison.

2   This insurance covers general average and salvage charges, adjusted or determined according to the contract of affreightment and/or the governing law and practice, incurred to avoid or in connection with the avoidance of loss from any cause except those excluded in Clauses 4, 5, 6 and 7 or elsewhere in this insurance.   **General Average Clause**

3   This insurance is extended to indemnify the Assured against such proportion of liability under the contract of affreightment "Both to Blame Collision" Clause as is in respect of a loss recoverable hereunder. In the event of any claim by shipowners under the said Clause the Assured agree to notify the Underwriters who shall have the right, at their own cost and expense, to defend the Assured against such claim.   **"Both to Blame Collision" Clause**

EXCLUSIONS

4   In no case shall this insurance cover   **General Exclusions Clause**

   4.1   loss damage or expense attributable to wilful misconduct of the Assured

   4.2   ordinary leakage, ordinary loss in weight or volume, or ordinary wear and tear of the subject-matter insured

   4.3   loss damage or expense caused by insufficiency or unsuitability of packing or preparation of the subject-matter insured (for the purpose of this Clause 4.3 "packing" shall be deemed to include stowage in a container or liftvan but only when such stowage is carried out prior to attachment of this insurance or by the Assured or their servants)

   4.4   loss damage or expense caused by inherent vice or nature of the subject-matter insured

   4.5   loss damage or expense proximately caused by delay, even though the delay be caused by a risk insured against (except expenses payable under Clause 2 above)

   4.6   loss damage or expense arising from insolvency or financial default of the owners managers charterers or operators of the vessel

4.7 deliberate damage to or deliberate destruction of the subject-matter insured or any part thereof by the wrongful act of any person or persons

4.8 loss damage or expense arising from the use of any weapon of war employing atomic or nuclear fission and/or fusion or other like reaction or radioactive force or matter.

Unseaworthiness and Unfitness Exclusion Clause

5 5.1 In no case shall this insurance cover loss damage or expense arising from

unseaworthiness of vessel or craft,

unfitness of vessel craft conveyance container or liftvan for the safe carriage of the subject-matter insured,

where the Assured or their servants are privy to such unseaworthiness or unfitness, at the time the subject-matter insured is loaded therein.

5.2 The Underwriters waive any breach of the implied warranties of seaworthiness of the ship and fitness of the ship to carry the subject-matter insured to destination, unless the Assured or their servants are privy to such unseaworthiness or unfitness.

War Exclusion Clause

6 In no case shall this insurance cover loss damage or expense caused by

6.1 war civil war revolution rebellion insurrection, or civil strife arising therefrom, or any hostile act by or against a belligerent power

6.2 capture seizure arrest restraint or detainment, and the consequences thereof or any attempt thereat

6.3 derelict mines torpedoes bombs or other derelict weapons of war.

Strikes Exclusion Clause

7 In no case shall this insurance cover loss damage or expense

7.1 caused by strikers, locked-out workmen, or persons taking part in labour disturbances, riots or civil commotions

7.2 resulting from strikes, lock-outs, labour disturbances, riots or civil commotions

7.3 caused by any terrorist or any person acting from a political motive.

DURATION

Transit Clause

8 8.1 This insurance attaches from the time the goods leave the warehouse or place of storage at the place named herein for the commencement of the transit, continues during the ordinary course of transit and terminates either

8.1.1 on delivery to the Consignees' or other final warehouse or place of storage at the destination named herein,

8.1.2 on delivery to any other warehouse or place of storage, whether prior to or at the destination named herein, which the Assured elect to use either

8.1.2.1 for storage other than in the ordinary course of transit or

8.1.2.2 for allocation or distribution,

or

8.1.3 on the expiry of 60 days after completion of discharge overside of the goods hereby insured from the oversea vessel at the final port of discharge,

whichever shall first occur.

Continued

551

8.2 If, after discharge overside from the oversea vessel at the final port of discharge, but prior to termination of this insurance, the goods are to be forwarded to a destination other than that to which they are insured hereunder, this insurance, whilst remaining subject to termination as provided for above, shall not extend beyond the commencement of transit to such other destination.

8.3 This insurance shall remain in force (subject to termination as provided for above and to the provisions of Clause 9 below) during delay beyond the control of the Assured, any deviation, forced discharge, reshipment or transhipment and during any variation of the adventure arising from the exercise of a liberty granted to shipowners or charterers under the contract of affreightment.

9 If owing to circumstances beyond the control of the Assured either the contract of carriage is terminated at a port or place other than the destination named therein or the transit is otherwise terminated before delivery of the goods as provided for in Clause 8 above, then this insurance shall also terminate *unless prompt notice is given to the Underwriters and continuation of cover is requested when the insurance shall remain in force, subject to an additional premium if required by the Underwriters,* either

9.1 until the goods are sold and delivered at such port or place, or, unless otherwise specially agreed, until the expiry of 60 days after arrival of the goods hereby insured at such port or place, whichever shall first occur,

or

9.2 if the goods are forwarded within the said period of 60 days (or any agreed extension thereof) to the destination named herein or to any other destination, until terminated in accordance with the provisions of Clause 8 above.

10 Where, after attachment of this insurance, the destination is changed by the Assured, *held covered at a premium and on conditions to be arranged subject to prompt notice being given to the Underwriters.*

CLAIMS

11 11.1 In order to recover under this insurance the Assured must have an insurable interest in the subject-matter insured at the time of the loss.

11.2 Subject to 11.1 above, the Assured shall be entitled to recover for insured loss occurring during the period covered by this insurance, notwithstanding that the loss occurred before the contract of insurance was concluded, unless the Assured were aware of the loss and the Underwriters were not.

12 Where, as a result of the operation of a risk covered by this insurance, the insured transit is terminated at a port or place other than that to which the subject-matter is covered under this insurance, the Underwriters will reimburse the Assured for any extra charges properly and reasonably incurred in unloading storing and forwarding the subject-matter to the destination to which it is insured hereunder.

This Clause 12, which does not apply to general average or salvage charges, shall be subject to the exclusions contained in Clauses 4, 5, 6 and 7 above, and shall not include charges arising from the fault negligence insolvency or financial default of the Assured or their servants.

13 No claim for Constructive Total Loss shall be recoverable hereunder unless the subject-matter insured is reasonably abandoned either on account of its actual total loss appearing to be unavoidable or because the cost of recovering, reconditioning and forwarding the subject-matter to the destination to which it is insured would exceed its value on arrival.

Termination of Contract of Carriage Clause

Change of Voyage Clause

Insurable Interest Clause

Forwarding Charges Clause

Constructive Total Loss Clause

14   **14.1**   If any Increased Value insurance is effected by the Assured on the cargo insured herein the agreed value of the cargo shall be deemed to be increased to the total amount insured under this insurance and all Increased Value insurances covering the loss, and liability under this insurance shall be in such proportion as the sum insured herein bears to such total amount insured.   *Increased Value Clause*

In the event of claim the Assured shall provide the Underwriters with evidence of the amounts insured under all other insurances.

14.2   **Where this insurance is on Increased Value the following clause shall apply:**
The agreed value of the cargo shall be deemed to be equal to the total amount insured under the primary insurance and all Increased Value insurances covering the loss and effected on the cargo by the Assured, and liability under this insurance shall be in such proportion as the sum insured herein bears to such total amount insured.

In the event of claim the Assured shall provide the Underwriters with evidence of the amounts insured under all other insurances.

BENEFIT OF INSURANCE

15   This insurance shall not inure to the benefit of the carrier or other bailee.   *Not to Inure Clause*

MINIMISING LOSSES

16   It is the duty of the Assured and their servants and agents in respect of loss recoverable hereunder   *Duty of Assured Clause*

16.1   to take such measures as may be reasonable for the purpose of averting or minimising such loss, and

16.2   to ensure that all rights against carriers, bailees or other third parties are properly preserved and exercised

and the Underwriters will, in addition to any loss recoverable hereunder, reimburse the Assured for any charges properly and reasonably incurred in pursuance of these duties.

17   Measures taken by the Assured or the Underwriters with the object of saving, protecting or recovering the subject-matter insured shall not be considered as a waiver or acceptance of abandonment or otherwise prejudice the rights of either party.   *Waiver Clause*

AVOIDANCE OF DELAY

18   It is a condition of this insurance that the Assured shall act with reasonable despatch in all circumstances within their control.   *Reasonable Despatch Clause*

LAW AND PRACTICE

19   This insurance is subject to English law and practice.   *English Law and Practice Clause*

NOTE:— It is necessary for the Assured when they become aware of an event which is "held covered" under this insurance to give prompt notice to the Underwriters and the right to such cover is dependent upon compliance with this obligation.

CL. 254.   *Sold by Witherby & Co. Ltd., London.*

APPENDIX H

The War Risks Policy Form for Cargo*

Institute War Clauses (Cargo) 1/1/82

* Available from Witherby & Co., London.

1/1/82

(FOR USE ONLY WITH THE NEW MARINE POLICY FORM)

INSTITUTE WAR CLAUSES (CARGO)

RISKS COVERED

1   This insurance covers, except as provided in Clauses 3 and 4 below, loss of or damage to the subject-matter insured caused by   *Risks Clause*

  1.1   war civil war revolution rebellion insurrection, or civil strife arising therefrom, or any hostile act by or against a belligerent power

  1.2   capture seizure arrest restraint or detainment, arising from risks covered under 1.1 above, and the consequences thereof or any attempt thereat

  1.3   derelict mines torpedoes bombs or other derelict weapons of war.

2   This insurance covers general average and salvage charges, adjusted or determined according to the contract of affreightment and/or the governing law and practice, incurred to avoid or in connection with the avoidance of loss from a risk covered under these clauses.   *General Average Clause*

EXCLUSIONS

3   In no case shall this insurance cover   *General Exclusions Clause*

  3.1   loss damage or expense attributable to wilful misconduct of the Assured

  3.2   ordinary leakage, ordinary loss in weight or volume, or ordinary wear and tear of the subject-matter insured

  3.3   loss damage or expense caused by insufficiency or unsuitability of packing or preparation of the subject-matter insured (for the purpose of this Clause 3.3 "packing" shall be deemed to include stowage in a container or liftvan but only when such stowage is carried out prior to attachment of this insurance or by the Assured or their servants)

  3.4   loss damage or expense caused by inherent vice or nature of the subject-matter insured

  3.5   loss damage or expense proximately caused by delay, even though the delay be caused by a risk insured against (except expenses payable under Clause 2 above)

  3.6   loss damage or expense arising from insolvency or financial default of the owners managers charterers or operators of the vessel

  3.7   any claim based upon loss of or frustration of the voyage or adventure

  3.8   loss damage or expense arising from any hostile use of any weapon of war employing atomic or nuclear fission and/or fusion or other like reaction or radioactive force or matter.

4   4.1   In no case shall this insurance cover loss damage or expense arising from   *Unseaworthiness and Unfitness Exclusion Clause*

      unseaworthiness of vessel or craft,

      unfitness of vessel craft conveyance container or liftvan for the safe carriage of the subject-matter insured,

      where the Assured or their servants are privy to such unseaworthiness or unfitness, at the time the subject-matter insured is loaded therein.

556

Transit
Clause

4.2   The Underwriters waive any breach of the implied warranties of seaworthiness of the ship and fitness of the ship to carry the subject-matter insured to destination, unless the Assured or their servants are privy to such unseaworthiness or unfitness.

DURATION

5   **5.1**   This insurance

5.1.1   attaches only as the subject-matter insured and as to any part as that part is loaded on an oversea vessel

    and

5.1.2   terminates, subject to 5.2 and 5.3 below, either as the subject-matter insured and as to any part as that part is discharged from an oversea vessel at the final port or place of discharge,

    or

    on expiry of 15 days counting from midnight of the day of arrival of the vessel at the final port or place of discharge,

    whichever shall first occur;

    nevertheless,

    subject to prompt notice to the Underwriters and to an additional premium, such insurance

5.1.3   reattaches when, without having discharged, the subject-matter insured at the final port or place of discharge, the vessel sails therefrom,

    and

5.1.4   terminates, subject to 5.2 and 5.3 below, either as the subject-matter insured and as to any part as that part is thereafter discharged from the vessel at the final (or substituted) port or place of discharge,

    or

    on expiry of 15 days counting from midnight of the day of re-arrival of the vessel at the final port or place of discharge or arrival of the vessel at a substituted port or place of discharge,

    whichever shall first occur.

5.2   If during the insured voyage the oversea vessel arrives at an intermediate port or place to discharge the subject-matter insured for on-carriage by oversea vessel or by aircraft, or the goods are discharged from the vessel at a port or place of refuge, then, subject to 5.3 below and to an additional premium if required, this insurance continues until the expiry of 15 days counting from midnight of the day of arrival of the vessel at such port or place, but thereafter reattaches as the subject-matter insured and as to any part as that part is loaded on an on-carrying oversea vessel or aircraft. During the period of 15 days the insurance remains in force after discharge only whilst the subject-matter insured and as to any part as that part is at such port or place. If the goods are on-carried within the said period of 15 days or if the insurance reattaches as provided in this Clause 5.2

5.2.1   where the on-carriage is by oversea vessel this insurance continues subject to the terms of these clauses,

    or

5.2.2   where the on-carriage is by aircraft, the current Institute War Clauses (Air Cargo) (excluding sendings by Post) shall be deemed to form part of this insurance and shall apply to the on-carriage by air.

Continued

557

5.3 If the voyage in the contract of carriage is terminated at a port or place other than the destination agreed therein, such port or place shall be deemed the final port of discharge and such insurance terminates in accordance with 5.1.2. If the subject-matter insured is subsequently reshipped to the original or any other destination, then *provided notice is given to the Underwriters before the commencement of such further transit and subject to an additional premium*, such insurance reattaches

5.3.1 in the case of the subject-matter insured having been discharged, as the subject-matter insured and as to any part as that part is loaded on the on-carrying vessel for the voyage;

5.3.2 in the case of the subject-matter not having been discharged, when the vessel sails from such deemed final port of discharge;

thereafter such insurance terminates in accordance with 5.1.4.

5.4 The insurance against the risks of mines and derelict torpedoes, floating or submerged, is extended whilst the subject-matter insured or any part thereof is on craft whilst in transit to or from the oversea vessel, but in no case beyond the expiry of 60 days after discharge from the oversea vessel unless otherwise specially agreed by the Underwriters.

5.5 *Subject to prompt notice to Underwriters, and to an additional premium if required*, this insurance shall remain in force within the provisions of these Clause during any deviation, or any variation of the adventure arising from the exercise of a liberty granted to shipowners or charterers under the contract of affreightment.

(For the purpose of Clause 5

"arrival" shall be deemed to mean that the vessel is anchored, moored or otherwise secured at a berth or place within the Harbour Authority area. If such a berth or place is not available, arrival is deemed to have occurred when the vessel first anchors, moors or otherwise secures either at or off the intended port or place of discharge

"oversea vessel" shall be deemed to mean a vessel carrying the subject-matter from one port or place to another where such voyage involves a sea passage by that vessel)

6 Where, after attachment of this insurance, the destination is changed by the Assured, *held covered at a premium and on conditions to be arranged subject to prompt notice being given to the Underwriters.*

7 **Anything contained in this contract which is inconsistent with Clauses 3.7, 3.8 or 5 shall, to the extent of such inconsistency, be null and void.**

CLAIMS

8 **8.1** In order to recover under this insurance the Assured must have an insurable interest in the subject-matter insured at the time of the loss.

8.2 Subject to 8.1 above, the Assured shall be entitled to recover for insured loss occurring during the period covered by this insurance, notwithstanding that the loss occurred before the contract of insurance was concluded, unless the Assured were aware of the loss and the Underwriters were not.

9 **9.1** If any Increased Value insurance is effected by the Assured on the cargo insured herein the agreed value of the cargo shall be deemed to be increased to the total amount insured under this insurance and all Increased Value insurances covering the loss, and liability under this insurance shall be in such proportion as the sum insured herein bears to such total amount insured.

In the event of claim the Assured shall provide the Underwriters with evidence of the amounts insured under all other insurances.

9.2 **Where this insurance is on Increased Value the following clause shall apply:**

The agreed value of the cargo shall be deemed to be equal to the total amount insured under the primary insurance and all Increased Value insurances covering the loss and effected on the cargo by the Assured, and liability under this insurance shall be in such proportion as the sum insured herein bears to such total amount insured.

In the event of claim the Assured shall provide the Underwriters with evidence of the amounts insured under all other insurances.

BENEFIT OF INSURANCE

10 This insurance shall not inure to the benefit of the carrier or other bailee.

Not to Inure Clause

MINIMISING LOSSES

11 It is the duty of the Assured and their servants and agents in respect of loss recoverable hereunder

Duty of Assured Clause

11.1 to take such measures as may be reasonable for the purpose of averting or minimising such loss,

and

11.2 to · ensure that all rights against carriers, bailees or other third parties are properly preserved and exercised

and the Underwriters will, in addition to any loss recoverable hereunder, reimburse the Assured for any charges properly and reasonably incurred in pursuance of these duties.

12 Measures taken by the Assured or the Underwriters with the object of saving, protecting or recovering the subject-matter insured shall not be considered as a waiver or acceptance of abandonment or otherwise prejudice the rights of either party.

Waiver Clause

AVOIDANCE OF DELAY

13 It is a condition of this insurance that the Assured shall act with reasonable despatch in all circumstances within their control.

Reasonable Despatch Clause

LAW AND PRACTICE

14 This insurance is subject to English law and practice.

English Law and Practice Clause

NOTE:— It is necessary for the Assured when they become aware of an event which is "held covered" under this insurance to give prompt notice to the Underwriters and the right to such cover is dependent upon compliance with this obligation.

CL. 266. *Sold by Witherby & Co. Ltd., London.*

The Strikes Risks Policy Form for Cargo*

Institute Strikes Clauses (Cargo) 1/1/82

* Available from Witherby & Co., London.

1/1/82   (FOR USE ONLY WITH THE NEW MARINE POLICY FORM)

INSTITUTE STRIKES CLAUSES (CARGO)

RISKS COVERED

1   This insurance covers, except as provided in Clauses 3 and 4 below, loss of or damage to the subject-matter insured caused by   Risks Clause

  1.1   strikers, locked-out workmen, or persons taking part in labour disturbances, riots or civil commotions

  1.2   any terrorist or any person acting from a political motive.

2   This insurance covers general average and salvage charges, adjusted or determined according to the contract of affreightment and/or the governing law and practice, incurred to avoid or in connection with the avoidance of loss from a risk covered under these clauses.   General Average Clause

EXCLUSIONS

3   In no case shall this insurance cover   General Exclusions Clause

  3.1   loss damage or expense attributable to wilful misconduct of the Assured

  3.2   ordinary leakage, ordinary loss in weight or volume, or ordinary wear and tear of the subject-matter insured

  3.3   loss damage or expense caused by insufficiency or unsuitability of packing or preparation of the subject-matter insured (for the purpose of this Clause 3.3 "packing" shall be deemed to include stowage in a container or liftvan but only when such stowage is carried out prior to attachment of this insurance or by the Assured or their servants)

  3.4   loss damage or expense caused by inherent vice or nature of the subject-matter insured

  3.5   loss damage or expense proximately caused by delay, even though the delay be caused by a risk insured against (except expenses payable under Clause 2 above)

  3.6   loss damage or expense arising from insolvency or financial default of the owners managers charterers or operators of the vessel

  3.7   loss damage or expense arising from the absence shortage or withholding of labour of any description whatsoever resulting from any strike, lockout, labour disturbance, riot or civil commotion

  3.8   any claim based upon loss of or frustration of the voyage or adventure

  3.9   loss damage or expense arising from the use of any weapon of war employing atomic or nuclear fission and/or fusion or other like reaction or radioactive force or matter

  3.10 loss damage or expense caused by war civil war revolution rebellion insurrection, or civil strife arising therefrom, or any hostile act by or against a belligerent power.

4   4.1   In no case shall this insurance cover loss damage or expense arising from

       unseaworthiness of vessel or craft,

       unfitness of vessel craft conveyance container or liftvan for the safe carriage of the subject-matter insured,

       where the Assured or their servants are privy to such unseaworthiness or unfitness, at the time the subject-matter insured is loaded therein.

   4.2   The Underwriters waive any breach of the implied warranties of seaworthiness of the ship and fitness of the ship to carry the subject-matter insured to destination, unless the Assured or their servants are privy to such unseaworthiness or unfitness.

(margin note: Unseaworthiness and Unfitness Exclusion Clause)

DURATION

5   5.1   This insurance attaches from the time the goods leave the warehouse or place of storage at the place named herein for the commencement of the transit, continues during the ordinary course of transit and terminates either

   5.1.1   on delivery to the Consignees' or other final warehouse or place of storage at the destination named herein,

   5.1.2   on delivery to any other warehouse or place of storage, whether prior to or at the destination named herein, which the Assured elect to use either

   5.1.2.1   for storage other than in the ordinary course of transit or

   5.1.2.2   for allocation or distribution,

       or

   5.1.3   on the expiry of 60 days after completion of discharge overside of the goods hereby insured from the oversea vessel at the final port of discharge,

       whichever shall first occur.

   5.2   If, after discharge overside from the oversea vessel at the final port of discharge, but prior to termination of this insurance, the goods are to be forwarded to a destination other than that to which they are insured hereunder, this insurance, whilst remaining subject to termination as provided for above, shall not extend beyond the commencement of transit to such other destination.

   5.3   This insurance shall remain in force (subject to termination as provided for above and to the provisions of Clause 6 below) during delay beyond the control of the Assured, any deviation, forced discharge, reshipment or transhipment and during any variation of the adventure arising from the exercise of a liberty granted to shipowners or charterers under the contract of affreightment.

(margin note: Transit Clause)

Continued

563

6 If owing to circumstances beyond the control of the Assured either the contract of carriage is terminated at a port or place other than the destination named therein or the transit is otherwise terminated before delivery of the goods as provided for in Clause 5 above, then this insurance shall also terminate *unless prompt notice is given to the Underwriters and continuation of cover is requested when the insurance shall remain in force, subject to an additional premium if required by the Underwriters,* either

6.1 until the goods are sold and delivered at such port or place, or, unless otherwise specially agreed, until the expiry of 60 days after arrival of the goods hereby insured at such port or place, whichever shall first occur,

or

6.2 if the goods are forwarded within the said period of 60 days (or any agreed extension thereof) to the destination named herein or to any other destination, until terminated in accordance with the provisions of Clause 5 above.

Termination of Contract of Carriage Clause

7 Where, after attachment of this insurance, the destination is changed by the Assured, *held covered at a premium and on conditions to be arranged subject to prompt notice being given to the Underwriters.*

Change of Voyage Clause

CLAIMS

8 8.1 In order to recover under this insurance the Assured must have an insurable interest in the subject-matter insured at the time of the loss.

Insurable Interest Clause

8.2 Subject to 8.1 above, the Assured shall be entitled to recover for insured loss occurring during the period covered by this insurance, notwithstanding that the loss occurred before the contract of insurance was concluded, unless the Assured were aware of the loss and the Underwriters were not.

9 9.1 If any Increased Value insurance is effected by the Assured on the cargo insured herein the agreed value of the cargo shall be deemed to be increased to the total amount insured under this insurance and all Increased Value insurances covering the loss, and liability under this insurance shall be in such proportion as the sum insured herein bears to such total amount insured.

In the event of claim the Assured shall provide the Underwriters with evidence of the amounts insured under all other insurances.

Increased Value Clause

9.2 **Where this insurance is on Increased Value the following clause shall apply:**
The agreed value of the cargo shall be deemed to be equal to the total amount insured under the primary insurance and all Increased Value insurances covering the loss and effected on the cargo by the Assured, and liability under this insurance shall be in such proportion as the sum insured herein bears to such total amount insured.

In the event of claim the Assured shall provide the Underwriters with evidence of the amounts insured under all other insurances.

BENEFIT OF INSURANCE

10 This insurance shall not inure to the benefit of the carrier or other bailee.

Not to Inure Clause

MINIMISING LOSSES

11 It is the duty of the Assured and their servants and agents in respect of loss recoverable hereunder

11.1 to take such measures as may be reasonable for the purpose of averting or minimising such loss, and

Duty of Assured Clause

564

11.2   to ensure that all rights against carriers, bailees or other third parties are properly preserved and exercised

and the Underwriters will, in addition to any loss recoverable hereunder, reimburse the Assured for any charges properly and reasonably incurred in pursuance of these duties.

12   Measures taken by the Assured or the Underwriters with the object of saving, protecting or recovering the subject-matter insured shall not be considered as a waiver or acceptance of abandonment or otherwise prejudice the rights of either party.   Waiver Clause

AVOIDANCE OF DELAY

13   It is a condition of this insurance that the Assured shall act with reasonable despatch in all circumstances within their control.   Reasonable Despatch Clause

LAW AND PRACTICE

14   This insurance is subject to English law and practice.   English Law and Practice Clause

NOTE:— It is necessary for the Assured when they become aware of an event which is "held covered" under this insurance to give prompt notice to the Underwriters and the right to such cover is dependent upon compliance with this obligation.

CL. 256.   *Sold by Witherby & Co. Ltd., London.*

APPENDIX K

The War Risks Additional Expenses Form for Cargo*

Institute Additional Expenses Clauses (Cargo—War Risks) 1/7/85

* Available from Witherby & Co., London.

1/7/85

(FOR USE ONLY WITH THE NEW MARINE POLICY FORM)

INSTITUTE ADDITIONAL EXPENSES CLAUSES
(CARGO-WAR RISKS)

This insurance is only to cover additional expenses incurred in consequence of War Risks, and only to the extent and subject to the conditions set forth in the following clauses:—

1   In the event of interruption or frustration of the voyage or adventure by arrests, restraints, detainment or acts of Kings, Princes and Peoples in prosecution of hostilities or by blockades or by belligerent or otherwise operations, whether there be a declaration of war or not, and whether by a belligerent or otherwise, or by reason of the exercise by the carrier of any liberty granted by any "War Risks" clause in the contract of affreightment, and the goods being discharged at a port other than the port of destination specified in this insurance or, where a country or district is specified in this insurance as the destination of the voyage, being discharged outside the limits of such country or district, the Underwriters shall pay (subject to the limit stated below) their proportion of additional expenses (including additional marine and war risk premiums and duty, if any) reasonably incurred by the Assured, in consequence of such interruption or frustration and discharge, for landing and/or warehousing charges and/or for transhipment to original destination or for returning the goods to the point of origin of the shipment or for transhipping to a substituted destination.

2   The additional expenses for returning the goods to the point of origin of the shipment or for transhipping to a substituted destination referred to in Clause 1 shall be considered reasonably incurred only if

   2.1   the approval thereto of the Underwriters hereon has been first obtained, or

   2.2   the sum for which the goods could have been sold there at the time the decision to transport the goods was made, less all necessary charges incurred in transporting the goods, including duty, if any, *exceeds* the sum which could have been realised by a sale at the place where the voyage or adventure was interrupted or frustrated, less duty, if any, which would have become payable in event of sale there, *and is not less than* the sum which could have been realised at some other place to which the Assured might reasonably have sent the goods, less all necessary charges which would have been incurred in transporting the goods, including duty, if any.

3   Subject to the provisions of Clause 2, if the goods are returned to the point of origin of the shipment or transhipped to a substituted destination, and the sum realised or which could be realised there, by the sale of the goods, exceeds the sum insured hereunder, the Underwriters' liability hereunder for additional expenses in respect of transport and duty shall be limited to the amount by which the said additional expenses incurred exceed the difference between the sum realised or which could be realised by the sale of the goods and the sum insured hereunder.

4   This insurance does not cover any expenses

   4.1   incurred as a result of physical damage to vessel or cargo,

      4.1.1   which may be recoverable under Marine or War Risk insurances on the goods, or

      4.1.2   which may not be recoverable under such insurances by reason of insufficiency of the sum insured thereunder,

   4.2   incurred subsequent to and in consequence of prohibition by the Government of the United Kingdom or of any of its Allies whereby the Assured is prevented from removing the goods from the port or place or country of discharge.

568

5 Warranted that the goods are covered by insurance against War Risks and against Marine Risks to an extent not less than the cover provided by the Institute Cargo Clauses (C).   37 38

6 Risk to commence at times of sailing and it is warranted that when the vessel sails the contract of carriage provides for discharge of the goods at the destination named in this insurance.   39 40

7 Where the vessel has the option under the contract of carriage to discharge the goods at any specified port or ports, or any port or ports in a specified range, no liability shall arise hereunder by reason of discharge at any such port or ports.   41 42 43

8 Underwriters shall not be liable for   44
8.1   warehousing charges after a period of six months,   45
8.2   any expenses incurred more than twelve months after the goods were discharged unless the goods were in course of being forwarded, returned or transhipped to a substituted destination, before the expiry of the said twelve months.   46 47 48

9 Unless otherwise agreed the sum insured hereunder shall be that for which the goods are insured against Marine Risks or the C.I.F. value whichever be the greater. The sum insured by this insurance shall be the limit of liability hereunder.   49 50 51

10 Warranted that the goods are not at any time during the voyage, the property of any government or of any person, firm or corporation (including those domiciled in neutral territory) who are alien enemies of the United Kingdom or its Allies.   52 53 54

11 This insurance excludes loss damage or expense arising from any hostile use of any weapon of war employing atomic or nuclear fission and/or fusion or other like reaction or radio-active force or matter.   55 56

12 This insurance is subject to English law and practice.   57

CL.322   *Sold by Witherby & Co. Ltd., London.*

The Marine Policy Form for Containers

Institute Container Clauses—Time (1/1/87)

1/1/87

(FOR USE ONLY WITH THE NEW MARINE POLICY FORM)

INSTITUTE CONTAINER CLAUSES — TIME

This insurance is subject to English law and practice

RISKS COVERED

1   This insurance covers all risks of loss of or damage to the subject-matter insured, except as provided in Clauses 4, 5, 6, 7 and 8 below.   Risks Clause

2   This insurance covers general average salvage and salvage charges, adjusted or determined according to the contract of affreightment and/or the governing law and practice, incurred to avoid or in connection with the avoidance of loss from any cause except those excluded in Clauses 5, 6, 7 and 8 or elsewhere in this insurance.   General Average Clause

For the purpose of claims for general average contribution salvage and salvage charges recoverable hereunder the subject-matter insured shall be deemed to be insured for its full contributory value.

3   This insurance is extended to indemnify the Assured against such proportion of liability under the contract of affreightment "Both to Blame Collision" Clause as is in respect of a loss recoverable hereunder. In the event of any claim by shipowners under the said Clause the Assured agree to notify the Underwriters who shall have the right, at their own cost and expense, to defend the Assured against such claim.   "Both to Blame Collision" Clause

4   The Underwriters shall only be liable under Clauses 1 and 2 above for loss of or damage to the machinery of the container   Machinery Clause

4.1   when the container is a total loss (actual or constructive)

4.2   when such damage is caused by

4.2.1   fire or explosion originating externally to the machinery

4.2.2   vessel or craft being stranded grounded sunk or capsized

4.2.3   overturning derailment or other accident to land conveyance or aircraft

4.2.4   collision or contact of vessel or craft with any external object other than water

4.2.5   general average sacrifice.

EXCLUSIONS

5   In no case shall this insurance cover   General Exclusion Clause

5.1   loss damage or expense attributable to wilful misconduct of the Assured

5.2   ordinary wear and tear, ordinary corrosion and rust, or gradual deterioration

5.3   mysterious disappearance, unexplained loss and loss discovered upon taking inventory

5.4   loss damage or expense caused by inherent vice or nature of the subject-matter insured

5.5   loss damage or expense proximately caused by delay, even though the delay be caused by a risk insured against (except expenses payable under Clause 2 above)

5.6   loss damage or expense arising from insolvency or financial default

5.7   loss damage or expense arising from

    unseaworthiness of vessel or craft,

    unfitness of vessel craft or conveyance for the safe carriage of the subject-matter insured,

    where the Assured or their servants are privy to such unseaworthiness or unfitness.

6   In no case shall this insurance cover loss damage liability or expense caused by   *War Exclusion Clause*

6.1   war civil war revolution rebellion insurrection, or civil strife arising therefrom, or any hostile act by or against a belligerent power

6.2   capture seizure arrest restraint or detainment (barratry and piracy excepted), and the consequences thereof or any attempt thereat

6.3   derelict mines torpedoes bombs or other derelict weapons of war

6.4   confiscation nationalisation requisition or pre-emption.

7   In no case shall this insurance cover loss damage liability or expense   *Strikes Exclusion Clause*

7.1   caused by strikers, locked-out workmen, or persons taking part in labour disturbances, riots or civil commotions

7.2   resulting from strikes, lock-outs, labour disturbances, riots or civil commotions

7.3   caused by any terrorist or any person acting from a political motive.

8   In no case shall this insurance cover loss damage liability or expense arising from any weapon of war employing atomic or nuclear fission and/or fusion or other like reaction or radioactive force or matter.   *Nuclear Exclusion Clause*

SCOPE OF INSURANCE

9   Each container is covered, including whilst on deck, within the sea and territorial limits specified in the Schedule below. Breach of these limits held covered at a premium to be agreed, subject to prompt notice being given to the Underwriters.   *Limits Clause*

10   If a container insured hereunder is sold leased or hired to a party not named as an Assured, the insurance of that container shall terminate automatically unless the Underwriters agree in writing to continue the cover.   *Sale or Hire Clause*

This Clause 10 shall prevail notwithstanding any provision whether written, typed or printed in this insurance inconsistent therewith.

CANCELLATION

11   This insurance may be cancelled by either the Underwriters or the Assured giving 30 days' notice (such cancellation becoming effective on the expiry of 30 days from midnight of the day on which notice of cancellation is issued by or to the Underwriters).   *Cancellation Clause*

11.1   In the event of cancellation by the Underwriters, they shall allow pro rata daily net return of premium to the Assured.

11.2   In the event of cancellation by the Assured, the Underwriters shall allow such return of premium as may be agreed.

(Continued)

ASSIGNMENT

12   No assignment of or interest in this insurance or in any moneys which may be or become payable hereunder is to be binding on or recognised by the Underwriters unless a dated notice of such assignment or interest signed by the Assured, and by the assignor in the case of subsequent assignment, is endorsed on the Policy and the Policy with such endorsement is produced before payment of any claim or return of premium thereunder.   *Assignment Clause*

CLAIMS

13   In order to recover under this insurance the Assured must have an insurable interest in the subject-matter insured at the time of the loss.   *Insurable Interest Clause*

14   In the event of accident whereby loss or damage may result in a claim under this insurance, prompt notice shall be given to the Underwriters or, if the container is abroad, to the nearest Lloyd's Agent so that a surveyor may be appointed to represent the Underwriters should they so wish.   *Notice of Claim Clause*

15   Where a claim is payable under this insurance for a container which is damaged but is not a total loss, the measure of indemnity shall not exceed the reasonable cost of repairing such damage.   *Partial Loss and Deductible Clause*

   15.1   The Underwriters only to be liable for the excess of the deductible specified in the Schedule below in respect of each container any one accident or series of accidents arising from one event but this deductible shall not apply to

     15.1.1   total loss (actual or constructive)

     15.1.2   general average salvage or salvage charges

     15.1.3   charges incurred under Clause 18 below.

   15.2   In respect of each container the Underwriters shall not be liable

     15.2.1   in respect of unrepaired damage for more than the insured value at the time this insurance terminates

     15.2.2   for unrepaired damage in the event of a subsequent total loss (whether or not covered by this insurance) sustained during the period covered by this insurance or any extension thereof.

16   16.1   In ascertaining whether a container is a constructive total loss, the insured value of that container shall be taken as the repaired value and nothing in respect of the damaged or scrap value shall be taken into account.   *Constructive Total Loss Clause*

   16.2   No claim for constructive total loss based upon the cost of recovery and/or repair of a container shall be recoverable hereunder unless such cost would exceed the insured value of that container. In making this determination, only the cost relating to a single accident or sequence of damages arising from the same accident shall be taken into account.

BENEFIT OF INSURANCE

17   This insurance shall not inure to the benefit of any carrier or bailee other than the Assured.   *Not to Inure Clause*

MINIMISING LOSSES

18   It is the duty of the Assured and their servants and agents in respect of loss recoverable hereunder   *Duty of Assured (Sue and Labour) Clause*

   18.1   to take such measures as may be reasonable for the purpose of averting or minimising such loss, and

   18.2   to ensure that all rights against carriers, bailees or other third parties are properly preserved and exercised and the Underwriters will, in addition to any loss recoverable hereunder, reimburse the Assured for any charges properly and reasonably incurred in pursuance of these duties.

19   Measures taken by the Assured or the Underwriters with the object of saving, protecting or recovering the subject-matter insured shall not be considered as a waiver or acceptance of abandonment or otherwise prejudice the rights of either party.   *Waiver Clause*

IT IS A CONDITION OF THIS INSURANCE THAT EACH CONTAINER BEARS CLEAR MARKS OF IDENTIFICATION.

SCHEDULE

Subject-Matter Insured

Type & Size	Identification Mark	Value

Sea and Territorial Limits
(which are deemed to include normal flying routes between points within these Sea and Territorial Limits)

Oversea Vessels

Deductible

or as per schedule attached

CL. 338   *Sold by Witherby & Co. Ltd., London*

APPENDIX M

The War and Strikes Policy Form for Containers*

Institute War and Strikes Clauses Containers—Time 1/1/87

---

* Available from Witherby & Co., London.

1/1/87   (FOR USE ONLY WITH THE NEW MARINE POLICY FORM)

INSTITUTE WAR AND STRIKES CLAUSES
CONTAINERS — TIME

This insurance is subject to English law and practice

RISKS COVERED

1   This insurance covers, except as provided in Clause 5 below, loss of or damage to the subject-matter insured caused by   *Risks Clause*

   1.1   war civil war revolution rebellion insurrection, or civil strife arising therefrom, or any hostile act by or against a belligerent power

   1.2   capture seizure arrest restraint or detainment, and the consequences thereof or any attempt thereat

   1.3   derelict mines torpedoes bombs or other derelict weapons of war

   1.4   strikers, locked-out workmen, or persons taking part in labour disturbances, riots or civil commotions

   1.5   any terrorist or any person acting from a political motive

   1.6   confiscation or expropriation.

2   This insurance covers general average and salvage charges, adjusted or determined according to the contract of affreightment and/or the governing law and practice, incurred to avoid or in connection with the avoidance of loss from a risk covered under these clauses.   *General Average Clause*

   For the purpose of claims for general average contribution salvage and salvage charges recoverable hereunder the subject-matter insured shall be deemed to be insured for its full contributory value.

INCORPORATION

3   The Institute Container Clauses — Time 1/1/87, except Clauses 1, 2, 4, 5, 6, 7, 8, 9 and 11, are deemed to be incorporated into this insurance in so far as they do not conflict with the provisions of these clauses.   *Incorporation Clause*

DETAINMENT

4   In the event that the container shall have been the subject of capture seizure arrest restraint detainment confiscation or expropriation, and the Assured shall thereby have lost the free use and disposal of the container for a continuous period of 12 months then for the purpose of ascertaining whether the container is a constructive total loss the Assured shall be deemed to have been deprived of the possession of the container without any likelihood of recovery.   *Detainment Clause*

EXCLUSIONS

5   This insurance excludes   *General Exclusion Clause*

   5.1   loss damage liability or expense arising from

   5.1.1   any detonation of any weapon of war employing atomic or nuclear fission and/or fusion or other like reaction or radioactive force or matter, hereinafter called a nuclear weapon of war

   5.1.2   the outbreak of war (whether there be a declaration of war or not) between any of the following countries:

United Kingdom, United States of America, France, the Union of Soviet Socialist Republics, the People's Republic of China

5.1.3 requisition or pre-emption

5.1.4 capture seizure arrest restraint detainment confiscation or expropriation by or under the order of the government or any public or local authority of the country where the Assured have their principal place of business

5.1.5 arrest restraint detainment confiscation or expropriation under quarantine regulations or by reason of infringement of any customs or trading regulations

5.1.6 the operation of ordinary judicial process, failure to provide security or to pay any fine or penalty or any financial cause

5.1.7 piracy (but this exclusion shall not affect cover under Clause 1.4),

5.2 loss damage or expense arising from the absence shortage or withholding of labour of any description whatsoever resulting from any strike, lockout, labour disturbance, riot or civil commotion,

5.3 loss damage or expense proximately caused by delay, even though the delay be caused by a risk insured against (except expenses payable under Clause 2 above),

5.4 loss damage or expense arising from insolvency or financial default,

5.5 loss damage liability or expense covered by the Institute Container Clauses — Time 1/1/87 or which would be recoverable thereunder but for Clause 15.1 thereof,

5.6 any claim for any sum recoverable under any other insurance on the container or which would be recoverable under such insurance but for the existence of this insurance.

SCOPE OF INSURANCE

6 6.1 Except as provided in Clauses 6.2 and 6.3 below, the subject-matter insured is covered only whilst on board an oversea vessel (including whilst on deck) or on board an aircraft, within the sea and territorial limits specified in the Schedule below.

6.2 The insurance against the risk of mines and derelict torpedoes, floating or submerged, is extended whilst the container is on board any vessel or craft.

6.3 The insurance against the risks covered under Clauses 1.4 and 1.5 is extended whilst the container is on board any vessel or craft or whilst ashore, including loading and unloading, except where the loss or damage arises from war civil war revolution rebellion insurrection, or civil strife arising therefrom, or any hostile act by or against a belligerent power.

6.4 This insurance excludes loss damage liability or expense arising whilst the container is not on board an aircraft or oversea vessel, except as provided in Clauses 6.2 and 6.3 above.

(For the purpose of this Clause 6 an "oversea vessel" shall be deemed to mean a vessel carrying the container from one port or place to another where such voyage involves a sea passage by that vessel.)

Anything contained in this insurance which is inconsistent with Clause 6.4 shall to the extent of such inconsistency be null and void.

Limits Clause

(Continued)

TERMINATION

7   7.1   This insurance may be cancelled by either the Underwriters or the Assured giving 7 days notice (such cancellation becoming effective on the expiry of 7 days from midnight of the day on which notice of cancellation is issued by or to the Underwriters). The Underwriters agree however to reinstate this insurance subject to agreement between the Underwriters and the Assured prior to the expiry of such notice of cancellation as to new rate of premium and/or conditions and/or warranties.

7.2   Whether or not such notice of cancellation has been given this insurance shall TERMINATE AUTO-MATICALLY

7.2.1   upon the occurrence of any hostile detonation of any nuclear weapon of war as defined in Clause 5.1.1 wheresoever or whensoever such detonation may occur and whether or not the container may be involved

7.2.2   upon the outbreak of war (whether there be a declaration of war or not) between any of the following countries:

United Kingdom, United States of America, France, the Union of Soviet Socialist Republics, the People's Republic of China

7.2.3   in the event of the container being requisitioned, either for title or use.

7.3   In the event either of cancellation by notice or of automatic termination of this insurance by reason of the operation of this Clause 7, or of the sale of the container, pro rata net return of premium shall be payable to the Assured.

This insurance shall not become effective if, subsequent to its acceptance by the Underwriters and prior to the intended time of its attachment, there has occurred any event which would have automatically terminated this insurance under the provisions of Clause 7 above.

IT IS A CONDITION OF THIS INSURANCE THAT EACH CONTAINER BEARS CLEAR MARKS OF IDENTIFI-CATION.

SCHEDULE

Subject-Matter Insured			Sea and Territorial Limits
Type & Size	Identification Mark	Value	(which are deemed to include normal flying routes between points within these Sea and Territorial Limits)
			Oversea Vessels
Deductible			

or as per schedule attached

SPECIMEN

CL. 340   *Sold by Witherby & Co. Ltd., London*

The British War Risk Rules

RULE 2

PART A—QUEEN'S ENEMY RISKS

2A.1 An Insured Owner who has entered his ship for insurance under Rule 2 is insured against the losses, liabilities, costs and expenses caused by any of the following risks (hereunder called "the Queen's Enemy Risks") which are specified in Rules 2A.2 to A.7; PROVIDED ALWAYS that:–

2A.1.1 the losses, liabilities costs or expenses caused by the risks specified in Rules 2A.2 to 2A.7 must have arisen out of war or other hostilities involving the United Kingdom; and

2A.1.2 the Queen's Enemy Risks shall not extend to cover any risks which are not war risks as defined by Section 10(1) of the Marine and Aviation Insurance (War Risks) Act 1952.

2A.2 Loss of or damage to an entered ship

Loss, whether partial or total, of the entered ship's hull, materials, machinery and all other parts and equipment thereof when caused by any of the following risks:–

2A.2.1 war or any hostile act by or against a belligerent power;

2A.2.2 capture, seizure, arrest, restraint or detainment and the consequences thereof or any attempt thereat;

2A.2.3 mines, torpedoes, bombs or other weapons of war, including derelict mines, torpedoes, bombs or other derelict weapons of war.

2A.3 Detention following capture, seizure, arrest, restraint or detainment

In the event of the entered ship being captured, seized, arrested, restrained or detained, the Insured Owner shall be entitled to recover from the Association:–

2A.3.1 the daily running expenses of the entered ship during the period of the detention, save for the first seven days thereof;

2A.3.2 the expenses, other than the expenses insured by Rule 2A.3.1 incurred in respect of the capture, seizure, arrest, restraint or detainment and the recapture, release and restoration of the entered ship, including claims for damage to property arising in respect of the entered ship during the period of capture, seizure, arrest, restraint or detainment which are recoverable in law from the Insured Owner;

2A.3.3 if the detention of the entered ship should last for a continuous period exceeding 90 days, in addition to any sums recoverable under Rules 2A.3.1 and 2A.3.2, a sum calculated at the rate of 10 per cent per annum of the insured value of the entered ship as specified at paragraph (1) of the Certificate of Entry and applied pro rata to the whole of the detention.

PROVIDED ALWAYS that:–

2A.3.3.1 unless the directors in their discretion otherwise determine, the Insured Owner shall give credit against the said amount payable under Rule 2A.3.3 for any claim paid or payable by the Association for damage received by the entered ship during such period.

2A.4 The sums recoverable under Rule 2A.3 shall be limited as follows:–

2A.4.1 No sum shall be recoverable, in an Insured Owner's claim for detention of an entered ship, in respect of any period during which that entered ship is:–

2A.4.1.1 delayed solely because a decision on the part of the Insured Owner, his servants or agents, is awaited on the disposal, repair or movement of the entered ship, or

2A.4.1.2 awaiting repairs or is being repaired, irrespective of whether the need for such decision or repairs has been created by damage caused to the entered ship by any of the risks specified in Rule 2 Part A or otherwise howsoever.

2A.4.2 If the Insured Owner shall have received any hire or other contractual reward payable on a time basis (whether under a demise or time charter party or otherwise howsoever) for the period in respect of which a claim is made hereunder, he shall give credit for such hire or other reward in making his claim under Rules 2A.3.1 and 2A.3.3 and if he shall have any right to receive such hire or other reward but shall not have received the same he shall assign his rights therein to the Association.

2A.4.3 Unless the directors in their discretion otherwise determine, no sum shall be recoverable from the Association in respect of any period after the entered ship has become or been accepted as an actual or constructive total loss (whether under the terms of a policy or contract against marine risks or under the cover specified in these Rules), or after the Association has accepted notice of abandonment or after the Association has notified the Insured Owner in writing, whether or not he has given any notice of abandonment, that the Association has decided to treat the entered ship as a constructive total loss.

2A.5 Collision Liability

Any losses, liabilities, costs and expenses incurred by an Insured Owner by way of damages for:–

2A.5.1 loss of or damage to any other ship or property thereon;

2A.5.2 delay to or loss of use of any such other ship or property thereon;

2A.5.3 salvage of, or salvage under contract of, any such other ship or property thereon and general average expenditure incurred by such other ship.

2A.5.4 PROVIDED ALWAYS that:–

2A.5.4.1 such losses, liabilities, costs or expenses arose in consequence of the entered ship coming into collision with any other ship; and

2A.5.4.2 such losses, liabilities, costs or expenses arose from one or more of the risks referred to in Rule 2A.2.

2A.6 Wreck liability

Any losses, liabilities, costs and expenses incurred by an Insured Owner:–

2A.6.1 relating to the raising, removal, destruction, lighting or marking of an entered ship, when such raising, removal, destruction, lighting or marking is compulsory by law or the costs thereof are legally recoverable from the Insured Owner;

2A.6.2 arising as the result of any such raising, removal, destruction, lighting or marking of the wreck of an entered ship as is referred to in Rule 2A.6.1 or any attempt thereat;

2A.6.3 arising as the result of the presence or involuntary shifting of the wreck of the entered ship or as the result of the Insured Owner's failure to raise, remove, destroy, light or mark such wreck including liability arising from the discharge or escape from such wreck of oil or any other substance.

2A.6.4 PROVIDED ALWAYS that:–

such losses, liabilities, costs or expenses arose in consequence of the entered ship becoming a wreck as the result of a casualty or event occurring during the period of that ship's entry in the Association and the entered ship became a wreck as the result of one or more of the risks referred to in Rule 2A.2.

2A.7 Requisitioned and chartered ships

2A.7.1 If the Secretary of State and the Insured Owner so desire an entered ship which is requisitioned or chartered on behalf of the Government of the United Kingdom shall be insured against the losses, liabilities, costs and expenses caused by the following risks:–

2A.7.1.1 the risks specified in Rules 2A.2 to 2A.6;

2A.7.1.2 civil war, revolution, rebellion, or civil strife arising therefrom;

2A.7.1.3 piracy;

2A.7.1.4 any liability to pay a contribution in general average or salvage on the net hire or freight at risk receivable by the Insured Owner under any charterparty under which the entered ship is running whilst on requisition and/or charter but only where the liability to contribute in general average or salvage arises out of one or more of the risks listed or referred to in Rules 2A.7.1.1 to 2A.7.1.3.

2A.7.2 PROVIDED ALWAYS that:–

2A.7.2.1 if the entered ship is a British ship, the provisions of Rule 2A.1.1 shall not apply to any insurance provided under Rule 2A.7;

2A.7.2.2 if the entered ship is not a British ship, the provisions of Rule 2A.1.1 shall not apply during the continuance of any war or other hostilities involving the United Kingdom to any insurance provided under Rule 2A.7;

2A.7.2.3 no sum shall be recoverable under Rule 2A.7 to the extent that the losses, liabilities, costs or expenses incurred thereunder are recoverable from the Government of the United Kingdom under the terms of the requisition or the charterparty by which the entered ship is engaged, or by the terms of any statute.

2A.8 Sue and labour

2A.8.1 Extraordinary costs and expenses reasonably incurred on or after the occurrence of any casualty, event or matter liable to give rise to a claim upon the Association within any of Rules 2A.2 to 2A.7 and incurred solely for the purpose of avoiding or minimising any losses, liabilities, costs or expenses against which the Insured Owner is insured under any such Rule.

2A.8.2 PROVIDED ALWAYS that:–

The following costs or expenses shall not be recoverable whether as sue and labour expenses or otherwise howsoever:–

2A.8.2.1 any fines, penalties or other impositions such as are specified in Rule 4F.4;

2A.8.2.2 any other sum of money paid in consideration of the release of an entered ship from any capture, seizure, arrest, detainment, confiscation or expropriation.

PART B—INSURANCE OF HULL, MACHINERY, ETC. (NON-QUEEN'S ENEMY RISKS)

2B.1 Loss, whether partial or total, of the entered ship's hull, materials, machinery and all other parts and equipment thereof when caused by any of the following risks:–

2B.1.1 war, civil war, revolution, rebellion, insurrection, or civil strife arising therefrom, or any hostile act by or against a belligerent power;

2B.1.2 capture, seizure, arrest, restraint or detainment, and the consequences thereof or any attempt thereat;

2B.1.3 mines, torpedoes, bombs or other weapons of war, including derelict mines, torpedoes, bombs or other derelict weapons of war;

2B.1.4 strikers, locked-out workmen, or persons taking part in labour disturbances, riots or civil commotions;

2B.1.5 any terrorist or any person acting maliciously or from a political motive;

2B.1.6 piracy or violent theft by persons coming from outside the entered ship;

2B.1.7 confiscation or expropriation.

2B.1.8 PROVIDED ALWAYS that:–

there shall be no insurance under Rule 2 Part B for any losses, liabilities, costs or expenses for which an Insured Owner is insured by Rule 2 Part A.

PART C—DETENTION OR DIVERSION EXPENSES

2C.1 This Part of the cover insures an Insured Owner against loss sustained through the detention or diversion of an entered ship caused:–

2C.1.1 by war, civil war, warlike operations, revolution, rebellion, insurrection, civil strife, any hostile act by or against a belligerent power or by conditions brought about as a result of any of the foregoing;

2C.1.2 as a result of compliance with orders, prohibitions or directions by the directors or by any Department of the Government of the United Kingdom or any other government having the right to give such orders or any British Military or Naval Authority given in order to avoid loss of or damage to the entered ship by any of the risks referred to in Rule 2 Part A or Part B;

2C.1.3 by any government or department or agency thereof or by the armed forces of any government or by any persons acting or purporting to act on behalf of any government or any department or agency thereof where the detention or diversion is considered by the directors in their discretion to have been caused, instigated, incited or encouraged by such government or department or agency in furtherance of its political aims;

2C.1.4 by any group of persons which in pursuit of its political aims maintains an armed force;

2C.1.5 by terrorists, pirates, bandits or rioters;

2C.1.6 in order to avoid loss of or damage to the entered ship by any of the risks insured under Rule 2 Part A or Part B but only where and to the extent that the directors in their discretion determine that the loss should be recoverable from the Association.

2C.1.7 PROVIDED ALWAYS that:–

2C.1.7.1 a loss caused by strikers, locked-out workmen or persons taking part in labour disturbances, or as a result of strikes, lock-outs or labour disturbances, or in order to avoid loss of or damage to the entered ship by any of the said risks, shall not be insured under this Rule 2 Part C;

2C.1.7.2 there shall be no recovery under Rule 2 Part C if the Insured Owner intended to detain or divert the entered ship before the commencement of loading cargo or passengers for, or clearing in ballast on, the voyage during which the detention or diversion shall have occurred;

2C.1.7.3 in the case of Rule 2C.1.2 the orders, prohibitions or directions were given after the commencement of the voyage.

2C.2 The sums recoverable from the Association in respect of a loss specified in Rule 2C.1 shall be as set out in Rules 2C.3 to 2C.5.

2C.3 In the event of the detention or diversion of an entered ship in any of the cases referred to in Rule 2C.1, the Insured Owner shall be entitled, subject to Rule 2C.5, to recover:–

2C.3.1 in the case of the detention of the entered ship, the daily running expenses of the entered ship during the period of the detention;

2C.3.2 in the case of the diversion of the entered ship, the net extra running expenses of the entered ship incurred by the Insured Owner in consequence of the diversion over and above those which would have been incurred but for the same.

2C.3.3 PROVIDED ALWAYS that:–

2C.3.3.1 no sum shall be recoverable from the Association under Rule 2 Part C in respect of loss of profit or in respect of the amortization of the capital cost of the entered ship or in respect of the depreciation thereof, or in respect of any payments of principal or interest made under any mortgage or other financial arrangements concluded in connection with the entered ship;

2C.3.3.2 from each claim there shall be deducted a sum equivalent to seven days' daily running expenses of the entered ship or, in the case of a claim for net extra expenses only, a sum equivalent to the net extra expenses for seven days; and

2C.3.3.3 no expenses shall be recoverable under Rule 2 Part C to the extent that they have either been paid or are recoverable under Rule 2A.3.

2C.4 In the event of the detention of an entered ship by any of the causes referred to in Rules 2C.1.1, 2C.1.3, 2C.1.4 or 2C.1.5 and lasting for a continuous period exceeding 90 days, the Insured Owner shall be entitled, subject to Rule 2C.5, to recover from the Association in respect of such detention, in addition to any sums recoverable under Rule 2C.3, a sum calculated at the rate of 10 per cent per annum of the insured value of the entered ship as specified in paragraph (1) of the Certificate of Entry and applied pro rata to the whole of the detention.

PROVIDED ALWAYS that:–

2C.4.1 unless the directors in their discretion otherwise determine, the Insured Owner shall give credit against the said amount for any claim paid or payable by the Association for damage received by the entered ship during such period;

2C.4.2 the Insured Owner shall give credit for any sum recoverable under Rule 2A.3.3.

2C.5 The sums recoverable by an Insured Owner under Rules 2C.3 and 2C.4 shall be limited as follows:–

2C.5.1 no sum shall be recoverable, in an Insured Owner's claim for detention of an entered ship, in respect of any period during which that ship is:–

2C.5.1.1 delayed solely because a decision on the part of the Insured Owner, his servants or agents, is awaited on the disposal, repair or movement of the entered ship, or

2C.5.1.2 awaiting repairs or is being repaired, irrespective of whether the need for such decision or repairs has been created by damage caused to the entered ship by any of the risks specified in Rule 2 Part B or otherwise howsoever.

2C.5.2 If the Insured Owner shall have received any hire or other contractual reward payable on a time basis (whether under a demise or time charterparty or otherwise howsoever) for the period in respect of which a claim is made under Rule 2C.3 and Rule 2C.4, he shall give credit for such hire or other reward in making his claim under Rule 2C.3.1 and 2C.4 and if he shall have any right to receive such hire or other reward but shall not have received the same he shall assign his rights therein to the Association.

2C.5.3 Unless the directors in their discretion otherwise determine, no sum shall be recoverable from the Association in respect of any period after the entered ship has become or been accepted as an actual or constructive total loss (whether under the terms of a policy or contract against marine risks or under the cover specified in these Rules), or after the Association has accepted notice of abandonment or after the Association has notified the Insured Owner in writing, whether or not he has given any notice of abandonment, that the Association has decided to treat the entered ship as a constructive total loss.

PART D—PROTECTION AND INDEMNITY COVER

2D.1 An Insured Owner who has entered his ship for insurance under Rule 2 is insured against the Protection and Indemnity losses, liabilities, costs and expenses specified in Appendix D paragraphs D.1 to D.12.

    2D.1.1 PROVIDED ALWAYS that:–

        2D.1.1.1 the losses, liabilities, costs or expenses referred to in each paragraph (save in paragraphs Appendix D.4.2, D.5 and D.10) must, irrespective of whether a contributory cause of the same being incurred was any neglect on the part of the Insured·Owner or on the part of the Insured Owner's servants or agents, have arisen or been incurred in respect of loss or damage, injury, illness or death or accident caused by:–

            2D.1.1.1.1 war, civil war, revolution, rebellion, insurrection or civil strife arising therefrom, or any hostile act by or against a belligerent power;

            2D.1.1.1.2 capture, seizure, arrest, restraint or detainment (barratry excepted), and the consequences thereof or any attempt thereat;

            2D.1.1.1.3 mines, torpedoes, bombs, rockets, shells, explosives or other weapons of war, save for those losses, liabilities, costs and expenses which arise solely by reason of the transport of any such weapons whether on board the entered ship or not.

            2D.1.1.1.4 strikers, locked-out workmen, or persons taking part in labour disturbances;

                2D.1.1.1.4.1 PROVIDED ALWAYS that:–

there shall be no recovery of the losses, liabilities, costs or expenses referred to in Appendix D, paragraph D.9 to the extent that they arise out of delay to the entered ship or her cargo.

            2D.1.1.1.5 any terrorist, or any person acting maliciously, or from a political motive;

            2D.1.1.1.6 piracy or violent theft by persons coming from outside the entered ship.

2D.2 There shall be no recovery of the losses, liabilities, costs or expenses referred to in Appendix D paragraphs D.1, D.2, D.3 and D.4.1 which arise out of the terms of any crew agreement, save the Agreements of the National Maritime Board of the United Kingdom, or other contract of service or employment, or under an indemnity or contract, unless the terms of such crew agreement, contract of service, indemnity or contract as the case may be have been previously approved by the Managers in writing. In giving such approval the Managers may impose any terms or conditions as they may think fit, including the imposition of a premium.

2D.3 The maximum recovery from the Association for claims under Rule 2 Part D in respect of any one accident shall be limited to whichever is the higher of the following:–

    2D.3.1 such limit of liability as may have been specified in or endorsed on the Certificate of Entry; or

    2D.3.2 such limit of liability as shall have been determined by the directors before or at the beginning of any policy year and notified by the Managers to the Insured Owner.

2D.4 Different limits of liability may be specified for different classes or types of risk whether by the Certificate of Entry or by the directors.

2D.5 If no other limit shall have been so fixed, the limit of liability for the purposes of Rule 2 Part D shall be the sum or sums for which the Association is reinsured in respect of the relevant claim otherwise than by virtue of a pooling agreement made with other like Associations.

2D.6 Such limit or limits shall be independent of and in addition to the sums insured for the purposes of the risks specified in Rule 2 Parts A and B.

2D.7 Unless the Directors otherwise determine, it shall be a condition precedent of an Insured Owner's right of recovery from the Association in respect of each of the liabilities and expenses enumerated in Rule 2 Part D that the Insured Owner shall first have paid the same.

PART E—SUE AND LABOUR

2E.1 Rule 2 Part E does not apply to the Queen's Enemy Risks.

2E.2 Extraordinary costs and expenses (not being the running expenses of the entered ship referred to in Rule 2C.3 or the liabilities and expenses referred to in Appendix D paragraphs D.1 to D.12) reasonably incurred on or after the occurrence of any casualty, event or matter liable to give rise to a claim upon the Association and incurred solely for the purpose of avoiding or minimising any losses, liabilities, costs or expenses against which the Insured Owner is insured by the Association.

    2E.2.1 PROVIDED ALWAYS that:–

        unless the directors in their discretion shall otherwise determine, the following shall not be recoverable whether as sue and labour expenses or otherwise howsoever:–

        2E.2.1.1 any fines, penalties or other impositions such as are specified in Rule 4F.4;

        2E.2.1.2 any other sum of money paid in consideration of the release of an entered ship from any capture, seizure, arrest, detainment, confiscation or expropriation.

PART F—DISCRETIONARY COVER

2F.1 Losses, liabilities, costs and expenses not otherwise recoverable under these Rules which the directors may decide to be within the scope of the Association. Claims under Rule 2 Part F shall be recoverable to such extent only as the directors may determine.

RULE 3

3.1 An Insured Owner who has entered his Ship for insurance under Rule 3 is insured against:–

    3.1.1 Loss of Freight and/or Disbursements and/or Premiums and/or Increased Values and/or other interests when the loss has been caused by any of the following risks:

    3.1.1.1 war, civil war, revolution, rebellion, insurrection, or civil strife arising therefrom, or any hostile act by or against a belligerent power;

    3.1.1.2 capture, seizure, arrest, restraint or detainment, and the consequences thereof or any attempt thereat;

    3.1.1.3 mines, torpedoes, bombs or other weapons of war including derelict mines, torpedoes, bombs or other derelict weapons of war;

    3.1.1.4 strikers, locked-out workmen or persons taking part in labour disturbances, riots or civil commotions;

3.1.1.5 any terrorist or any person acting maliciously or from a political motive;

3.1.1.6 piracy or violent theft by persons coming from outside the Entered Ship;

3.1.1.7 confiscation or expropriation.

3.1.1.8 PROVIDED ALWAYS that:–

    3.1.1.8.1 there shall be excluded from the risks insured under Rule 3 any risks which arise out of war or other hostilities involving the United Kingdom or threat of such war or other hostilities.

    3.1.1.8.2 there shall be no insurance under Rule 3 for any losses, liabilities, costs or expenses for which an Insured Owner is insured under Rule 2 Part A.

APPENDIX O

Agreement on War Risks Reinsurance with Her Majesty's Government[1]

New agreements for the reinsurance of British owned ships against war risks arising from hostilities involving the United Kingdom were announced on 18th February, 1988, by Paul Channon Secretary of State for Transport.

In answer to a Parliamentary Question from Eric Forth, MP, (Worcestershire, Mid) Mr Channon said:

"I have today entered into separate agreements with 10 British mutual war risks insurance associations under the Marine and Aviation Insurance (War Risks) Act 1952 to provide reinsurance against war risks to shipping. They replace agreements entered into in 1954 and 1959, and provide similar cover for the reinsurance of British-owned ships against war risks arising from hostilities involving the United Kingdom.

They include however an important new provision, that ships on foreign registers may be covered when I give my consent. This will allow the benefits of government reinsurance for war risks to shipping to be extended to shipping beneficially owned by British interests and registered in foreign states. The new agreements are in line with the new rules that the Associations have this year adopted, the rules and the agreements both reflecting the changes that have in recent years taken place in the marine insurance market. They are though more closely integrated with the rules and considerably simpler than those they replace."

TEXT OF THE AGREEMENT

AN AGREEMENT made this Eighteenth day of February 1988 BETWEEN the Secretary of State for Transport (hereinafter referred to as "the Secretary of State") of the one part and the United Kingdom Mutual War Risks Association Limited (hereinafter referred to as the "Association") of the other part.

WHEREAS:

(A) the Association insures ships entered in the Association against war risks but would be unable to continue to do so in the event of war or other hostilities or threat thereof involving the United Kingdom;

(B) the Secretary of State under section 1(1) of the Marine and Aviation Insurance (War Risks) Act 1952 is empowered with the approval of the Treasury to enter into agreements with any authorities or persons for the reinsurance by him of any war risks against which any ship is for the time being insured subject to the conditions therein appearing;

(C) the Secretary of State and the Association consider it expedient that the present Agreements dated 18th February 1954 and 26th May 1959 (hereinafter referred to as "the present Agreements") whereby the Secretary of State presently gives reinsurance to the Association should be terminated and replaced by this Agreement;

1. Department of Transport Press Notice No. 88, 18th February, 1988.

591

IT IS HEREBY AGREED between the Secretary of State and the Association that in consideration of the obligations hereby assumed by each party to the other:—

Reinsurance by the Secretary of State

1. The Association provides and will continue at all times to provide insurance against Queen's enemy risks (hereinafter referred to as "Queen's enemy risks") as defined by the Rules of the Association effective from noon GMT on 20th February 1988 as from time to time amended.

2. The Secretary of State reinsures the Association against 95 (ninety-five) per centum of any losses, liabilities, costs or expenses arising from Queen's enemy risks.

3. The Association undertakes to make no changes to its Rules which affect this Agreement without the prior consent in writing of the Secretary of State.

Reinsured Ships

4. Of the ships insured by the Association against Queen's enemy risks, those that are reinsured by the Secretary of State are British ships and such other ships as the Secretary of State has stated that he is prepared to accept for reinsurance. Such ships are referred to in this Agreement as the "reinsured ship" or "reinsured ships".

5. The Secretary of State may withdraw his acceptance of a reinsured ship, other than a British ship. Notice of such withdrawal shall be given to the Association. If such notice is given:

    (a) before the service of a general premium notice, the obligations of the Secretary of State to give reinsurance in respect of that reinsured ship shall terminate forthwith;

        provided always that if at the time the Secretary of State gives such notice of withdrawal the reinsured ship is within an area specified by a special premium notice and is being insured by the Association against Queen's enemy risks at an additional premium, the reinsurance given by the Secretary of State shall continue until the end of the current period for which such insurance is being given, and shall then terminate; save that in all cases such reinsurance shall not terminate in less than seven days;

    (b) after the service of a general premium notice, the reinsurance given by the Secretary of State hereunder shall continue until the end of the premium period as defined by the Association's Rules in which it is given, or at the end of any subsequent premium period as the Secretary of State may require, and shall then terminate; save that in all cases such reinsurance shall not terminate in less than seven days.

Insured Values

6. Subject to the provisions of clauses 7 and 8, the insured value of each reinsured ship shall be the total marine insured value, that is to say the total sum for which she is insured for total loss under marine policies.

7. The insured value of any reinsured ship may be altered as follows:

    (a) The Secretary of State and the Association may agree on a different insured value for insurance against Queen's enemy risks, or

    (b) The Secretary of State may, after consultation with the Association, require that an insured value for insurance against Queen's enemy risks shall be altered to such sum as he shall determine. If the Association does not accept such determination, the dispute shall be referred to arbitration in the manner provided by clause 32.

8. If it shall appear to the Secretary of State that a substantial increase of Queen's enemy risks has occurred or is likely to occur, he may, after consultation with the Association,

determine that the insured values of all reinsured ships shall not thereafter be changed without his consent in writing.

Conversion into Sterling

9. Before the service of a general premium notice, the provisions of this clause shall apply in respect of any reinsured ship which is insured by the Association in a currency other than sterling. Any additional premium payable by the Association under clause 14 shall be paid in sterling at the rate of exchange prevailing at the date that the Association receives payment of the additional premium from the owner of the reinsured ship. Any claim made by the Association under this Agreement shall be converted into sterling at the rate of exchange prevailing on the date that the Association pays the owner of the reinsured ship in respect of that claim and shall be paid by the Secretary of State in sterling.

10. Upon the service of a general premium notice, the values of all reinsured ships that are insured by the Association in currencies other than sterling shall be converted into sterling and such reinsured ships shall thereafter be insured by the Association in that currency. Such conversion shall be effected by using the average of the daily rates of exchange for the previous 90 days based on the average daily rate supplied by the Bank of England.

11. After a general premium notice has been served, the Association shall accept insurance of further reinsured ships only in sterling.

Reinsurance Premiums

12. The reinsurance given by the Secretary of State is given on terms that no premium is payable by the Association unless the Secretary of State shall serve on the Association a general premium notice or a special premium notice.

13. If it shall appear to the Secretary of State that reinsured ships are, or may be, exposed to Queen's enemy risks generally (and not in a particular area or areas) he may serve on the Association a general premium notice. If it appears to him that such exposure is likely to be confined to a particular area or areas he may serve on the Association a special premium notice which shall define the area or areas to which it applies.

14. The Association shall pay to the Secretary of State 95 (ninety-five) per centum of the premium which the Secretary of State determines shall be charged to the owners of the reinsured ships under clauses 15 and 16.

General Premium Notices—Premium Periods and Premiums

15. The following provisions shall apply in respect of a general premium notice:

(a) at the time that a general premium notice is served the Secretary of State shall declare a premium period. If the general premium notice has not been withdrawn and is still in force at the time of the expiry of the first premium period, the Secretary of State shall declare further premium periods in succession to one another. All premium periods shall be of such length and duration as the Secretary of State shall determine;

(b) an advance premium, and if necessary a supplementary premium, shall be charged by the Association to the owners of all reinsured ships during each premium period at such rates as the Secretary of State shall, from time to time, reasonably determine. The advance premium shall be expressed as a percentage of the insured value of each reinsured ship, and any supplementary premium as a percentage of the advance premium to which it relates;

(c) no such premium shall be levied in respect of any reinsured ship until Queen's enemy risks premiums in respect of that ship become payable in accordance with the Association's Rules;

(d) if any reinsured ship shall be insured for on y part of a premium period, the Secretary of State may determine that the premiums payable in respect of that reinsured ship shall be payable on a pro rata basis representing the time that such ship is reinsured during the relevant premium period;

(e) the Association may make a separate charge, approved by the Secretary of State, to the owners of all reinsured ships in respect of its expenses other than those which are taken into account in the calculation of the premiums under sub-paragraph b.

Special Premium Notices

16. Where a special premium notice has been served, an additional premium shall be charged by the Association to the owner of any reinsured ship which enters or remains within the area or areas defined by such notice and which is insured for Queen's enemy risks by the Association whilst within that area or those areas, at such rate or rates, and for such period or periods, as the Secretary of State shall, from time to time, reasonably determine. Such additional premium shall be expressed as a percentage of the insured value of any such reinsured ships.

Consultation

17. In exercising their respective powers under clauses 15 and 16 of this Agreement, the Secretary of State and the Association shall consult each with the other and seek the other's guidance.

Settlement of Claims

18. Before the Association accepts for payment or pays any claim by an owner of a reinsured ship in respect of any Queen's enemy risks, the Association shall first obtain the consent in writing of the Secretary of State. The Secretary of State may authorise any claims to be paid without such consent upon such terms as he shall stipulate in writing.

19. If the Secretary of State shall withhold his consent, or shall not have given his consent within a reasonable time, and the owner of the reinsured ship shall have obtained a final judgment against the Association, then the Secretary of State shall accept such judgment as determining the issues to which it refers.

Subrogation

20. If, after payment of any claims for which the Association is reinsured by the Secretary of State under the terms of this Agreement, it is desired that a claim shall be made by way of subrogation to seek recovery from any third party:

(a) the Association may, with the consent of the Secretary of State, exercise its rights of subrogation. In the event of any recovery from any third party this recovery shall be divided between the parties to this Agreement in the same proportions as the Association and the Secretary of State under this Agreement shall respectively bear of the claim for which recovery was sought. Legal and other costs of making any such recovery shall be similarly apportioned;

(b) the Secretary of State may, if the Association shall decline or shall fail to exercise its powers of subrogation within 30 days of being required to do so by the Secretary of State, institute such proceedings in the name of the Association and/or the name of the owner of the reinsured ship as the circumstances may require. In this event the Association shall execute such formal assignment or such formal deed of subrogation of all or any rights, and shall take all reasonable steps generally, including production of all information documents and evidence, as the Secretary of State may require. There shall be no apportionment of any recovery that the Secretary of State may make or of any legal or other costs that he may incur.

Discretion under the Rules

21. Where the directors of the Association have any discretion in respect of the insurance against Queen's enemy risks given by the Association's Rules, such discretion shall not be exercised in favour of the owner of the reinsured ship without the consent in writing of the Secretary of State.

Accounting between the Parties

22. As between the Secretary of State and the Association, all monies payable to the Association under this Agreement shall be debited in account to the Secretary of State and all monies payable by the Association under this Agreement shall be credited in account to the Secretary of State.

23. The accounts between the Secretary of State and the Association shall be rendered monthly by the Association to the Secretary of State within 14 days after the close of each calendar month and the balance due on either side shall be paid within seven days after the expiry of the said period of 14 days; save only that if at the end of any week the balance due on either side shall exceed £250,000, the Association shall notify the Secretary of State and the excess shall be paid within seven days of the said notification.

Information to be Supplied to the Secretary of State

24. The Association shall keep the Secretary of State advised of:

   (a) the names and current insured values of all reinsured ships; and
   (b) the names of all reinsured ships which are within an additional premium area and which are insured for Queen's enemy risks whilst within that area; and
   (c) such further information which the Secretary of State shall reasonably require for the purposes of this Agreement.

Representatives of the Secretary of State

25. The Secretary of State may appoint not more than two representatives who shall be entitled to attend all meetings of the Association and of its board of directors and of any committee thereof at which any matter relating to the insurance of Queen's enemy risks is considered.

26. The Association shall permit the said representatives or any of their assistants and representatives of the Comptroller and Auditor-General at all convenient times to examine the books and documents in the possession of the Association relating to the insurance against Queen's enemy risks provided by the Association, or to any losses, liabilities, costs or expenses thereunder and to take extracts therefrom. The Association shall also give all information in the possession of the Association relating thereto and, so far as lies in its power, shall produce or procure the production of all books and documents of which the Association is entitled to have production in connection with the said insurances or any losses, liabilities, costs or expenses thereunder for examination by such representatives.

Expenses

27. The Secretary of State shall bear and pay his rateable proportion of any expenses including legal costs and expenses not otherwise provided for by the terms of this Agreement which are reasonably incurred by the Association in connection with any losses, liabilities or claims under any insurance reinsured by the Secretary of State in pursuance of this Agreement.

Unpaid Premiums

28. If, after the service of a general premium notice or a special premium notice, the owner of a reinsured ship shall have failed to pay when due and demanded by the Associ-

ation a Queen's enemy risks premium, or an additional premium as defined by the Association's Rules, the Secretary of State may, after consultation with the Association, require the Association to give that owner the notice required by the Rules to cancel the insurance of the reinsured ship against Queen's enemy risks or to take such other steps as are provided by the Rules.

29. If any Queen's enemy risks premium or additional premium in respect of any reinsured ship is not paid by the owner of that ship before the expiry of any notice to cancel the insurance then, until such time as the said Queen's enemy risks premium or additional premium is paid in full or, in the case of a Queen's enemy risk premium, is otherwise secured as provided by the Association's Rules:

(a) the Association shall not accept for payment or pay or otherwise commit itself to pay any claim for losses, liabilities, costs or expenses caused by Queen's enemy risks to the owner of that reinsured ship, and shall not seek any recovery in respect thereof from the Secretary of State under the terms of this Agreement, and

(b) the Association shall not be under any liability to pay the proportion of any reinsurance premium which relates to that reinsured ship.

Notices between the Parties

30. A notice or other document requiring to be served by the terms of this Agreement shall be validly served if sent by hand, by post, by telex or by any other means by which written messages may be transmitted and addressed to the Secretary of State or to the registered office of the Association, as the case may be, or to such other address as may from time to time be notified by one party to the other as the address for service of such notices.

Disputes between the Parties

31. If any dispute shall arise between the parties to this Agreement in connection with its terms or the obligations of each to the other (other than disputes for which provision is made in clause 32), it shall be decided by the High Court of Justice (Commercial Court) in London which shall have exclusive jurisdiction over the matter.

32. If, following a determination by the Secretary of State under clause 7b, a dispute shall arise on the proper insured value of a reinsured ship, the dispute shall be referred to arbitration:

(a) by a sole arbitrator experienced in the valuation of ships for war risks purposes, or

(b) if no agreement can be reached on the appointment of a sole arbitrator, then by two arbitrators, one to be appointed by the Secretary of State and one by the Association. Such arbitrators, and any umpire they may appoint, shall be similarly experienced.

Any arbitrator, arbitrators or umpire shall consider and take into account any case which the owner of the reinsured ship may wish to present. The award of an arbitrator, arbitrators or umpire shall be conclusive and binding for all the purposes of this Agreement.

Commencement of this Agreement

33. This Agreement shall commence and take effect at noon GMT on 20th February 1988.

34. The present Agreements shall terminate and cease to have effect at noon GMT on 20th February 1988 except in respect of any event which occurred prior to noon GMT on 20th February 1988.

Termination of this Agreement

35. Unless otherwise agreed, this Agreement may be terminated by one party giving to the other a written notice of termination not later than noon GMT on 20th November in any

year to take effect at noon GMT on 20th February next following. If such a notice shall be given, the reinsurance of reinsured ships given by the Secretary of State in pursuance of this Agreement shall terminate at noon GMT on 20th February next following. The parties to this Agreement shall however remain liable each to the other under its terms in respect of any event which occurred prior to noon GMT on 20th February next following, but shall be under no such liability in respect of any event occurring thereafter.

IN WITNESS whereof the Association has caused its Common Seal to be hereunto affixed and the Secretary of State has caused his Corporate Seal to be hereunto affixed the day and year first before written.

The Common Seal of the United Kingdom Mutual War Risks Association Limited was hereunto affixed in the presence of [the Chairman and Secretary]

The Corporate Seal of the Secretary of State was hereunto affixed in the presence of [a person] authorised by the Secretary of State

[L.S.]

We approve the making of the Agreement by the Secretary of State. [Two of the Lords Commissioners of Her Majesty's Treasury].

[L.S.]

APPENDIX P

The Hellenic (Bermuda) War Risk Rules

RULE 2

2A.1 Risks insured

2A.1.1 Unless the Terms of Entry provide otherwise, every Owner of an Entered Ship is insured against loss of or damage to its Hull and Machinery when caused as specified in Rule 2A.2.

2A.1.2 If the Terms of Entry expressly so provide (but not otherwise), the Owner of an Entered Ship is insured against loss of Freight and Disbursements when caused as specified in Rule 2A.2.provided, in the case of the causes specified in Rules 2A.2.4 to 2A.2.8, that the loss arises from loss of or damage to the Entered Ship.

2A.1.3 The insurance provided under Rule 2A.1.1 and 2A.1.2 includes the proportion of general average, salvage and/or salvage charges attaching to the Entered Ship or freight at risk of the Owner (as the case may be), provided that:

> 2A.1.3.1 In case of general average sacrifice of the Entered Ship, the Owner may recover in respect of the whole loss without first enforcing his right of contribution from other parties.
>
> 2A.1.3.2 No claim shall be allowed under this Rule 2A.1.3 unless the loss was incurred to avoid or in connection with the avoidance of a risk insured against.

2A.2 Causes of loss

The Owner of an Entered Ship is insured as provided in Rule 2A.1 if the loss, damage or expense as the case may be is caused by:

> 2A.2.1 war, civil war, revolution, rebellion, insurrection, or civil strife arising therefrom, or any hostile act by or against a belligerent power;
>
> 2A.2.2 capture, seizure, arrest, restraint or detainment, and the consequences thereof or any attempt threat;
>
> 2A.2.3 mines, torpedoes, bombs or other weapons of war (whether any of the aforesaid are derelict or otherwise);
>
> 2A.2.4 strikers, locked-out workmen, or persons taking part in labour disturbances, riots or civil commotions;
>
> 2A.2.5 any terrorist or any person acting maliciously, or from a political motive;
>
> 2A.2.6 piracy and violent theft by persons from outside the ship;
>
> 2A.2.7 confiscation or expropriation;
>
> 2A.2.8 save in cases where the Entered Ship is insured for marine risks on the terms of the Standard Form of American Hull Policy with the American Institute Hull Clauses attached, the risks excluded from the Standard Form of English Marine Policy (Hulls) by Clauses 23 (the War Exclusion Clause), 24 (the Strikes Exclusion Clause) and 25 (the Malicious Acts Exclusion Clause) of the Institute Time Clauses—Hulls;

2A.2.9 where the Entered Ship is insured for marine risks on the terms of the Standard Form of American Marine Hull Policy with the American Institute Hull Clauses attached, the risks excluded by conditions (a), (b), (c), (e), (f), (g), and (h) set out in the War Strikes and Related Exclusions Clause therein.

2A.3 General average and salvage

2A.3.1 General average and salvage shall be adjusted according to the law and practice obtaining at the place where the adventure ends, as if the contract of affreightment contained no special terms upon the subject, but where the contract of affreightment so provides, the adjustment shall be according to the York-Antwerp Rules.

2A.3.2 When the ship sails in ballast, not under charter, the provisions of the York-Antwerp Rules 1974 (excluding Rules XX and XXI) shall be applicable and the voyage for this purpose shall be deemed to continue from the port or place of departure until arrival of the vessel at the first port or place thereafter other than a port or place of refuge or a port or place of call for bunkering only. If at any such intermediate port or place there is an abandonment of the adventure originally contemplated, the voyage shall thereupon be deemed to be terminated.

2A.3.3 A claim by the Owner of an Entered Ship for reimbursement of general average, salvage and/or salvage charges, is subject to the following conditions:

2A.3.3.1 If the Agreed Value is the same as or more than the Contributing Value, then subject to condition 2A.3.3.3, the sum recoverable shall be the full amount of the claim.

2A.3.3.2 If the Agreed Value is less than the Contributing Value, then subject to condition 2A.3.3.3, the sum recoverable shall be reduced in the proportion which the Agreed Value bears to the Contributing Value.

2A.3.3.3 If the insurance is given on the basis of a proportion of the Agreed Value, then the sum recoverable shall be limited to an equivalent proportion of the sum recoverable under condition 2A.3.3.1 or 2A.3.3.2 as the case may be.

2A.3.3.4 Notwithstanding condition 2A.3.3.2, the Directors may determine that even if the Agreed Value is less than the Contributing Value, the claim shall not be reduced to the extent provided in condition 2A.3.3.2 or that no reduction shall be applied.

In the above conditions:

—"Contributing Value" means the value used in the relevant adjustment to calculate the proportion of general average, salvage and/or salvage charges payable by the ship, and

—in any case in which the insurance is based on the Insurable Value of the ship, in accordance with Rule 2A.4.1.2, references to "Agreed Value" shall be construed as references to "Insurable Value".

2A.3.4 Should the Entered Ship receive salvage services from another ship belonging wholly or in part to the same Owner or under the same management, the Owner of the Entered Ship receiving those services shall have the same rights of recovery from the Association as if the other ship had been entirely the property of an Owner not interested in the Entered Ship but in any such case the amount payable for the services rendered shall be referred to a sole arbitrator to be agreed upon between the Owner and the Managers.

2A.4 Additional terms and conditions applicable only to insurance under Part A against loss of or damage to the hull and machinery of an entered ship

2A.4.1 Value on which the insurance is based

2A.4.1.1 Insurance against the risks referred to in Rule 2A.1.1 is given by the Association on the basis of the Agreed Value of the Entered Ship, except that when, by agreement between the Association and the Owner, only a proportion of the Agreed Value is insured, the insurance is given on the basis of that proportion.

2A.4.1.2 If in relation to any Entered Ship there is no Agreed Value, such insurance is based on the Insurable Value of the ship.

2A.4.1.3 The Agreed Value and, where applicable, the proportion of the Agreed Value on which the insurance is based, will be recorded in the ship's Certificate of Entry.

2A.4.2 Exclusion of risks insurable under Marine (non-war) Policies

2A.4.2.1 Subject to Rules 2A.4.2.2 and 2A.4.2.3, the Association shall not be liable to the Owner of an Entered Ship for any loss, damage, or expense wholly or partially covered by the Standard Form of English Marine Policy (Hulls), or which would have been wholly or partially covered thereby if, at the time of the incident giving rise to such loss, damage or expense, the Entered Ship had been insured under such a policy.

2A.4.2.2 Subject to Rule 2A.4.2.3, where the Entered Ship is covered for marine risks on the terms of a Hull Policy with the American Institute Hull Clauses attached the Association shall not be liable to the Owner of an Entered Ship for any loss, damage, or expense wholly or partially covered thereby.

2A.4.2.3 Loss, damage or expense which is caused by piracy or by violent theft by persons from outside the ship, and which is within the scope of the insurance otherwise afforded to the Owner of an Entered Ship, is not excluded from the insurance by Rule 2A.4.2.1 or where applicable Rule 2A.4.2.2 notwithstanding that claims for such loss, damage or expense are also recoverable under the Standard Form of English Marine Policy (Hulls) or recoverable under a Hull Policy with the American Institute Hull Clauses attached.

2A.4.3 Reduction in amount recoverable

2A.4.3.1 If an Entered Ship becomes, or under Rule 3.11.5 is treated as, an actual or constructive total loss the sum payable by the Association in respect of any claim for such actual or constructive total loss (hereinafter referred to in this Rule as "the sum payable") shall be subject to the limits specified in paragraphs 2A.4.3.2 and 2A.4.3.3 of this Rule.

2A.4.3.2 If the Entered Ship is

(a) insured by the Association on the basis of an Agreed Value or a proportion of an Agreed Value, and
(b) insured under a Hull Policy,

the sum payable shall be limited to and shall not exceed whichever is the lower of

(i) the Agreed Value or the proportion of the Agreed Value as the case may be, and
(ii) a sum equivalent to 125 per cent of the aggregate value on the basis of which the ship is, at the time of the incident giving rise to the claim for actual or constructive total loss, insured under the terms of its Hull Policy, including any amount insured in respect of increased value whether in the Hull Policy or any other policy in force at that time.

2A.4.3.3 If the Entered Ship is insured by the Association on the basis of an Agreed Value or a proportion of an Agreed Value but is not insured under a Hull Policy, the sum payable shall be limited to and shall not exceed whichever is the lower of

(i) the Agreed Value or the proportion of the Agreed Value as the case may be, and
(ii) a sum equivalent to 125 per cent of the Insurable Value at the time of the incident giving rise to the claim for actual or constructive total loss.

2A.4.3.4 In paragraph 2A.4.3.2 of this Rule the words "value on the basis of which the ship is, at the time of the incident giving rise to the claim for actual or constructive loss, insured under the terms of its Hull Policy" shall mean the agreed value under the Hull Policy or if there is no such agreed value the Insurable Value irrespective of whether the insurance is given on such agreed value or Insurable Value or on a proportion of such agreed value or Insurable Value.

2A.4.4 Average payable

Average is payable without deductions new for old, whether the average be particular or general.

2A.4.5 Unrepaired damage

2A.4.5.1 The measure of indemnity in respect of claims for unrepaired damage shall be the reasonable depreciation in the market value of the ship, at the end of the Policy Year in which the damage occurred, arising from such unrepaired damage, but not exceeding the reasonable cost of repairs.

2A.4.5.2 The Association shall not be liable for unrepaired damage if the ship becomes, or under Rule 3.11.5 is treated as, an actual or constructive total loss during the Policy Year in which such damage occurred (whether or not such total loss falls within the scope of the insurance of the ship, under her Terms of Entry).

2A.4.5.3 The Association shall not be liable in respect of unrepaired damage for more than the aggregate of:

    (a) the value on which the insurance is based in accordance with Rule 2A.4.1, and
    (b) the sum (if any) insured in respect of Freight and Disbursements.

2A.4.6 Freight Waiver

In the event of actual or constructive total loss no claim shall be made by the Association for freight whether or not notice of abandonment has been given, but this restriction shall not apply if the Owner is insured under this Part against loss of Freight and Disbursements.

2A.5 Additional terms and conditions applicable only to insurance under Part A against loss of freight and disbursements relating to an entered ship

2A.5.1 Sum insured and limit of recovery

2A.5.1.1 Insurance against the risks referred to in Rule 2A.1.2 is given by the Association on the basis of the sum (referred to in this Rule 2A.5 as the "sum insured") agreed between the Association and the Owner of an Entered Ship as the sum insured in relation to those risks.

2A.5.1.2 The sum insured will be recorded in the Certificate of Entry.

2A.5.1.3 The maximum liability of the Association in respect of any claim for loss of Freight and Disbursements shall be an amount equivalent to the sum insured.

2A.5.1.4 If an Entered Ship becomes, or under Rule 3.11.5 is treated as, an actual or constructive total loss, the amount recoverable shall be the sum insured in respect of Freight and Disbursements whether the ship be fully or partly loaded or in ballast, chartered or unchartered. If, however, an Entered Ship becomes a constructive total loss but the Owner's claim against the Association be settled as a claim for partial loss, this provision shall not apply.

2A.5.1.5 In relation to a claim which does not arise out of the actual or constructive total loss of an Entered Ship, the liability of the Association shall, subject to Rule 2A.5.1.3, be limited to the amount of the Freight and Disbursements which, as a result of the incident giving rise to the claim, is not recoverable by the Owner under a contract existing at the date of such incident.

2A.5.1.6 Except where Rule 2A.5.1.4 applies the amount recoverable for loss of Freight and Disbursements shall not exceed the amount actually lost.

2A.5.2 Exclusion of claims for loss or frustration of voyage or adventure

The Association shall not be liable to an Owner of an Entered Ship for any claim arising out of loss or frustration of any voyage or adventure.

2A.5.3 Exclusion of claims relating to loss of time

The Association shall not be liable to an Owner of an Entered Ship for any claim consequent on loss of time of that ship, whether arising from a peril insured against or otherwise.

2A.5.4 Exclusion of risks insurable under freight policies

2A.5.4.1 Subject to Rule 2A.5.4.2 the Association shall not be liable to the Owner of an Entered Ship for any loss or expense covered by the Standard Form of English Marine Policy (Freight) with the Institute Time Clauses Freight (Edition of 1.10.83) attached, including the War Exclusion Clause, the Strikes Exclusion Clause and the Malicious Acts Exclusion Clause or which would have been covered thereby if, at the time of the incident giving rise to such loss or expense, the Entered Ship had been insured under such a policy.

2A.5.4.2 Loss or expense which is caused by piracy or by violent theft by persons from outside the ship, and which is within the scope of the insurance otherwise afforded to the Owner of an Entered Ship is not excluded from the insurance by Rule 2A.5.4.1 notwithstanding that claims for such loss, damage or expense are also recoverable under the Standard Form of English Marine Policy (Freight).

PART B—DETENTION AND DIVERSION LOSSES AND EXPENSES

2B.1 Risk insured

Every Owner of an Entered Ship is, unless the Terms of Entry of the ship provide otherwise, insured to the extent of the amounts recoverable under this Part of Rule 2 when the Entered Ship is detained or diverted in the circumstances specified in Rule 2B.2.

2B.2 Causes of loss

The Owner of an Entered Ship is insured as provided in Rule 2B.1 if the detention or diversion which causes the loss or expense is:

2B.2.1 caused by war, warlike operations, civil war, revolution, rebellion, insurrection, civil strife, any hostile act by or against a belligerent power, or by conditions brought about as a result of any of the foregoing;

2B.2.2 caused by compliance with any order, prohibition or direction:

2B.2.2.1 the object of which is to avoid any loss, damage or expense arising from a cause specified in Rule 2A.2.1, 2A.2.2 or 2A.2.3, and

2B.2.2.2 which is made or imposed by:

(a) the Directors; or

(b) any Government department or military authority of a country in which the ship is owned, managed or registered; or

(c) any Government department or military authority of a country having the right or de facto power to do so;

2B.2.3 in the opinion of the Directors, caused, instigated, incited or encouraged in furtherance of the political aims of any Government, by:

2B.2.3.1 that Government or any department or agency thereof;

2B.2.3.2 any person acting or purporting to act on behalf of such Government, department or agency;

2B.2.3.3 the armed forces of that Government;

2B.2.4 caused by any group of persons which in pursuit of its political aims maintains an armed force;

2B.2.5 caused by terrorists, pirates, bandits or rioters;

2B.2.6 for the purpose of avoiding any loss or damage to the ship which is insured under Rule 2, Part A, provided that in any such case the Owner is only insured if and to the extent that the Directors so decide.

2B.3 Exclusions

2B.3.1 Exclusion of the consequences of the actions of strikers and others

An Owner shall not be entitled to any recovery from the Association in respect of detention or diversion of an Entered Ship when such detention or diversion is directly or indirectly caused by:

2B.3.1.1 strikes, lockouts, industrial action or labour disturbances;

2B.3.1.2 the action or activity of strikers, locked-out workmen or persons taking part in industrial action or labour disturbances;

2B.3.1.3 action taken to avoid loss of or damage to or financial or other loss in connection with an Entered Ship caused by any of the events or persons referred to in Rules 2B.3.1.1 and 2B.3.1.2.

2B.3.2 Exclusion of delays relating to repairs and other matters

An Owner shall not be entitled to any recovery from the Association in respect of a period during which the Entered Ship is:

2B.3.2.1 delayed solely by the failure of the Owner, his servants or agents to give or comply with instructions for the disposal, repair or movement of the ship, or

2B.3.2.2 awaiting or undergoing repairs,

irrespective of whether such instructions or repairs are necessitated by damage caused to the ship by any of the risks specified in Rule 2, Part A or any other reason whatsoever.

2B.3.3 Exclusion of claims relating to periods which are subsequent to the termination, cesser or cancellation of insurance

An Owner of an Entered Ship is not insured in respect of any period subsequent to the date when the insurance of that ship by the Association has expired or, in accordance with the Rules, has terminated, ceased or been cancelled.

2B.4 Amount recoverable

Subject to Rules 2B.5 and 2B.6 and the proviso to Rule 2B.2.6, the amounts recoverable by an Owner of an Entered Ship insured under this Part are as follows:

2B.4.1 in the case of detention of the ship caused by a cause specified in Rule 2B.2, a sum calculated at the rate of 10 per cent per annum of the aggregate of:
   (a) the value on which the insurance is based in accordance with Rule 2A.4.1, and
   (b) the amount (if any) insured in respect of Freight and Disbursements,
   that sum being applied pro rata to the whole period of the detention (subject to the exclusions in Rule 2B.3);

2B.4.2 in the event of detention of the ship in any of the circumstances specified in Rule 2B.2.1, 2B.2.3, 2B.2.4 or 2B.2.5, and lasting for a continuous period exceeding 90 days, a sum calculated at the rate of 5 per cent per annum of the aggregate of:
   (a) the value on which the insurance is based in accordance with Rule 2A.4.1, and
   (b) the amount (if any) insured in respect of Freight and Disbursements,
   that sum being applied pro rata to the whole period of the detention (subject to the exclusions in Rule 2B.3) and being recoverable in addition to any amounts recoverable under Rule 2B.4.1.

2B.4.3 in the case of diversion of the ship caused by a cause specified in Rule 2B.2 a sum calculated at the rate of 10 per cent per annum of the aggregate of:
   (a) the value on which the insurance is based in accordance with Rule 2A.4.1, and

(b) the amount (if any) insured in respect of Freight and Disbursements,

that sum being applied pro rata to the length of time by which the voyage of the Entered Ship during which the diversion takes place is prolonged as a consequence of the diversion.

2B.5 Deductible, and reductions of amounts recoverable

2B.5.1 Deductible

From every claim under Rule 2B.4.1 in respect of detention of an Entered Ship and from every claim under Rule 2B.4.3 in respect of diversion of an Entered Ship shall be deducted a sum equivalent to the sum payable by the Association to the Owner of such ship in respect of seven days of the detention or as the case may be of the period by which the voyage of the Entered Ship is prolonged as a consequence of the diversion.

2B.5.2 Reduction relating to damage claims

From each claim for detention under Rule 2B.4.2 there shall be deducted a sum equivalent to any claim paid or payable by the Association under Rule 2, Part A for damage to the detained ship during the period of detention, unless the Directors decide that this deduction should be reduced or not applied.

2B.5.3 Reduction relating to hire and other earnings

From each claim for detention under Rule 2B.4.1 and, if applicable, Rule 2B.4.2 and from each claim for diversion under Rule 2B.4.3, there shall be deducted an amount equivalent to any hire or other contractual reward which is payable on a time basis (whether under a demise or time charter or otherwise howsoever) for the period in respect of which the claim for detention or diversion is made and which is received by the Owner before the time when such claim is paid by the Association.

2B.6 Assignment to the Association of owner's claim for hire

If an Owner is or may be entitled to claim any hire or other contractual reward referred to in Rule 2B.5.3 but at the time when the claim for detention or diversion is paid by the Association he has not received that hire or reward, the Association shall be entitled to exercise rights of subrogation in respect of such hire or reward and the Owner shall assign its rights thereto to the Association which may pursue the claim and shall be entitled to any eventual recovery in respect of it.

PART C—PROTECTION AND INDEMNITY

2C.1 Risks insured

2C.1.1 Subject to Rule 2C.1.2, an Owner is insured against liabilities, costs and expenses which fall within the categories specified in Appendix A and which the Owner incurs in the circumstances specified in Rule 2C.2, unless the Terms of Entry provide otherwise.

2C.1.2 Liabilities, cost and expenses

2C.1.2.1 relating to the Crew of an Entered Ship; or

2C.1.2.2 which the Directors may from time to time decide are to be insured only by special agreement and on payment of a Premium

are not insured under this Part unless the Terms of Entry expressly provide for such insurance.

2C.1.3 Insurance under this Part is subject to the exclusions and qualifications set out in Appendix A.

2C.2 Causes of loss

The Owner of an Entered Ship is insured as provided in Rule 2C.1 if the incurring of the liability, cost or expense is caused by:

> 2C.2.1 war, civil war, revolution, rebellion, insurrection, or civil strife arising there-from, or any hostile act by or against a belligerent power;
>
> 2C.2.2 capture, seizure, arrest, restraint or detainment (barratry excepted) and the consequences thereof or any attempt thereat;
>
> 2C.2.3 mines, torpedoes, bombs, or other weapons of war (whether any of the afore-said are derelict or otherwise);
>
> 2C.2.4 strikers, locked-out workmen, or persons taking part in labour disturbances, riots or civil commotions;
>
> 2C.2.5 terrorists or any person acting maliciously, or from a political motive;
>
> 2C.2.6 piracy and violent theft by persons from outside the ship.

2C.3 Limit of recovery

2C.3.1 The Directors may, by decision made before the beginning of any Policy Year, limit the maximum liability of the Association under this Part in respect of any description or descriptions of claim whatsoever.

2C.3.2 The maximum liability of the Association in respect of any claim under this Part which is not subject to any such limit as mentioned in Rule 2C.3.1 shall be a sum equal to the limit up to which the Association is reinsured in respect of such claim.

2C.4 Payment first by the owner

Unless and except to the extent that the Directors decide otherwise, it shall be a condition precedent of an Owner's right of recovery under this Part that he shall first have discharged the liability or paid the costs and expenses which are the subject of his claim on the Association.

PART D—SUE AND LABOUR

2D.1 Risks insured

Unless the Terms of Entry provide otherwise, every Owner of an Entered Ship is insured against extraordinary costs and expenses (not being costs or expenses insured under any other Part) which the Owner:

> 2D.1.1 reasonably incurs at or about or after the time of the occurrence of any casualty, event or matter which is likely to or which may give rise to a claim on the Association, and
>
> 2D.1.2 incurs solely for the purpose of avoiding or minimising any loss, damage, liability, cost or expense against which the Owner is insured by the Association at that time.

2D.2 Prior agreement of the managers

Unless and except to the extent that the Directors decide otherwise, it shall be a condition precedent of an Owner's right of recovery under this Part that the costs or expenses which are the subject of his claim on the Association were incurred with the prior approval of the Managers.

2D.3 Exclusions

2D.3.1 Exclusion of fines, penalties etc.

Unless and except to the extent that the Directors decided otherwise, an Owner is not insured against fines, penalties or other impositions.

2D.3.2 Exclusion of sums paid to release a ship

Unless and except to the extent that the Directors decide otherwise, an Owner is not insured against any sum paid in consideration of or for the purpose of the release of an Entered Ship from any capture, seizure, arrest, restraint, detainment, confiscation or expropriation.

PART E—DISCRETIONARY INSURANCE

2E.1 Risks insured

Unless the Terms of Entry provide otherwise, every Owner of an Entered Ship is insured against such losses, liabilities, costs and expenses, not otherwise recoverable and not expressly excluded under the Rules, as the Directors in their discretion decide to be within the scope of the Association.

2E.2 Amount of recovery

If the Directors in their discretion decide that a payment should be made to an Owner under this Part, they may decide that the Owner's claim shall be paid in full or that only a proportion of the amount claimed shall be paid.

PART F—OPTIONAL ADDITIONAL INSURANCE

2F.1 Insurance by special agreement

If the Terms of Entry expressly so provide (but not otherwise), the Owner of an Entered Ship may be insured against any risks in respect of which insurance has been authorised by the Directors.

2F.2 Terms and conditions

The terms and conditions of any insurance given by the Association under this Part shall be such as have been agreed in writing by the Managers.

Index

NATO War Risks Insurance Scheme—*cont.*
  1982–1992, evolution, 41.54, 41.55
  background, 41.39–41.43
    structure, 41.43, 41.44
  improved basic principles, 41.63, 41.64
  improved valuation scheme, 41.62
  policy, resemblance to new War Hull Clauses,
    41.56
  question of success, 41.65, 41.66
  scope, 41.2
  structure, 41.58–41.61
  underwriting methods, 41.57
Non-Queen's Enemy Risks insurance
  evolution, 41.5
  termination in time of war, 41.36
  see also Queen's Enemy Risks insurance
Norway
  Mutual War Risks Association, 2.5
  and war risks insurance in time of war, 41.2
Notice of Abandonment
  and actual total loss, 27.6
  and capture, 11.5
  circumstances where not necessary,
    27.57–27.67
  and constructive total loss, 27.8, 27.11, 27.15,
    27.17–27.27
    and cargo, 36.59
  evolution, 27.28
  question of, 27.29
  timing, 27.40–27.47
  and T.T. Club Rules, application of Marine
    Insurance Act 1906, 39.140
  and underwriters
    disadvantages to, 27.30–27.34
    replacement device, 27.35, 27.36
  see also Capture, apprehension of; Seizure, and
    presence of force
Novus actus interveniens, see Proximate cause,
    simultaneous events
Nuclear risks
  detonation
    and Cancellation and Automatic
      Termination Clause, 4.15–4.28
    and Mutual War Risks Associations' need
      for reinsurance, 4.39, 4.40
    prospects, 4.46, 4.47
  and new Cargo Marine Clauses, 33.29, 35.9,
    36.15–36.24
  and new Marine and War Hull Clauses, 32.22,
    32.30, 32.33, 36.11–36.14
  and new War Freight Clauses, 32.58
  and new War and Strikes Clauses, 34.11,
    38.10–38.12
  and old Cargo Clauses, 33.13, 33.14, 33.23
  and old Container Clauses, 37.16, 37.17, 37.34,
    37.35
  and old War Hull Clauses, 32.15
  and T.T. Club Rules, 39.25, 39.27,
    39.96–39.98, 39.105

Oil, bulk
  and piracy, 36.9
  and special cargo insurances, 35.17–35.20

Oils, seeds and fats
  and piracy, 36.9
  and special cargo insurances, 35.24–35.29,
    36.36
  and unseaworthiness, 36.41
One-ship companies, and total loss, 27.38

P. & I. Associations, *see* Protection and
    Indemnity Associations
Partial loss
  compared with total loss, 27.77
  and Marine Insurance Act 1906, 27.3
  and T.T. Club Rules, application of Marine
    Insurance Act 1906, 39.134, 39.135
Particular Average, and pre-1982 Cargo Marine
    Clauses, 33.7
Particular charges, and salvage charges, 24.29
Piracy, 20.1–20.41
  Cargo Marine Clauses, post 1982, and special
    cargo insurances, 35.6–35.8
  characteristics, 20.40
  criminal concept compared with insured peril,
    5.3
  definitions, 20.2, 20.16
  early treatment of, 20.4–20.15
  as insured peril, 20.3
    evolution, 20.1, 20.17–20.38, 20.41,
      36.3–36.10
  and missing ships, 27.13
  and new Container War and Strikes Clauses,
    38.18
  and new Marine Hull Clauses, 32.21, 32.26
  and new War Clauses, 32.42, 32.55
  question of, 12.51, 12.67
  and T.T. Club Rules, 39.22, 39.23
Political motive, effect on insured peril, 19.12,
    19.13
Pollution
  and new War Clauses, 32.47–32.49, 32.63
  and T.T. Club Rules, 39.106
Port authorities
  and T.T. Club Rules, 39.58–39.67
  see T.T. Club Rules, and port authorities
Ports, unsafe
  war or hostilities in, 31.1–31.29
  and war risk, 23.19
Power
  defined in F.C.& S. Clause, 10.3
  see also Belligerent power
Pre-emption
  characteristics, 21.37
  as defined in T.T. Club Rules, 39.7
  and new War Hull Clauses, 32.37
  scope, 21.31, 21.32
  and T.T. Club Rules, 39.13, 39.14
Premiums, 3.1–3.22
  additional, 3.6, 3.11–3.21
Princes, restraint of, *see* Restraint of Princes
Prize and search cases, scope, 11.53–11.63
Prize Courts
  and abandonment to underwriters, 27.28
  jurisdiction, 25.5

INDEX

Prize Courts—*cont.*
see also Capture, insured peril, cases; Prize and
search cases; Recovery, unlikelihood of,
meaning, cases
Proof, and proximate cause, 30.74, 30.78–30.80,
30.90, 30.100
Protection and Indemnity Associations
compared with Mutual War Risk Associations,
2.4
and court fines, 25.9
responsibility for wreck, 27.31
and salvor's expenses, 24.32
and South Atlantic War 1982, 41.70
Protection and Indemnity insurance
and constructive total loss, 27.37
and fines, 32.41
and War Risks, 23.10, 23.13
Proximate cause, 30.1–30.100
bad becoming worse, 30.37–30.66
casualty's cause not established, 30.67–30.91
drawbacks, 30.67
recent occurrences, 30.92–30.99
scope, 30.1–30.4, 30.13
simultaneous events, 30.15–30.36
tests applied, 30.5–30.12
and war risk insurance, 5.1
and War Risks, 30.14

Quarantine regulations, and new War Hull
Clauses, 32.39, 32.40
Queen's Enemy Risks insurance, 32.1, 41.4–41.19
and consultation regarding reinsurance
premiums, 41.26
criteria, 41.12–41.17
evolution, 41.5–41.8
insured perils, 41.15–41.18
and requisition, 23.38
and South Atlantic War 1982, 41.68, 41.69
see also Non-Queen's Enemy Risks insurance

Radioactivity, *see* Nuclear risks
Ransom, and sue and labour provisions,
24.36–24.38
Reasonable despatch, and new cargo War and
Strikes Clauses, 34.34, 34.36–34.38, 34.40
Rebellion
compared with other perils, 8.5, 8.19, 8.24,
8.31, 8.32, 10.11
defined, 8.4, 8.20
gradations between levels of insured peril, 8.1,
8.2
question of lesser perils embracing greater, 8.3
scope, 8.1–8.34
see also Civil Commotion; Insurrection;
Revolution; Riot
Recklessness
compared with wilful misconduct, 29.4, 29.5,
29.14
and imprudent conduct, 29.19
and T.T. Club Rules, 39.107
Recovery
amount of, 27.68–27.77
unlikelihood of, 11.31–11.36

Reinsurance
Agreement on War Risks Reinsurance with
Her Majesty's Government, text,
Appendix O
and London market, 2.1, 2.3
Requisition, 4.29–4.37
characteristics, 4.29, 4.30, 21.24, 21.33, 21.37
and ending insurance, 4.30, 21.23
and modification of Hellenic (Bermuda)
Association Rules, 23.37
and Mutual War Risks Associations, 4.39,
4.42, 4.43
and new Clauses, 32.37, 32.38, 38.27, 38.28
requisition for title compared with requisition
for use, 4.29
of ships, 21.19–21.22
and Royal Prerogative, 21.13–21.18
and T.T. Club Rules, 39.12–39.14
Restraint
characteristics, 13.76
compared with other perils, 12.2, 13.1, 13.4
as insured peril, 13.17–13.26, 13.63–13.72
and cargo, 36.26–36.29
evolution, 13.7
Mutual War Risks Associations' practice,
13.51–13.62
smuggled goods, 13.35–13.44
see also Arrest; Consequences and attempt
provisions; Detainment
Restraint of Kings, Princes and people, *see*
Restraint of Princes
Restraint of people
as insured peril, 13.12–13.16
see also Restraint of Princes
Restraint of Princes
as insured peril, 13.1–13.34, 13.65
contrasted with ordinary judicial process,
25.3, 25.4
defined, 13.2, 13.21
and freight delays, 22.29, 22.46–22.51
question of proximate cause, 30.62–30.66
and seizure, 12.3, 12.4, 12.30, 12.31
Revolution
compared with other perils, 8.5, 8.31
definition, 8.4, 8.32
gradations between levels of insured peril, 8.1,
8.2
question of lesser perils embracing greater, 8.3
scope, 8.1–8.34
see also Civil Commotion; Insurrection;
Rebellion; Riot
Riot, 17.1–17.16
characteristics, 17.36
compared with other perils, 8.31
criminal concept compared with insured peril,
5.3
definition/terms, 17.2–17.6
gradations between levels of insured peril,
8.1–8.3
and T.T. Club Rules, 39.18–39.20
and War Risks Policy, scope, 16.4
see also Civil Commotion; Insurrection;
Rebellion; Revolution

617